Understanding Psychology

FOURTH EDITION

ANILA R. RAGADE

R. H. ETTINGER

Text Design and Composition: Archetype Book Composition

Cover Design: Linda Price

Illustrations: Joey C. Wu and Misty Canyon Designs

Typesetter: Linda Price

ISBN: 978-1-62751-253-4

Table of Contents

PART II: Biological Foundations, Perception, and Sleep

PART IV: The Nature and Treatment of Psychological Disorders

Preface

We live in an age in which science and technology have revolutionized the way we view the world, yet many students fail to realize that scientific methods can also be applied to the study of human behavior. While many students have no difficulty mastering numerous facts and theories, their behavior appears to be little changed by this experience. That is, there is little evidence that a first course in psychology has changed the way they interpret behavioral events. Perhaps this is because it is so difficult to remain objective about behavior—and perhaps it is due, in part, to the ways in which texts present and support principles of psychology.

If psychology is a science, then it should be presented as a science. Throughout this text we have attempted to involve students actively in the discovery process by inviting them to question assumptions and to participate in the scientific process of supporting or refuting ideas. Although the text is rich with content, it endeavors to bring students, and their own behavior, closer to the scientific process of observation and control. We have tried to make the reading of the chapters a rewarding experience for the students because we think learning should be fun.

The major goal of this textbook is to be able to successfully demonstrate to students how the science of psychology has evolved and continues to develop. We wanted to create a textbook that engaged students in the scientific process by asking stimulating questions and demonstrating how scientific research proceeds to answer them. In addition, we wanted to introduce students to several contemporary and influential psychologists in order to show them how researchers think about important issues as well as to illustrate how controversy still surrounds much of this important discipline. We believe that it is important to show students how we know what we know by discussing facts of psychology in terms of the scientific context in which they are demonstrated. More importantly we discuss the methods of research throughout the text as we display hundreds of classic and contemporary experiments in detail. There are more than 2500 references to published research, much of it published since 2000 and some as recent as May of 2013!.

Special Features

In this 4th edition old information which was no longer valid due to the discovery of other relevant facts has been weeded out and fresh new information that replaces it has been introduced with the caveat that time alone will allow us to gauge its validity as others try to replicate the work. This text-book makes it clear that the study of the human mind is a very complex task and what we once thought was correct might be found wanting whereas what we once discarded might be found to be correct and in this rests the strength of science because science is founded on hard evidence.

What makes this text different from others that are also well grounded in current research is the way in which research is presented. We attempt to demonstrate how research evolves from simple questions about behavior. We then show how research answers these questions and how theories of psychology develop from research. In many cases we discuss how both the questions and the research are influenced by individual personalities and the political climate of the time. Psychology, like any other science, is a dynamic, social process within which our knowledge continually changes.

Throughout each chapter there are numerous questions that students are asked to consider and attempt to answer. Immediately following many of these questions are descriptions of research designed to answer them. Students are thus led through the research process so that they become accustomed to how questions lead to research and research provides answers. In many cases research does not lead to clear answers and we discuss how to evaluate both sides of an issue critically.

Supplements

Study Guide Each chapter consists of learning objectives, a chapter summary, matching exercises, true/false statements, multiple choice questions, and review diagrams and charts. Additionally, the study guide contains application exercises which challenge students to apply chapter content to "real life" situations and/or problems, and critical thinking exercises that encourage students to analyze and evaluate psychological research and concepts.

Acknowledgments

It is with great pride and joy that I am writing this preface to the 4th edition. I had not expected to work on one and I took on the task only because Nate Shankles from BVT Publishing urged me to take it on. Once I accepted the task, I found that working on it was very rewarding! We know so much more about the brain now than we did just a couple of years ago that it is simply astounding! I relished learning about the new discoveries in the various sub-disciplines within psychology and hope that my students will share the joy that new discoveries bring.

Writing a book, even if it is as a Co-author is a Herculean task. It is impossible to do it without the cooperation of many people. I sincerely want to thank my Co-author, Dr. R. H. Ettinger, for writing the initial scholarly manuscript. I also want to thank Nate Shankles, Textbook Specialist at BVT, Linda Price, our typesetter, Amanda Crocker Custom Publishing Coordinator at BVT and Janai Bryand, Production and Full-time Manager at BVT Publishing. I also want to thank all the people I worked with from Horizon Textbooks before it became BVT. Thanks are also due to my colleagues from Jefferson Community & Technical College who take pride in my accomplishments, especially Ms. Catherine Wright, my Division Chair and Mr. Byron Tharpe, our Program coordinator and Mary Sloan our Division Secretary and Judy Dial our book-store manager for being extremely willing to cooperate with me in changing the ISBN numbers, working with the dead-lines etc.

I also want to thank Mrs. Seema Gupte, a good friend of mine who not only goaded me to walk every morning which kept my energy levels up as I taught full-time at Jefferson Community College and researched material for revising this text-book, but also provided home-made Indian flat-bread for me and my husband to free me from my kitchen duties!

Finally, I also want to express my gratitude to my dear husband, Dr. Rammohan Ragade, for putting up with endless inconvenience due to my work on my project and helping me deal with technical problems as I worked on the manuscript. If not for the help of all these good people, I would never have had the joy of saying "I am working on the 4th edition of my text-book" and it was a delightful task!

Anila Ragade Ph.D.
Professor of Psychology
Behavioral & Social Sciences Division
Jefferson Community College
Louisville, KY 40272
September 21, 2013

PART I:

Origins and Methods of Psychology

CHAPTER 1

What Is Psychology?

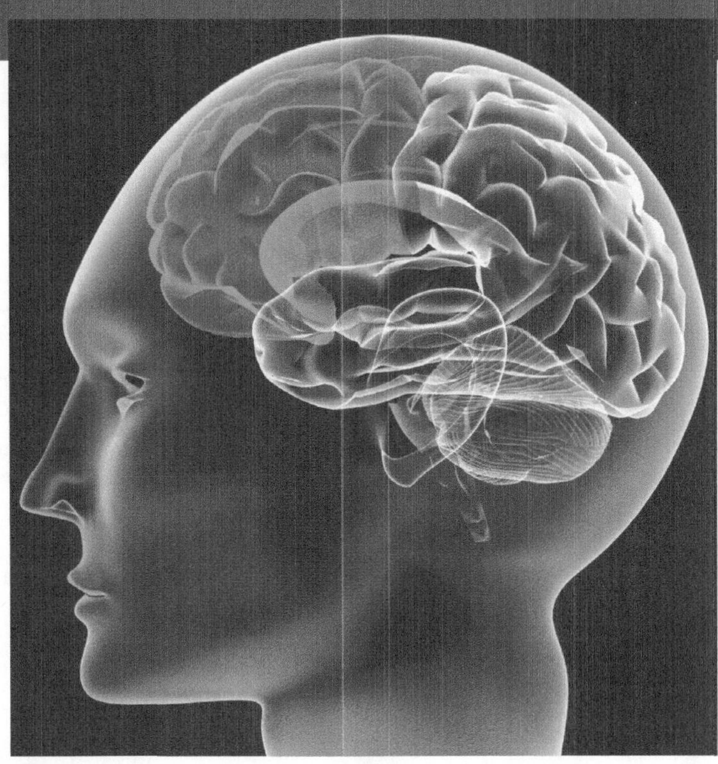

iStock

Definition of Psychology

History of Psychology

Structuralism
Functionalism
Psychoanalysis
Behaviorism
Gestalt Psychology
Humanistic Psychology

Contemporary Psychology

Current Perspectives in Psychology
Pryshology Professionals

"Man, Know Thyself…and thou shalt know the gods." states an inscription on the wall of the inner sanctum at the Egyptian Temple of Luxor, dated circa 1400 BCE. About 700 years later, around 700 BCE, in India, a sage named Uddalaka said "Tat Tvam Asi", or "Thou Art That!" in response to his son's inquiry about the "Self". Uddalaka taught that the "Self" his son was searching for, was none other than "That", where "That" stood for an "All- Pervading- Consciousness". (Nikhilananda, pg. 327).

About another 400 years later, Socrates, the famous Greek Philosopher said, "Know thy self." So…what is this "Self" that we routinely talk about? What is this "consciousness" that allows us to be aware of "ourselves" as separate from the world around us? How did we acquire this consciousness? Is "Consciousness" the same as "The Mind" or a background against which the "mind" operates? What does it do for us? Do lower animals have it? What happens to our consciousness when we die…does it cease at death? Such questions have been asked since time immemorial, and Mankind is still asking and trying to answer these same questions! The pursuit of valid answers to such profound questions gave rise to the subject we now call Psychology.

We humans have pondered our own existence and asked and answered questions regarding our own minds since time immemorial. We have tried to figure out which of our organs is responsible for our mental activities. Some people thought the mind was housed in the heart and some thought it was in the liver.

In any case, the first known incidence of a written statement indicating that the brain was the seat of the mind was drawn by the Egyptians, around 1600 BCE. The Greeks had reached the same conclusion by the time of Pythagoras, circa 500 BCE (Halonen, Santrock, Schneider & Ragade, 1996). Today we believe that all "mental" phenomena are generated by and in the brain.

As a person journeys through life, he/she asks more or less the same questions that others before him/her have asked. The only difference is that in the past, people relied only on their own logic and judgment to discern the correctness of their answers. Today's scientists rely on **objective evidence** in addition to their reasoning. Today, we have a body of knowledge based on **scientific facts gathered via direct experiment, i.e., empirically**. It allows us to answer the same age old questions but with the confidence that we have evidence to support our statements. **This body of empirical knowledge about behavioral and mental processes is known as Psychology**.

What will studying Psychology do for me you say? Well … Although we admit to some bias, we do believe that knowledge of psychology is helpful even to people

continued

who do not plan to pursue it as a career. Studying psychology provides insights into why people behave as they do. It also helps us to better understand our own thoughts, feelings, behaviors, and attitudes—and, hopefully, it can strengthen our appreciation of and tolerance for the wide differences that exist among people. Understanding yourself might allow you to live a healthier, happier life both by accepting those aspects of you that you cannot do anything about and transforming those aspects of yourself that you can change for the better.

DEFINITION OF PSYCHOLOGY

Psychology is an evolving subject and as such, its definition has gone through several changes and we will trace the history of psychology through these changing definitions. An appreciation of where psychology has been will help you to see where it is going.

First Definition (19th century): *Psychology is the scientific study of the human soul.*

The roots of the first definition of psychology lie in European philosophy. Many early philosophers had tried to study the soul in a systematic scientific way, in the 18th and 19th centuries. The most popular idea in those days was that a man's mind was allowed to him by his God-given soul, and that the soul was a non-material entity. In contrast, a man's body was a material object, and did not have consciousness without its soul residing in it. This idea that a God-given soul animated the separate but otherwise lifeless body was known as **mind-body dualism**.

Willhelm Wundt, a Professor of Physiology at the University of Leipzig, Germany, in the 19th century, is considered to be **the founder of Psychology**. Wundt believed in **psycho-physical parallelism**. Psycho-physical parallelism held that although the mind and body operated in different worlds, the non-material mind and the material body were tightly linked and operated in tandem. Though they did not have a causal relationship, they could still reflect each other's states as in the saying "Healthy body—healthy mind" (Boring, 1957). So Psychology, the name Wundt conjured up for the study of this relationship, was coined from two Greek words, *psyche*, which stood for the mind or the soul, and *logos*, which stood for systematic knowledge.

Although the founder of the subject, Wilhelm Wundt, believed in psycho-physical parallelism he decided to focus on the activity and contents of the mind rather than its metaphysical aspects (Rieber & Robinson, 2001 pp128). Wundt and his students did not study animal behavior because the European philosophers of that time thought that animals did not have souls and therefore did not have minds. There was also little inquiry into the minds of children.

Second Definition (19th century): Psychology is the scientific study of human and animal minds or mental processes.

Although the Wundtian psychology had allowed many wonderful discoveries about the human mind, it was soon replaced by a different type of psychology. This change was brought about by a philosopher named **William James,** who was a professor at Harvard University in the United States. James investigated psychic phenomena in order to verify the existence of the soul but was disillusioned and drew inspiration from Charles Darwin's theory of evolution (a new and controversial theory at the time). *James concluded that the mind was a process that had evolved to allow an animal to adapt to its circumstances or environment, so it could survive.* Psychology came to be defined as the scientific study of human and animal mental processes. So the idea of a "God-given soul" was replaced by this concept that the mind was a "process" developed in response to evolution. In turn, psychology became the study of those processes for both humans and animals.

> ***Third Definition (Early 20th century):*** *Psychology is the scientific study of human and animal behavior.*

This second definition served well, till the early 20th century, when John Watson of Chicago decided that mental processes were hidden and therefore they were not a proper target for a subject that claimed to be a "science". *The focus shifted to observable behavior which can be documented and verified.* Psychology was defined as the scientific study of human and animal behavior. This new ideology or school of thought was called Behaviorism.

These re-inventions served to effectively discard the word "mind" from being the central purpose of Psychology, in favor of focusing on the relationships between external events or stimuli, and the responses or behaviors from animals and humans.

Behaviorism though founded by Watson, was championed by a Harvard Professor of Psychology, **B. F. Skinner** (1904–1990). Skinner wrote several influential including the most influential book, "About Behaviorism" published in 1976. Skinner's work provided excellent experimental evidence in favor of Behaviorism. This type of Psychology flourished till the 1950s, when a group of psychologists now known as Humanistic psychologists criticized Behaviorism because Behaviorism did not allow for free will or the influence of choice making.

> ***Fourth Definition (1970s, Late 20th century):*** *Psychology is the scientific study of human and animal behavior and mental processes.*

In the 1970s, another group of psychologists, now known as Cognitive Psychologists, also joined in criticizing Behaviorism because it had rejected the study of mental processes. The Cognitive psychologists argued that the human mind probably worked very much like chess playing computer programs did, and that it would be possible to study mental processes by using surveys, developing models and studying artificial intelligence. So these two groups, one of the Humanistic psychologists and the other of the Cognitive psychologists, jointly brought about a change in the definition, reintroducing the concept of mental processes.

So the word mind, thrown out by the Behaviorists, was effectively put back in, by the Humanistic and Cognitive psychologists. As psychologists continued their work, a tremendous amount of research in biology, paleontology, medicine, etc., made it clear that humans were primates; they had evolved and were the latest creatures in the animal kingdom. As such, it seemed redundant to say "animal and human" behavior or "animal and human" mental processes, because humans were animals! So beginning in the 1980s, those words were dropped from the definition.

Fifth Definition (1980s, Late 20th century): *Psychology is the scientific study of behavior and mental processes.*

This fifth definition held for about a decade or so, until it was changed to reflect the concern that behavior must be understood in the context of some framework of culture as well as other factors. Psychologists recognized that although humans from all over the world did indeed belong to the same species, there were tremendous differences in behavior and mental processes that arose due to culture, as well as tremendous similarities in behavior and mental processes that arose despite those cultural differences. So to catalog something as strange, bizarre or abnormal in the context of American culture would limit our understanding of man's psychology on a global scale.

Sixth & Current Definition: *Psychology is the study of behavior and mental processes in context.*

In the early to mid 1990s, the definition was changed as stated above, with the word "context" referring to the historical, social, cultural and economic influences that affect behavior and mental processes (Halonen & Santrock, 1999).

Thus, psychology started as a scientific, empirical study of the human soul, discarded the soul and started on the study of human and animal minds or mental processes. It then went on to discard the study of the mind, and focused exclusively on **outward behavior** of animals and humans. It then decided to re-study the mind, and viewed the "mental process" as generated by brain activity rather than by an "other-worldly soul". It then decided that the word animal in the definition was unnecessary, because, other sciences and a type of psychology named Evolutionary Psychology had substantiated evolution, which meant that *humans were animals,* so the word animal was dropped, and finally, because behavior and mental processes take place in a given context, and make sense only in that context, the word context was introduced in the current, and hopefully, the final definition.

You now have a pretty good idea of where the subject began and how it morphed over the years to come to be what it is today, in terms of a definition. Now let us learn a little bit more about some of the early schools of thought and their founders, or The History of Psychology.

HISTORY OF PSYCHOLOGY

Structuralism

WILHELM WUNDT (1832–1920) Has been called "The Father of Experimental Psychology". Wilhelm Wundt was the first to establish a laboratory to study adult human minds and that marked the birth of this subject. **This laboratory was established at the University of Leipzig in Germany in the year 1879.**

Wundt defined the task of psychology as the systematic study of the *structure* of the conscious adult mind. Historically, philosophers had thought of the mind as a non-physical entity distinctly different from the material body. Wundt, however, wanted to study the mind, not as a metaphysical entity, but as a natural phenomenon. Even so, he believed that the mind and the body were two completely different realms, which were related and linked, a belief known as **psychophysical parallelism** (Rieber & Robinson, 2001 pp 128).

Wundt believed that the conscious mental processes involved in such things as perceiving colors, reacting to stimuli, and experiencing emotions could be understood best by breaking them down into their basic elements and then analyzing how the elements were connected with one another, much as one contemplates how the pieces of a jig-saw puzzle fit together to yield a complete picture.

Wundt borrowed a tool of philosophy, ***introspection*** (looking inward), for studying mental processes. For example, subjects listening to music might be asked to break their perceptual experience down into its basic elements of pitch, volume, timbre, and so forth. Subjects were trained in introspection so that they could provide clear reports of their inner experiences. Wundt also believed that introspection needed to be supplemented by experiments. Therefore, he would systematically vary some physical dimension of a stimulus, such as the volume of a particular sound, to see how sensations changed. This approach came to be known as experimental self-observation. Throughout Wundt's career, he continued to emphasize gaining information about the mind from observable, measurable events.

Because Wundt and his colleagues used metaphors like jig-saw puzzles, or walls composed of brick, etc., to explain their idea of how the mind was made up of elements put together, this approach to psychology was called **structuralism**.

Structuralism

Approach to psychology that attempted to break down experience into its basic elements or structures, using a technique called introspection, in which subjects provided scientific reports of perceptual experiences.

PROBLEMS WITH STRUCTURALISM Structuralism enjoyed only short-lived popularity. Psychologists soon discovered that introspection, the major research tool of structuralism, often altered the nature of the conscious mental processes they wished to analyze. An even more damaging flaw became apparent when a number of researchers who were using introspection independently of one another discovered that their results were often different. Finally, many American psychologists criticized structuralism as impractical; they thought psychology should offer solutions to the problems of everyday life. This movement toward a more pragmatic psychology culminated in the *Functionalist school.*

Functionalism

WILLIAM JAMES (1842–1910) Known as "The Foremost American Psychologist" (Boring, 1950), was one of the greatest of all American psychologists. James, a professor of physiology at Harvard, distinguished himself as a writer of psychology by his new approach to investigating the mind. He agreed with the Structuralists that psychology should study mental processes. However, he felt that the science would be better served by attempting to understand the fluid, functional, continually changing, personal nature of conscious experience. He was particularly interested in trying to understand mental processes that helped humans and other animals adapt to their environments. Because of his emphasis on the functional, practical nature of the mind, his conception of psychology's proper task became known as **Functionalism**. In 1890 James published his landmark book titled "Principles of Psychology" a book that is still considered to be one of the most important psychological texts of all time.

Functionalism

An approach to psychology that emphasized the function of the mind rather than its structure or contents. Influenced by Darwin's theory of natural selection, functionalists attempted to learn how mental processes, such as learning, thinking, and perceiving, helped people adapt.

James was greatly influenced by Charles Darwin's theory of evolution by natural selection. According to Darwin, characteristics of a species change or evolve over time as environmental conditions change. Those characteristics that aid in the survival and reproduction of the species are maintained while others are eliminated. For instance, the protective coloration of some types of moths or the opposable thumbs of humans was a trait that was preserved because it helped that species adapt to its environment. Similarly, functionalists concluded that psychological states or processes such as consciousness also evolved because they served particular functions, such as guiding the activities of the individual. Functionalists wanted to learn how various mental processes, such as perceiving, learning, and thinking, helped people adapt. To accomplish this purpose, they continued to use introspection in their research. However, they also introduced another research method: collecting data from observations of human and animal behavior.

Both structuralism and functionalism played important roles in the development of psychology as a science. Structuralism brought psychology into the laboratory by demonstrating that mental processes were a legitimate focus for scientific research. Functionalism broadened psychology to include the study of nonhuman animals, and it expanded the data of psychology to include observations of behavior. James's contributions have had enduring effects on both psychology and education.

Psychoanalysis

SIGMUND FREUD (1856–1939) A brilliant physician and neurological therapist from Vienna, made waves by coming up with his unique new theory of unconscious sexual desires or unhappy childhood memories as being the instigators of disturbing adult behavior. Freud's theory, psychoanalysis, was named after the procedure employed in interviewing patients with neurotic symptoms.

Early on, it became apparent to Freud that most of his patients' symptoms had a sexual basis. Many of Freud's views, particularly his belief that sexual urges were powerful energizers of human behavior, shocked both professionals and laypeople. His emphasis on the unconscious mind, with its irrational urges and drives beyond the control of conscious rational processes, upset many people; it was a blow to human pride to be told that we are often not the masters of our own lives.

Freud's school of though is more widely recognized among non-psychologists than is any other school of psychological thought. However, psychoanalysis has been widely criticized, in part because its assertions cannot be tested in the laboratory.

Despite these criticisms, Freud's impact on psychology was profound. He provided important insights into understanding the emotional lives of people and helped to legitimize the study of human sexuality. Although psychoanalysis is not a major force in contemporary psychology, the practice of psychoanalysis continues. You will learn a little bit about this perspective in the Behavioral Disorders chapter and also in the Treatment of Behavioral Disorders chapter.

Behaviorism

The change in psychology from structuralism to functionalism in the United States was both gradual and incomplete. Certainly functionalism did not completely replace the methods of structuralism and both schools agreed that mental processes were the subject of psychology. However, in 1913 a revolution against both of these schools occurred. This revolution, initiated by John Watson, was both sudden and quite dramatic. The new and revolutionary approach to psychology was called **behaviorism**.

Behaviorism

An approach to the study of behavior that emphasizes the relationship between environmental events and an organism's behavior.

JOHN WATSON (1878–1958) In the spring of 1913, John Watson, who was a graduate of the University of Chicago and was in charge of Animal Psychology at the university, essentially founded behaviorism with a paper titled "Psychology as the Behaviorist Views It" (Boring, 1950, pp. 643). Watson proclaimed a new psychology, free of introspection, whose task was simply to observe the relationship between environmental events (stimuli) and an organism's responses to them. This stimulus-response (S-R) approach to psychology was a ***radical departure*** from Watson's predecessors' focus on mental processes.

The early goal of behaviorism was to discover the rules of association and how combinations of simple associations lead to complex behavior. Watson's work was greatly influenced by the work of the Russian physiologist, Ivan Pavlov (1849–1936).

Behaviorism quickly caught on, and soon many younger American psychologists were calling themselves behaviorists. Behaviorism continues to exert a profound influence on contemporary American psychology due mainly to the monumental contributions of Harvard's B. F. Skinner (1904–1990). Skinner's major contributions to psychology include his important work in operant conditioning, in which he systematically investigated the effects of consequences on behavior. You will learn more about this perspective when you study a chapter titled "Learning".

Gestalt psychology

Approach to psychology that argues that the whole of an experience is different from the sum of its parts. Gestalt psychology is an active force in current investigations of perceptual processes and learning as well as therapy, where it emphasizes the whole person.

Gestalt Psychology

MAX WERTHEIMER (1880–1943) A German, was a professor of psychology at Frankfurt, when he discovered the Phi phenomenon in which a series of stationary lights rapidly turned on and off, seem to be in motion. It was this discovery that allowed Wertheimer to criticize the Wundtian school and found his own school of thought (Boring, 1950). Wertheimer criticized Wundtian psychology on grounds that when we perceive our environment, we don't perceive it in terms of component elements or parts, but as a "Gestalt" or a "whole". Gestalt psychologists popularized the paradox: "The whole is greater than the sum of its parts" and proved their point by studying perceptual illusions and trying to discover principles of perception. You will get a chance to study Gestalt Psychology in the latter half of a chapter titled "Sensation and Perception."

Humanistic Psychology

Humanistic psychology

Approach to psychology that emphasizes the role of free choice and our ability to make conscious rational decisions about how we live our lives.

ABRAHAM MASLOW (1908–1970) A professor of psychology at Brandeis University in the 1950s, was famous for starting what he called the "Third Force" in psychology. He strongly criticized the way human behavior was being portrayed as strictly controlled either by unconscious sexual motivations, as the Freudians did, or as controlled by its consequences, as the Behaviorists did. Maslow argued that neither type of psychology left room for choice based behavior or free will. Maslow was famous for his theory of self-actualization, according to which, once biological needs are met, a human is motivated to fulfill his potential, or be all that he can be. Abraham Maslow's ideas will be presented to you in a chapter titled "Motivation".

CONTEMPORARY PSYCHOLOGY

The previous section briefly introduced the major historical contributions to modern psychology. Many of those approaches have endured and even thrived into the present. Modern psychology, however, is not dominated by any single theoretical approach. Rather, there are many specialties within the field of psychology, and each emphasizes a particular theoretical approach. The following section describes several major areas of specialization that, together with the enduring historical perspectives, define modern psychology.

Cognitive perspective

Approach to psychology focusing on the ways in which organisms process information. Investigates processes such as thinking, memory, language, problem solving, and creativity.

Current Perspectives in Psychology

COGNITIVE PERSPECTIVE The word "cognition" stands for mental activity or process by which knowledge is acquired. This contemporary perspective is a psychological approach that tries to understand how information is organized and interpreted by the mind. Thinking, remembering, forgetting, etc., are some of the mental actions that are experimentally investigated by cognitive psychologists. A chapter titled "Memory" and another titled "Cognition: Thinking and Language" will shine a light on this perspective.

Life-span development (Developmental Psychology)

Field of specialization in psychology concerned with factors that influence development and shape behavior throughout the life cycle, from conception through old age.

LIFE-SPAN DEVELOPMENT Psychologists in this field are interested in factors that influence development and shape behavior throughout the life cycle, from conception through old age, ending with death. They study patterns of physical, intellectual, emotional and social growth, or decline in an age-related or chronological fashion. Life-span development, also known ad **developmental psychology**, is a very useful type of psychology, especially for those who wish to raise psychologically healthy children, or who plan to use psychology as a guide to direct their futures.

Social psychology

Field of specialization concerned with understanding the impact of social environments and social processes on individuals.

SOCIO-CULTURAL PERSPECTIVE **Social psychology** is concerned with understanding the impact of social environments on the individual. Social psychologists are interested in attitude formation and change, social perception, conformity, social roles, prejudice, interpersonal attraction, and aggression, while cultural psychology studies the influence of ethnic groups, and nationality on human behavior and mental processes. You will learn a little of this in a chapter titled "Social Psychology".

Biological psychology

Branch of neuroscience that focuses on the relationship between behavior and physiological events within the nervous system.

BIOLOGICAL PERSPECTIVE Studies the biological basis of behavior. **Biological psychologists** investigate such things as the association between behavior and drugs, hormones, genes, and brain processes. They also investigate the brain processes involved in emotion, learning, memory, and disordered behaviors. This type of psychology is at the forefront of science because of advances in neurosciences, and medicine. The third chapter titled "The Biology of Behavior" will give you a very good idea of this perspective.

EVOLUTIONARY PERSPECTIVE In 1975, E. O. Wilson, an entomologist, published a work titled "Sociobiology: The New Synthesis", which argues that there is a biological basis for the social behavior of all social animals and even social insects like ants. Darwin's theory of evolution forms the bedrock of this perspective, but higher human behaviors such as altruism, and despicable behaviors such as ethnocide, are both explained

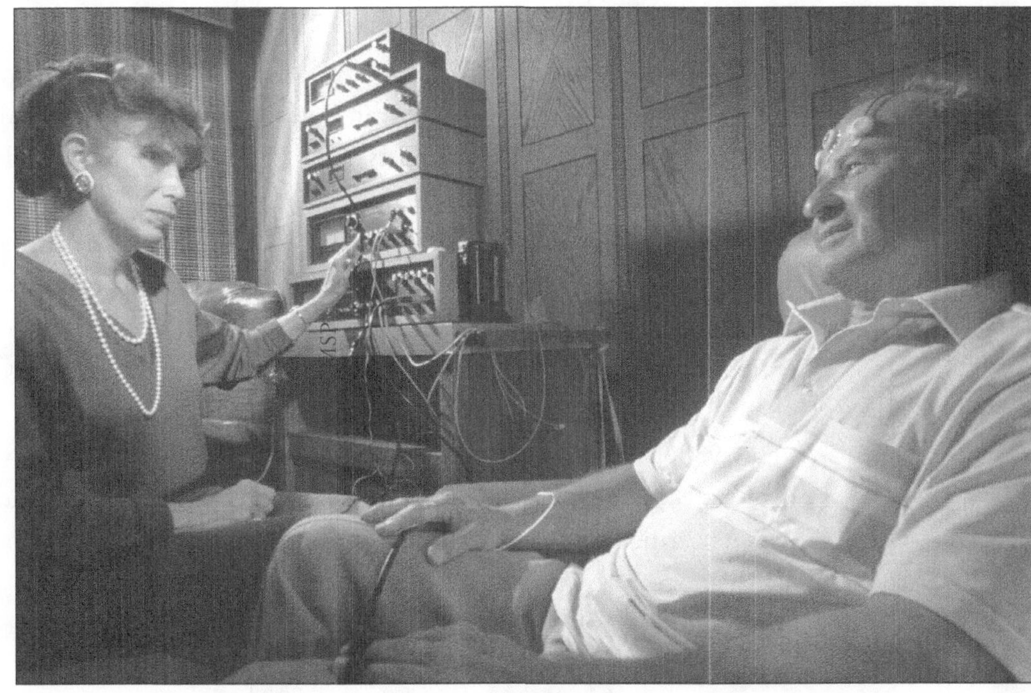

Biological psychologists attempt to explain behavior in terms of physiological or biological process.

on the basis that it is the survival of the gene pool, that is important, not the survival of individual organisms, and that organisms do what they do, in order to allow the continuation of their genes.

Psychology Professionals

There are several varieties of Psychology professionals, but they can be sub-divided into two main groups. One is that of the Experimental Psychologists and the other of the Clinicians. Experimentalists conduct research and try to discover fundamental facts about human and animal nature. Clinical Psychologists treat patients on the basis of the fundamental facts about human nature discovered by the Experimentalists.

By the time you are done with this course, you will get a pretty good idea of the variety of sub-disciplines in which experimental psychologists conduct research. They are generally employed at a University, and teach students in addition to conducting research.

There are three different types of Clinicians who deal with mental health. **The Clinical psychologist** is trained by a Psychology department and he/she treats patients who are sane but have severe behavioral or emotional problems.

A Counseling psychologist is generally trained not by a Psychology department but either by a School of Social work, or by a School of Education. Counseling psychologists help normal, sane people cope with temporary behavioral or emotional problems caused by difficult circumstances, such as the death of a loved one, or the bitter divorce of parents, etc.

The third mental health professional is a **Psychiatrist**. A Psychiatrist is a physician with a M.D. degree, and specializes in drug therapy as well as other talk therapies. A psychiatrist is licensed to prescribe mind-altering drugs, which in most States of the United States, a Clinical psychologist or a Counseling psychologist is not allowed to do.

PSYCHOLOGICAL ASSOCIATIONS During its brief history, psychology has grown by leaps and bounds. The American Psychological Association (APA), the major professional organization of psychologists in the United States, was founded in 1892 by 31 charter members. The APA now has 134,000 members. The APA presently recognizes 54 divisions or specialties within psychology. Even with an increasing number of divisions within the APA, many members believe that the mission of APA is directed more towards clinical applications than towards basic research. As a result, a new psychological association was organized.

American Psychological Association (APA)

The major professional organization of psychologists in the United States.

American Psychological Society (APS)

Professional group of academic and research psychologists founded in 1988.

In 1988 the **American Psychological Society (APS)** was founded with the stated purpose of better representing the academic and research interests of psychology. It is now known as Association for Psychological Science (APS) and maintains a web-site with research articles and resources for Teaching Psychologists.

SUMMARY

DEFINITION OF PSYCHOLOGY

1. Formally defined, psychology is the scientific study of behavior and mental processes in context.
2. The theories and facts of psychology emerge from the careful application of scientific methods.

HISTORY OF PSYCHOLOGY

3. Psychology has roots in both philosophy, which posed many of the important questions, and physiology, which provided the tools for careful, scientific examination of these questions.
4. The establishment of Wilhelm Wundt's laboratory at the University of Leipzig in 1879 marks the formal beginnings of psychology as a scientific discipline.
5. Wundt employed the methods of introspection and experimental self-observation to pursue what he considered to be the task of psychology—the systematic study of the structure of the conscious adult mind. This school of thought was later labeled structuralism.
6. Structuralism soon gave way to the more practical psychology of William James, who emphasized the functional nature of the mind. James accepted evolution and professed that the mind had evolved because it helped organisms to adapt to their environment. His school of thought was called functionalism.
7. Sigmund Freud, a neurologist, developed his highly subjective psychoanalytic approach around 1902, or early 20th century. Freud put great emphasis on the unconscious mind and repressed irrational urges and drives, based on his experience with patients who complained of abnormal symptoms.
8. In the first few decades of the twentieth century, a new force in psychology called behaviorism emerged. This approach, championed by John B. Watson, and later greatly expanded by B. F. Skinner, disregarded internal mental events and focused exclusively on observed behaviors, their antecedents and their consequences. Behaviorism was sometimes derided as Stimulus-Response psychology.
9. Gestalt psychology was contemporary to behaviorism. Max Wertheimer pointed out that internal events such as perception were important and that we perceived things as a "whole" rather than as parts put-together and that the whole was greater than the sum of its parts, as in Phi phenomena and other perceptual illusions.
10. Humanistic psychology de-emphasized the impact of both stimulus-response events and unconscious processes in determining human behavior. Instead, it focused on the role of free choice and our desire to fulfill our dreams and better ourselves (self-actualization) as we go through life.
11. Social Psychology studied the influence of peer-group, leadership style, and such other social factors that influence behavior and mental processes.

CONTEMPORARY PSYCHOLOGY

12. Cognitive psychology is an important sub-discipline in psychology that has led to a refocusing of attention on processes such as memory, language, thinking, problem solving, and creativity.
13. Social psychologists seek to understand the impact of social environments and social processes on the individual.
14. Biological psychologists study the relationship between physiological processes and behavior.
15. Life Span psychologists or developmental psychologists study age-related changes in physical growth and psychological development from conception to death.
16 Evolutionary Psychology: A perspective that explains social behavior of humans and animals as biologically based behavior that is initiated to allow the continuation of their gene pool.
17. Both clinical and counseling psychologists are involved in the diagnosis and treatment of psychological problems. Individuals specializing in counseling psychology tend to focus on less serious problems of adjustment than do their counterparts in clinical psychology.
18. While psychologists in every area of specialization usually conduct research at some point in their careers, experimental psychologists devote their primary efforts to conducting research and are not licensed to treat patients.
19. There are two major Professional organizations for psychologists. One is the American Psychological Association or APA and the other, newer one, which caters more to the experimental psychologist, is the Association for Psychological Science or APS.

TERMS AND CONCEPTS

psychology
scientific method
structuralism
functionalism
behaviorism
Gestalt psychology
humanistic psychology
cognitive psychology
developmental psychology
social psychology
personality psychology
experimental psychology
biological psychology
evolutionary psychology
clinical psychology
counseling psychology
educational psychology
artificial intelligence (AI)
American Psychological Association (APA)
American Psychological Society (APS)

CHAPTER 2

The Methods of Psychology

Corbis

Examine the following statements and decide whether they are typically true or false. Base your conclusions on both your personal experiences and your assumptions about human behavior.

- Sleepwalking most often occurs during a dreaming phase of sleep.
- Punishment is not as effective as reinforcement is in changing behavior.
- Humans are the only organisms that use symbolic language to communicate.
- Couples who live together before marriage generally experience happier and more stable marriages than couples who do not live together before getting married.
- The most beneficial way to treat severe mental disorders is to have people relive traumatic childhood experiences through psychoanalysis.

Most students evaluate all or most of the above statements as true. You may be surprised to find that they are all false. Indeed, many of the things people presume to be true about behavior are fallacies. To safeguard against the fallibility of common sense, psychologists have developed a number of tools or methods for systematically collecting data about behavior. These scientific methods have disproved many widely held beliefs about human behavior; they have also verified some other common assumptions. In this chapter we outline the methods that psychologists use.

RESEARCH AND RESEARCH METHODS

The Goals of Psychology

Although Psychology was founded as a "science" by Wilhelm Wundt, the goals of the subject were first articulated by John Watson, the founder of Behaviorism. Of course, the goals he stated were in terms of observed behavior. Today, they have been expanded to include mental processes. The goals of psychology are:

1. To describe behavior and mental processes with precision
2. To predict behavior and mental processes
3. To understand or explain behavior and mental processes
4. To be able to modify or influence behavior and mental processes

The first goal, to describe behavior or a mental process with precision is done to reduce controversy when two or more psychologists are observing the same general phenomena. They define the behavior under consideration as specifically as possible. For example, even though a very large variety of behaviors from using foul language to physical violence indicate aggression, a psychologist studying aggression might define it as the number of times a child grabbed a toy from another child, during the time interval in which the child was observed. Or a psychologist studying the effects of Social class of a person on his health, might define Social class as the number of years of schooling beyond high-school that a person has received. Such a clear-cut and exact specification of a behavior, mental process, or concept under study, is known as an **Operational Definition.**

The second goal, prediction, is a goal that is fairly easy to meet. You will soon see how psychologists determine if one phenomenon can be predicted on the basis of another observed phenomena. If you do not know the methodology, it seems like magic. However, we will let you in on that magic in just a little bit, when we explain the methods.

The third goal, to explain or understand behavior, actually means to be able to answer what, how, when, where and why a behavior occurred. Of these questions, the question as to WHY a certain behavior or mental process occurred is considered to be the most important, because, once that question is answered satisfactorily, one knows the cause of the behavior or mental process.

Once the cause of a behavior is known, it is easier to devise ways to prevent the behavior or mental process from occurring or to make it occur, if that is what is desired. In other words, once the cause is known, the psychologists are on their way to meeting the fourth and final goal of their discipline, which is to influence or modify behaviors and mental processes.

The above goals of psychology are met by using certain scientific methods, but before we study the methods themselves, let us take a quick look at the criteria that a subject has to meet in order to be considered a science, rather than an art.

The Demands of Science

In order to be called a *Science* a subject has to meet the following requirements. Science demands that:

1. Professed theories must be testable.
2. Evidence provided to substantiate theories must be "objective".
3. The methodology and results of research studies must be published to allow scrutiny by other scientists.
4. Experimental research studies must be replicable

Let us consider each of these demands in a little more detail:

Theory

A scientific theory is a logical explanation for all of the relevant data or facts scientists have observed regarding certain natural phenomena.

An essential aspect of scientific theories is that they must be both testable and refutable, not to be confused with the common usage of the term used to signify a hunch, a speculation, or an opinion.

Hypothesis

Statement proposing the existence of a relationship between variables, typically as a tentative explanation for cause and effect. Hypotheses are often designed to be tested by research.

Objective evidence

Evidence that can be documented, measured, and verified.

TESTABILITY OF THEORIES: A theory is a position statement taken by a scientist. The statement offers a tentative explanation of a phenomenon under study, and is based on the scientists own logic and knowledge regarding the subject. A theory is also very broad in scope, and therefore, it is not possible to test a theory with one experiment.

Generally, psychologists will select a slice of the phenomena under study and come up with a specific if-then statement based on a theory. This if-then statement is much narrower in scope, and specific enough to be tested experimentally, and is known as a **hypothesis**. A scientist tries to create the if conditions in his laboratory and waits to see if the "then conditions" or effects, fit in with the expectations generated by the theory.

Some perspectives lend themselves more easily to such testing than others because not all theories are testable. The Biological perspective is an example of a very testable perspective. The theory that guides biological psychologists is that the biological mechanisms of the brain account for mental phenomena and behavior. Based on this theory, it is logical to conclude that if brain mechanisms are altered, corresponding mental phenomena and/or behavior should change. This can easily be tested by actually altering various brain mechanisms, especially in lower animals and observing corresponding behavioral changes, or by temporarily altering brain chemistry by means of drug administration and assessing mental phenomena of humans via tests, to assess changes brought on by the administered drug.

On the other hand, there are some theories that are essentially un-testable because it is not possible to create the "if" conditions. For example Sigmund Freud's theory that unconscious sexual urges experienced by children influence their adult behavior, is essentially an un-testable theory because there is no way to manipulate unconscious sexual urges and create them on demand, or to measure them because they are unconscious, which means a person is unaware of having them.

OBJECTIVE VERSUS SUBJECTIVE EVIDENCE: **Objective Evidence** is evidence that can be documented, measured and verified. Outward behavior and some physiological events such as changes in blood pressure, or heart-rate or pulse, etc., are measurable, and can be documented and verified. **Subjective evidence** on the other hand, is evidence that only the person experiencing it has. There is no recordable, measurable event. For example, a person who is visiting the U.S. for the very first time in his life, might go into a building, and feel like he has been there before! Such an experience is known as a *Déja vu.* No matter how strongly he feels he has seen all this before, his travel records indicate that he has never been to the U.S. before this trip, which means all he has, is his feeling, and that could be due to a faulty memory. No matter how authentic his self-reports are, scientists will not take him seriously because of the lack of any objective evidence.

PUBLIC VERIFICATION OF RESULTS: Once a psychologist has conducted a study and obtained certain results, she is expected to publish her research in a peer-reviewed journal. Such a peer-review offers scrutiny of her methods, logic and findings, which puts the theory she is operating under, on a firmer scientific footing.

REPLICATION OF EXPERIMENTAL STUDIES: Once a new or ground-breaking study is published in a peer-reviewed journal, other scientists take an interest in the subject and try to replicate or reproduce the experiment. If they too get very similar results, then the theory on which the work was based is said to be supported. Typically, hundreds of different psychologists, hailing from very different Universities or laboratories try to replicate interesting studies. If several such studies report consistent findings, the theory becomes more strongly established.

Science is a process. Scientists recognize that any theory might have to be modified or discarded as new evidence or new knowledge becomes available. Thus every scientist scrutinizes the work of those who have studied the subject before him, and tries to uncover what has been left unaddressed, so it can be addressed in his own research. Thus, slowly but surely, useless theories get weeded out, and those that have substantial objective evidence supporting them, continue to get taught and be explored further.

RESEARCH METHODS

Psychologists use a number of methods to study behavior, ranging from measuring behavior in highly controlled laboratory environments to producing detailed case studies of specific individuals.

Table 2.1 summarizes the major research methods used by psychologists. Each of these strategies has advantages or disadvantages for investigating different types of questions about behavior and some of them are presented in Table 2.1.

TABLE 2.1 A Summary of Research Methods

METHOD	BRIEF DESCRIPTION	ADVANTAGES	LIMITATIONS
Experimental Method	Subjects are presented with specific stimuli under precisely controlled conditions. Researchers using this method directly manipulate a particular set of conditions (independent variable), and then observe its effect on behavior (dependent variable).	Design of laboratory experiments provides control over relevant variables and opportunities to draw conclusions about cause-and-effect relationships.	Artificial nature of the laboratory setting may influence subjects' behaviors. Also, some questions posed by psychologists do not lend themselves to experimental investigation.
Survey Method	A representative group of people are questioned, using interviews or written questionnaires, about their behaviors and attitudes.	Survey allows researchers to obtain information from more people than is practical to study in the laboratory and also may require less investment of time and financial resources than laboratory research.	Do not allow cause-effect inferences to be drawn and provide only limited insights about factors that contribute to behaviors and attitudes of people.
Observational Method	Researchers observe their subjects as they go about their usual activities, which often take place in a natural setting.	Often provides a wealth of information, which may generate hypotheses for further research in a more controlled environment. Also, there are some clear advantages to seeing and recording behavior firsthand instead of relying on reports made by others.	Subjects' behavior may be altered by the presence of an observer. Furthermore, the reliability of recorded observations may sometimes be compromised by preexisting observer biases.
Case Studies	Involve in-depth explorations of either a single case or a small group of subjects who are examined individually.	Many different methods can be used to gather data (direct observation, testing, etc.), and this flexibility provides researchers excellent opportunities for acquiring insight into specific behaviors.	Lack of investigative control of important variables, potential for subjective observer bias, and poor sampling techniques often limit generalization of findings to other people in the clinical category being investigated.
Correlational Method	Statistical methods are used to assess and describe the amount and type of relationship between two variables of interest.	Can be used to answer questions about some kinds of relationships that cannot be clarified by other research methods. Findings expressed in mathematical values provide a strong basis for making predictions about behavior.	This technique, by itself, does not allow researchers to conclude that a demonstrated relationship between two variables means that one is causing the other.

Non-experimental Research Methods

CASE STUDIES A **case study** is an in-depth exploration of either a single subject or a small group of subjects who are examined individually. This method is not used to study normal behavior. Only individuals who manifest behaviors which are considered to be

Case study

Method of research that involves in-depth study of one or more subjects who are examined individually using direct observation, testing, experimentation, and other methods.

abnormal are studied this way. The therapist who is treating the person writes an in-depth life-story of the person, along with the therapy used, results on personality tests, and other such relevant and useful information, in order to allow insights into the most likely reasons for the manifestation of the abnormality.

Much of our current information about criminal behavior, incest victims, disorders such as multiple personality, and other unusual conditions has been obtained using this approach. Case studies have provided valuable insights into such conditions, and have led to other methods of studying them. The case Study Method is also known as the Clinical Method, and is considered to be a descriptive method which allows insight into the behavior but does not allow cause-effect connections to be drawn.

Survey

Research method in which a representative sample of people are questioned about their behaviors or attitudes. The survey provides descriptive information.

SURVEYS AND QUESTIONNAIRES A second important research method is the **survey**, in which a representative group of people is questioned about their behaviors or attitudes. Psychologists use this method when they are interested in obtaining information from more people than it is practical to study in the laboratory—for instance, to find out how college students feel about men and women sharing domestic chores at home or to determine the television viewing habits or shopping habits of people in a certain age group, or to determine attitudes about controversial issues, etc.

A carefully constructed questionnaire is likely to reveal trends that exist in the general population even though only a small percentage of that population is surveyed. Surveys and interviews primarily allow description of the behaviors or processes under study and do not allow cause-effect connections to be drawn. Hence they are considered to be descriptive methods.

Sample

Selected segment of a larger population that is being studied in psychological research. Two kinds of samples are the representative sample and the random sample.

Random sample

Sample group of a larger population that is selected by randomization procedures. A random sample differs from a representative sample.

Representative sample

Sample in which critical subgroups are represented according to their incidence in the larger population that the researcher is studying.

How Samples are Selected for Survey Most research questions relate to a population much too large to be studied in its entirety. For example, if you wished to find out how the use of marijuana affects adolescent problem-solving ability and scholastic achievement, your relevant population would include teenagers from all over the world. Even if you decided to limit your observations to American adolescents, your target group would still be prohibitively large; you could never evaluate all its members.

Psychologists get around this difficulty by gathering data from a relatively small **group** or selected segment of the entire population that interests them but apply the results to the population as a whole. For the results derived from a small group of subjects or a **sample**, to be applicable to, i.e., to **generalize** to a population, the sample must meet two criteria. These criteria are, one, it must be a **random sample** and second, it must also be a **representative sample.**

REPRESENTATIVE SAMPLES A sample in which all the various sub-groups within a population are equally represented (McCall, 1980). For example, if a researcher is interested in the average IQ of Americans, and he is going to actually administer IQ tests to a couple of thousand people, then he must make sure that along with the majority group he also has subjects from the various ethnic minorities, such as African-Americans, Native-Americans, Japanese-Americans etc. in the same proportion, as in the population at large. In short, if 15% of the population is African –American and 10% is Native American, then 15% of his sample will be made up of African Americans and 10% of the sample will be composed of Native Americans.

RANDOM SAMPLES A random sample is a sample in which the subjects participating in the study were selected by chance rather than because of any particular attribute. Selection by chance affords any member of the population an equal opportunity to participate in the study, in comparison with any other member of the population (McCall, 1980).

Suppose you wanted to conduct a phone survey, and wanted a random sample, you might say, "I will phone every third person listed on every page of the telephone directory of my city". If you do that, you will have a random sample, but not necessarily a representative sample. To get a representative sample you will have to put in much more work, and might have to filter your randomly selected subjects in terms of their ethnicity, till you get your random and representative sample.

If the sample is not gathered by random selection or is not representative of the population, the conclusions reached by the researcher are often incorrect. A famous example illustrating the danger of demographic bias was the 1936 survey poll of more than 2 million people that led to a prediction that Republican presidential candidate Alf Landon would defeat Democratic incumbent Franklin Roosevelt by a landslide. In fact, the reverse happened.

The poll was dead wrong because the survey sample was selected by picking names from telephone directories, which gave them a random sample, but did not yield a representative sample because, in those Depression years, only the well-to-do had telephones, and the wealthy favored Landon. Since then, political survey techniques have been greatly refined so that such errors rarely happen nowadays.

Observational method

Method of psychological research in which subjects are observed as they go about their usual activities. The observational method provides descriptive information.

Still another caution in using the survey method concerns the design of the questions themselves. Psychologists have learned, often to their dismay, that *even very minor changes in the wording of a question can alter people's responses.* For example, Elizabeth Loftus (1975) found that subjects who were asked, "Do you get headaches *occasionally* and if so, how often?" reported an average of 0.7 headaches a week; a comparable group of subjects who were asked, "Do you get headaches *frequently* and if so how often?" reported a weekly average of 2.2 headaches. Clearly, a considerable amount of thought and careful attention must be applied in constructing survey questions.

Finally, surveys are not appropriate for every research project. A survey can provide a broad profile of attitudes and behaviors of a large group, but it cannot look closely at specific individuals to understand their behaviors or attitudes. Psychologists must use other methods to provide that kind of information.

THE OBSERVATIONAL METHOD A third research method is the **observational method** wherein researchers observe their subjects as they go about their usual activities.

Corbis

Dr. Jane Goodall observing a family of chimpanzees is an example of naturalistic observation.

Naturalistic observation

Psychological research using the observational method that takes place in a natural setting, such as a subject's home or school environment.

This research method often takes place in a natural setting and is called **Naturalistic observation**. If the observation is conducted in the laboratory, as in the case of animals, it is called Contrived or **Laboratory observation**, and yields different results as compared to naturalistic observation of the same animals.

Like the survey method, the observational method provides descriptive information. For instance, in the study of children's aggressive behavior discussed earlier in this chapter, researchers might observe that when children become aggressive, adults pay more attention to them. This observation might lead to the hypothesis that aggressive behaviors in children are likely to increase in keeping with the amount of adult attention they produce. This hypothesis cannot be tested by using the observational method, since it does not provide any way of controlling variables. Nevertheless, such observations could serve as an excellent starting point for further research in a more controlled environment.

Limitations of the Observational Method Like the case studies and the survey, direct observation is not appropriate for every research question.

Observer bias

Tendency of an observer to read more into a situation than is actually there or to see what he or she expects to see. Observer bias is a potential limitation of the observational method.

One potential problem of the observational method is the risk of subjectivity, or **observer bias**: An observer may have certain expectations or beliefs which may predispose him to neglect phenomenon that does exist, or even perceive phenomenon that does not exist. Psychologists conducting observational research generally try to avoid making biased interpretations by keeping very careful records of their observations. Sometimes audiovisual records that can be evaluated by independent observers are also used in the effort to minimize observer bias.

Another potential problem is that the presence of a human observer may affect the behavior being observed. For example, children on a playground may behave less aggres-

Observer effect

Tendency of subjects to modify behavior because they are aware of being observed.

sively simply because they are being watched by a strange adult. *Most psychologists will hide themselves to prevent or conduct covert observation, to prevent* ***observer effect.***

Despite its potential disadvantages, direct observation often produces valuable information when it is carefully conducted. In addition, there are some clear advantages to seeing and measuring behavior firsthand instead of relying on reports given by others. In addition, direct observation can provide some important insights into relationships that may exist in a particular behavioral area.

CORRELATIONAL METHOD Some types of questions cannot be answered by surveys, direct observation, or case studies. For instance, because you know that colleges use Scholastic Aptitude Test (SAT) scores to determine admissions, you might wonder if SAT scores are related to success in college. You could define "success in college" as a high Grade Point Average (GPA) and collect the SAT scores and first-year GPAs of a large sample of college freshmen. The SAT scores collected by you would be termed variable X and the GPA scores would be termed variable Y. You would then use a statistical formula in which you would plug the values of all the Xs and the Ys to analyze the data and determine the relationship between these two variables. This research technique is called the **correlational method**, and the statistic used to describe the amount and type of relationship is called the **coefficient of correlation.**

Correlational method

Research method that uses statistical techniques to determine the degree of relationship between variables.

Coefficient of correlation

Statistic used to describe the degree of relationship between two or more variables. Positive correlations indicate that variables vary together in the same direction; negative correlations indicate the opposite.

A coefficient of correlation is designated as "r" and always falls somewhere between +1.00 and –1.00. The plus and minus signs show the direction in which the changes are linked and the number indicates the strength of the relationship. A plus sign indicates a positive correlation, which means that as X increases, so does Y. A minus sign indicates a negative correlation, which means that as the value of X increases, the value of Y decreases. A correlation coefficient of r = 1, indicates a perfect correlation, or that the two variables are very tightly linked, so if one is known, the other can be predicted with 100% accuracy or confidence. A value of r = zero indicates a weak or nonexistent relationship between the two variables so it is not possible to predict the value of one variable based on the value of the other.

If the data you collected on SAT scores and GPA scores yielded a positive correlation coefficient, especially one that was closer to number 1 than to zero, then the use of SAT scores to limit admissions to college would make sense. If the value of r was closer to zero, one would not have used SAT scores to determine admission, because there would be no relationship at all between doing well on the SAT and doing well in college. On the other hand if the value of r was a negative number, it would indicate that the two variables, X and Y or SAT scores and GPA respectively, are related, but vary in opposite directions, or that those who do well on one of the two variables do poorly on the other

In fact, college administrators use SAT scores because it is known that SAT scores are positively correlated with college GPA. Students who obtain high SAT scores tend to achieve high GPAs and those with low SAT scores tend to have lower grades. This relationship is far from a perfect 1.00, however. In the real world, correlations between variables are virtually never perfect.

TABLE 2.2 Positive Correlation Between SAT Scores and Freshman GPA for Five Students

SUBJECT	SAT SCORE	GPA
1	595	2.15
2	621	2.67
3	650	3.45
4	652	3.20
5	712	3.85

FIGURE 2.1 Positive Correlation Between SAT Scores and Freshman GPA for Five Students

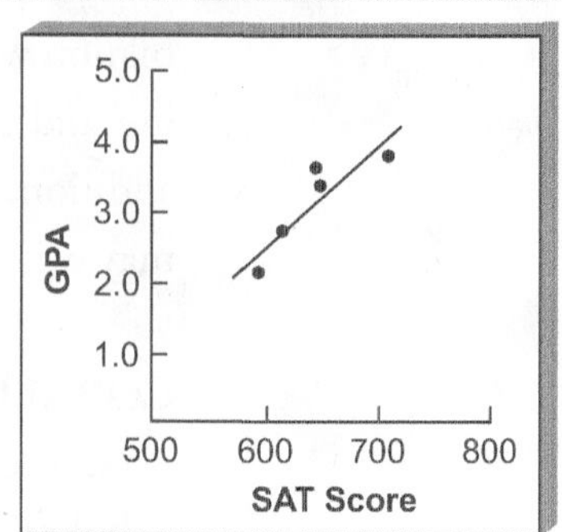

Table 2.2 provides the raw data on both the variables for five students, and also shows the variables plotted on a graph. Had all the points fallen directly on the straight line the correlation would have been 1.00. As the points get further from the line the correlation gets closer to 0.

Limitations of Correlational Studies Correlational studies help us discover relationships between variables, but it is important not to read more into them than is there. One of the most *common mistakes* people make in interpreting correlational studies *is to conclude that because two factors are related, one causes the other.* Certainly, this is sometimes the case. Observations of drivers negotiating obstacle courses under the influence of alcohol, for instance, reveal a positive correlation between error scores and blood alcohol levels (the higher the level, the greater the number of errors). This correlational relationship is a causal one, since alcohol is known to impair the brain's ability to perceive, interpret, and respond to stimuli.

On the other hand, a consistent relationship between two factors is not always causal. In some cases *a third factor,* related to each of the other two, may account for the apparent causal relationship. For example, years ago, scientists in California had observed that a small marine creature named **Aplysia** burrowed itself into the sand a few hours before a high tide and would burrow itself out in time for a low tide. The Aplysia continued this behavior linked to California tides even when transported to a laboratory on the Florida coast! The scientists could actually predict the occurrence of high and low tide in California by observing the Aplysia in the Florida laboratory. Obviously, the creature was not causing the California high tide or low tide any more than the tide was causing the creature's behavior in the Florida lab. Although correlated to each other, there was no causal relationship in this case. In sum, it is dangerous to read causal effects into correlational studies. You will find a more in-depth discussion of statistical correlation in the Appendix.

The problem with the research methods just discussed is that they do not allow for precise control over the various factors that may influence the behavior being studied. One research technique that does allow this control is the experimental method. All things considered, this is often the research approach preferred by psychologists and is described next.

Experimental Research Methods

Experimental research
Research conducted in precisely controlled laboratory conditions in which subjects are confronted with specific stimuli and their reactions are carefully measured to discover relationships among variables.

Independent variable
Condition or factor that the experimenter manipulates in order to determine whether changes in behavior (the dependent variable) result.

Dependent variable
In experimental research, the behavior that results from manipulation of an independent variable.

Experimental group
In experimental research, a group of subjects who are exposed to different varieties of independent variables, so that resulting behaviors can be compared.

Control group
In experimental psychology, a group of subjects who experience all the same conditions as subjects in the experimental group except for the key factor (independent variable) the researcher is evaluating.

THE EXPERIMENTAL METHOD In **experimental research**, subjects are presented with specific stimuli under precisely controlled conditions that allow their reactions to be reliably measured. The major advantage of the experimental method is that it allows the researcher to control conditions, ruling out all possible influences on subjects' behaviors other than the factors that are being investigated.

A research psychologist using this method directly manipulates a particular set of conditions, termed the **independent variable**. The researcher then observes its effect on behavior. The effects are termed the **dependent variable** because their occurrence depends on the presentation of the Independent Variable. All of the other variables, which could affect the behavior being studied, and which are either controlled or eliminated by the researcher, are known as **"Extraneous Variables"**.

Suppose a researcher suspects that Marijuana use is linked to poor memory and is interested in determining whether the use of Marijuana diminishes recall. The researcher's first step would be to recruit a group of subjects who are as similar as possible in age, educational background, IQ, etc., to ensure a homogenous subject pool, for example, freshmen students at a particular college. He would then use a procedure that ensures **random selection of subjects for a random sample**, from that pool of subjects. After recruiting the subjects, the researcher would **randomly assign** them to one or the other of two different groups. The two different groups would be the **experimental group** and the **control group**.

The Experimental Group, would receive "the independent variable" or pills containing Marijuana (or its active chemical ingredient), which is the suspected cause. The Control Group, which is a comparison group, would not receive pills with Marijuana in them, but might receive inert pills, or placeboes. Both groups would then be given the same paper and pencil questionnaire to test their recall. The researcher would then compute the average score on the test for each of the two groups. If the average score of the Experimental group was much lower than the average score of the Control group, the researcher could conclude that since they come from the same college, with the same SAT cut-off, have very similar educational backgrounds, their scores on the test should have been similar. The only thing that could account for the poor performance of the Experimental group would be the Marijuana they had received at the start of the experiment.

The similarity of the subjects in terms of their SAT scores, etc., would have controlled some **extraneous variables** that influence test scores. There would be other variables, such as use of a drug privately by some participants, fatigue, or lack of sleep that some participants might have experienced the day of the test, etc. A good researcher will eliminate these by giving specific directions as to what a subject may do and not do, eat, or not eat, etc., before the experiment. The researcher would also make sure that the subjects complied with the directions before allowing them to participate in the experiment.

The experimental design explained above is known as a **between subjects design**. Not all experiments involve comparisons between two different groups of subjects who form the experimental and control groups, as described above. In some cases it is more desirable to compare individual subjects to themselves under different conditions. For example, a psychologist might compare the scores of a group of subjects on one test of recall, to their scores on another similar or equivalent test, given to them after they have been administered the Independent Variable. In this case the same subject serves in both the experimental and control conditions, but at different times, generally before and after the administration of the Independent Variable or the treatment. This type of design is known as a **within subjects design**.

Most researchers will repeat their own studies with variation in design, subject pools, intensity of the Independent variable, etc. Even so, no researcher bases his final conclusions in support of his theory based on a few experiments that he has conducted. As explained earlier, several scientists have to replicate the study and the results before such results are accepted by the scientific community as a whole.

Limitations of the Experimental Method We have discussed some of the positive aspects of experimental laboratory research. The experimental method also has some limitations. One limitation is simply that not all questions posed by psychologists lend themselves to experimental investigation. For instance, we might be interested in the effects of severe malnutrition on learning and memory. These kinds of data could not be gathered by manipulating variables in a laboratory setting. Instead, you would need to take your investigation to real families or natural settings. Such methods are called quasi-experimental methods, and psychologists do use them, with full understanding of their limitations.

The appropriateness of the experimental method has sometimes been questioned for another reason besides its artificial nature: A number of experimental studies have been criticized on ethical grounds.

Ethics in Psychological Experiments

In past years, several controversial studies have prompted serious questions about the ethics of some psychological experiments. Consider the following example and decide whether you think any ethical principles were violated.

THE STANLEY MILGRAM SHOCK EXPERIMENT In 1963 Stanley Milgram a son of European Jews, who had immigrated to the United States, published the results of his experiments and created shock waves in the world of academia. Milgram was an Assistant Professor of Psychology at Yale University, and had given much thought as to how and why the Holocaust could have happened. Milgram had wondered if people in any part of the world, would similarly obey authority and perpetrate unjust and cruel acts. He created an experiment where subjects were divided into "teachers" and "learners".

The teachers were to teach and test the student from behind a panel which had a range of electric shocks, clearly marked as "slight" "medium" "intense" and "very dangerous". With every error made by the student, the teacher had to administer the next higher shock. The teacher was made aware of how painful the shocks might get, by allowing the teacher to experience the lowest shock at the start of the experiment. The shocks ranged from 15 to 450 volts, but the panel was not actually connected to a shock generator (Milgram, 1963).

In reality, the "learners" were stooges of the experimenter and were never given a shock. They were provided with a script and were asked to vocalize their pain, in increasing intensity every time a light came on, indicating that a shock had been given to them by their "teacher". The "teachers" who heard the learner in pain, often wondered whether they should give the next higher intensity shock with the next error, however, the "authority" in the room, who was the experimenter in a lab coat, would say "continue teacher" in a stern voice.

Stanley Milgram discovered that under these conditions, almost 65% of the subjects who served as teachers, went all the way to 450 volts, or used the shock clearly marked as "Danger severe shock" to punish the learner! In other words, *Milgram had provided evidence that the pressure to obey authority can take precedence over one's own conscience and judgment.*

Milgram was criticized by his colleagues and the newspapers for deceiving the subjects who served as teachers and for causing them anguish. Milgram's study was replicated in other areas of the world, and the results were similar. Milgram left Yale and was invited to teach at Harvard, but was denied tenure at Harvard, partly because of the negativity generated by the deception used in the experiment (Blass, 2002).

Was it unethical of Milgram to deceive his subjects? Could he have obtained similar findings without deception, in a more ethical way? What do you think?

THE STANFORD UNIVERSITY PRISONER STUDY (Please see the following Web site hosted by Dr. Zimbardo, for astounding details and a slide show, of this controversial study: http://www.prisonexp.org/). The now famous Stanford University prisoner study was conducted in the summer of 1971, by social psychologist Philip Zimbardo and his colleagues (Haney & Zimbardo, 1977; Zimbardo, 1975).

These investigators had real Palo Alto police search, hand-cuff and arrest people as their neighbors, and other on-lookers watched. These people had no idea that they were about to be arrested and taken to a jail on the Stanford campus. They had, though, previously answered an advertisement regarding an experiment on prison life and had given an "informed consent" to being locked up in a jail on the Stanford campus, for which they would be paid at the rate of $15.00 per night.

Zimbardo and his colleagues were investigating this phenomenon because they had wondered about the cause of the atrocities committed by the guards in Hitler's camps. They also had a former prisoner serve as a consultant in the construction of their jail, etc. Even so, they say they had not anticipated the profoundly disturbing impact of this experience on students cast as guards or prisoners in their study.

The guards soon became so cruel that several of the prisoners suffered emotional reactions ranging from depression to anxiety and even extreme rage (not unlike the responses of many inmates in genuine penal institutions). As soon as Zimbardo and his associates became aware of the severe impact their study was having on their subjects, they terminated the experiment. Should this experiment have been conducted? Was it unethical to place humans in a situation that could have led to hostile confrontations?

Ethical Guidelines for Research

Nevertheless, such studies generated a debate about ethics in research that ultimately culminated in the American Psychological Association's (APA) adopting a list of ethical guidelines in 1973. Since then, researchers are required to meet stringent guidelines to ensure that subjects don't come to any physical or psychological harm. *Subjects are told of* ***their right to an informed consent****, and experimenters are required to disclose all the treatments that the participator will be subjected to.*

Some researchers seemed relatively satisfied with Milgram's response to his critics. The issue of deception in research remains controversial. Some studies would lose their effectiveness if participating subjects knew in advance exactly what the experimenter was studying. *The APA's guideline provides that if deception must be used, a post-experiment debriefing must thoroughly explain to participants why it was necessary.* At such time, subjects must be allowed to request that their data be removed from the study and destroyed.

Sometimes it is hard for researchers to objectively weigh the potential benefits of a study against the possibility of harming its subjects. Recognizing the difficulty of this task, virtually every institution conducting research in the United States has established ethics committees or Institutional Review Boards that review all proposed studies. If they perceive that subjects' welfare (humans or other animals) is insufficiently safeguarded, the proposal must be modified or the research cannot be conducted.

The APA's list of ethical principles, together with the activities of institutional review boards, makes it very unlikely that subjects in a research study would be harmed in any way. Researchers who do not adhere to this strict code of ethics risk serious professional and legal consequences.

STATISTICAL CONCEPTS FOR RESEARCH

Regardless of the research method used, psychologists generally end up with data that must be described and interpreted. Usually the data are in the form of numbers that can be analyzed by **statistics**, via mathematical methods for describing and interpreting data. There are essentially two kinds of statistics: descriptive and inferential.

Descriptive statistics summarizes large amounts of data into a form that is easily interpreted. Providing bar graphs, averages, etc., are ways of summarizing data. Once data have been described, psychologists often draw inferences or conclusions about their findings based on special statistical procedures that allow conclusions to be drawn. Such statistical tests form **inferential statistics**.

You might recall the experiment where one group received pills containing Marijuana and the other group that served as the Control group received an inert pill. Even if the researcher finds that the Marijuana group performed poorly on the test as compared to the placebo group, the researcher cannot be absolutely sure that the lower average of the Marijuana group was indeed due to Marijuana, because it could have been a fluke. It might reflect the same difference in averages you might get, if you randomly picked two sets of numbers and worked out their averages.

The problem for the researcher is to determine whether differences between the two groups are due to the independent variable or simply due to chance.

A variety of tests have been devised by statisticians to answer this question. *Such procedures are called tests of* ***statistical significance***. Statisticians have documented the slight differences that occur, when a bunch of numbers are picked at random and subjected to comparison of the means. When scientists conclude that a research finding is statistically significant, they are stating that they are confident the difference in the means of the two groups is large enough, that it could not have occurred if there was no consistent difference in the scores of the two groups.

Evaluating Opinions, Beliefs, and Scientific Evidence

We have seen in this chapter that psychological research can be hindered by a number of factors, including difficulties in obtaining representative samples, ethical considerations, experimenter bias, and a variety of other problems. We have also seen that research psychologists have shown remarkable versatility in their efforts, collecting data in many different ways. Thus, a major strength of psychological research is its reliance on a wide assortment of methodological techniques.

A major goal of this textbook is to teach you to think critically and to ask questions about how we have come to conclusions about behavior. Some of the questions that will help you evaluate the quality of the research are:

What type of methodology was used? Were sufficient scientific principles adhered to?

Is there any reason to suspect bias in the selection of subjects?

Can the results be applied to individuals other than those in the sample group? How broad can these generalizations be and still remain legitimate?

Is it possible that the method used to obtain information may have biased the findings? For instance, did the questionnaire promote false replies? Is it likely that the artificial nature of the laboratory setting influenced subjects' responses?

Have there been any other published reports that confirm or contradict the particular study in question?

Keeping questions such as these in mind is helpful in finding a middle ground between absolute trust and offhand dismissal of a given research study.

Throughout this text we will be discussing research findings related to a wide variety of topics. It will be useful for you to remember some of the advantages and limitations of different research methods as we discuss this research. In addition, this brief review of statistical methods will provide you with a better understanding of how research is interpreted to be either supportive of, or contradictory to, a particular perspective or theory.

SUMMARY

THE GOALS OF PSYCHOLOGY

1. The goals of psychology are understanding, predicting, and influencing behavior.
2. For the most part, our understanding of behavioral phenomena is expressed in the language of theories. Theories are tentative attempts to provide a logical framework for relevant data or facts regarding certain phenomena.
3. Good psychological theories generate hypotheses, which are expectations about how people should respond under certain conditions, assuming the overall theory is correct.

THE SCIENTIFIC METHOD AND BEHAVIOR

4. Three of the most common reasons why psychologists conduct research are to test a hypothesis, to solve a problem, and to confirm findings of previous research.
5. A hypothesis is a testable statement that proposes a relationship between two or more variables. A hypothesis is based on a theory and is formulated to test the theory or its applications.
6. When psychologists publish new research findings they include details so that others may repeat the experiment to verify the results. The replication of prior research is the backbone of good science.

RESEARCH METHODS

7. Psychologists use a number of methods to study behavior. These techniques include surveys, the observational method, case studies, the correlational method, and the experimental method.
8. An important research method is the survey method, in which a representative group of people are questioned in face-to-face interviews or by using written questionnaires about their behaviors or attitudes.
9. Surveys are often conducted with a representative sample—that is, a sample in which critical subgroups are represented according to their incidence in the larger population about which one wishes to draw conclusions.
10. Another kind of sample, called a random sample, is selected by randomization procedures. A random sample might not yield a representative sample.
11. Potential limitations of the survey method include demographic bias, improperly worded questions that bias responses, and a tendency to provide only limited insights.
12. Researchers employing the observational method observe their subjects as they go about their usual activities. When this research takes place in a natural setting it is called naturalistic observation.
13. A potential problem with the observational method is the risk that an observer may read more into a situation than is actually there. This phenomenon is called observer bias.
14. Another possible limitation of the observational method is the problem of observer effect, in which the presence of a human observer may affect the behavior being observed.
15. The case study is an in-depth exploration of either a single subject or a small group of subjects who are examined individually.
16. Shortcomings of the case study method include lack of investigative control of important variables, a potential for subjective observer bias and a lack of proper sampling techniques that limit the generalization of findings.
17. The correlational method utilizes statistical methods to assess and describe the amount and type of relationship between two variables of interest,

such as the SAT scores of high school seniors and their GPAs during the first year of college.

18. One major limitation of the correlational method is that this technique, considered alone, does not provide any evidence regarding a cause-effect connection between the correlated variables.
19. In experimental research, subjects are presented with specific stimuli under precisely controlled conditions that allow their responses to be reliably measured. The purpose of the experimental method is to discover causal relationships among independent and dependent variables.
20. An independent variable is a condition or factor that the experimenter manipulates because the experimenter hypothesizes that it is the cause of the phenomenon under study; the resulting behavior that is measured and recorded is called the dependent variable because its occurrence depends on the receipt of the causal treatment or the Independent Variable.
21. A formal experiment uses at least one Experimental Group and one Control group. A researcher can, if he so wishes, use two or more Experimental groups and compare them to one Control group, where each of the experimental group receives a different treatment or a different level or dose of the Independent Variable.
22. Special advantages of the experimental method include control over relevant variables and opportunities to draw conclusions about cause-and-effect relationships.
23. A limitation of the experimental method is that some questions posed by psychologists do not lend themselves to experimental investigation because it is not possible to create the Independent Variable or causal conditions in the laboratory. Such questions are answered by using quasi-experimental methods.
24. The APA has adopted ethical guidelines for research that require that a subject be fully informed of the procedures used in the experiment and that the subject give an informed consent to allow the researcher to administer the procedures. These guidelines also require that the research procedures not pose any threat to the mental or physical well-being of the subject and that they protect confidentiality of the data and respect a subject's right to refuse to participate at any time during the course of a study.

STATISTICAL CONCEPTS FOR RESEARCH

25. There are two kinds of statistics: descriptive and inferential. Descriptive statistics provide succinct descriptions by reducing a quantity of data to a form that is more understandable. Inferential statistics include a variety of statistical procedures to draw conclusions about the meaning of data.
26. Inferential statistics allows researchers to make judgments about whether their research findings are statistically significant. When scientists conclude that a research finding is statistically significant, they are stating that obtained differences in

TERMS AND CONCEPTS

operational definition
hypothesis
replication
case study
survey
sample
representative sample
random sample

observational method
naturalistic observation
observer bias
observer effect
correlational method
coefficient of correlation
experimental research
independent variable
dependent variable
experimental groups
control group
statistics
descriptive statistics
inferential statistics
statistical significance

PART II:

Biological Foundations, Perception, and Sleep

CHAPTER 3

The Biology of Behavior

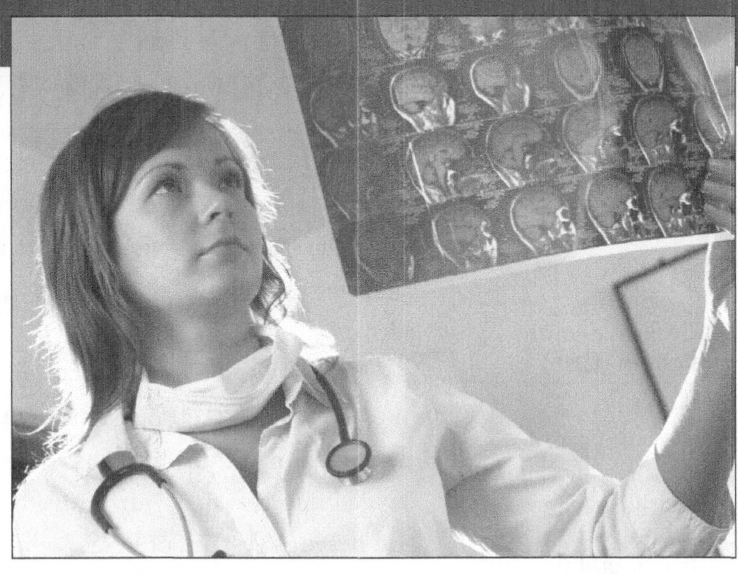

iStock

Although the brain has been viewed as the seat of consciousness for several centuries, some people believe that a soul or a spirit animates the body and allows us our consciousness. Most scientists, however, believe that it is the brain itself that allows us consciousness as it functions.

In this chapter, we will focus on the mechanisms that allow the brain to function as it does.

OVERVIEW OF THE NERVOUS SYSTEM: ORGANIZATION AND FUNCTION

All of our activities—sensing, perceiving, moving, feeling, thinking, or remembering—depend on the functioning of our brain since the brain is a major part of our nervous system. Our nervous system is actually a complex communication system that allows messages to flow from one part of the body to another, via specific pathways known as nerves.

Central nervous system (CNS)

The part of the nervous system that consists of the brain and the spinal cord

Peripheral nervous system (PNS)

Portion of the nervous system that transmits messages to and from the central nervous system. The PNS consists of the somatic nervous system and the autonomic nervous system.

Somatic nervous system

Division of the peripheral nervous system that transmits messages to and from major skeletal muscles as well as from sensory organs to the CNS.

Autonomic nervous system (ANS)

Division of the peripheral nervous system that transmits messages between the central nervous system and the endocrine system as well as the smooth muscles of the heart, lungs, stomach, and other internal organs that operate without intentional control.

Although this nervous system is one continuous, system, scientists artificially divide it into divisions and sub-divisions to make its workings easier to comprehend.

Divisions of the Nervous System: (See Figure 3.1). The nervous system (NS) is subdivided into two major divisions: the **central nervous system**, or **CNS**, and the **peripheral nervous system**, or **PNS**.

The CNS consists of the brain and the spinal cord, and they are the most protected organs of the body. Both are encased in bones and surrounded by protective membranes called meninges. *The CNS plays a central role in coordinating and integrating all bodily functions.* It acts as an intermediary between the stimuli, such as sounds, smells, and touches, etc., which we receive from our environment and our responses to those stimuli. For example, if your bare foot comes in contact with something hairy and wiggly when you put on a shoe, a message of alarm will travel from the nerves in your foot it will go up your leg, go up your spinal cord and reach your brain, and trigger a rapid response that will travel to other internal organs in the brain and back down the spine eventually ending in the muscles of that foot, causing you to experience horror or pain depending on whether or not the hairy thing's fangs have pierced your foot, and to jerk your foot to dislodge the thing!

In the situation just described, the CNS acts as a processor of the incoming "icky" touch message and the generator of the "kick the shoe off" outgoing message. However, the brain also sends commands directly to various parts of our bodies without first receiving an incoming stimulus. For instance, the decision to put on your shoes in the first place may have been the result of a decision to go outdoors—a decision that was unrelated to any immediate environmental stimulus.

Our brains also send commands to glands and internal organs, which allows us to regulate various internal states such as hunger, thirst, etc.

Although the CNS occupies the commanding position in the nervous system, it could neither receive stimuli nor carry out its own directives without the nerves in your leg which are part of the peripheral nervous system (PNS). *The peripheral nervous system transmits messages to and from the central nervous system.* The PNS is subdivided in two functional parts, the *somatic nervous system and the autonomic nervous system.*

The **somatic nervous system** consists of nerve fibers known as ***afferent sensory fibers.*** These carry messages from the body, messages such as touch or pain *to* the spine and ***efferent motor fibers*** which carry messages *from* the brain and spine, or the CNS *to* the muscles of the body, which allow the appropriate part, such as your foot in the above scenario, to move.

FIGURE 3.1 Divisions of the Nervous System

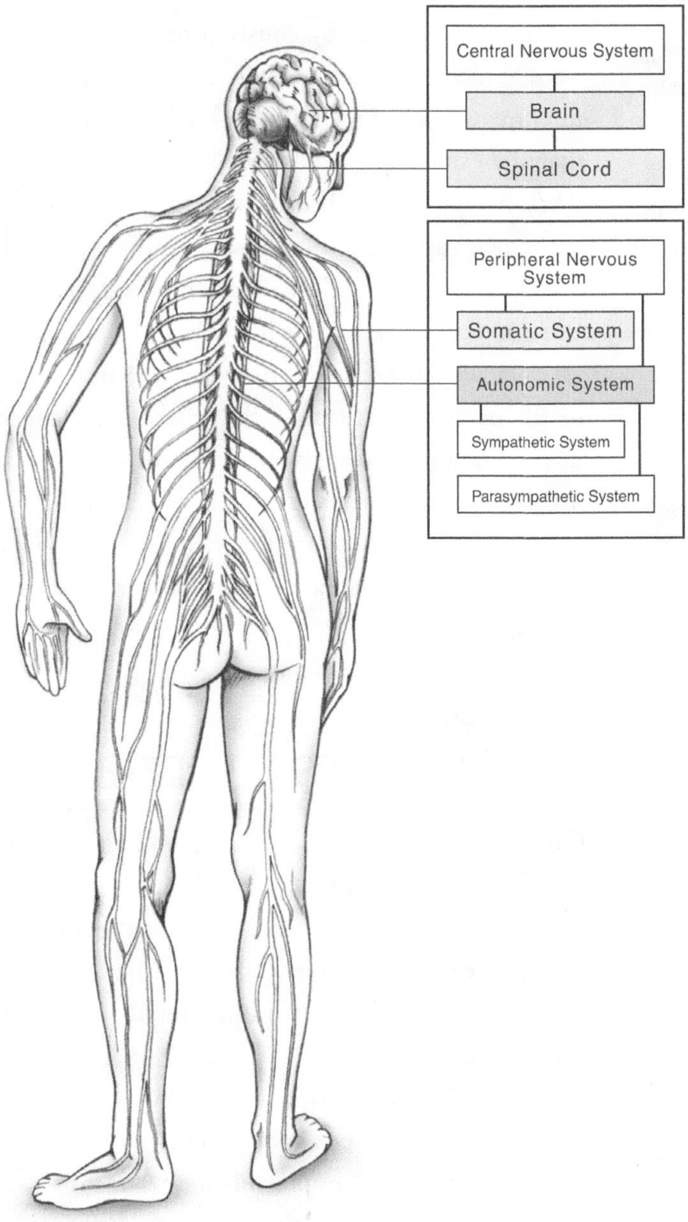

Sympathetic nervous system

Division of the autonomic nervous system that functions to produce emergency responses such as increased heart rate, pupil dilation, and inhibited digestive activity. The sympathetic nervous system works in tandem with the parasympathetic nervous system.

The other division of the PNS is known as the **autonomic nervous system**, or **ANS**. The ANS consists of two functional parts, one is known as the **sympathetic nervous system**, and the other is known as the **parasympathetic nervous system**. These two functional units work hand in hand to allow you to take quick action when you face a threat of some sort, like a threat to your life or your money or your good name.

Of the two units, ***the sympathetic nervous system is an arousal system***, and it alerts you and fires you up as soon as a threat of any kind is perceived. In so doing, it produces several physiological changes such as rapid respiration, to get more oxygen to your brain to enhance its function, dilated pupils to help you to see to a greater distance, opened bronchial passages, and diversion of available glucose to your arm and leg muscles, so the

Parasympathetic nervous system

Division of the autonomic nervous system that functions to conserve energy, returning the body to normal from emergency responses set in motion by the sympathetic nervous system.

Neuron

Type of cell that is the basic unit of the nervous system. A neuron typically consists of a cell body, dendrites, and an axon. Neurons transmit messages to other neurons and to glands and muscles throughout the body.

muscles can function better, etc. *These changes signify arousal and help you escape from the threat or to cope with it.* Once the threat is over, the parasympathetic nervous system brings you back to normal, by constricting the dilated pupils, returning the breathing to your normal rate, etc. The two systems are complementary to each other and the feeling of a mixture of joy and relief that overtakes someone who has escaped a major threat is a sign that the excitement and anxiety producing adrenaline rush is over and the parasympathetic nervous system has taken over.

The **sympathetic nervous** system is termed the "**fight or flight**" system. It actually comes on in any situation where you need to fight, or to flee, or are frightened enough to faint, and any time you are involved in love-making and are aroused.

The **parasympathetic nervous system** is known as the "**housekeeping system**," primarily because it returns all the aroused mechanisms back to normal, which is termed as maintaining **homeostasis**. It also returns the flow of glucose to the internal organs allowing digestion, excretion, etc., which accounts for its name. (See Figure 3.2.)

Now that you have some idea as to the divisions of the nervous system and their functions, let us take a deeper look into the very building blocks of the nervous system, neurons.

NEURONS: BASIC UNITS OF THE NERVOUS SYSTEM

Sensory neuron

Neuron that carries messages to the CNS from receptors in the skin, ears, nose, eyes, and other receptor organs. Also known as afferent neuron.

Motor neuron

Neuron that transmits messages from the CNS to muscles or glands.

Interneuron

Neuron of the central nervous system that functions as an intermediary between sensory and motor neurons.

Our bodies are made up of trillions of living cells including blood cells, skin cells, muscle cells, bone cells and the special cells of the nervous system, which are known as **neurons.** The major difference between all these other cells and *neurons is that the neurons generate their own electricity.* This electricity mediates everything that the brain and our entire nervous system do and the main function of a neuron is to transmit information to its neighboring neurons.

Neurons vary in shape, size, and other characteristics according to their location and function in the nervous system. The brain, for instance, contains the most concentrated mass of neurons. It is impossible to say how many neurons it contains, but estimates range around 100 billion (Fischbach, 1992). Although this is an extraordinarily large number, sheer number alone does not account for the extreme complexity of the brain. An average neuron forms about 15000 connections with other neurons, and it is these connections or neural networks that account for much of the brain's complexity.

There are three major types of neurons. One type, called **sensory** or **afferent neurons,** carries messages to the CNS from receptors in the sense organs, e.g., the skin, ears, nose, eyes, and so forth. The brain and sometimes the spinal cord interpret these messages and send appropriate responses through a second type of neuron called **motor** or **efferent neurons,** which carry information from the brain and spinal cord to muscles and glands. A third type of neuron, known as an **interneuron**, resides only within the central nervous system and it connects a sensory neuron to a motor neuron. Without these connecting interneurons, sensory messages would not result in appropriate bodily responses.

FIGURE 3.2 Functions of the Sympathetic and Parasympathetic Nervous System

These two systems work together to allow our bodies to react quickly to our environments, and to relax.

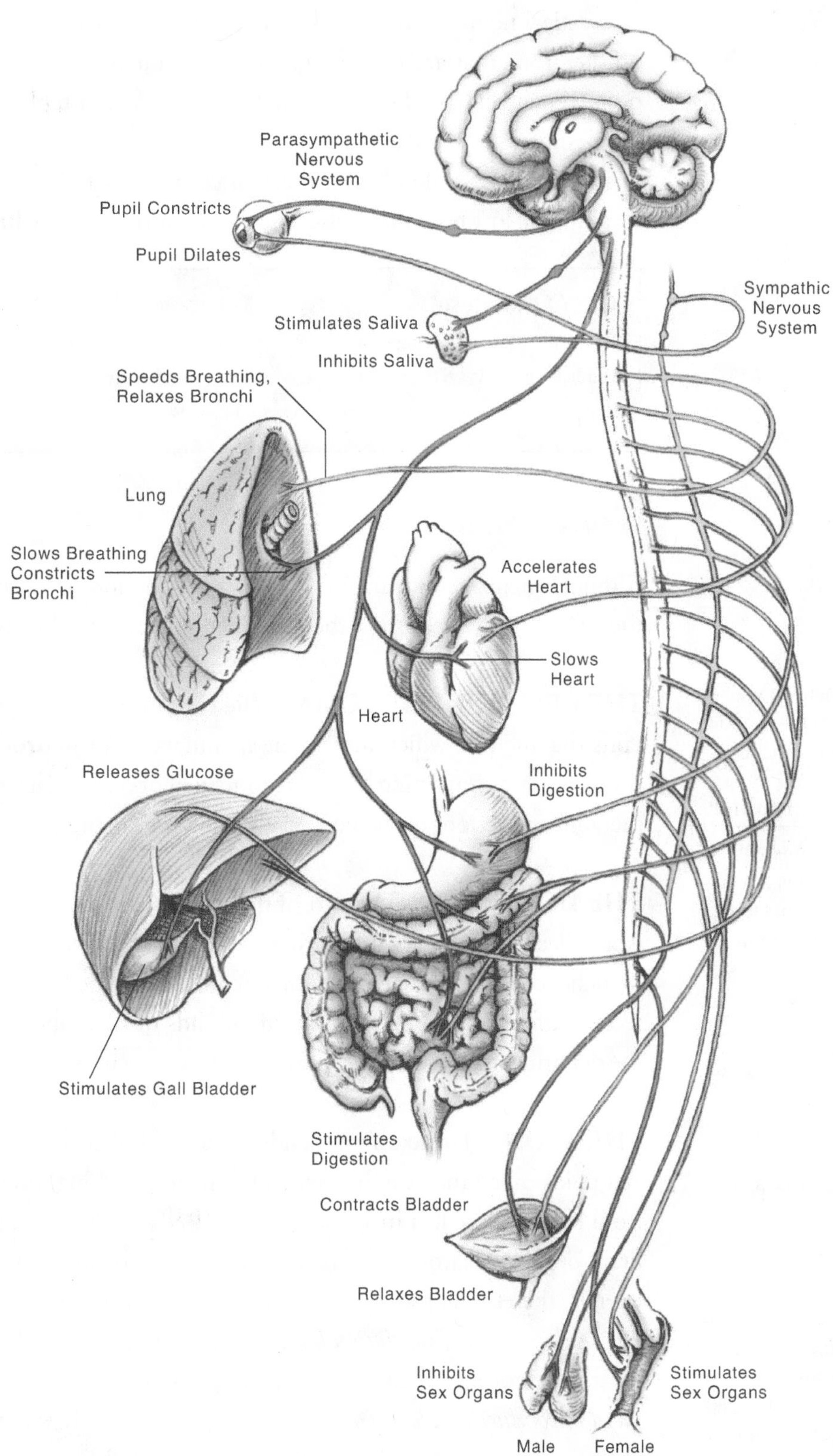

Neuronal Plasticity

The brain's ability to change in response to learning, or produce adaptive changes to internal or external stimuli is called "Plasticity". A baby comes to birth with all of its neurons in place. New neurons are not created after birth, but in fact, neurons that are not used die off. Neurons that are in use as a baby sees touches or hears things form denser connections. If neurons that were put to use die, they are not replaced, but sometimes existing living neurons send collaterals from their axons to form denser networks, in place of the missing neurons and take over their function. This ability of the brain to adapt in order to regain some lost function is also known as plasticity of the brain.

> **Get Outta Here!**
> Did you know that fasting or maintaining a long interval between meals enhances the plasticity of the brain and helps prevent ageing related changes such as those seen in Alzheimer's? As long as you eat your breakfast, skipping lunch now and then might be a good idea! ☺ (Mattson, Duran & Guo, 2003).

Neuron Structure

Cell body

The largest part of a neuron, containing the nucleus as well as structures that handle metabolic functions.

Neurotransmitter

Chemical messenger that transmits an impulse across the synaptic gap from one neuron to another.

Dendrite

Branch-like extensions from a neuron with the specialized function of receiving messages from surrounding neurons.

Axon

Extension of a neuron that transmits an impulse from the cell body to the terminal buttons on the tip of the axon.

Although neurons vary in size, shape, and function, they share four common structures: the cell body, the dendrites, the axon, and the terminal buttons (see Figure 3.3).

THE CELL BODY OR SOMA The **cell body** is the largest part of the neuron. It contains the nucleus, which directs the manufacture of **neurotransmitters**, which that neuron will use in imparting messages to its neighboring neurons. The soma also handles the metabolic functions of the neuron allowing it to maintain life.

THE DENDRITES The part of the neuron that receives most of the transmitted signals is a collection of fibers called **dendrites**, which extend out from the cell body like the branches of a tree. (The word *dendrite* comes from the Greek word for tree.) Dendrites may receive information from a few to thousands of surrounding neurons. Signals received by the dendrites are passed on to the cell body, which in turn passes them on through the axon.

THE AXON The **axon** is a slender, extended fiber that takes a signal from the cell body at a point called the axon hillock and transmits it along its entire length, which may range from two or more feet in spinal cord and PNS neurons to a tiny fraction of an inch in the brain or CNS neurons. The axon may divide into two or more major branches called collaterals, thereby increasing its capacity to communicate with other neurons. *Many axons have a thick layer of insulation known as myelin.* Most peripheral axons are myelinated, and most (but not all) of the axons in the brain are unmyelinated. *Myelination increases the speed of conduction along the axon.* It is myelin that gives the grayish brown brain tissue a glistening white color. Hence, a collection of cell bodies looks gray, but a collection of axons or *nerve fibers* looks white.

FIGURE 3.3 Neuron Structure

Neural messages from surrounding neurons are received by the dendrites and then passed down to the cell body, the portion of the neuron in which metabolic functions take place. The neural signal then moves along the axon, the transmitting fiber of the neuron. Terminal buttons at the end of the axon release chemicals called neurotransmitters that activate adjacent neurons, thereby allowing the message to continue.

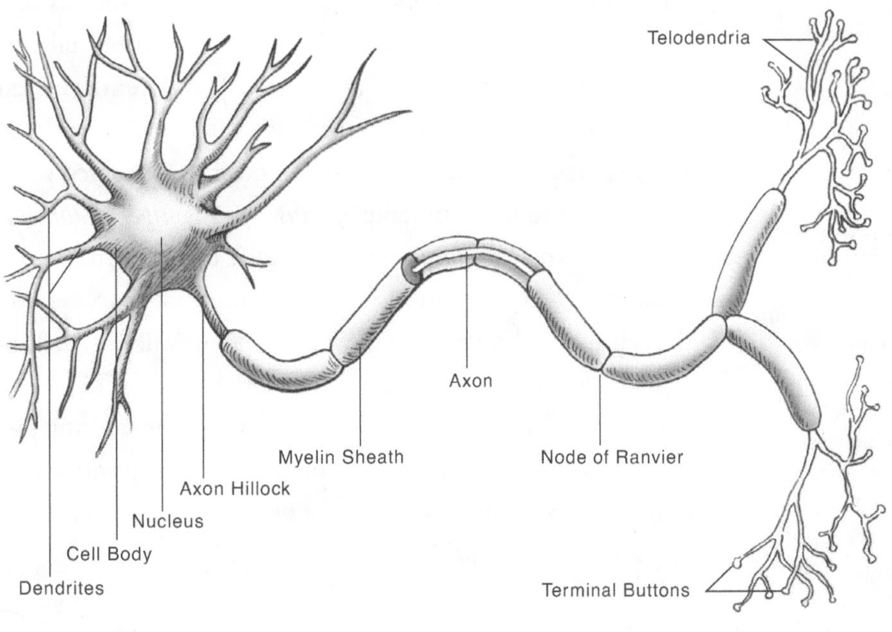

Terminal buttons

Swollen bulb-like structure on the end of a neuron's axon that releases chemical substances known as neurotransmitters.

THE TERMINAL BUTTONS The transmitting end of the axon consists of small bulb-like structures known as **terminal buttons**. Chemicals known as **neurotransmitters *are manufactured in the body of the neuron*** *and stored in these terminal buttons. Then, these stored neurotransmitters are released from the terminal buttons to enable the signals received by one neuron to be passed on to a neighboring neuron.* In the next section we will take a closer look at this complex process.

Neural Transmission

People often think of the nervous system as a vast, complex network of interconnected wire-like structures. However, instead of a continuous filament, as in a copper wire, neural circuits are made up of hundreds of thousands of individual neurons. *In order for a message to travel from neuron to neuron, it must move from the terminal buttons at the end of one neuron's axon to the dendrites of an adjacent neuron.* The process by which impulses are transmitted in the CNS is not just electrical, as it is in the wiring system of a house; it also involves chemical substances called neurotransmitters, and *the entire process is called **neural transmission**.*

The Generation of Neuronal Electricity

(See http://faculty.washington.edu/chudler/ap.html for further elucidation).

The billions of neurons that form your nervous system literally float in a liquid known as ***the extracellular fluid***. Each individual neuron is made up of a double-walled semipermeable membrane. The neuron maintains its shape and form partly due to the liquid that is held inside it. The *liquid inside* the neuron is known as ***the intracellular fluid***. Both the extracellular fluid and intracellular fluid contain several charged particles known as **ions** but their ionic compositions are drastically different. The Extracellular fluid is very rich in Sodium ions (Na++) and Chloride ions (Cl-), whereas Intracellular fluid is rich in negatively charged protein ions (An-) and positively charged potassium ions (K+).

Ions
Charged particles found within extra- and intracellular fluid.

The neuronal membrane, *because of its semipermeable nature,* permits the cell to maintain an internal environment that is quite different from that of the extracellular fluid. The membrane acts as a barrier for the Sodium ions (Na++) preventing them from entering the cell and it also prevents the large protein Anions (An-) from leaving the cell.

The neuronal membrane allows some ions, for e.g. Na++ ions inside the neuron only when a "gate" or "channel" is open. Sodium ions carrying positive charges accumulate outside the neuron making the neuronal membrane positively charged on the outside, relative to its inner side, and *this difference in voltage is known as "**The Resting Potential**" and it is the "default setting" of the neuron.*(Okami, P. 2013).

Resting potential
State in which a neuron is not transmitting a nerve impulse. A neuron in this state has a net negative charge relative to its outside environment, and this state of potential energy prepares it to be activated by an impulse from an adjacent neuron.

RESTING POTENTIALS A neuron that is displaying the default setting, is a neuron at rest that is one that is not transmitting a nerve impulse at that time. A resting neuron or an "undisturbed neuron" contains a net negative charge of about –70 millivolts (70/1,000 of a volt) relative to its outside and this 70 mv of potential energy is known as "The Resting Potential".

Maintaining this resting potential allows the neuron to store the energy that it utilizes when it transmits an impulse (Kolb & Whishaw, 1985). This Resting Potential comes to an end when the neuron receives excitatory signals called *"generator potentials"* form its dendrites. The Na++ ions which carry these electrical charges accumulate in the soma of the neuron, at a point close to the beginning of the axon and known as "**The Axon Hillock**". If enough positive charge bearing sodium ions have come in, to cause a "Sodium channel" or "Gate" at the axon hillock to open, we say the "Threshold" has been reached.

Graded potential
Voltage change in a neuron's dendrites that is produced by receiving an impulse from another neuron or neurons.

Threshold value
The minimum voltage change sufficient to activate a response.

Axon hillock
A specialized region of the cell body near the base of the axon.

ACTION POTENTIALS Once the arrival of enough sodium ions allows a neuron to reach its threshold and the "Gate" at the Axon hillock or the "Voltage-dependent-ion channel" opens, a whole lot of sodium ions gush into the axon and change its resting potential from negative to positive, and this change is called "depolarization".

*An **action potential** is initiated when the axon is depolarized to its threshold level (approximately –55 millivolts).* When the membrane reaches this threshold level, a sudden complete depolarization results due to the opened gate and the axon goes from about –55

Action potential
Electrical signal that flows along the surface of the axon to the terminal buttons, initiating the release of neurotransmitters.

FIGURE 3.4 Neuron Electrical Activity

A. Neuron at rest. Resting membrane potential is maintained by distribution of charged ions on either side of cell membrane. B. Initiation of action potential. Action potential is initiated at axon hillock by movement of sodium (Na+) ions to inside of cell. C. Movement of action potential. Action potential moves (propagates) along axon as Na+ ions enter cell. After an action potential occurs, membrane potential is restored by movement of both potassium (K+) and sodium (Na+) ions from the cell.

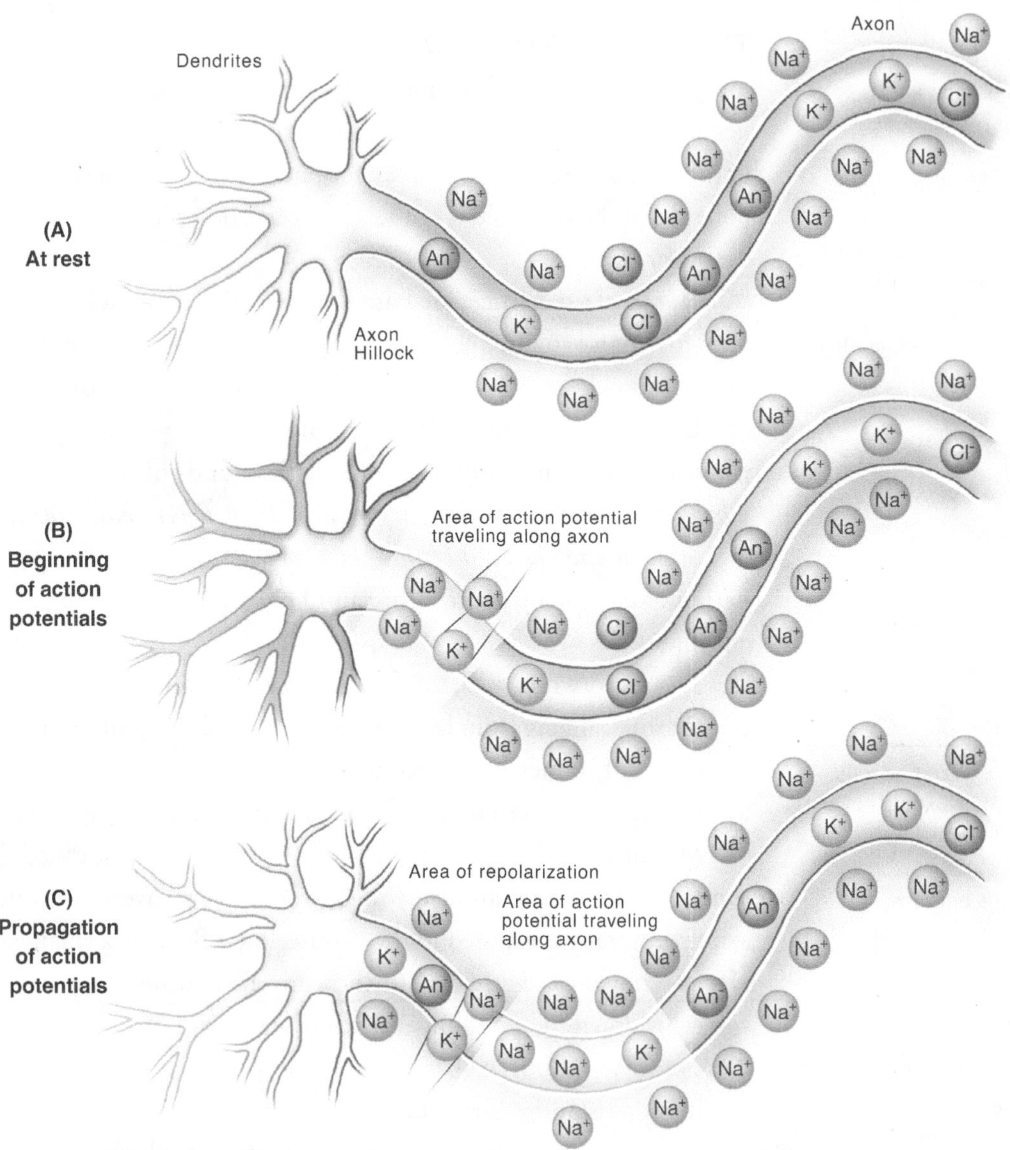

millivolts to approximately +55 millivolts instantaneously. This "Action Potential" or depolarization now begins to travel down the length of the axon towards the terminal buttons, opening subsequent "Na++-ion-channels" and causing depolarizations of membrane segments. As soon as the action potential moves to the next segment, the previous segment gets restored to its resting potential. This continuous rapid change that proceeds down the axon is actually a flowing electrical signal and it is known as ***"The Action***

Potential" or ***"The firing of the neuron"*** and it is the ***"information"*** that is carried over that axon, to the next one in the circuit! The action potential is also known as the **nerve impulse** or the **neural impulse**. The entire process of the generation of an action potential takes about 1 millisecond (1/1,000) of a second and *it is this event that results in the release of the stored neurotransmitter from the terminal buttons of the neuron, allowing it to send a "message" to the next neuron in the circuit!*

Nerve impulse/ neural impulse

See Action Potential.

All-or-none law

An action potential will be passed through a neuron's axon as long as the sum of graded potentials reaches a threshold. The strength of an action potential does not vary according to the degree of stimulation. See also, graded potential.

THE ALL-OR-NONE LAW Once a nerve impulse is triggered within an axon, it is transmitted the entire length of the axon with no loss of intensity. Partial action potentials or nerve impulses do not occur; thus, an axon is said to conduct without decrement. If the sum of the graded potentials (i.e. generator potentials) reaches a threshold, there will be an action potential; if the threshold is not reached, an action potential will not occur. This is known as the **all-or-none law**.

Our final experiences are based on several factors including the total number of neurons firing and the frequency at which they are firing, due to a given stimulus. Intensities of various stimuli are distinguished not on the basis of the firing of one neuron, but on the response of many. Weak stimuli may trigger impulses in only a few neurons, whereas very strong stimuli may cause thousands of neurons to fire. *The frequency with which neurons fire can also vary greatly, from fewer than 100 times per second for weak stimuli to as often as 1,000 times per second for extremely strong stimuli.* Thus, the combination of how many neurons fire and how often they fire allows us to distinguish different intensities of stimuli.

The speed with which an impulse travels through a neuron varies with the properties of the axon, ranging from less than one meter per second in unmyelinated very thin fibers to as fast as 100 meters per second (roughly 224 miles per hour) in larger and well myelinated fibers. The speed of neural transmission is greatly enhanced by its myelination.

Glia

Specialized cells that form insulating covers called myelin sheaths around the axons of some neurons, increasing conductivity.

Myelin sheath

Insulating cover around some axons that increases a neuron's ability to transmit impulses quickly. Myelin sheaths are made of specialized cells called glia cells

Node of Ranvier

Small gap or exposed portion of the axon of a neuron between the glia cells that form the myelin sheath.

Myelination of the axons is done by specialized cells, called **glia**, which wrap around some axons, forming an insulating cover called a **myelin sheath**. Between each glia the axon membrane is exposed to the extra-cellular fluid by a small gap called a **node of Ranvier**, as shown in Figure 3.3. In these myelinated neurons, nerve impulses do not travel smoothly down the axon. Instead, they jump from node to node, in a process called *saltatory conduction* (from the Latin *saltare,* meaning to leap).

In a devastating disease called multiple sclerosis (MS), loss of myelination short-circuits or delays the transmission of signals from the brain to the muscles of the arms and legs. As a consequence, a person with MS often experiences a weakness or loss of control over the limbs.

Neurotransmitters and the Synapse

The transmission of an electrical impulse from one end of a neuron to the other provides only a partial explanation of how messages are transmitted. When an electrical nerve impulse reaches the end of an axon, it cannot flow directly into other neurons.

This is because there is a space between neurons. This space is known as the synaptic gap and it contains extracellular fluid. The space is minuscule, and generally it is no more than five-millionths of an inch across, but the electrical impulse does not bridge it alone. A chemical process is necessary in bridging the synaptic gap. Figure 3.5 illustrates a **synapse**, which includes the membrane on the terminal button (the presynaptic membrane), the synaptic gap, and the membrane on the dendrite or receiving neuron (the postsynaptic membrane).

Synapse

Includes the synaptic gap and a portion of the presynaptic and postsynaptic membranes that are involved in transmitting a signal between neurons.

STEPS IN NEURAL TRANSMISSION The action potential generated in one neuron, is conducted to its terminal buttons, where *it discharges on little vesicles found inside the terminal buttons.* These vesicles are little packets of neurotransmitter molecules, encased by a membrane. On the discharge of the action potential, these vesicles fuse with the membrane of the terminal button and the membrane ruptures spilling the neurotransmitter molecules into the synaptic gap or junction.

The neurotransmitter molecules then float across the synaptic gap and bind to specialized receptors in the dendritic membrane of the receiving neuron in the circuit. The binding of the neurotransmitter causes the specialized receptor to open ion channels and ions which were previously not allowed into this neuron by its semi-permeable membrane, now enter it.

FIGURE 3.5 Synapse

Illustration of an active synapse depicting neurotransmitter being released into the synaptic gap.

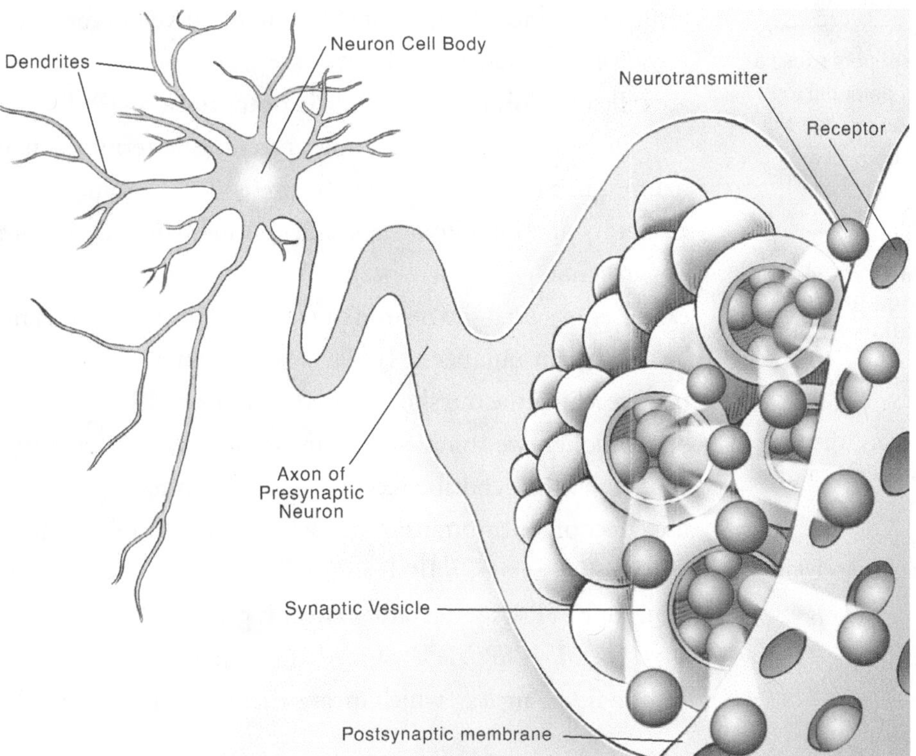

This opening of ion channels via dendritic receptors by a neurotransmitter, depends on the shape and size of a neurotransmitter molecule. Any chemical molecule which has a similar shape and size can open the same channel via the same receptor much like similar keys can open cheap locks. This fact is known as the Lock and Key Principle. Or, in other words, a synapse works on the **Lock and Key Principle**.

Once the dendritic ion-channels are opened and ions enter the neuron at the dendrite, graded potentials (generator potentials) are generated, as mentioned earlier. These graded potentials are summated at the axon-hillock of this second neuron, and if the membrane near the axon-hillock reaches its threshold of excitation, voltage-dependent sodium ion channels open, Na++ ions gush into the cell, and cause an action potential in the second neuron. Thus the process that caused an action potential in the first neuron of a circuit repeats itself in a contiguous neuron in the circuit, after neurotransmitters have allowed the discharged message to be regenerated via synaptic action.

Excitatory and Inhibitory Effects

As described above, neurotransmitters exert their effects by opening gates or channels in the postsynaptic membrane, letting ions of one kind or another pass through. ***If positively charged sodium ions enter, the membrane is excited or depolarized and graded potentials are caused in the receiving neuron.*** Neurotransmitters that cause these changes are called excitatory neurotransmitters, and their effects are referred to as **excitatory postsynaptic potentials**, or **EPSPs**. Conversely, if the action of the neurotransmitter causes positively charged potassium ions to pass outside of the postsynaptic membrane, or causes *negatively charged chloride ions to enter, the membrane is inhibited* and the graded potential results in making the membrane more negative (a process called hyperpolarization). Neurotransmitters that act in this way are called inhibitory neurotransmitters, and their effects are called **inhibitory postsynaptic potentials, or IPSPs**.

Excitatory postsynaptic potentials (EPSPs)

Effects that occur when excitatory neurotransmitters cause a graded potential to occur on the dendrite or cell body of a receiving neuron.

Inhibitory postsynaptic potentials (IPSPs)

A transitory state of hyperpolarization that occurs when inhibitory neurotransmitters inhibit the postsynaptic membrane of a receiving neuron.

Since hundreds or even thousands of axon terminals may form synapses with any one neuron, EPSPs and IPSPs may be present at the same time. The combination of all these excitatory and inhibitory signals determines whether or not the receiving neuron will fire. For an action potential to occur EPSPs must not only predominate, they must do so to the extent of reaching the neuron's threshold. To prevent this from happening, there needs to be a sufficient number of IPSPs present to prevent the algebraic sum of EPSPs and IPSPs from reaching the threshold of depolarization.

Although we think of a neurotransmitter as excitatory or inhibitory based on what happens at the dendritic receptor, it is the postsynaptic receptor site that determines what the effect of a neurotransmitter will be. Thus, a neurotransmitter may have an inhibitory effect and generate an IPSP at one synapse and an excitatory effect at another, thus generating an EPSP. If an excitatory effect is generated the chances that the next neuron will fire are higher. If IPSPs are generated after synaptic transmission then, the chances of the next neuron firing are less, which means that neuron is inhibited or prevented from firing.

NEUROTRANSMITTER BREAKDOWN AND REUPTAKE What keeps the supply of neurotransmitters from being exhausted? There are several answers to this question. First, the raw materials used in the manufacture of neurotransmitters are constantly being replenished by the cell body. Second, some neurotransmitters are broken down by enzyme action once they have accomplished their function. Their breakdown products then reenter the terminal buttons to be recycled for further use. Third, in many cases the transmitter substance is retrieved intact, in a process called reuptake. Finally, neurons contain regulatory mechanisms that prevent depletion and regulate their sensitivity to neurotransmitters.

IDENTIFYING NEUROTRANSMITTER SUBSTANCES Neurotransmitters are released only within the small area of the synapses they operate in and they often occur in very small quantities. It is therefore quite difficult to identify how many different substances work as neurotransmitters. Table 3.1 presents a list of several important substances known to be neurotransmitters, as well as the functions they are thought to perform. ***For a substance to be considered a neurotransmitter it must meet the following criteria:*** (a) It must be contained in the axon terminal buttons, (b) it must be released into the synapse when the neuron fires, and (c) it must cause a postsynaptic effect after it interacts with the receptor.

NEUROTRANSMITTER SUBSTANCES Although the list of substances so far identified as neurotransmitters is quite large, we will discuss a few that are well understood and play important roles in behaviors that will be discussed in later chapters.

Acetylcholine (ACh)

The neurotransmitter that is released from motor neurons onto muscle fibers to make them contract. Appears to also be involved in learning and memory.

Cholinergic

Circuits containing acetylcholine.

Acetylcholine (ACh) **Acetylcholine** was the first neurotransmitter discovered. It plays an important role in muscular movement, because it is the neurotransmitter released from motor neurons onto efferent muscle fibers to make them contract. Circuits containing this neurotransmitter are known as **cholinergic** circuits and compounds that work on this circuit are called cholinergic compounds. In the PNS, cholinergic circuits mediate muscular movement, but in the CNS, cholinergic circuits play a role in memory, learning and possibly some mood disturbances (McKim, 1991).

Since synapses work on the lock & key principle as explained before, chemical compounds which are similar in size and shape to ACh can cause neurons to fire, or prevent them from firing by blocking the receptor site.

There are some disorders that people suffer because of malfunction of the ACh circuits. Alzheimer's is one well known dementia due to malfunction of CNS cholinergic circuits due to lack of acetylcholine in the vesicles of the terminal buttons and Myasthenia Gravis, is an illness in which the muscles become weak due to the blockage of the postsynaptic receptors in the cholinergic neuromuscular junction.

Increasing dietary Choline in-take is thought to enhance cholinergic functions. Choline is a precursor of acetylcholine that is found in peanuts, eggs, and lentils and chocolates which are rich in lecithin. Lecithin and choline are sold as tablets in health food stores and are thought to enhance memory and thinking.

TABLE 3.1 Chemicals Known to Be Major Neurotransmitters

Neurotransmitter Effects	Location	Functions
Acetylcholine (ACh) *Excitatory*	Cortex, spinal cord, target organs activated by parasympathetic nervous system	Excitation in brain. Either excitation or inhibition in target organs of PNS. Involved in learning, muscular movement, and memory.
Norepinephrine (NE) *Excitatory*	Spinal cord, limbic system, cortex, target organs of sympathetic nervous system	Arousal of reticular system. Involved in eating, emotional behavior, learning, and memory.
Dopamine (DA) *Inhibitory*	Limbic system, basal ganglia, cerebellum	Involved in movement, emotional behavior, attention, learning, memory, and reward.
Serotonin (SE) *Inhibitory*	Raphe System, Brain stem, most of brain	Involved in emotional behavior, arousal, sleep.
Gama-amino butyric acid (GABA) *Inhibitory*	Most of brain and spinal cord	Involved in regulating arousal; major inhibitory neurotransmitter in brain.
Endorphins *Inhibitory*	Spinal cord, most of brain, reward system, MFB	Functions as a natural analgesic for pain reduction; involved in emotional behavior, eating, learning.
Glutamate *Excitatory*	Brain and spinal cord	Major excitatory neurotransmitter in brain. Involved in learning.

Get Outta Here!

Once upon a time, women from several ancient cultures, including those of Egypt, India, Rome, and Greece, put a few drops of the juice of a certain plant named Belladonna, (Atropa), to dilate their pupils. Apparently their dilated pupils made them appear more attractive to prospective suitors!

Sometimes, they also fed this juice to their enemies, to drive them insane! Belladonna contains potent ACh blockers and the victims suffered from memory loss, disorientation, and finally, death (McKim, 1986). Likewise, it is thought that sorcerers from Haiti use plants with similar compounds to create Zombies (Davis, 1986). Although ACh or its mechanisms were unknown in ancient times, people had stumbled upon unique uses for compounds that influenced ACh circuits.

Norepinephrine

A major excitatory neurotransmitter in the brain. It is distributed throughout the central and peripheral nervous systems and is important in emotional arousal and stress.

Norepinephrine (NE) **Norepinephrine**, also known as noradrenaline (NA), is distributed throughout the central and peripheral nervous systems. It is important in emotional arousal, stress, impulsivity, learning and memory. Norepinephrine is a major excitatory neurotransmitter in the brain. Drugs such as amphetamine and cocaine stimulate these circuits, by releasing NE into the synapse or by blocking its reuptake for recycling, partly accounting for the feeling of energy or well-being that a low dose of these drugs produces. *Deficiencies in norepinephrine activity are linked to depression, attention disorders, and some eating disorders.*

Increasing the dietary intake of cheese, fish, tofu, nuts, etc., which contain Tyrosine can enhance the levels of NE and help balance the levels and improve the functioning of processes dependent on this neurotransmitter.

Get Outta Here!

Several Mexican Indian groups, including the Aztecs, used Peyote, a cactus, as part of their religious ceremonies. Modern science isolated Mescaline, a hallucinogen, also known as an "entheogen," i.e., "that which makes a person to be in God" from the cactus. A Winnebago tale talks of a man who eats the cactus and then "a holy spirit entered him and taking the spirit of the Indian carried it away to the regions above" (McKim, 1991, pp 306). Mescaline is very similar to the neurotransmitter NE and is said to be a Noradrenergic compound.

Dopamine

A neurotransmitter involved with the initiation of motor movement, attention, and learning and memory. The dopamine system mediates reward and pleasure and it is the substance of addiction.

Dopamine (DA) **Dopamine** is located primarily in the brain; it is involved with the initiation of motor movement, attention, and learning and memory. In addition, the dopamine system mediates reward and pleasure, and it is thought to be involved in addiction. Death of dopamine generating cells in a certain area of the brain called substantia nigra results in Parkinson's disease a severe motor disorder. Parkinson's disease is most effectively treated with a drug that is converted into dopamine in the brain (levodopa). On the other hand schizophrenia a major psychotic disorder, appears to be associated with an *excess* of dopamine in certain regions of the brain. Drugs that block DA circuits are useful as medicines in reducing the symptoms of schizophrenia. Dopamine is manufactured from phenylalanine and tyrosine we get from food, and once DA is manufactured it is converted into NE in the neurons that use NE. Some of the foods that help manufacture both DA and NE are nuts, lentils, fish and cottage cheese.

Get Outta Here!

Witches of old used to toss toads in their brew, primarily to produce hallucinations in themselves and their victims. Toad skin, from a specific species of toads, has been found to contain a chemical known as Bufotenin, which augments the firing of DA circuits and produces hallucinations. Bufotenin causes feelings of floating, which probably led to the belief that witches can fly. Bufotenin is also found in fish known as dreamfish caught in Norfolk Islands, a territory of Australia. Apparently, the eating of dreamfish causes vivid dreams (McKim, 1991). People, who are afraid to eat the dreamfish at night for fear of nightmares, eat them for breakfast!

Serotonin

A neurotransmitter involved in the control of the sleep/wake cycle, mood, and appetite. Deficiencies in serotonin are associated with sleep disorders, aggression, and depression.

Serotonin (5-HT for 5-hydroxy tryptophan) **Serotonin** is distributed throughout the brain and spinal cord and is involved in mediating mood, appetite, and the sleep/wake cycle. Deficiencies in serotonin are associated with sleep disorders, aggression, and depression. The most widely prescribed antidepressants are a class of drugs called *selective serotonin reuptake inhibitors*, or SSRIs; some neurons conserve neurotransmitter by allowing it to re-enter the pre-synaptic membrane and re-encasing it in a vesicle after releasing it due to an action potential. A drug that inhibits this re-uptake allows the neurotransmitter to linger much longer in the synapse, so its action in the synapse continues. Prozac is a prime example of such an SSRI antidepressant.

Dietary intake of tryptophan, an amino-acid, enhances Serotonin levels. Tryptophan is found in proteins, but tryptophan enters the brain in larger quantities when the meal is accompanied by high carbohydrate foods. Hence a combination of bananas and milk, or turkey with mashed potatoes, etc., is thought to help lift serotonin levels and lift mood or induce sleep.

Gamma-amino butyric acid (GABA)

GABA is the major inhibitory neurotransmitter in the brain and spinal cord. It plays an important role in regulating arousal and anxiety.

Gamma-Amino Butyric Acid (GABA) **GABA** is the major inhibitory neurotransmitter in the brain and spinal cord. It plays an important role in regulating arousal and anxiety. Drugs such as Valium, Xanax, Halcion, etc., increase the activity of GABA, producing a calming effect and even sleep. Increase in dietary intake of sun-flower seeds, sesame seeds, lean beef or pork can help ease ADHD symptoms which correlate with low levels of GABA.

Endorphins

A class of neurotransmitter substances that function to inhibit the transmission pain information. Morphine and other opiates act by facilitating endorphin transmission.

Endorphins: **Endorphins** and enkephalins are a family of neurotransmitters chemically similar to opiates such as morphine. They are widely distributed throughout most of the brain. Extensive research has linked the endorphins to an array of behavioral and mental processes, including inducing a sense of well-being and euphoria, counteracting the influence of stress, modulating food and liquid intake, and reducing pain. Dietary intake of green leafy vegetables, Lima beans, etc., is thought to enhance endorphin and enkephalin levels.

Glutamate (glutamic acid)

An amino acid derived from glucose. This neurotransmitter plays an important excitatory function. MSG contains glutamate.

Glutamate: **Glutamate** or **glutamic acid** is an amino acid derived from glucose. Glutamate is one of the most important excitatory neurotransmitters in the brain. It is said to increase the speed of neural transmission and increase the efficiency of learning and memory (Okami 2013). Glutamate is thought to be the most abundant amino acid in the diet and there is no known evidence of brain damage in humans caused by a dietary deficiency of glutamate (Meldrum, 2000).

Oxytocin: Although better known as a hormone, it is also serves as a neurotransmitter in the hypothalamus, an organelle of the brain which is involved in allowing the experience and expression of emotions. Oxytocin circuits are thought to mediate emotions and feelings such as fear, trust, generosity and Oxytocin is released when a person is hugged or touched in a loving relationship. Oxytocin also reduces blood-pressure and other indicators of stress and may be involved in mother-infant bonding (Kosfeld M et al. 2005,Kirsch P. et.al, 2005; Okami, 2013).

The above discussion is only a brief review of several of the most important neurotransmitter substances. New neurotransmitters and other neuro-active chemicals are still being discovered and investigated.

THE BRAIN AND BEHAVIOR

Now that you have a pretty good idea of how the nervous system is structured, and how its individual units, the neurons communicate, and the "mental" functional qualities of the various neurotransmitters, let us take a look at the divisions of the CNS and their functions.

Divisions of the CNS

The CNS is subdivided into the brain and the spinal cord. ***The brain is further sub-divided into the hindbrain, the midbrain and the forebrain.*** The hindbrain consists of the cerebellum and the brain stem. The brain stem consists of the medulla and the pons. The midbrain is not further subdivided. *The forebrain has several organelles, such as the hippocampus, the hypothalamus, the thalamus, the basal ganglia and finally the cortex and they are all involved in allowing us our "mental" or inner experiences.* (See Figure 3.6).

We will look at the functions of the CNS beginning with the Spinal cord, and make our way up towards *the cortex, which is considered the seat of our consciousness or higher mental functions.*

The spinal cord is housed within a hollow tube-like structure composed of a series of bones called vertebrae. Along the length of the spinal cord are spinal nerves that branch out between pairs of vertebrae. These nerves connect with various sensory organs, muscles, and glands served by the peripheral nervous system.

Because the brain occupies the commanding position in the CNS, the spinal cord is often overlooked in discussions of the biological bases of behavior. However, the spinal cord fills the very important function of conveying messages to and from the brain. In addition, *the spinal cord controls reflexes,* which are simple circuits of sensory and motor neurons that initiate responses to specific stimuli without any input from conscious awareness and usually serve a protective or survival function. The brain is not directly involved in controlling these simple reflexive responses, but it is clearly aware of what action has transpired (see Figure 3.7).

The Medulla

Medulla

Structure low in the brain that controls vital life support functions such as breathing, heartbeat, and blood pressure; it also regulates many reflexive functions such as coughing or sneezing.

The **medulla** is the continuation of the spinal cord and also the lowest part of the brain. This structure is protected by the skull because *it contains centers that control many vital life-support functions such as breathing, heart rate, and blood pressure.* Even the slightest damage in a critical region of the medulla can cause death. The medulla also mediates other reflexive behaviors, such as sneezing, coughing, and vomiting. There is a special area in the medulla that is called the CTZ or Chemo-receptive Trigger Zone. This CTZ is a life-saving mechanism. When it detects toxic molecules in the blood, it forces the emptying of the stomach via vomiting, to prevent any more of the toxic molecules from the food from entering the blood. Nausea and vomiting experienced after a dose of opiates or other drugs

Pons

Brain structure located just above the medulla that functions in fine-tuning motor messages, programming species-typical behaviors, processing sensory information, and controlling respiration.

Cerebellum

Brain structure located beneath the overhanging back part of the cerebral hemispheres which functions to coordinate and regulate motor movements.

is due to the CTZ which detects them and sends a signal to the Vomiting Center, another nearby area in the medulla, to initiate vomiting.

The Pons

The **pons** is a large bulge just above the medulla. It has some *autonomic functions* and is also involved in sleep and arousal. It is involved in regulating the body during sleep and is very responsive when you perceive a threat, especially to your life. (Okami, 2013).

The Cerebellum

The **cerebellum** is a distinctive structure about the size of a fist, tucked beneath the back part of the cerebral hemispheres. It consists of two wrinkled hemispheres covered by an outer cortex. *The cerebellum's primary function is to coordinate, regulate, and execute well-learned muscular movements without the need for constant attention to them.*

FIGURE 3.6 Bisected View of the Human Brain, Showing the Locations of Major Structures and Areas

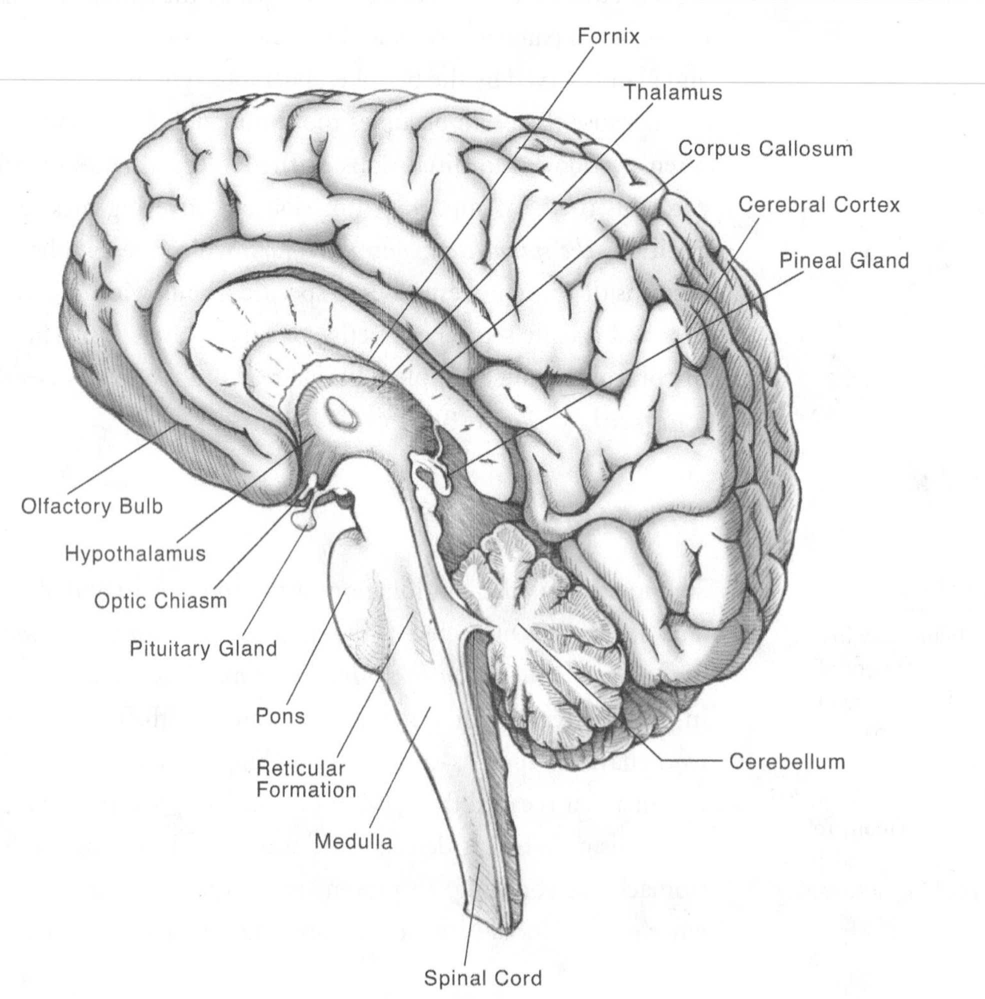

Damage to the cerebellum results in awkward, jerky, uncoordinated movements and may even affect speech. Professional boxers are especially susceptible to slight damage to the cerebellum, which results in a condition called punch-drunk syndrome.

The Reticular Formation

Reticular formation

Set of neural circuits extending from the lower brain up to the thalamus that play a critical role in controlling arousal and alertness. Also known as the reticular activating system.

The **reticular formation** consists of a set of neural circuits that extend from the hindbrain to the midbrain (refer back to Figure 3.6). The reticular formation plays a critical role in consciousness and in controlling arousal or alertness and is known as *the* ***reticular activating system, or RAS or ARAS for Ascending Reticular Activating System****. This system filters out noises and stimuli that are a regular part of our environment but alerts the cortex when an unusual stimulus is present, thus awakening us when someone coughs at night, for example.* CNS depressants like alcohol or barbiturates dampen the function of the RAS while noradrenergic stimulants like amphetamine increase arousal, because the neurons of the RAS are primarily noradrenergic.

The Limbic System

Limbic system

Collection of structures located around the central core of the brain that play a critical role in emotional expression as well as motivation, learning, and memory. Key structures of the limbic system include the amygdala, the hippocampus, the septal area, and parts of the hypothalamus.

The ***limbic system*** *is the portion of the brain most closely associated with emotional experiences and expression and with basic drives such as hunger, thirst and sex;* it also plays a role in motivation, learning, and memory. The limbic system is a collection of structures located around the central core of the brain, along the innermost edge of the cerebral hemispheres. Figure 3.8 shows some *key structures of the limbic system,* such as the hypothalamus, the hippocampus and the amygdala. Damage to or stimulation of sites within this system may profoundly affect some very basic drives and emotional experiences and expressions.

Get Outta Here!

In 1970, one of the authors of this text (Ragade) lived in Waterloo, a small town in Ontario, Canada. One day, there were headlines in the *Kitchener-Waterloo Record,* the local newspaper, which read "Woman Jailed for Cruelty to Shrimp." Yes, to shrimp, the all-you-can-eat shrimp!

According to the newspaper, the woman worked in a fish packing plant in the neighboring town of Kitchener. She would drop a handful of shrimp on the sides of the hot stove, rather than in the boiling water as instructed. The shrimp would blister, and in so doing, they would pop and jump and that somehow amused this woman.

Her co-workers had filed the suit against her because they could not stand to see the shrimp suffer. In court, the woman's lawyer argued that shrimp were insects and did not have a limbic system, which meant that they could not experience emotion, much less show it! If the shrimp could not experience emotion, how could his client have been cruel to them?

The judge in the case sent the woman to jail under the Cruelty to Animals Act, and said, "I don't care whether shrimp can experience emotions or not. Her co-workers certainly can feel emotions. They were distressed, they begged her to stop and she did not, which is why they filed a suit. As far as I am concerned, they are animals, so I am sentencing this woman under the Cruelty to Animals Act!"

FIGURE 3.7 Neural Control of Simple Reflexes

A simple reflexive response involves the interaction of a sensory neuron, an interneuron, and a motor neuron. Interneurons functions to both convey sensory information to the brain and to stimulate motor neurons to activate the withdrawal reflex.

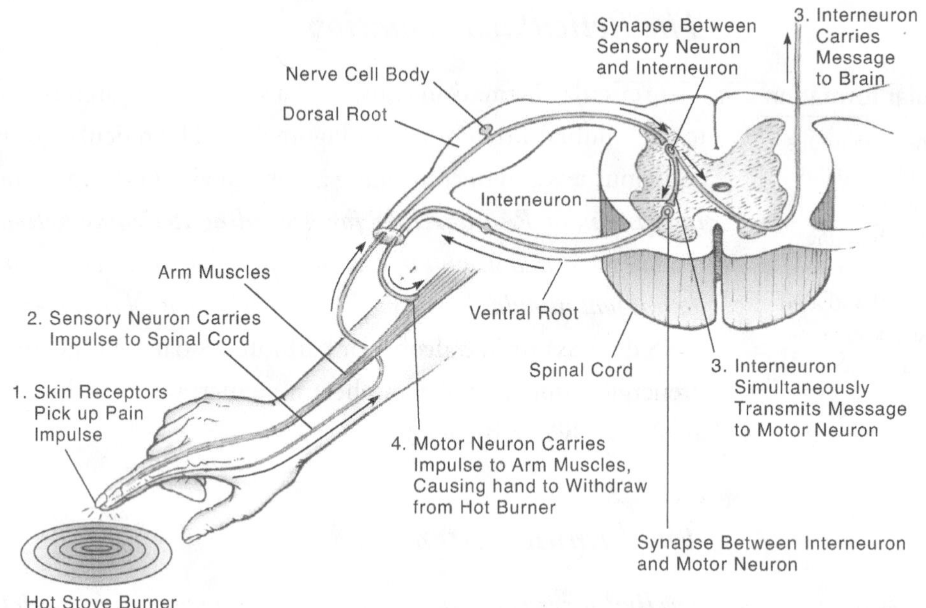

The Amygdala

Amygdala

A small limbic system structure located next to the hippocampus in the brain that plays an important role in the expression of anger, rage, fear, and aggressive behavior.

The **amygdala**, a small almond-shaped structure next to the hippocampus, plays an important role in the expression and understanding of anger, rage, and aggressive and fear-motivated behavior. Amygdala damage in humans results in the inability of thoughts or memories to trigger emotional states. These emotional states are essential to normal social functioning and decision-making (Bechara et al., 2003; Damasio, 1995). It is also thought that the Amygdala underscores traumatic memories, allowing them to be stored as very vivid memories (McGaugh, 2003).

The Hippocampus

Hippocampus

Structure in the brain's limbic system that seems to play an important role in memory.

Another limbic-system structure, the **hippocampus** consolidates new information in memory. There are two of them and they are referred to as hippocampi to indicate both. Individuals who experience damage to this structure have difficulty storing new information in memory. They can however learn motor skills, but have no recollection of doing so. The hippocampus is also thought to be involved in recalling stored memories, imagination and in visualizing future events (Bird, Capponi King et.al, 2010).

FIGURE 3.8 The Limbic System

Major limbic structures include the amygdala, the septum and septal nuclei, the fornix, the hypothalamus, and the cingulate gyrus.

SOURCE: Adapted figure of "Primary Areas of the Motor Cortex and Somatosensory Cortex," article from "Specializations of the Human Brain" from *Scientific American,* September 1982, p.182 by Norman Geschwind. Copyright © 1979 by Scientific American, Inc. All rights reserved.

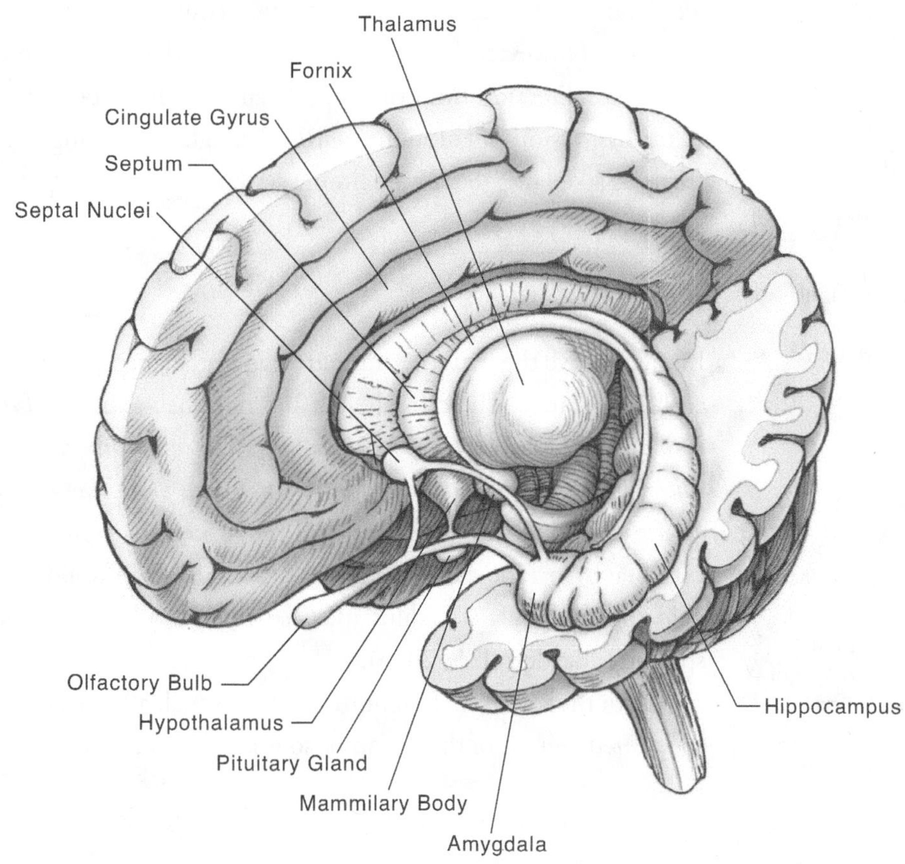

Get Outta Here!

Psychologist Brenda Milner (Milner, 1985) describes the sad case of a man named H.M. who sort of froze in time, unable to remember anything that had transpired after his hippocampi had been removed. He had some types of memory, though, because, according to Milner, although his eyes revealed a gleam of recognition for her, he did not know who she was, even after working with him every day for 15 years. Milner had to start her day by saying "Hello Mr. H.M., I am your psychologist, Brenda Milner."

Hypothalamus

Small structure located below the thalamus in the brain that plays an important role in motivation and emotional expression, as well as controlling the neuroendocrine system and maintaining the body's homeostasis. The hypothalamus is part of the limbic system.

The Hypothalamus

As its name **hypothalamus** indicates (hypo means below in Greek), this grape-sized structure lies below the thalamus. The hypothalamus contains control mechanisms that detect

Thalamus

Structure located beneath the cerebrum in the brain that functions as a relay station, routing incoming sensory information to appropriate areas in the cerebral cortex. Also seems to play a role in regulating sleep cycles.

Basal ganglia

Neural structures involved in the initiation of motor movement and emotion. Includes the caudate nucleus, putamen, and the substantia nigra.

Caudate nucleus

A component of the basal ganglia involved with the control and initiation of motor movement. An area of the brain affected by Huntington's disease. Located adjacent to the putamen.

changes in body systems and *regulate internal environment or maintain homeostasis.* The hypothalamus is also critical to motivation. It contains nuclei (densely packed concentrations of specialized cell bodies) that govern eating, drinking, and sexual behavior.

The hypothalamus is also the hub of the neuroendocrine system, which is discussed later in this chapter. You may have heard the brain's pituitary gland described as the master gland, since it secretes substances that control the activity of other glands throughout the body. However, the term *master* is somewhat a misnomer, since the pituitary gland itself takes direction from the hypothalamus. The hypothalamus plays an integrative role in the expression of emotions, partly through interacting with the endocrine system and partly as a key member of the limbic system.

The Thalamus

Located above the hypothalamus are two egg-shaped structures that lie side by side, one in each hemisphere. These are the left and right halves of the ***thalamus**, a structure that relays incoming sensory information to appropriate areas within the cerebral cortex. Many of the cell nuclei in the thalamus also perform initial data processing before relaying information to the cortex.* The thalamus also acts on input received from the cerebral cortex as to which information can be relayed and which information should be blocked, so attention can be paid to a particular stimulus more so than another, such as one voice when many are speaking (Bartlett, E.L, 2013).

With the sole exception of the sense of smell, all sensory information is routed through specialized regions of the thalamus so it is primarily seen as a relay station.

THE BASAL GANGLIA

Putamen

A component of the basal ganglia involved with the control and initiation of motor movement. An area of the brain affected by Huntington's disease, located adjacent to the caudate nucleus.

The **basal ganglia** consist of several subcortical brain structures, including the **caudate nucleus**, the **putamen**, and the **substantia nigra**. These structures receive messages from the cortex and the thalamus. *The primary function of the basal ganglia is in the control and initiation of voluntary muscular movement.* People with damage to the basal ganglia have great difficulty in initiating movement. In addition, movement is often weak and poorly coordinated. One of the most common disorders of the basal ganglia is a condition referred to as Parkinson's disease. *Parkinson's disease results from the destruction of the dopamine-containing neurons of the substantia nigra.*

THE CEREBRAL CORTEX

A major structure of the human brain is the **cerebral cortex**, the thin outer layer of the brain. This portion of the brain is also called the neocortex, or new cortex, since it was the last part of the brain to develop during evolution. (See Figure 3.9.)

Substantia nigra

A region of dark colored neurons in the upper brainstem that sends axons to the caudate nucleus and to the putamen. An area of the brain effected by Parkinson's disease.

Cerebral cortex

Thin outer layer of the brain's cerebrum (sometimes called the gray matter) that is responsible for movement, perception, thinking, and memory.

You may wonder why the cortex is wrinkled and convoluted. The answer has to do with the economics of space. The cortex's folds and wrinkles are nature's solution to the problem of cramming the huge neocortical area into a relatively small space within the skull.

The cortex is gray in color, which is why it is often referred to as the gray matter of the brain. The gray color comes from the lack of the whitish myelinated coating that insulates the neural fibers of the inner part of the brain. The cortex is mainly composed of the unmyelinated fibers and cell bodies of billions of neurons, and it is the part of the brain responsible for higher processes such as perceiving, thinking, and remembering and allowing us to KNOW that we indeed perceive, think, and remember!

LOCALIZATION OF CORTICAL FUNCTIONING To facilitate studying and describing the brain, researchers have found it convenient to divide each of the cortical hemispheres into four separate regions called lobes. These four regions are the frontal, parietal, occipital, and temporal lobes, are shown in Figure 3.9. Two long valleys, called sulci, within the surface of the cortex separate these four lobes, and also serve as landmarks.

FIGURE 3.9 Localization of Cortical Functions in the Four Lobes of the Left Cerebral Cortex

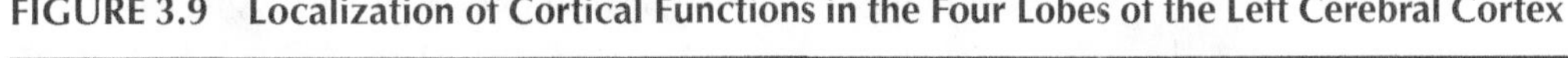

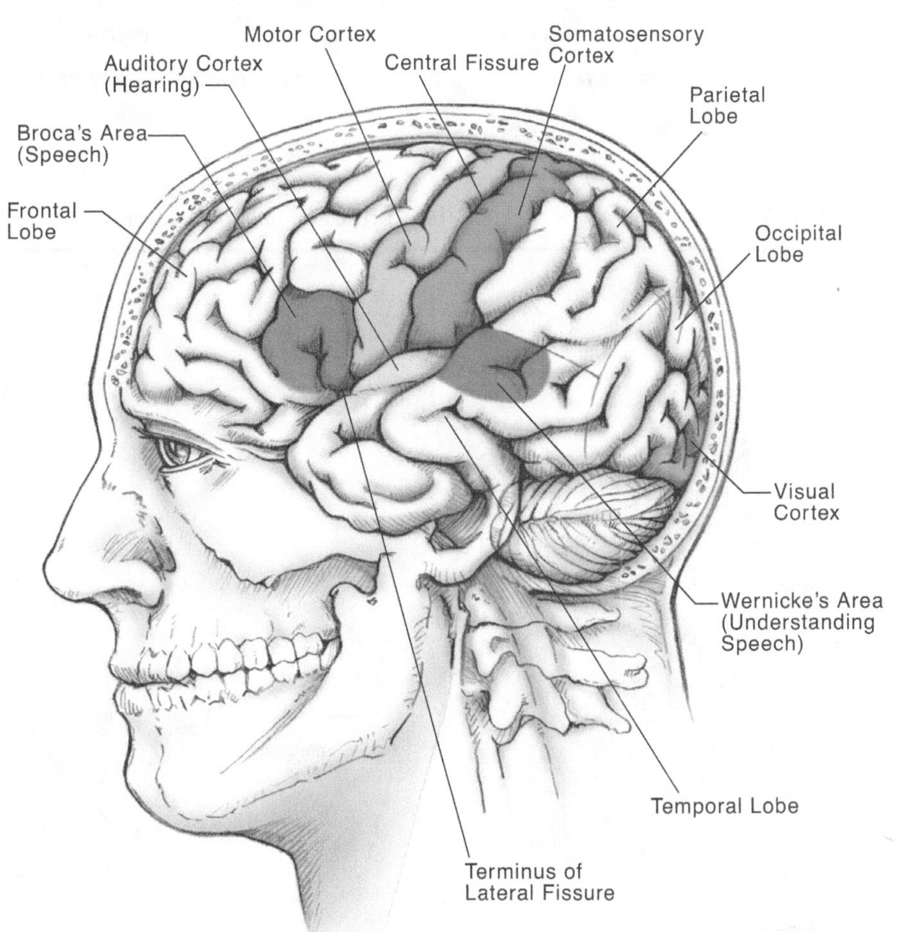

Frontal lobe

Largest, foremost lobe in the cerebral cortex; an important region for movement, emotion, and memory.

Motor cortex

Region of the cerebral cortex that transmits messages to muscles. The motor cortex controls virtually all intentional body movement.

Broca's area

Region of the left frontal lobe that is the primary brain center for controlling speech.

The Frontal Lobe The **frontal lobe** is the largest of the four lobes in each hemisphere and is an important center for both the motor and association cortex. The **motor cortex**, a narrow strip just in front of the central sulcus along the back of the frontal lobe, ***contains neurons that contribute to the control, planning, and execution of motor movement.*** Virtually all body movement, from throwing a ball to wiggling a small toe, involves the motor cortex. Newest information indicates that the actual planning of motor movement and the decision to move a body part might be ***subconscious*** or ***unconscious*** rather than conscious and might not be made by the motor cortex but by other areas in the frontal lobe, ***raising the question of the existence of something called "free will"!*** (Hallett, M. 2007; Lang Obrigg, et.al, 1990).

The body is represented in an upside-down fashion along the motor cortex; that is, neurons controlling facial muscles are at the bottom of the motor cortex, and those that control movement of the toes are at the top part. (Refer to Figure 3.10.) Larger areas of the motor cortex are devoted to the muscles involved in talking and moving the fingers, reflecting the critical role of speech and tool use in human behavior.

Nerve fibers that descend from the motor cortex in one side of the brain activate muscles on the opposite side of the body. *That is, the right motor cortex controls movements of the opposite, or contralateral, side of the body.*

In the nineteenth century, a French neurosurgeon, Pierre Paul Broca, reported that damage to another area of the left frontal lobe caused difficulty in speaking. Subsequent research has confirmed that this frontal lobe region, called **Broca's area** ***after its discoverer, is the primary brain center for controlling speech.*** (Refer back to Figure 3.9.) Peo-

FIGURE 3.10 Primary Areas of the Motor Cortex and the Somatosensory Cortex

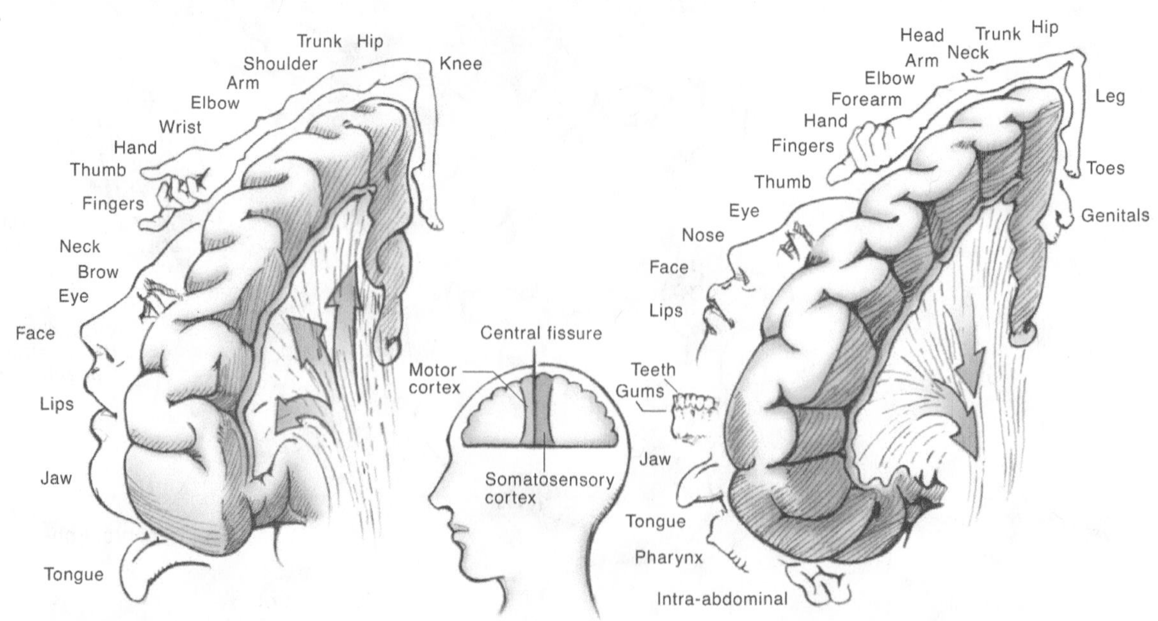

Parietal lobe

Region of the cerebral cortex located just behind the central fissure and above the lateral fissure. The parietal lobe contains the somatosensory cortex as well as association areas that process sensory information received by the somatosensory cortex.

Somatosensory cortex

Area of the parietal lobe, directly across from the motor cortex in the frontal lobe, which receives sensory information about touch, pressure, pain, temperature, and body position.

Occipital lobe

Region at the rear of the cerebral cortex that consists primarily of the visual cortex.

Visual cortex

Portion of the occipital lobe that integrates sensory information received from the eyes into electrical patterns that the brain translates into vision.

Temporal lobe

Region of the cerebral cortex located below the lateral fissure that contains the auditory cortex.

Auditory cortex

Region of the temporal lobe located just below the lateral fissure that is involved in responding to auditory signals, particularly the sound of human speech.

ple who have been injured in this critical area typically have trouble articulating the right words to describe things, even though their comprehension of what they hear or read is unaffected. This condition is called *motor or expressive aphasia.*

The Parietal Lobe The **parietal lobe** lies just behind the frontal lobe. At the front of the parietal lobe, *directly across from the motor cortex in the frontal lobe, is an area called the* ***somatosensory cortex***. This portion of the parietal lobe receives sensory information about touch, pressure, pain, temperature, and body position. ***Like the motor cortex, the somatosensory areas in each hemisphere receive sensory input from the opposite sides of the body***. Thus, when you stub your left toe, the message is sent to your right somatosensory cortex. As in the motor cortex, the body is represented in an upside-down fashion, with the largest portions receiving input from the face and hands, as shown in Figure 3.10.

The parietal lobe is involved in relating visual and spatial information. *The parietal lobe is also involved in complex visuospatial tasks such as mental rotation.* Mental rotation is the imaginary rotation of a familiar object in your mind. People with damage to their parietal lobes also suffer a peculiar deficit referred to as ***sensory neglect***. Sensory neglect occurs to the contralateral side of the body. *That is, a person with damage to the left parietal lobe may neglect the right side of the body* by failing to dress it as neatly as the left side, or he or she may draw a self-portrait with the right side either missing or drawn with a marked lack of detail. While reading, a person with sensory neglect may read only the left side of a page. Such persons also have difficulty following directions, either from instructions or from a map. (For sad but amusing and true stories of patients with parietal lobe damage, see *The Man Who Mistook His Wife for a Hat* by Dr. Oliver Sacks (Touchstone, 1998, ISBN: 0684853949). One of the authors of this textbook [Ragade] cannot recommend it enough!)

The Occipital Lobe The **occipital lobe** lies at the rear of each hemisphere. This lobe consists primarily of the **visual cortex**, a complex network of neurons devoted to vision. Most people think they see with their eyes, but although the eyes receive sensory information, it is the visual cortex that integrates this information into vision. *The visual cortex of each hemisphere receives sensory messages from both eyes. Nerve fibers from the right visual field of each eye go to the right hemisphere; fibers from the left visual field send impulses to the left hemisphere.* In addition to receiving primary visual information, the visual cortex is also responsible for the processing of color, shape, three-dimensional form, and motion of objects. As you can imagine, damage to the occipital lobe results in varying degrees of visual impairment, ranging from the inability to perceive shapes, colors and motion, to complete blindness.

The Temporal Lobe Again, there are two temporal lobes, one in each hemisphere, behind each temple. A primary function of the **temporal lobe** is hearing. The **auditory cortex**, located on the inner surface of the temporal lobe in a region below the lateral sulcus, receives information directly from the auditory system. These auditory signals are then

Wernicke's area

Area of the left temporal lobe that is the brain's primary area for understanding speech.

Agnosia

An inability to know or recognize objects through the senses usually caused by brain injury or disease. Visual agnosia is the failure to recognize or identify objects visually even though they can be seen.

transmitted to an adjacent structure, known as ***Wernicke's area****, which is involved in interpreting sounds, particularly the sound of human speech* (refer back to Figure 3.9). This area was named after Germany's Carl Wernicke, who reported that patients who were injured in the rear portion of the *left* temporal lobe often had trouble understanding the speech of others. Another major function of the temporal lobe is object recognition and identification. Damage to either temporal lobe can cause peculiar disorders referred to as ***agnosia****, a condition in which patients cannot name or identify familiar objects.* Often patients can copy the simple object of a drawing, e.g., a cat, say things like it is a small animal, eats mice, etc., but cannot say it is a "cat." When asked to name it, they behave as if they do not know what it is called.

Lateralization of Function

You may have noticed in a preceding discussion that both Broca's area and Wernicke's area were identified in the left hemisphere. Indeed, in most people (approximately 96 percent of right-handed people and 70 percent of left-handers), verbal abilities such as the expression and understanding of speech are governed more by the left hemisphere than the right hemisphere, and there are other differences as well. Furthermore, the right side of the brain seems to be more specialized for spatial orientation, including the ability to recognize objects and shapes and to perceive relationships among them (Gordon, 1986; Patterson et al., 1989).

Lateralization of function

Degree to which a particular function, such as the understanding of speech, is controlled by one rather than both cerebral hemispheres.

The term **lateralization of function** is used to describe the degree to which a particular function is controlled by one rather than both hemispheres. If, for example, a person's ability to deal with spatial tasks is controlled exclusively by the right hemisphere, we would say that this ability is highly lateralized in this person. In contrast, if both hemispheres contribute equally to this function, the person would be considered bilateral for spatial ability.

Studies have shown that the two hemispheres are asymmetrical, differing in anatomical, electrical, and chemical properties. Although each hemisphere is specialized to handle different functions, they are not entirely separate systems. Rather, our brains function mostly as an integrated whole. *The two hemispheres constantly communicate with each other through a broad band of millions of connecting nerve fibers called the* ***corpus callosum***, shown earlier in Figure 3.6. And while in most people a complex function such as language is controlled primarily by regions in the left hemisphere, interaction and communication with the right hemisphere also play a role. Furthermore, if a hemisphere that is primarily responsible for a particular function is damaged, the remaining intact hemisphere may take over the function. For example, if a person were to experience an injury to the language-processing area of the left hemisphere, the right hemisphere might develop a greater capacity to handle verbal functions. This is particularly true if the damage occurs early in life, as was witnessed in the case of an adolescent girl who underwent hemispherectomy, but gained the lost skills considerably due to plasticity of the brain (Patterson et al., 1989).

Corpus callosum

Broad band of nerve fibers that connects the left and right hemispheres of the cerebral cortex.

Get Outta Here!

Lateralization of Brain Function became a topic of research interest after Dr. Michael Gazzaniga observed the rather bizarre behavior of a patient who had undergone Callosotomy (severing of the Corpus Callosum) in order to alleviate his uncontrollable epilepsy. Dr. Gazzaniga reports the following incident in his lucid book "The Bifurcated Brain" (Gazzaniga, 1970).

One day, when Gazzaniga stopped by the patient's home one Sunday morning, **he saw the patient in the backyard, hitting and choking his wife with his *left hand* while his *right hand* was trying to prevent the left from beating and choking her!** Gazzaniga stopped the patient and asked him what was going on. In a very puzzled tone the patient explained that all of a sudden his left hand had started beating on his wife and was choking her! He loved her, so he was trying to stop that hand from hitting and choking her!

Gazzaniga reported this behavior to his seniors and soon they arranged to have him tested in the laboratory and discovered that *because of the severing of the Corpus Callosum, each half of the brain was now unable to share information with the other half, so it directed its desired action via the hand it controlled.* The right hemisphere which mediates emotion was mad at the wife, so the left hand which receives input from it was directed to hit her. *But the right hemisphere is mute, so the patient could not tell Gazzaniga that it/he was mad with his wife.* The left hemisphere that could talk, and controlled the right hand was not mad, and had no idea as to what was going on in the right hemisphere, so it was puzzled with the left hand's independent action, and tried to prevent the beating, like it said. It/he was able to talk about why the right hand did what it did, because the left hemisphere contains the Broca's area which mediates speech production and controls the right hand!

So, for people who have undergone a Callosotomy, the right hand really does not know what the left hand is doing!

How the Brain Is Studied

SURGICAL LESIONS Some of the earliest clues about how the brain functions came from observations of people with head injuries, and via *lesion production* in nonhuman subjects. Today, there are many ***non-invasive techniques*** that are just as if not more useful in studying the brain. Some of these techniques are as follows.

Lesion production

Technique for studying the brain that involves surgical damage to a precise region of the brain.

Electroencephalography (EEG)

Technique used to measure and record electrical activity of the cortex.

ELECTROENCEPHALOGRAPHY (EEG) Electroencephalography (EEG) has been around for quite some time. Because the brain constantly generates electrical activity, electrodes placed on the scalp can be used to record the electrical activity of the cortex. *The electroencephalograph amplifies these very small electrical potentials thousands of times and records them on paper in patterns called brain waves.* Brain waves vary according to a person's state—whether they are alert and mentally active, relaxed and calm, sleeping, or dreaming. The EEG has been used to diagnose such conditions as epilepsy, brain tumors, and a variety of other neurological disorders that generate abnormal brain-wave patterns.

COMPUTERIZED AXIAL TOMOGRAPHY (CAT) Was developed in the early 1970s. It is a refined X-ray technique that provides an accurate image of the brain. An X-ray

Computerized axial tomography (CAT)

A procedure used to locate brain abnormalities that involves rotating an X-ray scanner around the skull to produce an accurate image of a living brain.

Positron emission tomography (PET)

Technique for studying the brain that involves injecting a subject with a glucose-like sugar tagged with a radioactive isotope that accumulates in brain cells in direct proportion to their activity level.

Magnetic resonance imaging (MRI)

Procedure for studying the brain that uses radio waves to excite hydrogen protons in the brain tissue, creating a magnetic field change.

Functional magnetic resonance imaging (*f*MRI)

A method of magnetic resonance imaging that measures energy released by brain cells that are active during a specific task.

Endocrine system

System of ductless glands, including the pituitary, thyroid, parathyroids, adrenals, pancreas, and gonads, that secrete hormones directly into the bloodstream or lymph fluids.

scanner is rotated in a circular path around the skull, sending a thin beam of X-rays through the brain. A detector measures the amount of radiation that reaches the other side. Because different brain tissues absorb different amounts of radiation, the CAT scanners produce excellent pictures that can be used to locate tumors, lesions, and a variety of neurological abnormalities. In the past this information could only be obtained on autopsy.

POSITRON EMISSION TOMOGRAPHY (PET) A third noninvasive technique, the **PET scan** takes advantage of the fact that glucose is utilized at higher rates in active cells.

The technique works as follows. A patient receives an intravenous injection of a glucose-like sugar that has been tagged with a radioactive fluoride isotope. Active brain cells metabolize the sugar, but they cannot metabolize the radioactive component. Thus, the isotope accumulates within the cells in direct proportion to their activity level. As it decays, it emits charged particles called positrons. Instruments scanning the brain detect the radioactivity and record its location, and a computer converts this information into colored biochemical maps of the brain.

The PET scan has proved to be a useful tool in mapping the brain, pinpointing locations involved in movement, sensation, thinking, and even memory (Altman, 1986; Depue & Iacono, 1989; Fox et al., 1986).

MAGNETIC RESONANCE IMAGING (MRI) This fourth noninvasive technique uses harmless radio waves to excite hydrogen protons in the brain tissue, creating a magnetic field change that is detected by a huge magnet that surrounds the patient. The information is fed into a computer, which compiles it into a highly detailed, three-dimensional colored picture of the brain. The images created are much sharper and more detailed than those provided by the CAT scan. The MRI can pinpoint tumors and locate even the slightest reduction in blood flow in an artery or vein. It can also provide biochemical information, distinguishing between cancerous and noncancerous cells. In addition, MRI has been shown to be particularly helpful in diagnosing various diseases associated with brain abnormalities, such as multiple sclerosis (a degenerative disease of the CNS characterized by tremors and impaired speech), spinal cord abnormalities in children, and brain lesions associated with epilepsy.

A version of magnetic resonance imaging called **functional magnetic resonance imaging (*f*MRI)** provides high-resolution three-dimensional images of the brain during specific tasks. Regional changes in cerebral blood flow can be measured during a visual task, for example, and mapped onto an image of the brain's visual cortex. *Researchers using fMRI can actually watch the brain as a subject is engaged in specific cognitive or motor tasks to determine the relative contributions of various brain areas to these activities.* Currently, the fMRI technique is being used by Cognitive Neuroscientists to study decision making by normal college students (Caltech Media Relations, 2005).

MAGNETOENCEPHALOGRAPH (MEG) This is the latest non-invasive technique and recordings of the magnetic field generated by the brain are made. This technique is

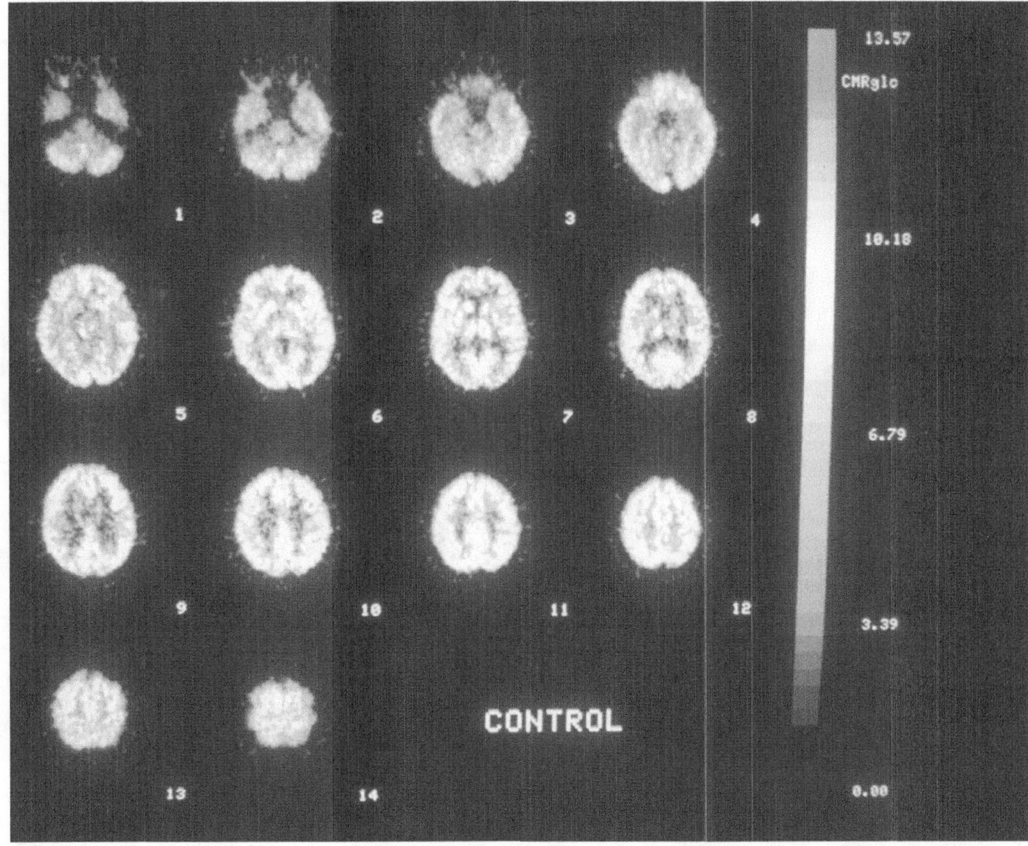

CMSP

Computer screen of a series of PET scans. PET stands for Positron Emission Tomography. PET scans identify areas of the brain that are most active in response to a variety of tasks.

being used to provide evidence for the plasticity of the human brain. It has advantages over other techniques because it provides ongoing measurements of change millisecond by millisecond and the exact areas of the brain in which the changes are taking place (http://ilabs.washington.edu/what-magnetoencephalography-meg; Okami, 2013).

THE ENDOCRINE SYSTEM

Up to this point in this chapter, we have covered only the nervous system. However, the nervous system is not the only biological system that governs behavior. To be complete, a discussion of biological foundations of behavior should also consider the role of the endocrine system, which is illustrated in Figure 3.11.

The **endocrine system** consists of several glands located throughout the body. Glands in the endocrine system are *ductless;* that is, they have no external excretory ducts but rather *secrete internally directly into the bloodstream or lymph fluid (the lymph system is a system of vessels and organs that makes up your immune system).* ***The major endocrine glands include the pituitary, the thyroid, the parathyroid, the adrenals, the pancreas, and the gonads.*** The location of the various endocrine glands is shown in Figure 3.11. Each of these glands produces **hormones**, which are secreted directly into the bloodstream. A single gland may produce several different hormones.

Hormones

Chemical messengers secreted by the endocrine glands that act to regulate the functioning of specific body organs.

FIGURE 3.11 The Major Glands of the Endocrine System

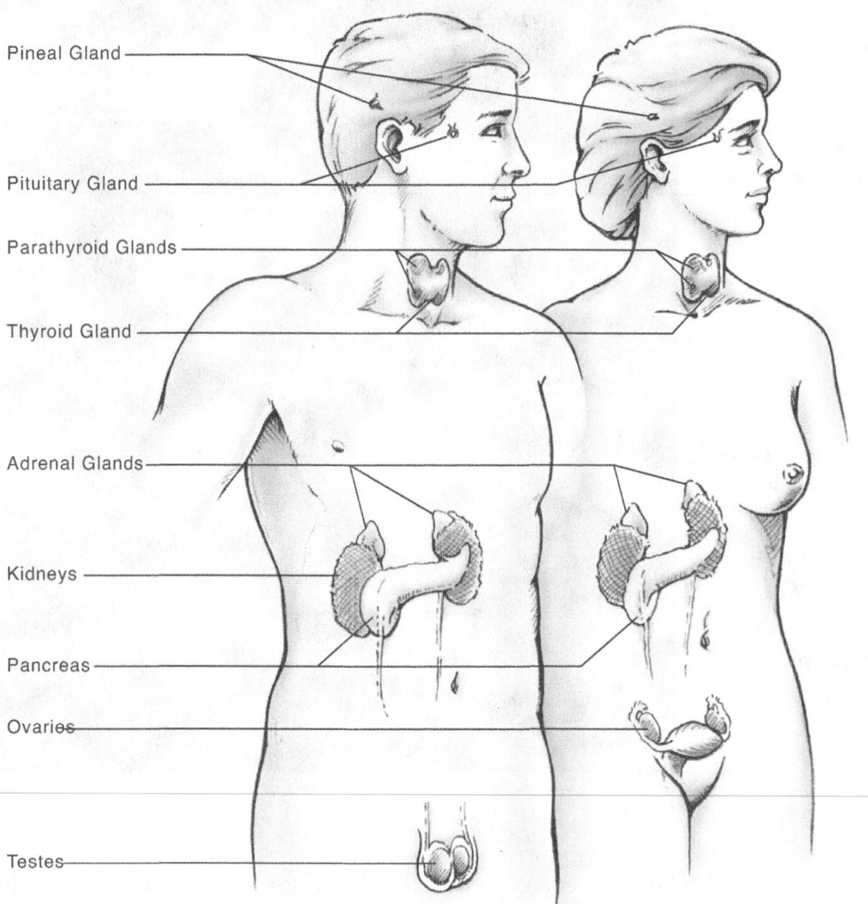

Like neurotransmitters, hormones act as chemical messengers. There is, however, a key difference. *Neurotransmitters have local action, limited to the synapse in which they are secreted, whereas hormones are released into the blood stream so they can influence several distal targets.*

The endocrine system often works in tandem with the nervous system. For example, when a person is suddenly exposed to a fearful stimulus, heart rate increases instantly in response to sympathetic nervous system input. *At the same time, the adrenal glands secrete epinephrine, which has a similar effect on heart rate.* In this fashion, the two major regulating systems of the body often work together.

The hypothalamus is a key interface between the nervous system and the endocrine system. As noted earlier, this region of the brain controls the activity of the pituitary gland through production of a group of chemicals known as *hypothalamic-releasing factors.* These chemicals in turn stimulate the pituitary to produce hormones that stimulate other glands.

Once an endocrine gland releases a hormone into the bloodstream, the substance travels throughout the body. However, each hormone exerts its primary influence only on certain specific organs and cells, often referred to as *target organs.* Some hormones, called trophic hormones, affect only the activity of another endocrine gland. For example, hormones called gonadotropins stimulate only the gonads.

Endocrine glands do not produce a steady stream of hormones. Instead, target organs signal the secreting glands either to increase or decrease secretions. Hormones are secreted until the target organ is stimulated; at this point, the target organ releases another substance that circulates back through the system to regulate hormonal activity in the initiating gland. This *negative-feedback mechanism* provides an internal control that limits extremes of hormone production.

Through these general mechanisms, the endocrine system influences many important physiological functions including metabolism, emotional responses, and motivation. A number of these effects are of particular interest to psychologists.

The Pituitary Gland

Pituitary gland

Gland in the endocrine system, located directly below and connected to the hypothalamus. The pituitary gland produces a number of hormones, many of which trigger other endocrine glands to release hormones.

Known as the master gland, the **pituitary gland** located below the hypothalamus, receives "releasing hormones" from the hypothalamus, and produces the largest number of different hormones, some of which trigger other glands to release hormones.

The pituitary also produces a number of huge protein molecules called neuropeptides. Neuropeptides act as neurotransmitters, and they influence a number of functions such as eating and drinking, sexual behavior, sleep, temperature regulation, pain, and responses to stress.

The Thyroid Gland

Thyroid gland

Endocrine gland located in the neck that influences metabolism, growth, and maturation. Produces the hormone thyroxine.

Thyroxine

The major hormone produced by the thyroid gland that regulates metabolism.

The **thyroid gland**, located within the neck, responds to pituitary stimulation by releasing the hormone **thyroxine**. This substance affects a number of biological functions, the most important of which is the regulation of metabolism. Because metabolism is in turn closely linked to motivational and mood states, the thyroid has an important impact on behavior. Low levels of thyroxine (hypothyroidism) can cause depression (Denicoff et al., 1990) and excessive thyroxine output (hyperthyroidism) may have just the opposite effect, causing hyperactivity, weight loss, anxiety, and excessive tension (Houston & Hay, 1990).

The Adrenal Glands

Adrenal glands

Glands within the endocrine system, located just above the kidneys, that influence emotional state, energy levels, and responses to stress by releasing hormones.

The **adrenals** are a pair of glands, located just above each kidney, that influence our emotional state, level of energy, and ability to cope with stress. They consist of two distinct parts: an inner core called the adrenal medulla and an outer layer called the adrenal cortex. The adrenal medulla produces epinephrine and norepinephrine, both of which prepare the body to respond to emergencies by making the heart beat faster, diverting blood from the stomach and intestines to the voluntary muscles, and enhancing energy resources by increasing blood sugar levels. The adrenal medulla is able to act quickly in threatening situations because it is stimulated directly by neural impulses.

The Gonads

Gonads

Glands within the endocrine system (ovaries in females and testes in males) that produce sex hormones that influence development of sexual systems and secondary sex characteristics as well as sexual motivation.

The **gonads**—ovaries in the female and testes in the male—produce several varieties of sex hormones. The ovaries produce two classes of hormones: the estrogens (the most important of which is estradiol), which influence development of female physical sex characteristics and regulation of the menstrual cycle; and the *progestational compounds* (the most important is progesterone), which help to regulate the menstrual cycle and prepare the uterus for pregnancy. Estradiol also contributes to sex differences in the cerebral cortex and the hypothalamus.

The primary output of the testes is the *androgens*. The most important of these hormones is testosterone, the function of which is to influence the development of both male physical sex characteristics and sexual motivation. In both sexes, the adrenal glands also secrete sex hormones, including small amounts of estrogen and greater quantities of androgen (this is where females get testosterone).

Around the onset of puberty, the sex hormones play a critical role in initiating changes in the primary sexual systems (the growth of the uterus, vagina, penis, and so forth) and the secondary sex characteristics, including body hair, breast development, and voice changes. They also exert strong influences on the fertility cycle in women and contribute to sexual motivation.

DRUGS AND BEHAVIOR

Not all drugs directly affect behavior and mental processes. Only psychoactive drugs directly affect behavior and mental processes.

For example, if you were ill due to Montezuma's curse or Delhi-belly (traveler's diarrhea caused by impure water) and felt miserable and weak, but took something like Pepto-Bismol, which put an end to your woes and your spirits were lifted, does that mean Pepto-Bismol caused the lift in mood? Yes and no.

Psychoactive drug

A drug that produces changes in behavior and mental processes by entering CNS tissue and modifying its actions.

Pepto simply cured the ailment, and *that* led to the improvement in mood. Hence Pepto-Bismol is not considered to be a **psychoactive drug**. ***A psychoactive drug is defined as a drug that produces changes in behavior and mental processes by entering CNS tissue and modifying its actions (Hansen et. al, 2000).***

Solomon Snyder, an expert on neurotransmitters, stated that "virtually every drug that alters mental function does so by interacting with a neurotransmitter system in the brain" (Snyder, 1984, p. 23). This interaction may happen in a variety of ways. Some drugs release neurotransmitters from the presynaptic vesicles; some mimic the action of neurotransmitters; other drugs prevent transmission by binding to receptors on the postsynaptic membrane, effectively preventing the contact between the neurotransmitters and postsynaptic receptors that is necessary to trigger the changes. Still other drugs interfere with the conservation of the neurotransmitters, leading to their depletion. In this section we examine some of the more common drugs used to alter behavior.

It is not uncommon for people in our society to have a few glasses of wine at a party, and then follow through the next morning with a few cups of coffee or tea to help clear the cobwebs. Such substances, as well as nicotine, marijuana, sleeping pills, cocaine, and narcotics, are psychoactive drugs.

Drug abusers

People who are addicted to drugs.

Although ***people who are addicted to drugs are*** commonly called "drug users," they are ***drug abusers***, because there are differences between the use of a drug, misuse of a drug, and abuse of a drug. ***Use of a drug is to correct a defective function, misuse is unwarranted use and abuse is continued ingestion when the drug is causing harm to the person taking it.***

Tolerance

When a person no longer gets the same effect from the same dose of a drug, and thus usually ends up taking a larger does to get the same effect.

Continued ingestion of many of the psychoactive drugs tends to lessen their effects, because the CNS tries to keep its normal level of function in spite of the drug, so that the user develops a **tolerance** to the drug. Development of tolerance means that a person no longer gets the same effect from the same dose of that drug, and he/she usually ends up taking a larger dose to get the same effect. For example, repeated injections of opiates such as heroin result in the development of tolerance, which means the user, must continually increase the amount of drug taken to get euphoric effects.

Psychological dependence

Intense craving for the drug without concomitant physiological withdrawal symptoms or changes in neural mechanisms

Along with tolerance, **physiological dependence** on the drug also develops over time. If a person has developed physiological dependence on a drug, abrupt stopping of the drug causes symptoms which tend to be opposite the effects produced by a drug and are known as "withdrawal symptoms" (Hansen et. al., 2000, p. 123). In the case of opiate dependence withdrawal symptoms such as cramps, nausea, tremors, headaches, and sweating occur with the drug's abrupt stoppage of use. One of the most ironic things about drug dependence is that the original reason for taking the substance may be replaced by a desperate need to maintain adequate levels of the drug just to avoid withdrawal symptoms.

The three major groups of drugs, classified by their effects, are depressants, stimulants, and hallucinogens. The remainder of this chapter looks at these types of drugs and their effects on people.

Depressants

Psychoactive drugs, including opiates, sedatives, and alcohol, that have the effect of slowing down or depressing central nervous system activity.

Depressants:

Drugs that tend to slow or depress activity in the central nervous system are classified as **depressants**. Substances in this category include sedatives and alcohol. Some researchers include Marijuana in this group while others consider Marijuana to be a Hallucinogen rather than a Depressant.

Sedatives

Class of depressant drugs including tranquilizers, barbiturates, and nonbarbiturates that induce relaxation, calmness, and sleep.

SEDATIVES: **Sedatives** are drugs that induce relaxation, calmness, and sleep. This group of drugs includes tranquilizers, such as Halcion, Xanax, and Ambien, barbiturates, such as Seconal, and the non-barbiturates like Quaalude. Many of these drugs are prescribed by physicians as remedies for anxiety, insomnia, and gastrointestinal disorders.

The tranquilizers are considered to be much safer than the barbiturates or non-barbiturates, and other than for epilepsy where barbiturates are still prescribed, most physicians prefer to prescribe the tranquilizers for sedation etc. Sedative drugs increase the sensitivity of postsynaptic receptors for *gamma-amino butyric acid (GABA)*, which acts to inhibit neural transmission. By increasing the inhibition generated by GABA, sedative drugs reduce neural activity in the circuits involved with emotional arousal, thus allowing a sense of calmness at low doses and sedation and sleep at higher doses.

Alcohol, a CNS depressant, is a "teratogen". It causes birth defects when abused by pregnant women especially during the embryonic stage as organogenesis takes place at that time. Alcohol crosses the Blood-Brain-Barrier and because the placental barrier is similar, it enters the blood supply of the embryo. Once in the developing embryo's system, it can prevent organs from forming or cause malformations or birth defects.

There are two well recognized syndromes. One is called Fetal Alcohol Syndrome, which causes severe mental retardation and the other is called Fetal Alcohol Effects (FAE). FAE is a milder syndrome and is seen in babies of women who consume as little as two glasses of an alcoholic drink like wine or beer, throughout the pregnancy. The babies look normal, but have an IQ that is lower than normal by ten to fifteen points.

Narcotics (opiates)

Also known as opiates, a class of depressant drugs that includes opium, morphine, codeine, and heroin.

OPIATES: Opiates *or narcotics* are another category of drugs that produce sedation. *Opium* is derived from a sticky resin secreted by the opium poppy and *morphine* and *codeine*, two commonly prescribed painkillers are found in opium. *Heroin*, another opiate, is obtained by chemically treating morphine.

Heroin is snorted or injected directly into the veins, which is known as intravenous use. When injected in the veins, the almost immediate effect is a "rush," which users describe as an overwhelming sensation of pleasure. Shortly after it is injected, heroin decomposes into morphine, which produces other effects commonly associated with opiate usage: a sense of well-being, contentment, and drowsiness. However, the intravenous abuser quickly acquires tolerance and physical dependence and psychological dependence on the pleasure, which gets him addicted to the drug. The long-term effects of this addiction can be devastating. People addicted to heroin do almost anything to ensure their supply of the drug—steal, prostitute themselves, or even crawl through a sewer and beg to buy it (White, 1985, p. 149).

What happens when an addict tries to break the habit? After a few hours without heroin, the user begins to experience withdrawal symptoms which are like a terrible flu with severe diarrhea along with an insatiable craving for the drug! So quite often, the addict prefers to succumb to the addiction.

Stimulants: Caffeine, Nicotine, Amphetamines, and Cocaine

Stimulants

Psychoactive drugs, including caffeine, nicotine, amphetamines, and cocaine, that stimulate the central nervous system by increasing the transmission of neural impulses.

Drugs that stimulate the central nervous system by increasing neural transmission are called **stimulants**. The most widely consumed of these drugs are caffeine and nicotine, which are legal, and the amphetamines and cocaine, which are illegal but more potent than caffeine or nicotine.

CAFFEINE The psychoactive ingredient found in chocolate, coffee, tea, and colas has long provided people with a quick lift. Within a few minutes after it is consumed, heart and respiration rates and blood pressure increase. Most feel mentally stimulated; some experience a brief burst of energy. Despite its reputation as "the milk of chess players" because it supposedly enhances intellectual ability, it does not enhance performance on intellectual tasks, unless fatigue had set in (McKim, 1999, p. 192). People who routinely consume six or more cups of coffee, or equivalent amounts of caffeinated soft drinks, may suffer from *caffeinism,* which produces symptoms such as irritability, headaches, the jitters, and sleep disturbances, etc., *which could be misdiagnosed as anxiety neurosis.* People can become physically dependent on caffeine, as evidenced by the countless number of people who just cannot function without their daily quota of coffee, tea, or cola.

Caffeine exerts its effects on the nervous system by blocking adenosine receptors. Adenosine is an inhibitory neurotransmitter that produces behavioral sedation and regulates the dilation of blood vessels (Julian, 2001; Hsu, Wang, & Chiu, 2010).

NICOTINE: Nicotine is second only to caffeine on the list of widely used stimulants. Found in tobacco, nicotine increases heart rate, blood pressure, and stomach activity, and constricts blood vessels. Paradoxically, it may have either a relaxing or a stimulating effect on the user, depending on the circumstances and the user's expectations. Nicotine produces physiological dependence and psychological dependence, and people who stop smoking may experience a variety of withdrawal symptoms including craving for tobacco, increased appetite, stomach cramps, headaches, restlessness, irritability, insomnia, anxiety, and depression.

The long-term effects of smoking have been well publicized: Over 500 thousand people die every year from coronary heart disease, cancer, respiratory diseases, and other diseases caused by smoking. There is also evidence that women who smoke while pregnant have a higher incidence of miscarriages, stillbirths, low birth-weight babies, and babies who die from sudden infant death syndrome (SIDS) than women who do not smoke (Zotti, 2003) and there is new evidence that childhood Asthma is linked to maternal grandmother's smoking, in children of non-smoking mothers, so here are multi-generational ill-effects! (Leslie F.M. 2013).

Amphetamines

A group of powerful stimulants, including Benzedrine, Dexedrine, and Ritalin, that dramatically increase alertness and promote feelings of euphoria.

AMPHETAMINES: **Amphetamines** are very potent stimulants, sold under the trade names Benzedrine, Dexedrine, and Methedrine (speed) or methamphetamine, which is a slightly altered version of amphetamine. These drugs tend to dramatically increase alertness and activity, counteract fatigue, and promote feelings of euphoria and well-being by increasing the activity of norepinephrine (NE) and dopamine (DA) circuits (Cooper, 2003). Tolerance, physical and psychological dependence occurs with repeated amphetamine ingestion.

When amphetamines are abused intravenously for the rush they produce, they can cause muscle and joint aches, weight loss, tremors, and feelings of paranoia that are indistinguishable from paranoid schizophrenia (McKim, 199, p. 211).

COCAINE: Cocaine is a powerful central nervous system stimulant that is extracted from leaves of the coca shrub. It is often sniffed (snorted) through a straw into the mucous membranes of the nasal passages. A solution of the drug may also be injected into the vein. Crack is the street name given to cocaine that has been processed from cocaine hydrochloride (the crystalline derivative of the coca leaf that is sold on the street as coke) into freebase by using ammonia or baking soda and water and heating the mixture. The baking soda causes a crackling sound when the base is heated, thus giving rise to the street name.

No matter which form is used, many of cocaine's effects are similar to those of amphetamines. They include increased alertness and abundance of energy, feelings of euphoria, and a sense of well-being. There is good evidence that cocaine blocks the reuptake of dopamine and norepinephrine, increasing the time these chemicals actively stimulate their receptors.

The craving produced by intravenous Cocaine use is said to be very powerful, and is said to be occasionally triggered by environmental cues (Hansen et. al. 2001, pg. 273). Although there is no known cure for cocaine addiction, research in Dr. Ettinger's laboratory has resulted in a cocaine vaccine. Rats vaccinated with the cocaine antibody preparation were resistant to cocaine's reinforcing and analgesic effects (Ettinger et al., 1997; 2000).

Get Outta Here!

In the late 19th century Angelo Mariani, a Corsican chemist, isolated the psychoactive ingredient of the coca leaves chewed by Andean Indians, and added it to a special Bordeaux wine and named it ***Vin Mariani***. This wine was so appreciated by the **Pope Leo the XIII, that he presented a gold medal to Angelo Mariani for his fine work!** (Hansen et al., 2001, p. 265).

Hallucinogens

Class of psychoactive drugs, including LSD and ecstasy, that alter sensory perceptions, thinking processes, and emotions, often causing delusions, hallucinations, and altered sense of time and space.

LSD (Lysergic acid diethylamide)

Hallucinogenic drug derived from a fungus that grows on rye grass that produces profound distortions of sensations, feelings, time, and thought.

Hallucinogens: LSD, Ecstasy, and Marijuana

LSD Derived from the ergot fungus that grows on rye grass, **LSD** became recognized for its extreme potency and psychoactive properties in the 1940s. Throughout the 1950s and early 1960s, researchers experimented with it as a tool for treating behavioral and emotional disorders, to allow spiritual insights to patients who were terminal, and as a drug that might have possible military applications. It soon became a popular drug of misuse and was made illegal.

Although the exact mechanism of action of LSD is not known, it is a serotonergic drug. The hallucinations probably result from disinhibition of the neural circuits responsible for dreaming so they operate even though the user is wide awake (Julien, 2001).

ECSTASY: Ecstasy or MDMA is a hallucinogenic that is less potent as compared to LSD. The most prominent effects of ecstasy are mood enhancement, euphoria, a sense of depersonalization, and thought disturbances. In addition, users commonly experience hyperthermia, rapid heart rate, high blood pressure, muscle rigidity, and convulsions. Of the recreational drugs discussed here, ecstasy is by far the most toxic to the nervous system

Marijuana

Drug derived from the hemp plant *Cannabis sativa,* containing the chemical THC (delta 9-tetrahydrocannabinol), which is commonly classified as a hallucinogen, although it also may have depressant and stimulant effects.

Anandamide

A naturally occurring substance that binds to THC receptors in the brain. Marijuana contains THC, which also binds to these receptors.

and repeated use appears to irreversibly destroy serotonin-containing neurons (NIDA, 2001; Julien, 2001). Despite these adverse effects there is an ever-increasing use of ecstasy, especially in dance clubs and "raves." Most recently, researchers from Harvard received FDA permission to administer ecstasy to terminally ill cancer patients to test it for psychotherapeutic anxiety-mitigating effect (Weiss, 2004).

MARIJUANA As a recreational drug, **marijuana** is the most widely used of the illegal psychoactive drugs, second in popularity only to alcohol.

Marijuana is derived from the flowering top of the Cannabis sativa, a hemp plant once known primarily as an excellent material for making rope. The mind-altering component of marijuana is the chemical THC (delta 9-tetrahydrocannabinol). Marijuana is classified as a hallucinogen because relatively high doses of THC can produce hallucinations however it is not typically hallucinogenic.

Until recently, researchers did not know how marijuana altered the activity of the brain to produce its euphoric effects. However, William Devine and his coworkers identified receptors for THC in the brain, as well as a natural substance that binds with these THC receptors. The brain's natural THC has been named **anandamide** (Devine et al., 1992) from the Sanskrit word ananda, meaning bliss, and amide for its chemical nature. It

When Coca-Cola first appeared on the market in 1885 it contained cocaine. Cocaine was removed from soft drinks in 1903.

is now believed that anandamide plays an important role in regulating mood, pain, movement, and appetite.

Two physiological effects of marijuana use are increased heart rate and enhanced appetite. Small doses often produce euphoria and enhance some sensory experiences, such as listening to music. Marijuana impairs reaction time and the ability to concentrate on complex tasks, and some people become confused, agitated, or extremely anxious under its influence. Marijuana impairs a person's perceptual skills and motor coordination, thus significantly increasing his or her risk of having an accident while driving an automobile. Recall may also be impaired while under the influence of marijuana.

Medical practitioners have discovered that marijuana can be therapeutic in some situations. For example, it can be helpful in epilepsy and glaucoma (a disease that can cause blindness). It has been shown to reduce the nausea that often accompanies chemotherapy treatment for cancer patients, and it may now be used to prevent some of the weight loss associated with AIDS diseases. Because of these legitimate medical uses, marijuana can be legally obtained for these purposes in some states. Controversy still surrounds the issue of marijuana legalization in the United States and it is likely to continue for some time.

Get Outta Here!

Approximately 4000 years ago, a legendary Chinese Emperor, Chen Nung or Shen Nung, first recognized the properties of hemp or marijuana. He correctly prescribed it for glaucoma, gout, malaria, gas pains, and absent mindedness! (Hansen et al., 2001, p. 367). Likewise, Chen Nung was also the first to warn that consuming its fruits would make one "see devils," and if used over a long period of time, it would allow communication with spirits and lighten one's body (McKim, 1991, p. 277).

SUMMARY

OVERVIEW OF THE NERVOUS SYSTEM: ORGANIZATION AND FUNCTION

1. The nervous system of humans and other vertebrates consists of two major parts: the central nervous system (CNS) and the peripheral nervous system (PNS).
2. The CNS consists of the brain and the spinal cord. It occupies the commanding position in the nervous system, as it coordinates and integrates all bodily functions.
3. The PNS transmits messages to and from the CNS. It is subdivided into the somatic nervous system and the autonomic nervous system.

NEURONS: BASIC UNITS OF THE NERVOUS SYSTEM

4. There are three major classes of neurons: sensory neurons that carry messages to the CNS; motor neurons that transmit messages from the CNS to muscles and glands; and interneurons that connect other neurons to each other.
5. Neurons have four common structures: the cell body, which handles metabolic functions; the dendrites, which receive neural messages; the axon, which conducts a message to the end of the neuron; and the terminal buttons at the end of the axon, which release transmitter substances.
6. The transmission of a neural message involves both electrical and chemical aspects. Electrical processes are activated when the dendrites (or cell body) of a neuron respond to an impulse from neighboring neurons by undergoing a change in permeability of the cell membrane. Voltage changes then occur, due to an influx of positive sodium ions through the more permeable membrane. These voltage changes are called graded potentials. When the sum of graded potentials reaches a sufficient magnitude, an electrical signal or action potential is generated that flows along the length of the neuron.
7. Neural impulses are transmitted from one neuron to another, across the synaptic gap, via chemical messengers called neurotransmitters. These transmitter substances may act either to excite or inhibit action potentials in the receiving neuron.
8. Variations in neurotransmitter levels, or in responsiveness to these chemical messengers, have been linked with various psychological disorders and the action of numerous drugs.

THE PERIPHERAL NERVOUS SYSTEM

9. The PNS, which transfers information to and from the CNS, has two divisions: somatic and autonomic.
10. The somatic nervous system serves the major skeletal muscles that carry out intentional movements. It also contains nerves that transmit sensory information from the skin, muscles, and sensory organs of the body.
11. The autonomic nervous system controls the glands and smooth muscles of internal organs. The two subdivisions of the autonomic nervous system, the sympathetic and parasympathetic system, operate in an integrative fashion to allow the body to function optimally when either relaxed or highly aroused. The sympathetic system is particularly active during emotional emergencies. The parasympathetic system, which provides a braking mechanism for organs activated by the sympathetic system, is more involved during relaxation and body restoration.

THE CENTRAL NERVOUS SYSTEM

12. The spinal cord conveys messages to and from the brain, helps coordinate the two sides of the body,

and mediates certain basic reflexive behaviors (such as the quick withdrawal of a hand from a hot stove).

13. The medulla, the lowest part of the brain, contains centers that control many vital life-support functions such as breathing, heartbeat, and blood pressure.
14. The pons, a large bulge in the lower brain core, plays a role in fine-tuning motor messages and in processing some sensory information in addition to having some autonomic functions.
15. The cerebellum, tucked beneath the back part of the cerebral hemispheres, coordinates and regulates motor movements.
16. The reticular formation or reticular activating system, a set of neural circuits extending from the lower brain up to the thalamus, plays a role in controlling levels of arousal and alertness.
17. The limbic system, a collection of structures located around the central core of the brain, is closely associated with emotional expression.
18. The hypothalamus, located beneath the thalamus, helps to maintain homeostasis within the body's internal environment. In addition, it plays a key role in mediating emotional experiences and their expression and serves as the hub of the neuroendocrine system.
19. The thalamus, located beneath the cerebral cortex, plays a role in routing incoming sensory information to appropriate areas within the cerebral cortex and receives input from the cortex which allows selectivity of attention to sensory stimuli.
20. The basal ganglia consist of several structures involved in motor movement, including the caudate nucleus, putamen, and substantia nigra.

THE CEREBRAL CORTEX

21. The cerebral cortex, the thin outer layer of the cortex, is the part of the brain responsible for higher mental processes such as perceiving, thinking, and remembering.
22. To some degree, researchers have been able to localize a variety of functions within various regions or lobes of the cortex of the two hemispheres. The frontal lobe contains the motor cortex, a narrow strip of brain tissue that controls a wide range of intentional body movements. The primary brain center for controlling speech is also in the frontal lobe. The parietal lobe contains the somatosensory cortex, which receives sensory information about touch, pressure, pain, temperature, and body position from various areas of the body. The occipital lobe consists primarily of the visual cortex, devoted to the business of seeing. A primary function of the temporal lobe, hearing, is localized in the auditory cortex.
23. A number of techniques such as electroencephalography (EEG), computerized axial tomography (CAT), positron emission tomography (PET), and magnetic resonance imaging (MRI) and *f*MRI (Functional MRI) and Magnetoencephalograph or MEG.

THE ENDOCRINE SYSTEM

24. The endocrine system is composed of several ductless glands that secrete hormones directly into the bloodstream. The endocrine system often works in tandem with the nervous system to regulate a variety of bodily responses. The hypothalamus functions as a key interface between the nervous system and the endocrine system.
25. The endocrine system influences many important physiological functions, mental processes, and behavior patterns, including disease regulation, metabolism, emotional responses, and motivation.
26. The pituitary gland produces hormones that trigger other glands to action. It produces growth

hormone, which controls the rate of growth, and neuropeptides, which influence such things as eating, drinking, sexual behavior, sleep, pain reduction, and responses to stress.

27. The thyroid gland produces thyroxine, which helps to regulate metabolism. Lethargy and hyperactivity are related to too little or too much thyroxine, respectively.
28. The paired adrenal glands produce a variety of hormones, including epinephrine and norepinephrine, which prepare the body to respond to emergencies and cope with stress.
29. The gonads secrete several varieties of sex hormones that influence development of physical sex characteristics, sexual reproduction, and sexual motivation.

DRUGS AND BEHAVIOR

30. Sedative drugs such as Halcion, Xanax, and the barbiturates induce relaxation and sleep. They are often prescribed for anxiety and sleep disorders.
31. Opiates or narcotics such as morphine and heroin induce a state or euphoria and are highly addictive. Opiates are prescribed to control pain.
32. Alcohol acts as a central nervous system depressant in the cerebral cortex and cerebellum. Alcohol is the nation's number one drug problem and is also a teratogen, or producer of deformed babies, when abused by a pregnant woman.
33. The major stimulants include caffeine, nicotine, amphetamine, and cocaine.
34. Amphetamine and cocaine are potent stimulants that are highly addictive.
35. Hallucinogens such as LSD, ecstasy, and marijuana produce changes in perception and mood.
36. Marijuana has few if any a long-term effects on cognition, but it does disrupt cognitive functioning (including memory) when a person is under its influence. A number of states have legalized marijuana for medical purposes.

TERMS AND CONCEPTS

central nervous system (CNS)
peripheral nervous system (PNS)
neuron
sensory (afferent) neuron
motor (efferent) neuron
interneuron
cell body
dendrites
axon
terminal buttons
resting potential
graded potential
action potential
all-or-none law
Lock & Key Principle
glia cells
myelin sheath
node of Ranvier
synapse
neurotransmitters
excitatory postsynaptic potential (EPSPs)
inhibitory postsynaptic potentials (IPSPs)
acetylcholine
norepinephrine
dopamine
serotonin

Gamma-amino butyric acid (GABA)
endorphin
glutamate
somatic nervous system
autonomic nervous system
sympathetic nervous system
parasympathetic nervous system
cerebral hemispheres
medulla
pons
cerebellum
reticular activating system (RAS)
limbic system
amygdala
hippocampus
hypothalamus
thalamus
basal ganglia
caudate nucleus
putamen
substantia nigra
cerebral cortex
sensory cortex
motor cortex
association cortex
frontal lobe
Broca's area
parietal lobe
somatosensory cortex
occipital lobe
visual cortex
temporal lobe
auditory cortex
Wernicke's area
agnosia
lateralization of function
corpus callosum
lesion production
electroencephalography (EEG)
computerized axial tomography (CAT)
positron emission tomography (PET)
magnetic resonance imaging (MRI)
magnetoencephalograph (MEG)
functional magnetic resonance imaging (*f*MRI)
endocrine system
hormones
pituitary gland
thyroid gland
thyroxine
adrenal glands
gonads
depressants
organogenesis
teratogen
sedatives
narcotics (opiates)
stimulants
amphetamines
hallucinogens
LSD (lysergic acid diethylamide)
marijuana
anandamide

CHAPTER 4

Sensation and Perception

Corbis

A soft kiss, a heady perfume, a lilting melody, a beautiful sunrise; what allows you to experience these things? Have you ever wondered how something out there in the world becomes a part of your inner experience? If you did, this chapter will help you understand how stimuli from the outer world become sensations and perceptions.

PRINCIPLES OF SENSATION AND PERCEPTION

All perceptions begin with a *stimulus,* some type of physical energy such as a sound or a flash of light, to which we can respond. *The process which allows the detection of external stimuli by converting stimulus energy into neural impluses is known as* ***sensation****. The organization and interpretation of these sensations lends a unique meaning to them, and that subjective experience of meaning is referred to as* ***perception****.*

Sensations

Basic, immediate experiences that a stimulus such as a sound elicits in a sense organ such as the ear.

Perception

Process of interpreting, organizing, and often elaborating on sensations.

Although the two processes are difficult to distinguish they are different. For example, if you step out on a cloudless, star-lit night and try to identify the constellations, all you might see at first are a bunch of stars. However, with a little patience you might be able to spot the Big Dipper or The Great Bear, etc. *Once you begin to see the pattern, the sensation of the light from the stars has been given a meaning, or it has been perceived.* However, for you to even see the light emitted by the stars, that light, which is an electro-magnetic energy, has to be converted to the electric signals that our nervous system is capable of processing. *This process of conversion of other forms of stimulus energy into usable electric signals is known as* ***transduction****.* We will study transduction in a little more detail after learning a little more about the general phenomena of sensation and perception.

What Do We Perceive?

Transduction

Process by which sensory organs transform mechanical, chemical, or light energy into the electrochemical energy that is generated by neurons firing.

The fact that sensations result from the **transduction** of physical energy in the environment into neural impulses raises an interesting question: Since noises, smells, sights, and sounds surround us, why are we not equally aware of all these sensations? For instance, as you are reading, your nervous system is being bombarded with stimuli from numerous different sources. Besides the visual stimuli this book provides, there are other sounds, sights, smells, and tactile sensations. Your world is full of different kinds of physical energy.

Although many of these stimuli are transformed into sensations and ultimately perceptions, many also go unheeded. Three factors which determine whether a stimulus is perceived or not, are *sensory thresholds, attention,* and *adaptation*. The investigation of these factors can be traced from the very beginnings of psychology to the present in a field of psychology called psychophysics. **Psychophysics** is the part of psychology that focuses on the relationship between physical aspects of external stimuli and our perceptions of them.

Psychophysics

Study of the relationship between the physical aspects of external stimuli and our own perceptions of these stimuli.

Psychophysics

SENSORY THRESHOLDS The psychological world constructed by our brain is much simpler than the physical complexity of the world around us because our sense organs do not inform our brains about all of the events that take place. Only those stimuli which are intense enough to reach a certain level of intensity called "the threshold" are perceived. For example, our sense of smell is activated only when an adequate number of chemical molecules are present in the air.

Threshold

Minimum level of intensity or strength of a stimulus that is sufficient to activate a sensory process (for instance, the minimum number of molecules that must be present in the air for us to smell a substance).

One of the most important reasons we do not respond to many stimuli, therefore, is simply the biological limitations of our senses. Two kinds of sensory thresholds operate to limit our perception of sensation: *absolute thresholds* and *difference thresholds.*

ABSOLUTE AND DIFFERENCE THRESHOLDS Imagine yourself waiting at a restaurant for a special person with whom you will dine. When the person arrives and takes a seat at your table you perceive a subtle scent of perfume or cologne but you're not quite sure. For several minutes you wonder whether you are imagining the scent or if you really do smell it. As you begin talking you move closer and suddenly you recognize the scent. It is not strong, but detectable enough to distinguish it clearly. How intense did the scent need to simply notice it and how much more intense did it have to be to recognize it clearly? Both of these questions are about sensory thresholds. The first question pertains to what psychologists call an absolute threshold and the second question refers to a difference threshold.

Absolute threshold

Minimum physical intensity of a stimulus that can be perceived by an observer 50 percent of the time.

Thresholds: When you first noticed the perfume or cologne but couldn't be sure what it was its intensity was at your **absolute threshold**. *An absolute threshold is defined as the minimum physical intensity of a stimulus that can be perceived by an observer 50 percent of the time.* Table 4.1 lists some absolute thresholds for the five major senses. These values are average and represent ideal conditions in a laboratory. Clearly, you could not hear a watch ticking 20 feet away under normal circumstances.

Difference threshold

The minimum difference in intensity that we can distinguish between two stimuli 50 percent of the time. Also known as the just noticeable difference (JND).

Difference Thresholds As your friend moved closer and you could now distinguish the scent, this change in intensity was sufficient to reach your difference threshold. A **difference threshold** *is the minimum increase in the intensity of a stimulus necessary to just notice a change 50 percent of the time.* This increase in intensity is also referred to as a **just noticeable difference** or **jnd**.

The cut-off value of 50% is based on probability of occurrence of any one possibility when only one of two possibilities can occur. For example, in coin tossing where you can either have a head or a tail, you will get a head in roughly half of the coin flips, or 50% of the time, due to pure chance. *So anything above 50% indicates something other than chance is influencing the coin-toss.* In the case of the detection of the perfume or any other stimu-

TABLE 4.1 Absolute Sensory Thresholds

Sense	Absolute Threshold
Smell	One drop of perfume dispersed in a three room apartment
Taste	One teaspoon of sugar dissolved in a gallon of water
Hearing	Ticking of a watch at 20 feet, under quiet condition
Touch	Wing of a bee falling on your cheek from a distance of one centimeter

lus, *if it is detectable on more than 50% of the trials, then the intensity of the stimulus, rather than chance is attributed for its detection.*

WEBER'S LAW AND THE JUST NOTICEABLE DIFFERENCE Our perception of a particular stimulus is always relative to its background level or its context. Thus, the degree of increase or decrease in intensity that is necessary to produce a jnd (just noticeable difference) depends on the original strength of the stimulus. In 1834 a German scientist named E. H. Weber conducted a classic experiment that revealed one of the first major principles of sensation. *He discovered that the difference threshold for various stimulus intensities tends to be a constant fraction of the original stimulus intensity.* Thus, as the strength of the original stimulus increases, the magnitude of the change must also increase in order for a jnd to be perceived. This relationship is known as **Weber's law.**

Weber's law

One of the major principles of sensation, based on the fact that for various stimulus intensities, the difference threshold tends to be a constant fraction of the stimulus. As the strength of the original stimulus increases, the magnitude of the change must also increase in order for a just noticeable difference to be perceived.

In mathematical form, Weber's law is expressed as the following equation:

$$\Delta I = kI$$

(Where ΔI is the change in stimulus intensity necessary for a jnd, I is the initial stimulus intensity, and k is a value known as Weber's constant.)

Although this sounds complicated, it is really quite simple to apply. In a psychophysics experiment you might be asked to judge the difference between two weights; say one 10 lb. weight and another 10.10 lb. weight. The difference of .10 lbs. is not enough to tell the difference (.10 lbs. is less than 1 jnd for 10 lbs.). However, if the second weight were increased to 10.20 lbs., you could now detect a noticeable difference. The ratio of stimulus intensity for a jnd of weight is 1/50th of the original weight. Using this ratio and Weber's Law, how many pounds would have to be added to a 100 lb. weight for you to just notice a difference? If you answered 2 lbs. this would be correct. The fraction, 0.02 or 1/50, is called a *Weber's constant.* Weber discovered that this constant remains the same for each dimension of sensation, but changes for different stimulus dimensions. For instance, Weber's constant for brightness of light is 1/60, and for the taste of salt, 1/3 (Schiffman, 2000), so our sense of vision is more sensitive than our sense of taste.

ATTENTION Another factor influencing how much of the outside world we perceive is attention. In most situations, it is impossible to be aware of all the stimuli around us, even if we are biologically capable of responding to them. Instead, we pay attention to some but not to others. For example, returning to the scenario of your dinner date, you may not have been aware of the music in the background because you were listening to your friend. After your friend stops, however, your attention might shift so that you hear the next song.

Attention

A cognitive mechanism that determines which stimuli, from a pool of available stimuli, an organism responds to or perceives.

Attention is a selective psychological process in that we are aware of certain stimuli and not others at any given moment. Attention does not block the physical and biological response of our sense organs to these stimuli; it simply increases or decreases our psychological perception of these events. Of course, some stimuli are difficult to overlook, for example, someone mentioning your name in a conversation at the next table. At other times attention to one stimulus interferes with our perception of another. Later in this chapter we consider several characteristics of stimuli that are particularly effective in capturing our attention.

Sensory adaptation

In perception, the decrease in the response of sensory receptors to stimuli when exposed to continual, unchanging stimulation.

SENSORY ADAPTATION **Sensory adaptation** describes the decrease in the response of sensory receptors when they are exposed to continual, unchanging stimulation. Sensory adaptation occurs in all of the sensory organs, but some adapt more quickly than others. In fact, perception is actually dependent on stimulus change. If stimuli remain constant we adapt to them and they are no longer perceivable.

Our receptors for smell are the quickest to adapt, which is fortunate for people who live near industrial plants or have jobs requiring them to work in foul-smelling environments. Most of our other senses adapt fairly quickly to constant stimulation. For example, you are probably not aware of background noises in your room until they actually change. You may only notice that your refrigerator is quite noisy when it shuts off.

The following sections will describe the mechanism underlying each of the sense organs to help you understand sensation and perception.

VISION

In many ways, vision is our most important sense. It contributes enormously to our awareness of the surrounding environment, and it provides extremely valuable information that we can use to change our location or actions. Much of what we do depends on an adequately functioning visual system. The primary importance of vision is reflected in the fact that a greater portion of our brains is devoted to vision than to any of the other senses.

Our visual systems are composed of three major parts: the eyes, which capture and respond to light energy; the neural circuits that transmit signals from the eye to the brain; and the visual centers within the brain that interpret these messages.

Light: The Stimulus for Vision

We see things because they reflect light. Light is a form of electromagnetic radiation. Virtually all matter consists of oscillating, electrically charged particles that discharge many forms of electromagnetic radiation, only one of which is light. Other varieties include cosmic rays, gamma rays, X rays, ultraviolet rays, infrared rays, microwaves, and TV and radio waves.

Electromagnetic radiation travels in waves, and different forms of this energy have different wavelengths. A wavelength is precisely defined by how far the radiation travels between oscillations. Wavelength is measured in nanometers, abbreviated nm. A nanometer is equal to a billionth of a meter.

Figure 4.1 shows the full range of the electromagnetic spectrum. Note humans can perceive wavelengths ranging from roughly 400 to 750 nm, which is a small portion of the electromagnetic spectrum. All living things do not share our own blindness to other seg-

FIGURE 4.1 The Electromagnetic Spectrum

This figure shows the full range of the electromagnetic spectrum. Visible light represents only a small part of the complete spectrum. The visible spectrum can be obtained by passing white light (such as sunlight) through a prism. Visible light ranges from about 400 nm. to 750 nm.

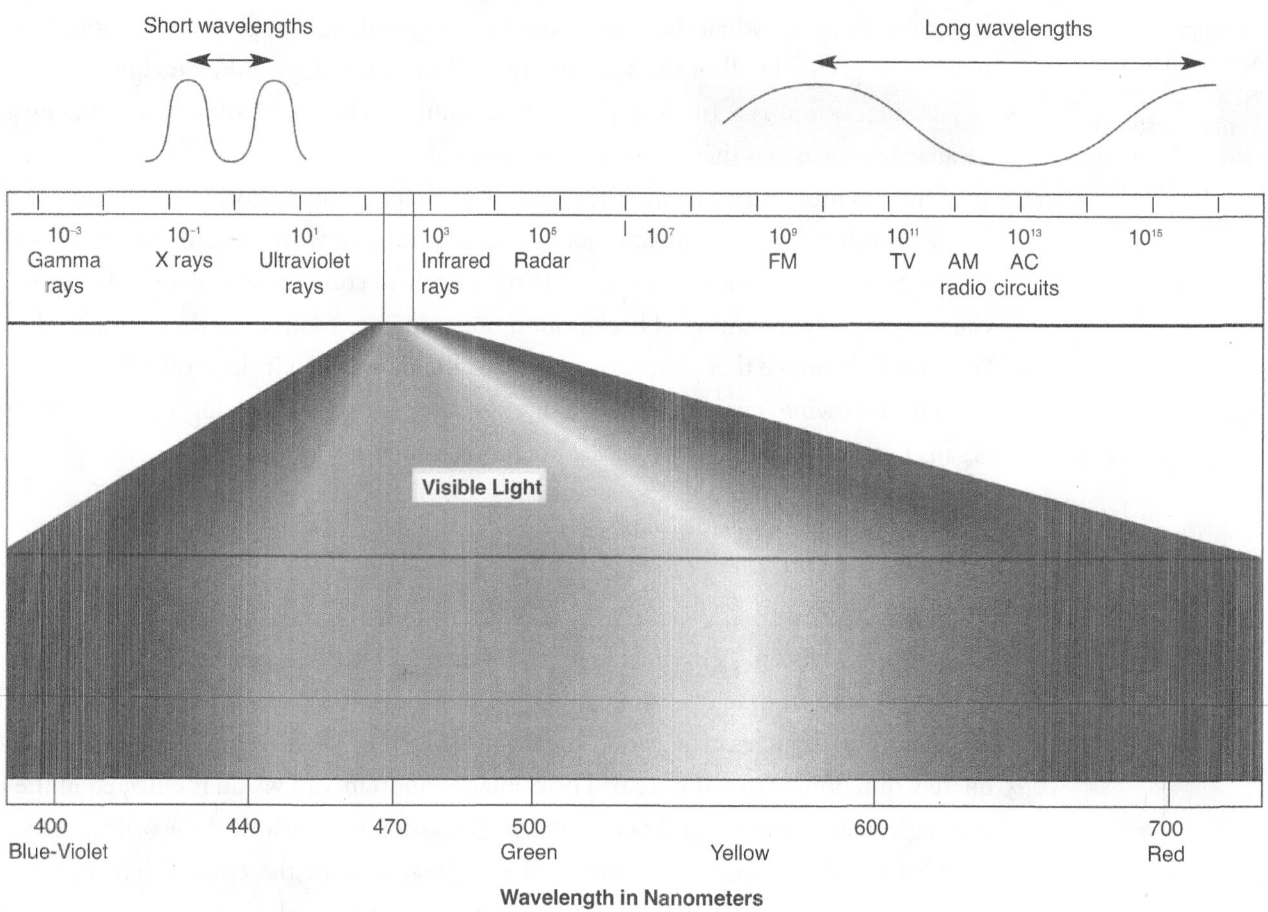

Brightness

Intensity of light, measured by the number of photons or particles of electromagnetic radiation emitted by a light source.

Hue

The color we perceive, determined partly by the wavelength of light and partly by the complex process by which an organism's visual system mixes wavelengths.

ments of the full spectrum. For example, some insects can discern ultraviolet light, and some predatory birds use infrared radiation to detect their prey.

PROPERTIES OF LIGHT Brightness, hue, and saturation are three properties of light that are particularly important in the psychological study of vision. **Brightness**, or the intensity of light, is measured by the number of *photons* (particles of electromagnetic radiation that we see as light). In general, the more intense the light source, more the number of photons emitted, the brighter the appearance of the light, and the higher the amplitude of the light wave.

Hue, or the color we perceive, is determined partly by the wavelength of light. To people with normal eye-sight, a wavelength of 400 nm. appears violet, 500 nm. appears blue-green, 600 nm. appears as yellow-orange, and 700 nm. looks red. The perception of color is not just a matter of wavelength, however. Several colors, such as purple and white, are not even in the spectrum of visible light. A complex process in which the visual system mixes various wavelengths produces the broad variety of colors that we see.

Saturation

Proportion of colored or chromatic light to noncolored or nonchromatic light, which determines how colorful light appears.

A third dimension of light, **saturation**, determines how colorful the light appears. White corresponds to a completely colorless state; the more white is present in color, the less saturated it is.

Structure and Function of the Eye

Brightness, hue, and intensity describe the stimulus of light, but our primary concern is how we receive that stimulus. For that, we must have some understanding of how our eyes work.

Figure 4.2 illustrates several key structures of the human eye. *Two components of the eye are most relevant to our discussion.* One is the image-focusing part, roughly comparable to a camera. Major structures within this unit are the cornea, lens, iris, and pupil. *The other primary component of the eye's visual system is the image-recording part, called the retina. The film in a camera is roughly analogous to the retina.*

Visual sensations result when patterns of light that enter the eye are focused on the light-sensitive retina. When a light beam first enters the eye, it passes through the cornea, a thin, transparent membrane that bends or refracts light waves to bring them into sharper focus on the retina. Light then passes through the *aqueous humor,* a watery fluid that helps nourish the cornea.

Light next passes through a small opening in the *iris* called the *pupil.* The iris is a pigmented set of muscles that constrict or expand to control the amount of light that can enter. *The pupil dilates to let more light in when illumination is low, and it constricts in response to a bright light.* Eye color is determined by the amount of pigmentation in the iris. Heavy pigmentation produces brown eyes; little pigmentation results in blue eyes.

After light passes through the pupil, it enters the *lens,* an oblong elastic structure that further refracts and focuses the light beam into an image that is projected through the *vitreous humor* (a clear fluid that supplies nutrients to the interior of the eye) onto the retina. The focusing power of the lens resides in its ability to adjust its shape from flat to more rounded, depending on the distance between the object viewed and the eye. *This focusing process is called **accommodation**.* If the lens is functioning properly, a clear image is projected onto the retina. However, abnormalities in eye shape often make it impossible for the lens to accommodate correctly. When this happens, a person may be either nearsighted or farsighted. (A nearsighted person is able to see distinctly for only a short distance; someone who is farsighted can see distant objects clearly but cannot see near objects in proper focus.)

Accommodation

In vision, the focusing process in which the lens adjusts its shape, depending on the distance between the eye and the object viewed, in order to project a clear image consistently onto the retina.

Retina

Thin membrane at the back of the eye containing photoreceptors called rods and cones. The retina functions to record images.

THE RETINA Most of the structures of the eye function to focus light onto the **retina**, a thin layer of tissue at the back of the eye that records images. The inset in Figure 4.2 shows ***the key parts of the retina: rods, cones, bipolar cells, and ganglion cells***. Light focused on the retina passes through several layers of neurons on its way to the primary ***photoreceptor cells* known as the rods and the cones**. Once light passes through the retina, excess light not absorbed by the receptor cells is absorbed by the backmost part of

FIGURE 4.2 Structure of the Eye

A cross-sectional drawing of the eye illustrating several key structures, including the image-focusing structures—the cornea, lens, iris, and pupil—and the image-recording structure known as the retina. The retina consists of several layers of cells as shown in the magnified inset. Visual information leaves the retina through the optic nerve, which travels to several brain structures which mediate vision.

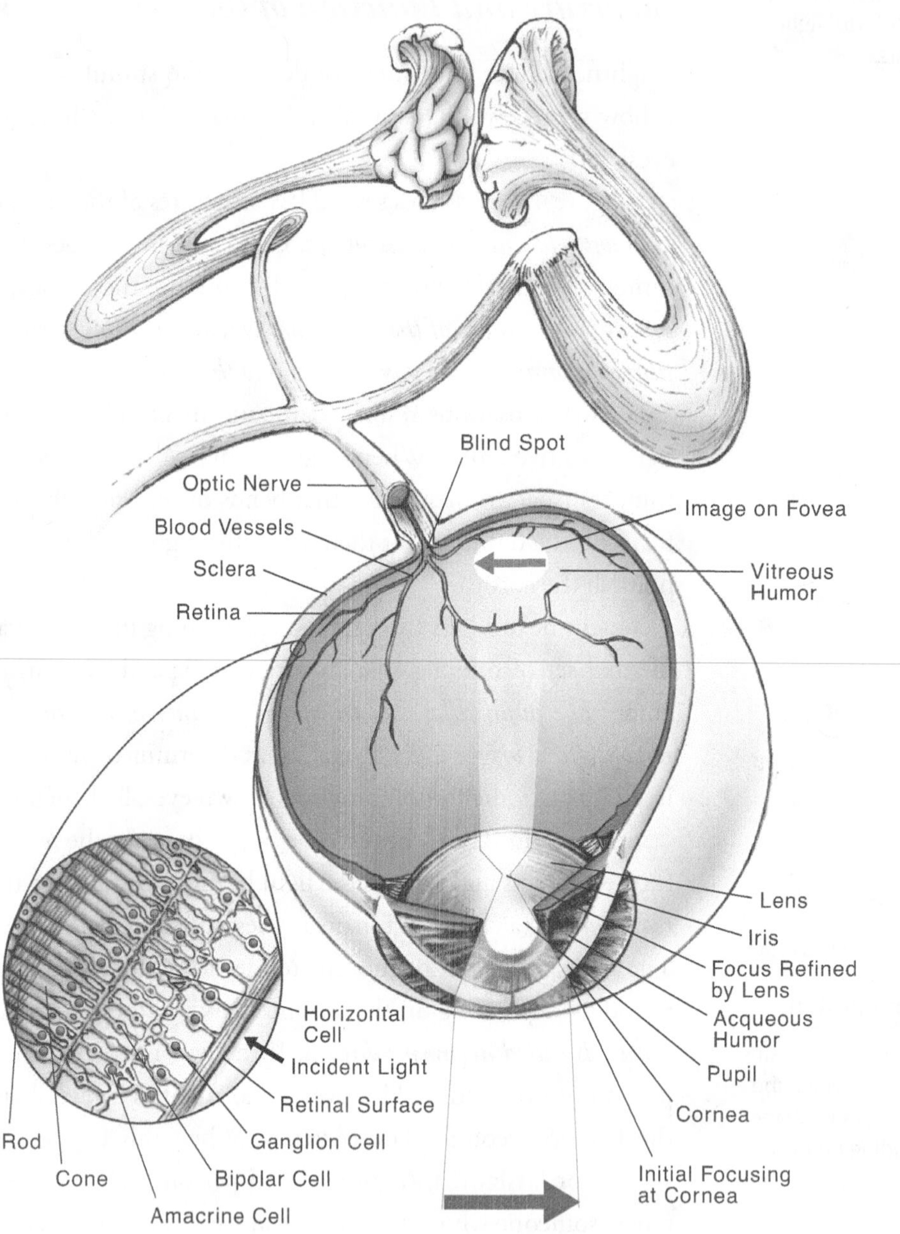

the eye called the pigment epithelium. In humans the pigment epithelium is quite dark, allowing it to absorb most of the light not absorbed by photoreceptors. If this light were to be reflected back into the retina and not absorbed, vision would be distorted because of the scatter of light inside the retina.

Not all animals have dark-colored pigment epithelium, however. Animals that forage at night rely more on sensitivity (the ability to detect light) than on *acuity (the ability to finely focus light)* and their eyes reflect light off of the pigment epithelium rather than absorb it. This reflected light is absorbed by the photoreceptors on its second pass through the retina. Light reflected off of the pigment epithelium is what you see when your car headlights catch an animal at night. This kind of reflection occurs in human eyes when more light than can be absorbed enters the eye. For example, the "red eye" in flash photography is caused by red light being reflected off your pigment epithelium.

Rods

Photoreceptor cells distributed across the inner layer of the retina that are important in peripheral vision and seeing in dim light.

Cones

Photoreceptor cells distributed across the inner layer of the retina that play an important role in the perception of color.

Rods and Cones There are approximately 120 million rods and 6 to 7 million cones in each of our eyes. The rods and cones are distributed in an orderly fashion across the inner layer of the retina. ***The densest concentration of cones occurs in a region of the retina called the fovea*** (see Figure 4.2). Because our vision is sharpest when images are focused on the fovea, *we move our eyes around until the image is projected to the fovea when we wish to focus clearly on an object.*

Our perception of color depends largely on the cones. Different cones respond to different wavelengths of light. However, *the cones are relatively poor light sensors as compared to the rods.* A considerable amount of light must be projected on a cone before it responds by transducing this energy to neural signals. Thus, the cones are not much good at night, which is why your friend's colorful sweater is hard to see in a dark theater and why that great paint job on your car is hardly noticeable at night.

Rods are extremely sensitive photoreceptors, allowing us to see in dim light. Our peripheral vision (vision away from the center of focus) depends primarily on the rods, which are concentrated around the edges of the fovea and elsewhere on the surface of the retina. (No rods are in the fovea and only a relatively few cones are located outside the fovea.)

You can demonstrate for yourself some of the distinguishing features between the rods and cones next time you are outside on a clear night. Pick out a distant object that is barely discernible, such as a faint star. If you look slightly to the side of the object, it is easier to detect because you have moved the image away from your fovea to the outer part of your retina, which is filled with light-sensitive rods.

Both the rods and the cones contain *photopigments* that respond to light. *Rods contain Rhodopsin and Cones contain Iodopsin.* Both Rhodopsin and Iodopsin are made up of a chemical similar to Vitamin A and known as Retinal and another protein molecule known as opsin. *When light falls on the Rhodopsin or Iodopsin molecules, the opsin absorbs the photons and breaks away from the Retinal molecule, thus allowing an electrical change known as a generator potential in the membrane.* Summed up together, these generator potentials produce an Action Potential or a neural signal. These neural signals are then passed on from the rods and cones to the *bipolar cells,* which in turn pass information to the *ganglion cells. The axons of the ganglion cells travel across the inner surface of the retina and converge to form the optic nerve, which carries visual messages to the occipital lobe.*

The part of the retina where the optic nerve exits the eye is known as the ***optic disk***. *There are no photoreceptor cells at this point. Consequently, the **optic disk** region corresponds with the a **blind spot** in the visual field:* An image that is projected there will not be recorded. We are usually unaware of our blind spot, for a number of reasons. For one, our

FIGURE 4.3 Finding Your Blind Spot

Because there are no photoreceptors where the optic nerve exits the eye, this leaves a blind spot on your retina. To find your blind spot, close your left eye and focus your right eye on the black cross. Then, move the book to about 12 inches directly in front of your face. The picture of the telephone will disappear but the vertical lines will not.

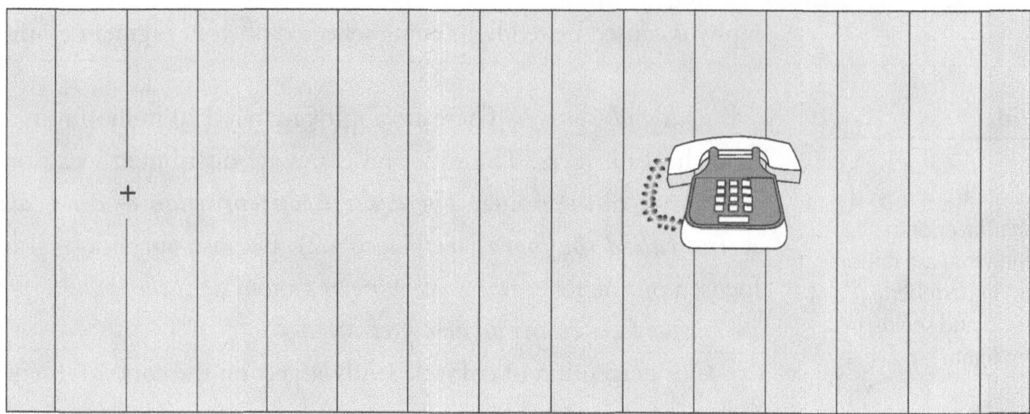

eyes are constantly moving, allowing us to pick up the image in another part of the retina. Furthermore, an image that falls on the blind spot of one eye is focused somewhere else in the other eye, thus compensating for the momentary blindness. *To see your blind spot in action, try the exercise in Figure 4.3. When the image in the figure falls on your blind spot it will disappear.*

In summary, visual information is passed through a three-cell chain, from rods and cones to bipolar cells to ganglion cells. Two other kinds of retinal cells, *horizontal cells* and *amacrine cells* do not transmit visual signals toward the brain. Instead, they transmit signals laterally across the retina, allowing interaction between adjacent photoreceptor, bipolar, and ganglion cells. This interaction, termed *lateral inhibition,* functions to enhance our perception of images by "turning off" neighboring photoreceptors. See the Mach bands in Figure 4.4.

NEURAL PROCESSING OF VISION: Visual signals from the retina are projected to the brain along the *optic nerve.* Before reaching the visual cortex at the back of the brain, visual information from the two eyes converges in a region of the thalamus called the *lateral geniculate nucleus.* The thalamus acts as a relay station, directing incoming sensory information to appropriate areas within the cortex. The two lateral geniculate nuclei, located in the left and right hemispheres of the thalamus, combine information from both eyes before sending it on to the cortex. From the lateral geniculate nuclei, this information is then sent to the visual cortex in the right and left hemispheres of the occipital lobe.

Research has yet to determine exactly how these neural signals are translated into the three dimensional, colorful world we perceive. Perception of the three-dimensional world is

FIGURE 4.4 Mach Bands

The bands in this figure are uniformly shaded, but they appear to either lighten or darken at the borders. This illustrates the contour-enhancing effects of lateral inhibition.

a complex phenomenon and is a product of information from the other senses such as sense of touch, and hearing, etc., and experience. The brain's association areas seem to compile, organize and interpret the incoming information to allow us the 3-D, moving, colorful world we see.

Color Vision

Among mammals, only primates (humans, apes, and monkeys) are able to perceive a full range of colors. Cattle have no color vision (the colorful cape of the matador is merely a prop for human observers). Most color vision experts think that dogs do not see color either, although some evidence suggests that they may have some limited capacity to discern colors (Jacobs, 1983). Surprisingly, simpler organisms such as fish, birds, reptiles, and insects have excellent color vision (Nathans, 1987).

THEORIES OF COLOR VISION Two major theories have been proposed to explain how we see colors: the trichromatic theory and the opponent-process theory.

Young-Helmholtz theory (Trichromatic theory of color vision)

Also known as the Young-Helmholtz theory, the postulation that the human eye contains three types of color receptors (for red, green, and blue), which form the basis for our perception of all colors.

The Trichromatic Theory of Color Vision In 1802 Thomas Young, an English physicist and physician, demonstrated that various combinations of red, green, and blue light can produce all the other colors in the spectrum. He suggested that the human eye contains three types of color receptors corresponding to these three distinct hues, and that the brain somehow creates our perception of color by combining the information transmitted by each type of receptor. Half a century later, Young's theory was modified and expanded by the German physiologist Hermann von Helmholtz. Their combined theory became known as the **Young-Helmholtz theory**, or the **Trichromatic theory of color vision**.

Neither Young nor Helmholtz was aware that the retina contained distinct photoreceptor cells. *Over a century later, their theory was supported when research revealed that there are three distinct kinds of cones in the human retina, each containing a slightly different photopigment. These cones are maximally sensitive to light of three wavelengths: 435, 540, and 565 nm. Figure 4.5 reveals that these wavelengths correspond to blue, green, and yellow-green.* Although the photopigments in each of these types of cones respond most effectively to light in the wavelengths we have listed, light of a particular wavelength stimulates more than one type of receptor.

The Trichromatic theory explains the effects of mixing colors of different wavelengths. However, it does not explain some other phenomena, such as negative afterimages (discussed in the following section) and the fact that color-blind people almost always fail to distinguish pairs of colors rather than just one color. A second theory, the opponent-process theory, helps to explain these phenomena.

The Opponent-Process Theory of Color Vision In the 1870s a German physiologist, Ewald Hering, proposed a theory of color vision asserting that yellow is as basic or primary a color as red, blue, and green; that is, that yellow is not a mixture of other colors. Hering believed we see six primary colors (red, green, blue, yellow, black, and white) rather than the three proposed by Young and Helmholtz. He further theorized that these six colors are grouped into three pairs, which form three types of receptors. One receptor, the black-white pair, contributes to our perception of brightness and saturation; the other two receptors, a red-green and a blue-yellow pair, are responsible for our perception of color.

Hering believed that the two members of each pair tend to work in opposition to each other, one inhibiting the other (hence the name **Opponent-process theory of color vision**). According to this viewpoint, if our eyes are struck by light containing more red wavelengths than green, the red inhibits the green and we perceive red. The blue-yellow system works similarly, which is why we never perceive such shades as greenish red or bluish yellow.

Opponent-process theory of color vision

Theory that explains color vision based on six primary colors, which are grouped into three pairs (red-green, blue-yellow, black-white). Receptors in the eye are sensitive to specific pairs, and the presence of one member of a pair inhibits vision of the other.

Hering's opponent-process theory is consistent with what we know about color blindness. Approximately 8 percent of males and .05 percent of females exhibit some form of color blindness, but only rarely are individuals totally blind to color. *Most people with color-vision problems have difficulty detecting pairs of colors. Red-green color blindness is the most common.* People with red-green color blindness cannot see either red or green, but they can see other colors. Yellow-blue color blindness is much less common.

Most contemporary vision experts believe that both the trichromatic theory and the opponent-process theory are correct. In fact, our color perception may be a product of both mechanisms. *The trichromatic system operates at the level of the photoreceptors, with three kinds of light-sensitive pigments in the cones.* The opponent-process system has been identified in ganglion cells of the retina and in the lateral geniculate nuclei. Researchers using *f*MRI have found a large number of brain cells that respond in an opponent manner to red-green and blue-yellow stimuli in the *visual cortex* (Engel et al., 1997; Schluppeck, 2002). *Thus, color vision results from interplay between a trichromatic system operating at the level of the photoreceptor cells and an opponent-process mechanism working at later stages* (Shiffman, 2000).

AUDITION

People who become deaf after years of normal hearing often report feeling a great deal of stress and a profound sense of isolation (Sekuler & Blake, 1985). Audition allows us to enjoy perhaps the richest form of communication. A deaf person cannot easily engage in conversation with others, whereas a blind person can converse with people either person-to-person or over the phone. Thus, while our ears may bring us less information than our eyes, they convey a special type of *social communication* that is exceedingly important to our appreciation of life.

Sound: The Stimulus for Audition

Most of the sounds we hear consist of physical energy in the form of rhythmic pressure changes in the air. When an object vibrates to produce sound, it sets air molecules in motion. The vibrating motion of the sound source alternately pushes air molecules together and pulls them apart. The forward thrust of the vibrating object as it moves toward you *compresses* the air, making it denser; as the vibrating object moves away from you, it pulls the molecules farther apart, thus *rarefying* the air, making it thinner. *These changes in air pressure constitute sound waves, and they travel at a speed of approximately 1,100 feet per second.*

When the compressed-air portion of the sound wave arrives at your ear, it bends the *tympanic membrane* (your eardrum) inward. The negative pressure of the following rarefied portion of the sound wave causes your eardrum to bend out. *These movements or vibrations of the eardrum begin the complex process of transducing the energy of sound waves into the neural signals that carry auditory messages to the brain.*

Sound waves most commonly travel through the medium of air. However, other media such as the ground, water, wood, or metal also convey sound waves. Perhaps you have listened to a conversation in the next room with your ear against the wall, have heard an approaching train by pressing your ear against a metal rail, or have heard sounds while swimming under water.

Loudness

In hearing, the intensity of a sound as measured by decibels. Loudness is determined by the amplitude of a sound wave.

Pitch

Dimension of hearing that determines how high or low a sound is, measured in hertz. Pitch is determined by the frequency of a sound wave.

PROPERTIES OF SOUND WAVES Two properties of sound waves influence our perception of sound: amplitude and frequency. The *amplitude* or intensity of a sound wave determines the **loudness** of a sound. Loudness is measured in *decibels* (dB.). A decibel is not a linear unit like a pound or an inch; rather, it is a point on a sharply rising curve of intensity. For example, 10 dB. is 10 times greater than 1 dB., but 30 dB. is 1,000 times greater than 1 dB., and 100 dB. is approximately 10 billion times greater than 1 dB. To most people, a sound at 10 dB. is quite soft, whereas one as loud as 130 dB. is painful. Figure 4.5 shows the decibel levels of a number of common sounds.

A second important property of a sound wave is its *frequency*, which determines the **pitch** that we perceive. Sound wave frequency is measured in *Hertz* (Hz.), or cycles per second. The higher the pitch, the shriller we perceive a sound to be. *The average human ear can perceive sound waves within the range of 20 to 20,000 Hz. We are most sensitive to*

FIGURE 4.5 Decibel Levels of Several Common Sounds

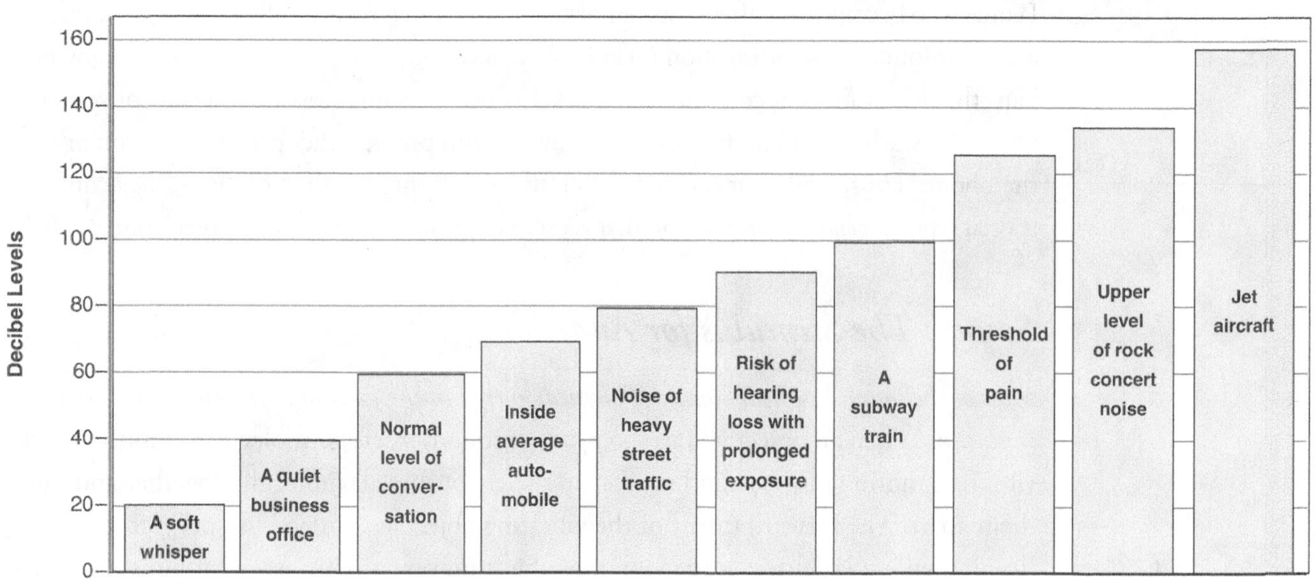

sound waves in the range of 100 Hz. to 3,500 Hz., which is, conveniently, the range within which most human speech falls. Women tend to have high pitched voices while men tend to have low pitched voices. To understand how we discern pitch, you will have to know how the transduction of a sound wave takes place, so we will discuss pitch perception after elaborating on the transduction of sound.

DISTINGUISHING DIFFERENT SOUNDS OF THE SAME PITCH You may have noticed that the same notes sound different when produced by different instruments. Middle C played on the piano sounds quite different from the same note played on the violin, in spite of the fact that both instruments produce sound waves with exactly the same frequency.

Neither the violin nor the piano produces a pure note of a single frequency. In fact, very few of the sounds we hear are pure tones. Most are a combination of a *fundamental frequency* and a unique set of additional frequency components called *overtones*. Combined with the fundamental frequency, these overtones add a characteristic quality called **timbre** to complex sounds. *Our ability to distinguish between the sounds of various musical instruments depends on differences in timbre.* If sound filters were used to screen out all overtones, it would be impossible for a person to identify various instruments just by hearing them.

Timbre

Quality of complex sound that is a product of the combination of fundamental frequency and additional frequency components called overtones.

Figure 4.6 summarizes the three properties of sound waves. Before reading on, see if you can tell how samples *A, B, C,* and *D* would be perceived.

Structure and Function of the Ear

THE OUTER EAR The ear has three major parts: the outer ear, the middle ear, and the inner ear (see Figure 4.7). What most of us call our ears are merely the pinnas, the odd-

FIGURE 4.6 **Physical Properties and Perceptual Dimensions of Sound Waves**

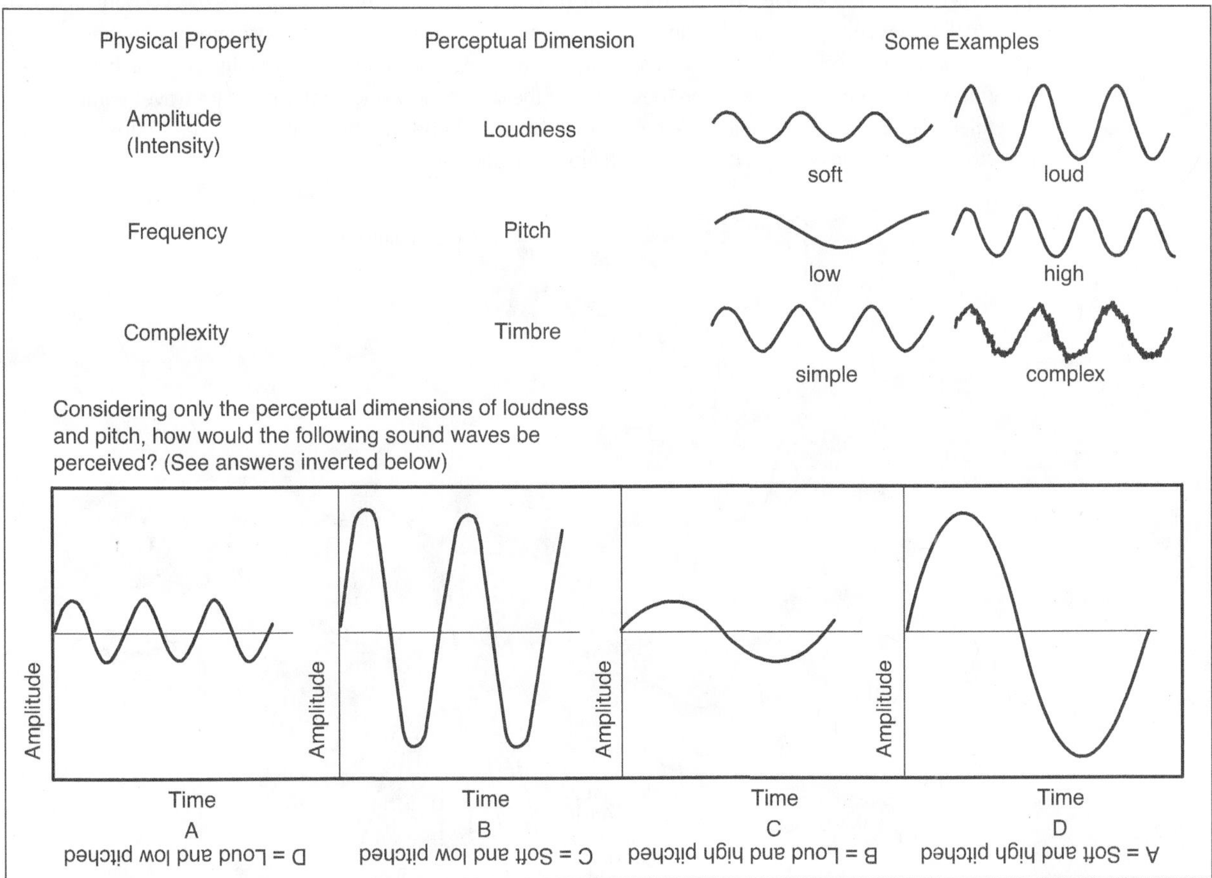

shaped, flesh-covered cartilage that protrudes from the sides of our heads. *The function of the pinna is to collect and funnel sound waves down the auditory canal, which, along with the pinna, forms the outer ear.* Both the pinna and the auditory canal serve to funnel the sound wave into the middle ear.

THE MIDDLE EAR Consists of the eardrum or **tympanic membrane** and three tiny linked bones (**ossicles**), consisting of the hammer (*malleus*), the anvil (*incus*), and the stapes (*stirrup*). The funneled sound wave causes the tympanic membrane to vibrate, which in turn sets the malleus vibrating. The malleus passes its vibrations to the incus, and the incus sets the stapes in vibration. The stapes is in contact with a membrane called the oval window, which forms the beginning of the inner ear. The ossicles act like a system of levers that transfer and amplify (or dampen) the intensity of a sound stimulus.

THE INNER EAR When the ossicles vibrate in response to sound waves, the last bone in the series, the stapes, pounds against an opening to the inner ear called the oval window.

Tympanic membrane

Membrane stretched across the end of the auditory canal that vibrates in response to sound waves. Also known as the eardrum.

Ossicles

Set of three tiny linked bones (the malleus, incus, and stapes) in the middle ear that receives a sound stimulus from the tympanic membrane and transfers it to the oval window of the inner ear.

FIGURE 4.7 Anatomy of the Human Ear

The outer ear, consisting of the pinna and auditory canal, collects and funnels sound waves to the eardrum, which cause it to vibrate. The eardrum, which serves as the opening to the middle ear, is connected to three small bones called ossicles that amplify the intensity of movement as it is transmitted to the inner ear. The last bone in the series, the stapes, pushes against a membrane called the oval window, which separates the middle ear from the inter ear. The movement of the oval window generates pressure waves within the fluid-filled cochlea, causing the flexible basilar membrane to bend. The bending of hair cells in the organ of Corti causes neural messages to be transmitted along the auditory nerve to the brain.

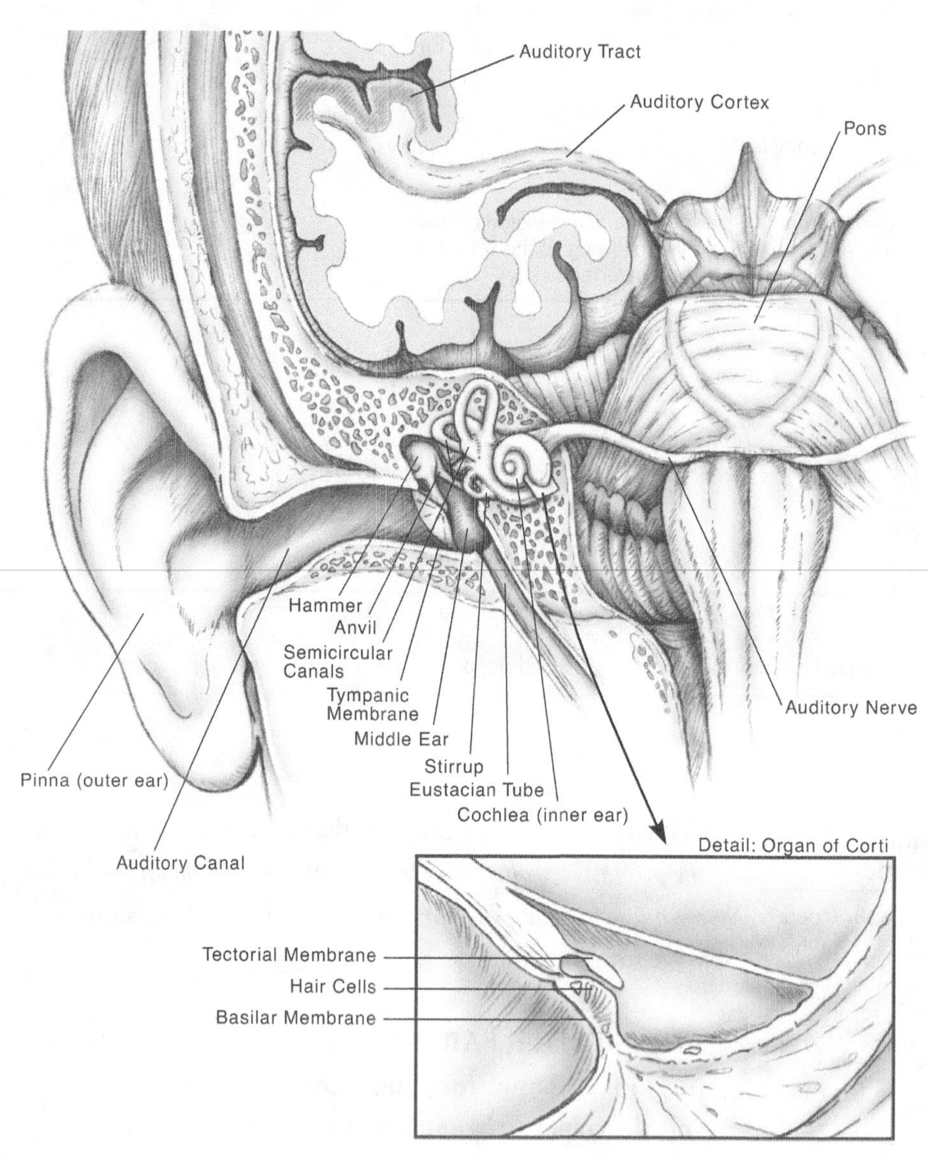

Cochlea

Coiled, fluid-filled chamber in the inner ear with two flexible surfaces: the oval window and the round window.

The inner ear consists of three main parts, known as ***the oval window****, the* ***cochlea*** *and* ***the organ of Corti****.* The cochlea is a snail-shaped, coiled chamber, which is filled with fluid. The **cochlea** consists of three wedge-shaped chambers: the *vestibular canal,* the *cochlear duct,* and the *tympanic canal* (see Figure 4.8). The tympanic canal and cochlear duct are separated by a rubber-like flexible membrane known as the **basilar membrane**. The **organ of Corti** lies on the basilar membrane and contains about 15,000 *special receptors* known as *hair cells.*

FIGURE 4.8 The Cochlea of the Inner Ear

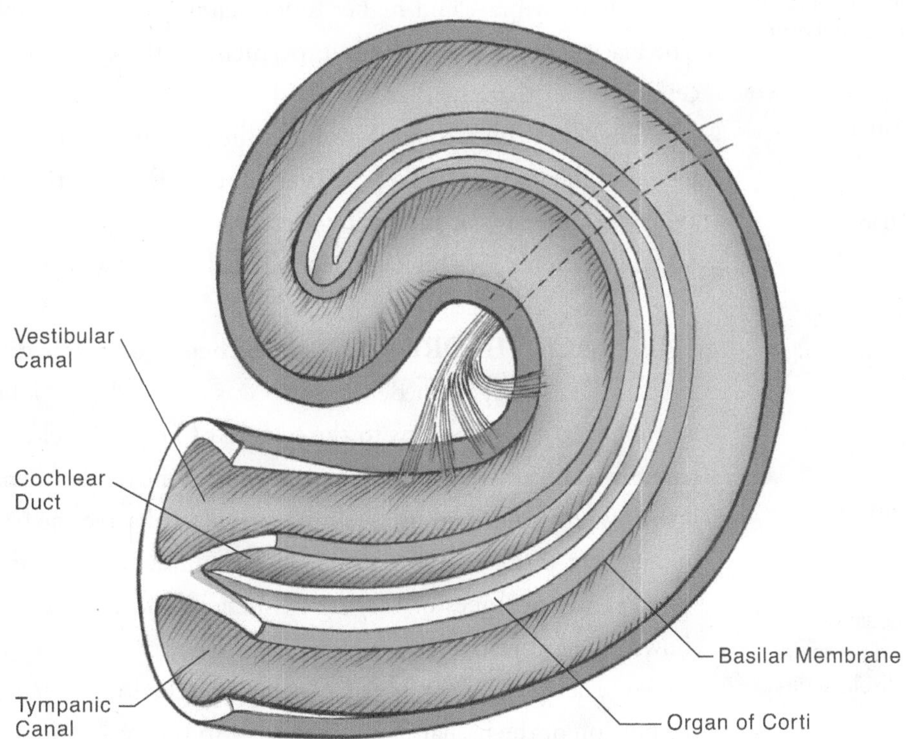

Basilar membrane

Membrane in the cochlea of the inner ear that vibrates in response to pressure waves, causing auditory hair cells on the adjoining organ of Corti to release neurotransmitters that activate neurons of the auditory nerve.

Organ of Corti

Structure in the inner ear located directly above the basilar membrane, consisting of auditory hair cells, a tectoral membrane, and cilia.

Except for two locations where it is covered by flexible, elastic material, the cochlear wall consists of hard bone. The two flexible spots are the *oval window* and the *round window* at the base of the tympanic canal. These two flexible surfaces allow pressure waves to be generated within the fluid that fills the vestibular and tympanic canals. *The movement of the oval window (caused by the movement of the stapes) generates pressure waves within the fluid-filled cochlea, causing the flexible basilar membrane to bend. The bending of hair cells in the organ of Corti causes* ***stimulation of the hair cells which generates action potentials,*** *which get transmitted as neural messages along the auditory nerve to the brain, allowing the perception of the sound* that first caused the eardrum or tympanic membrane to vibrate.

In summary, sound waves are converted into mechanical movements of the ossicles in the middle ear, which in turn act on the inner ear to produce pressure waves that travel through the fluid of the cochlea, flexing the basilar membrane and activating hair cells of the organ of Corti, which in turn activate neurons of the auditory nerve. In this complex manner, the physical energy of sound waves is converted into neural impulses that our minds perceive as sounds.

Theories of Pitch Perception

There are two major theories explaining how we discriminate pitch: the place theory and the place-volley theory.

Volley theory

Related to the frequency theory of pitch discrimination. Postulates that since single auditory neurons cannot fire rapidly enough to enable us to perceive tones in the 1,000 to 4,000 Hz range, pitch perception is made possible by groups of interrelated neurons firing in concert.

Place theory of pitch discrimination

Theory that we discriminate different pitches because sound waves of different frequency displace different regions on the cochlea's basilar membrane.

Frequency theory of pitch discrimination

Theory that perception of low tones depends on the frequency with which auditory hair cells in the inner ear's organ of Corti trigger the firing of neurons in the auditory nerve.

Auditory localization

Ability to locate the origins of sounds by differences from ear to ear in variables such as intensity and the time the sound arrives at each ear.

The Place theory states that our perception of the pitch depends on the area of the Basilar membrane that vibrates, with high pitched sounds making the area close to the oval window vibrate and higher tones making areas away from the oval window vibrate. The Place-Volley theory is an improvement on the Place Theory. It explains low pitch perception better than the Place theory does.

The Place-Volley theory combines the idea of the Place theory and a theory called the temporal theory which takes the timing of the firing of the cochlear neurons into account along with the area of the basilar membrane that is vibrating, and this combination helps explain all the various high and low pitched sounds we can hear.

THE PLACE THEORY The **place theory of pitch discrimination** was developed primarily by George von Békésy, who was awarded the Nobel Prize in recognition of his monumental contributions to the science of hearing. Békésy theorized that waves of different frequencies activate different regions of the basilar membrane. He conducted experiments with guinea pigs using a microscope to observe the basilar membrane through tiny holes cut in various locations along the cochlea. Békésy noted that when the guinea pigs were exposed to tones of varying frequencies, different regions of the basilar membrane showed the greatest.

For example, Békésy noted that high-pitched tones caused the most displacement in the portion of the basilar membrane close to the oval window, whereas intermediate-range tones caused the greatest response farther along the basilar membrane. Unfortunately, Békésy's theory applied well only to frequencies above 4000 cps. And did not hold up as well for low-frequency tones, below 4,000 Hz. The manner in which tones below this level displace the basilar membrane is largely indistinguishable (von Békésy, 1960). Subsequent research confirms that the place theory holds up well for all but tones in the lower frequency range (Lewis et al., 1982).

Auditory Localization

People are usually able to locate the origins of sounds rather well. Infants can identify which side a sound comes from very early, and within a few months learn to localize sounds in their environments (Castillo & Butterworth, 1981). This ability, called **auditory localization**, is the result of the difference in the sounds that arrive in each of our two ears (Goldstein, 1989). One key difference is in the intensity of loudness of the sounds. If someone sitting to the left of you blows a whistle, the sound wave reaching your left ear is more intense than the sound striking your right ear. This occurs because a large object like the human head does not transmit high-frequency sounds very well; your right ear is in a *sound shadow*. By the time the sound wave circumnavigates your head to reach your right ear, its intensity diminishes somewhat. *Our brains use this information about differing intensities to determine the origin of a sound* (Semple & Kitzes, 1987).

In addition to intensity difference, another important auditory localization cue has to do with the time a sound arrives. As we learned earlier, sound waves travel through the air at the relatively slow rate of approximately 1,100 feet per second. Thus, a sound originating from the left strikes the left eardrum fractions of a second before it completes the somewhat longer journey to our right ear. *Here again, our brains utilize information about these minuscule time differences to help us localize sounds.*

Hearing Loss

Roughly 20 million people in the United States suffer some hearing loss, making it the most common of all physical disabilities. Chronic exposure to extremely loud noise, drug side-effects, middle ear infections, etc., can all cause deafness. *In terms of neural mechanisms hearing loss can occur due to damage to the hair-cells found in the organ of Corti. Such loss is termed sensorineural hearing loss and chronic exposure to loud noise can produce it* (Goldstein, 1989). Hearing loss can also be caused by hardening of the bones of the middle ear, which prevents them from vibrating. This type of hearing loss is termed *conduction hearing loss.*

Conduction hearing loss

Hearing loss caused by the failure of the outer and middle ear to conduct sound energy to the inner ear's receptors, sometimes due to infection or to buildup of ear wax.

Conduction hearing loss does not produce total deafness, as is often the case with severe forms of sensorineural impairment. One reason is that sounds can be transmitted directly through the bones of the skull to the inner ear. Many hearing aids, designed to amplify sound transmission via bone conduction, can markedly reduce the effects of conduction hearing loss.

Sensorineural hearing loss

Hearing loss caused by damage to either the hair cells of the inner ear or the auditory nerve.

SENSORINEURAL HEARING LOSS Damage to either the hair cells of the inner ear or the auditory nerve can cause **sensorineural hearing loss**. The most common example of this type of impairment is the gradual loss of sensitivity to high frequencies that occurs with aging, a condition called *presbycusis.*

Exposure to excessively loud noises can also cause permanent damage to the sensitive structures of the inner ear (Goldstein, 1989). This type of hearing loss is often accompanied by an annoying condition called *tinnitus,* a continuous ringing in the ears. The effects of exposure to loud noises may accumulate over a person's life, thereby contributing to a steady loss of hearing with advancing age. Young people who spend a great deal of time listening to extremely loud music can suffer permanent damage to the hair cells.

Gustation

The sense of taste, which, like olfaction, is activated by chemical senses in the environment.

GUSTATION AND OLFACTION

Olfaction

The sense of smell, which, like taste, is activated by chemical substances in the environment.

The senses of taste, or ***gustation****, and smell (****olfaction****) are classified as chemical senses because chemical substances in the environment activate both.* Taste and smell are often called minor senses because, relatively speaking, humans utilize vision and audition more than these other senses. We may not rely as much on the senses of smell and taste as do many other animals. However, these minor senses contribute greatly to our experience. The smell of the air after a spring rain, meat sizzling on the barbecue, the sensuous smell of perfume, all of these senses contribute immeasurably to our zest for life. Sometimes smells and flavors provide crucial information. Odors such as the smell of gas or smoke signal danger, for instance, and taste may have evolved as a signal for both toxic and particularly nutritious foods.

Gustation

The sense of taste is actually a mix of messages from special *transducers* known as *taste buds* and from receptors for touch, pain, and thermal properties of the food, in addition to messages regarding its appearance, odor, etc., from vision and olfaction.

The taste buds, housed in protrusions on the tongue and known as *papillae*, are taste receptors that distinguish only five different sensations: sweetness, saltiness, sourness, and bitterness and "umami". Umami is a Japanese word which means "Savory taste" and this particular sensation is experienced when glutamate is present in the food and it enhances the overall palatability of the food.

The "hot," as in chili-pepper hot in Mexican or Indian cuisine, is not a "taste" message but a message of "burning sensation," even though the gestalt is one of taste. The burning sensation on eating chili peppers, the cool sensation produced by mentholated candy, and the stinging of carbonated drinks in the nose are all due to sensations produced by receptor mechanisms for other senses, such as those involved in pain, touch, and thermal perception found in the nose, mouth, throat, and even the eye.

The sense of smell contributes greatly to our ability to perceive differences in flavors. In fact, without the sense of smell, you could not distinguish many of the flavors you recognize. You have probably noticed that things taste flat when you have a bad head cold that plugs up your nose.

The receptors for taste are located in the little bumps on the tongue called papillae. Each papilla contains as many as 150 taste buds, which in turn contain a number of receptor cells called microvilli. The microvilli are hair-like projections that extend into the saliva that coats the tongue. When we take ingestible material into our mouths, food particles (chemical molecules) chemicals that are dissolved by saliva stimulate the receptor cells, which transduce this chemical energy into electrochemical energy or neural signals that are transmitted to the brain.

As Figure 4.9 shows, historically, different parts of the tongue were thought to be most sensitive to different taste qualities, however, research using newer techniques has not substantiated it. Currently, it is thought that a given solute activates a receptor by causing Ca++ channels to open, and the information is passed to the cortex via the Gustatory nerve. The cortex takes information from the other cranial nerves such as the trigeminal, and olfactory nerve, etc. and the combined information is perceived as a particular "taste" (Small & Prescott,2005; McCaughey, et al., 1998). In general, compounds high in sodium ions are perceived as "salty," while those high in hydrogen ions are perceived as sour. Carbohydrates are generally perceived as sweet, while alkaloids like caffeine and quinine, etc., taste bitter. Protein-rich foods such as meat as also tomatoes are thought to have "umami". Monosodium glutamate, a

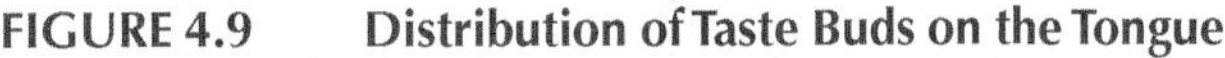

FIGURE 4.9 Distribution of Taste Buds on the Tongue

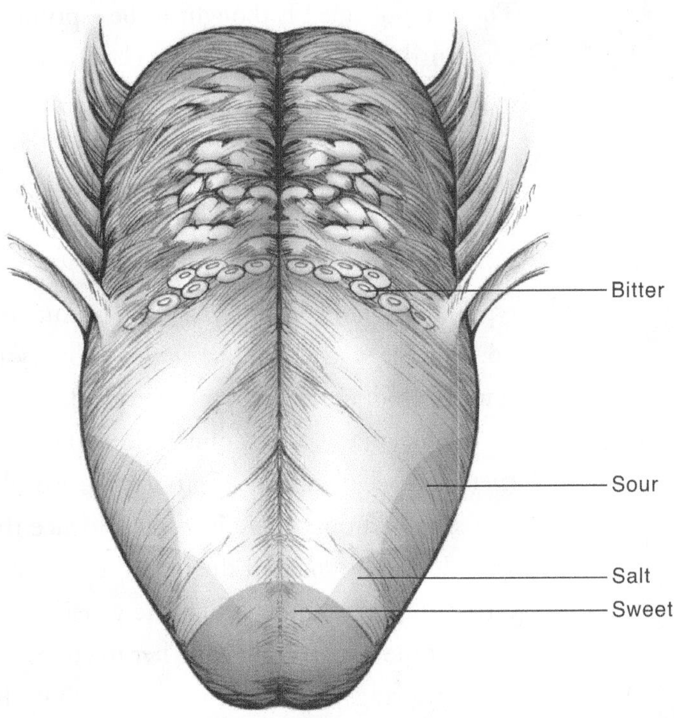

flavor enhancer used in Oriental cooking is thought to enhance the umami of foods and give them a brothy, savory, meaty or fuller taste.

There is evidence that taste sensitivity undergoes considerable change over the course of our lives, which may account, in part, for changes in taste preferences. For example, most children prefer sweetness to other tastes, but this preference often does not hold up in the adult years. Unfortunately, as we grow older, our taste buds become less sensitive, which is why many older people often complain that food does not taste as good as it once did (Shiffman, 1999).

Unique Application of Science Facts

Do squirrels eat up the birdseed you bought for birds? A birdseed company has created special "hot" birdseed to allow birds to consume the seed and prevent squirrels from getting at it!

All mammals have gustatory receptors for capsaicin, a natural ingredient of chili peppers. When activated by capsaicin, these receptors send a message of "burning pain" to the brain. Birds do not have these receptors, so they can consume these hot seeds with no problems. The squirrels, however, experience the pain from the hot seeds, suffer temporarily, but remember the experience, so they do not eat those seeds again! (One more fact in favor of operant conditioning!) For further information check out: http://www.hotbirdseed.com/html/faq.html

Olfaction

The sense of smell is thought to be a primitive sense, or a sense that came into existence early in the course of evolution,because lower animals have a keener sense of smell and depend on it far more than we humans do. Also, the transducers of the olfactory system happen to be free nerve endings of the olfactory nerve, and they lie exposed to the environment in the nasal mucosa. *In all the other sense organs the transducers are encapsulated and are not exposed to the environment.* Even so, there are literally thousands of different receptors in the human Olfactory System, where as there are only three different types of cones and one type of rods in the Visual system! So primitive or first to evolve though it may be, it surely is not a simple system and *is the only* sensory system where stem cells in nasal epithelium continually produce new cells to replace old ones, throughout life (Axel, R. 1995).

Unlike many other animals, humans do not depend on the sense of smell to identify friends, repel enemies, and attract mates or do they? Humans can detect 10,000 different odors! In addition, there is some evidence that females may be influenced albeit unconsciously, by the smell of the man they choose to mate with. The odor of the man's sweat carries information regarding the genetic compatibility of the man's chromosomes with those of the woman's allowing her to choose a mate that is best in terms of the viability of their offspring! (Roberts & Gosling, 2003; Thornhill et. al, 2003).

With advances in evolutionary and biological psychology, we now have evidence that newborns locate their mother's breast because of the pheromones released in the secretions from the areolar gland in the mother's nipples and that very pheromone upsets childless females when they are exposed to it! (Hadhazy, A. 2012)

Nevertheless, odors do enhance our enjoyment of life, particularly those smells connected with the food we eat. *Odorous substances emit chemicals that vaporize and enter the nasal cavity as airborne molecules, either through the nostrils or through the back of the oral cavity. The receptor cells for odors lie in the epithelium layer of the olfactory mucosa or mucous membrane that lines the nasal cavity (see Figure 4.10). Tiny hair-like projections (cilia) extend outward from the receptor cells, catching the airborne molecules.*

We do not know exactly how the chemical energy of various odors is converted to neural signals that carry differing smell messages to the brain. Humans have approximately one thousand different types of receptors in the nasal mucosa and each type responds to a family of odorous chemicals, i.e., chemicals which are similar in shape, size and structure, and generally have similar chemical properties and similar odor (Axel, 1995; Shiffman, 2000). In other words, the sense of olfaction works on the lock and key principle, where the odorous molecule serves as the key, and the receptor in the nasal mucosa serves as the lock, but there is more to it as one air-borne chemical molecule can open more than one type of lock, so the pattern of neurons that are firing is taken into account when perceiving the smell. Once the odoriferous molecules bind to receptors, a pattern of neural firing travels first to the olfactory bulb and then via the hypothalamus to the primary olfactory cortex which lies along the olfactory nerve to higher brain centers in the limbic system, and frontal lobe. How this information is perceived as "a pleasant" or "unpleasant" odor is not known at this time.

FIGURE 4.10 The Olfactory System

When we smell something, molecules of its fragrance enter the nasal passage from the nose and/or throat. Receptor cells in the olfactory mucosa transduce these stimuli into neural messages that are transmitted along the olfactory tracts to the brain.

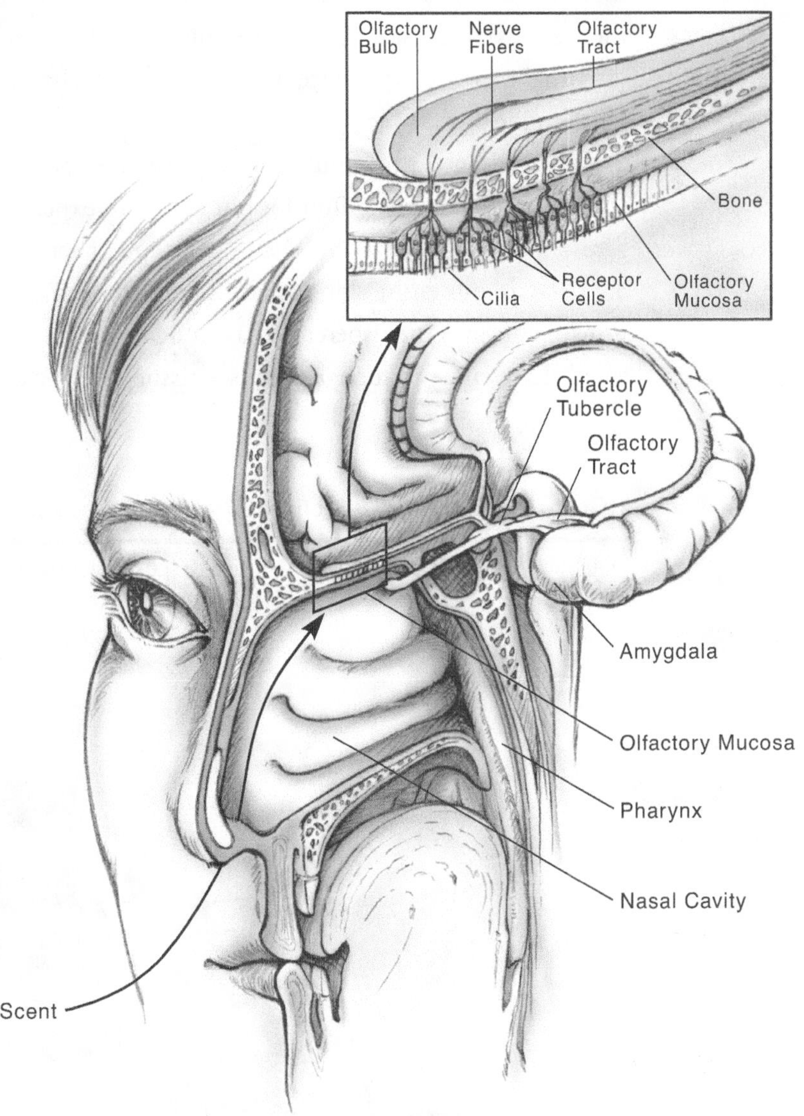

Get Outta Here!

In southwestern Ethiopia there live a group of people known as the Dassanetch. Some of the Dassanetch raise cattle and others are fisher-folk. Apparently, raising cattle is considered a prestigious livelihood in Dassanetch territory, while fishing is looked down upon. So people smear themselves with the smells associated with the raising of cattle. For example, the women smear liquid clarified butter (ghee) on their skin to show off their aristocracy and attract suitors, while the men smear cow dung on themselves to alert others to their profession and ensure suitors! Still think women are not as smart as men? ... *Think again!* (Franzoi, 2002 pg. 128)

THE SKIN SENSES

Our skin not only serves to demarcate the boundary between ourselves and the world, but it also allows us to experience the joys of the sifting sand beneath our feet, the sharpness of the shells and pebbles we might step on, the warmth of the sun's rays on our bodies and the wetness of the sea, as the waves play with our feet on a sunny beach! Later, that very skin might let you experience horrible itch, if the beach you visited had certain types of jellyfish in the waters!

Approximately one million receptors are found beneath our skin and distributed throughout our skin account for our ability to experience three basic skin sensations: *pressure*, *pain*, and *temperature*. The fourth type of sensation is the sense of touch. As Figure 4.11 shows, our entire skin surface is embedded with receptors for the various skin sensations. Light pressure is perceived as "touch," whereas heavy pressure is perceived as "pressure." Excessive pressure that causes tissue damage is perceived as "pain.". In addition,

FIGURE 4.11 A Cross-Sectional Drawing of the Skin

Different receptors in the skin are sensitive to specific kinds of stimuli.

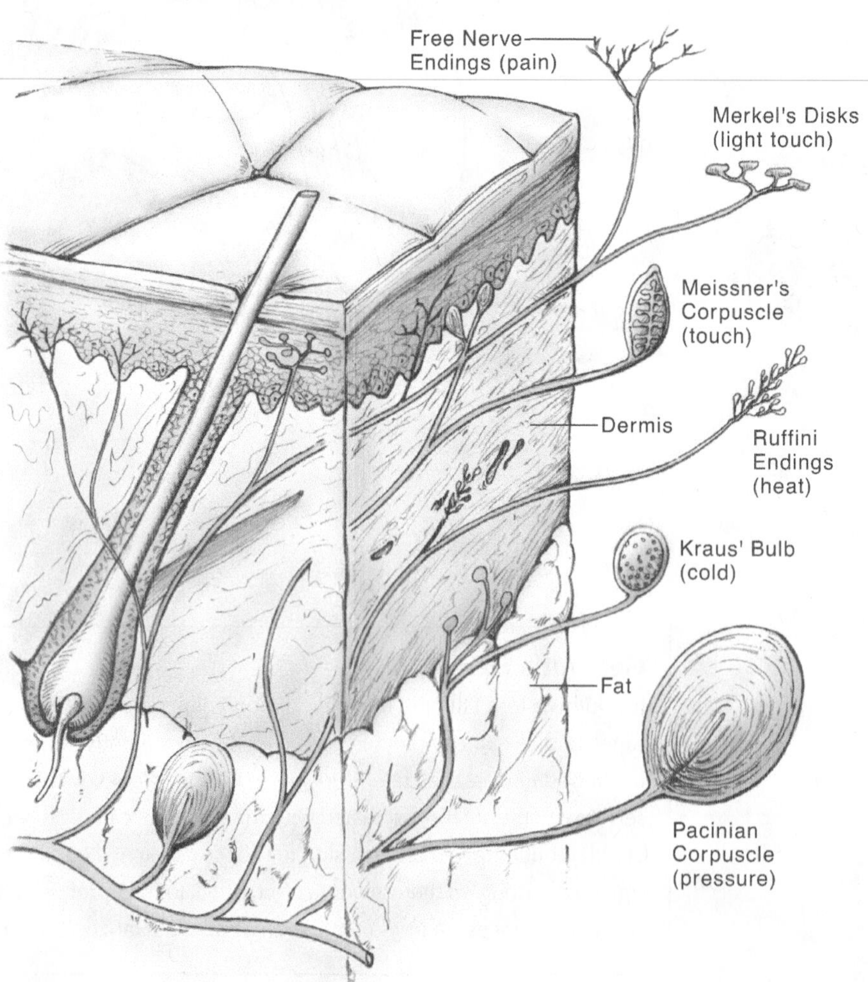

recent information shows that the skin cells themselves might also be involved in transducing temperature and touch (Lumpkin, E.A. & Caterina, M.J., 2007).

All of these various receptors are the dendrites of neurons: Unlike vision, hearing, and taste, our skin senses use no specialized receptor cells other than neurons. These neurons do have specialized dendritic endings, however, that modify the manner in which they transduce physical energy into a neural firing.

Receptors for the different kinds of skin senses are distributed unevenly over the body. For example, our faces are much more sensitive to touch than our backs because the receptors are more densely packed in the skin of the face than that of the back. However, another reason as to why our faces are more sensitive to touch is because the signals get to the brain a fraction of a second faster than from other parts of the body, the face being much closer to the brain. Researchers have attempted to link particular kinds of skin receptors to specific sensory experiences, with only limited success.

Our Experience

The sense of touch is actually a composite of three different sensations: pressure, temperature, and pain. Special receptors known as pacinian corpuscles, embedded in deeper layers of the skin, are credited with transduction of pressure and *Merkel's discs or tactile discs,* which are relatively closer to the top layers of the skin, are credited with transduction of light touch or very slight pressure (see Figure 4.11). Other receptors such as Krause's end-bulbs, etc. are said to transduce radiant heat and *naked or free nerve endings are thought to transduce tissue damage, which is perceived as pain.* More complex sensory experiences such as tingling, itching, tickling, or wetness are produced from combinations of these three basic sensations.

Pressure

We experience the sensation of pressure when a mechanical force causes a displacement of the skin. Sensory adaptation occurs very quickly, which is why we are soon unaware of the pressure of tight-fitting pants or snug shoes. (If you continue to be aware of your tight shoes, it is probably because you are feeling the sensation of pain rather than pressure.) Some parts of our bodies are much more sensitive to pressure than others. The most sensitive regions are the face and fingers; the least sensitive are the back and the legs. Pressure is mediated by a specialized receptor known as the Pacinian Corpuscle.

Temperature

The detection of changes in body temperature is of great importance because most animals cannot survive when body temperature either falls below or exceeds certain values. As body temperature decreases, organisms can adapt by seeking warmth or insulation. As it rises, organisms may, for example, seek a cooler environment or water immersion. Certain highly localized areas of the skin seem to be sensitive to cold but not to warmth; other spots show just the opposite sensitivity. This observation is consistent with general agreement among researchers that different specialized dendrite endings, called *free-nerve endings,* respond to cold and heat. Receptors for warm temperature respond more rapidly as the temperature increases while receptors for cold respond in an increasing manner as temperature decreases. Detectors for cold appear to be located closer to the skin's surface than are heat detectors. Some chemicals produce the sensations of cold and warmth. For example, menthol produces cold sensation by stimulating cold receptors while methyl salicylate (found in ointments like Ben-Gay) or capsaicin increase peripheral blood flow, thereby causing a warm sensation (Shiffman, 2000).

The Sensation of Pain

As much as we dislike pain, it is essential. Pain acts as a warning that something is harming us, and it drives us to seek necessary medical attention. Despite its importance relatively little is known about what causes pain and how to relieve it. Approximately 33% of America's adult population complains of chronic pain! *Chronic pain lasts far beyond the stimulation of peripheral nerve fibers and the tissue damage responsible for the message.* Hence, some researchers talk of a motivational or an emotional dimension of pain that is separate from the sensory dimension.

Fortunately a very small number of people suffer from a condition known as *congenital pain insensitivity* in which they do not have pain sensations at all. These individuals often experience serious accidental self-inflicted injuries to the skin and bones (Rassmusen, 1996) and most do not survive past the age of 25.

One fact that makes understanding pain so difficult is that no specific physical stimulus exists for pain as it does for the other sensory processes we have been discussing. *Virtually any excessive stimulus can cause pain.* A sound that is too loud, a light too bright, or a temperature too hot or cold can all produce pain sensations. Some pain researchers maintain that pain results from overstimulation of any sensory receptors; others believe that pain results when *damaged tissue releases chemicals that stimulate free-nerve endings in the skin,* which then transduce the chemical energy to neural signals that carry pain messages to our brains. Chemicals believed to be involved in this process include *prostaglandins, bradykinins,* and *substance P* (P for pain protein). Many known pain-killing medicines reduce pain by blocking prostaglandins, e.g., aspirin (Ophardt, 2003).

Substance P

A peptide neurotransmitter that signals pain from peripheral nerve fibers to the spinal cord.

Pain researchers have identified nerve fibers that transmit pain signals from the point of injury to the spinal cord and then on to the brain. One set of rapidly transmitting, myelinated fibers convey a message of localized, sharp, pricking pain, probably the only sensation we feel when the pain begins and ends quickly (as when our skin is pierced by a needle). However, if the pain stimulus is more severe, as might result from a burn or a damaging body blow, we perceive a second sensation within a second or two. This message, which is conveyed by unmyelinated slow nerve fibers, induces an awareness of a burning, searing, throbbing, or aching pain that is usually more diffuse.

Gate-control theory

Theory that neural gates in the spinal cord allow passage of pain signals to the brain; these gates may be closed by the simultaneous firing of non-pain nerve fibers, so that pain is not perceived.

GATE-CONTROL THEORY OF PAIN For centuries mid-wives have given light abdominal and leg massages to women undergoing labor pains and the technique is still used in Lamaze method of birthing. In 1965, a possible mechanism explaining why the massages might reduce labor pain became available. The **gate control theory** proposed in 1965 by Melzack and Wall states that small diameter nerve fibers carry pain stimuli, while large diameter fibers carry "touch" messages, and messages from both fibers pass through a 'gate mechanism' which is handled by interneurons in the spinal cord. This gate receives input from the brain which guides it as to whether or not it should allow the input from the pain fibers through. This in turn explains why peripheral sensory inputs, cognitive factors and emotional factors modulate our perception of pain (Melzack, 1992). If many touch messages are flowing in simultaneously with pain messages from the thinner fibers, the touch messages flowing on the thicker fibers block the pain messages, provided there are cognitive reasons to disregard the pain, and the "gate" closes to the pain messages.

The gate-control theory also suggests an explanation for why people are often unaware of pain when they are injured under conditions of high stress and intense emotions. For instance, a woman who cuts herself while rescuing a child from a broken window may not notice her own injury until the crisis has passed. It seems plausible that intense emotions can create competing stimuli that overload the neural circuits, thereby blocking the pain pathways.

A device known as TENS unit or trans-cutaneous electrical nerve stimulation unit, which is used to alleviate some types of chronic pain, delivers low-level electrical pulses through the skin to block the transmission of pain messages to the brain. Pain relief can be induced in both humans and other animals by electrical stimulation of certain areas within the spinal cord (Besson & Chaouch, 1987; Devulder et al., 1990; Meilman et al., 1989).

Endorphins

A class of neurotransmitter substances that function to inhibit the transmission of pain information. Morphine and other opiates act by facilitating endorphin transmission.

Periaqueductal gray area (PAG)

A region of the brain stem that controls pain signals sent to higher brain centers. The PAG also receives signals from endorphin-containing neurons for pain analgesia.

NEUROTRANSMITTERS AND PAIN *Two neuropeptides play important roles in the transmission of pain signals from sensory neurons to the brain. The first,* ***substance P****, is found throughout the midbrain, pons, and medulla, as well as in the spinal cord.* In the spinal cord, substance P appears to be the neurotransmitter released by incoming sensory neurons that signal pain. *Another group of neuropeptides, called endorphins, possess painkilling (analgesic) properties similar to opiate drugs.* The term endorphin means internal morphine. The part of the brain in which the endorphins are believed to inhibit pain is an area of the brainstem called the **periaqueductal gray area (PAG)**, which is believed to be the center of the pain circuit. Currently, researchers are using a combination of yoga techniques and biofeedback to alleviate chronic pain and endorphins are thought to mediate the pain-relief.

As sensory neurons transmit pain signals to the spinal cord they excite afferent neurons that ascend to the brainstem and the thalamus of the brain (see Figure 4.12). In the brainstem periaqueductal gray region these afferent neurons cause the release of endorphins, which (through the involvement of several other neurons) results in the excitation of descending neurons. These descending neurons release serotonin at the original sensory neuron synapse in the spinal cord inhibiting the afferent neurons signaling pain. There-

FIGURE 4.12 The Periaqueductal Gray Region of the Brainstem

Pain messages are transmitted through the spinal cord to the periaqueductal gray (PAG) region of the brainstem. Endorphin and GABA-containing neurons interact to cause the release of serotonin in the spinal cord, inhibiting pain transmission. Pain messages are also transmitted to the thalamus and other brain areas in which pain is perceived (from Groves and Rebec, 1992).

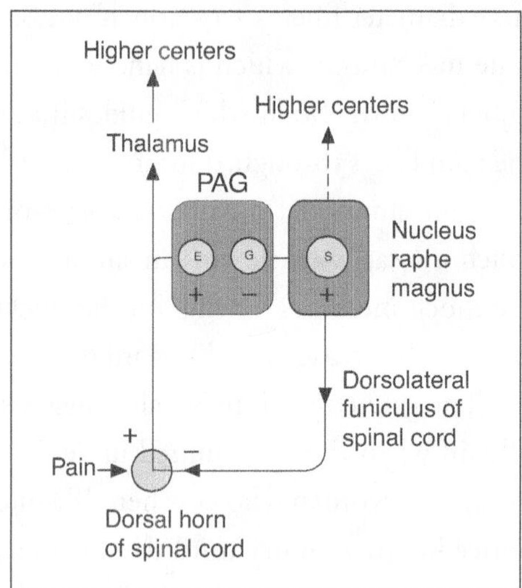

Equilibrium

The sense of balance, localized within the inner ear and comprising two sensory receptors: the semicircular canals and the vestibular sacs.

fore, serotonin appears to be involved in the inhibition of pain signals to the brain. It is for this reason that physicians may prescribe certain SSRIs (antidepressants) for management of chronic pain.

KINESTHESIS AND EQUILIBRIUM

Body senses

Term used to describe the two interrelated sensory systems of kinesthesis and equilibrium.

Kinesthesis

Bodily sense that provides information about perceptions of the location of various body parts in relation to other parts and about the position of the body in space.

Try closing your eyes and moving your hand to various positions. You will have no trouble keeping track of where your hand is. With your eyes still closed, try touching your nose. Again, you will have no problem. Finally, eyes closed, try standing on one foot. This task is a little tougher, but you will probably find you can maintain your balance reasonably well.

All of these simple exercises are accomplished without the aid of the senses discussed so far in this chapter. Rather, *these tasks are aided by two interrelated sensory systems called kinesthesis and equilibrium.* These two **body senses**, working in concert, tell us the orientation of our bodies in space, the relative position of the various body parts, and the movement of any parts of the body.

*The sense of **kinesthesis** is diffuse throughout the entire body. It consists of specialized nerve endings embedded in the muscles, tendons, and joints that tell the brain whether muscles and tendons are being stretched, contracted, or relaxed.* The cortex translates this sensory information into perceptions about locations of various parts of the body in relation to other parts. Kinesthesis allows us to throw a ball without watching what our arms are doing, and it helps us take appropriate corrective action when we stumble or slip.

Semicircular canals

Three ring-shaped structures in the inner ear that provide information about the body's equilibrium or balance.

*The sense of **equilibrium**, or balance, is localized within the inner ear.* It comprises two sets of sensory receptors: the semicircular canals and the vestibular sacs. The **semicircular canals** are three ring-shaped structures, oriented at right angles to each other so that they lie roughly in each of the three dimensions of space (see Figure 4.13). Each is filled with a fluid (endolymph) that moves when the head is rotated. *The lining of the semicircular canals contains hair cells that bend in the direction of the fluid flow.* When you move your head, the fluid flows in the canal along the plane in which your head is moving. *This movement is transduced to neural messages, which tell your brain that your head is either accelerating or decelerating. If velocity is kept at a constant rate (in an airplane for example) motion is not usually detectable.* The viscosity of endolymph fluid is apparently changed by alcohol consumption, which contributes to the "spins" when you've consumed too much.

Vestibular sacs

Structures at the junction of the semicircular canals and cochlea of the middle ear that provide information about the head's position in space.

Another source of information comes from the **vestibular sacs**, located at the junction of the semicircular canals and the cochlea. *These sacs contain hair cells weighted with crystals of calcium carbonate. When the head is tilted, gravitational forces cause the weighted cilia to shift, and this action in turn triggers neural activity in adjacent nerve fibers.* This information, in conjunction with information received from the semicircular canals (as occurs in a swaying car or a boat on a rough sea) sometimes produces motion sickness. Motion sickness is the result of unusual vestibular stimulation in which motion information signaled by the visual system is mismatched with vestibular information.

FIGURE 4.14 The Semicircular Canals

These fluid-filled canals contain specialized receptor cells that are stimulated by head movement.

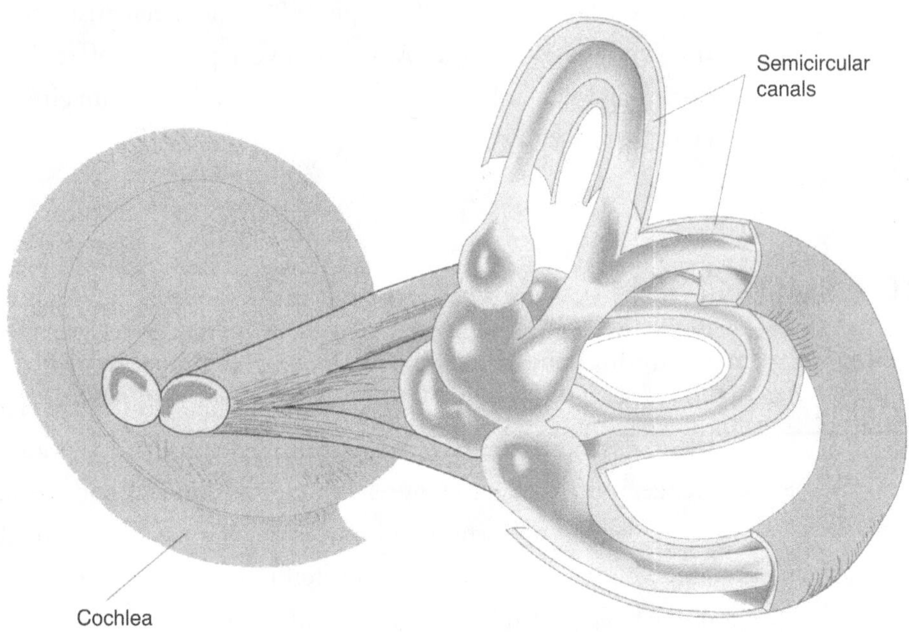

SYNESTHESIA

Synesthesia

A condition in which one type of sensory stimulation evokes the sensation of another as when, for example, the hearing of a sound produces the visualization of a color.

***Synesthesia** is the unusual and bizarre, and quite rare, condition in which sensations from one modality cause perceptions in another.* For example, an individual with synesthesia might experience a vivid green color while tasting lemonade, see black numbers in different colors, or even see distinct colors while listening to different musical notes. Scientists have long known about these experiences, and Francis Galton, a cousin of Charles Darwin, even wrote about them in 1880.

Although long thought to be a mere curiosity, fakery, or a strange memory, synesthesia may actually shed light on understanding normal brain organization and function. *It is believed that synesthesia is the result of cross wiring between cortical brain areas.* The processing of colors and numbers, for example, occurs in adjacent cortical regions where the temporal, parietal, and occipital lobes converge. In a series of brain-imaging experiments, this cross-wiring idea was supported. Upon presenting black numbers on a white background to a synesthiasic, both the number area and the color area showed increases in activity—something that does not occur with normal subjects (Nunn, et al., 2002). Synesthesia appears to run in families, suggesting a genetic disposition, and it occurs more frequently in women and creative people. It is estimated that there are about 50 distinct types of synesthesia and it occurs in 1 in 200 people (Ramachandran et al., 2003).

Some hallucinogens such as *mescaline, the psychoactive ingredient of the peyote cactus* used in religious rituals by peoples of Mexico such as the Huichols and the Aztecs, *is known for its synesthesia producing ability.* For example, people who have consumed a sizable dose of mescaline claim to see vibrant rainbow colors when water droplets from the shower hit their skin! Likewise, LSD is claimed to make people hear colors and see sounds (Hansen et. al, 2000; pg 340). The mechanism via which mescaline produces this synesthesia is not known. It is a very puzzling effect because these effects are temporary and last only as long as the drug molecules are circulating in the blood in sufficient amounts.

PERCEIVING THE WORLD

Up to this point, we have been looking at the processes by which we receive sensations about the physical world through our various sense organs. How we interpret or perceive these sensations depends on other processes. Our perceptions are much more than what we see, hear, smell, taste, or sense with our skin and body senses. Our brains organize and give meaning to the constant input of sensory messages through an active process of selecting, ordering, synthesizing, and interpreting. In the rest of this chapter we consider some of the basic principles that govern our perceptions.

FIGURE 4.14 Perceptual Organization

Perceptual organization is the process whereby we organize structural elements into objects.

Perceptual Organization

Look at the illustration in Figure 4.14. Rather than meaningless dots, lines, and colors, you no doubt perceive a familiar animal. Virtually everything we perceive with our eyes is made up of elementary sensations in the form of points, lines, edges, brightness, and varied hues. The process by which we structure these elementary sensations into the objects we perceive is called **perceptual organization.**

Perceptual organization

Process by which we structure elementary sensations (such as the sight of lines, brightness, and points) into the objects we perceive.

Gestalt psychologists identified the major principles of perceptual organization in the first half of this century. This group of influential German psychologists included Max Wertheimer, Kurt Koffka, and Wolfgang Köhler. They theorized that we perceive figures and forms as whole patterns that are different from the simple sum of individual sensations. They outlined several principles that influence how people organize sensations into whole patterns called *gestalts and some of those principles will be discussed next.*

THE FIGURE AND GROUND PRINCIPLE Is considered a fundamental principle of organization. One feature of perceptual organization identified by the Gestalt psychologists is our tendency to differentiate between **figure** (the part of an image on which we focus our attention) and **ground** (the background against which the figure stands). For example, the black words on this page stand out as figure against the white background.

Figure

In perception, the part of an image on which we focus our attention.

Ground

In perception, the background against which the figure that we focus on stands.

Figure 4.15 illustrates an ambiguous figure-ground relationship. At first glance, you may see either two light face profiles as a figure against a darker ground, or a dark vase as the figure against a lighter ground. Such figures are called "Reversible Figures" and many interesting ones can be seen on web-sites which show perceptual illusions. You may want to see some at: **http://dragon.uml.edu/psych/**

FIGURE 4.15 The Rubin Vase

The Rubin Vase is used to illustrate the figure-ground principle of perceptual organization. The illustration is ambiguous because either the dark grey or the light grey can serve as figure or ground.

Perceptual grouping

Tendency to organize patterns of stimuli into larger units according to proximity, similarity, and good continuation.

Proximity

Perceptual grouping principle whereby, all else being equal, we tend to organize perceptions by grouping elements that are the nearest to each other.

Similarity

In perception, the principle that we tend to group elements that are similar to each other. In social psychology, similarity of beliefs, interests, and values is recognized as a factor attracting people to one another.

Good continuation

Perceptual grouping principle that we are more likely to perceive stimuli as a whole or single group if they flow smoothly into one another than if they are discontinuous.

Reversible figures demonstrate the distinction between sensation and perception. *The pattern of sensory receptors activated in our retinas remains constant while our perceptions shift between the two figure-ground patterns.* The manner in which our brains organize these constant sensory stimuli allows us to perceive either the faces or the vase, but not both at the same time.

The figure and ground organization principle also applies to senses other than vision. For example, when you listen to music, the melody may stand out as the figure against a background of chords that serve as ground. However, a sudden change in tempo, rhythm, or volume may suddenly bring a chord to the forefront, where it becomes the central figure. Perhaps you are listening to a friend describe some important political event when a voice on the TV set behind you mentions your favorite athletic team. Suddenly the TV announcement becomes the focal point of your attention, and your friend's voice becomes background noise. You cannot focus on your friend's voice and the TV announcer at the same time: One must be figure, and the other the ground.

PRINCIPLES OF PERCEPTUAL GROUPING Gestalt psychologists also demonstrated the role of **perceptual grouping** to explain how we organize sensory input into meaningful wholes. Patterns of stimuli are grouped into larger units in three major ways: by **proximity**, **similarity**, and **continuation**.

Figure 4.16 illustrates these three perceptual grouping principles. ***The principle of proximity*** suggests that, all else being equal, we tend to organize our perceptions by grouping elements that are the nearest to each other.

The principle of similarity suggests that we group elements that are similar to one another. A final grouping principle, good continuation, suggests that we are more likely to perceive stimuli as a whole or single group if they flow smoothly into one another as opposed to being discontinuous.

The principle of closure *explains* our inclination to perceive incomplete figures as complete. A careful examination of Figure 4.17 reveals that what appear to be two overlap-

FIGURE 4.16 Perceptual Grouping Principles

Part A illustrates the principle of proximity: The pattern on the left can be seen as either columns or rows because the dots are spaced equally. The patterns to the right are seen as columns because of the horizontal spacing. Parts B and C demonstrate the grouping principle of similarity (in B we see rows and in C we see columns). Pattern D illustrates the principle of continuity, in which stimuli that flow smoothly into one another form a group.

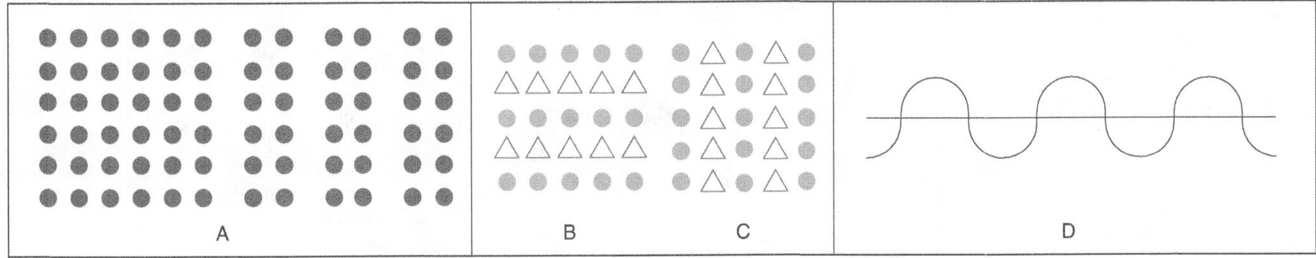

ping triangles are actually incomplete figures. Furthermore, the solid white triangle does not exist; it is merely an illusion. The perceptual process that allows us to see these as complete figures is referred to as **closure**. *The non-existent figures are known as* ***subjective contours*** *and are produced because of closure.* This phenomenon of closure allows us to read hand-writing where people don't always write the letters correctly and completely.

Closure

Perceptual organizing principle that we tend to perceive incomplete figures as complete.

ATTENTION AND PERCEPTION Another basic principle of perceptual processing is selective attention, the process of focusing on one or a few stimuli of particular significance while ignoring others. In general we do not attend equally to all of the stimuli we re-

FIGURE 4.17 The Principle of Closure

We can see two overlapping triangles in this illustration because of our tendency to fill in missing perceptual information. The solid white triangle is merely an illusion induced by closure.

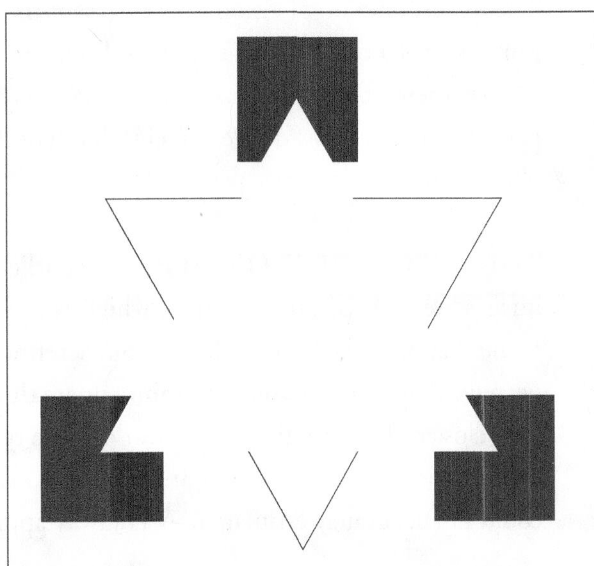

FIGURE 4.18 Binocular (Retinal) Disparity and Convergence

Part A illustrates that the closer an object is the greater the retinal disparity. Part B illustrates the convergence of the eyes that is necessary to view nearby objects. Both binocular (retinal) disparity and convergence are important depth cues for perception.

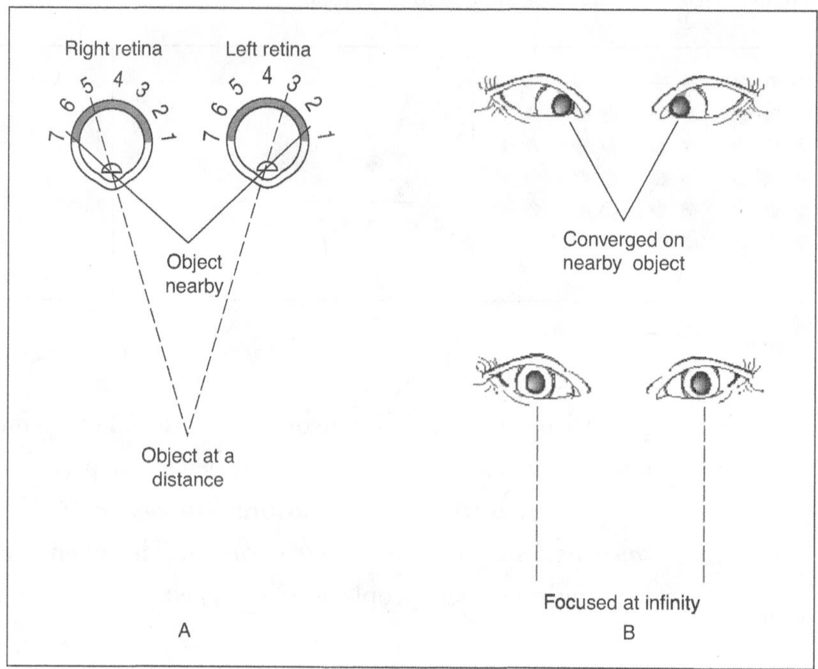

Selective attention

The process of focusing on one or a few stimuli of particular significance while ignoring others.

ceive at any given point in time. If we did, our nervous systems would become hopelessly overloaded. Instead, certain stimuli are focused on, and the other events fade into the background. Through this process of **selective attention** our perceptual ability is enhanced.

Spatial Perception

The major function of vision is to represent the spatial arrangement of objects in our environment. Objects are seen at varying distances and from different perspectives, yet we recognize their form and size quite accurately. This poses two related problems for perception. First, how do we perceive depth or distance? And second, how do we recognize objects from different perspectives?

THE PERCEPTION OF DEPTH Earlier in this chapter, we learned that visual images are focused on the retina, which is essentially an image-recording layer of neural tissue that lines the back of the eye. Since retinal images are two-dimensional, how can we perceive that objects in our environment are three-dimensional, and how do we determine how close or far away they are? Clearly, these types of discrimination are essential for normal functioning. Can you imagine what it would be like to walk through a busy city if you could not accurately estimate how far away approaching cars happened to be? A variety of

Binocular cues

Visual cues for depth or distance, such as binocular disparity and convergence, that depend on both eyes working together.

Monocular cues

Distance cues such as linear perspective and height on a plane that can be used with just one eye.

Binocular (retinal) disparity

The difference in the retinal image of an object as seen from each eye, due to the difference in viewing angles, that provides an important binocular cue for depth. Also known as retinal disparity.

Convergence

Binocular distance cue based on the fact that the two eyes must converge or rotate toward the inside to perceive objects closer than about 25 feet. The closer the object, the more rotation is necessary and the more muscle tension created.

perceptual cues allow us to judge the distance of objects accurately. Some of these cues, called **binocular cues**, depend on both eyes working together; others, called **monocular cues**, can be used with just one eye.

Binocular Cues Seeing with both our eyes provides important binocular cues for distance perception (Foley, 1985). Perhaps the most accurate of these is **retinal disparity.** Retinal disparity is based on the fact that since the eyes are a couple of inches apart, each eye has a slightly different view of the world. To demonstrate this phenomenon, stare at this page and alternately close one eye at a time. Note that the page appears to shift its position slightly. Normally our brains fuse these two images into a single three-dimensional image. At the same time, the brain analyzes the differences in the two images to obtain information about distance.

There is greater binocular disparity when objects are close to our eyes than when they are far away. This can be demonstrated with the ***Jumping Finger demonstration,*** as follows: Hold the index finger of one hand very close to your face and align it with the same finger of the other hand as far away as possible. Now alternately close each eye. Your closest finger seems to leap back and forth, while the far one shifts only slightly. Figure 4.19a shows why close objects create more significant disparity whereas those that are far away create only minor disparity: The difference in the angle of the two eyes to the far object is much slighter than the difference for the close object. The ability of the visual system to utilize binocular disparity is quite impressive. The minimum disparity required to detect a depth difference is 1 micron (1 millionth of a meter). This is less than the diameter of a photoreceptor!

Another important binocular distance cue is called convergence. When we look at an object that is no more than 25 feet away, our two eyes must converge (rotate to the inside) in order to perceive it as a single, clearly focused image. This rotation of the eyes is necessary to allow them to focus on the same object, but it creates tension in the eye muscles. As Figure 4.18b shows, the closer the object, the greater the tension. Objects far away require no convergence for sharp focusing. Consequently, *muscular feedback from converging eyes becomes an important cue for judging the distance of objects within roughly 25 feet of our eyes.*

Although, as explained by the Jumping Finger demonstration, each eye receives a slightly different picture of the same object due to retinal disparity, the brain *fuses* the two images and lets us perceive one image of the object when both the eyes are open. ***A demonstration known as the Hole in the Hand Illusion, shows off fusion very nicely.***

To view fusion, roll a sheet of paper into a narrow, hollow tube. With both eyes open, take the tube close to one eye, and make sure it is close enough to touch the eye. Then bring the palm of your other hand (the one that is not holding the tube to the eye), alongside the tube and close to its lengthwise center. Look with both eyes open. *If you do this correctly, you will see a round hole going right through the middle of your palm,* and what's more, you will see whichever object happens to be behind your palm, through the hole!

Monocular Cues If objects that are far away create little retinal disparity and no convergence, how can we judge their distance? A number of one-eye, or monocular, cues provide that information. *These* monocular cues *are also known as pictorial cues because artists use them to create three-dimensional painting on a two dimensional canvas.* They are also known as *experiential cues,* because most of these ways of reckoning depth are learned as you explore the world in infancy and early childhood.

Height on a plane

Important monocular depth cue based on the fact that objects that are highest on one's plane of view appear to be farthest away.

Figure 4.19 illustrates several important monocular cues for distance perception. One of these is elevation, or **height on a plane**. Note that the objects in Figure 4.19 that appear to be farther away are higher on your plane of view. This cue is always present. If you look around your room or gaze out the window, you will see that the farther away an object is, the higher it will be on your plane of view and the more you have to lift your gaze to perceive it.

Overlap

Important monocular distance cue based on the fact that objects close to us tend to block out parts of objects that are farther away. Also known as interposition.

Another distance cue, called **overlap** or superposition, describes the phenomenon in which objects close to us tend to block out parts of objects that are farther away from us. If you look around your room again, you will notice that your textbook blocks your view of the desk under it, that the desk in turn blocks your view of the floor, and so forth.

Linear perspective

Important monocular distance cue based on the fact that parallel lines converge when stretched into the distance.

A third distance cue, called **linear perspective**, is based on the fact that parallel lines converge when stretched into the distance. For example, when you look at a long stretch of road or railroad tracks, it appears that the sides of the road or the parallel tracks converge on the horizon.

If we know how large objects are, we can judge their distance by their apparent size in relation to each other. If you look out your window and see two people, one 50 yards away

FIGURE 4.19 Monocular Cues for Depth Perception

Many monocular cues also contribute to depth perception. Objects faraway tend to be higher on our plane of view A, objects closer to us block objects that are further away B, when you look at this stretch of the rood the sides (lines) of the rood converge C, and objects that are closer tend to be larger than similar objects at a distance D.

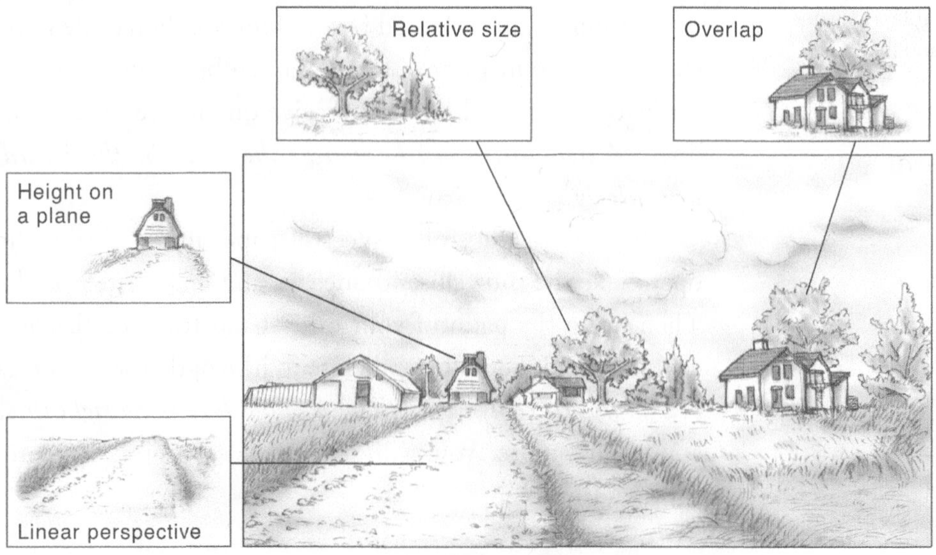

Relative size

Monocular distance cue based on the fact that objects of the same size appear to be smaller the farther they are from the viewer.

Texture gradients

Monocular distance cue based on the fact that textured surfaces (such as a grassy lawn) appear to be smoother, denser, and less textured when they are far from the viewer than when they are close.

Aerial (atmospheric) perspective

Monocular distance cue based on the fact that distant objects tend to appear more fuzzy and less clear than those close to the viewer due to dust and haze.

Relative motion (motion parallax)

Monocular distance cue based on the fact that moving objects appear to move a greater distance when they are close to the viewer than when they are far away.

and the other 200 yards away, you notice a great difference in their **relative size**. Instead of concluding that one person is a dwarf and the other a giant, you take this cue as evidence that the smaller person is a greater distance from you.

Another monocular cue, **texture gradient**, involves perceived change in the texture of surfaces as they extend farther from our eyes. For example, if you look at a textured surface such as an expanse of grassy lawn or a rock-strewn field, the elements close to you seem to be farther apart or less dense than those that are farther away. The close elements are also clearer. A striking illustration of this phenomenon is provided in Figure 4.20.

Objects that are far away appear fuzzier than those that are close by because as distance increases, smog, dust, and haze reduce the clarity of the projected image. This depth cue, called **aerial perspective** or **atmospheric perspective**, can sometimes cause us to judge distance inaccurately, especially if we are accustomed to the smoggy atmosphere of urban areas.

A final monocular cue for distance may be demonstrated if you gaze at the scene outside your window and move your head from side to side. You will notice that objects nearby seem to move a much greater distance than objects farther away. This cue, called ***relative motion*** *or* ***motion parallax***, is particularly noticeable when you look out the window of a moving car and observe nearby objects moving much more rapidly than distant ones.

PERCEIVING DEPTH: THE VISUAL CLIFF EXPERIMENT There can be little doubt that many distance cues are enhanced by experience. In fact, before a classic experiment over 30 years ago, many psychologists believed that distance or depth perception

FIGURE 4.20 Texture Gradients

The fine texture in the foreground of this picture fades away in the distance.

Corbis

depended on learning. However, Eleanor Gibson and Richard Walk (1960) provided convincing evidence that *some aspects of depth perception are inborn or innate, at least in some species.*

Visual cliff

Device that produces the illusion of a cliff, allowing researchers to test the ability of animals to perceive and respond to depth cues.

The device created by Gibson and Walk is called the visual cliff. The **visual cliff** is an elevated glass surface. A checkerboard-patterned plane lays just under half of the glass surface; there is nothing under the other half except for the checkerboard painted on the floor, roughly three and one-half feet below. This design produces the illusion of a deep side and a shallow side.

Infants of many species that can walk immediately after birth were tested on the apparatus. All of these newborn animals, including kittens, puppies, lambs, chickens, piglets, and kids, refused to cross over to the deep side, suggesting that depth perception is innate in these species. Even chicks whose initial visual experience occurred on the visual cliff would not step over the deep side. Evidence also suggests that depth perception in this case is based on the monocular cue motion parallax, which is the dominant cue for depth perception in most animals.

Size constancy

One form of perceptual constancy. Although the retinal image of an object becomes smaller as the object recedes into the distance (or larger as it approaches), the viewer adjusts for this change and perceives the object to be constant in size.

Since human babies could not be tested until they were able to crawl (usually around the age of six months), their depth perception was more difficult to interpret. Obviously, a lot of learning can take place in the first six months of life. Most of the infants tested would not spontaneously crawl onto the deep side, something that infants of other species would never do. Yet some infants, especially those who began crawling at a very young age, can be enticed to crawl over the cliff.

Some researchers argue that by the time human infants can be tested on the visual cliff, they may have already learned to avoid drop-offs. Others have argued that the kind of depth perception required for the cliff is an innate capacity in humans that emerges at about six months after birth, the age at which most infants begin to need this capability (Richards & Rader, 1981). Which explanation is correct? At this point, we can say with confidence that depth perception is an innate ability in many species of animals. In humans it is either innate, or it is learned very early in life. Human infants are clearly not living in a visual world that is "one great blooming, buzzing confusion" as stated by William James in 1890. Rather, their world appears to be perceived much like our own.

Brightness constancy

An element of perceptual constancy. We perceive objects that we see at night or in poor lighting to be the same brightness as they appear during the day.

SIZE, COLOR AND SHAPE CONSTANCIES Are part of Gestalt principles of organization. The retinal image of the object changes in size but the brain allows us to perceive it as if there was no change in the object to allow continuity to our experience.

Color constancy

An element of perceptual constancy. We perceive objects that we see in the dark to be the same color as they appear during the day even though their retinal images change.

Size Constancy Perceiving an object as if there was no change in size, when its retinal image has indeed changed in size because it has moved away or moved closer, is known as "Size Constancy". Size constancy is illustrated in Figure 4.21. In this illustration the man walking is the same size in both pictures. However, as he approaches the foreground, he appears to shrink.

FIGURE 4.21 Size Constancy

The man who is walking in these pictures is the same size in each shot. As he moves closer he appears to shrink.

Brightness and Color Constancy **Brightness constancy** and **color constancy** also help us perceive our world as constant. When you look out your window at night, the trees, grass, and bushes do not appear to be the same color or brightness as they are during the daytime. Since you already know that the leaves of the bushes are a dark green and the grass and trees are brighter green, however, you perceive these qualities to be constant even under conditions of different illumination.

Perceptual constancy

The fact that objects are normally perceived to be constant in size, color or brightness, and shape, despite the fact that their retinal images change according to different conditions.

Shape Constancy Another element of **perceptual constancy** is **shape constancy**. When we look at objects from different angles, the shape of the image projected to our retinas is different in each instance. Nevertheless, we perceive the object as unchanged (see Figure 4.22). When we view a door from straight on, it appears rectangular in shape. When the door is opened, we still perceive it as rectangular despite the fact that the image projected on our retinas is trapezoidal.

Shape constancy

Element of perceptual constancy. We perceive objects as maintaining the same shape even though their retinal images change when we view them from different angles.

In summary, we perceive our dynamic environment as essentially stable and containing constant stimulus properties. This occurs even though our visual system receives a varied array of stimulus properties including changes in size, brightness, color, and shape. However, as we noted for depth perception, perceptual constancies have been demonstrated very early on in human development and early on in the development of other animals suggesting that some perceptual constancies may be innate.

Throughout this chapter we have emphasized that our perceptions of physical stimuli are not exactly the same as the properties of the physical stimulus. Some of this discrep-

FIGURE 4.22 Shape Constancy

We perceive the opening door as being rectangular despite the image projected on our retinas.

ancy is produced by our nervous system during the process of transducing the physical sensation. Other discrepancies are more related to the perceptual organization of stimuli. In the next section we will examine stimuli that produce considerable perceptual ambiguity because of these discrepancies.

Visual Illusions

Illusion

False or inaccurate perception that differs from the actual physical state of the perceived object.

Visual **illusions** are of interest to psychologists because they provide insights into normal perception, not because they are errors in perception. The illusions discussed here are important because of their relation to spatial perception.

THE AMES ILLUSION Perhaps one of the most vivid illusions is provided by the *Ames room,* shown in Figure 4.23. A person standing on one side of the room appears to be a giant; someone on the other side appears to be a dwarf. It is even more amazing that when people cross the Ames room, they steadily appear to grow or shrink, depending on the direction in which they are walking. This illusion is produced by conflicting environmental cues.

The Ames room was designed to fool the observer into thinking it is shaped like a normal rectangular room. However, as you can see from the diagram in the figure, the room is definitely not rectangular. Both windows are trapezoidal, and one is much larger than the other. In addition, the floor is uneven so that one end of the Ames room is higher on the plane than the other. The relationships between the various objects in the room were altered in this manner to change relationships that we are accustomed to perceiving between people and their environments. Since we have not experienced this kind of arrangement before, however, our perceptual constancy processes cause us to perceive the room as rectangular and the windows as equal in size and rectangular in shape. Recent research has shown that the Ames room illusion persists (although in somewhat dimin-

FIGURE 4.23 The Ames Room

In the Ames room people appear to change sizes as they move about. As you can see from the diagram, the person on the left is twice as far away as the person on the right. The illusion occurs because the depth cues are not apparent to the viewer.

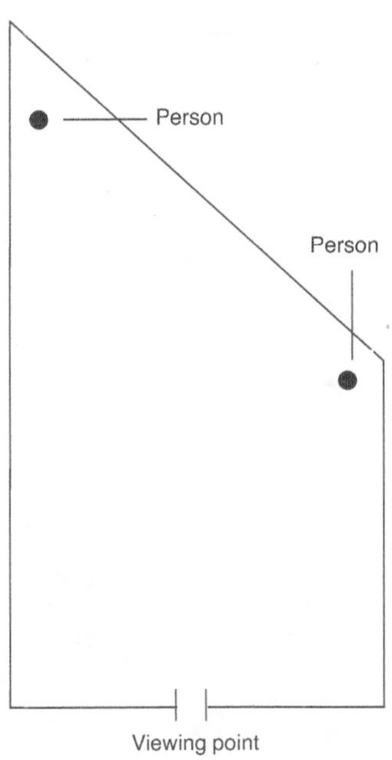

ished form) even when subjects are allowed to leave the viewing point indicated in the figure and move about the room (Gehringer & Engel, 1986).

THE MÜLLER-LYLER ILLUSION One of the most widely analyzed visual illusions is the *Müller-Lyler illusion,* illustrated in Figure 4.24. Ignoring the angled lines (arrowheads) at the ends of each vertical line, decide which line is longer. Most people see the line on the right as longer, but actually the two are of equal length. How can the Müller-Lyler illusion be explained? It seems as though depth cues and size constancy both play a role. Think back to what you have learned about perceptual constancy in this chapter, and try to formulate an answer before reading on.

Actually, psychologists do not agree as to why the Müller-Lyler illusion fools us. According to one interpretation that enjoyed popularity for a period of time, the illusion is created by the fact that the outward-turned angles draw the viewer's eyes farther out into space; the inward-turning angles draw the eyes back toward the center.

One study cast serious doubt on this interpretation, however. In this experiment an apparatus was designed to hold a subject's eyes and head very still while the lines of the Müller-Lyler illusion were flashed into one eye and the arrowheads into the other. When these sensations were combined in the subject's brain, the same illusion resulted (Gillam, 1980). This finding indicates that the illusion is created by something more than the movement of the eyes.

FIGURE 4.24 The Müller-Lyler Illusion

The two vertical lines are equal in length.

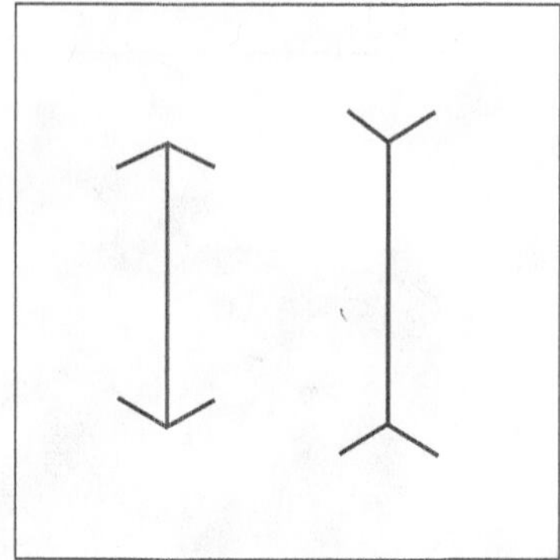

A British psychologist, R. L. Gregory (1978), has proposed a more likely interpretation—that the Müller-Lyler illusion is the result of size constancy. According to Gregory, the angled lines provide linear perspective cues. As Figure 4.25 shows, the vertical line on the left, enclosed by the inward-turning angled lines, is perceived as being closer than the line with the outward-turning angled lines. We have already learned that if two objects appear to be the same size, and we think one is closer, then size constancy causes us to assume that the farther one is bigger (Gregory, 1978).

Gregory's theory is supported by research demonstrating that the Müller-Lyler illusion is either very weak or absent in cultures in which people have little exposure to angles (Seagall et al., 1966). For example, the Zulus of southeast Africa, who live in circular huts with few straight lines and corners, do not judge distance from such linear cues as effectively as we do. These people respond only minimally to the Müller-Lyler illusion.

THE MOON ILLUSION An illusion you are probably familiar with is the *moon illusion.* Most people have had the experience of looking at a full moon on the horizon and thinking how huge it looks. When the moon is low on the horizon, it appears larger than when it is overhead, yet the actual size of the moon's image on the retina is the same regardless of its position in the sky. Why does this illusion occur?

The moon illusion also seems to result from size constancy. When the moon is low, it appears to be farther away than when it is overhead. This effect results from the presence of visual cues for distance, such as overlapping structures and relative size. Compared to the trees or buildings on the horizon, we perceive the moon to be very far away. In contrast, when we look at the moon overhead, we have no visual cues for distance. (Yantis, 2000). But since the retinal image of the moon is actually the same size, our minds make it look bigger when it is near the horizon to compensate for the perceived increase in distance.

FIGURE 4.25 What Causes the Müller-Lyler Illusion?

This illustration suggests that the Müller-Lyler illusion results from depth cues and size constancy.

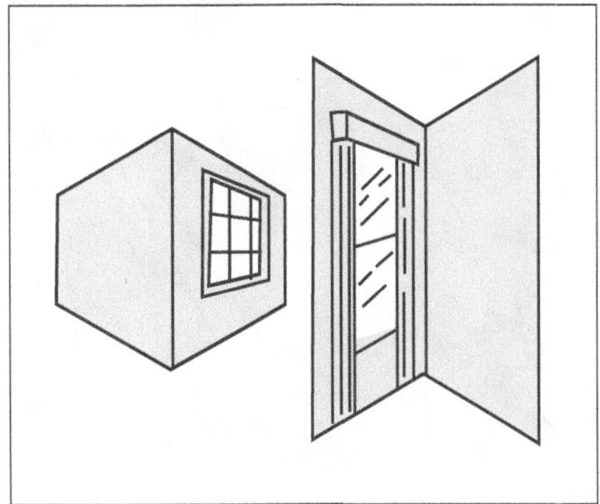

THE PONZO ILLUSION The *Ponzo illusion* is illustrated in Figure 4.26. The two horizontal lines are equal in length although we perceive the "distant" line as longer. The Ponzo illusion is an illusion of perspective. The converging lines at the top of the figure are associated with distance, falsely suggesting that the top horizontal line is farther away. An object that is farther away and yet occupies the same visual angle as an object that is closer to us must then be longer.

THE POGGENDORFF ILLUSION Another interesting illusion is the *Poggendorff illusion,* shown in Figure 4.27a. It appears that if the diagonal lines were continued toward each other, the one on the right would pass above the left line. In reality, they would join, as you can determine by laying a straight edge along their projected paths. Many psychologists believe this illusion results from our inclination to maintain shape constancy. Figure 4.27b illustrates one possible example of something we have experienced that influences our perception of the Poggendorff illusion. Clearly, if lines *A* and *B* were the leg and back support, respectively, of an overturned chair, they could never meet.

The illusion created in part of this figure gives us the impression that if line *A* were extended it would pass below line *B,* when in fact they would meet. This illusion may result from our inclination to maintain shape constancy.

Perceptual Sets

In addition to the cues we have been discussing, our perceptions are also influenced by many subjective factors such as our tendency to see (or hear, smell, feel, or taste) what we expect or what is consistent with our preconceived notions of what makes sense.

FIGURE 4.26 The Ponzo Illusion

The two horizontal lines are of equal length.

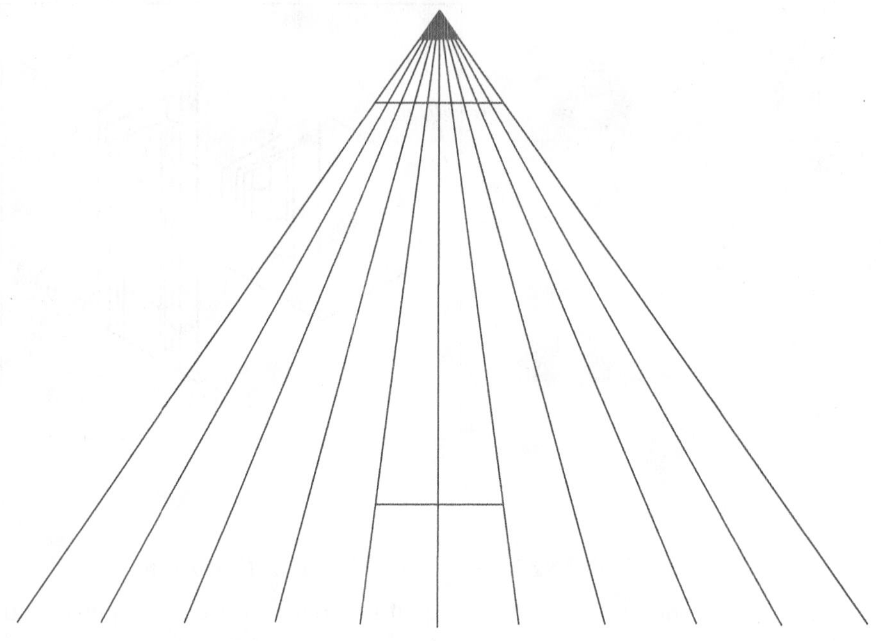

FIGURE 4.27 The Poggendorff Illusion

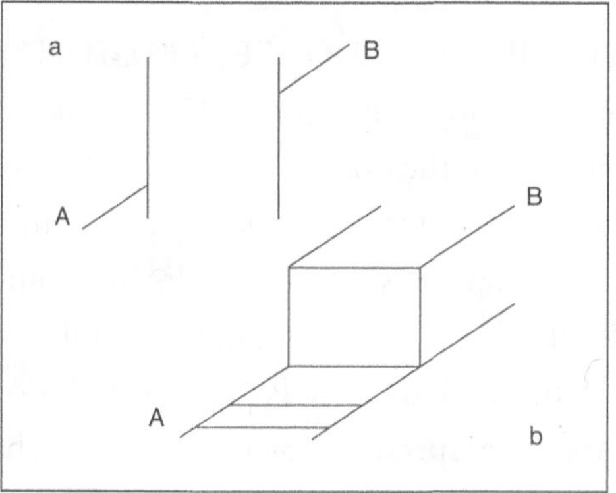

Perceptual set

Tendency to see, hear, smell, feel, or taste what we expect or what is consistent with our preconceived notions.

This phenomenon is known as a **perceptual set**, and it is illustrated in Figure 4.28. You can try this demonstration out on two friends. Show one friend picture *A* (keep *B* and *C* covered), and ask what is seen. The response will probably be an old woman. Then show picture *C* while covering *A* and *B*. Again, an old woman is likely to be seen. Next, repeat the procedure with a different friend, but this time start with picture *B* followed by *C*. In this situation, your friend is likely to report seeing a young woman in both pictures. The difference is explained by the fact that the particular image seen in picture *C* depends on the viewer's previous experience. *Since the first friend was initially exposed to the picture of the old lady, he*

FIGURE 4.28 A Demonstration of Perceptual Set

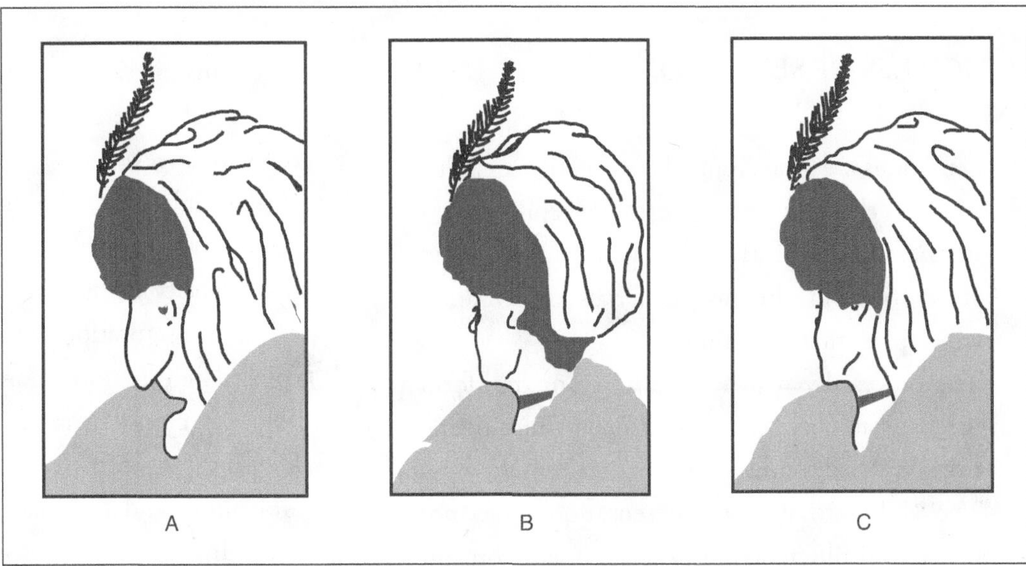

or she ***developed a perceptual set*** *to see an old lady in picture C.* In contrast, the second friend's perceptual set was geared toward seeing the youthful image in picture *B.*

Motivational state can also have a strong impact on how we perceive our environments, presumably by the mechanism of establishing perceptual sets. For example, if you drive down a main thoroughfare while feeling hunger pangs, you probably notice almost every sign advertising food. You may even misread signs so that an ad in the window of the local garden store seems to say steaks instead of stakes.

Selective perception

A form of perceptual set; the tendency to perceive stimuli that are consistent with expectations and to ignore those that are inconsistent.

Another form of perceptual set is the tendency to perceive stimuli that are consistent with our expectations, and to ignore those that are inconsistent. This phenomenon is frequently referred to as **selective perception**. For example, if you believe that all neatly dressed elderly women are honest, you might not even think twice about the elderly woman at the next table when your wallet disappears in a restaurant, even if she is the most obvious suspect. Likewise, people who distrust groups of people because of their appearance, religion, or ethnic background are unlikely to recognize the good qualities of an individual who is a member of one of those groups. We're sure if you think about it for a while you can recognize instances where your behavior was influenced by a perceptual set of this sort.

In this chapter we examined the process of sensation where some aspect of the physical environment is transduced into neural activity. This neural activity is interpreted by the nervous system as vision, audition, olfaction, gustation, or one of the skin senses. The way we organize this information into useful representations of our environment was described as perceptual organization. We discussed a number of these organizational processes and showed how conflicting processing cues can lead to illusions. Although experience can clearly influence these organization processes, much of perceptual organization appears to be either innate or learned very early in development.

SUMMARY

PRINCIPLES OF SENSATION AND PERCEPTION

1. Sensations are basic, immediate experiences that a stimulus elicits in a sense organ. Perception refers to the process of interpreting, organizing, and elaborating on the raw materials of sensation which gives them meaning.
2. The process by which sensory organs transform mechanical, chemical, or light energy into neural firing is called transduction.
3. The ability to distinguish sensations does not depend on differences between the sense organs, but rather on what part of the brain is activated by the sensory messages.
4. Many of the physical events surrounding us go unheeded. The most important variables determining whether or not we perceive things happening around us are sensory thresholds, attention, and adaptation.
5. Our perception of various sensory inputs occur only when the strength of a stimulus reaches a minimal or threshold level of intensity sufficient to activate a sensory process. Weber's law describes the relationship between stimulus intensity and our perception of stimulus change.
6. Attention refers to the control of our conscious behavior by specific stimuli or stimulus situations.
7. Adaptation refers to the decrease in the response of sensory receptors when they are exposed to continual, unchanging stimulation.

VISION

9. The most important parts of our visual system are: the eyes, which capture and respond to light energy; the photosensitive receptors which transduce light into neural signals; the neural circuits that transmit signals from the eye to the brain; and visual centers within the brain that interpret these messages.
10. Visible light, the stimulus for vision, has three particularly important properties: brightness, or the intensity of light; hue, or the color we perceive; and saturation, which is the proportion of colored light to non-colored light.
11. Two key components of the eye are the image-focusing part, consisting of the cornea, lens, iris, and pupil; and the image-recording part, called the retina.
12. The primary photoreceptor cells in the retina, the rods and cones, contain photopigments that respond to light. Our perception of color is largely dependent on the cones; the rods are extremely sensitive photoreceptors that allow us to see in dim light.
13. Two major theories of color vision have been proposed: the trichromatic theory and the opponent-process theory. Most vision experts believe that color vision may result from interplay between a trichromatic system operating at the level of photoreceptor cells and an opponent-process mechanism in the thalamus.

AUDITION

14. Most of the sounds we hear consist of physical energy in the form of rhythmic pressure changes in the air.
15. Three characteristics of sound waves that influence our perception of sound are loudness (amplitude), pitch (frequency), and timbre (a combination of a fundamental frequency and additional frequency components called overtones).
16. Auditory perception results when sound waves are converted into mechanical movement of the ossicles in the middle ear, which in turn act to

produce pressure waves within the fluid of the inner ear that stimulate hair cells, which transduce the physical energy of sound waves into neural impulses that our brains translate into sounds.

17. The best available evidence suggests that our perception of pitch is determined by both the place of maximal excitation on the basilar membrane and the frequency with which auditory nerve fibers fire.
18. Auditory localization is the result of differences in both the loudness and the time of arrival of sounds reaching each of our ears.
19. Hearing loss may result from either damage to the neural structures that transmit auditory messages to the brain (sensory neural hearing loss) or inability of the outer and middle ear to conduct sound energy to the receptors in the inner ear (conduction hearing loss).

GUSTATION AND OLFACTION

20. Our taste receptors, located on little bumps on the tongue called papillae, can distinguish only five different sensations: sweetness, saltiness, sourness, bitterness and umami. In addition, the tongue will sense touch, temperature, movement, and pain via other receptors.
21. The receptors for odors lie in the mucous membrane that lines the nasal cavity and airborne chemical molecules that dissolve in the nasal mucosa serve as stimuli. Molecules that are similar in shape and size generally have similar smells.

THE SKIN SENSES

22. The mechanism of the sense of touch is a composite of three different senses: pressure, temperature, and pain. Specialized receptors housed in and under the skin mediate the various sensations.
23. The sensation of pressure occurs when a mechanical force causes a displacement of the skin.
24. Different specialized dendrite endings respond to cold and heat.
25. Some pain researchers maintain that pain results from over stimulation of any sensory receptor; others believe that pain occurs when damaged tissue releases chemicals that stimulate specialized nerve endings in the skin.

KINESTHESIS AND EQUILIBRIUM

26. The two body senses of kinesthesis and equilibrium, working in concert, tell us the orientation of our bodies in space, the relative position of the various body parts, and the movement of any parts of the body.

SYNESTHESIA

27. Synesthesia is the unusual and bizarre, and quite rare, condition where sensations from one modality cause perceptions in another. Hallucinogenic drugs such as mescaline, LSD, etc., are known to produce temporary synesthesia, where one sees music or hears colors.

PERCEIVING THE WORLD

28. The process by which we structure elementary sensations into the objects we perceive is called perceptual organization.
29. Three important principles that influence how people organize sensations into whole patterns, called gestalts, are figure and ground, perceptual grouping, and closure.
30. Figure and ground refers to our tendency to differentiate between the parts of an image we focus on (figure) and the background against which the figure stands (ground).

31. According to the principle of perceptual grouping, we tend to group patterns of stimuli into larger units in three major ways: by proximity, similarity, and good continuation.
32. Another organizing principle is our inclination to perceive incomplete figures as complete, a process known as closure. Sometimes, we perceive nonexistent figures due to closure of incomplete figures. Such figures are called subjective contours.
33. Selective attention refers to the process of focusing on one or a few stimuli of particular significance while ignoring others.
34. Characteristics of stimuli that tend to capture attention almost automatically include sudden change, contrast and novelty, intensity, repetition, and stimulus difficulty.
35. Key stimuli capture attention by activating motivational systems.
36. Binocular cues for perceiving distance include retinal disparity and convergence.
37. Important monocular cues for distance perception include height on a plane, overlap or interposition, linear perspective, relative size, texture gradients, aerial perspective, and relative motion.
38. Research has revealed that depth perception is clearly an innate ability in many species of animals, and that in humans it is either innate or is learned very early in life.
39. Perceptual constancy allows us to adjust for varying conditions and changing patterns as we perceive the world. When we look at objects at different distances and angles and under different levels of illumination, we are able to make the necessary adjustments to maintain a degree of constancy in our perception of size, shape, brightness, and color.
40. A perceptual illusion is a false perception in that it differs from the actual physical state of the perceived object.
41. A tendency to perceive what we expect or are inclined to see, a phenomenon known as perceptual set, may have a strong impact on how we perceive our environments.

TERMS AND CONCEPTS

sensations
perception
transduction
psychophysics
threshold
absolute threshold
difference threshold (just noticeable difference [jnd])
Weber's law
attention
sensory adaptation
brightness
hue
saturation
accommodation
retina
rods
cones
Young-Helmholtz theory (trichromatic theory of color vision)
opponent-process theory of color vision
loudness
pitch
timbre
tympanic membrane
ossicles
cochlea
basilar membrane
organ of Corti

volley theory
place theory of pitch discrimination
frequency theory of pitch discrimination
auditory localization
conduction hearing loss
sensorineural hearing loss
gustation
olfaction
substance P
gate-control theory
endorphins
periaqueductal gray area (PAG)
equilibrium
body senses
kinesthesis
semicircular canals
vestibular sacs
synesthesia
perceptual organization
figure
ground
perceptual grouping
proximity
similarity
good continuation
closure
selective attention
binocular cues
monocular cues
binocular (retinal) disparity
convergence
height on a plane
overlap
linear perspective
relative size
texture gradients
aerial (atmospheric) perspective
relative motion (motion parallax)
visual cliff
size constancy
brightness constancy
color constancy
perceptual constancy
shape constancy
illusion
perceptual set
selective perception

CHAPTER 5

Consciousness: Sleep, Dreaming, Hypnosis, and Meditation

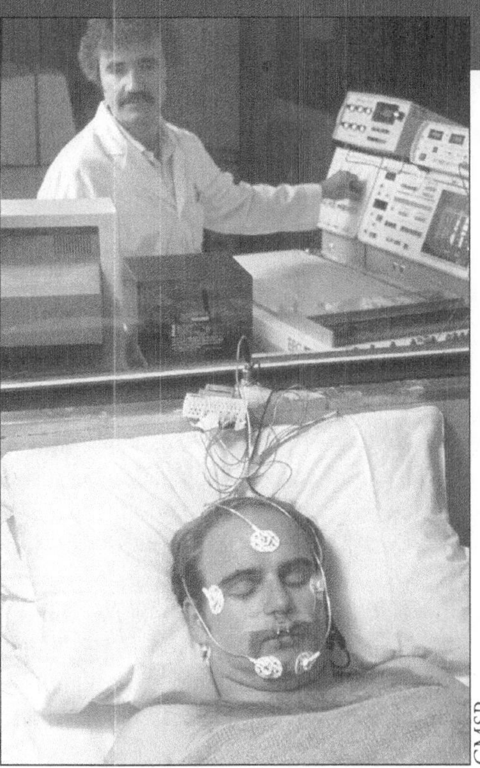
CMSP

Get Outta Here!

"Woman in Coma Plays Tennis" wrote Maggie Fox, in her September 8, 2006, article about a comatose woman who followed commands to play tennis, albeit, only in her imagination! Several articles on the fMRI scan of this woman's brain reported that her brain lit up in the correct areas when given verbal commands.

In November 2012, that same fMRI technique used on that woman was used on a young Canadian comatose patient, by the same Cognitive Neuroscientist, Dr. Adrian Owen, to get answers to Yes/No questions! Believe it or not, the comatose patient answered them by imagining the specific situations he was requested to imagine for a yes or no answer!

There is no doubt that this line of research will revolutionize the field of consciousness! Looks like the debate about when life support should be switched off will take on a life of its own!

See the full articles at the following web sites:

Woman in Coma Plays Tennis by Maggie Fox: http://www.abc.net.au/science/news/stories/2006/1735888.htm

Unconscious Man Talks
http://www.the-scientist.com/?articles.view/articleNo/33264/title/An--Unconscious--Man-Talks/

From Karen Anne Quinlan, who collapsed into a coma in 1975, to Terri Schiavo, who went into a coma in 1990 and stayed in it until 2005, people have debated the switching off of life-support systems in comatose people. In Terri Schiavo's case there was a very bitter public battle between her husband, who wanted her feeding tubes removed, and her parents, who did not. Her case was even debated in the United States Congress. However, Terri's feeding tubes were finally removed on March 18, 2005, by order of the Miami High Court.

In Terry Schiavo's days there was no way to assess whether or not there was any awareness or consciousness in the vegetative patient, but just a couple of years later, *Dr. Adrian Owen, a Canadian Cognitive Neuroscientist and his team, showed that a comatose patient who was in a vegetative state had cognitive abilities and could process auditory information and follow simple commands*. When asked to "imagine playing tennis" she did exactly that and her fMRI images were very similar to that of normal volunteers, when they played tennis in their imagination! (Owen, A. et.al, 2005).

On the thirteenth of November, Dr. Owen made head-line news again, when he asked yes/no questions of Scott Routley, a comatose patient in a vegetative state, and read his answers on the fMRI!

Dr. Owen instructed the patient to imagine specific images for yes and no responses. The patient's fMRI corresponded to those specific images, for example, when the answer was "No" the patient consistently imagined "Going down a path", the specific image he was asked to imagine for a negative response! (Mole, 2012).

The technique of using fMRI of a living brain in a "normal" person has revolutionized this field! How the tales we have in this chapter will change as more information comes in is anybody's guess. Gone will be the days of the "Lie Detector" that people could cheat! Hooking up a liar to the fMRI and looking at the brain area that is activated will tell the fMRI operator exactly what the person is lying about! (Gannis, G. Kosslyn, S.M. et.al, 2003).

Science has lmade fantastic discoveries about consciousness, *but the debate as to what it is, how it comes into existence, when and whether it ceases to exist, are still hotly debated.*

Consciousness is generally defined as our awareness of external and internal stimuli and is thought to be produced by the functioning of our cortical neurons. Those who have it react and respond to stimuli in a purposeful way, while those who do not have it, do not respond purposefully to stimuli, but may have some inner awareness and experience, that is some form of consciousness!

Perhaps you recall that unlike Wilhelm Wundt who believed that consciousness was a static structure, William James, the founder of functionalism, had argued that consciousness was not static, and in fact, it was a constantly changing stream. In this chapter we will look at various changes in consciousness, i.e., states of consciousness and the methods which people use to produce them.

In order to be able to talk effectively about consciousness, psychologists define the state of awareness or ***alertness you experience/exhibit when you first awaken in the morning, as your normal everyday awareness or NEA***. This NEA consists of a range of states of alertness that you experience. Sometimes however, your consciousness is distinctly different from NEA, because it has shifted beyond the normal everyday range. These large shifts in consciousness make up *the altered states, and they range from tranquility to states of extreme agitation*. In this chapter, we will look at some special states such as daydreaming, sleeping, meditating, and hypnosis. We will also take a look at the methods used to produce them and the biological or neural underpinnings of altered states of consciousness and the main reasons as to why people seek these altered states.

Methods of Producing Altered Sates: Extremely vigorous physical activity, prolonged fasting, intense prayer, meditation, sensory deprivation, hypnosis, and use of psychoactive drugs, have all been used since ancient times to produce altered states of consciousness, also known as "trance states". The major difference between people who reported using these methods themselves and scientists, who studied these people, was that those who underwent the experience often reported paranormal, magical or mystical experiences.

Scientists studying such often dismiss the mystical and the magical, as self-deception, hallucinations or outright deception. Today, neuroscience has allowed the scientists to look at the brains of people while they are in a trance state and scientists are beginning to recognize that different areas of the brain are involved in producing the various states brought on by these differing methods. We will briefly touch upon a few of the ancient methods and the effects claimed for them.

Extremely Vigorous Physical Activity: Anthropologists report that just about every primitive society or tribal group they have studied uses some form of extreme physical activity to produce a trance state. Siberian Shamans used dance to trance, the Lakota Indians are well known for their "Sun dance" in which they maintained a fast and ran or danced around a sacred tree till the rope that tied them to that tree snapped or the skin through which they were attached to it, sloughed off and they fell to the ground in an ecstatic state. The Shakers of Kentucky, so named because they danced till they trembled and fell to the ground, and Arab Dervishes, who twirl and whirl, all have one thing in common...they all claimed that they experienced an "ineffable" joy, a joy they have no words to describe, a joy that made them forget their hunger, thirst, and bodily pain, a type of joy they were all sure was due to their being in contact with a "Higher Power", "God" or "Spirit". Andrews, E.D. 1967; Erzen, J. 2008).

Get Outta Here!

In December 2004, scientists from the University of Florida grew a *"brain"* in a *petri dish!* What was even more amazing was that this "brain," grown from a few cortical neurons extracted from a single rat embryo, *learned to fly an F-22 jet simulator!*

At first the plane kept crashing, but soon the neural network adapted and learned to control it and kept the plane horizontal under various conditions, based on information about the direction of the nose and wing tips of the plane, which the "brain" received as input.

In other words, *by demonstrating that it could control the plane and had learned to make it stay horizontal, the neural network or petri-dish brain, had indicated that it was conscious?! Did this little piece of rat brain "know" that it existed and was doing something?*

For more information check out the following Web sites:

http://edition.cnn.com/2004/TECH/11/02/brain.dish/

Or insert the key words "brain," "petri-dish," and "flight simulator" in any Internet search engine for several articles on this exciting topic.

MEDITATION

MEDITATION Is a very ancient traditional spiritual technique of achieving calmness and tranquility. It was known to and has been practiced by Yoga adepts or Yogis in India for over three thousand years. Meditation was introduced in Tibet by Gautama Buddha, the founder of Buddhism, circa 500 BCE and the Buddhist monks of Tibet developed it further and made tremendous contributions. Meditation was also known to the ancient Chinese, as the Taoist techniques of *jing* (quiet stillness) and *ding* (concentration, focus) although the methods of achieving them were quite different from the Indian ones.

The term *meditation* covers a variety of mental exercises which alter the normal flow of the stream of consciousness. Although there are many ways of meditating such as staring at a candle flame or a dot on a wall, etc. the most common and easiest method is to sit comfortably with your eyes closed, hands resting in your lap, palms facing upwards and saying a "Mantra" with every exhalation.

There are many Mantras but the simplest ones are "OM" from Hindu meditation and "Hum" for Tibetan meditation. The word "OM" stands both for a simple affirmative, i.e. "Yes" and also stands for The Universe itself and The Consciousness that is All Pervading. The "OM" sound is produced as a low pitched hum as the breath is exhaled. Meditation was claimed to allow one to acquire various "Siddhis" where "Siddhi" stood for miraculous or paranormal powers.

Scientific evidence was sought in the 1970s by the Americans, when *meditation was first introduced to the United States by Maharishi Mahesh Yogi, a guru or spiritual teacher of meditation, from India.* The Maharishi introduced a special type of meditation known as *Transcendental Meditation (TM).*

The first few scientific studies on TM were reported by Dr. Herbert Benson (Benson, 1976) of Harvard University Medical School, who reported that TM, when practiced for 15 to 20 minute sessions, induces the *"Relaxation Response" which in turn reduces reaction time, improves short-term memory, enhances recall from long-term memory, lowers blood pressure, and reduces psychosomatic illnesses (Benson, 1985; Gelderloos, et al., 1991; Alexander et al., 1989).*

The basic premise of most of the meditative techniques is to hone selective attention by limiting attention to one sound, one image or even one action.

Although there are several meditative states and yogis have demonstrated amazing abilities in being able to control their heart-rate, body temperature, etc. (Green E. & Green A. 1977), most researchers refer to a state with the alpha or theta wave as being predominant during meditation and research continues, especially at the Maharishi International University in Iowa, established by Mahesh Yogi himself.

At the University of Massachusetts Medical Center, Dr. Jon Kabat-Zinn has instituted a very effective program for the reduction of chronic pain by the use of "Mindfulness" or "Vipassana" meditation, a Tibetan Buddhist technique. This technique has also been shown to enhance mood, *induce a more positive immune profile in breast and prostate cancer patients, and improve the overall quality of life* (Carlson et al., 2003). Vipassana meditation, in which a person focuses on one's own breathing without changing it in any way, is also taught to develop the feeling of compassion for all life forms. This type of meditation has also been shown to reduce violence in prisons where Vipassana meditation has been taught. Recent research shows that Mindfulness Meditation brings about the beneficial effects by increasing self-regulation and neuroimaging studies indicate that neuroplastic changes in the frontal lobe, temporal lobe and hypothalamus are involved in bringing about the change in self-regulation (Holzer B.K., Lazar, S.W. et.al, 2011).

SENSORY DEPRIVATION A method of producing an ASC by floating in an isolation tank full of salt water was created by Dr. John Lilly, a physician, a marine biologist, and researcher in consciousness and its altered states. John Lilly discovered that floating in that tank with almost no information coming in from any of the sense organs because light, sound, and even temperature messages were cut off as the water was at body temperature, produced an altered "expanded state" of consciousness.

Get Outta Here!

Are you a lark or a night owl? Psychologists have identified two different types of adults based on their circadian rhythm. One type, the lark, falls asleep as soon as it is dark, and sleep induction is very quick. In contrast, the night owl does not go to bed early, but stays up until much later at night. On retiring to bed, the night-owl tosses and turns for some time because sleep induction is slow.

In the morning, the larks wake up as soon as sunlight hits their room and they jump right out of bed, ready to launch into activities of the day. Night-owls on the other hand linger in bed, wanting to snooze, and get up much after light has brightened their room. The larks tend to have long lives and most centenarians are larks! Night owls on the other hand, tend to die off in their sixties or seventies.

Research also indicates that adolescents go through a phase where they are night owls because of their biological clock, and their school performance suffers if their schools start early in the morning, as most schools in the United States do.

Research indicates that simply starting the school a little later in the morning allows the grades of adolescents to go up, and their behavior improves. Some schools in Minnesota switched to a later start for high schools and found that the later start improved grades and dropped the rates of misbehavior (Santrock, 2003, pg 237). New research indicates that there are genetic differences between Night-owls and Larks, but behavior can influence the biological clock, so biology is not destiny! (Cavallera &Giudici, 2008).

Lilly also discovered that the complete rest that the procedure allowed reduced stress-related neurochemicals in the brain and the person undergoing the deprivation felt a sense of great well-being. Floatation tanks and sensory deprivation machines were in fashion for a while in the 1970s and some floatation tanks are still sold for the purpose of producing brief periods of sensory deprivation for stress-reduction, A type of therapy known as REST of Restriction of Environmental Stimulation Therapy has been shown to provide relief from illnesses which are due to chronic stress (Lilly, J.C. 1977; Turner, J.W. & Fine, T.H. 1983).

BIOLOGICAL RHYTHMS

Biological rhythms

Natural variations in biological functions, hormonal activity, temperature, and sleep that typically cycle every 24 to 25 hours. Also called circadian rhythms.

All biological systems (plants and animals) are influenced by cycles or **biological rhythms** of physiological activity. Several human physiological processes show significant fluctuations, which change at the periodic rate of a day. Rhythms that reflect this day/night rhythm or a 24 hour cycle are known as Circadian, for "circa" meaning around, and "dia" meaning day and rhythms which repeat many times in one day are called ultradian (Monk & Folkard, 1983).

Circadian rhythms are clearly seen in plants that have flowers that open in the day and close at dusk like daisies do, or open at night and close during the day, like some varieties of evening primroses do. Likewise, behavior, body temperature, and many other physiological processes show *these rhythms which are controlled by* ***internal biological clocks*** *and are influenced by external illumination.*

Suprachiasmatic nucleus (SCN)

An area of the hypothalamus that is located above the optic chiasm. The SCN exerts the main control over biological rhythms. The SCN is also referred to as the biological clock because damage to this area disrupts daily cycles in sleep and other biological functions.

Researchers have identified the **suprachiasmatic nucleus (SCN)** of the hypothalamus as the location of the biological clock in all mammals. The SCN is vital for our daily well-being. It prepares us for our daily period of activity by anticipatory raises in heart rate, body temperature, and certain hormone levels, thereby synchronizing our endocrine and autonomic nervous system with the time of day (Buijs, et al., 2003). When biological clocks are in mismatch with artificially induced light/dark time intervals, such as induced by shift work and jet lag, human performance and health suffers (Monk & Folkard, 1983).

Daydreaming is now known to be a mental activity which coincides with an ultradian rhythm that is in cycles which repeat many time in a day. Daydreaming occurs every 9o minutes (Lavie, P. 1980).

If you are like most people, you spend a great deal of time fantasizing. If you are studying, you daydream about making the dean's list. If you are an athlete, you imagine winning medals and cups, and if you are an aspiring actor or actress, you probably daydream about receiving an Oscar! While you are paying rapt attention to your internal make-believe, you have neglected some aspects of your external world, even if it is only for a couple of minutes.

Such daydreams are mild shifts from a state of alertness, in which your thoughts move from external focal points to internal stimuli. When you daydream, you create pictures in the "mind's eye" that are akin to night time dreams. The content of daydreams is not as bizarre or disjointed as the content of night dreams is.

Young people, such as college students, spend a significant portion of their waking hours, about one-third of their time, daydreaming (Bartusiak, 1980). Comparatively, older adults spend considerably less time daydreaming perhaps because most daydreams relate more to formulating goals regarding future course of action, which has more relevance to the lives of the young (Greenwald & Harder, 1997.) In fact, a linear decrease in daydreaming occurs with aging and the content of daydreaming shifts from wishful grand scenarios to mundane problem solving.

Sleep

Natural, periodically occurring state of rest characterized by reduced activity, lessened responsiveness to stimuli, and distinctive brain-wave patterns.

In general women daydream more than men do. Men daydream less than women do but the content of their daydreams is about sex far more often than the content of women's daydreams is!(Giambra, M. 1974; Giambra, M. 1980.)

THE SCIENCE OF SLEEP AND DREAMING

At least once every day, we experience a dramatic shift in consciousness when we go to sleep; we experience still another state of consciousness when we dream while sleeping. We spend roughly one-third of our lives sleeping, and the question of what happens when we sleep and dream has fascinated people for ages.

Stages of Sleep

REM sleep

State of sleep characterized by rapid eye movements, and often associated with dreaming.

NREM sleep (Non-rapid eye movement sleep)

Stages of sleep during which rapid eye movements typically do not occur. Dreaming occurs far less frequently during NREM sleep than during REM sleep.

Research since the 1950s has confirmed the connection between REM sleep and dreaming. However, we have also learned that dreaming is not limited to REM sleep and that REM is not synonymous with dreaming. There is widespread agreement among sleep researchers that *dreams reported during REM sleep are usually much more vivid, tend to last longer, and are more visual* than the thought-like processes that occur during NREM sleep. These differences are perhaps due to different physiological processes mediating REM and NREM sleep and dreaming (Takeuchi, et al., 2003). Likewise, nightmares might be different from dreams, because recent research on the neuro-pharmacology of Nightmares indicates that the neuro-chemicals that affect the REM mechanism are different from the neuro-chemicals that influence dreams (Pagel, 2006).

In the 1970s, William Dement, one of the first few researchers to set up a sleep laboratory, introduced the "scanning hypothesis" of REM. Dement reported that the direction in which the eyes moved was correlated to the scene witnessed in the dream (Dement, 1978). This scanning hypothesis was *not* completely supported by later research, as later research findings indicated that scanning movements of the eyes correlate only for the last couple of seconds of a much longer dream interval.

Psychologists, for example, Gestalt psychologists, believe that dreams can be programmed to help you solve problems. Others, such as Freud, believed that dreams reveal repressed thoughts or the workings of our subconscious, while some humanistic psychologists and some parapsychologists believe that dreams can herald future events and such dreams are called Pre-cognitive dreams (Ullman & Krippner, 1973).

THEORIES OF DREAMING: Man has wondered about the meaning and function of dreams for ages! One of the earliest known theories of dreaming is evident in the Epic of Gilgamesh, a Sumerian myth, dated to 2700 BCE in oral tradition and inscribed in stone around 600 BCE. Dreams, they theorized, served as a form of communication with the Sumerian gods and goddesses and allowed a glimpse into alarming events that were to take place in the future. Likewise, roughly 2000 BCE, the Egyptians were interpreting dream symbols (a distant crowd, for example, was seen as a warning of death), and dream diaries existed long before the emergence of psychology as a science. However, systematic sleep and dream research was not possible until the technological breakthroughs of the past half-century.

There are many theories that profess a purpose or a function for dreams. These proposed functions range from maturation of the brain of the new-born, to the maintenance of a brain activity in an idling brain. Dreams are also thought to allow the consolidation of memories, cross-filing memories which allows the narration of a continuous life-story via episodic memory, linking memories in order to do problem-solving, to identify environmental threats and prepare to meet them, and a relatively new one, to help forget some episodic memories! (Winson, 2002).

In contrast, Hobson & McCarley (1977) proposed a purely physiological theory known as the **Activation-Synthesis Theory of REM sleep and dreams**. ***To Hobson & McCarley dreams are meaningless!*** They say that the rapid eye movements are comparable to the occasional muscle twitches that occur during dreaming, and that *dream content is just a byproduct of an idling brain. Since all mammals and even birds and fetuses have REM sleep, they do not see how dreams could have any psychological or para-psychological meanings.* Research indicates that rapid eye movements have little if anything to do with dream content. For example, people who have been blind for over 50 years and cats raised in the dark who have never seen anything still show rapid eye movements during sleep (Webb & Bonnet, 1979), although people born blind do not have rapid eye movement sleep.

During a night's sleep, body activity may vary from lying very still to thrashing and twisting in bed. In extreme cases, some people may talk in their sleep, sleepwalk, or have sleep terrors. These behaviors do not take place during REM sleep in which there is dream content, **because there is profound loss of muscle tone during REM sleep**. *Thus, sleepwalking and sleep terrors almost invariably occur during NREM sleep.*

Though most of us cannot move during REM sleep, sleep researchers have discovered that some humans, when they enter REM sleep, thrash violently about, leap out of bed, and may even attack their bed-partners; they are not paralyzed during REM as most people are (Chase & Morales, 1990). This abnormality is called *REM behavior disorder* (Mahowald & Schenck, 1989).

MEASURING STAGES OF SLEEP Sophisticated measuring devices such as the electroencephalogram (EEG); the *electroculogram (EOG)*, which measures movements of the eye; and the *electromyograph (EMG)* which measures electrical activity in the muscles, and the *f*MRI or functional MRI which allows one to view live cortical action, have allowed us to distinguish between the various stages of sleep. Research using such devices has revealed systematic changes in the brain wave patterns, muscular activity, levels of breathing, and heart rate during the course of a night's sleep. These measures have not only clarified the differences between REM and NREM sleep; ***they have also allowed researchers to identify four distinct stages of sleep in addition to REM sleep***. Figure 5.1 demonstrates characteristic brain wave patterns of each of these stages, as well as REM sleep and wakefulness.

CHARACTERISTICS OF WAKING AND SLEEP STATES When we are awake and alert, the EEG reveals low-amplitude, high-frequency waves called *beta waves*. (The two key characteristics of brain waves are their *amplitude*, or height, and their *frequency*, measured in cycles per second.) When we are relaxed and drowsy, just before falling asleep, our brain waves show an *alpha* rhythm of higher amplitude and slower frequency (8 to 12 cycles per second). In this drowsy state, breathing and heart rate also slow down, body temperature drops, and muscles relax. The different brain waves associated with different states of arousal are shown in Figure 5.1.

Get Outta Here!

As you just read, REM, sleep stages and alterations in consciousness during sleep were identified *only after Eugene Asrinsky's dramatic discovery of REM-Dream connection, in the 1950s,* although changes in brain-wave patterns had been demonstrated in the late 1930s, after the development of EEG. You also read that your consciousness goes from light sleep to deep sleep and then you enter the REM stage or active sleep in which you dream. After the REM period, your brain starts to slow down again, taking you to deep sleep, again and again, four or five times, in the course of a night. *Now would you believe that ancient peoples of India knew this roughly 900 years B.C.E.?*

In a treatise called Brahadaranyaka Upanishad, circa 900 BCE, Rishi (Seer) Yajnyavalkya, when asked what happens to the "self" when sleeping, answers:

"Just as a great fish swims alternately to both the banks of a river, so does the infinite Self move to both these states of deep sleep and of awareness. After enjoying himself and roaming and merely seeing good and evil (in dreams) he, (the self) stays in a state of profound sleep and *comes back in the reverse order* to his former condition in the dream sleep." (Ragade, 1996, Madhavananda, 1975).

How could Yajnyavalkya have known and described the alterations in consciousness reflected and supported by modern EEG techniques? This is a very puzzling piece of information, It definitely gives you something to think about.

Stage 1 The light sleep that occurs just after dozing off is known as **Stage 1 sleep**. It is characterized by low-frequency (3 to 7 cycles per second), low-amplitude brain waves called theta waves. Stage 1 sleep may be accompanied by some slow eye movements, irregular breathing, and muscle relaxation. People are easily awakened during Stage 1 sleep, and often they do not realize they have been sleeping. This stage typically lasts from about one to ten minutes.

Stage 1 sleep
Light sleep that occurs just after dozing off, characterized by brain waves called theta waves.

Stage 2 After a period of Stage 1 sleep, we gradually drift into the deeper **Stage 2 sleep**. Stage 2 sleep is characterized by brief bursts of brain activity called sleep spindles (12 to 14 cycles per second), as well as another brain wave pattern called the *K complex,* The K complex is a low-frequency, high-amplitude wave that occurs in response to either an external stimulus, such as the sound of a voice, or an internal stimulus, such as stomach cramps. Eye movements are minimal during Stage 2, and muscular activity often decreases to an even lower level.

Stage 2 sleep
Stage of sleep that typically follows Stage 1 sleep, characterized by brief bursts of brain activity called sleep spindles as well as K-complex responses to stimuli such as noises.

Stage 3 About 30 to 45 minutes after falling asleep, the cycle progresses into an even deeper level of sleep, and there is a gradual increase in the incidence of low-frequency (0.5 to 2 cycles per second), high-amplitude delta waves. When these waves account for 20 percent to 50 percent of the EEG tracing, a person is in **Stage 3 sleep**.

Stage 3 sleep
Stage of sleep that typically follows Stage 2 sleep, characterized by an EEG tracing 20 to 50 percent of which consists of delta waves. There are virtually no eye movements during Stage 3 sleep.

FIGURE 5.1 Different Stages of Sleep and Characteristic Brain Patterns

SOURCE: Figure of "Stages of Sleep and Characteristic Brain Wave Patterns" from *The Sleep Disorders* by Peter Hauri. Copyright © 1977 by Peter Hauri. Reprinted by permission of The Upjohn Company and the author.

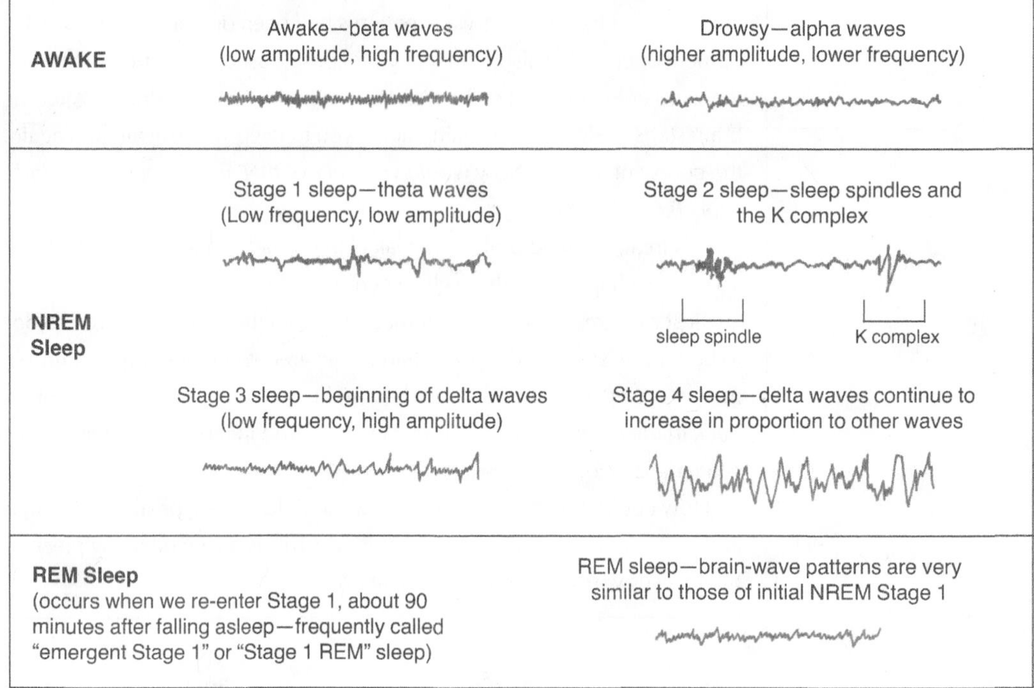

Stage 4 As sleep continues, delta waves continue to increase in proportion to other brain waves. When they exceed 50 percent, a person is said to be in Stage 4 sleep, the deepest level of sleep. It is difficult to arouse a person from **Stage 4 sleep**. If suddenly awakened from this stage of sleep, you will feel disoriented and confused. During Stages 3 and 4 there are virtually no eye movements, and the EEG patterns become much more synchronized.

Stage 4 sleep

Deepest level of sleep, characterized by an EEG tracing exceeding 50 percent delta waves and virtually no eye movements.

The Sleep Cycle

It takes roughly 45 minutes to reach Stage 4 sleep after first dozing off. People typically remain in Stage 4 for about 30 to 40 minutes, *then return gradually through Stages 3 and 2 to Stage 1 again.* ***The first period of REM sleep occurs when we reenter Stage 1, about 90 minutes after falling asleep.*** During this period, which is frequently called emergent Stage 1 or Stage 1 REM sleep, brain-wave patterns are very similar to those of the initial NREM Stage 1, with the exception that "saw-tooth like" waves are present.

In a night's sleep, we move through successive cycles, drifting up and down between the various phases of REM and NREM sleep. These cycles last about 90 minutes, and we generally complete about five of them during the course of a night. After the first cycle of sleep ends, we return to Stage 2 and then re-enter the REM stage of the next 90 minute

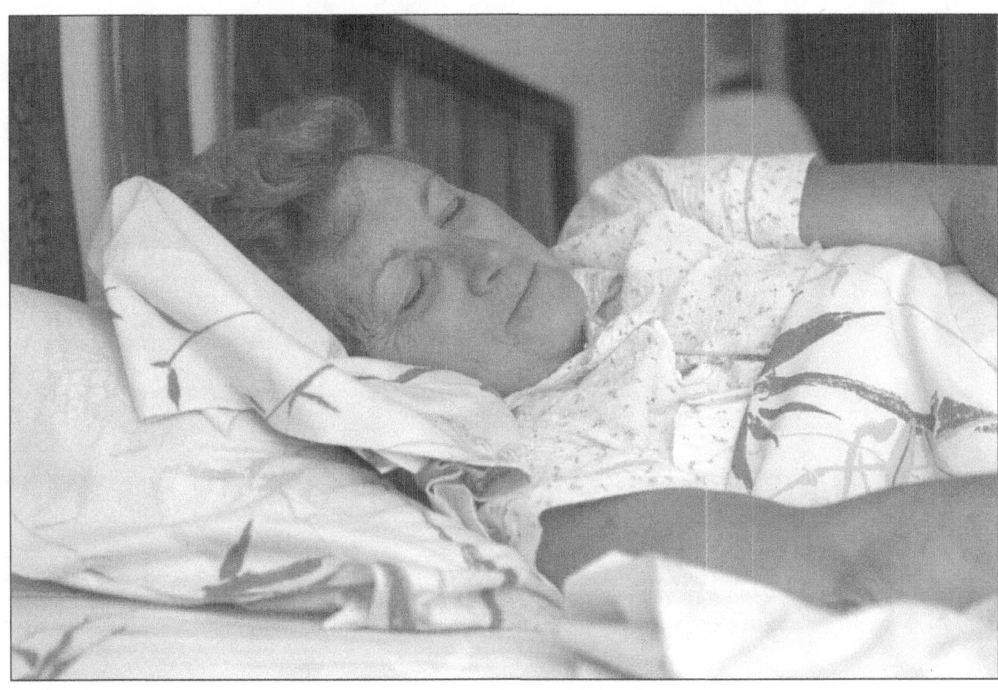

We sleep through roughly one-third of our lives.

cycle. The first episode of REM sleep may last only 5 to 10 minutes. However, with each subsequent cycle, the REM periods become progressively longer and deep sleep stages become shorter (Lavie, 1987). Figure 5.2 demonstrates the typical sequence of sleep stages.

Changes in Sleep Patterns with Age

Sleep patterns are not stable throughout our lives. The percentage of the night's sleep that is spent in a REM state decreases throughout the life cycle. Newborn babies may sleep an average of 16 hours per day, with roughly 50 percent of that time spent in REM sleep but by the age of 60 to 70, a person is likely to sleep only about six hours and be in a REM phase only 15 percent (approximately one hour) of this time.

The amount of time spent in Stage 4 sleep also changes with age, so that by the time we are in our 60s, deep sleep (Stage 4) is likely to disappear altogether. As a consequence, older people are more easily *awakened*.

Figure 5.3 shows the major brain areas involved in sleep and wakefulness. The **reticular activating system (RAS)** is primarily responsible for our awakened state. Damage to the RAS can lead to a marked lack of activity and an increase in sleep.

Another brain area involved in sleep is the **raphe system**. This pathway originates below the RAS in the brainstem and ascends through the pons and the medulla to the midbrain. The raphe system becomes most active at the time of sleep onset. This increase in raphe system activity acts to inhibit the RAS, thus decreasing arousal and promoting sleep onset.

Reticular activating system (RAS)

Set of neural circuits extending from the lower brain up to the thalamus that play a critical role in controlling arousal and alertness. Also known as reticular formation.

Raphe system

A group of serotonin-containing neurons extending from the raphe nuclei, located in the pons and medulla, throughout the limbic system and forebrain.

FIGURE 5.2 Typical Sequence of Sleep Stages

Sleep grows progressively less deep throughout the sleep cycle and REM periods tend to lengthen throughout the night. S1 refers to Stage 1.

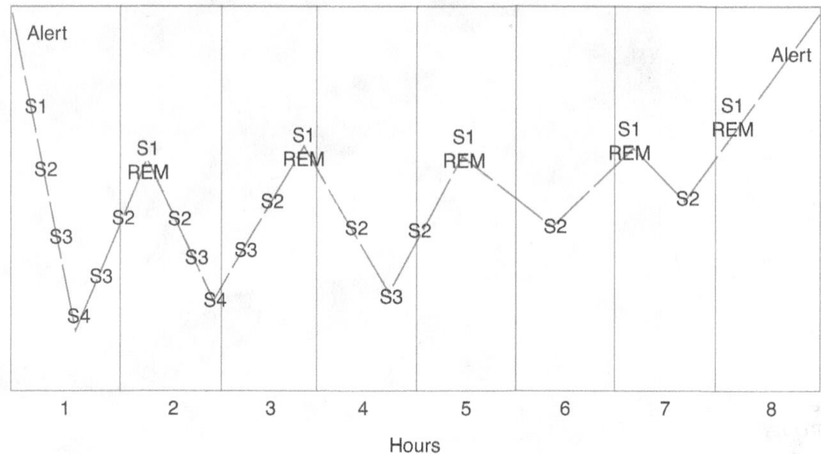

NEUROTRANSMITTERS AND SLEEP The primary neurotransmitter of the RAS is norepinephrine. And, as you might expect, drugs that increase the activity of these norepinephrine neurons, such as amphetamine, increase alertness and activity. On the other hand, serotonin appears to be the neurotransmitter of sleep. Research has shown that destruction of the raphe nucleus (serotonin neurons), or disruption of serotonin synthesis, results in insomnia, which can be reversed by restoring serotonin.

Although serotonin is believed to be involved in sleep onset, its role in maintaining sleep and dreaming is less certain. The serotonin system is virtually silent during REM sleep (Jacobs, et al., 2003). Other hormones and neurotransmitters are probably involved to a greater extent once sleep is initiated. In fact, the neurotransmitter acetylcholine is directly involved in dreaming and REM sleep. Injections of acetylcholine into the pons of animals can cause REM sleep; this fact leads one researcher to remark, "Acetylcholine is the stuff of which dreams are made" (Palca, 1989). Research indicates that several neurotransmitters such as GABA, Histamine and Acetylcholine might be involved in producing sleep and related phenomena, so it is a complex process.

The Function of Sleep

IS SLEEP NECESSARY? In the 1960s and 70s researchers wondered whether sleep was necessary and what would happen if a person was deprived of sleep. Two famous reports, one by Peter Tripp and the other of a youngster named Randy Gardner reported by Dr. William Dement, differed widely. The New York disc jockey Peter Tripp staged a wake-a-thon, remaining awake for 200 hours, but alas, he also became increasingly paranoid and hallucinated (Luce, 1965).

FIGURE 5.3 Major Brain Areas Involved in Sleep and Arousal

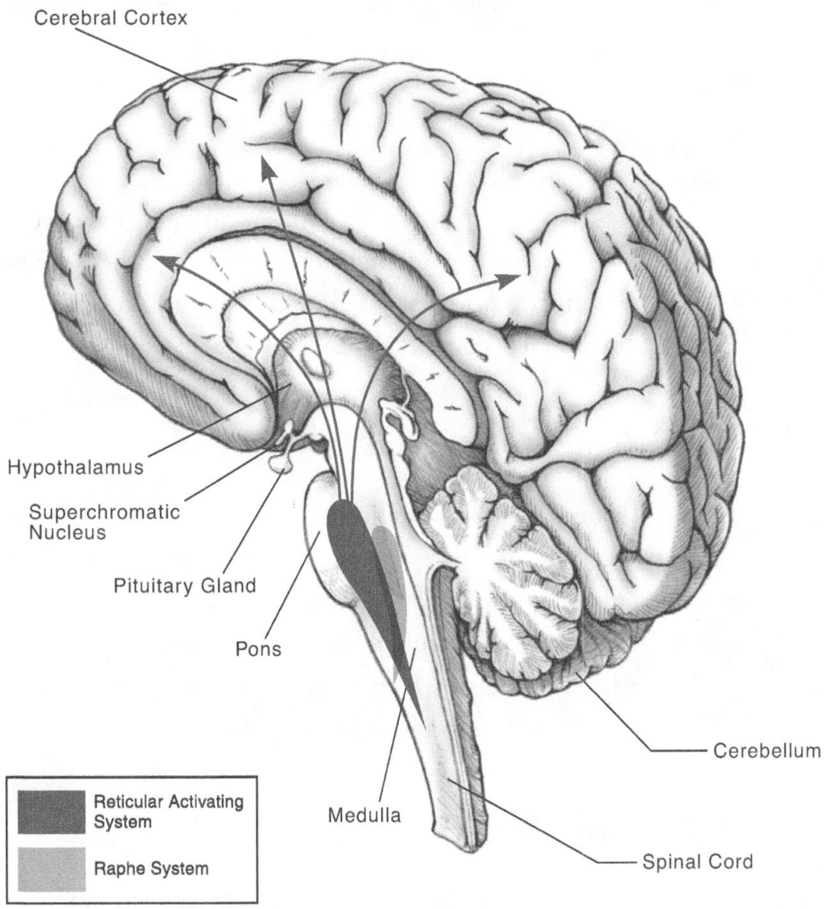

In contrast, William Dement reported that Randy Gardner remained awake, alert and lucid enough to play chess and win the game after eleven days of sleep deprivation (Dement, 1972). Sleep laboratories have conducted systematic research on sleep deprivation since then, and today most scientists subscribe to the restoration theory of sleep, which means they accept that sleep is necessary for physiological and psychological health.

There is tentative evidence that certain kinds of tissue restoration, such as cell repair etc. may occur during sleep (Mackiewicz,. et.al, 2007). Growth hormone, which promotes tissue growth, is secreted at higher levels in Stage 4 sleep. Some researchers also believe that neurotransmitters are refilled during sleep and that the amount of sleep we need is related to the levels of these chemicals present when we fall asleep.

There is also some evidence that sleep aids in memory consolidation. In a study conducted by Avi Karni (1992) people were trained to recognize patterns portrayed on a computer screen before going to sleep. Karni found that performance on a pattern recognition task was poorer if they were awakened during REM sleep than if they were awakened during NREM sleep. All of these studies suggest that sleep may promote the storage of newly learned information. *Perhaps you could use this to your advantage by studying psychology just before you sleep as opposed to just after waking!*

SLEEP DISORDERS

Sleep disorders

Class of disorders that interfere with sleep, including insomnia, sleep apnea, sleep terrors, nightmares, and sleepwalking.

Generally, people who have been busy and have worked hard all day fall fast asleep at night and get a good night's rest. However, there are people who suffer from sleep disorders and do not get a good night's rest. Although there are many sleep disorders, we will discuss a few common ones here.

Insomnia

Insomnia

Sleep disorder characterized by a consistent inability to get to sleep or by frequent awakenings during sleep.

Insomnia is the inability to sleep. It is more common among the elderly, women, and depressed or stressed people. Sedatives and tranquilizers are prescribed for insomnia but not as frequently as they used to be prescribed in the 1970s, primarily because research has uncovered many problems such as overdose, side-effects, dependence, etc., which are related to use of sedatives. Stress reduction and overall improvement of health habits is thought to be the key to getting a good night's rest.

Sleep Apnea

Sleep apnea

Sleep disorder characterized by irregular breathing during sleep.

A second sleep disorder is a disturbing condition known as **sleep apnea**. People with this disorder do not breathe regularly during sleep. In fact, their breathing actually stops for as long as a few seconds to a minute or two. As the need for oxygen becomes acute, the person briefly awakens, gulps in air, and then settles back to sleep, only to repeat the cycle when breathing stops again.

Some researchers believe that sleep apnea may be one cause of *sudden infant death syndrome (SIDS),* commonly called crib death. (Franco, 1999). There is speculation that breathing centers in the brainstem malfunction, causing susceptible infants to stop breathing (Sawaguchi, 2002).

Extreme cases of apnea used to be treated surgically. However, a nonsurgical approach to treating severe sleep apnea has been developed. A continuous flow of air is applied to the nostrils through a nose mask. This technique, called nasal continuous positive airway pressure (nCPAP), is now the treatment of choice for this disorder (Mohsenin, 2003).

Narcolepsy

Narcolepsy

Sleep disorder characterized by falling asleep suddenly and uncontrollably.

A peculiar sleep disorder called **narcolepsy** manifests itself as uncontrollable sleep attacks in which a person falls asleep suddenly, perhaps while talking, standing, or driving. The attack may last only a few minutes, or it may last half an hour or more. *EEG monitoring* *reveals that these sleep attacks involve the immediate onset of REM sleep. Since REM sleep produces a loss of muscle tone, most victims collapse the moment they lapse into sleep.* For this reason, narcoleptic attacks can endanger a person's life, particularly if they occur while driving or operating dangerous machinery.

Researchers have linked narcolepsy to a neurodegenerative disorder in the brain mechanisms that control sleep and waking. This disorder may involve inadequate production of the hypothalamic hormone orexin, which is believed to play a role in arousal and the inhibition of REM sleep (Scammell, 2003). Although physicians sometimes prescribe stimulants such as amphetamine to reduce the frequency of sleep attacks, there is no effective treatment yet.

Nightmares

Nightmare
Bad dream that occurs during REM sleep.

A **nightmare** is a bad dream that occurs during REM sleep. Nightmares typically leave a strong impression on the dreamer; people often awaken after a nightmare with vivid recall of the dream. Sometimes nightmares are repetitive. Many dream theorists once believed that repetitive nightmares reflected areas of conflict or sources of emotional turmoil in a person's waking life. Recent research, however, suggests that there is a strong genetic contribution the occurrence of nightmares, which tend to run in families, with a greater prevalence in females. In addition, nightmares tend to occur throughout one's life and are frequently associated with psychiatric disorders (Hublin, 2003).

Sleep Terrors

Sleep terror
Sleep disorder in which a person suddenly awakens from Stage 4 sleep in a panic, typically with no recollection of a bad dream.

People often confuse sleep terrors with nightmares. **Sleep terrors**, like nightmares, are frightening experiences associated with sleep—but sleep terrors occur during Stages 3 and 4 of NREM sleep, not during REM sleep. Typically, the sleeper screams, sits up, stares unseeingly, and perhaps gasps or hyperventilates. Occasionally he or she jumps out of bed. Full awakening doesn't always occur following a sleep terror. In fact, it is more common for the individual to lie down and continue sleeping. People awakened by a sleep terror usually recall a sense of intense fear but do not recall the content of a dream. They go back to sleep easily and do not recall the experience when they awaken the next morning.

Sleep terrors, unlike nightmares, seem to be related to daytime stress and fatigue. *Following the September 11, 2001, attacks in New York and Washington D.C., the incidence of sleep terrors rose sharply in the United States.* Although sleep terrors may be associated with some personality disorders, they are not themselves evidence of an underlying disorder or considered abnormal.

Sleepwalking

Sleepwalking
Sleep disorder, also known as somnambulism, characterized by walking in one's sleep during Stage 3 or 4 of NREM sleep.

For many years it was believed that people who sleepwalk (called somnambulists) are acting out dream events. We now know that **sleepwalking** *occurs during Stage 3 or 4 of*

Get Outta Here!
Murder by Sleepwalking!

Kenneth Parker of Toronto, who drove a good 14 miles to his in-laws home and stabbed both his in-laws to death, claimed he had done so while sleepwalking and was unaware of what he had done. The Canadian Supreme Court upheld the acquittal given him by a lower court.

However, Falater, another Arizona man who beat his wife, pushed her into their swimming pool and held her head underwater till she died, was unsuccessful in using the sleepwalking defense. Falter had pushed his wife in the swimming pool after beating her and had held her head under the water till she died. He had then stashed his soiled clothes and tools in the trunk of his car. He claimed he had done all this while sleepwalking. However, an Arizona jury refused to buy into his "sleepwalking automaton" theory, even though his psychiatrist testified that sleep laboratory EEG indicated that Falter might be suffering from somnambulism (sleepwalking). Falter was sentenced to life without parole (Source: CNN.com http://www.cnn.com/US/9905/25/sleepwalk.defense/).

Sleepwalking or not . . . can any person who violently beats a loved family member to death be considered sane? Should that person be allowed to live as a free person in society?

NREM sleep, when the body is capable of movement. The duration of sleepwalking can vary from a few minutes to over half an hour. During this time it is very difficult to awaken the person. If awakening occurs the individual is typically disoriented but does not recall the episode. Contrary to popular belief there is no danger involved in awakening a sleepwalker. After awakening, the person typically returns to sleep. Approximately 20 percent of the population has experienced sleepwalking with the majority of episodes occurring between 6 and 12 years of age (Anch et al., 1988).

Sleepwalkers can negotiate obstacles, although they move quite clumsily and often fall down or bump into things. Occasionally sleepwalking may subject a person to extreme danger. Parents can reduce the possibility of their child being injured during sleepwalking by adjusting the environment. Frequent sleepwalking in adults, particularly elderly adults, is considered serious because of the consequences of falling.

Sleep Talking

Sleep talking

The production of speech or speech sounds associated with sleep without subjective awareness.

Practically everyone talks during sleep on occasion, but it is much more prevalent in children than adults. Unlike sleepwalking, **sleep talking** appears to occur equally across periods in the sleep cycle. In some individuals, however, sleep talking can occur during both NREM and REM sleep. When sleep talking occurs during REM sleep it may reflect dream content. Contrary to myth, sleep talkers rarely reveal secrets.

In contrast to sleepwalking, talking while asleep is usually purposeless and unrelated to stress or other events that occur during the waking state. There is usually no recollection of sleep talking if the person is awakened during talking or when they awaken the following morning. Sleep talking is not considered a symptom of any underlying disorder, nor is it of any clinical significance.

PROBLEMS RELATED TO THE SLEEP–WAKE SCHEDULE People who continually change their sleep-wake schedule because of rotating shifts, frequent travel, or other interruptions from a consistent schedule often have difficulty with sleep and alertness later during the day. No matter what the cause of the disturbance in the schedule, the severity of the sleep problem is proportional to the size of the disturbance. For example, we have no difficulty adjusting to a one-hour shift that occurs during changes from standard time to daylight savings time. However, an eight-hour shift that results from a changing work schedule or a long flight can cause difficulty.

Because the normal sleep-wake cycle is slightly longer than 24 hours (approximately 25 hours) it is generally less disruptive to travel from east to west than west to east; that is, *it is easier to delay than to advance sleep-wake behavior*. This explains why it is easier to adjust to forward rotations in shift work. For example, it is easier to adjust to schedules rotating clockwise (from an 8:00 a.m. to 4:00 p.m. schedule to a 4:00 p.m. to 12:00 p.m. schedule) than the reverse.

HYPNOSIS

Hypnosis

State of altered consciousness characterized by a deep relaxation and detachment as well as heightened suggestibility to the hypnotist's directives.

Hypnosis is a fascinating phenomenon that has aroused considerable controversy within the discipline of psychology. Hypnosis, known as **Mesmerism** in nineteenth century Europe, was named after Anton Mesmer. Mesmer, a Viennese physician, claimed to have serendipitously discovered the phenomenon when treating a neurotic patient and playing with magnets! In reality, the phenomenon was known to people who were into witchcraft, or magico-religious cults. In fact, Mesmer's own habit of dressing in a wizard's robe, complete with a pointed hat and a magic wand filled with magnets, sort of proves that he did not "discover" it as such, but might have had some insights into it, which allowed him to use it successfully in treating some disorders. Even so, Mesmerism acquired a bad name because a panel of scientists known as **The Blue Ribbon Commission investigated Mesmer and declared that although the cures people claimed under mesmerism were genuine, they were temporary and *magnetism was not a part of the phenomenon*.** Later, because of the bad reputation Mesmer had acquired, a neurologist named James Braid changed the name of the phenomenon to Hypnosis. Braid coined the word Hypnosis after Hypnos, the Greek God of Sleep, because at the time people mistakenly thought that mesmerism put people to sleep. Sigmund Freud was one of the most famous neurologists to have used hypnosis to help women suffering from imaginary illnesses or women who were considered to be "neurotic."

In India, a phenomenon similar to Mesmerism, where one person could charm another into seeing or doing whatever the charmer directed the other person to do or see, was known as Indrajaal (a net of illusions cast by the God Indra) and was mentioned in a sixth century play named *Ratnavali* (Siegel, 1991). In modern times many stage magicians claim to use hypnosis as a form of entertainment in which members of the audience who are "hypnotized" do almost anything the stage magician has told then to do, much to the amusement of the on-lookers!

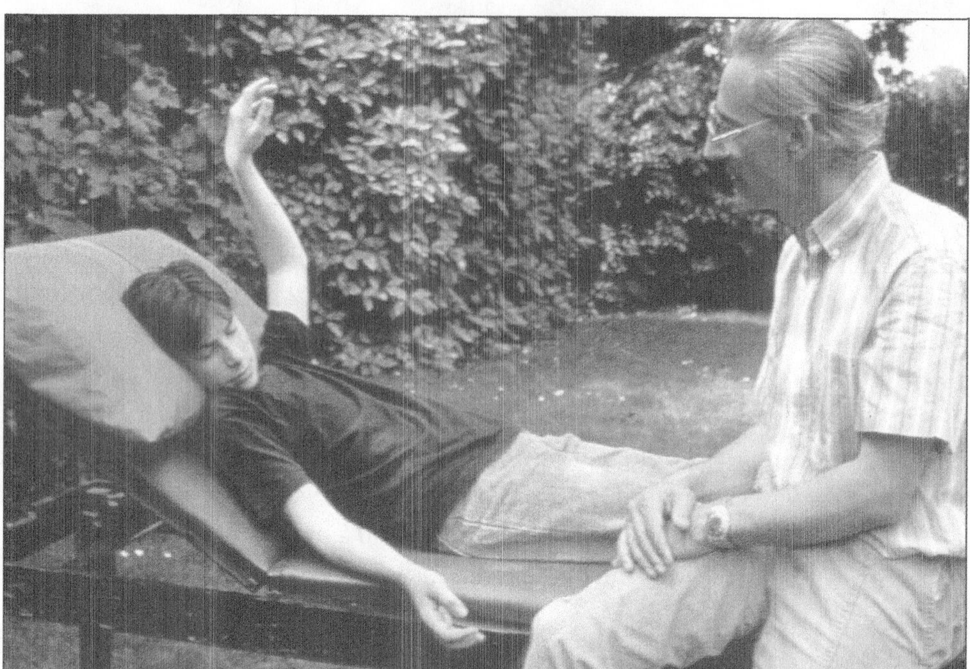

CMSP

Hypnotherapist with a patient in a trancelike state.

Much of the credibility afforded to hypnosis stems from the thoughtful research and writings of the renowned psychologist Ernest Hilgard (Hilgard & Hilgard, 1983). According to Hilgard, hypnosis represents a state of dissociated awareness. Hilgard proposed a theory known as the Special Process Theory of Hypnosis, which states that hypnosis creates a "hidden observer" which is part of a person's consciousness that is aware of what is happening during hypnosis, but remains passive, while the other part engages in non-voluntary behaviors as directed by the hypnotist. Even so, Hilgard maintained that the hypnotist did not control the hypnotized person, but the hypnotized person put cognitive effort into complying with the hypnotist because of the special state of dissociation. Hilgard also claimed that the brain created special filters which prevented the recall of the contents of the hypnotic episode or post-hypnotic amnesia (Hilgard 1977).

In contrast, T. X. Barber and many others, such as Nicholas Spanos (1996), held the view that *hypnosis was not a special altered state of consciousness* and that one could do anything that one did under hypnosis without being under hypnosis. In other words, if a subject complied with the hypnotist, he/she did so because they wanted to, or their behavior was voluntary and there was no partition of consciousness that would prevent them from recalling what they had done when hypnotized (Spanos, 1988).

T. X. Barber has most recently published a paper titled "Hypnosis: A Mature View" (Barber, 1999). In it, Barber states that hypnosis is a multidimensional phenomenon. He states that along with three different types of subjects, one type is fantasy prone. This type of individual fantasizes constantly, and has a life-long history of fantasizing. The other type is Amnesia-prone. These people are very forgetful and have experienced amnesia in childhood. The third type of subject, is a good hypnotic subject, but is neither fantasy prone or amnesiac, but has a positive attitude, or positive motivation or positive expectations or all three, regarding hypnosis. The other dimensions of the phenomenon are effects produced by loose experimental protocol, experimenter bias, etc. How this multi-dimensional theory will add to our knowledge of hypnosis remains to be seen.

Advances in Cognitive Neuroscience which allow neuroscientists to peer in the living, working brain of a hypnotized person both when not hypnotized and when hypnotized indicate that the brain areas that light up *indicate that the two states are different* and that there is enhanced self-regulation (Cojan, Y., Waber, L. et.al, 2009) and "top-down inhibition" meaning the cortex inhibits other lower areas of the brain when hypnotized and allows reinterpretation of perceptual experiences (Rainville, P. Hofbauer, R.K. et.al, 2006). *Thus, Cognitive Neuroscience has put an end to the controversy.* ***Hypnosis is an "Altered State"!***

Phenomena Associated with Hypnosis

Hypnosis has been linked to a number of phenomena, sometimes accurately and sometimes with a fair amount of hyperbole. Its reputed effects include improved athletic performance, symptomatic relief of physical ailments, pain reduction, enhanced memory, age regression, imaginary sensory experiences (hallucinations), and posthypnotic suggestions which the subjects carry out as if they were their own ideas. The evidence for these effects is evaluated in the following paragraphs.

HYPNOSIS AND ATHLETIC ABILITY You may have heard reports about people demonstrating amazing feats of strength or other outstanding athletic performances, allegedly as a direct result of hypnotic suggestion. Although many of the reports of performance are true, a caveat must be kept in mind: There is no evidence that hypnosis can increase a person's capacity to perform beyond natural limits.

HYPNOSIS AND RELIEF OF PHYSICAL AILMENTS Well-documented evidence shows that suggestions given to hypnotized people can help relieve the symptoms of a variety of stress-related illnesses, including asthma, ulcers, and colitis. Hypnotism has also been used to help clear up warts, psoriasis, and a variety of other skin ailments (Smith, 1985; Spanos et al., 1990). Hypnosis has not been very effective in treating self-initiated addictive disorders such as alcoholism, smoking, and overeating (Wadden & Anderton, 1982).

HYPNOSIS AND PAIN RELIEF Today, most medical practitioners acknowledge that hypnosis can be very effective in reducing the pain associated with childbirth, back problems, arthritis, dental procedures, burns, and even major surgery (Evans, 1988, 1989; James et al., 1989).

HYPNOSIS AND MEMORY ENHANCEMENT A few decades ago, about the memory enhancement capabilities of hypnosis led to its widespread use by police departments, often to help witnesses recall criminal acts. However, there is little substance to claims that it can enhance a person's recall of a criminal act (Kebbell et al., 1998). Furthermore, there may actually be danger to relying too heavily on hypnosis. Psychologists have also used hypnosis to investigate suspected cases of past child abuse. *However, it may well be that hypnosis actually planted false memories of abuse in clients rather than uncovering repressed memories of real abuse (Loftus et al., 1994; Stocks, 1998).* In summary, there is no reliable evidence that hypnosis enhances either distant or recent memory (Muzur et al., 1998).

Posthypnotic suggestion

Suggestion or instruction to a hypnotized person that motivates that person to perform an action or actions after returning to a normal state of consciousness.

POSTHYPNOTIC SUGGESTION **Posthypnotic suggestions** motivate people to perform a variety of actions after they return to a normal state of consciousness. Subjects typically carry out these suggestions without any recall of the instructions they received, and they often attempt to justify or rationalize the behavior in other ways. For example, in one classroom demonstration, a hypnotized student volunteer was given a posthypnotic suggestion to open a window when she observed her instructor loosen his tie. Right on cue, she raised her hand and asked if it would be OK to open a window, since the room seemed stuffy.

Can hypnosis be used to make you do something you would not ordinarily do? Could it be used to get you to commit a crime, disrobe in front of strangers, or engage in some type of act that you would normally consider unacceptable? Take a moment to evaluate this question based on what you have already learned about hypnosis before reading on.

A common misconception is that hypnosis cannot be used to motivate behavior in which a person would not ordinarily engage. It is true that most hypnotized people would not comply with direct suggestions to behave in an antisocial or inappropriate way. However, a hypnotist can alter the perceptions or awareness of a susceptible subject in such a way that such behaviors seem necessary or appropriate.

At present there is no universally accepted theory of hypnosis. This is in part because of our inability to describe a hypnotic state adequately and objectively. Until we can define hypnosis in objective terms—such as a particular physiological state—different investigators will not know whether they are indeed studying the same phenomenon. As a result, several conflicting theories are bound to exist. On the positive side, there is evidence that there is an increasing interest in hypnosis research from several related disciplines including medicine, dentistry, and psychology. And fMRI studies or other innovations may allow a definition in terms of a physiological state, for now, we do know that it is indeed a genuine phenomenon.

SUMMARY

BIOLOGICAL RHYTHMS

1. All biological systems are influenced by rhythms of physiological activity. When these rhythms are on a 24-hour cycle they are called circadian rhythms and if they repeat many times in one day, they are called ultradian rhythms.
2. Circadian rhythms appear to be controlled by the suprachiasmatic nucleus (SCN) of the hypothalamus. Sleep is a circadian rhythm but daydreaming is an ultradian rhythm.

THE SCIENCE OF SLEEP AND DREAMING

3. Sleep is a natural, periodically recurring state of rest, which is characterized by reduced activity, lessened responsiveness to stimuli, and distinctive brain-wave patterns.
4. Researchers distinguish between REM (rapid eye movement) and NREM (non-rapid eye movement) sleep. Dreaming is more likely to occur in REM than in NREM sleep. However, dreaming is not limited to REM sleep.
5. During a normal night's sleep we pass through four stages of sleep in naturally recurring, successive cycles. These stages range from very light sleep, characteristic of Stage 1, through Stage 4, the deepest level of sleep. Dreaming occurs most commonly during Stage 5 sleep.
6. During dreaming, muscular activity is inhibited. Sleepwalking almost invariably occurs during NREM sleep, Stage 3 or 4.
7. The major brain areas involved in sleep and waking are the ascending reticular activation system (RAS) and the raphe system.
8. Research suggests that sleep is necessary for a number of reasons. The Restorative function theory of sleep is now accepted as there is evidence of repair of tissue and cellular mechanisms during sleep.

DISORDERS OF SLEEP

9. Sleep disorders include insomnia, sleep apnea, narcolepsy, sleep terrors and nightmares, and sleepwalking.

HYPNOSIS

10. Hypnosis is a state of heightened suggestibility in which a person is unusually willing to comply with the hypnotist's directives.
11. Hypnosis can act as a powerful motivator, but it cannot increase a person's capacity to perform beyond natural limits.
12. Evidence suggests that hypnosis can help to alleviate pain and relieve the symptoms of a variety of stress-related illnesses. However, it has been shown to be only marginally beneficial when used to facilitate memory.
13. Explanations of hypnosis include dissociative theories.
14. Meditation is a very ancient, simple technique in which attention is limited to any one stimulus, such as a sound. Meditation has been shown to have beneficial effects on Psychosomatic, i.e. stress-related illnesses.

TERMS AND CONCEPTS

biological rhythms
suprachiasmatic nucleus (SCN)
sleep
REM sleep
NREM sleep
Stage 1 sleep
Stage 2 sleep
Stage 3 sleep
Stage 4 sleep
reticular activating system (RAS)
raphe system
sleep disorders
insomnia
sleep apnea
narcolepsy
nightmare
sleep terrors
sleepwalking
sleep talking
hypnosis
posthypnotic suggestion

PART III:

Learning, Memory, Cognition, Motivation, and Emotion

CHAPTER 6

Learning and Behavior

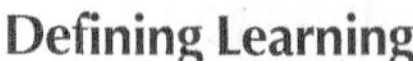

Puppy see, puppy do? We all are familiar with the phrase "monkey see monkey do," but as a matter of fact, several animal species learn by observing others, and even more so by observing their mothers. In a recent study on German Shepherds trained to sniff narcotics for detection of smugglers, pups who were allowed to observe their mothers at work when they were between six and eight weeks old did significantly better at detecting narcotics than a group of puppies that was not allowed to observe their mothers while sniffing out narcotics (Helton, 2003). The learning that these puppies demonstrated occurred because of the experience of seeing their mothers sniff out the narcotics.

Several different types of learning have been demonstrated in various animal species, including our own. Even individual neurons exhibit some forms of learning, so it should not surprise us to know that insects and animals have the ability to learn a wide variety of things. This chapter will focus on the various types of learning and the mechanisms of learning.

DEFINING LEARNING

Learning

Relatively enduring change in potential behavior that results from experience.

Learning *is defined as a relatively permanent change in behavior or potential behavior that results from experience.* This definition contains three important elements. The first element is lasting change. Most learning tends to produce lasting changes in the behavior of the learner.

Second, this definition excludes changes in behavior that are caused by diseases, injury, aging, drug use, or brain damage. Brain damage will result in numerous changes in your behavior, few of which are learned.

The third element of this definition speaks of *potential* behavior. Although learning causes changes in behavior, it is not always reflected directly in performance. The absence of observable behavior change does not necessarily mean that no learning has taken place. However, a change in behavior under the appropriate conditions must be observable at some point in time to claim that learning has occurred. Such learning is called *"Latent learning."*

For example, suppose a young boy often sees his father strike his mother during arguments. For the time being, the father's actions may have no apparent effect on the boy's behavior. When the boy becomes an adult, however, he strikes his wife during an argument. During the boy's childhood, we would have had no reason to believe that he had learned to be physically violent when frustrated. However, the potential for this behavior may have been acquired; it may have simply required similar circumstances for the learned behavior to be manifested.

Rats in a maze demonstrate another example of latent learning or learning that cannot be observed immediately. If there is no reinforcement (such as food) at the end of the maze, rats explore the alleys with no indication that learning is taking place. When food is placed at the end of the maze, however, they quickly negotiate the twists and turns to reach it. Some learning had taken place during the exploration, but it required a proper incentive to be reflected in actual performance.

Associative learning

Learning by making a connection or association between two events, through either classical conditioning or operant conditioning.

Classical conditioning

Learning that takes place when a neutral stimulus (CS) is paired with a stimulus (UCS) that already produces a response (UCR). After conditioning, the organism responds to the neutral stimulus (CS) in some way. The response to the CS is called a conditioned response (CR).

How Learning Takes Place

You should now have an understanding of what learning is. But how does it take place? Suppose you eat a particularly tasty new dish at a restaurant, but later that day you become quite ill and nauseous. This illness may be completely unrelated to the dish you had eaten earlier. Perhaps it's a touch of the flu. However, the *association* of illness with the dish leads to a dislike or aversion to this unique dish that you had liked earlier. Similarly, for patients undergoing radiation or chemotherapy, food aversions can be quite common and they are acquired in the same fashion. A meal that is followed by treatment that makes the patient ill will be less desirable than before.

This kind of learning is called **associative learning**. It describes the process by which we make a connection or an association between two events, such as the flavor of a particular food and illness. Associative learning takes place in two primary ways: through *classical conditioning* and through *operant conditioning*. Both of these processes contribute continually to your ongoing behavior.

E.L. Thorndike, a student of William James at Harvard, formulated a psychology he called "Connectionism." Thorndike studied animal intelligence by placing animals in puzzle boxes. Based on his observations of cats escaping from such puzzle-boxes, ***Thorndike formulated The Law of Effect in 1898.***

Operant conditioning

Behavior modification techniques that attempt to influence behavior by manipulating its consequences.

Social learning theory

Theory that emphasizes the role of observation in learning.

Observational learning

Learning process wherein an individual acquires a behavior by observing someone else performing that behavior. (Also known as modeling.)

Cognitive learning theory

Theoretical perspective that attempts to study the role of thinking and memory processes in learning.

Basically, Thorndike had observed that a boxed cat exhibits several behaviors as it tries to escape the box. Serendipitously, one of those many behaviors allows the cat to escape, and once the cat escapes it seems to remember the behavior that allowed the escape and uses it more frequently, which in turn, enables it to get out of the box more easily. This observation that a behavior that is effective in solving a problem is remembered and is more likely to be repeated when facing the same situation, is known as "The Law of Effect." *Thorndike pointed out that animals make a connection between a behavior and its consequence.*

Classical conditioning *involves learning a connection between two stimuli that results in a change in behavior,* such as when the flavor of the new dish and the illness that followed become associated. This type of learning is also known as *Pavlovian conditioning.* It contributes to your emotional states, the functioning of your digestive and immune systems, and even to the development of tolerance to drugs.

In **operant conditioning**, *people or other animals learn to associate their own behavior with its consequences,* which results in a change in behavior. Thus a child learns that pressing a button brings an elevator, or a college student learns that answering questions in a certain class produces praise, or a porpoise learns that jumping through a hoop nets him fish to eat! Orthodox Behaviorists such as B.F. Skinner believed that most kinds of learning can be described in terms of classical and operant conditioning. However, beginning with Albert Bandura's **Social Learning Theory** which gave importance to **Observational Learning**, the role of cognition and concept formation in learning became more prominent and **Cognitive Learning Theory** has dominated the field since then. The chapter of Cognition will elaborate on concept formation etc. so those topics will not be addressed in this chapter. We will discuss each of these learning techniques next.

CLASSICAL CONDITIONING

Pavlov's Discovery

Ivan Pavlov (1849–1936), a Russian physiologist, first reported a series of experiments that gave rise to the discovery of a type of learning now known as *Pavlovian conditioning* or *classical conditioning.* In the 1920s, Pavlov was investigating the salivation responses of dogs by placing the animals in a harness-like apparatus, in order to find out whether saliva aided digestion. A surgical procedure exposed each dog's salivary glands, which were connected directly to a device that measured the flow of saliva. Pavlov then presented meat powder as a stimulus. When food entered the dog's mouth, the immediate result was the natural, reflexive response of salivation.

However, Pavlov soon noted an unexpected occurrence. His dogs began to salivate to stimuli other than food in their mouths. For example, an animal might start salivating at the mere sight of the experimenter. The sound of Pavlov's footsteps or the sight of the food dish also caused salivation.

This discovery changed the course of Pavlov's study, for Pavlov now began to investigate how other stimuli could cause dogs to salivate. His experiments are generally recognized as the first systematic study of learning, and the processes that he outlined came to be called classical (as in "the first") conditioning. (Today classical conditioning is frequently called Pavlovian conditioning.) A basic outline of this model of learning follows.

A hungry dog, secured in Pavlov's apparatus, hears a bell. A couple seconds later, the dog is given meat powder; copious salivation results. This procedure is repeated several times, with one stimulus (the sound of the bell) followed consistently by another stimulus (food). Eventually, the dog salivates as soon as it hears the bell, even when no food follows. The dog has associated the bell with food. However, what is learned is more than a mere association between two stimuli. Rather, classical conditioning may be best described as the learning of relations among events so as to allow the organism to respond to its environment (Rescorla, 1988a). Or, put another way, Pavlov's dog learned something about important relationships existing in its environment, namely that the sounding of a bell signaled the availability of food. Consequently, when the bell rang the dog salivated *in anticipation* of eating food. *Many conditioned responses function to prepare the learner for a change in events.*

Unconditioned stimulus (UCS)

In classical conditioning, a stimulus that elicits an unlearned response or reflex.

Unconditioned response (UCR)

In classical conditioning, an unlearned response or reflex caused by a stimulus.

Conditioned stimulus (CS)

In classical conditioning, a neutral stimulus that elicits a response only after it has been associated with an unconditioned stimulus.

Conditioned response (CR)

In classical conditioning, CR is a learned response to a previously neutral stimulus.

The fact that a previously neutral stimulus (a stimulus, such as the sound of the bell, that does not elicit the to-be-learned response) eventually produces a response (salivation) ordinarily associated with another stimulus (food) is clear evidence that learning has taken place. Pavlov identified four key elements for classical conditioning.

1. *The unconditioned stimulus (UCS).* Meat causes dogs to salivate. Salivation to food is a wired-in or reflexive response and occurs automatically, without learning or conditioning. A stimulus that elicits an unlearned response or a reflexive response is called an **unconditioned stimulus (UCS).** Therefore, meat is a UCS.
2. *The unconditioned response (UCR).* Salivating at the presentation of meat is an automatic reflexive response that does not require learning. An unlearned response is called an **unconditioned response (UCR).** Thus salivation in response to meat is a UCR/UR.
3. *The conditioned stimulus (CS).* The bell initially is a neutral stimulus in that it does not elicit the to-be-learned response by itself. It causes salivation only when the dogs learn the association between the bell and the unconditioned stimulus, i.e., the food. A stimulus to which an organism learns to respond is called a learned or **conditioned stimulus (CS).** Therefore, the bell is a CS.
4. *The conditioned response (CR).* Pavlov's dogs were conditioned to salivate when a bell sounded. Such a learned response is called a **conditioned response (CR).** Thus salivation in response to the bell is a CR.

FIGURE 6.1 Pavlov's Conditioning Procedure

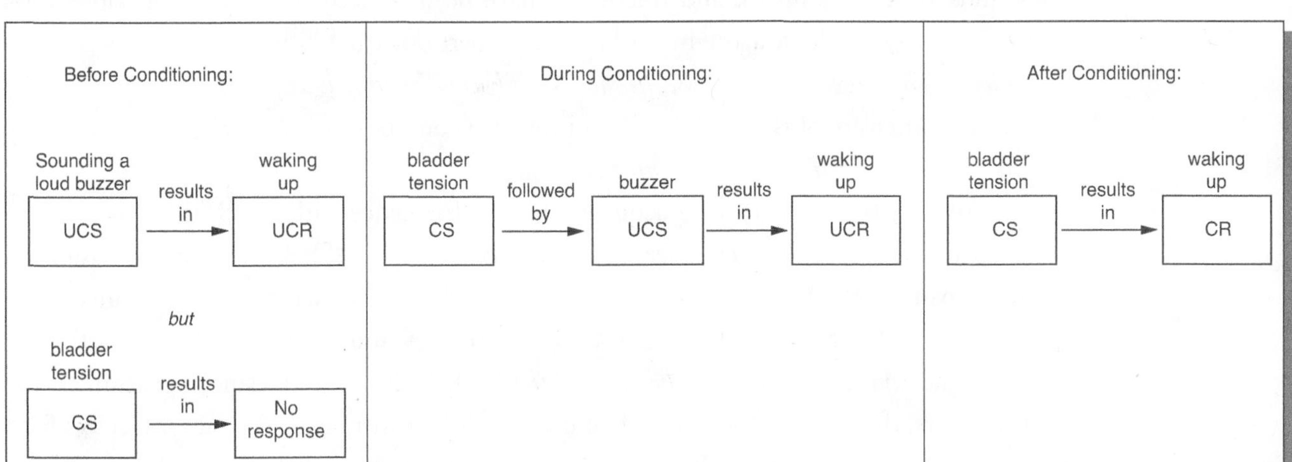

Figure 6.1 summarizes the steps by which conditioning took place in Pavlov's model.

The conditioning in Pavlov's dogs was measured by collecting saliva secreted following the presentation of the CS. Other conditioned responses may take place and be measured at a physiological level. For instance, in the Health, Psychology, and Life segment at the end of this chapter we discuss classical conditioning of the immune system, which could have far-reaching medical implications.

DIFFERENTIATING BETWEEN THE UCR AND THE CR At first glance, the unconditioned response and conditioned response often appear to be identical. The UCR in Pavlov's experiments occurred when the dogs salivated in response to meat and the CR was also salivation. However, the UCR and the CR may be quite different depending on both the nature of the CS and the UCS. In conditioned taste aversions, illness is the UCR but the aversion to food is the CR.

Unconditioned and conditioned responses also differ in their intensity and generally, a UCR is more intense than a CR. For example, dogs salivate more copiously when meat is actually placed in their mouths than they do when they either hear a bell or see the person who feeds them.

What do dogs salivating to a sound have to do with our lives as humans? As you will soon see, we humans learn several such associations and react in anticipation, just like the dogs do!

Acquisition

In classical conditioning, it is the process of learning to associate a conditioned stimulus with an unconditioned stimulus. In operant conditioning, it is the process of learning to associate responses with a reinforcer or a punisher.

Acquisition of Classical Conditioning

Several factors influence how easily a classically conditioned response is acquired. For example, conditioning takes place more easily when the neutral or conditioned stimulus is clearly different from other stimuli. Had Pavlov signaled the arrival of food by quietly humming a Russian ballad, his dogs might never have perceived the connection since such sounds are commonplace and might not have been noticed. In contrast, Pavlov's dogs could hardly overlook a ringing bell. This property of the CS is referred to as *stimulus salience. The more salient the CS, the more readily conditioning is acquired.*

The intensity of the UCS will also influence conditioning. *Typically, the more intense the UCS the more readily conditioning takes place.*

Another factor influencing acquisition is the frequency with which the CS and UCS are paired. *Frequent pairings generally facilitate conditioning.* If bells were only occasionally accompanied by feeding, Pavlov's dogs would have been less likely to be conditioned.

Yet another factor is the degree to which the CS and UCS are related. By this we mean the *contingency between the CS and the UCS.* If the UCS does not occur unless the CS occurs, then the UCS is contingent on the CS. In short, if the dog never receives food unless the bell is rung first, the dog will learn to salivate to the bell very easily.

CS-UCS Timing and Conditioning

Conditioning occurs most easily when the CS is presented ***just moments before*** *the UCS appears,* and it is continued until after the presentation of the UCS. For example, the bell rings before food is presented to Pavlov's dog, and it continues until the animal begins to salivate as food enters its mouth. Typically, CS-UCS delays between 0.5 and 2 seconds are optimal.

An exception to the rule that the delay between CS and UCS onset must be short is conditioned taste aversions.

CONDITIONED TASTE AVERSIONS Conditioned taste aversions (sometimes called the Garcia Effect) were first studied by John Garcia (1961). In his experiments rats were first exposed to a novel taste; in this case saccharine. Several hours later the rats were exposed to moderate doses of radiation, which made the rats ill. To test for conditioning the rats were given access to two drinking spouts, one containing plain water, the other, saccharine solution. Normally rats would prefer the saccharine solution to water, but these conditioned rats do not. The lack of a saccharine preference is called a **conditioned taste aversion**. Conditioned taste aversions reliably occur with long CS-UCS intervals. In numerous experiments the interval between the CS (the taste of saccharine) and the UCS (illness) has been as long as 24 hours. Nature has allowed such a long time interval in the case of learning taste aversion because learning which food is toxic is extremely vital. The animal's life depends on it.

Conditioned taste aversion

Is a learned aversion to a relatively novel taste that occurs if the novel taste is followed by an illness.

Preparedness and Selective Associations: All associations are not as readily learned as the association between a novel taste and illness. In fact, most learned associations require numerous trials containing CS-UCS presentations. When associations are learned quickly, like conditioned taste aversions, they are considered to be prepared. That is, animals may be *prepared biologically* to learn certain associations more quickly than others. The survival advantage for animals to learn quickly to avoid foods that have made them ill is fairly clear.

Extinction and Spontaneous Recovery

Extinction

In classical conditioning, the process by which a conditioned response is eliminated through repeated presentation of the conditioned stimulus without the unconditioned stimulus. In operant conditioning, it is the process of eliminating a learned response by discontinuing reinforcement for it.

Spontaneous recovery

In classical conditioning, the spontaneous reappearance of a conditioned response after extinction has taken place.

Would Pavlov's dogs have continued to salivate at the sound of the bell if it were no longer accompanied by food? The answer, of course, is no. They would salivate less and less at the sound until, without any additional presentations of the UCS, they eventually would cease salivating altogether and this process is known as Extinction..

Extinction occurs in classical conditioning when the CS is repeatedly presented alone, without the UCS. Extinction does not mean that a response is totally stamped out, however. Once extinguished, a conditioned response can be reactivated in much less time than it took to acquire it in the first place. For instance, the classically conditioned response of salivating to a bell may have been established only after several pairings or trials. *But after extinction, the conditioned response might be reestablished after only one or two pairings of the bell and the food.*

In fact, a conditioned response will sometimes reappear at the beginning of a session after extinction. For example, we might thoroughly extinguish the salivation response and then, after keeping the dog away from the experimental procedures for a few days, present the bell again. Even without food to help reestablish the old connection, the dog might salivate to the bell alone. This phenomenon is called **spontaneous recovery**.

As Figure 6.2 demonstrates, spontaneous recovery is not a complete recovery. A response does not come back to its previous level; it also extinguishes more rapidly if the CS is once more repeatedly presented alone.

FIGURE 6.2 Acquisition, Extinction and Spontaneous Recovery

This figure, based on data from Pavlov (1927), demonstrates rapid acquisition of the CR (salivation to the bell) after several trials in which the bell (CS) was paired with food (UCS). During extinction the UCS no longer follows the CS and the CR decreases. Later, some salivation (CR) occurs following the presentation of the CS. This is referred to as spontaneous recovery.

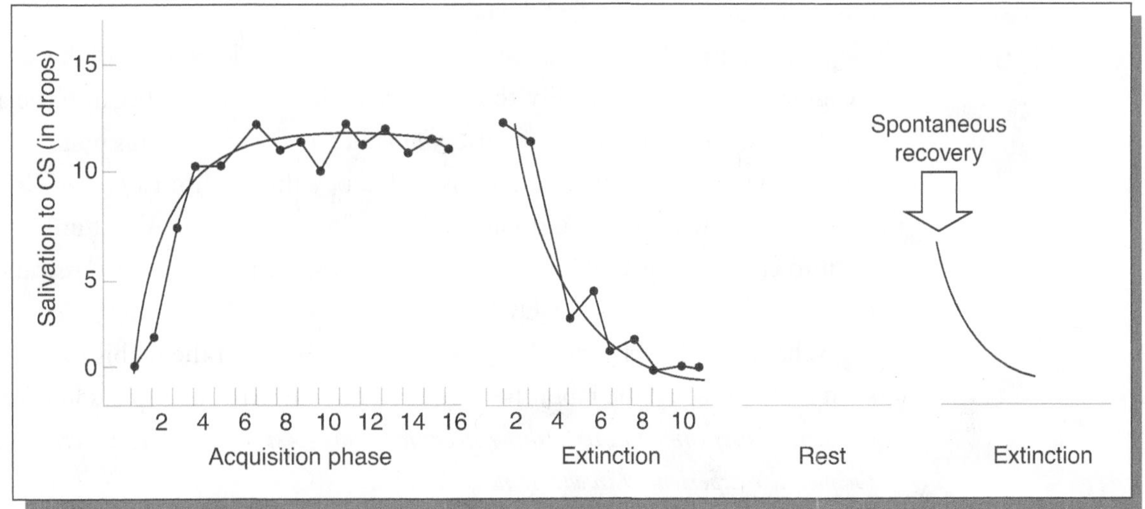

Stimulus Generalization and Discrimination

When a response has been conditioned to a particular stimulus, other stimuli may also produce the same response. For example, a war veteran who has been conditioned to dive for cover at the sound of gunfire may show the same response at the sound of a car backfiring. *The more similar a new stimulus is to the original CS, the more likely it is to elicit the CR.*

When people and other animals respond to similar stimuli without undergoing training for each specific stimulus, it is referred to as stimulus **generalization**. For example, Pavlov's dogs may have salivated to a variety of similar bell sounds.

Generalization

Process by which an organism responds to stimuli that are similar to the conditioned stimulus, without undergoing conditioning for each similar stimulus.

Discrimination

In classical and operant conditioning, the process by which responses are restricted to specific stimuli. In social psychology, the behavioral consequence of prejudice in which one group is treated differently from another group.

Just as a learned response may generalize to similar situations, it may also be restricted through the process of **discrimination**. Early in the conditioning process, stimulus generalization may cause a learner to respond to a variety of similar stimuli. However, with time he or she learns that only one of these stimuli, the CS, is consistently associated with the UCS. Once the learner discriminates between stimuli, he or she responds only to the CS. For example, if the war veteran experienced a variety of jarring loud noises without the accompaniment of bullets whizzing through the air, he would soon learn to discriminate between noises like a car backfiring and a gunshot.

Although Ivan Pavlov gets the credit for discovering classical conditioning, ***John Watson**, the founder of behaviorism gets the credit for explaining how humans learn to react emotionally to certain stimuli via classical conditioning.*

John Watson used classical conditioning to create fear of a rabbit in a toddler named Albert. Watson started with the naturally occurring UCS-UCR pair of sudden loud sound (UCS), which invariably produces the reflexive Moro Response or *startle response* in babies. On hearing a sudden boom, a baby brings its limbs close to the body, flings them out and starts crying in a high pitch, as if terrorized.

Watson used a rabbit, which ordinarily does not produce any fear in toddlers, as his CS. Basically, he brought the rabbit to the lab, made sure that the child saw it, and within seconds of the child's noticing the rabbit, he had an assistant fire a gun right outside the lab. The loud sound caused the baby to experience fear. With a few repetitions of this same sequence, the rabbit alone started producing the fear in the baby, so the baby was thus classically conditioned to fear the rabbit.

At first, little Albert was afraid only of the rabbit. However, soon his innate ability to recognize similarities or ability to *generalize* took over, and he began to be afraid of cats, poodles and any small furry animals, even ladies' fur purses. At this point, since the fear to these objects was irrational, Albert was said to be suffering from a *fur phobia.*

Fortunately, a psychologist named *Mary Cover Jones* made Albert unlearn his fear, and learn to enjoy seeing a rabbit, by using the very same principles of classical conditioning, but by using a different UCS-UCR pair.

What Mary Cover Jones did, was to bring Albert and the rabbit to her laboratory. As soon as Albert spied the rabbit he started crying, but Ms. Jones put some ice cream in his mouth. *Babies come to birth liking sweet food, or sweet food such as ice cream is a UCS and the pleasure experienced in eating it, is the UCR.*

Ms Jones thus paired the rabbit with the ice cream several times, and brought the rabbit closer every time. Soon, she presented the rabbit without presenting the ice cream or UCS, but baby Albert smiled, indicating that learning had taken place. The rabbit was now the new CS for joy! *This method, which removes classically conditioned responses, is known as* ***counter conditioning****.*

We have seen that classical conditioning is a form of associative learning that accounts for certain types of behaviors. However, classical conditioning does not explain all forms of learning. It is clearly involved in the learning of emotional and motivational states but it does not by itself account for why you are diligently (we hope) reading this textbook. What is the UCS that automatically causes you to study? Obviously, there is none. To learn why you study and why you engage in a host of other voluntary behaviors, we must examine the second kind of associative learning, known as operant conditioning.

OPERANT CONDITIONING

B. F. Skinner (1904–1990), a giant who towered over all behaviorists will be remembered for ever in psychology, as will the principles of operant conditioning that he professed and popularized.

B. F. Skinner talked of what he liked to call the ABCs of behavior. A stood for *antecedents*, or stimuli that an organism responded to, B stood for *behavior*, or the responses an organism produced because of having perceived that stimulus, and C stood for the *consequences* of the particular response or behavior the organism had manifested on perceiving the stimulus.

Skinner argued (and provided evidence beyond the shadow of a doubt) that an organism very quickly learns an association between its behavior and the consequences of that behavior. A behavior comes under the influence of its consequence and the probability of its occurrence changes as soon as the connection between them is learned.

We can trace the origin of the principles of operant conditioning to the American psychologist Edward Thorndike (1911) mentioned earlier.

Thorndike's puzzle box illustrates why the term operant has been applied to this type of learning. His cats learned to operate on their environment in a manner that resulted in satisfaction. Another way of saying the same thing is that their behaviors were instrumental in achieving a positive outcome. Thus, this conditioning model is sometimes called *instrumental conditioning.* B.F. Skinner used similar devices to provide more evidence via laboratory experiments on various species of animals and one such device is the famous Skinner box.

Operant Conditioning in a Skinner Box

A hungry rat is placed in a box similar to that shown in Figure 6.3. This chamber, called a Skinner box, is empty except for a bar protruding from one wall with a small food dish directly beneath it.

FIGURE 6.3 A Skinner Box Used for Operant Conditioning

After a short time in a Skinner box, the rat begins to examine its surroundings. As it explores, it eventually approaches the bar. When the rat is near the bar a food pellet is released into the dish. The next bar approach followed immediately by food delivery occurs after some additional exploration. Soon the rat spends most of its time around the bar. Next the rat must contact and exert some force on the bar before food is delivered. As with approaching the bar, this activity soon comes to predominate. The operant response of bar pressing is "selected" by the food it produces, and the rate of pressing steadily increases.

MEASURING OPERANT BEHAVIOR Perhaps the most common measure of operant behavior is its rate of occurrence. Skinner designed a device called a *cumulative recorder* that is used to measure operant behavior in a laboratory environment. A recording pen rests on paper that moves slowly at a fixed rate. Each time an animal makes an operant response, such as pressing a bar, the pen moves up a fixed distance and then continues on its horizontal path. The more frequently an animal responds, the more rapidly the pen climbs up the chart. The result, called a **cumulative record**, is a reliable measure of operant behavior.

Cumulative record

A chart recording of operant responses over time. Time increments are indicated along the horizontal axis and operant responses along the vertical axis. As response rate increases the slope of the record increases.

DISCRIMINATIVE STIMULI In his experiment, Skinner put a light above the bar. He used the light to introduce a new variable, setting the dispenser to deliver food only when both the bar is pressed and the light is on. When the light is off, no food is delivered.

Under these conditions of *differential reinforcement* (that is, reinforcement which takes place only under certain circumstances), the rat soon learns to make the appropriate discrimination: It presses the bar only when the light is on. In this circumstance, the light serves as a **discriminative stimulus**, that is, a stimulus that controls the response by signaling the availability of reinforcement.

Discriminative stimulus

In operant conditioning, a stimulus that controls a response by signaling the availability of reinforcement.

Skinner's experiments illustrate the primary features of operant conditioning. An animal's behavior is selected or controlled by the *immediate* consequences of that behavior. For Skinner's rats, bar pressing was controlled by the delivery of food. Unlike classical conditioning, in which the learner passively responds to a stimulus, operant conditioning occurs when the learner acts on the environment as a result of the consequences for that act. Sometimes response consequences are quite apparent as with Skinner's example. However, consequences may be much more subtle such as an approving nod by a parent for acting politely or a change in facial expression by a friend for a compliment.

Reinforcement

Operant conditioning stresses the effects of consequences on behavior. These consequences are described as reinforcement (or a reinforcer) and punishment (or a punisher). ***Reinforcement** is defined as a stimulus whose delivery following a response leads to an increase in either the frequency or probability of that response.* Punishment, on the other hand, is defined as a stimulus whose delivery following a response results in a decrease in the frequency or probability of that response. We shall first examine procedures used to study the effects of reinforcement, and then we will discuss punishment.

Reinforcement

A consequence that increases the probability of the occurrence of a particular response.

In studying operant conditioning, researchers have experimented with different types of reinforcers and different schedules for delivering reinforcement. Their findings help to explain how and why operant conditioning takes place.

Positive reinforcement

In operant conditioning, any stimulus presented after a response that increases the probability of the response.

POSITIVE AND NEGATIVE REINFORCEMENT **Positive reinforcement** is any stimulus presented following a response that increases the probability of the response. **Negative reinforcement** is *also* a stimulus that increases the probability of a response, but *through its removal* when the desired response is made.

Negative reinforcement

In operant conditioning, any stimulus that increases the probability of a response through its removal. For example, pounding on the wall (operant behavior) may be maintained by the termination of loud noise (negative reinforcer) in an adjoining room.

Introductory psychology students frequently misunderstand negative reinforcement; often confusing it with punishment assuming that it is used to stop a behavior. In fact, quite the opposite is true: Negative reinforcement, like positive reinforcement, increases the occurrence of a desired behavior. It is important to remember that the terms positive and negative refer only to whether a stimulus is presented (positive) or removed (negative), not its hedonic value. Since the previous examples in this chapter have illustrated positive reinforcement, we look here at some examples of negative reinforcement and the procedures used to study them.

ESCAPE AND AVOIDANCE PROCEDURES A rat is placed in a Skinner box, the floor of which consists of a metal grid that can be electrified. A mild current is activated and, as the rat tries to escape, it bumps into a bar and the shocking current immediately ceases. The pattern is repeated several times until the rat remains poised by the bar, ready to press it at the first jolt. This form of learning, called **escape conditioning** clearly involves negative reinforcement. The shock, an unpleasant stimulus, may be terminated only by the appropriate operant response. The removal of, or the escape from, the shock thus acts as the reinforcer for the bar press response. Taking aspirin to alleviate headache pain is essentially escape behavior maintained by the termination of the headache.

Escape conditioning

In operant conditioning, learning that takes place when an organism performs a response that will terminate an aversive stimulus.

The escape conditioning procedure can be modified slightly by introducing a warning signal that allows the rat to avoid the shock altogether. If the light goes on a few seconds prior to each shock, the rat soon learns to respond to this discriminative stimulus by pressing the bar in time to avoid the shock. This type of learning is called **avoidance conditioning**.

Avoidance conditioning

In operant conditioning, the learning of a response to a discriminative stimulus that allows an organism to avoid exposure to an aversive stimulus.

These examples bring to mind many parallels in our own lives. For instance, if you live in a dormitory or an apartment building you may find that you pound on the wall of an adjoining room to get your noisy neighbor to quiet down. Your pounding behavior is thus maintained by negative reinforcement, the removal of the noise. Much of human behavior is maintained by avoidance conditioning. In fact, our punitive legal system is a set of aversive consequences established to keep us in line. As long as we behave lawfully we avoid these aversive consequences. You may attend your classes not because of positive reinforcement, but to avoid the aversive consequences of failing exams. We pay taxes promptly to avoid the punitive consequences of not paying them on time. And, we obtain a flu shot to avoid the consequences of getting the flu.

PRIMARY AND CONDITIONED REINFORCERS: Reinforcers can be categorized into two groups, known as primary and secondary reinforces. ***Primary reinforcers*** *usually satisfy a biologically based need, such as hunger, thirst, sex, or sleep. However, some social events like parental contact may be primary reinforcers. It is obvious why food, water, sex, or sleep reinforce. But why do things like money reinforce? The answer lies in the concept of conditioned reinforcement. A variety of neutral stimuli associated with primary reinforcement can also become* ***conditioned reinforcers***, or ***secondary reinforcers***. In other words, money becomes a reinforcer because it allows access to the primary reinforcers such as food, water, sleep, and even a mate! Much of our behavior is influenced more by conditioned reinforcement than by biologically significant primary reinforcement. Social reinforcers, such as words of praise and pats on the back, may be biological, or they may be secondary, but money, status symbols, etc., are some of the conditioned reinforcers that influence our lives.

Primary reinforcer

In operant conditioning, a stimulus that satisfies a biologically based drive or need (such as hunger, thirst, or sleep).

Conditioned reinforcer

A stimulus that takes on reinforcing properties after being associated with a primary reinforcer.

Research suggests that the crucial factor that allows a secondary reinforcer to become one seems to be the reliability with which it predicts the availability of the primary reinforcer (Fantino, 1977; Rose & Fantino, 1978). For example, a coin that always produces raisins when inserted in a chimp-o-mat quickly becomes a strong conditioned reinforcer; coins that have less predictable results may be much weaker conditioned reinforcers for the chimp, no matter how often they have been paired with raisins. Thus, conditioned reinforcers acquire their reinforcing properties just like Pavlovian conditioned stimuli: through stimulus associations.

CONTINUOUS VERSUS PARTIAL REINFORCEMENT In addition to the type of reinforcer used, another factor that influences the effectiveness of reinforcement is the consistency with which a behavior is reinforced or *the schedule* on which an animal receives reinforcements.

Continuous reinforcement schedule

In operant conditioning, the presentation of a reinforcer for each occurrence of a specific behavior.

In laboratory demonstrations of operant conditioning, if a behavior is reinforced every time it occurs, the animal is said to be on a **continuous reinforcement schedule**. For example, a rat that receives a food pellet each time it presses a bar would be on this schedule. Outside the laboratory, particularly in the everyday lives of humans, continuous reinforcement is unusual. For example, smiling at the food server in your college cafeteria does not always produce an extra large helping of food, nor does getting out of the house 20 minutes early always ensure your favorite parking space on campus. But these behaviors persist because they are reinforced occasionally. When behavior is reinforced only part of the time or occasionally, the schedule is called a **partial reinforcement schedule**. There are striking differences between the effects of continuous and partial reinforcement schedules on behavior.

Partial reinforcement schedule

In operant conditioning, a schedule that reinforces behavior only part of the time, for example, a ratio or interval schedule.

Continuous reinforcement schedules almost always produce the highest rate of acquisition of a new behavior. For example, a rat learns to bar-press most rapidly when it receives food each time it makes the appropriate response. However, what happens when reinforcement is withdrawn? Extinction begins, and the rat quickly ceases its bar-pressing behavior.

Behaviors that are acquired on partial instead of continuous schedules of reinforcement are slower to be established. However, these behaviors are remarkably more persistent when no reinforcement is provided. *For example, a rat accustomed to only intermittent reinforcement for bar pressing continues to press long after the food dispenser has run dry.* This is particularly true when the partial reinforcement is delivered in an unpredictable fashion. This phenomenon is known as the **partial reinforcement effect**.

Partial reinforcement effect

Behaviors that are acquired on partial instead of continuous reinforcement schedules tend to be established more slowly, but are more persistent when no reinforcement is provided.

PARTIAL REINFORCEMENT SCHEDULES Partial reinforcement is typically delivered in either of two basic ways, known as ratio or interval schedules. On a *ratio schedule,* a certain percentage of responses receive reinforcement. For instance, a slot machine in a casino might be programmed to provide some kind of payoff on 10 percent of all plays. An *interval schedule,* in contrast, is time-based: Subjects are reinforced for their first response after a certain amount of time has passed, regardless of how many responses might occur during that period. *In many natural environments, an animal's foraging is maintained by an interval schedule.* Birds searching for food find it after the passage of variable amounts of time, not after a specific number of attempts. The same is true of a scavenger hunt.

Both ratio and interval schedules may be either variable or fixed. *Variable schedule* reinforcement is delivered unpredictably, with the amount of time or number of responses required varying randomly around an average. In contrast, *fixed schedule* reinforcement is always delivered after a constant number of responses or a fixed interval of time. These categories combine to form four basic partial reinforcement schedules: fixed ratio, variable ratio, fixed interval, and variable interval (see Figure 6.4).

FIGURE 6.4 Schedules of Reinforcement

Stylized cumulative records from several common schedules of reinforcement. Panel *A* shows a fixed ratio schedule with characteristic pauses in responding, panel *B* illustrates a variable ratio schedule with typical high response rates, panel *C* illustrates the scalloped pattern of responding observed on fixed interval schedules, and panel *D* shows the stable pattern of responding found on variable interval schedules.

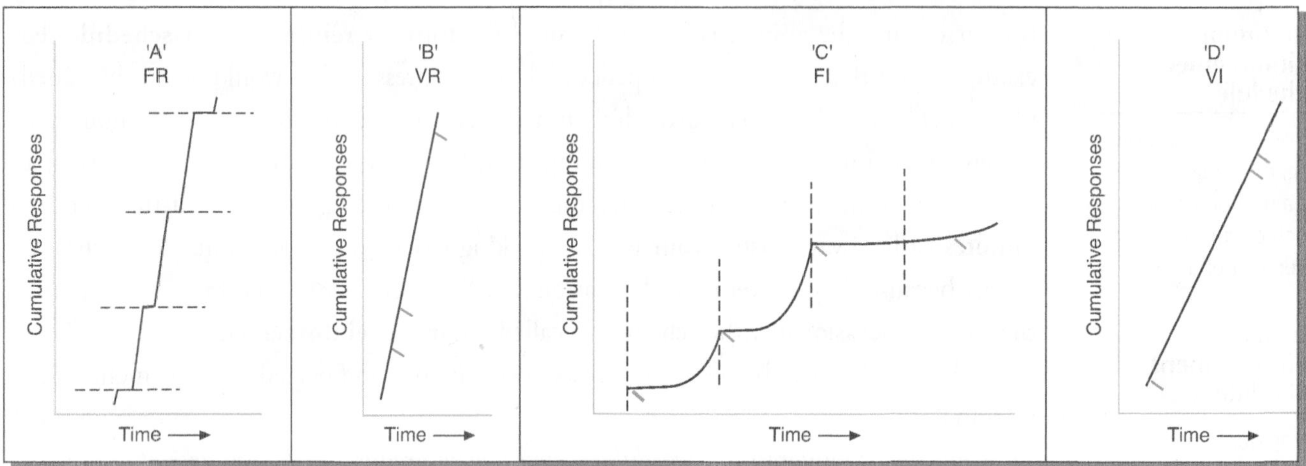

Fixed ratio (FR) schedule

Partial reinforcement schedule in operant conditioning wherein reinforcement occurs after a fixed number of responses.

Fixed Ratio Schedule On a **fixed ratio (FR)** schedule, reinforcement occurs after a fixed number of responses. For example, a rat receives a food pellet after 12 bar presses and a strawberry picker receives $1 after filling 12 small boxes with berries. Both are on an FR-12 schedule. This type of schedule tends to produce rather high rates of responding: The faster the rat bar-presses, the more pellets it gets, and the quicker the strawberry picker works, the more money she or he earns. Fixed ratio schedules are also used in programmed instruction where students proceed at their own pace and receive feedback after each section of work is completed. *Programmed instruction is often quite successful in generating high rates of academic work.* The fixed ratio schedule is illustrated in Panel A of Figure 6.4.

This fact explains why some factories and businesses pay workers (like the strawberry picker) on a piecework basis. However, there are some limitations to this practice. For example, if workers in an automobile assembly plant were paid only according to the number of cars they ran through the assembly line, the quality of their work might suffer. Another potential limitation of the fixed ratio schedule is that people and other animals often pause briefly after reinforcement is delivered, probably because they have learned that their next few responses will not be reinforced. The pause following reinforcement on a fixed ratio schedule is termed *post-reinforcement pause.* Post-reinforcement pause may be one reason why payday typically occurs on Friday.

Variable ratio (VR) schedule

Partial reinforcement schedule in operant conditioning where reinforcement is provided after an average of a specific number of responses occur.

Variable Ratio Schedule A **variable ratio (VR) schedule** of reinforcement also requires the occurrence of a certain number of responses before reinforcement is delivered. Unlike a fixed ratio schedule, however, the number of responses required for each reinforcement varies. For example, a rat on a VR-6 schedule receives a food pellet on the *average* of every six bar presses, so reinforcement may be granted after four bar presses in one run and after eight presses on the next run, as long as the rat receives reinforcement after six presses on the average. The pattern of behavior maintained by a VR schedule is illustrated in Panel B of Figure 6.4.

Variable ratio schedules produce high response rates. Furthermore, because of the unpredictable nature of reinforcement, there is typically no post-reinforcement pause, for it is possible that reinforcement will occur on the very next response. Behavior that is maintained on this schedule is often *very slow to extinguish.*

Gamblers are very familiar with variable ratio schedules. For example, a person who always bets on 13 at the roulette wheel is on a VR-38 schedule (the wheel has 36 numbers plus 0 and 00). On the average, number 13 comes up once in every 38 spins. However, during a hot streak 13 might occur three times in 20 spins (of course, it also might not occur at all). Similarly, a slot machine may be rigged to pay off once every 20 times a coin is deposited, on the average (a VR-20 schedule). The gambler does not know when it will return a few of the coins it has swallowed. *It is the unpredictable, highly variable nature of these payoffs that makes gambling so compelling to some people.* In fact, gamblers often put in much more than they get back, a result that doesn't occur on interval schedules. Experimental animals also show the tendency to respond at very high rates on VR schedules, sometimes at the cost of forgoing the food they've earned on previous ratios!

Fixed interval (FI) schedule

Partial reinforcement schedule in operant conditioning wherein reinforcement is provided for the first response after a specified period of time has elapsed.

Fixed Interval Schedule On a **fixed interval (FI) schedule**, reinforcement is provided for the first response after a specified period of time has elapsed. For example, a rat on an FI-30 schedule, whose bar press has just produced a food pellet, will receive its next reinforcer the first time it bar-presses after 30 seconds have elapsed.

The response rates of animals on FI schedules quickly adjust to this contingency. Because no reinforcements occur for a period of time, no matter how often an animal responds, it typically stops working after reinforcement is delivered and then begins to respond toward the end of the interval. Thus this pattern of reinforcement tends to produce regular, recurring episodes of inactivity followed by short bursts of responding. This is illustrated in Panel C of Figure 6.4.

Variable interval (VI) schedule

Partial reinforcement schedule in operant conditioning where opportunities for reinforcement occur at variable time intervals.

Variable Interval Schedule Finally, a **variable interval (VI) schedule** involves variable time intervals between opportunities for reinforcement. Thus an animal on a VI-45 schedule might receive reinforcement for a response after 30 seconds have elapsed, then after 60 seconds, and then after 45 seconds. This schedule averages out to reinforcement every 45 seconds. See Panel D of Figure 6.4.

As you might guess, the random, unpredictable occurrence of reinforcement on this schedule tends to produce more steady rates of responding than fixed interval schedules. The steady persistent pattern of behavior maintained by VI schedules makes them quite useful to researchers studying the effects of other variables on behavior. For example, a researcher interested in examining the effects of certain drugs on behavior might examine the pattern of responding on a VI schedule both before and after drug administration.

A woman rubbing off lottery tickets. Gamblers do not know when the lottery tickets will pay off. Their gambling behavior is maintained by a variable ratio schedule of reinforcement.

The reinforcement schedules we have been discussing share a common assumption: The learner will produce the desired behavior so that it can be reinforced. In operant conditioning, however, it is sometimes difficult to get an animal (humans included) to make the initial correct response so that it can be reinforced. The next section discusses methods for increasing the probability that a desired response will occur.

Reinforcing the Initial Operant Response

In operant conditioning, many responses occur spontaneously. For example, rats placed in Skinner boxes invariably get around to pressing the bar during the course of their explorations. In other circumstances, however, the behavior may not occur without some additional help. For instance, no matter how many times you say "roll over" to your untrained dog, the odds are remote that it will perform the trick so that you can reinforce it. Some special techniques can be used to encourage the desired response, however.

Shaping

In operant conditioning, a technique in which responses that are increasingly similar to the desired behavior are reinforced, step by step, until the desired behavior occurs.

SHAPING You may have wondered how researchers trained rats to press levers in several of the experiments already discussed in this chapter. The procedure used is referred to as ***the method of successive approximations, or shaping.*** **Shaping** involves a systematic process whereby responses that are increasingly similar to the desired behavior are reinforced step by step in combination with withholding reinforcement till a better approximation of the target behavior is reached, until finally the desired behavior occurs. For example, hungry rats are first reinforced for being near the lever. Later they must touch it, and finally they are required to exert sufficient force on the lever to operate it, before they receive the reinforcement.

Shaping is especially effective for establishing novel behaviors. For instance, the learning of speech by a young child is shaped from nonsensical babbling to closer and closer approximations of the appropriate sounds of words. The reinforcement during this process may be as subtle as a change in facial expression of the parent. Later, reinforcement may be the appropriate response of the listener to a command. Animals performing in circus acts are often trained this way.

MODELING Learning based on the observation of others performing a certain behavior, was first experimentally substantiated by Albert Bandura in the late 1970s and he considered this type of observational learning as cognitive learning as the viewer learned the behavior without experiencing the consequences directly. Bandura's theory is known as the Social Learning Theory or as the Cognitive Theory of Learning and is based on his experimental work on observational learning. Modeling as a way of influencing behavior became a part of Behaviorism since the advent of Bandura's influential Social Learning Theory.

Modeling

Learning process wherein an individual acquires a behavior by observing someone else performing that behavior. Also known as observational learning.

Modeling involves demonstrating the desired behavior to the learner. Many athletic skills, such as diving, hitting a tennis ball, or riding a skateboard, are more easily learned by watching someone else or watching your own performance on video. Videotape has been used successfully with both adults and children to model a variety of skills (Dowrick, 1999). Modeling can teach a wide range of behaviors, undesirable as well as desirable. For instance, a young child who observes a parent working hard, being kind, etc., might behave similarly. Remember the pups mentioned in the introduction to the chapter, the ones who learned how to sniff out narcotics by observing their mothers? Their mothers obviously served as models for them.

Punishment and Operant Behavior

Certainly punishment is widespread, from spanking misbehaving children to keeping students after school, meting out traffic fines, and incarcerating people in prisons. However, the fact that many people and institutions rely on punishment to control behavior does not necessarily mean that it is more effective than reinforcement. People have long debated the relative advantages and disadvantages of reinforcing desirable behavior versus punishing undesirable acts. There is no simple answer. Nevertheless, research has provided ample data that can help us make better informed choices as we confront this issue in our own lives. We begin by defining punishment.

Punishment

A procedure in which the presentation of a stimulus following a response leads to a decrease in the strength or frequency of the response.

Punishment (or a punisher) is defined as a stimulus whose delivery following a response results in a decrease in the frequency or probability of the occurrence of that response. We often think of punishment as an unpleasant or aversive stimulus, such as a spanking. However, punishment may also involve the withdrawal of positive reinforcers such as affection, playtime, watching TV, money, or the use of the family car each time the undesirable behavior was performed.

Limitations of Punishment

EXTINCTION OF PUNISHED RESPONSES One limitation of punishment is the longevity of its effectiveness. In some cases, punishment suppresses the unwanted behavior for a short time, but does not eliminate it. In fact, there is ample evidence that suppressed behavior may reemerge when the prospect of punishment is gone or sharply curtailed. When either reinforcement or punishment is discontinued, responding can return to its pre-reinforcement or pre-punishment level.

For example, a child who is punished by a parent each time she raids the cookie jar will probably learn to suppress this behavior. However, if punishment hasn't occurred for some time she is likely to raid again.

EMOTIONAL SIDE EFFECTS OF PUNISHMENT Another potential problem is that punishment may produce undesirable emotional side effects such as fear and aggression. This outcome is particularly true when punishment is severe. For example, a child who receives constant, severe punishment from a parent may learn to fear that parent. The process by which this fear response is learned is classical conditioning. In this case a parent who consistently punishes may become a conditioned stimulus for fear. The subject will learn to withhold the punished behavior but also learns to fear the punishing situation. This could lead to problems interacting with the parent that may generalize to other relationships. In fact, punishment may induce aggression against the punisher.

The negative emotional effects of punishment are often generalized to related behaviors. Thus a child who is singled out for harsh punishment in one class may begin to react negatively to school in general. *In contrast, people who are reinforced for desirable behavior generally feel good about themselves, are motivated to perform well, and are optimistic about future endeavors that they anticipate will lead to additional positive consequences.*

PHYSICAL PUNISHMENT AND MODELING Children are often punished by physical means, such as slapping or spanking. Considerable evidence suggests that youngsters who are punished physically learn to model or imitate these aggressive acts and often become more aggressive in their interactions with others (Bandura & Walters, 1959; George & Main, 1979). Thus parents who spank or hit misbehaving children may be teaching them more than is intended, namely, that physical aggression is acceptable.

Advantages of Punishment

While it is important to be aware of the limitations of punishment, most psychologists do not advocate total abolition of all punishment for controlling or modifying behavior. Although reinforcement is preferable in most cases, punishment is sometimes essential as a way to suppress undesirable actions so that a desirable alternative behavior may occur.

Punishment is effective only when it is delivered immediately after the undesirable behavior, it is strong, and it is meted out consistently. Otherwise, punishment becomes ineffective.

When punishment becomes ineffective, the punisher tends to escalate it, and an unhappy situation between the punisher and the punished gets set up. Hence it is best that parents and teachers reserve punishment only for those behaviors which are major violations of social norms or life threatening, etc., and use modeling or reinforcement of desired behaviors to raise children.

COMPARING CLASSICAL AND OPERANT CONDITIONING

In Classical Conditioning, the animal/subject learns an association between two environmental stimuli, where one of them has a biological reflexive response, whereas in Operant Conditioning the animal/subject learns the relationship between a voluntary behavior and the short term consequence of that behavior.

Operant Conditioning has several practical uses and is the mainstay of a therapy known as Behavior Modification. Comparatively, Classical Conditioning does not have many applications.

Two-factor theory of learning

A theory of avoidance learning that involves both classical and operant conditioning.

In the laboratory they can be isolated and studied but in real life both types of learning takes place simultaneously. Most learning situations combine both classical and operant conditioning in what is called two-factor learning.

Cognitive Processes in Learning

We have presented cognitive learning as separate from the associative types of learning, which is the traditional way of viewing learning. Pavlov, for instance, stressed that *temporal contiguity* (that is, closeness in time) of the CS and the UCS is essential for classical conditioning, and most learning theorists after Pavlov continued to view classical conditioning as a relatively automatic form of learning that is strengthened through repeated pairings of the CS and the UCS.

Recent evidence has caused some psychologists to question this view, however. According to their interpretation, *cognitive processes are involved even in classical conditioning* (Rescorla, 1988a, 1988b, 1999; Turkkan, 1989).

According to this cognitive perspective, the learner during classical conditioning first observes that the CS and UCS typically occur together and stores this information in memory. Later, when the CS appears by itself, the learner retrieves the information from memory and makes the conditioned response in anticipation that the UCS will occur. *In other words, it appears that the CS and UCS become associated not simply because they occur contiguously in time, but rather because the CS provides information about the UCS* (Rescorla, 1987, p. 121). Recent interpretations of Rescorla's experiments indicate that more informative or predictive the CS is the better conditioning will be.

Cognitive factors may be important in operant conditioning, as well. Although the operant conditioning emphasizes the consequences of behavior, those consequences do not automatically strengthen or weaken responses. Rather, they provide the learner with important information about the probable consequences of a given behavior under certain circumstances. *Cognitive theorists view individuals as information-processing systems that store this relevant information about consequences. Later, when confronted by similar circumstances, the learner retrieves this information from memory and acts accordingly. Thus, from the cognitive perspective, operant behavior is guided by expectations of probable outcomes* (Colwill & Rescorla, 1986; Rescorla, 1987; Rescorla, 1999; Williams et al., 1990).

The cognitive theorists stress the argument that the events occurring in classical and operant conditioning do not automatically stamp in behavior. Instead, they provide relevant information that helps to establish expectancies and it is these expectancies that form the basis for subsequent behavior.

If you recall the sequence of changes in definition of Psychology, you will realize that beginning with the 1970s Behaviorism waned and Cognitive Psychology was in the catbird seat. It still is and today's scientists are studying the neural mechanisms of learning. Even so, the facts discovered by the Behaviorists are correct and Classical conditioning, Operant conditioning, etc. do work when applied correctly to humans and animals.

Radical or Orthodox Behaviorism considered behavioral change due to learning but did not consider conceptual changes that occur, or how they make sense of and use of information especially when they solve novel problems with existing information! Cognitive Psychology addressed this issue and Cognitive Learning Theory came into existence.

The Cognitive Learning Theory is not the work of any one psychologist but is based on the input of many 20th and 21st century psychologists. They see the learner as an active agent in the learning process and they put emphasis on making the information provided to the learner meaningful and to make it relate to what the learner already knows or his/her prior learning and reframing the information in keeping with the learner's schema.

Teachers whose teaching is based on the Cognitive Learning Theory do not believe in giving reinforcers or punishers to their students. Instead they focus on providing unifying themes for the content, providing a context to activate existing schemas and encouraging students to organize the information within a suitable framework and asking probing questions to identify prior knowledge (Yilmaz, K. 2011). You will learn more about these information processing processes in a chapter titled "Cognitive Psychology".

SUMMARY

DEFINING LEARNING

1. Learning may be defined as a relatively permanent change in potential behavior that results from experience.
2. Associative learning, the process by which connections or associations are made between two events, may take place in two primary ways: through classical conditioning and through operant conditioning. Classical conditioning involves learned associations between two stimuli. Operant conditioning, involves learning to associate one's own behavior with consequences that follow the behavior.

CLASSICAL CONDITIONING

3. The four key elements in classical conditioning are the unconditioned stimulus (UCS), the unconditioned response (UCR), the conditioned stimulus (CS), and the conditioned response (CR). After pairing a previously neutral stimulus (CS) with a stimulus (UCS) that automatically elicits an unlearned, reflexive response (UCR) the CS will cause a similar response on its own.
4. Factors that facilitate the acquisition of a classically conditioned response include a CS that is clearly different from other stimuli, frequent pairings of the CS and the UCS, and the order and timing with which the CS is paired with the UCS.
5. The acquisition of classical conditioning depends on a predictive relation between the CS and the UCS called stimulus contingency.
6. When certain associations are acquired very quickly they are called selective associations. Conditioned taste aversions are examples of selective associations.
7. Extinction, or cessation of the CR, occurs in classical conditioning when the CS is repeatedly presented alone, without the UCS.
8. A CR sometimes reappears spontaneously after extinction, a phenomenon called spontaneous recovery.
9. When a response has been conditioned to a particular stimulus, other stimuli may also produce the same response. This principle is called stimulus generalization.
10. Early in the conditioning process, a learner may respond to a variety of similar stimuli (generalization). However, with time he or she learns that only one of these stimuli, the CS, is consistently associated with the UCS. This process of learning to make distinctions between the CS and similar but not identical stimuli is called discrimination.

OPERANT CONDITIONING

11. In operant conditioning humans and other animals learn to associate their behavior with either reinforcing or punishing consequences.
12. Reinforcement is defined as a procedure that increases the probability that a response will occur.
13. A positive reinforcer is any stimulus presented following a response and which increases the probability of the response. A negative reinforcer is a

stimulus that increases the probability of a response through its removal when the desired response is made.

14. In escape conditioning, an organism learns to produce a response that will allow termination or escape from an aversive stimulus (negative reinforcer). In avoidance conditioning the individual learns to emit an appropriate avoidance response, thereby averting any exposure to the aversive stimulus.
15. A primary reinforcer is a stimulus that satisfies a biologically based drive or need. Secondary reinforcers are stimuli that acquire reinforcing properties through association with primary reinforcers.
16. A continuous reinforcement schedule exists when behavior is reinforced every time it occurs. A partial reinforcement schedule exists when behavior is reinforced only part of the time.
17. Behaviors that are acquired on partial instead of continuous schedules of reinforcement are slower to be established, but they are remarkably more persistent when no reinforcement is provided.
18. Four varieties of partial reinforcement schedules include those based on a percentage of responses that are reinforced (fixed ratio and variable ratio) or passage of a certain amount of time before a response is reinforced (fixed interval and variable interval).
19. Methods used to encourage the occurrence of an initial desired operant response include shaping and modeling, verbal instruction, and increasing motivation.
20. Punishment can be defined as a procedure, which decreases the probability that a given behavior will occur.
21. The effectiveness of a punisher in producing a desired change in behavior depends upon its intensity, consistency, and the delay between a response and punishment.
22. Principles that may improve the effectiveness of punishment include immediacy, consistency, moderation, and combining it with positive reinforcement (always reinforcing acceptable alternatives to the punished behavior).

COMPARISON OF CLASSICAL AND OPERANT CONDITIONING

23. Classical conditioning involves learning associations between a CS and a UCS. Operant conditioning involves learning associations between behavior and its consequence.
24. Most learning situations combine both classical and operant conditioning in what is called two-factor learning.
25. Many human phobias are a result of two-factor learning. First an individual acquires a fear of a neutral stimulus (classical conditioning), and then acts to reduce or eliminate this fear by learning to avoid the frightening stimulus (operant avoidance conditioning).

COGNITIVE INFLUENCES ON LEARNING

26. Cognitive theorists suggest that we learn by forming a cognitive structure, or representation, in memory that preserves and organizes information relevant to a given situation.
27. The roots of cognitive learning theories go back many years to studies of insight in chimpanzees and latent learning in rats.
28 Latent learning refers to learning that is not demonstrated by an immediately observable change in behavior at the time of learning.
29. Cognitive theorists suggest that what is learned in classical conditioning is not a mere contiguity

between the CS and UCS, but rather an expectancy that the UCS will follow the CS.

30. From the cognitive perspective, operant behavior is also viewed as being guided by expectations of probable outcomes.
31. The role of observation and imitation in learning is explained in social learning theory. In some circumstances, learning by observation, or modeling, may be even more effective than operant conditioning in shaping our behavior.
32. The Cognitive Learning Theory is the work of several 20th and 21st century psychologists who see a learner as an active agent in the learning process and who see learning as acquisition of new information based on its meaningfulness, relatedness to prior knowledge, its context, relevance and usefulness to the learner.

TERMS AND CONCEPTS

learning
latent learning
associative learning
classical conditioning
operant conditioning
social learning theory
observational learning
unconditioned stimulus (UCS)
unconditioned response (UCR)
conditioned stimulus (CS)
conditioned response (CR)
acquisition
conditioned taste aversion
extinction
spontaneous recovery
generalization
discrimination
cumulative record
discriminative stimulus
reinforcement
positive reinforcement
negative reinforcement
escape conditioning
avoidance conditioning
primary reinforcer
conditioned reinforcement
continuous reinforcement schedule
partial reinforcement schedule
partial reinforcement effect
fixed ratio (FR) schedule
variable ratio (VR) schedule
fixed interval (FI) schedule
variable interval (VI) schedule
shaping
modeling
punishment
two-factor theory of learning

CHAPTER 7

Memory

Getty

The female digger wasp begins each day with an inspection tour of up to *15 separate nesting sites* where her larvae are kept in underground burrows. After this initial inspection tour the female wasp begins hunting for caterpillars to replenish her nests. Quite remarkably she returns to each burrow in turn with just enough food to replenish each nest. The female digger wasp not only remembers the condition of each nest as it was during her morning checkout visit, she must also remember where each burrow is located with respect to various landmarks. Her memory of nest condition and location serves to guide her behavior on return visits later in the day (Tinbergen, 1958). Compare the digger wasps ability to remember with the capacity of human short term memory about which you will learn a little later in this chapter. If a person who replenishes vending machines had to mentally note down the status of fifteen machines in fifteen different buildings on a campus, and then had to get those materials and return to each vending machine to replace the consumed items, do you think he would get it right if he did not use a smart phone or a notebook to make entries?

All but the most primitive responses require memory. Your very consciousness, perceiving, thinking, and feeling, all depend on your ability to store and use information about your past each day. In lower animals, like the digger wasp, primitive memories can lead to extremely complex patterns of intelligent behavior that would not be possible otherwise.

Psychologists have studied memory for years, but in many ways it is still a mystery. What changes take place in our brains that allow us to store memories, sometimes for a lifetime? By what process do we retrieve these memories from a brain cluttered with information? We explore such questions in this chapter.

Although we do not have all the answers, we will see that there is much that we do understand about what we remember, how we remember, why we forget—and even what we can do to improve memory. We begin with the definition of memory.

WHAT IS MEMORY?

Information Processing and Memory

Will you accurately remember what you have just read? The chances are very good that you will remember something of what you have read! The accuracy of your recall will depend on three separate processes (Crick, 1989; Murdock, 1974). First, you *encode* or translate incoming information into a neural code that your brain can process. Second, the encoded information becomes *stored* so that it can be retained over time. Finally, you must be able to *find and recover this stored information* when you need it later on, through the process of retrieval. These three processes together form your memory.

Memory is an internal process without which learning is impossible. It is also the storehouse of all your life-experiences. From the perspective of cognitive psychology the brain is a biological computer that processes information. The neural circuitry of the brain is the hardware, and psychological phenomena are the software, and *a life experience is "information."* Within the framework of this information processing perspective, *memory is defined as the process that involves encoding, storage, and retrieval of information.*

Encoding

In memory, the process of perceiving information, then categorizing or organizing it in a meaningful way so that it can be more easily stored and recalled.

Storage

Process by which encoded material is retained over time in memory.

Retrieval

Process by which information stored in memory is accessed.

ENCODING: **Encoding** involves categorizing or organizing information in some meaningful way. We encode information acoustically (in terms of sound), visually (as a mental image), and in terms of its meaning. When we encode material, it becomes associated or linked to what we already know.

STORAGE: **Storage** is the process by which encoded material is retained over time in memory. Exactly how memories are stored is the topic of some of the most important current research in psychology. We know that memories do not just float around in our brains waiting to be retrieved: Some changes must take place in the brain to allow memories to be stored for later use. We investigate this topic in some detail later in the chapter.

RETRIEVAL The final step in the process of remembering is **retrieval**. If you properly encoded and stored the information about the digger wasp and her incredible memory in the earlier example, you will be able to retrieve this information from memory at a later time. Generally speaking, the more effort we put into preparing information for storage, the more efficiently we can retrieve it.

A MODEL OF MEMORY

Historically, ***Hermann Von Ebbinghaus*** (1850–1909), a psychologist who was contemporary to Wilhelm Wundt, had *conducted experiments in which he memorized lists of words and tested his own recall of them.* He plotted graphs of his performance which yielded what was called *the learning curve.* Based on the learning curve, Ebbinghaus had postulated that we have two stores of memory, one, which holds memory for a short while as the process of storage is taking place, known as *short term memory* (STM), and the other, known as *long term memory* (LTM), which holds the information almost for ever once the processing is complete.

Today most psychologists believe that there are *three* distinct memory systems that allow us to process, store, and recall information. We first introduce these three systems and then go into much more detail describing research that supports each system's role in memory.

Sensory memory

First system in the three-system model of memory, in which brief impressions from any of the senses are stored fleetingly, disappearing within a few seconds if they are not transferred to short-term memory.

Iconic memory

Visual sensory memory, including fleeting impressions of what we see. Also known as visual memory.

Echoic memory

Auditory sensory memory; fleeting impressions of what we hear. Also known as auditory memory.

Short-term memory (STM) a.k.a. Working Memory

Immediate recollection of stimuli that have just been perceived; unless it is transferred to long-term memory, information in this memory system is usually retained only momentarily. Also called working memory.

Long-term memory (LTM)

The third memory system in the three-system model of memory. Information transferred from short-term to long-term memory may be stored for periods of time from minutes to years.

Three Memory Systems

MOVEMENT OF INFORMATION TO STM Research suggests that information that first comes to us through our senses is stored for a fleeting moment within **sensory memory**. Because of the highly transitory nature of this memory system, we usually are not consciously aware of sensory memory, nor do we actively organize or encode this information. The function of this memory system seems to be to hold or preserve impressions of sensory stimuli just long enough for important aspects of this information to be transferred to the next system, or short-term memory.

There is a fleeting store for every type of sensation we experience but we do not have special names for those stores other than for the visual and auditory sensory stores. Visual sensory memory is known as ***iconic*** memory, and *auditory sensory memory* is known as ***echoic*** memory. Research indicates that auditory sensory memory or echoic memory for language stimuli can last up to two seconds. This is considerably longer than the estimated 0.3-second capacity of iconic memory. This difference makes sense, however, when we consider the nature of the sensory messages received by our eyes and ears. When we look around us, we can almost always look back if we fail to process something important through our iconic memories. In contrast, if we miss something in an auditory message, we cannot listen back. Therefore, there seems to be a good functional reason why auditory sensations should last longer than visual sensations.

WORKING MEMORY/SHORT-TERM MEMORY **Short-term memory (STM)** comprises our immediate recollection of stimuli that we have just perceived. The amount of information this memory system can store is much more limited than that of sensory memory. Unless we repeatedly reinstate the information transferred to short-term memory, it will probably be retained only momentarily, perhaps for no more than about 20 seconds. If repeated, ore rehearsed, it can be held much longer in this short term store.

LONG-TERM MEMORY Information that is transferred from short-term memory into **long-term memory (LTM)** may remain for minutes, hours, days, or perhaps even a lifetime. When we retrieve information from long-term memory, it passes through short-term memory. Figure 7.1 presents a theoretical model of how information flows into and among these three memory systems. Although we have these three systems, most of us mean long-term memory when we talk about memory.

Want to Experience Sensory Memory? Try this!
To experience sensory memory for touch, cross your middle finger over your index finger, and briefly touch both fingers with a pencil, at the point where they cross. Pay attention to the fingers, as you quickly remove the pencil. You will find that you can feel the lingering sensation of touch for a fleeting second, *after* the pencil has been removed. The reason as to why you might perceive this sensory memory in this exercise, but might not in every day touch, is because it is unusual for you to experience touch simultaneously on the two sides you touched when the fingers were crossed, and of course, you were paying attention.

Any time we can recall information, no matter how recently it passed through our sensory/perceptual systems, we are tapping memory. Let us look more closely at how these three memory systems work.

Movement of Information to STM

Incoming sensory information, if paid attention to, moves into short-term memory, regardless of which sense modality it came over. Sensory information that is not attended to does not move to short-term memory and is lost for ever, at least according to cognitive psychologists.

Working Memory

Short-term memory, also called working memory, is an intermediate memory process sandwiched between sensory memory and long-term memory. *STM is often referred to as our*

Want to See If Your Friend's STM Lasts Longer? Try This:
Take a few 3x5 index cards. Write any three random letters (e.g., AXY) on the first line and write them large enough for someone four feet away to be able to see them clearly. On the last line of the index card, write a random number made of three digits, e.g., 379. Ask a friend to sit in front of you, and instruct him/her, to read the letters softly to himself/herself, then to immediately read the number out loud and start counting backward in threes from that number, out loud. Show the index card, as soon as you friend reads off the number, hide the card, and let him/her do the counting.

Stop your friend after he/she has counted down for about 15 seconds, and ask him/her as to what the letters were. Repeat with another similar card, with different random letters and a different number. Ask you friend what the letters were after he/she has counted for about 22 seconds. See if he/she can recall them. Chances are, that while they could report what the letters were the first time, they could not do so the second time. Both the times, your friend would have been unable to mentally rehearse the letters, because they were busy counting out aloud. However, the first time, 15 seconds was within the time interval in which STM can retain information, so your friend was able to recall the random letters, where as the second time, the interval was too long, and STM was unable to hold the information.

This task which allows you to determine how long STM can hold information without rehearsal is known as ***The Brown and Peterson task***, after the researchers who developed it (Bherer et al., 2001).

FIGURE 7.1 A Theoretical Model of Memory

SOURCE: Adapted figure of "A Theoretical Model of Human Memory System" from article "The Control of Short-Term" from *Scientific American*, Volume 225, August 1971, p. 82 by C. R. Akinson and R. M. Shiffrin. Copyright © 1971 by Scientific American, Inc. All rights reserved.

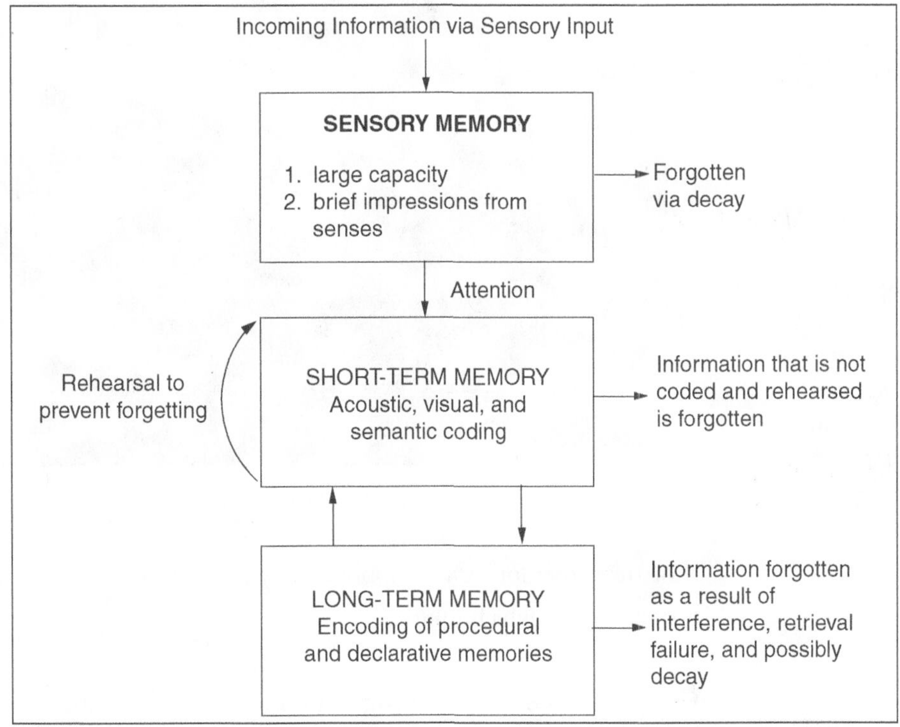

working memory because it is the memory system within which we actively process information, both as we transfer it from sensory memory and as we retrieve it from long-term storage.

As its name suggests, short-term memory has a short duration. If you look up a term in this book's index and see that it is used on pages 342 and 563, you will probably find that after searching page 342, you must check again for the second page reference. Unless we make an active effort to remember information, it fades from STM in about 20 seconds or less. However, we can retain information in our working memories for as long as we wish by active rehearsal—for example, by repeating the index references over and over.

Short-term memory has a limited capacity. You can test your STM capacity by reading the following list of numbers once, covering them, and writing down as many as you can in the order in which they appear.

9 2 5 7 6 1 3 7 8 4 5 6

If your short-term memory is like most people, you probably recalled about seven of these numbers. ***The capacity of STM is about seven items or chunks of unrelated information*** if the information has been encoded on the basis of how it sounds *(acoustic coding),* and about three or four chunks when items are encoded based on what they look like (visual coding) or what they mean (Gobet, F. & Clarkson, G.2004). Note that this STM capacity does not necessarily refer to seven numbers or letters. It refers to seven pieces of information that can be letters, words, or even meaningful sentences. The term chunk describes a meaningful unit of

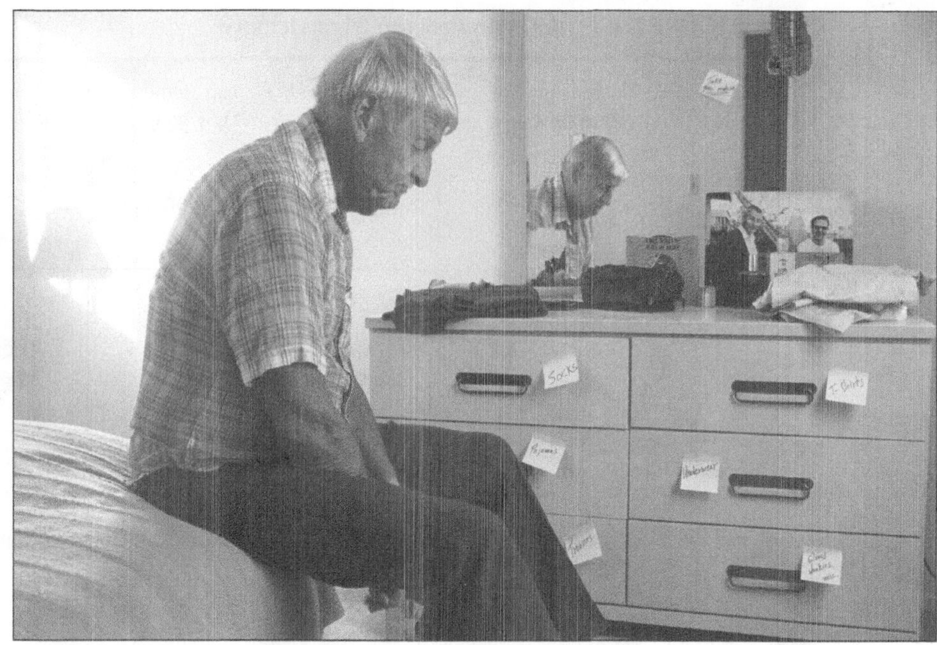

Getty

Male Alzheimer's patient resting on his bed. Due to his loss of short-term memory, he relies on post-it reminders on his dresser drawers to remind him how his clothes are organized.

short-term memory. One important way that we can increase the limited capacity of our STM systems is through chunking.

Chunking

Process of grouping items into longer meaningful units to make them easier to remember.

CHUNKING: **Chunking** is a mnemonic technique in which the items to be recalled are rearranged into longer, meaningful words or units, to make them easier to remember. For example, the sequence 1, 9, 4, 1 consists of four numbers that could be treated as four chunks. This would leave room for about three more chunks in STM. However, we could combine these four digits into one meaningful chunk 1941, a familiar calendar year. This method would leave space for at least five or six more chunks of information in STM.

You were probably unable to recall all 12 of the numbers in the previous short-term memory test. However, you might find it relatively easy to recall all 12 numbers by grouping or chunking them into four groups, a process that yields four individual numbers (925, 761, 378, & 456). Many of us routinely chunk telephone numbers by grouping the first three digits together, and then treating the final four as separate chunks, thereby reducing the original seven numbers into five chunks. We may further improve our retention of the last four digits by chunking them by twos for example, remembering 39 and 15 instead of 3-9-1-5.

We can also organize or chunk information held in STM according to its personal meaning, or we can match it with codes already stored in long-term memory. For instance, try reading once through the following list of letters and then recalling as many as possible from memory.

C P A N O W M A D D N B A

If you tried to recall these items as 13 separate letters, you probably remembered no more than seven. However, if you coded them into four well-known chunks (CPA, NOW, MADD, and NBA) you would have no trouble recalling them in proper sequence.

Long-Term Memory

The third memory system, long-term memory, is like a limitless storehouse that never quite fills up with the facts, feelings, images, skills, and attitudes that we keep accumulating. *Long-term memory allows us to do more than simply store information from past experiences. Faced with new problems and situations, information in LTM is made available to our working (short-term) memory thereby allowing us to deal with and process new information.* We may "live" in our short-term memory, but it is our long-term memory that allows us to understand and use the constant flow of new information we experience.

For example, suppose you are walking down the street and see a person lying prone next to a downed power line. In an instant, you would search your LTM to determine the significance of the scene. You have heard enough about the effects of high-voltage shock to guess that the person may be in cardiac arrest. Suppose this conjecture is confirmed by a pulse check. What next? If the person is lucky, your LTM also contains knowledge of cardiopulmonary resuscitation (CPR). You transfer this information into short-term memory and administer CPR. Then you search long-term memory for information you can use to keep the victim from going into post-trauma shock. This new information would displace the CPR information in short-term memory, which you no longer need. It is this constant, ongoing interaction between short- and long-term memory that allows us to reason, solve problems, follow schedules, see relationships between events, ride a bike, and so forth.

TYPES OF LONG-TERM MEMORY The abilities just mentioned are diverse, including not only what we can do but also what we know. Most psychologists categorize long-term memories along these lines, as either procedural or declarative memories.

Procedural memory

Recall for how to perform skills such as bicycle riding or swimming.

Procedural Memory **Procedural memories** are memories for how to perform skills. These memories can be highly complex. Suppose you enter a local golf competition. Before teeing off, a friend provides you with some specific information about course conditions. As you play your round, you draw upon a storehouse of knowledge about how to adjust your strokes to accommodate all these factors: the proper follow-through on a sand shot, how much muscle to put behind a stroke on wet turf, how to adjust for wind at the third hole, and so forth. All of these actions are specific skills acquired through practice and reinforcement, and they constitute procedural memory. Practice makes perfect because of procedural memory!

Declarative Memory Not all memory, of course, is based on recalling how to execute specific skills or procedures. For instance, your memory of what you have learned so far in

Declarative memory

Consists of episodic and semantic memories.

your psychology class is based primarily on lecture notes and your readings in this book. Recall of specific facts such as these is made possible by **declarative memory**.

Procedural memories are often hard to acquire. It may have taken months to perfect your golf swing. *Once established, however, these skill memories can be remarkably persistent.* Facts stored in declarative memory are often established more quickly, but they are much more susceptible to forgetting.

Another difference between procedural and declarative memory seems to be the location of their storage areas in the brain. One especially interesting source of information comes from an unfortunate accident in which *a fencing foil (narrow sword) was thrust through a young man's nostril into the left side of his* ***thalamus****. Since his injury, this person, known in the literature as* ***N.A.****, appears to be unable to store virtually any* ***new declarative knowledge*** *in LTM.* It is impossible for him to read a textbook and remember information on a previous page that the author might refer back to. Even watching TV or carrying on a conversation is hopelessly confusing, since words and plots don't appear to be registered in LTM. Interestingly, however, *N.A. is still able to store procedural knowledge. He can learn how to do things like ride a horse, swing a golf club, or swim.* These observations, as well as observations from many other patients with slight brain damage, seem to suggest that *factual knowledge and skill knowledge are stored in different parts of the brain.*

Procedural and declarative memories also seem to develop at different rates. Infants from a variety of species, including humans, develop the ability to remember skills well before they are able to remember facts. For example, in one study three-month-old monkeys were just as proficient in a skill task as mature adult monkeys. In contrast, tasks requiring memory for facts could not be totally mastered until the monkeys were two years old (Mishkin, 1982).

Episodic memory

Autobiographical memories about one's own experiences.

Semantic memory

General, non-personal knowledge about the meaning of facts and concepts.

Many psychologists divide *declarative memory into two distinct categories, episodic memory and semantic memory—a categorization that was proposed by Endel Tulving (1972, 1983).* **Episodic memory** contains ***autobiographical facts*** about a person's experiences stored in roughly chronological order. This type of memory includs your memories of your first kiss, the day you graduated from high school, what you had for breakfast this morning, and the sequence in which you consumed these food items. **Semantic memory** contains ***general, non-personal knowledge about the meaning*** of facts and concepts without reference to specific experiences. Knowledge about the principles of grammar, mathematical formulas, different kinds of food, and the distinction between afferent and efferent neurons are all examples of facts believed to be stored.

Dual-code model of memory

Theory that memories may be stored either in sensory codes or in verbal codes.

Semantic Memory Semantic memory is equivalent to an encyclopedic collection of facts about our world. In what form is this information stored in long-term memory? One widely discussed theory, the **dual-code model of memory** (Paivio, 1971; Paivio & Lambert, 1981), argues that memories may be stored either in *sensory codes* (for example, as visual images or sounds) or *verbal codes* (as words).

Some people appear to be able to use visual codes so efficiently that they can retain a vivid image of large amounts of visual material for several minutes. Research subjects with this ability claim they can close their eyes and see an entire picture or printed page from a book as if they were looking directly at it rather than scanning their memory. *This type of unusually long iconic memory is known as eidetic imagery.* It is a very rare talent that appears to be more common among children than adults. This difference may reflect the fact that children's memories are less cluttered with extraneous facts, thus allowing for clearer, less encumbered images.

Which type of coding, verbal or sensory, is most common? Do we even use two codes to store declarative memories? These questions have been the subject of much debate in psychology. To complicate matters further, it appears that we store some memories in the form of abstract codes that are neither strictly verbal nor sensory. For example, if you describe a movie you have just seen to a friend, you will not repeat word for word what you heard the actors say. Instead, you will have abstracted your impressions of the movie into a commentary that is your own creation, and it will often include your views on the cinematography, the acting, the plot, and the mood.

MNEMONIC TECHNIQUES Many memory experts draw an analogy between long-term memory and a set of file cabinets or the card catalog in a library. Encoding information for storage is like numbering books or files and using index cards to provide cues or access codes. The better we organize our file systems, the more quickly we can access information and the longer we can remember it. Therefore, a key to efficient long-term memory is in the organization of material. A number of ***memory aids*** or **mnemonic techniques** can help us to do this (Bower, 1970; Nield, 1987). The appropriateness or effectiveness of the various mnemonic devices outlined here varies from task to task. You may want to experiment with more than one approach for a given memory task.

Mnemonic technique

Memory system, such as clustering or acrostics, that organizes material in a meaningful way to make it easier to remember.

Clustering

Mnemonic device involving grouping items into categories.

Clustering: **Clustering** is a mnemonic technique in which items that are similar in some way or are used together, etc. are grouped together to facilitate recall. For example, suppose you want to memorize the following shopping list:

toilet paper	green beans	matches
hamburger	bacon	milk
asparagus	chicken	sour cream
corn	broom	cheese

These 12 items, if treated separately, include about five too many chunks for your short-term memory. Thus, you can probably forget trying to hold them in STM by repeatedly rehearsing the list all the way to the grocery store. If you treat the items as separate, without trying to organize the list in some meaningful way, your LTM recall is also likely to prove inadequate for the task. A far easier method is to *cluster or group the items under four subcategories:* dairy items, meat, vegetables, and household products. Remembering four categories, each with three items, is a much more manageable task.

Method of Loci The method of loci, developed by the early Greeks, involves forming pictorial associations between items you wish to recall and specific locations along a designated route you might travel (*loci* means locations or places in Latin).

The first step is to develop a route you are familiar with. Imagine, for example that you are walking from the campus library to your apartment. Pick out specific locations along the way that are easy to remember, such as a bus stop bench, a flagpole, a large oak tree, a broken-down van parked on the street, the sidewalk leading to your apartment house, and so forth. Then create a series of images that associates each item on your list with a specific location along your route.

For example, to use the loci method to remember the grocery list in the clustering discussion, you might imagine toilet paper strewn on the bus stop bench, cornstalks leaning against the flagpole, a chicken sitting in the oak tree, and so forth. Picture these associations as vividly as possible. Later, when you need to remember the list, take a mental walk along your route.

The Peg-Word System The peg-word or peg-board memory system involves first learning a series of words that correspond to a sequence of numbers to be used as a mental peg-board (Miller et al., 1960). Each word and corresponding number represents a peg in the system. The following 10 rhyming pairs is a popular example of this approach:

One is a bun	Six is sticks
Two is a shoe	Seven is heaven
Three is a tree	Eight is a gate
Four is a door	Nine is wine
Five is a hive	Ten is a hen

Once you have memorized these associations, you can use them to recall a list of 1 to 10 items. Create a series of visual images that allows you to hang the item you wish to remember on the appropriate peg. For instance, to remember the following list of building supplies—nails, masking tape, saw, electric sander, electric drill, wire, hammer, tape measure, pliers, and vise grips—you would imagine each item on your list interacting with one peg-word. Thus, you might imagine a hamburger bun stuffed with nails, two shoes taped together with masking tape, a large saw embedded in your mother's favorite fruit tree, and so forth.

Acrostics

Sentences whose first letters serve as cues for recalling specific information.

Acrostics: **Acrostics** are sentences in which the first letter of each word serves as a cue for recalling specific information. For example, the sentence, "Morphine Effects Aren't Solely Antitussive," a sentence one of the authors learned in a college biochemistry class decades ago, allows the author, Ragade, to recall several of morphine's effects, as follows: M stands for miosis (constriction of the pupils), E stands for euphoria, A for analgesia (removal of pain), S for sedation, and of course the last word, antitussive, stands for cough suppression. Likewise, if you took piano lessons at some point in your life it is a good bet that you used another acrostic, the sentence "Every Good Boy Does Fine" to help you memorize the notes on the lines of the treble staff.

Acronym

Meaningful arrangement of letters that provides a cue for recalling information; a mnemonic device.

Acronyms Still another memory system is the use of **acronyms**, or meaningful arrangements of letters that provide cues for the recall of material. For example, many people have learned the colors in a rainbow in their order of appearance by remembering Roy G. Biv (red, orange, yellow green, blue, indigo, and violet). Or the acronym HOMES for all the North American Great Lakes (Huron, Ontario, Michigan, Eerie, and Superior).

RETRIEVAL FROM LONG-TERM MEMORY The reason the mnemonic techniques just described work so well is that they provide cues or handles that help us access information. The more retrieval cues we can link to information, the more likely we are to recall it later on.

Retrieval Cues This phenomenon was demonstrated in an experiment conducted by Fergus Craik and Endel Tulving (1975). In the first phase of the study, subjects were given index cards containing single sentences with a word missing. After reading the sentence, they viewed a word flashed on a screen and pressed either a yes or no button to indicate whether or not the word fit the sentence. The sentence complexity varied from simple (She cooked the ____________.) to complex (The great bird swooped down and carried off the struggling ______________.).

Subjects saw a given word once. In some instances the word did not fit the sentence. In other cases it fit into a simple, medium, or complex sentence. For example, the word chicken would fit both of the sample sentences; house could fit neither. Subjects were told that the experiment was concerned with perceptions and speed of reaction time, so they made no special effort to store the words in their long-term memory.

After completing this phase of the experiment, subjects had a short rest period. They were then given the cards containing the sentences and asked to recall the word associated with each sentence.

Based on your understanding of memory processes described thus far, what kind of performance would you expect the subjects to exhibit on these retention tests? Would you predict that their ability to recall words was influenced by whether or not they matched with a sentence? Do you think that sentence complexity influenced recall, and if so, in what direction and why? Take a moment to formulate your answer before reading on.

Figure 7.2 demonstrates the results of this experiment. Subjects were much more likely to recall words that fit a sentence than words that did not. They were also considerably more likely to remember a word if it fit a complex sentence than if it fit a simple sentence.

It seems, then, that we remember things better if they are associated with specific cues. For example, we are more likely to remember the item "watch" if we can associate it with a visual cue, as suggested by the sentence, "He dropped the watch." We are even more likely to remember the item when it is used in a more complex sentence such as, "The old man hobbled across the room and picked up the valuable watch from the mahogany table." This complex sentence provides considerably more visual cues that can aid our retention.

FIGURE 7.2 Results of the Craik and Tulving Experiment

Subjects were more likely to recall words that fit into sentences than those that didn't. They were also more likely to recall words that fit complex sentences than those that fit simple ones.

SOURCE: Adapted figure of "Results of the Craik and Tulving Experiment" from *The Journal of Experimental Psychology*, 104, © 1975, pp. 268–294 by F. I. M. Creak and E. Tooling. Reprinted by permission of the authors.

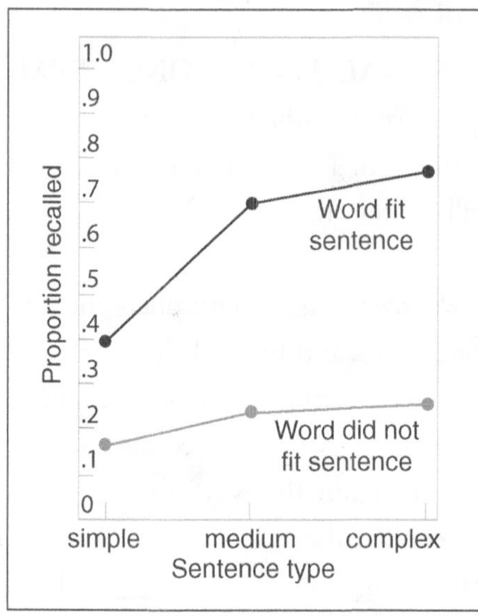

TESTING LONG-TERM MEMORY A number of methods have been used to measure our ability to store new material in long-term memory. The three most common techniques are recall tasks, recognition tasks, and relearning.

Recall

In memory tests, a subject's ability to reproduce information that he or she was previously exposed to. Fill-in-the-blank and essay questions test recall.

Recognition

In memory tests, a subject's ability to recognize whether he or she has been previously exposed to information. Multiple-choice and true-false questions test recognition.

Recall In a **recall** task, the subject is asked to reproduce information to which he or she was previously exposed. For example, a recall question designed to test your knowledge of the material in this chapter might ask you to name the three stores of memory. Fill-in-the-blank or essay questions are other examples of recall tasks.

Recognition A **recognition** task presents possible answers from which the subject must pick the correct one. Instead of having to pull information from memory, a recognition test simply involves realizing whether you have been previously exposed to a particular bit of information. For example, the familiar multiple-choice test used in classrooms is a recognition test rather than a test of recall.

Given the choice, most students prefer recognition tasks such as multiple-choice tests over recall tasks. This preference is not without justification, for research demonstrates that we can usually recognize much more than we can recall.

Explicit and Implicit Memory

Up to this point we have been discussing memories that are readily available to your consciousness. That is, through conscious effort you can recall a phone number, an answer to

Explicit memory

Memories that you can recall through conscious effort.

Implicit memories

Memories that are unavailable to conscious awareness, but contribute to explicit memories.

an exam question, or what you did on vacation last summer. These memories are referred to as **explicit memories** and they play an important role in your construction of a meaningful past. However, by themselves, these explicit memories are not enough. Memories of your past that are unavailable to conscious awareness also contribute to this construction. You experience these unconscious or **implicit memories**, when you have sense of familiarity with objects or places. For instance, when you encounter an old acquaintance you may at first sense that she is familiar and only later remember her name and the specific occasion when you met. *In this case the implicit memory served as a primer for the explicit memories of name and context.* Implicit memories provide us with a sense of knowing and familiarity that are essential to everyday functioning.

How do psychologists investigate memories that are unconscious? Harvard psychologist Daniel Schacter demonstrated that implicit memories could be studied using word completion tasks (Tulving & Schacter, 1990; Schacter, 1995; Schacter et al., 2007). In one such study, subjects are first shown a list of words and then later they are asked to complete a series of word fragments. Subjects do much better completing word fragments of words that were previously shown even though they cannot remember those words before the completion task. An example of a word completion task is shown in Figure 7.3. This research, and other research testing memory for nonverbal items, suggests that explicit and implicit memories are in fact distinct. More recent research using PET imaging to measure neural activity during explicit and implicit memory tasks has shown that these different memory systems rely on different neural structures (Uecker et al., 1997).

MEMORY AS A DYNAMIC PROCESS

We have seen that our ability to remember an event can be influenced by how that event was encoded or associated with earlier memories. What happens to those memories once stored? In this section we will see that memory is a dynamic process where our memories of events can change over time. For example, you may remember many details about the moment when you first saw the twin towers explosion, but a good friend who was in the same room with you may have a different memory. Indeed, our memories often vary significantly from the actual facts. Why does this occur?

Constructive Memory

Psychologists believe that memory is a dynamic process, not merely the collection of facts that remain unaltered by further experiences. For instance, we frequently add or delete details to make new information more consistent with the way we already conceive our world. Thus, remembering is often a process of reconstructing an event rather than simply searching long-term memory for a perfect copy of it. As a result, our memories are not necessarily accurate representations of what actually occurred. Instead, they may be accounts of what we think happened, or perhaps what we believe should have happened.

FIGURE 7.3 Word Completion Task

A typical word completion task to demonstrate implicit memory. Subjects are first shown a list of words and then, after a delay, asked to complete word fragments. Subjects are better at completing the words that were previously shown to them even though they cannot remember seeing them.

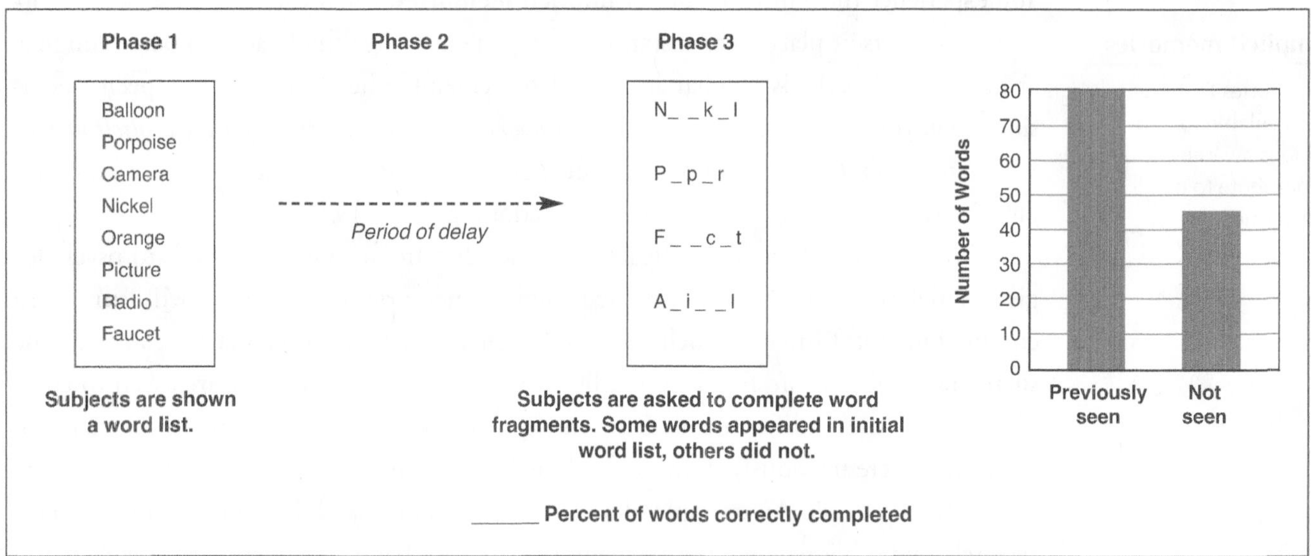

Serious investigations of constructive processes in memory did not catch on in psychology until the last couple of decades. However, this research was pioneered over 70 years ago by an English psychologist, Sir Frederick Bartlett (1932), who tested college students' memories of simple stories set in unfamiliar cultures.

Bartlett found that his subjects never recalled the material exactly as it had been presented. Rather, they stored a few primary facts and organized the rest of the story around these central themes. Bartlett's subjects tended to modify their memories of the original stories in several ways: by shortening and simplifying the story; by focusing on and overemphasizing certain details; and by altering certain details to make the story fit their own views more closely.

False Memories

In the previous section we saw how memories can change over time. Our biases, expectations, and even new learning can all contribute to reconstructions of our memories of the past. *But, can memories of events that never occurred to us be planted and appear as real?* Interest in these planted, or **false memories**, began to rise as reports from clinical settings suggested that *under hypnosis, or the direction of a therapist, adult patients claimed to recall instances of past child abuse.* Were these reports accurate recollections of actual child abuse or were they false memories unintentionally planted by the therapist?

False memory

A memory of an event that never occurred.

In an attempt to demonstrate the ease of planting false memories, psychologist *Elizabeth Loftus* designed the now famous ***Lost in the Mall*** experiment (Loftus, 1993, 1997). Her work has led to significant changes in the ways patients are interviewed about their past. In one version of her experiment, with the assistance of a willing family member playing "Remember when ______," subjects were asked if they remembered being lost in a shopping mall as a young child. False details about the incident were mixed in with actual events that occurred during this time in the subject's past. Several days later, subjects reported elaborate memories of the incident that never occurred. These false memories contained details of clothing worn, feelings of fear, and descriptions of people who assisted the subject in being reunited with family.

You might be thinking that false memories such as this are only the products of gullible people with vivid imaginations. Recent research suggests otherwise. For example, Roediger and his colleagues have shown that memories for previously seen words or scenes can be planted in college students during a memory recall test. In these experiments subjects were shown a list of words or pictures of familiar scenes and later asked to recall as many items as possible in collaboration with another subject. Unknown to the subject, the collaborator was really a confederate of the experimenter who deliberately recalled items that were not previously seen. Subjects typically report with confidence that the planted items were seen earlier (Roediger et al., 2001, Meade et al., 2002). It is easy to see from these experiments how false memories could be passed from person to person.

Schemas

Schemas

In reference to memory, conceptual frameworks that individuals use to make sense out of stored information. In Piaget's theory, the mental structures we form to assimilate and organize processed information.

The tendency to change details to fit our own cultural perspectives is consistent with recent findings on the impact of schemas on reconstructive memory processes. ***Schemas*** *are conceptual frameworks we use to make sense out of our world.* Because schemas provide us with preconceived expectations, they help make the world seem more predictable. However, they can also lead to significant distortions in our memory processes in that they often exert a strong impact on the manner in which memory for a particular event is encoded. Many memory distortions are consistent with our established schemas.

This idea was demonstrated in a classic study conducted over 40 years ago, in which subjects were shown a picture of two men engaged in an argument. One man was black and the other was white; the white man held a razor in his hand. After briefly viewing the picture, subjects were asked to describe the scene to someone who had not viewed the picture, who in turn passed the information on to someone else, and so on. As the information was passed from person to person, some of its features were altered. Most notably, the razor ended up in the hand of the black man (Allport & Postman, 1947). These findings suggest that the subjects' schemas (that is, their assumption that blacks were more prone to violence than whites) influenced the way they constructed and stored this information.

Some more recent studies have demonstrated another interesting point: When people remember information that is not consistent with their schemas, they are likely to distort the facts to make them fit better with their conceptual frameworks. For instance, in one study (Spiro, 1976) subjects read one of two different versions of a story about an engaged couple. In both versions, the male partner did not want to have

Get Outta Here!
How Ms. Cool Received a Cool 2.4 Million!

Dr. Elizabeth Loftus narrates the real life stories of Nadean Cool and others who sued their psychiatrists for planting false memories of child-hood sexual abuse, and won their court-cases!

Dr. Loftus also describes her own experimental work and findings regarding the creation of false memories. If you are interested in this topic please read this wonderful article that appeared in the September 1997 issue of *Scientific American,* in its entirety at the following web-site.

http://faculty.washington.edu/eloftus/Articles/sciam.htm

children. The difference between the stories was that in one version the woman did not want children either, whereas in the other version she was upset because she wanted children. Subjects were asked to read the story; when they were finished they performed some tasks involving paperwork. Then a postscript was added to the story: Some of the subjects were told that the couple married and lived together happily; others were told that they broke up and never saw each other again. Subjects were then asked to recall the story at a later date.

Can you predict the outcome of this experiment? Do you think that the relationship between the story version and the postscript influenced the way subjects remembered the story later on? Apply what you have learned about schemas and constructive memory processes to formulate a prediction before reading on.

If you predicted that subjects modified the story to fit their own views about men's and women's roles in the family, you were right. Subjects who heard a post scripted ending that did not seem to fit the rest of the story tended to "remember" information that resolved that contradiction. For example, those who read a version in which the couple disagreed about having children did not expect the couple to live together happily. When they remembered the story, they were likely to recall other facts that would make the ending fit the story, such as a compromise in which the couple had agreed to adopt a child instead of having one of their own.

Similarly, subjects who were told that the couple who agreed not to have children had broken up were likely to "remember" that this pair had other difficulties, such as parents who opposed the relationship. In contrast, subjects who read stories that matched the post-scripted endings did not add new facts to the story. They had no reason to, for the stories were consistent with their schemas.

Although schemas can lead to memory distortions, they also provide important association cues that can aid recall. Consider an experiment in which subjects were asked to study a list of behaviors of a hypothetical person. Some participants were told that they were subjects in a memory experiment and that they should attempt to remember as many of the behaviors as possible; others were told they were in an experiment designed to evaluate how people form impressions of others, and they were asked to try to form an impression (a schema) of the person. A later recall test revealed that subjects who attempted to fit the information into a schema demonstrated better recall than those who had merely attempted to memorize a list of behaviors (Hamilton et al., 1980).

We have seen that our memories may sometimes involve fiction as well as facts, a result of our tendency to fill gaps in our knowledge of previous events or to modify memories to match existing schemas. Such active constructive processes, which may occur in both the storage and retrieval stages of memory, may have a profound impact on a number of areas of human experience: for example, eyewitness testimony.

Eyewitness Testimony

The legal system places great value on the testimony of eyewitnesses. Police officers who file automobile accident reports, criminal investigators, and juries all tend to give considerable credence to the accounts of people who were on the scene. In recent years, however, several findings have raised questions about the reliability of eyewitness testimony.

Psychologist Elizabeth Loftus has been the leading investigator in this area of research. The accumulating evidence of memory as a constructive process prompted Loftus to wonder to what degree eyewitness testimony might be influenced by people's tendency to reconstruct their memory of events to fit their schemas. She also wondered whether information received after the fact might be integrated into witnesses' memories of what they had seen. Is it possible that subtle differences in the way questions are worded might cause a witness to remember the event in a different light? Can witnesses be misled into "remembering" things that did not actually occur?

A number of studies by Loftus and other researchers have investigated such questions. In one, subjects watched a film of a two-car accident and then filled out a questionnaire about what they had seen. There were four versions of the wording of one critical question. Some subjects were asked, "About how fast were the two cars going when they *contacted* each other?" In the three other versions, the words *hit, bumped,* or *smashed* were substituted for *contacted.* The word *contacted* yielded an average speed estimate of 32 mph, whereas the words *hit, bumped,* and *smashed* produced estimates of 34, 38, and 41 mph, respectively (Loftus & Palmer, 1974). The words used to describe the collision clearly influenced the way these subjects reconstructed their memories of the accident. It seems clear that the way witnesses remember an event can be influenced by the kinds of questions they are asked about the event.

After-the-fact information may do more than merely change our recollections. In some cases, it may cause people to incorporate completely false information into their memories. This idea was suggested in another study in which subjects watched a videotape of an automobile accident, and then were asked questions designed to introduce false information (Loftus, 1975). Half the subjects were asked, "How fast was the white sports car going when it passed the barn while traveling along the country road?" The remaining subjects were asked the same question, but without the words "when it passed the barn."

In point of fact, there was no barn in the videotape. When subjects were questioned again about the accident a week later, however, 17 percent of those who heard "when it passed the barn" reported seeing a barn in the videotape. In contrast, only 3 percent of the subjects who had heard nothing about a barn remembered seeing the barn.

Such findings are alarming when we consider what often happens to eyewitnesses. First a witness may be questioned repeatedly by police officers, some of whom may introduce erroneous information by asking leading questions. Friends and family members also ask questions and introduce new information. Later (probably much later), an attorney may question a witness on or off the stand. If intelligent college students can be misled into "remembering" erroneous information in controlled experiments such as those just described, how reliable are eyewitness accounts of real-world crimes and accidents?

Although such questions are valid, some researchers have disputed the findings of Loftus and her colleagues. Most notably, Maria Zaragoza and Michael McCloskey have suggested that flawed research techniques may have biased the Loftus team's findings, creating a high probability that misled subjects would exhibit poorer recall than control subjects even when the misleading information had no effect on memory for the original event (McCloskey & Zaragoza, 1985a, 1985b; Zaragoza et al., 1987). However, a study conducted by Barbara Tversky and Michael Tuchin (1989), which employed a slightly modified version of the original eyewitness research design, has corroborated the findings of Loftus and her colleagues. This study's results provided substantial support for the claim that misleading information affects memory for the original information.

Some controversy remains regarding the impact of misleading post-event information on memory. Researchers Zaragoza and McCloskey (1989) maintain that the misleading information to which eyewitnesses are often exposed may not actually impair memory for an earlier event. However, regardless of whether or not misleading post-event information actually alters memory for the original event, there is extensive evidence for a "misinformation effect"—that is, that misleading information presented after an event can lead people to erroneous reports of that misinformation (Ceci et al., 1988; Chandler, 1989; Geiselman, 1988; Gibling & Davies, 1988; Kroll & Ogawa, 1988; Register & Kihlstrom, 1988; Sheehan, 1988; Zaragoza & Koshmider, 1989).

A number of studies indicate that people exposed to violent events are especially likely to incorporate misinformation into their memory. Shocking events may interfere with our ability to store details accurately, even though we have vivid flashbulb memories of what we were doing or feeling at the time. Since an eyewitness's recall of a violent event may lack many details, he or she may be inclined to fill in the gaps with subsequent misinformation (Loftus & Burns, 1982). In contrast, others claim that in real life eyewitnesses had recalled the hair-color of the perpetrator correctly, especially in violent crimes and they suggest that caution must be exercised in generalizing laboratory findings to real life (Wagstaff, G., Macveigh, J., et.al, 2003).

It is clear from these cases that memory is a constructive process, involving much more than merely placing bits of data in storage and then retrieving them later on. In the next section we look at several additional factors that may affect the way we remember an event.

Flashbulb Memory

If you ask virtually any American who was an adolescent or older in 1963 what they were doing when they heard about John F. Kennedy's assassination, the odds are very good that they will be able to tell you an amazing number of details about where they were, what the weather was like, perhaps even what they were wearing. You may have a similar recall of what you were doing the moment you witnessed passenger jets crash into the twin towers in New York on September 11, 2001.

Flashbulb memory

An apparent vivid recall for an event associated with extreme emotion or uniqueness, such as the assassination of a president or the bombing of Iraq.

This kind of vivid recall for earlier events associated with extreme emotion, surprise, or uniqueness has been called ***flashbulb memory***. Such memories are so vivid that it is as if our brains had recorded them like a scene caught in the sudden glare of a camera's flashbulb. Our recall for such occurrences is not so precise for factual details surrounding the event itself, *but rather for the specific setting and manner in which we first heard about the event* hence the term flashbulb memory applies to the memory of the source of event information rather than the facts of the event itself and the brain areas that store the episodic information as to when you first heard the tragic information may be different from the area which stores the information on the event itself. Source information is stored in the Frontal lobe and event information in the Medial temporal lobe (Patrick, S.R. Cook, S.P. et.al, 2005) which could explain how one could remember source information better than event information. For example, you may have trouble remembering the sequence of the

A/P World Wide

Can you remember where you were when you first heard about the September 11 terrorist attacks on the World Trade Center?

two plane crashes, even though you may never forget where you were when you first witnessed the images of the explosions on the TV news broadcasts.

Are flashbulb memories more permanent than our memories for ordinary events? While it appears that flashbulb memories are more vivid and accurate than normal memories there is little evidence to support this perception. *Flashbulb memories are prone to distortion and forgetting, just like normal memories.* What appears to be different about flashbulb memories is not that they are more accurate, but that we are much more confident in their accuracy (Weaver, 1993).

FORGETTING

There is no single answer to the question "Why do we forget?" Forgetting seems to occur for many reasons. Among the explanations that psychologists have put forward to explain forgetting are the decay of the memory trace, problems with interfering material, a breakdown in the retrieval process, emotional and motivational conditions, and organic factors.

Decay of the Memory Trace

One explanation of why we forget is that the memory trace (the neurochemical and/or anatomical changes in the brain that encode memories) for some information simply deteriorates, fading away with the passage of time.

A number of psychologists believe that decay is at least partially responsible for forgetting. Some suggest that decay may cause us to lose material in short-term memory, but that any information in long-term memory is stored permanently and failure to recall it is due to a retrieval difficulty (Shiffrin & Atkinson, 1969; Tulving, 1977). Other psychologists do not agree that long-term information storage is forever. They maintain that some memories may decay over time and become lost (Loftus & Loftus, 1980). Since long-term memories must be stored through some type of physical change in the brain, it seems possible that these physical codes can sometimes break down with the passage of time.

Interference

There is evidence that forgetting is probably influenced more by what we do before or after learning than by the passage of time. According to the interference interpretation of forgetting, experiences that occur either before or after we learn something new interfere with our memory. There may be two types of interference: retroactive and proactive.

Retroactive interference

In memory, the phenomenon that occurs when a later event interferes with the recall of earlier information.

RETROACTIVE INTERFERENCE **Retroactive** (or backward) **interference** occurs when a later event interferes with recall of earlier information. Suppose, for instance, you look up a telephone number, and as you pick up the phone and prepare to dial, your roommate distracts you by asking what time it is. When you return to making the call, you discover that the number has slipped from your memory. This situation is an example of retroactive inhibition of memory.

Proactive interference

In memory, the phenomenon that occurs when earlier learning disrupts memory for later learning.

PROACTIVE INTERFERENCE In **proactive** (forward acting) **interference**, earlier learning disrupts memory for later learning. For example, if you learn a list of new vocabulary terms in your English class this afternoon, you may find that it is difficult to remember the psychology terms you review tonight. Figure 7.4 illustrates how psychologists study both types of interference effects.

THE SERIAL POSITION EFFECT Have you ever noticed that when you memorize a list of formulas, terms, or grocery items, you are more likely to remember those items at the beginning and end of the list than those in the middle? This phenomenon is called the **serial position effect**.

Serial position effect

Tendency to remember items at the beginning and end of a list more readily than those in the middle.

Why is it easier to remember items at the beginning and end of a long list? One possible explanation draws upon our knowledge of short- and long-term memory. Presumably, items at the beginning of a list move successfully into long-term memory because there is no competing information, that is, little proactive interference. As additional items move into memory, however, they may displace previously processed items because short-term memory can hold only a limited number of chunks. Items at the end of the list are remembered better than those in the middle because they have not been bumped or replaced by

FIGURE 7.4 Studying the Effects of Retroactive and Proactive Interference

When retroactive interference occurs, later learning (learning task *B*) interferes with the recall of information learned earlier (recall of task *A*). In proactive interference, earlier information (learning task *A*) disrupts memory for later learning (task *B*). If the control groups outperform the experimental groups in Step 3, interference has occurred.

Experimental Design for the Study of Retroactive Interference

	Step 1	Step 2	Step 3
Experimental Group	Learn A	Learn B	Test retention of A
Control Group	Learn A	Rest	Test retention of A

Experimental Design for the Study of Proactive Interference

	Step 1	Step 2	Step 3
Experimental Group	Learn A	Learn B	Test retention of B
Control Group	Rest	Learn B	Test retention of B

any additional material. In other words, retroactive interference is minimal at the end. In contrast, items in the middle of a list encounter interference from both earlier (proactive) and subsequent (retroactive) items.

The serial position effect shows up in a variety of situations. For example, when children learn the alphabet, letters in the middle are most difficult to remember. Similarly, students are more likely to miss test questions drawn from material in the middle of a lecture than information at the beginning or end.

Retrieval Failure

Suppose you are having trouble recalling the refrain of an old song you heard last week and had meant to tape. A friend drops by and comments that it is a beautiful, sunny day. Suddenly you remember the song you want to tape, "Let the Sun Shine In." It is clear that your memory for the song was intact, but it was just out of reach, waiting for the right retrieval cue.

Failure to recall information does not necessarily mean it is not there. It may simply be inaccessible because it was poorly encoded in the first place or *because we have inadequate retrieval cues.* Forgetting of long-term memories often reflects a failure of retrieval cues rather than decay or interference. Even memories that seem impossible to retrieve may pop into mind when the right cues are used. The recalled memories will not be exact replicas of the original experience but will have its essence or be essentially similar.

Motivated Forgetting

Sometimes we forget long-term memories because we do not want to remember them. Psychologists call this motivated forgetting: People often push certain kinds of memories out of conscious awareness because they are too embarrassing, frightening, painful, or degrading to recall.

Sigmund Freud's concept of repression is an example of motivated forgetting. Freud believed that we *repress* or forget certain ideas, feelings, and experiences because they are too painful to deal with on a conscious level. Repression thus lets us maintain a sense of self-esteem and avoid the anxiety that would result if this information were to surface in our awareness. There is some disagreement over the viability of Freud's concepts of repression and the unconscious mind as explanations of human behavior. However, psychologists agree that motivated forgetting does play a role in blocking at least some material stored in long-term memory. *There is experimental evidence indicating that individuals who use the "Defense Mechanism" of repression take longer to perceive threatening words as compared to neutral words, presented to them (Reisner, P. 1996). Experimental work using fMRI indicates that when recall is repressed the cortex of the anterior cingulate gyrus is activated, skin conductance increases, autonomic arousal takes place, indicating internal conflicts provoke repression. (Schmeing, J., Kehyayan, A. 2013)*

Organic Causes of Forgetting

Forgetting is not usually caused by organic pathology. However, certain physical illnesses or accidents can alter the physiology of the brain. Memory deficits caused by this condition are referred to as **organic amnesia**. There are many types of organic amnesia; in this section, we look at three main types: amnesia caused by disease, retrograde amnesia, and anterograde amnesia.

Organic amnesia
Memory deficits caused by altered physiology of the brain, which might result from an accident or certain physical illnesses.

AMNESIA CAUSED BY DISEASE OR TRAUMA Some diseases produce actual physical deterioration of brain cells, impairing memory as well as a variety of other functions. For instance, cardiovascular disease is characterized by decreased blood circulation, which sometimes limits the oxygen supply to the brain to the point that some brain cells die. Strokes are another common physical cause of memory impairment. Here, a vessel in the brain ruptures, with resulting damage to cells. Alzheimer's disease is another illness that produces progressive widespread degeneration of brain cells. This devastating disease produces severe memory deficits and other impairments of functioning.

RETROGRADE AMNESIA Sometimes a blow to the head may cause loss of memory for certain details or events that occurred *prior* to the accident. This condition is called **retrograde amnesia**. *In many of these cases, lost memories return gradually, with older memories tending to come back first.* In almost all cases investigated, memories for recent events have been shown to be more susceptible to disruption than older memories (Gold, 1987; Milner, 1989). This finding suggests that the amnesia reflects a temporary loss of access to information rather than an actual destruction of the memory trace.

Retrograde amnesia
Memory loss for certain details or events that occurred prior to experiencing brain trauma; a form of organic amnesia.

Retrograde amnesia is more likely to impair declarative memory, particularly the episodic type, than to interfere with procedural memory. For example, accident victims may not remember who they are or what they were doing prior to the accident, but they can remember old skills such as playing a musical instrument or speaking a foreign language.

ANTEROGRADE AMNESIA: Amnesia can also work in the reverse direction. Some victims of brain damage may be able to recall old memories established before the damage, but cannot remember information processed after the damage occurred. This condition is called **anterograde amnesia**. It may be caused by injury to a specific area of the brain; it may also be associated with certain surgical procedures and chronic alcoholism. Unlike retrograde amnesia, anterograde amnesia is often irreversible. The following section provides some clues about how and why injuries may be associated with memory loss.

Anterograde amnesia
Memory loss for information processed after an individual experiences brain trauma caused by injury or chronic alcoholism.

THE BIOLOGY OF MEMORY

We know that memories are not transitory events that float freely within our brains. When you learn the name of your psychology professor, your girlfriend's address, or how to play golf, some lasting changes take place within your brain. For decades, researchers have tried to understand the nature of these changes and to identify where they take place. A number of recent discoveries suggest that they are closing in on the answer.

The Hebbian Rule

Decades ago, physiological psychologist Donald Hebb (1949) suggested that short- and long-term memory have different physical bases. Short-term memory, he proposed, is maintained by the firing of a collection of neurons arranged in a specific circuit labeled a cell assembly. Our recall of a telephone number when we put down a phone book and begin to dial is thus kept alive by neurons firing in a repeated pattern that forms a briefly held memory trace. Hebb maintained that this brief electrical activity does not bring about changes in the physical structure of the brain; that is why short-term memory is transitory.

Hebb also suggested that information is transferred to LTM when physical changes take place, in the form of new connections between neurons. These changes are thought to involve structural changes in the synapses between neurons, which occur when cell assemblies are simultaneously activated.

Hebb's conception of short- and long-term memory as distinct phenomena has been supported by research. Of particular interest is mounting evidence indicating that structural changes take place in the synapses of neurons providing the formation of long-term memories. Simultaneous firings of nerve circuits appear to induce structural changes in specific neural connections. ***Hebb had stated: "neurons that fire together get wired together."*** In other words, the strength of the neural connections between two neurons strengthens if they are activated together. This prediction has become known as the **Hebbian Rule**. The mechanism underlying the Hebbian Rule is long-term potentiation (LTP).

Long-Term Potentiation

Long-term potentiation (LTP)

An increase in a neuron's sensitivity to fire following a burst of signals to that neurons dendrites.

Long-term potentiation (LTP) is defined as a change in the strength of a synapse resulting from simultaneous firing in both the presynaptic and postsynaptic neuron. Long-term potentiation has been observed in the sea slug *Aplysia* and in mammalian brain structures including the hippocampus and the cortex (Kandel et al., 1995). While considerable progress has been made in the understanding the molecular changes underlying memory, much remains to be learned.

Distributed Memory

Engram

A neural representation of something learned

Physiological psychologist Karl Lashley (1929, 1950) spent most of his research career searching for the **engram**, the place where memories are stored. His technique was to train rats in a variety of tasks, then surgically destroy selective regions of the cortex, and later test the rats' memories for the tasks. Lashley found that his rats could still perform learned tasks even after much of their cortex was removed. He never did succeed in pinpointing specific brain sites of memory. Lashley concluded that memories do not reside in precise locations in the brain, but rather involve large areas of cortical tissue (Lashley, 1950, p. 477). This conclusion has been supported by extensive evidence collected over the last several decades, suggesting that memories are represented by large networks of neurons distributed over broad portions of the brain, although some very specific memories may be stored in some specific areas of the brain.

Neural Structures for Long-Term Memory

Much of our information regarding the neural structures that are involved in the processing of memories used to come from studies of people who had experienced memory impairment through brain damage caused by stroke or injury. Modern brain imaging techniques have changed all that. Experimenters now devise experiments where they observe the brain as people do tasks which involve recall, recognition and directed forgetting. They report that the areas involved in these activities are different.

Encoding and retrieval of items to remember seems to be mediated by the entorhinal cortex, the hippocampus, the anterior medial prefrontal cortex, the left inferior parietal cortex, the posterior cingulate cortex and the precuneus. The precuneus, an area in the fissure of the Parietal lobe seems to be involved in self-regulation and is involved in active learning but not involved in implicit or passive learning. The above mentioned regions are also activated when recalling one's life experiences or retrieving one's episodic memory.

In directed forgetting tasks the **dorsomedial thalamus, the posterior intra-parietal sulcus and the anterior cingulate cortex, involved in attentional processes** are involved. One would think that the precuneus would be involved in directed forgetting because that cannot be a passive task but apparently other neural mechanisms involved in attentional processes are sufficient to conduct directed forgetting. (Bastin, C. Feyers, D., 2012).

As a person goes through life, he or she acquires many similar memories. Hence recalling relevant material from episodic memory must involve some mechanisms that inhibit or suppress other similar but non-relevant memories from surfacing. Experimental work using *f*MRI indicates that selective retrieval was associated with increased activity in the posterior temporal and parietal association cortices, in the hippocampi, and in the prefrontal cortex (Wimber, M. , Rutschmann, R.M. Et.al, 2009)

Even though we can look at the living working brain and see exactly which neuronal circuits are firing, etc. it still will be a while before reliable knowledge becomes available due to the very nature of the human mind which can and does shift attention from external to internal stimuli, both at will and at times, willy-nilly.

FIGURE 7.5 The Prefrontal Cortex

The prefrontal cortex, along with connections to other brain areas, is important for working memory.

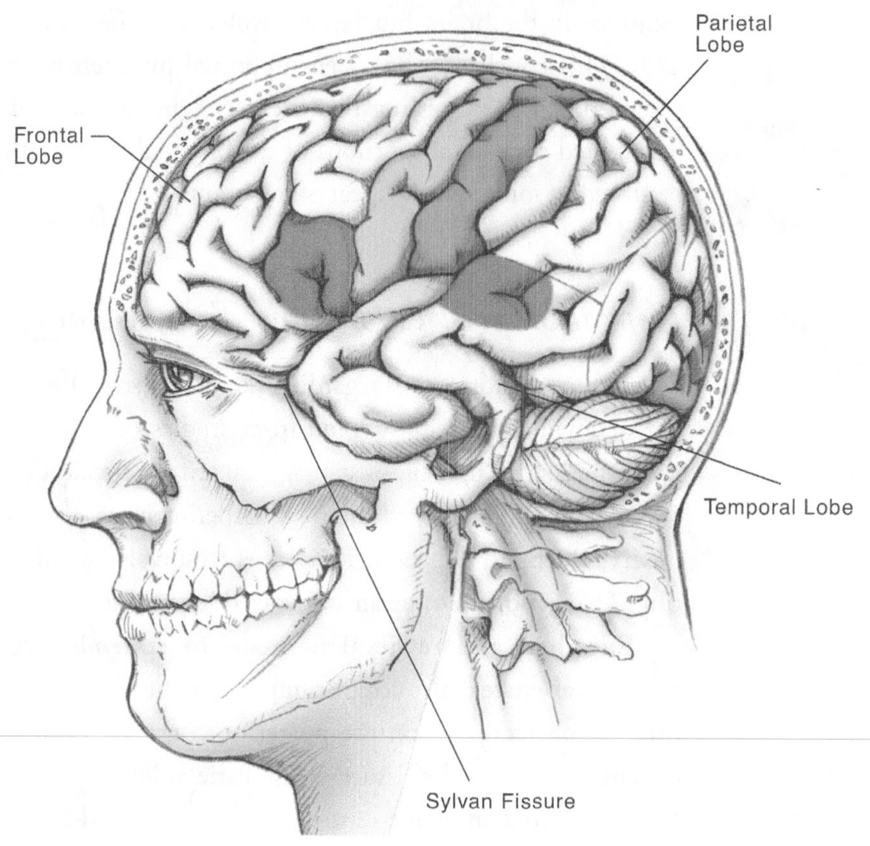

IMPROVING MEMORY

Professors are accustomed to hearing a sad refrain from students dismayed by poor test scores. It goes something like this: "I can't believe I did so poorly on the exam. I spent a lot of time studying, but I just couldn't remember the facts when it came to test time." In such cases, chances are that the problem was more a function of inefficient study methods than a bad memory. Research on learning and memory suggests a number of practical strategies that you may apply to improve your efficiency and therefore your performance as you study material assigned in your courses.

Effective Study Techniques and Strategies

Most psychologists recommend that students use what is now commonly known as the SQ4R method:

S stands for **Survey**. Even before you start to read the chapter the first time, just flip the pages and glance at the headings, pictures, inserts, etc. Then, go to Q.

Q stands for **Question**. Ask yourself what the major topic of the chapter seems to be, or what the author seems to be trying to teach you. Asking such questions will put you in a proper frame of mind to acquire the most pertinent information. Then go on to the first R.

R1 stands for **Read**. Read the entire chapter once through and underline or highlight anything that strikes you as important. Move on to R2

R2 stands for **Reflect**. Think about what you just read and elaborate or cogitate on the contents of the chapter and reduce the material to a compact manageable amount. Also note down the points that seem unclear to you, so you can seek clarification from the professor or fellow students.

R3 stands for **Recite**. Reread the most important points out aloud. Hearing them in your own voice will enhance their encoding. Recitation also involves recalling. Try to retrieve the points you have noted as important, and gauge your performance by testing your-self for recall. Repeat this till you are confident that you can recall the material. Then go on to R4.

R4 stands for **Review**. Review the main points quickly, especially just before a test.

MAKE USE OF STUDY BREAKS AND REWARDS People are often able to function at peak efficiency only so long before their concentration begins to break down. Such attention lapses interfere with learning, but they can be minimized with a routine of frequent but short study breaks. We suggest working 50 minutes, then taking a 10-minute break. Although some individuals may be able to work at peak efficiency for longer than 50 minutes, a 50 minute on and 10 minute off strategy seems to work well for many people.

To make the most of your 10-minute break, do something relaxing and enjoyable that provides a reward for 50 minutes of good effort: Stretch, call a friend, listen to a favorite piece of music, take a walk, or play with your dog. The key is to do something rewarding while avoiding heavy "mental" work, so that you can return to your studies refreshed.

SPACING STUDY SESSIONS Spreading your study sessions out over time is usually more effective than trying to learn a great deal of material all at once; that is, distributed practice is typically better than massed practice. For example, assume that you plan to spend six hours reviewing the material in this chapter after your initial reading. Your recall will probably be much better if you distribute your reviews over three two-hour sessions as opposed to cramming it all into one massed six-hour session. Considerable experimental evidence supports this advice.

AVOIDING INTERFERENCE Try to eliminate as much interference from competing material as possible. Earlier in this chapter we discussed the value of avoiding studying similar material on the same day (the more similar the material, the greater the interference with recall). If you must work on two or more subjects in the same time frame, make them as dissimilar as possible to reduce the impact of proactive and retroactive interference.

By all means, do not study for more than one test on the same day. You may think this suggestion is impossible, particularly during final exam season. However, if you plan in advance, and space your study sessions over time, you can probably avoid the need to double up your exam preparations on the same day. If you get in a bind and find that you must study for two tests on the same day, use the morning to study for one, followed by a nap, and then review the other subject before going to bed for your night's sleep. Sleep helps us avoid interference while information is being consolidated into long-term memory.

MANAGE YOUR TIME People often tend to put tasks off until suddenly they find themselves with too little time to do the job well. This human shortcoming is widely exhibited on college campuses.

One way to avoid the pitfalls of procrastination, while at the same time maintaining strong motivation in your college career, is to *develop a formal schedule to manage your time.* For a given week, first fill in all the slots of time that are already committed time spent in class, at meals, sleeping, at your part-time job, and so forth. Next, designate several of the available slots as study time, keeping in mind the principles of spacing your study sessions as well as the value of sleep after study. The remaining empty slots on your chart may be designated as open or free time.

Time management works only when you treat your designated study times as serious commitments. Similarly, you should treat your free time as something you deserve, a time for renewal, and *an opportunity to reward yourself for good effort.* Sticking to a formal schedule can break the binds of procrastination while allowing you to enjoy your free time without worrying about your studies.

SUMMARY

INFORMATION PROCESSING AND MEMORY

1. The term memory describes both the storage and retrieval of information.
2. Memory consists of three separate processes: encoding or translating incoming information into a neural code that the brain can process; storage of information over time; and, finally, the process of retrieval whereby stored information is located and recovered.

A MODEL OF MEMORY

3. One widely held perspective suggests that there are three distinct memory systems that allow us to process, store, and recall information: sensory memory, short-term memory (STM) which is also known as Working Memory, and long-term memory (LTM).
4. Sensory memories are brief impressions from any of our senses. Visual sensory memory and auditory sensory memory are referred to as iconic memory and echoic memory, respectively. Exceptionally strong iconic memory, seen mostly in children, is known as eidetic memory.
5. STM, frequently referred to as our working memory, is an intermediate memory process, sandwiched between sensory memory and LTM, within which we actively process information.
6 STM has both a short duration and a limited capacity. Chunking, the process of grouping items into longer meaningful units is an effective way to increase the limited capacity of STM.
7. Most of the information placed in STM is held there in an acoustic form, according to how it sounds. Information is also sorted in STM based on what it looks like or what it means (visual and semantic coding).
8. Long-term memories are composed of both procedural memories and declarative memories. Procedural memories are memories for how to perform skills. Recall of specific facts is made possible by declarative memory.
9. Memories that are made available to consciousness are called explicit memories. Implicit memories are associated with the feeling of knowing and familiarity and not available to consciousness.
10. It has been suggested that declarative memory may be further subdivided into episodic memory (autobiographical facts about a person's experiences stored in roughly chronological order) and semantic memory (general, non-personal knowledge about the meaning of facts and concepts without reference to specific experiences).
11. A number of memory systems or mnemonic devices can improve encoding of information in LTM. These include clustering, the method of loci, the peg-word system, acrostics, and acronyms.
12. The more retrieval cues that can be linked with information stored in LTM, the more likely we are to recall that information later on.
13. The three most common techniques for testing LTM are recall tasks, recognition tasks, and relearning.

MEMORY AS A DYNAMIC PROCESS

14. When we memorize a list of items, we are most likely to remember those items at the beginning and end of the list, a phenomenon known as the serial position effect.
15. It is often easier to recall a particular event or experience if we are in the same context in which the information was first encoded. Context includes external environment and internal state (physiological conditions, emotions, etc.). This phenomenon is referred to as state-dependent memory.
16. Flashbulb memory refers to an apparent vivid recall for earlier events associated with extreme emotion.

17. Memory is a dynamic and constructive process influenced by expectations and new information.
18. People may change details to reconstruct memories and make them consistent with their schemas, which are conceptual frameworks that they use to make sense out of their worlds.
19. Research has called into question the reliability of eyewitness testimony. Considerable evidence suggests that eyewitness testimony may be flawed by people's tendency to reconstruct their memory of events to fit their schemas.
20. A number of studies indicate that people exposed to violent events are especially likely to incorporate misinformation into their memory and that it is possible to plant false childhood memories especially in the minds of highly suggestible people, even so, others argue that results obtained in the laboratory might not be generalizable to real-life situations.

FORGETTING

21. Among the explanations put forth by psychologists to explain forgetting are the decay of the memory trace, interference, retrieval failure, motivated forgetting, and organic causes of forgetting.
22. According to the interference interpretation of forgetting, experiences that occur either before or after we learn something new interfere with our memory. Retroactive interference occurs when a later event interferes with recall of earlier information. Proactive interference occurs when earlier learning disrupts memory for later learning.
23. Failure to retrieve memory may occur because it was poorly encoded in the first place or because we have inadequate retrieval cues.
24. Sometimes we forget long-term memories because we do not want to remember them, a process called motivated forgetting.
25. Memory deficits caused by organic factors may be of three kinds: amnesia caused by disease (impaired brain circulation, Alzheimer's disease, etc.); retrograde amnesia (loss of recall for events occurring just before a brain trauma); and anterograde amnesia (inability to recall information processed after brain damage).

THE BIOLOGY OF MEMORY

26. Memory results from structural changes that take place in the synapses between neurons. These changes are called long-term potentiation. These synapses are referred to as Hebbian synapses.
27. Extensive evidence suggests that memories may be represented by large networks of neurons distributed over broad portions of the cortex.
28. Brain imaging techniques such as fMRI have allowed researchers to look at a working brain while it is working and the neural structures involved in encoding, retrieval, forgetting, etc. are being mapped. Hopefully the brain will soon yield all its secrets to our inquiring minds!

IMPROVING MEMORY

29. We can apply what we know about memory to improving study skills. Some of the most effective applications of the memory principles discussed in this chapter include using the SQ4R method or Survey, Question, Read, Reflect, Recite, and Review method of studying. Likewise, reducing the material to a manageable amount of important points, encoding material in a meaningful fashion, avoiding piecemeal studying, using active recitation in studying, taking study breaks, spacing study sessions over time, planning study sessions to minimize proactive and retroactive interference, and using time management techniques will all go a long way toward helping you achieve your desired educational goals.

TERMS AND CONCEPTS

encoding
storage
retrieval
sensory memory
iconic memory
echoic memory
short-term memory (STM)
long-term memory (LTM)
chunking
procedural memory
declarative memory
episodic memory
semantic memory
Dual-code model of memory
mnemonic devices
clustering
acrostics
acronyms
recall
recognition
relearning
explicit memory
implicit memory
false memory
schemas
flashbulb memory
retroactive interference
proactive interference
serial position effect
organic amnesia
retrograde amnesia
anterograde amnesia
long-term potentiation
engram

CHAPTER 8

Motivation

Corbis

The Nature of Motivation
- Defining Motivation
- Theories of Motivation
- Instinct Theory
- Drive-Reduction Theory
- Maslow's Hierarchy of Needs
- Cognitive Theories of Motivation
- Optimum Level of Arousal
- The Role of Physiological Needs in Motivation

Eating Disorders: Obesity, anorexia, and bulimia
- Obesity
- Anorexia Nervosa
- Bulimia

Sensation-Seeking Motivation
- Optimum Level of Arousal

Sexual Motivation and Behavior
- Biological Bases of Sexual Behavior
- Sexual Orientation: Homosexuality

On May 3, 2003, Aron Ralston, a young mountain climber from Colorado made history by surviving a *five day ordeal* in which he cut off his own trapped right arm with a dull, three-inch pen-knife, to save his own life. A huge falling boulder, described as weighing 800 pounds, had trapped the young man's arm as he climbed a remote mountain in Utah.

Even though he was bleeding profusely and was feeling faint with pain he kept sawing on his arm for hours, till he cut his arm free! Ralston then gave himself first-aid from the kit he carried with him and rappelled to the bottom of the canyon, a good 75 feet. He walked toward his truck, and that is when he met two hikers who phoned for help from their cell phones and was rescued by helicopter (Wapshott, 2003; Inbar, 2009; Walsh, 2011).

Since his accident, Ralston, who sports a prosthetic right arm, has kept himself busy addressing audiences about his ordeal, has authored a National Best-seller titled "Between a Rock and a Hard Place", and was featured in a movie titled "127 Hours" (Blevins, 2011). He has striven to keep the loss of his limb in perspective and is enjoying a full life. He climbed the last remaining peak of what is known as the Colorado's Fourteeners (Mutrie, 2005), his 59th peak, on March 10, 2005! What in the world possessed him to climb mountain after mountain, even after a life-threatening ordeal like that?

Each year 189 professional bicycle racers (21 teams of nine riders) from around the world participate in arguably the most arduous athletic event—the *Tour de France*. The tour, as racers know it, consists of 21 daily races or stages covering up to 150 miles, often in mountainous terrain. Most of these racers will never win a stage and most barely earn a livable wage racing as a professional. What keeps them going day after day suffering brutal climbs, frightening descents, and painful crashes?

These examples of highly motivated behavior reveal something about the role of motivation in determining our behavior. *Motivation* is a general term for the processes that influence and direct our actions. As we see in this chapter these processes are considerably more complex than this brief definition implies, and our behavior is often influenced by a combination of several motivating processes including our emotions. Indeed, without emotions our motivated behavior would reflect an air of indifference. Can you imagine how boring dating would be if it were not colored by feelings of excitement, happiness, and possibly love? Similarly, think how hard it might be to become motivated to study for a test if you never experienced fear of failure or the anticipation of success.

Emotions and motivation, then, are processes that are so intermingled, that it is often difficult to separate them. However, when we ask "why" a person did something or "what led" a person to do something, we are in effect inquiring about that person's motivation.

Get Outta Here!

Aron Ralston, the awe inspiring mountaineer whose story was featured in the opening paragraph of this chapter made big news again when he claimed that the vision of a little blond boy who was playing with a toy truck, a boy he took to be his ***future son***, gave him the *inner strength to hack at his own elbow bone and cut through his arm to free himself from the boulder that trapped him! Ralston's accident and vision happened in 2003. He got married a few years later and a blond-haired son was indeed born to them in 2010!*

*Ralston feels that it was a precognitive dream or prophecy of some sort. He thinks it was **the love for this unborn child of his dreams that motivated him**, gave him the push needed to take the ghastly actions to save his life. To him, seeing the vision of that three year old playing with a toy truck was a life-transforming, life-affirming incident! (Inbar, 2009; Blevins, 2011). Give some thought to Ralston's conclusions about his own actions as you read through the various theories of motivation that psychologists have professed through the years and see which theory if any, explains Ralston's behavior.*

THE NATURE OF MOTIVATION

In a sense, the entire study of psychology is concerned with the underlying causes of behavior. Thus far in this text, we have explored the biological foundations of behavior and the role that processes such as sensation, perception, and learning play in influencing our activities. However, these explanations still leave questions unanswered about our behavior.

One such question concerns inconsistencies or variations in behavior. Why do you dress to the hilt one day and go to class in a baggy sweatshirt the next? Why, when two people of comparable ability and training compete athletically, does one excel while the other fails? Motivation helps to explain both inconsistencies in a person's behavior over time and also variations between people's performance in the same situation, when these discrepancies cannot be attributed to differences in basic ability, training, or environmental conditions.

Besides explaining such inconsistencies, motivational concepts help to explain the distinction between learning and performance. Learning does not always lead directly to behavior. As a child your parents may have coaxed you to play the piano when their friends were visiting, and even though you knew how to play the piano, and had mastered a song, you might not have played it till your parent enticed you with the promise of something special for playing. What that enticement did, was change your motivation. Motivation is what often translates learning into overt behavior.

Defining Motivation

Motivation

Any condition that energizes and directs an organism's actions.

***Motivation** is defined as an inner state that energizes and directs our attention and our actions towards meeting a certain goal.* The inner state can include physiological factors, such as the bodily signals that tell us we are hungry, thirsty or tired, or psychological factors, such as cognitive conditions like a decision to meet a deadline or emotional issues such as a desire to be with a loved one or a thirst for vengeance.

Theories of Motivation

Over the years psychologists have generated several theories of motivation and emotion. We will consider a few theories of motivation in this section.

Instinct Theory

Instincts

Innate patterns of behavior that occur in every normally functioning member of a species under certain set conditions.

One of the earliest attempts to account for motivation was based on the notion of **instincts**. ***An instinct is an innate pattern of behavior that is essential for the survival of the species and occurs in every normally functioning member of a species under certain set conditions.*** For example, a salmon may swim thousands of miles through ocean waters and up a river system to reach the exact spot in a gravel bed to spawn where it was spawned several years earlier. Likewise, an arctic tern, hatched in the northland, will depart for the southernmost portion of South America when the arctic days grow shorter. Such behaviors occur in virtually identical fashion among all members of a species, generation after generation.

The attempt to explain human behavior in terms of instincts was the dominant force in psychology in the late 1800s and the early 1900s, due in large part to Functionalism. William James (1890) argued that humans were even more influenced by instincts than were lower animals because humans were motivated not only by biological instincts but also by a variety of psychosocial instincts such as play, sociability, jealousy, sympathy, etc. James proposed a list of 15 instincts. Not long after, other psychologists followed with longer lists of human instincts and the length of the lists soon swelled greatly to accommodate the tremendous number of behaviors that humans display. Soon, psychologists realized that there was a basic flaw in the instinct theory.

> *Instinct theory did not explain behavior;* it simply provided a "label" for existing behaviors. A label is not an explanation. Consider the following sentence as a commonplace example of labeling not being the same as an explanation: "John said, 'Harry could not sleep last night because he has insomnia." Insomnia is a label or the name given to the condition of not being able to sleep at night. It is not an explanation or a cause as to why a person does not feel sleepy. If instead John had said, "Harry cannot sleep well at nights because he drinks too much coffee by day," then the statement would have provided an explanation for the insomnia.
>
> Human behavior is very complex and it is very rare to see every human react in exactly the same way to a given stimulus, making it difficult to find examples of "instinctive" behaviors in humans. Language acquisition may be an exception and humans may have an "Instinctive" ability to acquire language based on fMRI studies which show that Broca's area gets activated when a foreign language is learned with correct grammatical rules but is not activated when the same words are taught using false or incor-

rect grammatical rules (Musso, M. Moro, A., 2003)As it stands though, the instinct theory became a thing of the past and the drive-reduction theory took is place.

Drive-Reduction Theory

The drive-reduction theory proposed by Clark Hull (1943) is based on an animal's tendency to *maintain homeostasis* or to keep internal physiological states constant by adjusting appropriately to change. According to the drive-reduction theory, *a deviation from homeostasis produces a physiological need.* If that physiological need is not met, the system collapses and may even cease to exist. Hence the physiological need must be met. *The unmet physiological need produces a drive.* The level of the need and the level of the drive are linked, so stronger the need, stronger the drive.

Drive

Term commonly used to describe motives that are based on tissue needs, such as hunger and thirst.

*A **drive** is any unpleasant internal state of tension, and it motivates an organism to engage in behaviors that meet the physiological need.* Meeting the physiological need automatically reduces the drive and returns the animal to its constant homeostatic state. *Survival needs, such as that for air, water, food, and sex (procreation) without which a sexually reproduced species will not survive, are all physiological needs.*

For example, an animal maintains a certain blood sugar level. If that level drops, the drop causes a need for sugar. The need produces a drive which gains strength as time lapses, if the need is not met. The drive state is an aversive state of tension and it motivates the animal to go in search of food, so as to lower the drive and replenish the sugar level, or maintain homeostasis.

Hull postulated that there are two kinds of drives: *primary drives* and *secondary drives. Primary drives are induced by internal biological needs, such as need for water and food, and they do not depend on learning.* While the underlying needs behind biological drives are inborn, and do not depend on learning, the *expression* of these drives is often learned. For example, a hungry person is motivated by a state of physiological food deprivation. Consequently, that person *learns* how to search for food in order to satisfy this basic need.

In contrast, *secondary or acquired drives are learned via association with primary drives.* For example the need for money is a secondary drive, acquired on learning that money allows access to food, water, and other similar biological needs and more.

Although the drive-reduction theory explains why we would want to reduce an aversive drive to meet a need, it does not explain why we would continue that behavior after the need was met, which we do, quite often. Consider the times when you left food on your plate because you couldn't eat another morsel, but readily ate something else like ice-cream or chocolate cake because you liked it even though you were full!

Incentive

An external stimulus that can motivate behavior even when no internal drive state exists.

Sometimes stimuli in our environments can energize or motivate us to behave in a certain way in the absence of an internal drive state. Such stimuli, which motivate behavior in the absence of an inner drive, are called **incentives**.

Still another problem with the drive-reduction theory has to do with the fact that many motivated behaviors do not decrease as they are expressed. According to the drive-reduction hypothesis, an internal need directs us to a goal, and reaching that goal reduces the tension of the drive. It follows, then, that when the drive is reduced, the motivated behavior should cease. However, sometimes a motivated behavior seems to be self-perpetuating.

Psycho-social motives such as the human need to achieve and the need for power typically continue to grow and expand as they are expressed rather than diminish, as drive theory would predict. For these and other reasons, the drive-reduction theory is inadequate to explain the wide range of human and animal behaviors we observe.

A number of other theoretical perspectives offer different explanations for motivation. One of these models is Abraham Maslow's hierarchy of human needs.

Maslow's Hierarchy of Needs

Humanistic psychologists have looked toward the role of motives such as love, personal fulfillment, the need to belong, and self-esteem in arousing and directing human behavior. The most influential of these humanistic perspectives was provided by a theory of human motivation developed by Abraham Maslow (1970). Maslow proposed that human needs exist on a multilevel hierarchy consisting of five stages, ranging from the "lowest," most basic biological needs to the "highest" need—to fulfill one's own unique potential (see Figure 8.1).

According to Maslow, we all start our lives at the lowest level of the motivational hierarchy. As infants we are dominated by basic *biological needs* for food, water, sleep, and so forth. (Drive-reduction theory operates at this level.) Relatively soon, however, we become concerned with our need to feel physically and psychologically safe, and so we are motivated by *safety needs* to secure some control over our environment. As we continue to develop, we move into the next two stages or levels on the hierarchy, where more complex

FIGURE 8.1 Maslow's Hierarchy of Needs

Maslow proposed a hierarchy of human needs ranging from the lowest, most basic biological needs to the highest need to become self-actualized.

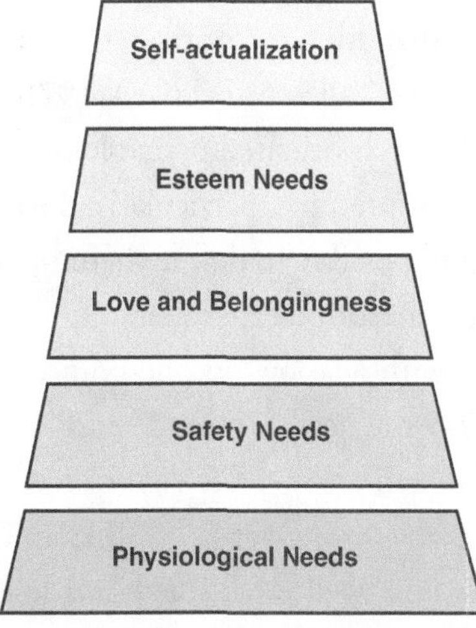

psychosocial motives become more important. We need to love, to be loved, and to feel a sense of belonging. These socially based *love and belongingness needs* are satisfied both by our family involvements and by the relationships we form with others outside the family. As we express our social affiliation with others, we are also likely to become motivated by *esteem needs.* These include the need to achieve and see ourselves as competent, and the desire to be recognized, appreciated, and held in esteem by others.

Finally, if we are successful in satisfying all of these needs, some of us may progress to the highest level in Maslow's hierarchy, where the need for *self-actualization* may become a dominant motivating force in our lives. ***Self-actualization is a complex concept, perhaps best described as the need to reach our own highest potential and to do the things we do best in our own unique way.*** Maslow characterized the self-actualized person as someone who is self-aware and self-accepting, one who strives to be individualistic and to meet one's own goals while striving to help others reach their goals and to fit in society. Maslow also described the self-actualized person as one who is open to new experiences and challenges, and engaging in activities that are commensurate with that individual's highest potential (for example, a musician making music or a poet writing). Maslow believed that although most people have the potential for self-actualization, circumstances beyond their control do not allow them to become self-actualized. In reality, the people we hold in high esteem for showing magnificent motivated behaviors overcome dire circumstances, much like the young man described at the start of our chapter. Figure 8.1 illustrates each of Maslow's need levels.

Maslow's conception that we must fulfill our basic needs before we can pursue needs at higher levels makes some sense. For example, if you are lost in the hills for days without food and then stumble upon a small mountain community, your desire to find food is likely to be much more powerful and immediate than your need to establish a sense of belonging. However, once your lower needs are satisfied, you are likely to be more concerned with higher needs such as those for belonging.

Yet Maslow's theory has also been criticized, especially his view that people's needs are precisely ordered in a five-level hierarchy with successive needs being satisfied only after those on a lower level have been met. This theoretical assumption is difficult to demonstrate by empirical research. Beyond the lowest level of the hierarchy, there is little evidence that human motives or needs are ordered in the exact sequence that Maslow proposed (Wahba & Bridwell, 1976).

Research-oriented psychologists have also criticized Maslow's theory because many of his major precepts, particularly the concept of self-actualization, are so vague that it is virtually impossible to define them operationally. Without operational definitions, Maslow's theory cannot be experimentally tested. One of the authors of this text, Dr. Ragade, disagrees with Maslow on one point. Maslow assigns "love and belonging" as a need that is felt *after* the need for "food" and "safety". There is documented evidence that infants who are fed, and are in a safe environment, but who are not loved and not allowed any interaction with a care-giver fail to thrive. The phenomenon was first described by John Bowlby and is now well established and known as "Social Dwarfism" (Bretherton, 1992. Thus, there are many criticisms of Maslow's theory but it is a theory that appeals to many people especially at an emotional level.

Cognitive Theories of Motivation

The cognitive perspective offers an alternative explanation of motivation. According to this view, our cognitions, expectancies, beliefs, and other mental processes play an important role in motivating our actions. In this section we will review some of the more influential cognitive theories of motivation. Cognitive theorists focus on the goals *consciously* selected by people, i.e., on the decision to pursue a goal and the thought they give to achieving it. ***Theories that look at thinking as a key factor in motivation are known as expectancy theories*** (Lefton & Brennan, 2005, pg. 421).

COGNITIVE EXPECTANCIES The idea that expectations are important motivators was championed in the 1930s and 1940s by Edward Tolman and later in the 1950s and 1960s by Julian Rotter (1954, 1966). Both Tolman and Rotter maintained that our likelihood of engaging in a given behavior depends on two factors: our expectations that a certain behavior will lead to a desired goal, and the value and location of that goal.

This view is exemplified by the role of expectations in both classical and operant conditioning. For example, when we study for an exam (an operant behavior), a consequence occurs (hopefully a good grade) that serves as a reinforcer. We form an association between the behavior and the reinforcement that follows. This association then generates an *expectation* that if the behavior is repeated, it will again produce positive consequences (Bandura, 1982). These **cognitive expectancies** can also be learned by observation. For instance, if a child watches another child behave aggressively with satisfactory consequences the child may come to expect similar positive consequences from aggressive behavior.

Cognitive expectancies

A learned expectancy of relationships between stimuli (in Pavlovian conditioning) and between responses and outcomes (in operant conditioning).

In real life, a behavior is not necessarily followed by the same consequence and hence the link between behaviors and their consequence becomes weak, thus weakening their expectancies. Under such conditions, Julian Rotter suggested that people either hold themselves responsible or hold external conditions responsible for the consequences of their behavior (Hock, 1999). For example, two students both make A's on a test. One says, "I worked super hard to ace this test," while the other says, "I got lucky; the professor questioned us mostly on the material I had studied, and there were very few questions from the content I had ignored." *The first student who claims responsibility is said to have an* ***internal locus of control,*** *while the second student who attributed his success to luck, has an* ***external locus of control.*** Rotter discovered that locus of control of a person tends to be a stable dimension of personality and that people with an internal locus of control don't take high risks in gambling, whereas people with an external locus are more apt to do so. Rotter also discovered that people with an internal locus of control tend to be more achievement oriented than those with an external locus of control.

PSYCHOSOCIAL MOTIVES In the 1960s, David McClelland (McClelland, 1987) proposed that there are psycho-social needs which are necessary for happiness and well-being but not survival as such. McClelland studied and outlined three needs, a need for achievement (nAch), a need for affiliation (nAffl) and a need for power (nPow), that motivate behavior. Other researchers talk of a need for novel stimulation, or the need to explore one's surroundings, but these two needs are seen in other animals, especially other mammals as well.

The psycho-social needs McClelland described are formed due to expectations that are formed in social situations and once formed those expectations direct and sustain behavior. If you are the kind of person who is not content unless you make top grades, and who is committed to being highly successful in your chosen career, psychologists would say that you have a high **need for achievement (nAch)**. The concept of achievement motivation was first defined in 1938 by Henry Murray as the need to "... accomplish something difficult. To overcome obstacles and attain a high standard. To rival and surpass others. To increase self-regard by the successful exercise of talent" (p. 164). Murray also developed the *Thematic Apperception Test (TAT)* to measure the need for achievement and other human motives. The TAT asks people to make up stories about a series of ambiguous pictures. The idea is that people will project into the stories their own motives, interests, and values.

Need for achievement (nAch)

Complex psychosocial motive to accomplish difficult goals, attain high standards, surpass the achievements of others, and increase self-regard by succeeding in exercising talent.

A number of studies show that people who score high in need for achievement differ notably from those with moderate or low nAch scores. Table 8.1 summarizes some of the traits that characterize people who have a high need for achievement.

INFLUENCING ACHIEVEMENT MOTIVATION Since the achievement need is a cognitive motivation, it is highly influenced by learning and experience. Indeed, ample evidence demonstrates that the way in which we raise our children may significantly influence their need to achieve (McClelland, 1985; McClelland & Pilon, 1983). One way to help instill a desire to achieve is to *encourage children to set reasonable goals and to provide ample reinforcements for their successes.* Being realistic about goals is especially important because reasonable goals are likely to be achieved, thus allowing children to experience success and develop cognitive expectancies for success in other situations.

TABLE 8.1 Characteristics of High nAch Individuals

1. Optimistic about personal prospects for success; feel personally in control of their destinies; and willing to delay gratification for the sake of achieving long-term goals (Kulka, 1972).
2. Tend to seek higher levels of socioeconomic success than parents, and are more often successful in achieving this than people with low nAch scores (McClelland et al., 1976).
3. Inclined to set realistic career goals that are neither too easy nor too difficult for their skills, whereas low nAch scorers tend to select career goals that are either too easy or unrealistic in light of their abilities (Mahone, 1960; Morris, 1969).
4. Attain higher grades in academic courses related to career goals than do low need achievers (Raynor, 1970).
5. Tend to be relatively independent and more concerned with succeeding on tasks than with how they affect other people (McClelland, et al., 1976).

Of equal importance is fostering independence. Little things like expecting a child to pick out what he or she is going to wear to school or *letting children have a vote in certain family decisions may encourage a sense of independence and motivate them to achieve success.*

STIMULUS MOTIVATION: ***Seeking Novel Stimulation*** Humans and other animals seem to require a certain amount of stimulation in order to feel good and function effectively. The need to manipulate and explore the environment and the need for sensory stimulation both fall under the category of **sensation-seeking motives**. These motives seem to be natural to a broad range of mammals. Observation of infants of many species, including humans, reveals a strong inclination to explore and manipulate the environment as soon as they are able. Animals have been shown to expose themselves willingly to various kinds of stimulation in the apparent effort to raise their level of physiological arousal. For example, young monkeys provided with mechanical puzzles, such as metal clasps used to seal a door, will tirelessly manipulate this object with no apparent reward beyond the opportunity to manipulate something

We can observe this same drive in ourselves. Very few of us are content with constant, never-changing environments. Sometimes we seek quiet and solitude, but after a time we are likely to seek the sounds and sights of people and activity. We turn on the television, jog, play tennis, talk on the phone, and so forth. We may thrive on challenging games, complex puzzles, or the opportunity to explore new things.

Some psychologists believe that the motivation to seek stimulation evolved in many species because of its survival value: Organisms that explore and manipulate their environment become more aware of its parameters of safety and danger. Beyond these evolutionary implications for species survival, sensation-seeking motives also seem to be related to how we feel. This notion is central to the optimum level of arousal theory.

Optimum Level of Arousal

Arousal is a general concept referring to a behavioral state; we experience arousal as the ability to process information effectively and to engage in motivated behavior. A certain minimum level of arousal is essential in order to express goal-directed behavior. Conversely, too much arousal may leave us over-stimulated, overloaded, and temporarily incapable of effective action. The **optimum level of arousal** seems to vary according to the type of task a person is performing. For instance, the high arousal level you need to compete successfully in a 100-meter race would be inappropriate and even counterproductive for some other tasks, such as writing a book review.

The Role of Physiological Needs in Motivation

BIOLOGICAL BASES OF HUNGER AND EATING Obesity in school-age children and related health problems is one of the main concerns of parents and educators today. Although we all experience hunger and growling stomachs when we have not eaten for some time, our stomachs are not the primary site for motivating eating behaviors. Research over several decades indicates that people whose stomachs have been removed continue to feel hungry, thus indicating that hunger is a brain-based experience. Today we know for a fact that the hypothalamus is involved in regulating hunger and fMRI studies indicate that under-activation or over-activation of para-ventricular hypothalamic (PVH) circuits co-exists with eating disorders. (Palmiter, R.D, 2012; Holsen, L M; Savage, C R; Martin, et.al, 2012). We also know that there are specialized gluco-sensing neurons in the hypothalamus (Poitry-Yamate, C., HongXia, L. & Gruetter, R., 2009) and that the hypothalamus is responsible for regulating the secretion of hormones necessary for glucose storage and release and for integrating sensory and metabolic information

Hypothalamic control theory

Theory that the ventromedial hypothalamus and the lateral hypothalamus operate together to maintain a relatively constant state of satiety.

Hunger is regulated on a daily basis by circuits connecting several different nuclei in the hypothalamus and cortical regions, but in addition, there are long-term control mechanisms that allow most of us to maintain our weight at a relatively constant level over time. Although some people seem to be perpetually losing and regaining the same 10 or 20 pounds, most animals including people maintain a relatively constant weight that may fluctuate by only a few pounds over the long term even though their food intake over this period of time exceeds many tons which leads us to believe that there is a biological body weight "Set Point" and that the hypothalamus is involved in maintaining this long term energy balance along with many other complex peripheral and central mechanisms.

EATING DISORDERS: OBESITY, ANOREXIA, AND BULIMIA

Obesity

Obesity

Condition in which an individual weighs 20 percent or more above the desirable weight for his or her height.

In July 2013 scientists from London reported that they had discovered a gene known as FTO gene (FTO for fat mass and obesity associated gene), mutations of which lead to obesity. People who have the mutated genes have not only have higher levels of a hormone named "Ghrelin" which has been termed a "hunger hormone" circulating in their blood but their brains are more sensitive to ghrelin! In addition to this, the FTO gene has been shown to bring on a craving for high fat foods! (Loos, R. J. F.[1] & Bouchard, C. 2008).

We are a nation that seems obsessed both by food and losing weight. The outcry about our children being overweight has even led popular fast food chains to offer fresh cut apples in their snack packs instead of French fries…but if obesity is due to gene mutations, will substituting apples for French fries make a dent in the size of the fat cells?

We tend to think that Americans are obese and in the past scientists have blamed it on lack of exercise and excessive TV viewing, but the fact of the matter is that obesity has increased world-wide, according to the World Health Organization (WHO)! The WHO report states that of the 191 countries studied, that while the prevalence rates for overweight and obese people are different in each region, the highest rates are seen in the Middle East, Eastern Europe, and North America (James, et.al, 2001).

How many people do you know who are on a diet? Perhaps you are one. According to a recent Gallup Poll, 4.9% of Americans are morbidly obese, another 26.2% are obese and 35.9% are normal weight (Brown, A. 2013). The economic impact of obesity in the U.S. is also staggering. It is estimated to cost well over $100 billion each year in direct and indirect medical expenses as well as losses in productivity. Most health professionals agree that obesity places a person at greater risk of developing one or more health problems. Obesity greatly increases the risk of high blood pressure, stroke, heart disease, diabetes, cancer, gall bladder disease, respiratory problems, and arthritis (CDC, 2003; Aballay, L.R., Eynard, A.R. et.al, 2013). Still another frequent consequence is the psychological burden of obesity. A number of studies have linked obesity with negative body image and depression (Cargill et al., 1999).

People try to get rid of excess weight by starving or sweating it off, but the grim fact is that in most cases fat wins. This is not to say that people cannot lose weight. Quite the contrary, many people lose and regain the same 10 or 20 pounds over and over again. Studies demonstrate that of those people who go on fad diets, approximately 95 percent regain all of their lost weight within one year. Furthermore, as many as 75 percent of individuals placed on medically supervised diets regain most if not all of their lost weight.

THEORIES OF OBESITY There are many theories about why people become overweight. Blame has been placed on genes, conditions of early development, i.e., fetal preprogramming due to nutritional deficiencies experienced as an embryo or as a fetus, metabolic factors, and learned responses to emotional stress. We briefly consider the evidence for some of these viewpoints.

Genetic Causes of Obesity Several studies have demonstrated that a child whose parents are both of normal weight has less than one chance in 10 of becoming obese. When one or both parents are overweight, however, the odds jump to approximately two out of five and four out of five, respectively.

Researchers have compared the concordance rate of obesity in identical twins with that of fraternal twins who do not share the same genes like identical twins do. Investigators have also compared the weight correlations between adopted individuals and their biological parents versus correlations between the weights of adopted individuals and their non-biological, adopting parents. Data from both of these kinds of studies have led obesity researchers to conclude that genetic influences have an important role in determining human obesity (Grilo & Pogue-Geile, 1991; CDC, 2003). And as stated earlier, scientists have found mutated genes which cause obesity. However, genetics is not the only factor contributing to obesity.

Early Childhood Experience It has been found that the fat cells of obese people are as much as 50 to 100 percent larger than those of lean people. In addition, obese people often have a greater number of fat cells. Many researchers believe that eating patterns during childhood and adolescence strongly influence the size and number of fat cells in the body of an adult, and this theory has been supported by research. Some research indicates that children who faced stressful lives, either because of child abuse or because of low Socio-economic status of their parents, tend to become obese as adults primarily due to lack of proper nutrition and medical care (Burkert, N., Rasky, E.et.al 2013).

Metabolic Factors Metabolic disturbances have often been blamed for obesity. Some people do seem to convert food into body tissue, primarily fat, at a faster rate than others, and they are likely to have trouble maintaining a desirable weight. Certainly variations in insulin secretion, as well as other hormones, can lead to obesity in humans. Most people who tend to be obese are found to be insulin resistant (Grundy, 2004).

Reactions to Emotional Stress: Many of us have a tendency to overeat when we are under stress. Campus cafeterias and local pizzerias seem to do a lot of business just before and during finals week. Some people who are chronically stressed, depressed, or anxiety-ridden tend to overeat as a matter of course. This tendency may be due to a number of factors.

One possible cause is experience. Unfortunately, some parents reinforce their children's good behavior with high-calorie goodies such as cookies or cake. This kind of experience helps a child learn to associate eating with feeling good, and food may also take on the symbolic meaning of love and acceptance. Again, parents often praise their children for eating lots of food—another experience that strengthens the association between food and feeling good. Later in life, these early experiences may show up as craving for food whenever a person feels rejected, depressed, disappointed, or unhappy.

Another factor that may contribute to the tendency to eat during emotional stress or depression is that certain foods, particularly those high in carbohydrates, produce a calming or sedative effect by altering levels of neurotransmitters. Foods high in carbohydrates indirectly increase levels of serotonin in the brain, which may alleviate symptoms of depression (Wurtman, 1982; Turner, J. 2011). Thus, eating may be maintained by reducing unpleasant emotional states (negative reinforcement) (Dallman et al., 2008).

Obesity is clearly a significant problem for a large number of individuals. Each year in the United States alone millions of dollars are spent trying to lose weight through diet and exercise programs and even more is spent on health problems related to obesity. While the review of causes of obesity presented here is fairly complete, there is no simple explanation for why an individual becomes obese and how to treat it.

DIETING TO CONTROL WEIGHT Regardless of the cause, it is often very difficult for overweight people to take weight off and keep it off. Many dieters have had the experience of losing a great deal of weight and then discovering, much to their chagrin, that they regain the weight while eating much less than before they started their diet. Why does this happen?

When people go on a diet, especially a starvation diet, there is a pronounced reduction in their resting metabolic rate, the energy the body uses when in the resting state. This change in metabolic rate occurs because the body actually resists the weight loss. Ironically, the dieter and his or her body are working toward opposite goals. Although a dieter wants to take off extra pounds and inches, *the dieter's body reacts to the sharp reduction in food intake as if it were protecting itself from starvation.* It slows down its metabolic rate to conserve energy, thus ensuring that the brain, heart, and other vital organs will have sufficient fuel.

This change in metabolic rate produces highly inconvenient results for the dieter. For instance, assume that you normally consume 3,000 calories per day and you suddenly begin an 800-calorie diet. At first, you may experience weight loss. Then your body will eventually lower its resting metabolic rate to conserve its fat stores with the result that you will likely hit a plateau. If you tough it out, you will be able to reach your weight goal.

At this point, you will want to begin eating a more reasonable diet again, but beware. Your body is now likely to play one of its cruelest tricks. Used to conserving energy, your metabolism will continue running in low gear. *Thus even a modest increase in calorie consumption (often well below your pre-diet level) may result in gaining the pounds back.* It may take weeks or months for your metabolism to readjust to a normal level, and by then you may have given up in disgust.

This scenario sounds discouraging, but, as with everything else, there are right ways and wrong ways of dieting. The "Health, Psychology, and Life" discussion at the end of this chapter provides additional information to keep in mind if you are trying to lose weight. Remember, however, that no safe method will work quickly and easily. All weight loss programs require considerable persistence.

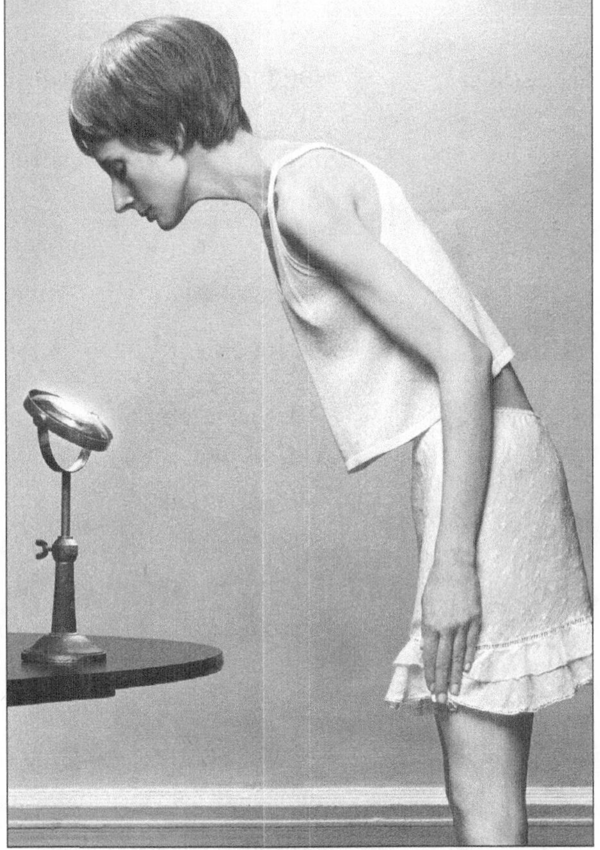

Anorexia is a serious disorder that can result in emaciation and death. (Corbis)

Anorexia Nervosa

Sometimes, dieting because of the fear of becoming obese can lead to excessive attention to the **body image**, which may become obsessive enough to cause other eating disorders such as anorexia or bulimia, which involve abnormal patterns of food intake (Pappalia et. al., 2004, pp. 396).

Anorexia nervosa

Eating disorder characterized by prolonged refusal to eat adequate amounts of food. This condition is most common among young females.

Anorexia nervosa affects adolescent girls more often than adolescent boys, but is a rare disorder and has been blamed on "The Clothes-hanger Culture" or a culture where very thin models are given way too much importance and exposure on television and other media. Anorexia is essentially self-starvation to the point of fatality and most of the young girls come from broken or dysfunctional families (Bruch, 2001). They are described by their parents as "good children" and quite often are depressed, obsessive and perfectionists (Pappalia et al., 2004, p. 396).

Bulimia

Bulimia

Eating disorder characterized by periodic episodes of binge eating followed by deliberate purging using either vomiting or laxatives.

Bulimia is a disorder in which a person, most commonly a young woman in her teens or twenties, engages in periodic episodes of binge eating, then uses either vomiting or a laxative to purge the body. Some bulimics maintain normal weight, and others are also anorexic. In one study, approximately half of the patients hospitalized for anorexia indicated that they periodically resorted to bulimic purges. The **percentage** of **women** who reported a history of **bulimia** with weekly binge eating and purging went from 1% in 1980 to 3.2% in 1983 and to 2.2%in 1991 indicating that the prevalence for this disorder may have peaked and may be declining (Pyle, R., Neuman, P.A. et.al, 1991).

Many people with bulimia frequently manifest depression, anxiety, sleep disturbances, poor body image, guilt, and substance abuse. In addition to these psychological problems, bulimia contributes to a variety of physical complications including cardiac complications resulting from the loss of potassium, gastrointestinal difficulties, extensive tooth decay and enamel deterioration from vomiting, and hair loss. Both anorexia and bulimia are serious disorders that may be fatal. A variety of therapeutic strategies have been shown to be effective in treating anorexia and bulimia including the use of antidepressants and counseling.

SEXUAL MOTIVATION AND BEHAVIOR

Another important source of motivation is sexual motivation. Our sexuality is a richly varied, highly individualized, and potentially enriching aspect of our lives. We express our sexuality in many ways, and the feelings, thoughts, and attitudes we bring to this area of human experience also vary widely.

In the remainder of this chapter we present a brief overview of selected topics, which provide an introduction to certain behavioral, biological, psychosocial, and cultural aspects of sexuality. We will see how human sexual behavior can be motivated by all of these factors.

We begin by exploring the question of how biology and psychosocial factors influence human sexual behavior. Sexual behaviors were once thought to be motivated primarily by a physiological drive, mostly because of the dominant role of physiology in animal sexual behavior. In non-primate mammals such as rats, for instance, hormones appear to be essential to sexual arousal and function. *However, there is now general agreement that learning, emotions, and social norms become more important as the complexity of the organism increases.* In humans, sexual interest and expression are controlled not only by hormones, but even more by the cerebral cortex, reflecting a combination of biological, psychological, and cultural factors.

All this is not to say that biology is irrelevant to human sexual motivation. In the following sections we compare the effects of biological and psychosocial factors to see how they contribute to sexual motivation and arousal.

Biological Bases of Sexual Behavior

Although Science does not know how or why life came into existence, it does know that the life that came into existence about 3.5 billion years ago (Gould, 2000), continues to this day because of an innate drive to procreate. This drive for procreation operates via a physiological need or desire for expressing sexuality and although this need is not a survival need for any individual animal, *it is a survival need in terms of the species as a whole.* It is difficult to distinguish between the effects of physiological processes and psychological processes on the sex drive. However, there is no doubt that our sexuality not only motivates us but also contributes to our self-perception in terms of our *gender identity* (our sense of whether we are male or female) and in terms of *our schemas of gender role* i.e. what we think we ought to be doing because we are males or because we are females. Our innate sexuality also influences our sexual orientation i.e. our proclivity to be attracted sexually to a particular sex, i.e., a male or a female.

Androgens

Male sex hormones, the most common of which is testosterone.

HORMONES AND SEXUALITY The primary male sex hormones are **androgens**. A number of lines of research have linked androgens with sexual activity. There is evidence that males who take *anabolic steroids* (e.g. testosterone) for building muscle mass may experience increased levels of sexual motivation. Testosterone is known to increase sexual motivation in males who have decreased libido resulting from low testosterone levels. However there isn't any consistent correlation between testosterone levels and sexual activity in human males.

Estrogens

Hormones that influence female sexual development.

Many people assume that the female sex hormones, **estrogens**, play a major role in female sexual motivation and behavior. We do know that these hormones help maintain the elasticity of the vaginal lining and contribute to vaginal lubrication (Walling et al., 1990). However, the role of estrogens in female sexual motivation is far from clear.

Estrogens are not the only sex hormones present in females, however. Both the ovaries and the adrenal glands produce androgens in females, and the connection between androgens and female sexual motivation seems somewhat more substantial. While androgens can be used to increase libido in both men and women, it is important to remember that interest in sexual behavior is dependent on many factors. Androgens by themselves are not sufficient to motivate sexual behavior in humans even though they are prescribed to treat sexual dysfunctions.

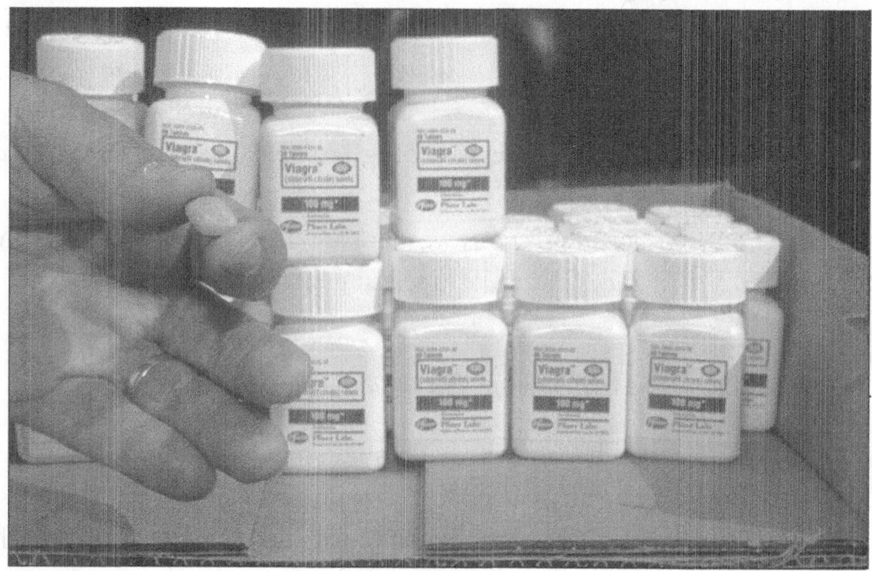
Corbis

Viagra pills sales have exceeded millions of dollars annually in the United States.

PSYCHOSOCIAL FACTORS IN SEXUAL BEHAVIOR Although hormones can, and do, influence human sexual motivation; our sexual behaviors are not strongly correlated with reproductive cycles and related biological events. Other animals stand in sharp contrast. Female sexual receptivity in other animals is governed by the reproductive cycle; biological cues (such as odors) are often necessary to instigate sexual activity; and hormone levels are closely tied to the ability to respond sexually.

In contrast, hormones are far from the only important factor influencing human sexuality. Indeed, it is likely that psychological and cultural conditions play a greater role in human sexual arousal and expression. Most of us continue to express our sexuality throughout much of our lives because sexual activity is reinforcing. This reinforcement takes many forms, including a sense of self-esteem that comes from being loved, erotic pleasure and gratification, reduction of feelings of anxiety, and a sense of closeness to another person. Sexual expression can even serve the function of providing a way of relieving boredom and increasing arousal levels. This variety of reinforcing effects that sexual expression allows, suggests that our incentives for sexual expression are largely psychosocial.

SOCIETAL INFLUENCES ON SEXUAL BEHAVIOR Social scientists have recorded the tremendous variation that occurs in human sexual behavior in different societies (Crooks & Baur, 1990; Ford & Beach, 1951). Societies exist in which individuals in their 60s are more active sexually than the typical 30-year-old American. In many societies, the marked gender differences in adolescent sexual behaviors that typify our own society are totally lacking.

Sexual social mores vary widely from society to society. On the Polynesian island of Mangaia for example, a high rate of sexual activity and extensive sexual instruction of youths is the norm, whereas on the Irish island of Inis Beag, sexual expression is discouraged from infancy through old age. Sexual misinformation is common, and female orgasm is practically unknown. Similarly, the Dani People of New Guinea demonstrate little interest in sexual activity and abstain from sex for years at a time which is quite in contrast to our own American culture. Likewise, the sexual mores of the same society can change over time. For example, contrast England in the Victorian period, where it is said that not even dining tables were allowed to expose their legs, with today's more sexually open and tolerant society, where magazines commonly expose far more of celebrities than their legs.

Such widespread fluctuations in sexual norms and behavior cannot be attributed to the influence of hormones. Nor can they be attributed to geographical factors. No other animal species have different sexual behaviors in different parts of the world. *Rats in Ethiopia copulate the same way and are triggered by the same stimuli as rats in Oregon.* The sexual patterns of dogs, cows, fowl, and higher primates are all highly similar, regardless of where they live. *Thus humans are unique in creating highly localized patterns of sexual behavior. This is perhaps the strongest evidence for the preeminence of psychosocial factors in human sexual motivation and expression.*

Many of us have our own ideas about what is "normal" sexual behavior and what is not, but *often the meaning of a given act (sexual or otherwise) cannot be fully understood without also understanding its cultural context.* For example, in our own North American society, we may attribute sexual overtones to the act of two men embracing each other. In Italy, however (and in many other societies), it is completely normal (and nonsexual) for men to hug one another.

Such diversity exists among the cultures of the world that the very definition of what is sexually arousing may vary greatly. In one society, exposed female breasts may trigger sexual interest in men, whereas in a different society this sight may induce little or no erotic interest. Furthermore, the acceptability of certain sexual activities varies widely from culture to culture. In some societies, such as the Mangaians of Polynesia, sex is highly valued and almost all manifestations of it are considered beautiful and natural. Other societies, such as the Manus of New Guinea, view any sexual act as undesirable and shameful (Crooks & Baur, 1990). Almost any sexual behavior is viewed in widely different ways in different societies.

Cultural mores

Established customs or beliefs in a particular culture.

The diversity of sexual expression tends to mask a fundamental generalization that can be applied without exception to all social orders: Within the **cultural mores** (established customs and beliefs) of all societies, the conduct of sexual behavior is regulated in some way. The rules vary from one society to the next, but in no social order is sexuality completely unregulated.

Homosexual

Primary erotic, psychological, and social interest in members of the same sex, even though that interest may not be expressed overtly.

Sexual Orientation: Homosexuality

A **homosexual** person is an individual whose primary erotic, psychological, emotional, and social interest is in a member of the same sex, even though that interest may not be overtly expressed. A homosexual person's gender identity agrees with his or her biological sex. That is, homosexual individuals perceive themselves as male or female, respectively, and are attracted to people of the same sex.

In our society, we tend to make clear-cut distinctions between homosexuality and heterosexuality. The delineation is not so clear-cut, however. At one end of a broad spectrum, a relatively small percentage of people consider themselves to be exclusively homosexual; at the other end, a greater number think of themselves as exclusively heterosexual. In reality, varying degrees of preference and experiences exist.

THE INCIDENCE OF HOMOSEXUALITY According to Alfred Kinsey et al. (1948), the proportion of exclusively homosexual individuals in our society is approximately 2 percent of women and 4 percent of men (or roughly 3 percent of the total U.S. population). Some writers have speculated that the actual number of predominantly homosexual people is closer to 10 percent of the population. This higher estimate is based partly on the assumption that social pressures cause many homosexual people to conceal their orientation.

Between the extremes on the continuum are many individuals who have experienced sexual contact with or been attracted to people of the same sex. Kinsey's estimate of this group's number was quite high. *Some 37 percent of males and 13 percent of females in his research populations reported having had overt homosexual experiences at some point in their lives,* and even more had been erotically attracted to members of the same sex.

ATTITUDES TOWARD HOMOSEXUALITY A monumental survey of 190 societies throughout the world, conducted by an anthropologist and a psychologist (Ford & Beach, 1951), found that homosexuality was accepted in approximately two-thirds of these societies. Homosexuality was also widely accepted in many earlier cultures. For example, over half of 225 Native American tribes accepted male homosexuality, and 17 percent accepted female homosexuality (Pomeroy, 1965).

The Judeo-Christian tradition, which is prominent in the United States, has had a far more negative view of homosexuality, primarily because of strong Biblical prohibition. For example, "You shall not lie with man as one lies with a female, it is an abomination" (Leviticus 18:22).

In recent years there has been a shift in attitudes toward homosexuality. The view that homosexuality is immoral has been replaced to some degree by a common belief that homosexuality is a sickness. Most current research, however, contradicts this notion. Studies comparing non-patient heterosexual and homosexual individuals have found no significant differences in adjustment between the two groups (Mannion, 1981; Wilson, 1984). Two noted researchers in this area, Alan Bell and Martin Weinberg, state that "... homosexual adults who have come to terms with their homosexuality, who do not regret their sexual orientation and who can function effectively sexually and socially, are no more distressed psychologically than are heterosexual men and women" (1978, p. 216). Attitudes towards homosexuality have changed toward more acceptance in recent years, especially as biological underpinnings of homosexuality are becoming clearer.

THEORIES OF HOMOSEXUALITY Several theories have attempted to explain the development of homosexuality. There is still no single clear answer, but recent research conducted by Alan Bell, Martin Weinberg, and Sue Hammersmith (1981) helps shed some light on the question. Bell and his colleagues used a sample of 979 homosexual people matched to a control group of 477 heterosexual people. All subjects were questioned about their childhood, adolescence, and sexual practices and their responses were analyzed using sophisticated statistical techniques. Much of the information presented in this discussion is based on this study's findings, to which we refer in evaluating both psychosocial and biological explanations of homosexuality.

Psychosocial Theories Some theories seek to explain homosexuality as the result of learning, personal experiences, parenting patterns, or the individual's own psychological attributes. For instance, one explanation for homosexuality is that it may be the result of unhappy heterosexual experiences or the inability to attract partners of the other sex.

Is homosexuality a learned response? Does homosexuality result from unhappy heterosexual experiences? This view is commonly voiced in the effort to explain lesbianism, which people often assume is based in resentment, dislike, fear, or distrust of men rather than an attraction toward women.

Perhaps the best way to evaluate this explanation of homosexuality is to turn the argument around: Is female heterosexuality caused by dislike and fear of women? The answer is no—just as lesbianism is not caused by unhappy experiences with men. In fact, research indicates that up to 70 percent of lesbian women have had sexual experiences with men, and many report having enjoyed them. However, they prefer to be sexual with women (Klaich, 1974).

Bell and his colleagues report that lesbianism is not related either to unpleasant heterosexual experiences or to a lack of such experience (1981, p. 176). Their research found that homosexual and heterosexual people had dated about equally in high school, a finding that contradicts the notion that homosexuality results from a lack of heterosexual opportunity. Both male and female homosexual subjects did tend, however, to feel differently about dating than did heterosexual subjects, for few of them reported enjoying it. These feelings probably indicate that these subjects were less interested in heterosexual relationships. For example, although the homosexual males dated as much as the heterosexual males in the study, they tended to have fewer sexual encounters with females. The researchers concluded that "unless heterosexual encounters appeal to one's deepest sexual feeling, there is likely to be little about them that one would experience as positive reinforcement for sexual relationships with members of the opposite sex" (p. 108).

Another myth dispelled by the Bell research team is that young men and women become homosexual because they have been seduced by older homosexuals. In reality, not only did most subjects (both male and female) report that their first homosexual encounter had involved someone of about their own age, but homosexual subjects were less likely than heterosexual subjects to have had initial sexual encounters with a stranger or an adult.

Some people may believe that homosexuality can be "caught" from someone else—for instance, that a homosexual teacher, especially one who is well liked and respected, will

HEALTH, PSYCHOLOGY, AND LIFE

Some Suggestions for Overcoming Obesity

Countless solutions have been proposed to deal with weight problems. This discussion presents a few suggestions based on the clinical experiences and experimental findings of weight loss specialists. Note that it is a good idea to consult a physician before embarking on a weight loss program.

1. *Determine your calorie intake.* Most adults of normal weight consume about 2,000 to 2,500 calories each 24-hour period, depending on their size, sex, and activity level. If you are overweight and convinced that you eat no more than your skinny friends, try keeping a record of everything you eat and drink for a period of a week or so. You can buy a convenient calorie counter to help you convert items consumed into average calories per day.

2. *Reduce food intake, if necessary.* If you are consuming more than a normal allotment of calories, it is helpful to reduce the amount you eat, particularly food high in fat and sugar content. Calories consumed as fat are converted into fat in the body more readily than the same number of calories consumed as carbohydrate or protein. Consult a physician, dietician, or authoritative textbook to be sure your reduced food intake provides a healthful, balanced diet.

Avoid crash diets that may reduce calories to only a few hundred a day. Your odds for success are much better if you cut back only moderately on daily calorie consumption.

Several tips may help you lower food consumption moderately. First, try stocking up on nutritious food that does not inspire lust in your taste buds. It is a good idea to allow for some interesting variety in your diet so that you will not end up feeling so deprived that you lose all control and binge.

Second, commit yourself to eating only at mealtime, and always in the same place. This helps eliminate the urge to snack that often results from learned associations between certain activities and food (for example, raiding the refrigerator during TV commercials). It can also be helpful to reduce access to foods that require no prepara-

become a role model for students. However, homosexual orientation appears to be established even before school age, and modeling is not a relevant factor (Marmor, 1980).

Another theory links homosexuality to certain patterns in family background. Sigmund Freud (1905) maintained that children's relationship with their parents was a crucial factor. Although Freud viewed men and women as innately bisexual, he thought that individuals normally passed through a "homoerotic" phase in the course of heterosexual development. Certain people could become "fixated" at the homosexual phase if some kinds of life experiences occurred, especially if a boy had a poor relationship with his father and an overly close relationship with his mother. Although Freud's theory is frequently cited, it has received little support from research. In fact, Bell and his colleagues found that no particular phenomenon of family life could be singled out as especially consequential in the development of either heterosexual or homosexual orientations.

Biological Theories of Homosexuality If psychosocial causes cannot explain homosexuality, does biology provide any more reliable answers? In the effort to answer this question, researchers have investigated a number of possible biological factors. The two most promising lines of research have explored genetic and hormonal factors contributing to brain development.

Some Suggestions for Overcoming Obesity, *continued*

tion. It is all too easy to nibble from an open box of crackers or cookies without even thinking about what you are doing.

3. *Exercise.* When used in conjunction with reduced food intake, regular, moderate exercise is probably the best strategy for losing weight.

If you can burn off 200 to 300 calories each time you exercise, you will obtain noticeable results in a reasonable amount of time (assuming, of course, that your food intake is held to a moderate level). Most specialists recommend exercise sessions that last a minimum of 20 to 30 minutes and occur at least three times a week. The activities you choose should be strenuous enough to raise your heart rate appreciably and to allow you to burn 200 to 300 calories per session. All kinds of exercise possibilities exist. Choosing one that is relatively enjoyable, or at least not unpleasant, will pay dividends in greater perseverance. Studies indicate that 30 minutes of brisk walking burns off about 150 calories, 30 minutes of bicycling on normal terrain burns off 200 calories, swimming, 275 calories, and jogging, 370. For many people, exercise actually seems to decrease appetite.

4. *Keep records and reward yourself.* It may be helpful to include others in your efforts to lose weight. Sometimes the first five or 10 pounds are the toughest because nobody seems to notice. However, having someone around to praise you for the pound or two you have lost can be very reinforcing.

Setting up little rewards along the way can also be helpful. Perhaps you can treat yourself to a professional massage after you drop the first five pounds. Maybe after 10 or 15 pounds you can take yourself to a beach resort where you can show off your gorgeous new body.

5. Buy a gorgeous out-fit one size smaller than the size you currently wear and hang it in your closet in a prominent place where you will see it daily. Seeing it will remind you of your desire and get you off to a good start in the morning.

According to one argument, a person's homosexuality may be determined by his or her genetic makeup. One study conducted by Franz Kallman (1952a, 1952b) tested this theory by comparing the sexual orientations of both fraternal and identical twins. In all cases, the twins had been reared together, so their prenatal (before birth) and postnatal environments were virtually identical. The primary difference between the two groups lay in their genetic makeup, which was identical for the identical twins but not for the fraternal twins.

Kallman reported an approximately 95 percent concordance rate for homosexuality among the identical twins. In contrast, the concordance rate for fraternal twins was only 12 percent. A more recent investigation reported concordance rates for homosexuality of approximately 75 percent and 19 percent, respectively, among identical and fraternal twins (Whitman & Diamond, 1986). However, other research has failed to find evidence of hereditary factors in homosexuality (Heston & Shields, 1968).

In the early 1990's Dr. Simon LeVay made headline news by publishing his discovery that one particular hypothalamic nucleus was undersized in exclusively homosexual males as compared to the size of the same nucleus in heterosexual males and was similar in size to that of heterosexual females (LeVay,S. 1991). Dr. LeVay also reviewed studies showing that the correlation in sexual orientation is higher for identical than for fraternal twins.

LeVay is cautious, however, in interpreting this as evidence for a "gay gene" (LeVay, 1993). If genes do contribute to sexual orientation they most likely do so by altering developmental processes resulting in differences in brain structure that mediate sexual motivation.

Some researchers speculate that prenatal hormone imbalances can alter the masculine and feminine development of the fetal brain. There is a critical period during which the fetus is particularly sensitive to levels of testosterone. How could brain levels of testosterone be altered during gestation? Research suggests that maternal stress during a critical period (perhaps between the second and the sixth months of pregnancy) results in decreased levels of fetal testosterone. The stress, which causes large amounts of adrenal hormones to enter the fetal bloodstream, inhibits the masculinization of the hypothalamus by testosterone. According to this theory, prenatal hormone imbalances during this period could contribute to homosexuality (Ellis & Ames, 1987; Roper, 1996; Swaab et al., 2002; Zuger, 1989). Laboratory research with animals has demonstrated that prenatal stress, which resulted in decreased levels of testosterone, also alters male sexual behavior. Prenatally stressed male rats responded to injections of testosterone with an increase in female sexual behavior (McLeod and Brown, 1988).

In conclusion, research seems to suggest that people may be biologically predisposed toward homosexuality either genetically or as a result of stress hormones during prenatal development. At this point, however, it seems most appropriate to think of sexual orientation as influenced by a variety of environmental and biological factors that are unique for each person, rather than trying to find a single cause.

SUMMARY

THE NATURE OF MOTIVATION

1. Motivation can be defined as any condition that energizes and directs behavior.
2. Motivation not only energizes or activates us to behave in a certain way; it also defines the direction of the resulting behavior. Motivation also has a direct impact on how vigorous or intense our behaviors are.

MOTIVATIONAL EXPLANATIONS OF BEHAVIOR

3. One of the earliest attempts to explain motivation was based on the notion of instincts or innate patterns of behavior that occur in every normally functioning member of a species under certain set conditions.
4. Instinct theories of motivation became obsolete when psychologists realized that instinct theories only provide a new label for a behavior, they do not explain it or provide guidance for further research.
5. According to the drive-reduction theory, motivation originates with a need or drive, experienced as an unpleasant aversive inner state that motivates us to act in a way that will reduce the aversive inner state. This theory also talks of drives brought on by unmet primary or biológical needs and secondary or learned needs. Secondary needs are generated after one learns that they allow better access to primary needs.
6. Maslow proposed that human needs exist on a multilevel hierarchy consisting of five stages ranging from the lowest, most basic biological needs to the highest need for self-actualization and a person whose lower needs are met gets motivated by the next higher unmet need.
7. Criticisms of Maslow's theory include the fact that there is little evidence that human motives or needs are ordered in the sequence that Maslow proposed and his theory is not a testable theory.
8. According to the cognitive perspective, our beliefs and expectations play an important role in motivating our actions.
9. One way to help instill a desire to achieve is to encourage children to set reasonable goals and to provide ample reinforcers for their successes. Serving as models for them to observe and learn from would be another excellent way of helping them achieve.
10. The need to manipulate and explore the environment and the need for sensory stimulation both fall under the category of sensation-seeking motives.
11. The hypothalamus in concert with other cortical areas seems to be regulating basic biological processes such as hunger, thirst, procreative drive, etc. Under- functioning or over-functioning of some of these circuits seems to be the underlying mechanism of some of these eating disorders.
12. Many researchers believe that our bodies may be programmed in some fashion to maintain a preferred level of body weight for each individual, a phenomenon known as Set Point.
13. Obesity places a person at risk for developing one or more serious health problems, such as high blood pressure, heart disease, and depression.
14. Genetic factors, conditions of early development, emotional stress, and metabolic factors have all been suggested as possible causes of obesity.
15. Suggested causes for anorexia nervosa and bulimia include a dysfunctional family, a culture that gives undue importance to slimness and physical beauty.
16. Psychological and cultural conditions probably play a greater role than hormones in human sexual motivation. This tendency is reflected in the role of reinforcement and psychosocial condition-

ing, which maintain and constrain sexual expression, respectively.

17. Ideas about what is sexually arousing vary greatly across the cultures of the world. Sexual conduct is regulated in some way in all societies, but the rules vary from one society to the next.
18. There are a number of psychosocial and biological theories that attempt to explain the development of homosexuality. Some of the psychosocial theories relate to parenting patterns, life experiences, or the psychological attributes of the person.
19. Theories of biological causation of homosexuality look to anatomical differences, genetic differences and prenatal influences on hormone levels and sexual differentiation of the brain.

TERMS AND CONCEPTS

motivation
instincts
drive
incentives
need for achievement (nAch)
cognitive expectancies
hypothalamic control theory
obesity
anorexia nervosa
bulimia
optimum level of arousal
androgens
estrogens
cultural mores
homosexual

CHAPTER 9

Emotion and Stress

Corbis

This chapter is all about your achy-breaky hearts or your emotions. Words such as, hearty, heart-broken, heart-throb, heartfelt, heartache, heart-rending, etc., indicate how most people in the world think that the seat of emotions is the heart, when in reality, it is in the brain. Since we do not have direct experiential access to the workings of the brain, we attribute emotion to the one part that seems to beat faster or slower, when we experience emotion ... the heart! In some parts of the world, people have attributed the experience of emotion to the workings of other organs, the workings of which are not directly available to us. For example, the Malaysians think of the liver as the organ that mediates emotion and prescribe drugs to affect the liver in order to cure emotional problems.

The Amhara of Ethiopia see the stomach as the seat of emotion. They blame feasting for emotional disorders and see fasting as a way to maintain emotional calmness (Schneider & Ragade, 1996, pp 119). The Tahitians believe that the stomach and the gut are the seat of emotions, which might make some sense to us, because we in the west do talk of a "gut feeling" or say "gut-wrenching" when describing a horrific emotional experience or describe a person as "gutsy" meaning bold and daring.

A bold and daring act requires strong motivation and the processes of motivation and emotion are very closely connected. Emotions can motivate behavior both by preceding it, as when a child's anger leads to kicking a bedroom wall, or by being a consequence of our actions, as when behaviors induce feelings of happiness, joy, excitement and pride.

Emotions do more than motivate our behavior, however. Can you imagine life without them? In this chapter we explore emotions in an effort to find out more about what they are, how they come about, what brain structures enable them, and how they influence our lives. We also explore a closely related topic: stress, the effect of stress on our lives, and the ways in which we can moderate some of the negative effects of stress.

THE COMPONENTS OF EMOTION

Emotions

An individual's subjective feelings and moods. The term applies to both physiological and behavioral responses to specific stimulus situations.

Although most people do not distinguish between an emotion and a feeling, psychologists do. To a psychologist human **emotions** have four integral components: ***cognitive processes,*** i.e., your thoughts, judgments etc.; affect or subjective ***feelings*** such as joy or sadness, which are either positive or negative; ***physiological changes*** such as a faster pulse, racing heart, and finally, concomitant ***behavioral responses*** such as punching someone out when angry at them or fleeing from someone due to fear.

THE RANGE OF HUMAN EMOTION

If you are asked to name some words that stand for an emotion, you are likely to come up with a long list, which is likely to cover most of the letters of the alphabet, if not all, beginning with admiration ending with perhaps, zeal. Some words will describe the same emotion, but at a different level of intensity, for example the words joy and ecstasy, while some words will describe a mixture of two or more emotions such as the word disgust which depicts a sense of outrage and revulsion. Some emotions will be so complex that the person experiencing them will describe them as ineffable or beyond words. Most Psychologists agree that there are eight primary emotions and each has various intensity levels. There are words that signify the emotion and words that signify its lowest and highest level of intensity. The primary emotion of Joy, for example, can be viewed as "Contentment" as depicting its lowest level and "Ecstasy" as depicting its highest level, or the primary emotion of Fear, being depicted by Apprehension at its lowest level and by the word Terror at its highest (Schneider & Ragade (1996):

Plutchik's Psychoevolutionary Theory of Emotions

Have you heard Tina Turner belt out "What's love but a second-hand emotion?" According to Robert Plutchik (1980), eight primary or basic human emotions are *wired in by evolution to specific stimuli* and there are some emotions which are not primary, but are experienced when two primary emotions are experienced simultaneously. *Love according to Plutchik is one such mixed-emotion* (see Figure 9.1). *Plutchik also states that each of the primarily emotion is wired-in as a response to a particular environmental stimulus situation,* for example, the emotion of joy is wired in to the stimulus of "mate" and the emotion of sadness to the stimulus of loss of a valued object such as a child or a parent, etc. Plutchik's wheel of emotions is given below in Figure 9.1. Plutchik assigns specific environmental stimulus situations (called Universal Situations) as producing specific primary emotions and lists the effects of the behavioral expression of that emotion on the survival of that individual animal.

FIGURE 9.1 Plutchik's Wheel of Emotions

According to Robert Plutchik, there are eight primary human emotions consisting of four opposite pairs. Adjacent emotions (such as joy and acceptance) blend to form more complex emotions (like love).

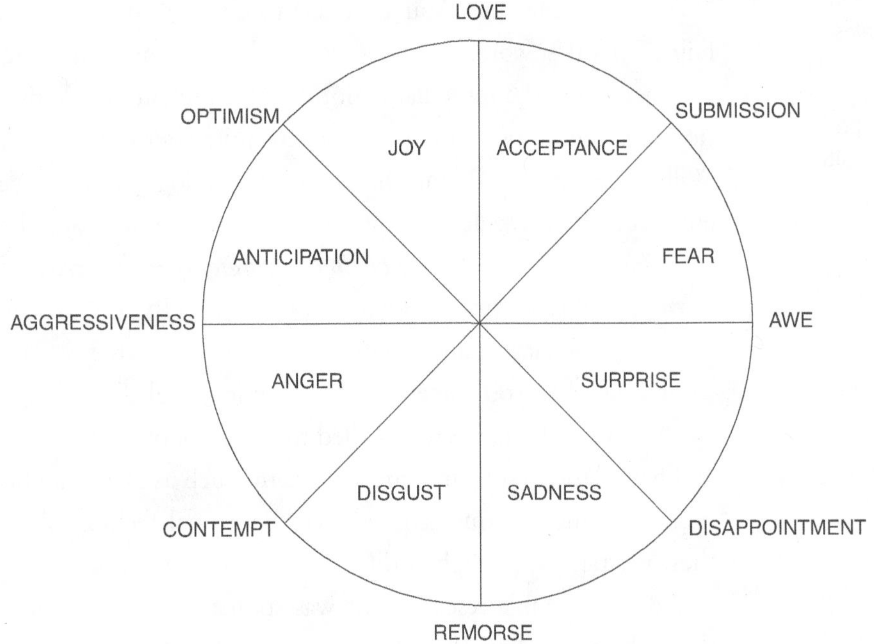

The Universal Stimulus Situation of spotting a predator, for example, produces the cognition of danger, the emotion of fear or terror, and the emotional facial expressions and the behavior of running away which then helps the animal survive! Or, take the example of a goal being blocked as a universal situation, the inferred cognition is "Now I will not reach this goal" or "get this much wanted object", the wired-in emotion is anger, and the behavior is fighting with the perceived blocker or "foe". Although this theory makes a lot of common sense it is not a theory that allows laboratory testing as such and hence science has moved on to other theories.

PERCEPTUAL/COGNITIVE EMBODIMENT THEORY OF EMOTION Is the newest theory, but it is a greatly improved version of the oldest theory or the 19th century James-Lange Theory. This new theory is based on integration of the information from Evolutionary Psychology, Cognitive Psychology, Neuropsychology and Neuroscience. Basically, the argument that this theory makes, is that we are conscious of an emotion when unconscious physiological cues produce a given inner state, and when we recognize someone else's emotion, we do so by reproducing or mimicking their body state. Electromyogram studies have shown that when people are asked to view a face and name the emotion on that face, they mimic the facial expression and it this embodiment that allows them the cognition of the emotion the face is displaying (Halberstadt, J.N., Winkielman, P., 2009).

Historical Theories of emotion

James-Lange theory

Theory that explains emotional states (such as fear) resulting from an organism's awareness of bodily responses to a situation, rather than from cognitions about that situation.

THE JAMES-LANGE THEORY Ordinarily, if someone saw you smiling and asked, "Why are you smiling?" you are likely to say "Because I am happy"; if that person said "Why are you happy?" You are likely to say "Because I made an A on a test I thought I'd failed." In other words, your cognition of the A generated the feeling of happiness, which in turn generated the muscular action involved in smiling. This "common-sense" interpretation of the activation of emotion seems quite logical. However, the American psychologist William James (1884), and the Danish physiologist Carl Lange (1885), writing independently of each other, subscribed to the view now known as the James-Lange Theory.

The James-Lange Theory of Emotion states that the perception of physiological states triggered by environmental stimuli produces emotion. In other words, the A on the test triggered some physiological changes such as an increased heart-beat and the muscular response of a smile, and when you perceived these physiological changes, you experienced happiness.

Many psychologists have called the James-Lange theory *the cart-before-the-horse theory,* and have derided it by making statements such as "I am sad because I cry" or "I am happy because I laugh." James argued that emotional feeling follows bodily reaction and that these reactions were slightly different for different emotions. The James-Lange theory generated considerable research but was soon replaced by other theories, the Cannon-Bard theory being the first of them.

Get Outta Here!

In Mumbai, India, a physician named Madan Kataria started a "Laughter Club" where club members gather outdoors in public parks or beaches or halls, to laugh out loud and *you can see for yourself* that the initial fake laughter turns in to genuine laughter and the participants begin to look happy and relaxed, if you log on to YouTube! (https://www.youtube.com/watch?v=yXE-fjVnYkqM).

Better yet, you can try laughing your head off every morning for a few weeks and see whether or not you experience any mood change or health benefits!
The James-Lange theory may be a "cart-before-the –horse" theory, but for all we know, it might be correct! Laughing out loud in a false laughter has shown to induce real laughter, joy and relaxation with real physiological benefits and enhancement in immune function and quality of life, although the results are still being debated and scientists are still weighing in (Nagendra, H.R.,Chaya, M.S., et.al,2007; Rip-Roll, M. 2010)

Cannon-Bard theory

Theory that emotions occur simultaneously with physiological changes, rather than deriving from body changes as the James-Lange theory suggests.

THE CANNON-BARD THEORY Walter Cannon and Philip Bard (1934) argued that autonomic and muscular changes are not the *cause* of emotion. *The* **Cannon-Bard theory** *states that emotional experiences and physical changes occur simultaneously.* Walter Cannon argued that on perception of environmental stimuli, the thalamus, which operates as the relay station, simultaneously forwards the message to the hypothalamus which produces autonomic changes and to the Cerebral cortex, which mediates the inner experience of emotion. In other words, the inner experience of emotion is independent of the autonomic changes such as the rise or fall of the heart-beat, etc. Walter Cannon had also raised the question as to how we distinguish between various emotions, because the heart-rate increases in both fear and anger, for example and autonomic changes are not very specific for every emotion.

In the 1960s, Stanley Schachter and Jerome Singer (1962) came up with an experiment that would help answer the question as to what allows us to distinguish between various emotions, because autonomic changes are often quite similar. The theory they proposed was known as the Cognitive theory of emotions.

Schachter-Singer theory

Theory that a given body state can be linked to a variety of emotions depending on the context in which the body state occurs.

THE SCHACHTER-SINGER COGNITIVE THEORY Is based on the Two-factor model. This model holds that emotion depends on two factors: 1) a general level of arousal and 2) a *cognitive interpretation* or labeling of the situation that is thought to cause the arousal (Schachter, 1971). Schachter and Singer proposed that when we sense internal changes caused by environmental stimuli, *we evaluate the circumstances* and label the arousal in accordance. The intensity of the emotion correlates to the intensity of internal arousal, ***but the specific emotion experienced depends on the evaluation of the circumstance or our cognitive appraisal of the situation.***

Schachter and Singer (1962) designed an ingenious experiment to test this theory. They injected some volunteers with adrenaline. Half the subjects were told that it was a vitamin and were given no other information (Uninformed group). The other half were told that it was adrenaline, and were informed about the physiological arousal they would experience (Informed Group). Then the subjects were sub-divided and half the subjects from each of the two groups were placed in a waiting room, with one of two confederates.

One group was exposed to a confederate who behaved as if the injection had made him very angry. The other group was exposed to another confederate who behaved as if the injection had made him feel very light-hearted and behaved like a joker. Schachter and Singer observed the subjects through a one-way mirror and also surveyed them about their drug experience. They found that uninformed subjects placed with the confederate who seemed happy and behaved like a clown, claimed that the vitamin injection had made them feel quite happy, whereas uninformed subjects that were placed with the angry confederate claimed that the drug made them angry. This "labeling" of the arousal did not work with the informed subjects who were told they were receiving adrenaline. Since they knew the correct cause of their arousal, they correctly attributed the inner changes to the drug and were relatively unaffected by the confederate's behavior, unlike the uninformed group.

Thus the researchers' hypothesis was supported by this experiment. Subjects, who had been uninformed, tended to use the confederate's behavior as a relevant cue for identifying and labeling their own unexplained arousal as either anger or euphoria. In contrast, subjects in the informed group or the control group who had an appropriate explanation for their arousal, tended not to share the confederate's emotional state.

The Schachter-Singer theory directed the attention of psychologists to the important role of cognitive interpretation in emotional experience. However, Schachter and Singer's theory and supporting research were not without critics. Several researchers have criticized the design of the classic 1962 experiment, and some attempts to replicate its findings have produced somewhat inconsistent results (Leventhal & Tomarken, 1986; Marshall & Zimbardo, 1979; Maslach, 1979). Furthermore, our own everyday experiences suggest that many emotions, particularly those that are triggered spontaneously and instantly by sudden stimuli, do not appear to result from interpreting and labeling unexplained arousal. For example, if you heard screeching tires as you were walking across a street, you would probably experience fear long before you had cognitively assessed why your heart was in your throat.

Facial feedback theory

Theory that specific facial displays are universally associated with the expression of the emotions of fear, anger, happiness, sadness, surprise, interest, disgust, and shame.

TOMKINS' FACIAL FEEDBACK THEORY Charles Darwin was one of the fist scientists to point out that even babies born blind smile, i.e. smiling is a wired-in behavior and not dependent on seeing someone else smile. According to Darwin, each emotional "state of mind" was associated with a stereotyped set of reactions that were common within each species. In addition, emotional states that were essentially opposite were associated with an opposite set of reactions. For instance, in greeting its master a dog displays a submissive posture like that shown in the top illustration in Figure 9.2a. This set of reactions is opposite to those displayed in the aggressive posture shown in the second image in Figure 9.2a.

Darwin believed that the advantage of opposite postures for opposite emotional states was that this minimized the possibility of emotional states being confused. Because there are few, if any, postural similarities between aggressive and submissive postures, they are unlikely to be treated similarly.

Darwin also believed that many human emotional expressions, particularly patterns of facial display, result from inherited traits that are universal in the human species. Enlisting the aid of missionaries and other people from all over the world, he conducted the first recorded study of facial expression of emotions. Darwin asked his recruits to observe and record the facial expressions of the local population in a variety of emotional contexts. Comparing their observations, he found a remarkable consistency in the facial expressions associated with such emotions as anger, fear, disgust, and sadness.

Darwin's findings were borne out a century later in studies by ***Paul Ekman*** and his associates (Ekman, 1982; Ekman & Friesen, 1984). *These researchers demonstrated that people in various parts of the world not only show emotion with similar facial expressions, they also interpret these expressions in the same way.* Ekman and his colleagues took photographs of American faces depicting happiness, anger, sadness, surprise, disgust, and fear. (Figure 9.3 shows examples of these six emotions.) They then asked people from several different cultures (including the United States, Japan, Brazil, Chile, Argentina, and the Fore and Dani tribes in remote regions of New Guinea) to identify the emotions shown in the photographs. People from all of these cultures were able to identify the emotion from the facial expression with better than 80 percent accuracy. Furthermore, American college students who viewed videotapes of emotions expressed facially by members of the Fore society were also able to identify these basic emotions, although they sometimes confused fear and surprise.

FIGURE 9.2 Emotional Expression in Animals

a. Emotional expression in dogs. Note that opposite postures represent opposing emotions.

b. Emotional expression in chimpanzees. These illustrations show the facial expressions of chimpanzees:

(a) glaring anger
(b) barking anger
(c) fear
(d) submission
(e) fear-affection
(f) affection
(g) frustration
(h) sadness
(i) crying
(j) excitement
(k) playfulness

A number of researchers have argued that facial muscles respond very rapidly and with sufficient differentiation to account for a wide range of emotional experience; some have theorized that feedback from our own facial expressions determines our emotional experiences. Perhaps the most influential proponent of this **facial feedback theory** is Sylvan Tomkins (1962, 1963). Like James and Lange, Tomkins argues that different kinds of physical actions precede different brain mechanisms linked to the emotions of fear, anger, happiness, sadness, surprise, interest, disgust, and shame. Tomkins also argues that a specific facial display is universally associated with each of these neural programs. Emotion, according to Tomkins, is independent of cognition and is part of one's genetic endowment. More current research with infants supports this contention (Demos, 1993).

Tomkins' notion of universal facial expressions was supported by the cross-cultural research just discussed, and further support was provided by an intriguing two-part experiment conducted by Paul Ekman and his associates (1983). Here, professional actors were employed as subjects. In the first part of the experiment, each subject was coached, with the aid of a mirror, to assume a specific facial expression corresponding to each of the six emotions in Figure 9.3. They were told exactly which muscles to contract, but they were not asked to feel or express a particular emotion. As a control measure, some actors were coached to move muscles not involved in a particular emotional expression. As the subjects molded their facial expressions, several physiological responses were measured, including heart rate, galvanic skin response, temperature of the hands, and muscle tension in the arms. In the second phase of this experiment, subjects were simply asked to think of

FIGURE 9.3 Facial Expressions Used by Paul Ekman

The faces, from left to right, were intended to represent happiness, anger, sadness, surprise, disgust, and fear.

Does Facial Feed-back induce emotion? Check it out!

Try this simple exercise and see for yourself as to what happens! Bite on a pencil lengthwise in your teeth, so that your lips are forced to part as if in a smile. After a few minutes, do you feel your mood lifting? According to the James-Lange theory, it should.

If that doesn't do it for you, go take a look at yourself in the mirror while still holding the pencil in your mouth. Perhaps seeing yourself with the pencil in your mouth will crack you up and make you happy!

emotional experiences in their lives that produced each of the six emotions. For example, subjects might recall a recent encounter that made them angry.

Two major findings emerged from this study. First, the researchers noted that each of the four negative emotions of anger, fear, disgust, and sadness, whether induced by facial modeling or thinking of an emotional experience, was accompanied by a distinct physiological "fingerprint" or pattern of physical responses. For example, heart rate was much greater in anger than in disgust and the hands were colder in fear than in anger. Table 9.1 shows the increases or decreases in heart rate and skin temperature for each of the six acted emotions. ***Ekman's findings indicate that different emotions are associated with distinct patterns of physiological response.***

The second and perhaps the most intriguing finding in this experiment is that when the subjects simply followed instructions to move their facial muscles to mirror a given emotion, they also experienced patterns of physiological arousal that were comparable to those recorded when they relived an actual emotional experience. In some instances, the physiological signs of emotion were more pronounced when the subjects merely moved their facial muscles than when they thought of an emotional experience.

Ekman's findings do have some practical implications. We have all heard the sage advice to "keep our chins up" or to "put on a happy face" when we are feeling sad or depressed, and this research suggests that there may be some validity to this advice. Sub-

TABLE 9.1 Heart Rate and Skin Temperature

Both heart rate and skin temperature were associated with different acted emotions in Ekman's experiment.

Specific Emotion	Change in Heart Rate (beats/min.)	Change in Skin Temperature (degrees C)
Anger	+8.0	+.16
Fear	+8.0	–.01
Distress	+6.5	+.01
Joy	+2.0	+.03
Surprise	+1.8	–.01
Disgust	–0.3	–.03

SOURCE: Figure of "Changes in Heart Rate and Skin Temperature for Six Emotions" from *Science,* Volume 221, © 1983 by Paul Ekman, et al. Reprinted by permission of Paul Ekman.

jects felt happy just by contracting the facial muscles associated with happiness. Perhaps if we make the effort to act cheerful, smile, and laugh when we feel down in the dumps, we will in turn feel more cheerful and less sad.

THE OPPONENT-PROCESS THEORY OF EMOTION In the chapter on Motivation, you read the incredible story of the Colorado mountain climber. What accounts for his continued participation in a sport that must arouse intense emotion at both ends of the scale—both high fear and ecstatic exhilaration? For that matter, why do people jump out of airplanes with a parachute strapped on their backs, ski off extremely steep mountain slopes, or return to a sport that almost killed them?

Opponent-process theory of emotion

States that when a strong emotional response to a particular stimulus disrupts emotional balance, an opposite emotional response is eventually activated to restore emotional equilibrium.

In the 1970s, psychologists Richard Solomon and J. D. Corbit (1974) proposed a theory of emotion that attempts to answer these questions. According to their **opponent-process theory of emotion**, people are inclined to maintain a relatively even keel or balance in their emotional lives. When a strong emotional response to a particular stimulus event disrupts this homeostatic balance, an opponent-process, or opposite emotional response, is activated to restore equilibrium in our emotional state. Thus, if our initial response to being confronted with Class 5 (wild water) rapids is sudden terror, we will probably subsequently experience elation after successfully negotiating the rapids—a positive or opposite emotion that cancels out the original negative emotion, thus restoring us to a neutral or balanced emotional state.

Solomon and Corbit also argued that when we repeatedly expose ourselves to a situation that arouses the same intense emotion, our initial emotional reaction will gradually weaken over time much like drug effects build tolerance while the opponent emotional reaction will grow stronger. Therefore, we could expect that with repeat exposure to the same dangerous stimuli our terror of heights would gradually diminish to a level of anxiety just sufficient to get the adrenaline pumping. In contrast, our euphoria after successfully negotiating a steep pitch could be expected to become more intense or powerful with subsequent successful climbs. *This weakening of the initial emotional response together with the eventual dominance of the opponent-process emotion, Solomon and Corbit thought, explains why rock climbers, skydivers, and other risk takers find that the more they engage in their thrilling sports the more enjoyable these activities become.* Solomon and Corbit also thought that the Opponent-Process theory explains drug abuse by explaining how the initial high becomes blunted with use due to tolerance where as the withdrawal effects of the drug, seen when the drug is withdrawn, become worse as the user increases his dose to combat tolerance. Opiates like Heroin, Morphine, etc. as drugs of abuse showed both tolerance with continued use and severe withdrawal symptoms on abruptly stopping the drug use. Hence for a while, the Opponent Process theory was thought to explain continued drug-abuse as a way of avoiding the severe withdrawal symptoms. However, over time psychologists recognized that tolerance does not occur to all drugs of abuse and not all drugs of abuse have sufficiently strong withdrawal symptoms to warrant repeat use. Hence the theory fell into disuse to explain drug abuse.

In some parts of India elderly women admonish young mothers not to tickle the baby and make it laugh too much, for fear that it may feel sad and cry later. Dismissed by the younger generation as an "old wives tale", perhaps the reproach is based on common-sense knowledge of the workings of the psyche, and perhaps the Opponent-Process theory applies to some naturally experienced emotions, if not to abuse of drugs.

In concluding our discussion of theories of emotion, we have traversed a full circle. We started with James Lange and have come to the Cognitive Embodiment Theory, which is very similar to that of William James and Carl Lange! We must acknowledge that many questions still remain unanswered. Each of the theories we have looked at helps to explain at least a part of the process whereby emotions are activated, and all of them are supported to some degree by research. New *f*MRI studies will add considerably to our knowledge and soon many of the unanswered questions be answered. In the next section we will examine the effects of stress and learn how to combat stress, anxiety and tension.

STRESS

We have all learned that negative emotions such as fear, anxiety, anger, and depression often exact a price in our lives in the form of impaired functioning, fatigue, symptoms of physical discomfort, and even illness. Disruptive, unpleasant emotions play a major role both in contributing to stress and as key components in the manifestation of reactions to stress. Thus we end this chapter with a somewhat detailed discussion of the topic of stress, including comments about the nature of stress and stressors, physiological and psychological responses to stress, and the relationship between stress and illness.

Physiological Responses to Stress

In the 1930s Canadian researcher **Hans Selye** was conducting research that he hoped would lead to the discovery of a new sex hormone. The leads were promising. When he injected rats with extracts of ovary tissue, the results were consistent: bleeding ulcers in the stomach and small intestine, enlargement of the adrenal cortex, and shrinkage of the thymus gland. Since no hormone was known to produce these effects, Selye was convinced that he was on the track of identifying a new one. His elation was quickly dampened, however, for when he injected extracts from other tissues, the effects were identical. Furthermore, the same thing occurred when he injected toxic fluids that were not derived from tissues.

Selye was devastated by this turn of events. But instead of giving up, he tried to determine what had happened. The answer occurred to him only when he stopped trying to relate his findings to the discovery of a new sex hormone. In his own words,

> It suddenly struck me that one could look at [my ill-fated experiments] from an entirely different angle. [Perhaps] there was such a thing as a single nonspecific reaction of the body to damage of any kind. (1976, p. 26)

Selye went on to study how animals responded to a wide range of stressful events other than injections. When Hans Selye was a medical student, he had noticed that many more of his class mates were sick, down with a cold or flu, just before a test. He had always wondered why, and eventually he figured out the connection between stress, distress and the immune system (Selye, 1976). Selye also learned that humans respond to stress with fairly consistent physiological patterns (1936, 1956, 1974, & 1976). The awareness that stress can have harmful effects on our bodies led to many more studies, as well as techniques for reducing the impact of stress on our own lives.

General adaptation syndrome (GAS)

Progressive responses to prolonged stress in which an organism mobilizes for action and compensates for stress.

Hans Selye's observations of how his rats responded to stressors led him to formulate the concept of the **general adaptation syndrome (GAS)**. According to this notion, when an organism is confronted with a stressor, its body mobilizes for action. This mobilization effort is mediated by the sympathetic nervous system, and it works primarily through the action of specific hormones on the body's muscles and organ systems. The response to stress is said to be *nonspecific,* because the same physiological reactions occur regardless of the type of stressor. Selye also noted that repeated or prolonged exposure to stress that is not adequately managed or reduced results in tissue damage (such as bleeding ulcers), increased susceptibility to disease, and even death in extreme cases.

ALARM, RESISTANCE, AND EXHAUSTION Selye described three phases of the general adaptation syndrome: alarm, resistance, and exhaustion (see Figure 9.4). When an organism is exposed to a stressful event, it first experiences an *alarm* reaction in which it mobilizes to meet the threat. A sudden arousal of the sympathetic nervous system pro-

FIGURE 9.4 Three Phases of Selye's General Adaptation Syndrome

SOURCE: Adapted from Selye, 1956

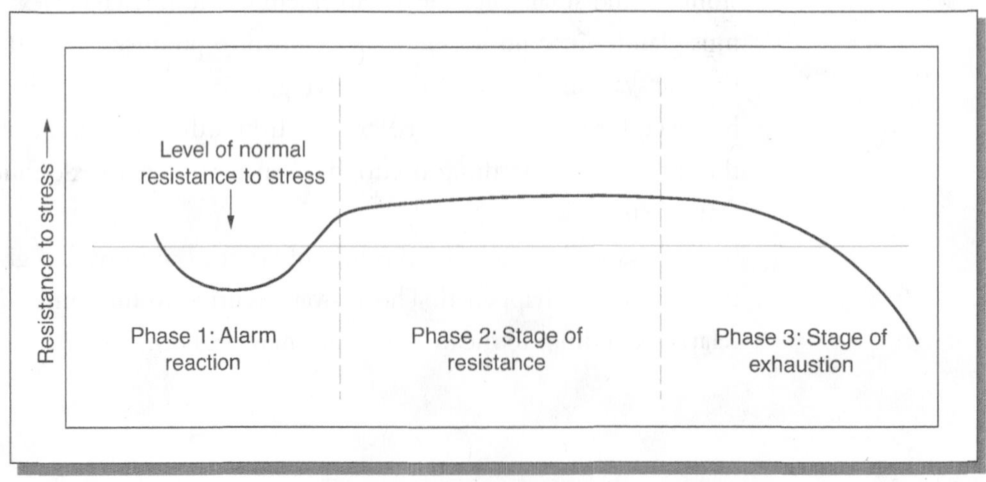

duces a flood of hormones—corticosteroids from the adrenal cortex and epinephrine (often called adrenaline) and norepinephrine from the adrenal medulla.

These hormones prepare the body for "fight or flight" by producing a number of physiological reactions. First, our heart rate is likely to increase, as is blood pressure. We experience this response as a pounding heart, like the rapid-fire thumping you may have felt after barely avoiding an accident on the freeway. Sugars and fats also flood the blood to provide fuel for quick energy. This emergency response provides extra reserves, with the result that people are often able to perform seemingly superhuman feats (such as lifting a heavy beam off a person trapped in a mine cave-in) that they could not otherwise perform. Digestion slows or ceases during the alarm stage, making more blood available to the muscles and brain.

Our breathing rate also accelerates to supply increased oxygen to muscles poised for greater than normal output. Thus people often have difficulty catching their breath after a severe fright. Still another response to stress is a tensing of the muscles in preparation for an adaptive response. This explains the stiff neck, sore back, and painful aching legs that many people experience after a long, hard exam or a rough day at work.

We also tend to perspire more when under stress—a response that acts as a kind of built-in air conditioner that cools our energized bodies. It also allows us to burn more energy (which produces heat) when we are faced with emergency situations. This is why many people find themselves drenched with perspiration after giving a speech or undergoing a stressful interview.

Finally, clotting agents are released into the blood when we are under stress, so that our blood will clot more rapidly if we are injured. One reason why we may not notice an injury we receive during an accident or fight is because the wound may have bled very little. Table 9.2 summarizes these responses to stress.

We are not able to maintain the alarm phase's high level of bodily response or sympathetic activity for very long. Eventually the parasympathetic nervous system comes into play, providing a braking mechanism for the organs activated by the sympathetic system. At this point the organism enters into the second stage of resistance. Now the body continues to draw upon resources at an above-normal rate, but it is less aroused than in the alarm state.

If the stress is prolonged or repeated, an organism is likely to enter the third stage of exhaustion. As a direct result of the continued drain on resources, the body tissues may

TABLE 9.2 Some Physiological Responses to Stress

- Heart rate and blood pressure increase, forcing blood to parts of the body that may need it for strenuous physical activity
- Digestion slows or ceases, so that more blood is available to other organs
- Breathing rate accelerates to provide increased oxygen to bloodstream
- Muscles tense in preparation for an emergency response
- Perspiration increases, acting to cool the body
- Clotting agents are released in the blood to prevent loss of blood in case of injury

begin to show signs of wear and tear during the exhaustion stage. Susceptibility to disease also increases, and continued exposure to the stressor is likely to deplete the organism's adaptive energy. The symptoms of the initial alarm reaction are likely to reappear, but resistance is now decreased and the alarm reaction is likely to continue unabated. If the organism is unable to develop strategies to overcome or cope with stress, serious illness or even collapse and death may result.

Selye's model has had a profound impact on our understanding of stress and its links to illness. However, Selye's theory has also been criticized on a few counts. One criticism is that Selye did not take the role of cognitive appraisal into account. Also, some newer evidence indicates that not all stressors produce a non-specific syndrome. For example, exercise stress produces a pattern of physiology quite different from that produced by emotional stress (Dimsdale and Moss, 1980).

Psychological Responses to Stress

Most of Selye's work focused on endocrine responses to stress in nonhuman animals, most notably rats. In recent years, however, increased attention has been directed to assessing the importance of psychological factors in stress reactions.

COGNITIVE RESPONSES TO STRESS If you think back to a situation in which you were under a great deal of stress—after breaking up with a partner, for instance, you might find that your cognitive responses stand out more clearly in your memory than your physiological responses. Typical cognitive responses may include reduced ability to concentrate, higher than normal levels of distractibility, impaired performance on cognitive tasks (such as reading or doing your homework), and sometimes a tendency to be plagued by disruptive or morbid thoughts. People who are under a great deal of stress often find that their attention wanders and that they are easily distracted. It is also common to be troubled by intrusive, repetitive thoughts such as "I'm worthless" or "I just don't have what it takes," especially after experiencing a setback such as the loss of a job.

Stress may also result in positive cognitive responses, as we learn new ways to cope with or neutralize the stressful event. For example, you may learn to cope with the stress of getting caught in rush-hour traffic by leaving for class earlier or not scheduling courses at times that coincide with heavy commuter traffic or you may take a basic course in auto mechanics to avoid the stress of a car that does not operate properly.

Why do some stressful situations produce negative effects, whereas others have a positive outcome? Psychologist Richard Lazarus (1999) proposes that our cognitive appraisal of a stressor makes a difference in our immediate response as well as our ability to cope with the stressor in the long run. Lazarus maintains that when we confront situations that may be potentially stressful, we first engage in a process of *primary appraisal* to determine if the event is positive, neutral, or negative. If we consider an event to be negative, we further appraise it to determine how harmful, threatening, or challenging the event is.

Once we complete the process of primary appraisal of potentially stressful events, Lazarus suggests that we engage in a *secondary appraisal* to determine whether or not our coping abilities and resources will allow us to overcome the harm or threat and successfully meet the challenge. The end result, in terms of the amount of stress we actually experience, represents a blending or balance between these two processes of primary and secondary appraisal. If we perceive the harm and/or threat to be very high, we are likely to experience a high degree of stress. On the other hand, if we think we can cope with the situation, we are likely to experience far less stress.

Some psychologists suggest that *taking a **task-oriented approach to stress** reduction is highly effective in coping with stressful events.* The steps they suggest for this task-oriented approach are:

1. Spot the source of the stress.
2. Ask yourself what you can do about it, and narrow down your choices
3. Draw out an action plan.
4. Execute your plan.
5. Evaluate the results.

Coming up with a battle plan in itself will relieve you of much stress right away, lifting your spirits and making you more able to cope.

EMOTIONAL RESPONSES TO STRESS Negative emotional states are strongly associated with stress. Emotional responses to stress include such feelings as anxiety, irritability, anger, embarrassment, depression, helplessness, and hostility.

Research indicates that people can talk themselves out of negative emotional states by making statements of hope to themselves, for example, saying "tomorrow will be another day" or "every cloud has a silver lining" helps people lift their mood (Lefton & Valvatne, 1988 pp 523).

BEHAVIORAL RESPONSES TO STRESS There are so many behavioral responses to stress that it is impossible to outline them all here. We have seen, however, that two general classes of adaptive behavioral responses are suggested by the fight or flight pattern. In some cases we take some kind of assertive action *(fight)* to confront stressors. For example, if you find that your home environment is stressful because of a room-mate who is constantly nagging at you, you may eventually confront the room-mate. By confronting the source of your stress, you may be able to clear the air and find mutually acceptable ways of reducing or eliminating this stressor in your life. Sometimes, however, people prefer to withdraw from a threatening or harmful situation *(flight)*. That is, you may decide you will experience less stress if you move into your own place.

Our strategies for coping with stress are not always either a clear confrontation or a clear withdrawal. A third alternative is to try to *adapt* to the stress. For example, assume you live near elevated train tracks and once every hour, at roughly the same time, you are disturbed by the loud noise caused by a passing train. If you are trying to study in your home, this intrusive noise could be a major source of stress in your life. You might neutralize this stressor simply by taking short hourly study breaks whenever a train passes. The Health, Psychology, and Life discussion at the end of this chapter proposes several physiological, cognitive, and behavioral strategies for reducing the effects of stress.

FACTORS THAT CONTRIBUTE TO STRESS Our cognitive assessments have a lot to do with the degree of stress an event will produce in our lives, but it is not true to say that all events have the same potential for eliciting stress. What characteristics increase the likelihood that we will perceive an event as stressful?

Lack of Control One important factor that contributes to the stressfulness of a situation is our perceived lack of control over the situation. Thus, it is much less stressful for you to stick a needle into yourself (for example, when removing a splinter) than to have a physician stick a needle into your arm. *Research reveals that uncontrollable or unpredictable events are generally more stressful than those we can control or predict.*

Suddenness A second variable influencing how stressful we perceive an event to be is the suddenness with which it overtakes us. When people experience accidents or an unexpected pink slip at work, they may find it very difficult to mobilize adequate coping mechanisms. In general, it is easier to cope with challenges that we can foresee. Thus a person who loses a loved one after a protracted illness, or who loses a job after expecting to be terminated for months, may be much less stressed by these aversive events.

Ambiguity In general, a stressor that we perceive as ambiguous is likely to induce more stress than one that is clear-cut. In well-defined situations we may be able to determine an appropriate course of action (fight, flight, or adapt), but ambiguity forces us to spend resource-depleting energy trying to figure out the nature of the stressor and possible strategies to cope effectively with it.

Socio-cultural Factors In addition to the above factors, social and cultural factors such as one's socio-economic status, ethnicity and corresponding acculturative stress i.e. stress experienced by a person who is adjusting to a new culture and gender role expectations also contribute substantially to stress. Quite often immigrant ethnic minority women face a low socio-economic status coupled with acculturative stress and gender role stress making them prone to stress-related illnesses.

Stress and Disease

Stress is widely recognized as a major factor in a wide range of physical illnesses. It has been estimated that as many as three out of four visits to physicians are prompted by stress-related problems (Charlesworth & Nathan, 1982). Furthermore, stress and stress-related behaviors may be the leading contributors to early death. Chronic Heart Disease,

Hypertension or High Blood Pressure, some types of Cancer (Moynihan, 2003), migraine headaches, frequent diarrhea and or constipation, digestive upsets such as acidity, excessive belching, suppressed immune system and even some birth defects have been said to be due to chronic stress experienced by a pregnant woman. In the next section, we will take a look at some techniques for coping with stress.

HEALTH, PSYCHOLOGY, AND LIFE

Stress Management Techniques

Evidence linking stress with a variety of illnesses has prompted many health professionals to turn their attention to developing techniques for managing stress. These techniques take aim not only at our physiological, cognitive, and behavioral responses to stress but also at behaviors and thought patterns that may induce or increase stress. The following paragraphs summarize some of the strategies that have been applied successfully in various stress-management programs offered at hospitals, clinics, and corporations.

MANAGING PHYSIOLOGICAL RESPONSES TO STRESS

Much of the physical damage associated with stress results from our bodies' physiological responses. These include the release of hormones and corticosteroids into the blood resulting in increases in metabolism, heart rate, blood pressure, and muscle tension, and a decrease in the ability of our immune system to respond effectively to invasion. Many techniques have been developed to minimize these reactions; three of the most effective are biofeedback, relaxation training, and exercise.

Biofeedback We are seldom aware of the subtle physiological changes that take place when we are under stress, such as rising blood pressure or increased heart rate. The theory behind biofeedback is that if we learn to recognize these changes we can also learn to control them. Biofeedback provides individuals with information about their bodily processes that they can use to modify these processes. For instance, people who suffer from high blood pressure might be hooked up to a biofeedback apparatus that constantly monitors their blood pressure, and emits a tone that changes in pitch as their blood pressure rises or falls. They then instruct themselves to relax and if the pitch goes down, they know they have succeeded in lowering their blood pressure. Through this process, they may eventually learn to recognize symptoms of high blood pressure even when they do not hear a tone, so that they can apply techniques to control this response. Although biofeedback is not a panacea for all stress-related disorders, it has been helpful in treating migraine headaches, tension headaches, muscle tension, high blood pressure, and chronic pain.

Relaxation Training Virtually every formal stress-management program teaches some kind of relaxation technique. One of these is *progressive relaxation,* in which a person first tightens the muscles in a given area of the body (such as the legs), then relaxes them and then progresses systematically to other body areas until the entire body is relaxed. The idea that physical relaxation can lead to mental relaxation has been supported by experience, and *progressive relaxation is now a key element in many stress-management programs.*

How effective is relaxation in controlling stress-induced effects such as muscle tension and high blood pressure? In one recent study, several hundred heart attack survivors were randomly assigned to one of two groups. One group received standard advice about proper diet and exercise; the other received the same advice, plus counseling on how to relax and slow down. In the ensuing three years, subjects in the group that received relaxation counseling experienced only half as many recurrent heart attacks as those who had received the standard medical advice (Friedman & Ulmer, 1984).

Relaxation training is also being used with some success in delaying the recurrence of some kinds of terminal cancer. It is believed that relaxation training may play a role in facilitating the body's immune system to fend off the rapid growth of cancer cells. A number of treatment programs have begun to adopt relaxation training as part of cancer treatment.

Exercise Have you ever noticed that some types of exercise, such as jogging a few miles or playing tennis, can help to relieve stress? Exercise helps to distract us from sources of stress, and it can also help to moderate

Managing Stress, *continued*

some potentially damaging physical effects of stress by lowering blood pressure, improving circulation, and strengthening the heart muscle. In addition, people who regularly engage in some form of exercise are more likely to adopt a healthful diet and be non-smokers.

Modifying Cognitive Antecedents of Stress People involved in stress-management programs learn to *pay attention to what they are thinking just before they experience stress.* One of the benefits of this *self-monitoring* is the awareness of how frequently our *own upsetting thoughts or negative self-talk trigger our feelings of stress.* Negative self-talk such as, "I'll never be able to pass this exam" can make the difference between good performance and failure; it can also help to bring on the elevated physical reactions typical of stress responses.

To modify these common cognitive antecedents of stress, Canadian psychologist Donald Meichenbaum (1993) suggests a technique he calls *stress inoculation,* in which we *learn to replace negative self-statements with positive coping statements.* For example, when faced with the stress of an exam, we might use positive self-talk such as, "There's no point in imagining the worst; I've prepared as well as anyone and I'll do the best I can." Although it may take some time to learn to alter negative self-talk successfully, the effect can be a reduction in anxiety and stress.

Modifying Behavioral Antecedents of Stress Many of us bring stress on ourselves by certain maladaptive behaviors. For instance, we may use our time poorly and then suddenly find ourselves under pressure, or we may habitually take on too many tasks to accomplish in the time we have. Stress management programs offer a variety of techniques for modifying such stress-producing behaviors. The following abbreviated list illustrates a number of these behaviors, as well as some strategies that are helpful in combating them.

- *Procrastination.* Time-management training can help people pace themselves to avoid leaving too much for the last minute.
- *The "super-person syndrome."* For some people, an important part of stress management is learning to say "no" and to delegate tasks to others. Time-management training can also help people recognize their limits so that they do not commit to more work than they can complete.
- *Disorganization.* Stress-management programs often help people deal with disorganization by providing training in how to set goals for each day, establish priorities, avoid wasting time, and become task-oriented.
- *Lack of assertiveness.* People who have difficulty standing up for their rights may be "boiling inside," generating tremendous amounts of stress. To combat this tendency, many stress-management programs incorporate *assertiveness training,* which teaches people to confront such situations rather than tiptoe around them.
- *Going it alone.* Facing stress alone is much more damaging than facing it with the support of people who care about us. Talking with others provides us with new perspectives; it may also boost our self-esteem and our sense that we are valued. Thus an important tactic in managing stress is to talk things over with someone. If friends or family members are not able to provide support, a campus counseling center, community health center, or private clinic may be a valuable resource.

SUMMARY

THE COMPONENTS OF EMOTIONS

1. Motivation and emotion are closely connected. Emotions often motivate our actions.
2. Emotions are composed of four integral components: cognitive processes, affect, physiological arousal, and behavioral reactions.

THE RANGE OF HUMAN EMOTION

3. According to Plutchik's Emotion Wheel there are eight primary human emotions, which consist of four pairs of opposites: acceptance and disgust, fear and anger, surprise and anticipation, and sadness and joy. Each of these emotions is wired-in to occur to certain environmental stimuli in order to ensure survival. Other emotions are a mixture of these primary emotions.
4. The newest theory is a come-back of the first historical theory (The James-Lange Theory) but with much more information and evidence from *f*MRI studies, EMG studies or other neuroimaging techniques. The theory is called Cognitive Embodiment Theory of Emotion.

HISTORICAL THEORIES OF EMOTION

5. According to the James-Lange theory, environmental stimuli trigger physiological responses from the viscera and muscle movements. These visceral and muscular responses then activate emotional states.
6. The Cannon-Bard theory suggests that internal physiological changes and muscular responses are not the cause of emotion, but rather that emotional experiences and physical changes occur simultaneously.
7. The Schachter-Singer theory combines elements from both the James-Lange and Cannon-Bard theories. Schachter and Singer maintained that emotions depend on a kind of double cognitive interpretation: We appraise the emotion-causing event while also evaluating what is happening physiologically with our bodies.
8. According to the facial feedback theory, facial muscles respond very rapidly and with sufficient differentiation to account for a wide range of emotional experience. Feedback from our own facial expressions helps determine our emotional experiences.
9. Solomon and Corbit's opponent-process theory maintains that when a strong emotional response to a particular stimulus event disrupts emotional balance, an opponent-process is eventually activated to restore equilibrium in one's emotional state. Repeated exposures to stimuli that arouse intense emotions result in a gradual weakening of the initial emotional reaction as the opponent process becomes stronger.

STRESS

10. There is a powerful relationship between emotion and stress. Stress may be defined as the process of appraising events (as harmful, threatening, or challenging), of assessing potential responses, and of responding to those events.
11. Selye's observation of organisms' physiological responses to stress led him to formulate the concept of a general adaptation syndrome (GAS) composed of three phases: alarm, resistance, and exhaustion. The alarm phase is characterized by a flood of stress hormones that prepare the body for fight or flight. In the resistance stage the body returns to a less aroused state, but one in which it continues to draw upon resources at an above-normal rate. If the stress is not alleviated, an

organism is likely to enter the third state of exhaustion in which its body tissues begin to show signs of wear and tear, and susceptibility to disease increases.

12. Typical cognitive responses to stress include reduced ability to concentrate, distractibility, impaired performance on cognitive tasks, and a tendency to be plagued by disruptive or morbid thoughts.
13. Emotional responses to stress include such feelings as anxiety, irritability, anger, embarrassment, depression, and hostility.
14. A myriad of possible behavioral responses to stress include assertive action to confront stressors, withdrawal from a stressful situation, and adapting to the source of stress.
15. Factors that contribute to the stressfulness of a situation include our lack of control over it, its sudden onset, and a degree of ambiguity that forces us to spend resource-depleting energy trying to figure out the nature of the stressor. Social factors such as socioeconomic status, ethnicity, acculturation stress, gender role expectations, etc., also cause stress.
16. Response to stress may be a major contributor to illnesses such as coronary heart disease, cancer, high blood pressure, and even birth defects if the mother is chronically stressed during pregnancy.
17. Stress hormones exert a pronounced effect on the immune system's ability to defend our bodies successfully against disease.

TERMS AND CONCEPTS

Emotions
James-Lange theory
Cannon-Bard theory
Schachter-Singer theory
Facial feedback theory
Opponent-process theory
general adaptation syndrome (GAS)

CHAPTER 10

Cognition: Thinking and Language

Corbis

Stumpf, Pfungst, and "Der Kluge Hans"

In Germany, around the turn of the century, there was a famous horse named Hans who performed amazing intellectual feats. When asked to solve spoken arithmetic problems, such as "What is the sum of 5 plus 1?" and even more complex arithmetic problems, Hans consistently signed the correct answer by tapping his hoof the correct number of times. Pretty soon, "Clever Hans" became a much talked about phenomenon, and was investigated by psychologist Carl Stumpf (Boring, 1950, p. 366) and systematically tested by a German psychologist named Oskar Pfungst (Wozniak, 1999).

Pfungst discovered that Hans had trouble solving math problems if the questioner either did not know the answer or was standing out of sight.

Pfungst provided evidence that Hans did not understand either the words or the math problems; instead, he had learned to respond to subtle body language cues of the questioners. Whenever his trainer or another questioner said something to him in an expectant tone of voice, then leaned forward and tensed up, Hans knew that he should start tapping his hoof on the ground. He would keep striking the ground until the trainer relaxed and stopped leaning forward. Hans knew that if he stopped tapping his hoof at this point, he would receive a carrot as a reward. In other words, *Hans was not solving the math problems with his independent thinking, but was relying on cues provided by humans who knew the answer.* Hans may not have been a thinker, but he sure was one clever horse!

In the following pages, we explore thinking, problem solving, reasoning and decision making, and the special qualities of human language and human intelligence. These processes constitute the core topics within the area of *cognitive psychology.* The abilities of Hans demonstrate that cognitive processes can be misinterpreted, and often complex behavior of humans and other animals can be reduced to simpler behavioral processes. The cognitive processes discussed in this chapter are not an exception.

THINKING

The term *think* has a variety of meanings. For example, we might remark to a companion, "I can't think of the name of that architectural style," or "I think that car is a terrific buy." Alternatively, if a neighbor asks your opinion about the best way to deal with the problem of cars speeding along your quiet street, you may respond, "Let me think about it for a while."

In the first two instances the word think is synonymous with remembering and belief, respectively; in the third example it implies a process of reasoning about a particular situation with the intent of solving a problem. Psychologists who study thought are interested primarily in this latter meaning. *Thus, we may define thought or* **thinking** *as a collection of internal processes directed toward solving a problem.* When we use symbols or concepts to imagine something internally, and to solve problems, we are said to be thinking.

Thought

Any cognitive processes directed toward problem solving, understanding language, memory retrieval, and perceiving patterns in sensory inputs.

Thinking

Is the mental manipulation of images, concepts and ideas that is done in order to solve a problem or to reach a goal.

Thinking is the process that lets us make sense out of our perceptions. Our ability to think also allows us to put what we have learned to use. Perhaps most importantly, thinking allows us to manipulate representations of objects, so that we can solve problems without actually going through any physical motions. For example, in a game of chess we might think about the consequences of several moves before actually moving a piece.

Cognitive psychologists who study thought are interested in determining how people transform and manipulate information to solve problems and make decisions. Before examining what research has revealed about how we accomplish these goals, we first consider a fundamental question: What are the basic components of thinking?

Components of Thinking

THINKING AS BEHAVIOR About half a century ago, many psychologists believed that thinking was essentially a matter of talking to ourselves, or simply covert behavior. Some early evidence supported this view. For example, when researchers used sensitive recording devices, they were able to record very subtle movements of the tongue and throat muscles that occurred when subjects were silently thinking about various problems (Jacobson, 1932). This prompted some Behaviorists to argue that subvocal speech and overt motor action was essential for thinking. Some, like John Watson, for example, went so far as to say that subvocal speech *was* thinking. Thus, thinking was seen as covert or hidden behavior, and laws of overt behavior were said to be sufficient to explain thinking.

However, others disagreed, and a member of a team of psycho-pharmacologists volunteered to have him-self injected with *curare*, a drug that temporarily paralyzes all of the skeletal muscles. Since the paralyzed subject could not move any muscles, he was unable to engage in subvocal speech, to breathe, or even to blink. He was placed on artificial respiration and other vital support services while temporarily immobilized. When the drug wore off, he reported that his mind had remained clear during the entire procedure, and that he had been able to think and solve problems when immobilized, so thinking was not the same as subvocal speech and did not need muscular movement (Smith et al., 1947).

Some psychologists interpreted these results as evidence that thinking can be independent of muscular movement, however most behaviorists were not convinced, and *B. F. Skinner (1974) termed this kind of* ***behavior covert*** *behavior and maintained that the same laws that govern any overt behavior also applied to this covert behavior called thinking.* However, cognitive psychologists persisted in their pursuit of learning more about thinking and defined thinking.

Covert Behavior

Behavior that is unobservable in another person. Thinking is an example of covert behavior.

MENTAL IMAGES If thinking is not solely covert behavior, what else is there? One additional component is mental imagery. Mental imagery may take the form of visual imagery, auditory, olfactory, or even tactile imagery. Most research however has focused on visual imagery.

For example, suppose you are trying to figure out how to assemble a new lawn mower after removing all the parts from the packing crate. You are likely to think about this task by manipulating visual pictures or mental images of the various parts. You might also use mental imagery to solve a mathematics problem, to picture the components of a perfect tennis swing, to compose or rehearse music, or to identify the correct rotation of a three-dimensional object.

However, what are these mental images? Certainly, they cannot be mere internal pictures, as this would require another "mind's eye" to interpret them, by perhaps another image. While some cognitive psychologists insist that mental images that represent the spatial properties of real objects exist just as vision exists, other psychologists argue that the picture image analog is misleading even though visual imagery and vision share some of the same neural mechanisms (Pylyshyn, 1984, 2002).

Although it appears that mental images of some sort are an element of thought, there is more to thought than representational images of sights, sounds, and touches. Most cognitive psychologists believe that there is another, more abstract or symbolic form of thinking that involves the use of *concepts*.

CONCEPTS Concept formation may be one of the most important cognitive functions that humans perform (Solso, 2000). Concept formation is mental categorization. In order to think and communicate about the objects, events, activities, and relationships, etc., that we encounter in our daily lives, we learn to simplify and provide order to our world by grouping them. Our mental representations of these categories are referred to as **concepts**. For example, you have a concept of an airplane, which refers to your representation of all cases of planes and it excludes other flying objects like insects and birds. Concepts thus represent categories or kinds of things and their rules of combination, not just individual cases. Most of our knowledge is in the form of concepts rather than independent, specific items or instances. Concepts may also represent more abstract ideas, such as *freedom, love, morality,* or *spirituality.*

Concepts

Cognitive categories for grouping events, objects, or processes.

Our ability to think and function efficiently would be greatly impaired if we were not able to form concepts. Without the general concept *car* we could never give our children simple instructions such as, "Watch out for cars when you cross the street." Instead, we would have to list every name of every automobile. Thus concept formation allows quick communication and comprehension.

Concepts range from broad to very specific. Examples of specific, narrow concepts are *sock, golden retriever,* and *red ball.* Examples of broader concepts are *footwear, dog,* and *ball.* We tend to organize concepts into hierarchies, with specific concepts grouped as subcategories within broader concepts. Thus, *airplane* represents a broad concept that may be subdivided into more specific lower-level categories, such as *propeller aircraft and jet aircraft.* Furthermore, *jet aircraft* may be subdivided into more specific concepts such as *jet fighters, commercial passenger jet,* and so forth.

Research has supported the idea that *we rely on basic-level categories most of the time.* When subjects are shown a picture of an object and are asked to verify (yes or no) that it illustrates a particular concept, they tend to react fastest at the basic level. For example, when shown a picture of a kitchen chair, subjects consistently classify it more quickly at the basic level (*chair*) than at either a subordinate level (*kitchen chair)* or a super-ordinate level (*piece of furniture*). As children develop and learn to think conceptually about their environments, basic-level categories are probably those they use first as they acquire the ability to name and classify events and objects. Many cognitive psychologists now believe that this dependence on basic levels of concepts continues to be a fundamental aspect of human thought throughout our lives.

But how do we form these concepts that are so essential to our everyday thought and decision-making processes? There are two theories of concept formation, one is known as the association theory and the other is the prototype theory.

ASSOCIATION THEORY was proposed by Clark Hull (1920). Hull described concept formation as the acquisition of stimulus-response (S-R) associations. According to this view, we learn to associate a single response (the concept) with a set of stimuli that share one or more common elements. Thus, we associate the concept response *bird* with a pattern of stimuli (has wings, flies, lays eggs, etc.). We form a representation of a concept that is broad enough to allow us to generalize the response to many different instances of the concept. When we encounter a novel instance of the concept, such as an exotic bird we have never seen before, we respond correctly ("it is a bird") on the basis of stimulus generalization.

The Prototype Theory of Concept Formation

Elanor Rosch (1976, 1978, 1988) proposed an alternative explanation of how we form everyday concepts. According to Rosch, the natural concepts that we learn in everyday life are represented in our memories by examples or **exemplars**. Thus, our concept of *fish* may be based on images of salmon, trout, or bass—*all examples of fish that we have seen rather than arbitrary rules such as "have fins," "breathe through gills," and "live in water."* Rosch pointed out that most natural concepts, such as *furniture, fish, bird,* and *game,* are not easily described as some well-defined combination of discrete attributes. Also, for any given concept category, some examples are more typical and some less typical. Rosch suggested

Prototype

Best or most typical representative of a category around which we often structure our concept of that category.

that we often structure our concepts around best instances, or most typical representatives of the category, i.e., **prototypes**. The more closely objects or events match our prototypes for a concept, the more readily we include them in the category.

Suppose, for example, you were asked, "Is a robin a bird?" and "Is a penguin a bird?" You would respond yes to both questions, but you would probably be slower to respond to the second question. The reason is that robin is more typical of the concept bird than is penguin.

Rosch demonstrated this in an experiment in which she asked people to rank different instances of a given category according to the degree to which the instance typified the concept. These rankings correlated with reaction time, with the most typical examples producing the fastest responses and the least typical examples resulting in the slowest responses. Regardless of how a concept is formed, we use concept formation for various types of cognition, such as planning, scheming, day-dreaming and of course, problem solving.

PROBLEM SOLVING

Problem solving is different from simply executing a well-learned response or series of behaviors, as a rat might do when it negotiates a maze to reach a food reward. It is also distinct from learning new information. The essence of all problems is that they require you to supply new or fresh knowledge or new skills that allow you to solve them.

In the 1980s, a method called the IDEAL method was developed for help with the attainment of a goal or problem solving, by two psychologists named John Bransford and Barry Stein (1984). The name IDEAL is an acronym, and its letters stand for:

I: Identify the problem: In order to solve a problem, it must be recognized as a problem in the first place. When there are too many traffic accidents at an intersection for example, complaints mount and the problem gets recognized.

D: Define the problem: Once recognized or named, the situation has to be verified and scrutinized for possible contributing factors. In the example selected, city officials might note whether the accidents occur at a certain time, like at dusk or dawn, or they occur because of poor visibility due to smog, inappropriate speed, or some other variable. Discerning the contributing variables will help define the problem. Well-defined problems are those in which the original state and goal state are clearly specified, as are the rules for allowable problem-solving operations.

E: Exploring Alternative Approaches: The next step is to generate several possible ways of curtailing the accidents such as a "speed monitored by radar" warning, or the posting of a notice declaring a very stiff fine for speeding through that intersection, a mile or so before it, or a four-way stop sign before the intersection to force all drivers to stop before driving through it, or some other suitable alternative and carefully considering all of them and selecting the most promising one.

A: Acting on the selected alternative is the next step. Unless some action is implemented, one will not be able to solve the problem.

L: Look at the effects or results, i.e., evaluate the effectiveness of the solution that was implemented. In other words, find out whether the number of accidents has dropped after the implementation of the selected measure. If yes, you have solved the problem, if no, you might have to reevaluate your definition of the problem and take a closer look at other workable solutions.

Whether a problem is clear-cut or vague, the way we approach it makes a critical difference in our ability to find a workable solution. A number of different strategies can be applied toward finding workable solutions. We consider four common strategies or approaches: trial and error, testing hypotheses, algorithms, and heuristics, each of which is suitable to certain types of problems.

Trial and error

Problem-solving strategy that involves trying possible solutions, one by one, to see which one is correct.

TRIAL AND ERROR Some problems have such a narrow range of possible solutions that we decide to solve them through **trial and error**. For example, suppose you return to campus late Sunday after a weekend trip, and an acquaintance in your dorm tells you that you had a call from a man who sounded distraught, insisting that you call immediately upon your return. Unfortunately, your dorm mate cannot find the slip of paper with his name and phone number, and has forgotten his name. The list of men who call you is somewhat limited, so you decide to call them one by one until you find out which one left the message. This trial-and-error process is not a bad strategy for solving the problem of the mystery caller, since the likely solutions are probably few in number. This very same strategy was used by E.L. Thorndike's caged cat to get out of it, thus allowing Thorndike to formulate The Law of Effect, described in Chapter 6.

Testing hypotheses

A problem-solving strategy that involves formulating specific hypotheses that generate relatively efficient approaches to solving a problem, then testing these hypotheses in a systematic fashion.

TESTING HYPOTHESES A somewhat more systematic approach to problem solving is provided by the strategy of **testing hypotheses**. In the above scenario, you may formulate specific hypotheses that generate a more efficient approach to solving your problem. For example, since your roommate described the man as "distraught," you might call those of your friends who might have some reason to be distraught, such as the friend whose father was hospitalized recently, before you call any other.

Algorithm

A problem-solving strategy that involves a systematic exploration of every possible solution; computers and people may use algorithms to find the correct answer.

ALGORITHMS A third possible problem-solving strategy is the **algorithm,** or rule-based problem solving. *Algorithms also involve a systematic exploration of every possible solution until the correct one is found.* This strategy originated in the field of mathematics, where its application can produce guaranteed solutions. Algorithms are especially well suited to computers, which can rapidly sort through hundreds, thousands, even millions of possible solutions without growing tired or suffering from boredom (both shortcomings of the human data processor).

Algorithms guarantee a correct solution if you are aware of all the possibilities or if you follow all the steps given to you by the formula or rule. You have used algorithms when you solved algebra problems or did long division, etc., in school. Sometimes, though, answers to problems simply spring to mind. When that happens, you have used heuristics.

Heuristics

Rule-of-thumb (quick-fix) problem-solving strategies such as means-ends analysis and working backward.

Means-ends analysis

A common heuristic problem-solving strategy that involves identifying the difference between an original state and a desired goal, then progressing through a series of subgoals to reach the solution.

Working backward

Common heuristic problem-solving strategy that starts with describing the goal, then defines the step that directly precedes that goal, and works backward in this manner until the steps needed to reach the goal are defined.

HEURISTICS: **Heuristics** refer to a variety of strategies or sets of empirical rules that may lead to solutions to problems. These are rough "rules-of-thumb" methods for approaching problems, *based on innate mechanisms* of gathering knowledge and remembering what worked in a similar situation, in the past. Cognitive psychologists have identified three different heuristic strategies: means-end analysis, subgoal analysis, and backward search.

Means-ends analysis is thought to be used by inventors. It involves asking yourself "why" a certain problem occurred so you can get to the source, or initial state, and then move toward reducing the difference between your initial or current state and final desired state or goal state.

Another common heuristic strategy is "**backward search**" or **working backward** from a clearly defined goal to the original state (Newell & Simon, 1972).

A puzzle known as the "Lilly Pond Puzzle" explains this strategy very well. According to the puzzle, there is a pond and this pond has a peculiar variety of lilies growing in it. These lilies double themselves every twenty-four hours. On day 30, the pond is full of lilies. On what day was the pond half-full of lilies?

Since you do not know anything as to the circumference of the pond or the lilies, etc., there is no way to solve this puzzle if you start on the first day. If, however, you say, on day 30, the lake was full, what was its condition the day before, you immediately realize that it was half-full on day 29, because the lilies would have doubled in 24 hours to fill the lake.

This backward search strategy is best used when you have to complete some work by a deadline. Start with the deadline in mind and then plan the stages of completion accordingly. If, for example, you have a manuscript due on a certain date; you might say, I must have the final draft ready one week before the deadline, a rough draft ready three weeks before the deadline, and all the material gathered at least one week before I start work on the first draft.

Yet another heuristic strategy is **subgoal analysis**. In this one, a major goal is broken down into **hierarchical** subgoals, *and each subgoal is worked on exclusively, till it is achieved, before moving on,* pretty much like you would climb a mountain, one step at a time, the lowest one first. If you outline the steps you need to take to attain a college degree this way, psychologists say that you are more likely to achieve your goal because focusing on one hierarchical goal at a time, semester by semester, one test at a time, reduces your anxiety and keeps you motivated.

Most of us are reasonably successful at solving the kinds of problems we encounter in our everyday lives. However, a number of relatively common situations can create obstacles to effective problem solving. Some of these obstacles have to do with the problem itself; others are the result of the way we approach the problem.

COGNITIVE INFLUENCES ON PROBLEM SOLVING Although complex and ill-defined problems tend to be inherently difficult, sometimes we have only ourselves to blame for the trouble we have solving problems. *Three common obstacles that we often create for ourselves that prevent effective problem solving are mental set, functional fixedness, and confirmation bias.*

Mental set

In problem solving, a tendency to approach a problem or situation in a predetermined way, regardless of the requirements of the specific problem.

Mental Set A **mental set** is a tendency to approach a problem in a set or predetermined way regardless of the requirements of the specific problem. When we operate under the influence of a mental set, we apply strategies that have previously helped us to solve similar problems, instead of taking the time to analyze the current problem carefully. Sometimes what we perceive as discrimination is simply the mental set operating in a person.

Functional fixedness

Tendency to be so set in our perception of the proper function of a given object that we are unable to think of using it in a novel way to solve a problem.

Functional Fixedness A second common obstacle to solving problems is **functional fixedness**, i.e., an inability to see a different use for an object commonly used for a given task. For example, suppose you are at a picnic and you open your picnic basket only to discover that you packed the bread and the butter, but forgot to pack a butter knife. Would you fail to make yourself a sandwich? If you looked around and used either the back of a spoon to spread the butter, or tore a piece of a Styrofoam cup and used that to spread the butter, you would have overcome functional fixedness. The ability to overcome functional fixedness is said to be linked to creative problem solving, and *using a different set of words to name a common object is said to help overcome functional fixedness.* For example, instead of saying, "Give me a fork," try saying "Give me that three-pronged steel eating utensil," or say "Where is that metal trident we use to pick up tender morsels of food with?"

Confirmation bias

The tendency to seek out evidence that confirms a hypothesis and to overlook contradictory evidence.

Confirmation Bias Another common obstacle to problem solving is our inclination to seek out evidence that will confirm our hypothesis, while at the same time overlooking contradictory evidence. This phenomenon, known as **confirmation bias**, was demonstrated in investigations conducted by British researcher Peter Wason (1968). Wason asked his subjects to discover what rule applied to a three-number series. Initially the subjects were provided with one example of a positive instance of the rule to be discovered, such as 2, 4, and 6. They were then told to propose additional series to the experimenter, who would indicate whether each did or did not conform to the rule.

Many of Wason's subjects tackled the problem we have just described by hypothesizing a specific rule, such as numbers increasing by two. They then proposed additional series, such as 4, 6, 8; 10, 12, 14; or 1, 3, 5, to verify their hypothesis. Wason responded that each of these series conformed to the rule. On this basis, many of Wason's subjects concluded that their hypothesis was correct and they were visibly frustrated when told that "numbers increasing by two" was not the general rule the experimenter had in mind. Can you figure out what they failed to do as they put their hypothesis to the test? Take a moment to consider this question before reading on.

The fact is Wason's unknown rule was very general—"numbers in increasing order of magnitude." Thus, if you had been a subject and your initial hypothesis had been "numbers increasing by two," any series that you proposed (4, 6, 8; 10, 12, 14; or 1, 3, 5) would also have conformed to the unknown rule. The point is that you would never be able to solve this problem if you continued to search only for evidence that would confirm your initial hypothesis. *The only way you could discover Wason's general rule would be to seek evidence that would disprove your hypothesis.* For instance, you might have proposed 4, 6, and 7 to disconfirm your "increasing by two" hypothesis. Discovering that this series also conformed to the rule would allow you to shift your thinking and quickly discover the correct solution.

People often have trouble with such problems for a simple reason: We are naturally more inclined to find instances that verify our hypotheses than those that disprove our theories. It is wise to keep in mind this confirmation bias, and to remember that finding solutions may require us to look not only for what might be correct, but also for what is incorrect.

DECISION MAKING

Decision making is a process that occurs whenever we are faced with an array of alternative choices and we choose one option while rejecting others.

Many of our everyday decisions are based on our *estimates of probabilities* of uncertain outcomes. Whether you decide to ask someone for a date, buy a lottery ticket, or plan a weekend camping trip, all depend on estimates of probabilities of success. In some cases our estimates may be based on mathematical probabilities, but in most cases our estimates are based on past experience. For instance, if the weather forecast predicts an 80 percent chance of rain for the weekend you may decide not to go camping. In this case your estimate of success was influenced by a mathematical probability of rain. Your decision to ask a person for a date, on the other hand, will more likely be influenced by your estimate of success based on past experience. There are several heuristics that appear to influence our estimates of probabilities; in this section we will examine two: representativeness and availability. In addition to these heuristics, we will see how the context in which a problem is formulated or framed influences our decision-making process.

REPRESENTATIVENESS HEURISTIC Consider the following passage, describing a woman who lives in Portland, Oregon. Based on the passage, which of the following two occupations do you think the woman is most likely to hold—that of police officer, or of the host of a local radio talk show oriented to solving relationship problems?

> She laughs easily and peppers her conversation with interesting questions. She is petite, soft-spoken, and very gentle. She likes to read about psychology and enjoys dealing with people on a personal level. She is sensitive to others' needs and always willing to listen to viewpoints that may not be her own and often ends up changing her mind when new information requires a change of opinion.

Representative heuristic

Strategy for categorizing an object or situation based on one's preconceived notion of characteristics that are typical of that category.

Did you choose "Radio talk show host"? If so you chose incorrectly because the woman in the scenario is actually a Police Officer! You chose "Talk show host" because the description is more representative of your preconceived notion of a person who solves personal problems than of a police officer. The **representative heuristic** strategy entails judging the likelihood of something by intuitively comparing it to our preconceived notion of a few characteristics that represent a given category to us.

For example, most people probably have a stereotype image of a police officer. You might associate characteristics such as "tough," "aggressive," and "non-emotional" with this job. The extent to which our mystery person fits these stereotypes indicates how representative she is of this category: Clearly, the fit is quite poor. On this basis alone, many people would be unlikely to guess that she is indeed a police officer. On the other hand, traits such as "peppers her conversation with interesting questions" "likes psychology," "laughs easily" etc. do match many people's image of someone who hosts a talk show that focuses on solving relationship problems.

Do you think you might have made a different choice if we had suggested that you consider *the relative proportion of police officers and talk show hosts in the general population?* Obviously, there are far more police officers than there are talk show hosts, so the probability of her being a police officer are stronger than her being a talk-show host! In one study, college students were presented with a series of brief personality profiles allegedly drawn at random from a sample of 100 attorneys and engineers (Tversky & Kahneman, 1973). They were asked to assign each profile to one job category or the other. Before the task began, they were told the relative proportions of attorneys to engineers in the sample, a proportion that the researchers varied with different groups of subjects, so that it might be 70 to 30 in some trials and 30 to 70 in others. Although you might expect this information about proportions to influence their decisions, it had virtually no impact. If a description stated that a person was politically active, argumentative, and articulate, subjects were likely to assign the profile to the attorney category no matter what the ratio. In this case the subjects overlooked the information about probabilities, basing their decisions instead on how well the profiles matched their own stereotypes.

Another common example of representativeness in estimating outcomes is our tendency to expect randomness in a short run of outcomes. For instance, suppose you observed four heads in four successive tosses of a fair coin. If you had to bet $10 on the fifth coin toss, how would you bet, heads or tails? Many people would bet on tails because "it's about time for tails." In other words, tails seems more representative of the random process than heads even though the outcome on the fifth toss is completely independent of the previous four. This bias in estimation of outcomes is referred to as the *gambler's fallacy*.

Availability heuristic

Approach to decision making based on information assessed from memory. It assumes that the probability of an event is related to how frequently it occurred in the past, and that events occurring more frequently are easier to remember.

AVAILABILITY HEURISTIC Another factor that influences our estimates is the degree to which we can access information relevant to a decision from our memories. This idea, called the **availability heuristic**, is based on two assumptions: first that the probability of an event is directly related to the frequency with which it has occurred in the past; and, second, that events occurring more frequently are usually easier to remember than less common events.

For example, our decision to serve hamburgers rather than calamari (squid) to a group of teenagers at a Sunday picnic is no doubt a wise choice based on past experiences with teenagers who enjoy hamburgers but dislike exotic seafood. Similarly, we decide to carry an umbrella on a gray, overcast day because we remember that clouds often bring rain.

On the other hand, the easiest events to remember are not always the most common ones. For example, after a tsunami people are afraid to take a cruise, or after a plane crash air travel decreases significantly despite the fact that the chances of similar attacks happening are statistically minute. This illustrates decision making is influenced by available vivid images rather than by the logical evaluation of probabilities.

This idea was tested in several experiments conducted by Tversky and Kahneman. In one experiment subjects were asked questions like the following:

> Are there more words in the English language that start with the letter "k" or those that have the letter "k" as their third letter?
>
> Which is the more likely cause of death in women—breast cancer or heart attack?

Think about your own answers to these questions before reading on.

In both cases subjects' answers to the questions were generally wrong. When asked about the letter "k," subjects reported that it occurred more frequently when starting a word, not in the third position. Actually the letter "k" occurs much more frequently in the third position but it is much more difficult to identify these words. Likewise, far more women die from heart attacks than from breast cancer, but breast cancer has received more attention in the media than heart attacks. This attention makes it more available to memory, thus influencing our estimate of true probability (Kahneman & Tversky, 1981).

FRAMING An additional factor that can influence subjective probabilities is the way in which a particular problem is formulated or framed. Consider the following joke to understand how framing works: A man was caught in a whirlpool, and was sinking fast, and crying for help. Two people were in a nearby boat, and one of them extended his hand and said, "Give me your hand. I will pull you out." However, the sinking man just kept yelling, "Help, help!" and made no move to extend his hand. At this, the other guy in the boat said, "I know this guy. He is a greedy miser. Don't say 'give me your hand,' say 'take my hand' if you want to save him."

According to cognitive psychologists, *framing* entails manipulating the reasoning process by increasing the representativeness or the availability of an outcome. It is the way in which alternatives are stated.

In the previous section we have seen how probability estimates affect our decisions. In some instances our probability estimates can be inaccurate, leading us to undesirable decision outcomes. Perhaps now that you are aware of the potential shortcomings of your decision processes you will be less likely to be influenced by faulty judgments. On the positive side, representativeness and availability can facilitate decision making and thus serve as heuristics in decision-making processes. In many cases they lead to quick and accurate decisions that serve us well most of the time. Now, we will turn to language, which plays a critical role in thinking.

LANGUAGE

Language is the primary means by which we humans communicate with one another. Whereas communication stands for an exchange of information, language stands for the use of abstract symbols combined in various ways according to commonly accepted rules, in order to exchange information. An animal on the prairie that emits a cry of warning as a predator approaches, or a bee signaling the direction of a food source, is also communicating messages. However, it is the ability to combine the same abstract symbols to convey numerous *original* messages that lifts human language to its heights and distinguishes it from the communication that lower animals also demonstrate. We will scrutinize human language and animal communication a little later to determine whether it too can be labeled "language," after discussing the properties of human language and its acquisition by humans.

Psycholinguistics

Psycholinguistics

Is the study of how sounds and symbols are translated into meaning, and of the cognitive processes that are involved in the acquisition and use of language.

Psycholinguistics is the study of how we translate sounds and symbols into meaning, and of what processes are involved in the acquisition and use of language. Psycholinguists have devoted considerable effort to studying the structure and rules of language. We begin our discussion at this level.

THE STRUCTURE AND RULES OF LANGUAGE The people we talk to each day are able to make sense out of what we say to them because we all string sounds together according to a common set of rules. There are actually four levels of rules—phonemes, morphemes, syntax, and semantics—and psycholinguists analyze languages at each of these four levels.

Phonemes

Individual sounds (such as those represented by s and sh in the English spelling system) that are the basic structural elements of language.

Phonemes The basic structural elements of spoken language are called **phonemes**. All languages are made up of individual sounds that are recognized as distinct or different. The English language has about 45 phonemes; other languages may have as few as 15 or as many as 85 (Solso, 1991). Most of the phonemes in the English language correspond to the consonant and vowel sounds. For example, in the word tap we may identify three separate phonemes, corresponding to the consonant sounds t and p and the vowel sound *a*. (The letter a represents four different vowel sounds, as in *tap, pray, care,* and *water*.) Some phonemes are represented by letter combinations, such as the *th* sound in *the* and the *sh* sound in *shout*. In some cases different letters represent the same sounds, such as the *a* in *bay* and the *ei* in *sleigh*. Thus, phonemes are not identical to the letters of the alphabet, even though individual letters correspond to many of the sounds unique to our language. Phonemes can be combined in numerous ways to create literally thousands of different words.

In order to represent ideas in our thought processes or to convey meaningful information, we must combine phonemes in ways that produce acceptable words. For instance, you quickly recognize that *dzashp* and *heeoiay* are not acceptable sound combinations in English even though they are pronounceable.

Morpheme

Smallest unit of meaning in a given language.

Morphemes A **morpheme** is the smallest unit of meaning in a given language. In the English language almost all morphemes consist of combinations of two or more phonemes (exceptions are the pronoun *I* and the article *a*). Many morphemes, like *book, learn,* and *read,* are words that can stand alone. Other morphemes must be attached as prefixes or suffixes to root words. For example, the word *replays* is a word that consists of three morphemes: *play,* which can stand alone; the prefix *re,* meaning "again" or "anew"; and the suffix *s,* which indicates "more than one."

The manner in which morphemes are formed and used also follows distinct rules. In the English language, for example, no more than three consonant sounds can be strung together in one morpheme. Rules also govern the manner in which suffixes can be added to form plurals. Thus, the plural forms of *hat* and *bus* are *hats* and *buses.* Morphemes also have fixed positions in the structure of language: A football broadcaster who repeats a critical play for home viewers is presenting a *replay,* not a *playre.*

Syntax

Language rules that govern how words are combined to form meaningful phrases and sentences.

Syntax Besides learning how to recognize phonemes and use morphemes, we also learn to use **syntax** (commonly known as grammar), the set of language rules that governs how words can be combined to form meaningful phrases and sentences. The sentence, "She purchased the dog small," is immediately recognizable as an improper sentence because one of the rules of English syntax is that adjectives generally precede the nouns they modify ("small dog"). If a Spanish-speaking person read this same sentence, translated word for word into Spanish, he or she would consider it to be grammatically correct, since adjectives normally come after nouns, according to Spanish rules of syntax.

Semantics

Study of the meaning in language.

Semantics Finally, language is also characterized by a system of rules that helps us to determine the meaning of words and sentences. The study of meaning in language is called **semantics**. For example, sentences may be syntactically correct but semantically incorrect. The grammatically correct sentence, "The dorm food is emotionally disturbed," is quite bizarre from the standpoint of semantics, for food cannot be emotionally disturbed (although some dorm food can lead to disturbed emotions!).

Theories of Language Acquisition

How do we learn all of these rules? A number of theories have been proposed to explain how we acquire language. Those explanations vary considerably in their emphasis on environment versus innate biological mechanisms.

THE LEARNING PERSPECTIVE According to behaviorist B. F. Skinner (1957) and social learning theorist Albert Bandura (1971), children learn to shape sounds into words and words into sentences through processes of selective reinforcement and imitation.

This learning perspective is supported by research evidence. For example, babies whose parents reinforce their early attempts at meaningful sounds do tend to vocalize more than institutionalized children who receive less attention (Brodbeck & Irwin, 1946).

Small children often imitate the words they hear their parents say, and this behavior is often reinforced. Selective reinforcement and behavioral modeling techniques have also been successful in teaching language to emotionally disturbed or developmentally delayed children (Lovass, 1973, 1987).

Parents play a very important role in shaping language acquisition in their children. Jean Berko Gleason (1990), a Boston University psychologist, is an authority on language development. Her primary research focus has been on how social interaction between children and adults (especially parents) shapes the acquisition of language. Gleason believes that social relationships may be necessary to activate the process of children learning to communicate through language and that social interactions provide children with important information about the functions of language (Ely et al., 2001).

The learning perspective does not explain all aspects of human language acquisition. For example, many of the words children spontaneously utter are their own inventions, not imitations of a model. Where do they come from if they are not learned? *Again, children typically do not imitate verbally exactly what they hear. Instead, they put words together in their own, often unique, way.* Furthermore, even though parents seldom correct their children's syntax, children usually begin to form grammatically correct sentences before formal schooling begins. Most importantly, it has been demonstrated that language acquisition follows an invariable sequence among children all over the world, under highly variable conditions. This finding suggests that there is something innate about language, which is exactly the position championed by psycholinguist Noam Chomsky.

THE GENETIC PERSPECTIVE: Just as children are genetically programmed to follow the developmental sequence of sitting, crawling, and walking, Chomsky (1965, 1968 & 1980) maintains that the human brain is also programmed to learn speech according to a sequential pattern. This view of language acquisition, sometimes referred to as nativism, does not suggest that our brains are programmed to learn a specific language such as English or French. Instead, it argues that a newborn's brain is organized with the ability to recognize phonemes and morphemes and to learn the basic rules of grammar and semantics. Chomsky labeled this innate ability to learn language the **language acquisition device (LAD)**. He believes that without this innate mechanism we would be overwhelmed by the virtually unlimited number of possible variations in combinations of sounds and words, and thus would be unable to understand the rules of language.

Language acquisition device (LAD)

According to the genetic or nativist view, the prewiring that gives humans the innate ability to learn and understand language.

How can we possibly understand this limitless number of creative sentences? For instance, how do we know that the meanings of the following sentences are the same: "The young boy chased the girl," and "The girl was chased by the young boy"? According to Chomsky our capacity to understand that these sentences have the same meaning is explained *not by learning or imitation, but by an innate capacity to grasp the rules that allow us to form sentences and transform them into other sentences with the same meaning.* These rules are referred to as *transformational grammar.* Our understanding of the meaning of these two sentences prevails even though the arrangement of the words or morphemes is altered. Chomsky argues that meaning is contained in the *deep structure,* or underlying form, of a sentence, not its surface structure. *Surface structure* refers to the superficial appearance of the sentence. In our example above, the surface structure of the sentences was altered but the deep structure remained the same. This genetic position has been supported by a variety of data, and "there is strong evidence that the process of learning human speech is largely guided by innate abilities and tendencies" (Gould & Marler, 1987) however, others argue that some seemingly innate mechanisms are actually abilities learned in early infancy and that general purpose mechanisms can account for language acquisition, so there is no need to theorize a special LAD (Behme, C., & Deacon, S.H., 2008)

Most contemporary psychologists believe that both learning and genetics supply pieces of the puzzle of human language acquisition. Learning appears to contribute more to our rich vocabularies than our genes do, but our genes appear to account more for the enormous complexity of language rules or structures (Ganger, 2000). While behavioral geneticists are attempting to parse out the relative contributions of learning and genes to language acquisition we are still a long way from agreeing on any firm conclusions.

Language Acquisition

Language acquisition is one of the most impressive human accomplishments. The average 6-year-old knows well over 10,000 words and can produce complex sentences that resemble adult speech (Gleitman et al., 1999). To accomplish this, children must learn about seven new words each day from the time they start speaking to age 6. If you have studied a foreign language you may appreciate the significance of this feat since most second-year language students know fewer than 1,000 foreign words. Language acquisition, however, is not merely the learning of a large vocabulary. Children must also learn to combine words into meaningful phrases and sentences using a vast set of complex rules. The sections that follow will briefly describe several stages in the acquisition of early language.

EARLY VOCALIZATIONS: *(Crying, Cooing and Babbling):* Infants begin to vocalize as soon as they are born and adults label that vocalization as "crying" but it actually is a type of communication. Roughly between four and six weeks, infants enter the second stage of vocalization, called cooing. While cooing, babies emit sing-song vowel sounds of pleasure when they are happy. At about six months, sometimes earlier, there is another significant stage referred to as *babbling*. The baby begins to utter repeatedly a variety of simple one-syllable consonant and vowel sounds like da-da-da, ba-ba-ba, or ma-ma-ma. In the first few months of babbling, the infant emits both sounds that are used in the adult language and those that are not.

At about nine or 10 months the babbling becomes intelligible, as babies begin to imitate the sounds of the speech of others more purposefully, even though they may not yet understand them. At this point in language development, these vocalizations begin to approximate the phonemes of the language they hear every day. Thus, cooing and babbling provide babies with a basic repertoire of sounds, laying the foundation for real speech.

For a young child, crying is a rudimentary form of communication.

CMPS

FIRST WORDS Children usually produce their first one-word utterances sometime around their first birthday and they have learned a vocabulary consisting of about 12 words. They have already learned that sounds can be associated with meanings, and now they begin to use sounds to convey meaning. First words are usually very simple, and they often refer to concrete things like familiar people ("mama," "dada"), toys ("ball"), consumables ("juice"), common implements ("cup"), animals ("da" or "dog"), words for greeting ("hi"), and a few action words ("eat," "up," "more"). These words may be oversimplifications of the actual words, but they nevertheless qualify as words if they are used consistently to refer to particular objects or events (thus "ba" for bottle or "nana" for banana).

A child may also use single words in a way that indicates much more. For example, a toddler who tugs on your leg and pleads "up" is probably conveying the meaning, "Pick me up," just as a child who points to a balloon and says "ba" with a rising inflection at the end is asking, "Is that a ball?" These single-word utterances designed to express a complete thought are called *holophrases*.

CONDENSED SPEECH At approximately 20 months of age children develop a vocabulary of about 179 words and sometime between 18 and 24 months they generally produce their first sentences, which usually consist of two-word utterances like "More milk," or "There ball." This type of speech is known as "telegraphic speech." These early primitive sentences typically leave out articles (such as "a" and "the"), prepositions ("to," "on"), conjunctions ("and"), and auxiliary verbs ("can," "will"). This pattern of condensed speech is simply a reduction of complex speech and it is typical of the first sentences spoken by children all over the world (Brown, 1973). Young children also have similar meaning in their short utterances, no matter what culture they belong to (Flavell, 1985).

EXPANDED LANGUAGE: Age two onwards, language development progresses rapidly. Children expand their vocabulary at the rate of several hundred words for every six months of age. Children seem to be remarkably adept at determining the meaning of new words they hear from the context in which the word was spoken (Boysson-Bardies, 1999; Markman, 1987). Two-word sentences give way to meaningful sentences that may lack absolutely correct grammatical structure but nevertheless display a syntax that approximates proper language structure (Valian, 1986). Children begin to make a shift from simple sentence grammar to a more complex syntax sometime between ages two and three. By age four or five, most children have learned most of the basic grammatical rules for combining nouns, adjectives, and verbs into meaningful sentences.

As they learn to combine morphemes into more complex words and into still more complex sentences, a number of errors typically occur regardless of which language is being learned. For instance, when children first learn the basic rules of grammar they may tend to overgeneralize these rules to instances where they do not apply. Thus, oxes may be used instead of *oxen, deers* instead *of deer*, and "I sleeped in the bed," instead of "I slept in the bed." Children may also overgeneralize by applying concept words too broadly. For instance, a child who learns to recognize police officers by their uniforms may call every person in uniform "police."

Another common error in the early stages of sentence usage is oversimplification—using just enough words to convey a message, without being syntactically correct. For example, when a three-year-old wants to play in the park she might say to her mother, "I go park." Later on she learns to add the articles, prepositions, and other parts of speech that are necessary to form grammatically correct sentences such as "I want to go to the park." Most children are quite successful at mastering these refinements: By the time they enter school, they usually have a good comprehension not only of the general rules of their language, but also of the exceptions.

PRAGMATICS OF LANGUAGE The rules of sentence structure are not the only rules children acquire as they develop language competency. In addition, there are a variety of extra-linguistic and pragmatic rules that are also necessary for conversation. For instance, along with sentence structure, a child needs to learn how to develop and maintain a conversation, adjust speech level, react to pauses in speech, and how to intonate speech sounds. Research suggests that children continue to develop these linguistic competencies through feedback from listeners as well as through listening to older models throughout their early school years (Wilkinson et al., 1984).

As children continue to grow and become more interested in their surroundings, we see the language interactions with their parents becoming necessarily more complex. The outcome of this interactive process is perhaps one of the most impressive developmental feats a child performs—that is, a child's ability to acquire and use language.

Brain Mechanisms for Language

In the preceding sections we have assumed that language exists at two levels: at the level of abstract language symbols in the external world, and at a level within the brain where these abstract symbols and their rules of combination are represented. In this section we will examine several of the major brain structures where language appears to be represented and processed.

Most of what we know about the role of the brain on language processing comes from patients who have suffered from brain injuries or strokes. Sometimes these lesions produce disturbances in the comprehension and formulation of speech referred to as *aphasias.* Aphasias can also occur in non-vocal sign languages. There are two major language areas that are involved in speech: Broca's area and Wernicke's area (see Figure 10.1).

Broca's area

Region of the left frontal lobe that is the primary brain center for controlling speech.

BROCA'S AREA Damage to **Broca's area**, a small part of the frontal lobe in the left cortex, results in the inability to speak fluently, and is referred to as *Broca's aphasia.* If the damage is more severe and includes parts of the thalamus and basal ganglia, a more severe long-lasting speech impairment is caused. This suggests that fluent speech involves all of these areas.

Another common characteristic of Broca's aphasia is the inability to organize words so sentences follow proper grammatical rules. In addition, patients underuse or fail to use conjunctions (*and, or, if*), prepositions (*to* and *from*) and auxiliary verbs (*will* and *did*). For instance a patient might say "Go I home tomorrow," instead of "I will go home tomorrow" (Damasio, 1992). Broca's area is also thought to be involved in language comprehension and to serve as a phonological short term memory resource (Rogalsky, C. & Hicock, G. 2011).

Wernicke's area

Area of the left temporal lobe that is the brain's primary area for understanding speech.

WERNICKE'S AREA Damage to **Wernicke's area**, located in the left temporal lobe cortex (see Fig. 10.1), on the other hand, does not disrupt the ability to produce speech, but it does *disrupt the ability to comprehend both verbal and written speech and to produce meaningful speech.* Modern fMRI studies show that Wernicke's area is active both while speaking and reading sentences confirming its role in understanding both speech and written sentences (Thickbroom, G.W., Byrnes, M.L., et.al 2003). Wernicke's aphasia is known to occur in alcoholics who also suffer from malnutrition and are deficient in thiamine (vitamin B1).

Other researchers have identified language disorders that appear to be much more specific. For instance, patients referred to as A.N. and L.R. have difficulty with some concepts; when shown pictures of objects like body parts, vehicles, animals, plants, tools, or human faces, *these patients recognize what they are looking at, but have difficulty retrieving names for these items.* They can even define the object's function, habitat, or value. If shown a picture of a raccoon, they might say, "Oh! I know what it is—it is a nasty animal. It will come and rummage in your backyard and get into the garbage. The eyes and the rings in the tail give it away. I know it, but I cannot say the name" (Damasio & Damasio, 1992).

FIGURE 10.1 The Left Hemisphere of the Brain

This illustration identifies several important language areas of the brain.

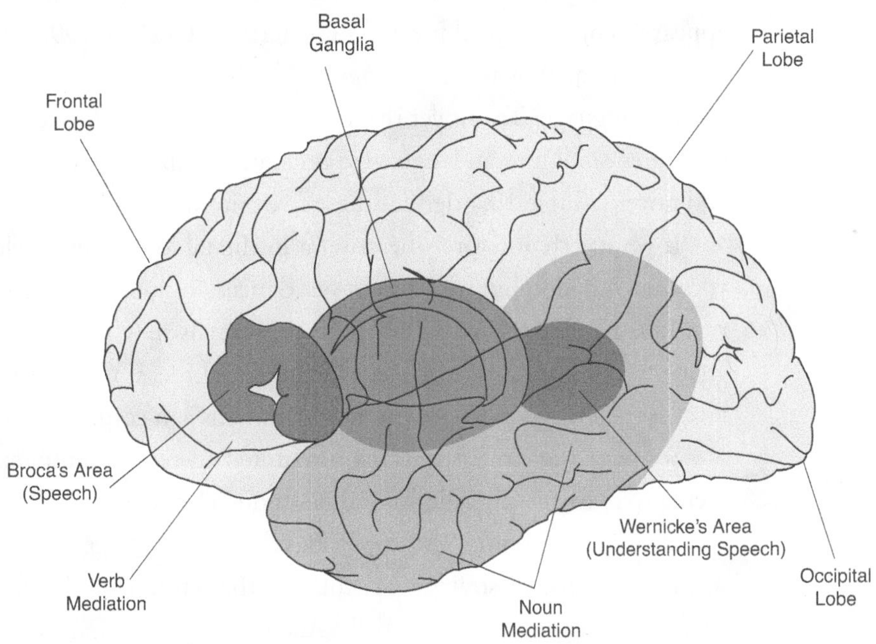

A.N. and L.R.'s, symptoms, as well as other patients' with similar problems with proper nouns, have been attributed to damage in the anterior and middle regions of the left temporal lobe.

We have briefly touched upon several important aspects of language processing including its structure, its acquisition, and neural bases. Research is currently studying the neural correlates of acquiring a second language and there is evidence that after an adult has studied a foreign language for over six months, the brain areas stimulated while conversing in it are the same areas that are activated in native speakers of the language. However, a topic of such importance to human behavior deserves much more than we can provide in this context. The analysis of language at all levels continues to be both an active and a vital aspect of psychology and neuroscience. Now we turn to the question we began with: do other animals possess language?

Is Language Unique to Humans?

We have been discussing human language, but nonhuman animals also have methods of communicating. A walk in any forest is likely to produce a cacophony of birdcalls that communicate danger. Monkeys have been shown to produce different sounds to indicate danger approaching from above, such as an eagle, versus danger from below, such as a prowling panther (Marler, 1967) and new research with chimpanzees and Macaque monkeys indicates that there is a similarity in the brain structures that are stimulated in them and humans (Petrides, M. & Pandya, D. N., 2009; Kelley, C., Uddin. L., et.al, 2010).

Bees communicate with each other about the nature and location of food sources by engaging in an intricate waggle dance (Moffett, 1990; von Frisch, 1974). Studies with vervet monkeys indicate that they have a rudimentary semantic system where specific calls appear to convey special meaning (Seyfarth & Cheney, 1992). Do these methods of communicating qualify as a true language in the sense that they contain the same features as human language? To answer this question, we first need to identify the primary criteria or attributes of all human languages: generativity, specialization, arbitrariness, displacement, and novelty. Table 10.1 defines these five criteria.

If we strictly interpret the criteria in the table, it is quite clear that birdcalls, monkey vocalizations, dolphin whistles, or bee dances do not qualify as language. But this does not rule out the possibility that nonhuman animals may have the ability to learn to use language to communicate abstract thoughts and ideas. Considerable research with apes, in fact, has challenged the view that only humans can communicate with abstract symbols.

Some of the earliest research attempted to teach chimpanzees to talk. These experiments were essentially failures, although one chimpanzee did learn to vocalize four words: "mama," "papa," "cup," and "up" (Hayes, 1951; Kellogg & Kellogg, 1933). Later experiments used another strategy. Speculating that chimpanzees simply did not have the vocal apparatus to communicate verbally, Allen and Beatrice Gardner (1969, 1975) took another route; they taught American Sign Language (ASL) to a chimpanzee named Washoe.

The Gardners began training Washoe when she was eight months old. They used a variety of methods, including modeling and physical guidance (actually moving her hands) and applying operant reinforcement. Washoe spent all of her waking hours with a trainer who communicated with her only through ASL. After four years of training, she could use 132 signs and after a few years had a vocabulary of about 350 signs.

Not only was Washoe adept at imitating her trainer's signs, but she also seemed to create her own communications. For example, when an aggressive rhesus monkey menaced her, she signed "dirty monkey," and when she saw a swan for the first time, she signed "water bird." Since she already knew the signs for water and bird, her trainer speculated that she understood the meaning of the words and was thus able to combine them creatively. Washoe passed away at the age of 42 in 2007. More recently the Gardners have trained several other chimpanzees to converse in signs. They present evidence that these chimpanzees initiate context appropriate conversations with each other (Bodamar et al., 2002; Jensvold et al., 2000).

Other studies have used varying approaches, also with success. Psychologist David Premack (1971) used operant and classical conditioning to teach a chimpanzee named Sarah to associate pieces of plastic with different aspects of her environment. The plastic pieces, which differed in size, shape, and color, had magnetic backing so that they could be placed on a metal "language board" to form vertical sentences. Sarah learned a large number of symbols indicating names of trainers, objects, properties of objects (like "color of"), and prepositions; she also learned to combine words in an apparently meaningful fashion (such as "Mary give apple Sarah"). Premack and his associates believed that Sarah could also learn concepts. For example, when she was asked to compare a banana and a yellow

TABLE 10.1 Attributes of Human Language

1. *Generativity:* The ability to provide for a huge variety of meanings in an unlimited number of utterances.
2. *Specialization:* The only purpose of the language is to communicate information to others.
3. *Arbitrariness:* The combinations of sounds selected to refer to objects or events is purely arbitrary. Thus, our English word *book* might just as well have been *zock.*
4. *Displacement:* Language can be generated in the absence of any eliciting stimulus. Thus, humans can talk about dangerous dogs when no dogs are present, whereas a monkey vocalizes a sound indicating danger only when a predator is observed. Displacement also refers to the ability to communicate about things in the past and future, not just the present.
5. *Novelty:* Humans are able to express themselves with novel phrases and sentences that they have never heard before. Thus, human language is more than mere memorization and repetition of word strings.

SOURCE: From, "The Origin of Speech," by C. Hockett from *Scientific American* 1960, v. 203, pp. 89–96. Reprinted by permission.

ball, she arranged symbols on the magnetic board to indicate "the same." (This correct answer requires an appreciation of the concept of color.)

At the Yerkes Primate Research Center in Atlanta, Georgia, another study attempted to teach chimpanzees "Yerkish," a computer language. The star pupil of this study, Lana, was raised in a room with a computer that she learned to use to obtain food, drink, and so forth. Each key was labeled with a particular symbol that stood for an object or action. (For example, a circle with a dot inside signified juice.) Lana and other chimpanzees learned to use the computer to type requests, answer questions, and even to engage in a complex game with another chimpanzee that required them to use the computer symbols to make statements. Some of Lana's keyboard talk was quite amazing. For example, one day she observed that her trainer had an orange that she wanted, but Lana did not have a symbol for orange in her language repertoire. So Lana improvised and typed "Tim give apple which is orange" (Rumbaugh, 1977; Savage-Rumbaugh et al., 1980, 1983).

Upon examination of Table 10.1, it appears that ape communication comes close to our criteria for language. For instance, the criteria of arbitrariness and perhaps novelty have been demonstrated in apes. *The criterion of displacement, generating language in the absence of a stimulus, however, has not been adequately demonstrated.* One criterion implied by displacement is that humans have a theory of "mind" and can attribute beliefs, knowledge, and emotions to others (Seyfarth and Cheney, 1992). In other words, people can talk about an object in its absence indicating we attribute knowledge of the object to another person. Our warning a child not to venture into the street until the light changes is prompted not by his or her behavior, but by a lack of knowledge about streets we attribute to them. Likewise children learn to attribute beliefs, knowledge, and emotions to others and behave in ways to change or maintain them. To date there have been no convincing studies to indicate that communication by other animals meets this criterion.

To do justice to this issue, we must return again to Clever Hans. According to some critics of ape language studies, the impressive results that we have just described simply show that chimpanzees can learn to respond to trainers in a manner similar to Clever Hans. Some support for this contention is provided by the frequent observation that when apes are tested by people who either are not familiar with the particular language symbols being used or do not know the correct answers, they consistently perform far more poorly than when they are tested by familiar trainers (Tartter, 1986). However, we cannot ignore the fact that this reduced performance may be no different from the common tendency of children to perform worse for strangers than for people they know.

Evidence that a chimpanzee's signs may be nothing more than imitations of a trainer's signs was provided by Herbert Terrace (1979). Dr. Terrace carefully analyzed videotapes of chimpanzees signing and concluded that his top performer, a chimpanzee named Nim Chimpsky (named after linguist Noam Chomsky), was able to use an impressive number of combinations of 125 basic signs, but only in imitative response to his trainer, and not as a means of creatively communicating new information.

It has also been suggested that language researchers, anxious to be vindicated for their enormous investments in time and effort in training their chimpanzees, may fall victim to what has been called the generous interpretation pitfall (Tartter, 1986). We all have a tendency to interpret the words of others as if we were emitting them ourselves. Thus, when Washoe signed "water bird" it was natural for a human observer to assume that she was being creative in naming a novel stimulus, a swan, by combining two other words. It has been pointed out, however, that a less generous interpretation would need to acknowledge the possibility that Washoe was first naming the water in which the swan was swimming, and then naming the animal, bird, both words with which she was familiar (Terrace et al., 1979).

You may agree that the accomplishments of Washoe and Sarah can probably be explained by the Clever Hans phenomenon or by their trainers' generous interpretations, but significant questions are still raised by the Yerkes Primate Research Center studies of computer communications. How can these results be explained? According to behaviorists such as B. F. Skinner and his colleagues at Harvard, the so-called language-driven behaviors of chimpanzees may be explained simply by common principles of learning, such as imitation and reinforcement. They see little difference between pigeons pushing buttons in sequence to get a grain reward and chimpanzees stringing together a series of symbols to obtain a payoff of juice or a tickling session. Epstein, Lanza, and Skinner (1980) used operant conditioning to train two pigeons, Jack and Jill, to perform language-like behaviors in which one pecked colored keys to answer a question selected by the pecks of its partner. These researchers noted, "We have thus demonstrated that pigeons can learn to engage in sustained and natural conversation without human intervention, and that one pigeon can transmit information to another entirely through the use of symbols" (p. 545).

In all, much of the data obtained from the ape language studies can be explained by simpler principles, such as the Clever Hans phenomenon or learning principles—none of which require us to assume that apes have language capabilities. Certainly if we confine our conception of true language ability to the criteria in Table 10.1, we must conclude that humans alone possess language. However, if we define language as the ability to convey meaning through the use of symbols, it is clear that apes and other animals also have this ability (Premack et al., 1991; Rumbaugh et al., 2000).

Perhaps another way to examine whether other animals have language abilities is to examine the neural structures required for both language production and comprehension. As mentioned above, in humans a number of specific neural structures, particularly in the left frontal cortex, have evolved for specific language related functions. As stated earlier, new fMRI studies indicate that homologous structures comparable to human ones become active in their brains when they communicate with each other.

THINKING AND LANGUAGE

As we discovered earlier, thinking is certainly more than mere silent language or talking to ourselves. It has also been conclusively demonstrated that thought can occur without language (Weiskrantz, 1988). However, the mental imagery we may use in thinking certainly involves language, and a great deal of thinking is in verbal form.

The two questions most widely pondered by cognitive psychologists as they consider the nature of the interrelationship between thinking and language are (1) Does language structure thought? And (2) Does thought structure language? We address both of these questions in the following paragraphs.

Does Language Structure Thought?

The fact that much of our thinking occurs at the abstract level of language symbols suggests the possibility that language might determine how we think. Anthropologists who study the cultures of different societies in the underdeveloped world have widely reported that languages spoken by people in these diverse societies often have little in common with the more familiar English and European languages. Furthermore, people in these societies are often described as thinking about their worlds in ways very different from Europeans and Americans. Linguist Benjamin Whorf (1956) argued that these variations in the way members of different societies view the world are a function of fundamental differences in the structure of language in these highly varied cultures. He formalized this theoretical conception in what has become known as *the* **linguistic-relativity hypothesis**—*the idea that the language of a particular culture determines the content of thoughts among members of that culture and the way these people perceive and think about their world.* For most Americans, who speak only English, language may seem to be more a vehicle for expressing our thoughts than a shaper of thinking. Nevertheless, Whorf maintained that people think differently in different languages.

Linguistic-relativity hypothesis

Notion that the language of a particular culture determines the content of thoughts among members of that culture, and the way these people perceive and think about their world.

One of the authors of this textbook, Ragade, speaks four different languages very fluently. From personal experience, she can testify that not only are cognitive processes different when using different languages, but even emotional processes are different. For example, this author had noticed that she was much more loving and nicer to her babies when speaking to them in her first language or mother tongue, than in English, which was her third language. It is possible that since one picks up a language alongside the mores that exist in a culture, the two go hand-in-hand. However, it may be more of a case of habitual behaviors and mental processes occurring together, than language shaping thought per se or a special case of "neurons that fire together wire together" as stated by Donald Hebb in 1949.

The above view is supported by the rare case of a Portugese person who had lived in England for many years and who was diagnosed as "schizophrenic" was found to be "sane" when speaking in Portuguese, when one of the psychiatrists who knew Portuguese serendipitously tried to speak in Portuguese to him! The patient apparently had not used Portuguese in many years, not since childhood, but remembered it well enough to be able to carry on a sane conversation with the psychiatrist, while remaining schizophrenic when speaking English (Zulueta et al., 2001).

Benjamin Whorf offered a number of observations to support his contention. For example, he suggested that the American Hopi Indians have difficulty thinking about the past because their language does not provide a past tense. Other evidence marshaled by Whorf is the difference in the ways in which Eskimos and English-speaking people view snow. There is only one English word for snow, whereas Eskimos use several different words, depending on whether the snow is slushy, packed hard, and so forth. Whorf argued that this broader range of descriptive terms, aside from demonstrating the survival value for Eskimos of recognizing snow conditions, illustrates that Eskimos can perceive different snow conditions more accurately than English-speaking residents of, say, California or Oregon.

On the other hand, just because residents of California or Oregon lack a rich vocabulary for describing snow does not necessarily imply that English-speaking non-Eskimos are any less capable of discriminating varied snow conditions. In fact, English-speaking skiers, who benefit from knowledge of different snow conditions, do use several descriptive terms for distinguishing types of snow, such as "sticky snow," "corn," and "powder." This latter example suggests that rather than having their thinking structured by language, Eskimos and skiers first learn to discriminate between varied snow conditions, and then *invent* a vocabulary for describing these differences.

Perhaps the most rigorous experimental test of Whorf's hypothesis was conducted as part of field research on how people learn natural color concepts. A comparison was made on memory for colors between people from the Dani society in New Guinea and college students in America. The Dani have only two words for colors—one for the darkest colors and one for light warm colors. In contrast, the vocabulary of the English-speaking students included words for 11 basic colors. Each subject was briefly shown a colored chip and then, after a delay of 30 seconds, was asked to pick out a chip of the same color among a set of 40 different colored chips.

If there is validity to Whorf's linguistic-relativity hypothesis, then a person's color vocabulary should influence memory for colors. Furthermore, we might logically predict that the Dani would have more difficulty with this task: They would be more likely to confuse similar colors of a slightly different hue that they had labeled with the same name than would the English-speaking subjects, whose broader color vocabulary would allow them to code the similar hues verbally into distinct categories. In actuality, the results did not support this prediction. While both American and Dani subjects made many mistakes, there were no significant differences in the rate at which people from each culture confused similar colors in spite of major differences in color vocabularies of the two languages (Heider & Oliver, 1972).

Today there is very little support for the notion that language rigidly structures or restricts thought as originally implied by the linguistic-relativity hypothesis. However, this is not to say that language has no influence on thought. Most cognitive psychologists and psycholinguists agree that languages influence the ease with which people are able to express a particular concept or idea or make distinctions about certain features of their environments. Put another way, it seems reasonable to conclude that it is often easier to express a particular concept or idea in one language as opposed to another. Furthermore, expanding our language comprehension through education and reading no doubt enhances our thinking processes. It does not follow from these observations, however, that our thoughts or perceptions are largely determined or structured by language.

Does Thought Structure Language?

A distinctly different viewpoint about the relationship between thinking and language is the idea that thought has some impact on the structure of language. Advocates of this theoretical position suggest that language takes on a form or structure that reflects, at least to some degree, the developing child's comprehension, of his or her world. Jean Piaget, a chief proponent of this interpretation, argued that certain words or phrases appear in the verbalizations of a child only after she or he has mastered certain intellectual skills during development (Piaget, 1972; Piaget & Inhelder, 1969).

One simple example here illustrates his viewpoint that language is structured by thought. By the age of two, most children have mastered the principle of *object permanence*—the realization that objects continue to exist, even when they are not immediately in view. Piaget would argue that prior to mastering "object permanence" a child's language would be devoid of references to objects not within view in the surrounding environment. Or, put another way, once children's thoughts (cognitions) embrace the understanding that hidden objects continue to exist, they are able to expand their language to conversations about these out-of-sight objects. This interpretation was supported by a study showing that child subjects were able to talk about absent objects only after demonstrating a firm grasp of object permanence (Corrigan, 1978).

Thus, we have some evidence that thought does influence the structure of language. However, just as it is incorrect to presume that language imposes a rigid structure on thought, it is inaccurate to presume that thought strictly structures language. Rather, in light of current knowledge, it seems more reasonable to conclude that the structure of language may bear some influence on how we think about our world just as our language reflects, to some degree, our understanding of our environment.

SUMMARY

THINKING

1. We may define thought or thinking as a collection of internal processes or behaviors directed toward solving a problem.
2. Research has demonstrated the inaccuracy of the early contention of behaviorists that subvocal speech was essentially equivalent to thinking and that it was a behavior, but covert behavior and was subject to the laws of behavior.
3. One component of thought is mental images of visual scenes and sounds that we manipulate in some systematic or logical fashion.
4. A more abstract or symbolic form of thinking involves the use of concepts. Concepts represent general categories into which we mentally group things (objects, activities, kinds of animals, and so forth) that share certain features even though they are not identical.
6. Formal concepts, employed by laboratory researchers, are logical and well-defined with clear, unambiguous rules specifying what features belong to that category.
7. In real life most of the natural concepts that we use to think efficiently about past and present experiences tend to be more ambiguous than formal concepts.
8. A number of different theories have been proposed to explain how people form concepts. These include association theory, hypothesis-testing theory, and exemplar theory.

PROBLEM SOLVING

9. A problem exists when there is a discrepancy between your present status and some goal you wish to obtain, with no obvious way to bridge the gap.
10. Problems consist of three components: the original state of the situation as it exists at the moment; the goal state, which is what the problem solver would like the situation to be; and the rules or restrictions that govern the possible strategies for moving from the original state to the goal state.
11. Problem-solving behavior generally involves three logical stages: representing or defining the problem, generating possible solutions, and evaluating how well a given solution works.
12. Algorithms involve a systematic exploration of every possible solution to a problem until a correct one is found.
13. Heuristics refer to a variety of rule-of-thumb strategies that may lead to quick solutions but are not guaranteed to produce results. Three commonly employed heuristic strategies are means-ends analysis, subgoal analysis, and backward search.
14. Common obstacles we often create for ourselves when engaged in problem solving are mental set, functional fixedness, and confirmation bias.
15. Mental set is a tendency to approach a problem in a set or predetermined way regardless of the requirements of the specific problem.
16. Functional fixedness is the tendency to be so set or fixed in our perception of the proper function of a given object that we are unable to think of using it in a novel way to solve a problem.
17. Confirmation bias refers to our inclination to seek evidence that will confirm our hypothesis at the same time that we overlook contradictory evidence.
18. Decision making is a process that occurs whenever we are faced with an array of alternative choices and we choose one option while rejecting others.
19. Subjective probabilities of outcomes influence our decisions. While these estimates can facilitate decision making, they can also lead to undesirable decision outcomes.

20. Two common rules-of-thumb or heuristic approaches to decision making include the representative heuristic and the availability heuristic.

LANGUAGE

21. The ability to use language is perhaps the most profound of all human behaviors.
22. Psycholinguistics is the psychological study of how we translate sounds and symbols into meaning, and of what processes are involved in the acquisition and use of language.
23. The basic structural elements of language are called phonemes.
24. A morpheme is the smallest unit of meaning in a given language.
25. Syntax refers to the set of language rules that govern how words can be combined to form meaningful phrases and sentences.
26. Language is also characterized by a system of rules that help us to determine the meanings of words and sentences. The study of meaning in language is called semantics.
27. Theories of language acquisition include the learning perspective, which emphasizes the role of experience in language acquisition, and the nativistic perspective, which maintains that the human brain is genetically programmed to learn speech. Most contemporary psychologists believe that genetics and environment interact in a complex fashion to provide us with the necessary foundations for learning language.
28. There appears to be a universal developmental sequence in which children learn language by progressing from babbling to one-word utterances to two-word utterances, and finally to expanded language using more complex sentences.
29. The major brain areas for language are located in the left hemisphere. These areas include Broca's area and Wernicke's area. Different components of speech and grammar appear to be mediated by specific regions within the brain.
30. Current fMRI studies indicate that similar brain areas fire when humans converse and chimps or macaque monkeys communicate, indicating that they too could have a "language" of some sort.
31. If we confine our conception of true language ability to the criteria of generativity, specialization, arbitrariness, displacement, and novelty, then we must conclude that humans alone possess language. However, if we define language as the ability to convey meaning through the use of symbols, it is clear that apes and other animals also have this ability.
32. According to Benjamin Whorf's linguistic-relativity hypothesis, people's language determines the content of their thought—so that, for instance, an Eskimo group that had several descriptive words for snow could perceive different types of snow more readily than could people whose language had only a few words for snow. Studies indicate, however, that while language may influence our ability to communicate ideas, it does not determine those perceptions or ideas.
33. Some theorists have argued that thought shapes language. The developmental psychologist Jean Piaget, for instance, noted that children do not develop a language to express concepts or ideas until they achieve mastery of these concepts.

TERMS AND CONCEPTS

thought
thinking
covert behavior
concepts
prototypes
trial and error
testing hypothesis
algorithm
heuristics
means-ends analysis
working backward
mental set
functional fixedness
confirmation bias
representative heuristic
availability heuristic
psycholinguistics
phoneme
morpheme
syntax
semantics
language acquisition device (LAD)
Broca's area
Wernicke's area
linguistic-relativity hypothesis

PART IV:

The Nature and Treatment of Psychological Disorders

CHAPTER 11

Psychological Disorders

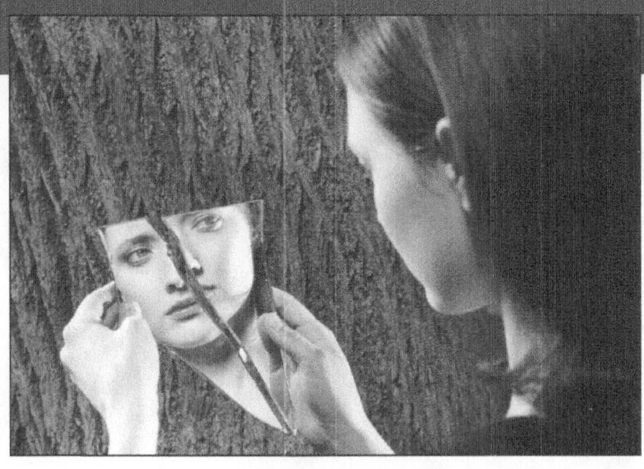

Getty

The term "mental illness" with which most people are familiar has not been used by psychology professionals for decades. People who used to be labeled "mentally ill" are now said to suffer from a "disorder," and in this chapter we will elaborate on several disorders.

The term "neurotic," once commonly used to describe people with mild psychiatric problems, is now obsolete. Instead, psychology professionals list several categories of "disorders." In this chapter we will discuss the models used by these professionals to come up with a diagnosis and also look at the symptoms that go with specific disorders.

To get some idea as to how different some of these behaviors are take a look at the letter in Figure 11.1 on the next page. It was written to the director of a state hospital by a patient who was being treated for "bipolar disorder," formerly known as manic depressive illness. This patient made repeated attempts for release as well as numerous claims that his psychologist was a communist who beat and starved patients. Notice that although there is evidence of distorted thought, the writing is mostly coherent and organized. The style of writing here is also characteristic of severe mood disorder in that it is forceful and directed off the page.

Figure 11.2 represents a sample of doodling made by a patient diagnosed with schizophrenia. Notice here that the writing is not very coherent and that there are numerous references to Christianity and sex. These kinds of references are not uncommon with schizophrenic disorders.

Although these samples of behavior are not sufficient for a diagnosis, it is not difficult to see that these patients are severely disturbed. In fact, when someone's behavior deviates extremely from the way people customarily behave or speak, it is rational to label their behavior as abnormal. But what about a university research scientist who *functions well in his everyday life* but confesses to her boyfriend, also a scientist that she converses with her dead father? (Schwartz, G. E. & Simon, W.L., 2003). Is this normal or abnormal? Or, a mother who devotes her entire life to nursing a chronically sick child at the expense of taking some time for herself and her other family members? Is she normal or is she suffering from a Psychological disorder known as Munchausen's by Proxy? Is she keeping her child sick so she can keep taking care of the child and be praised for it? Are these examples of abnormal behavior or simply of overly loving and caring people?

At this point, we don't have reliable answers but the newest neuroimaging techniques are offering up some unique answers. For example, most recently a woman accused of Munchausen's by Proxy was given a neurometric lie-detector test of sorts by conducting an *f*MRI

continued

Mood disorder

Class of disorders including major depression and bipolar disorder that are characterized by persistent depression (which in bipolar disorder is accompanied by intermittent episodes of mania).

on her as she answered questions about the poisoning of her infant. An fMRI study of her living, working brain was observed by researchers as she answered questions about the allegations that she had poisoned her own child. In this case, the researchers concluded that, based on the time taken to respond to questions and the brain circuits that were activated, she was telling the truth when she said that she had not poisoned her child. Apparently, her ventrolateral prefontal cortex and anterior cingulate cortex took longer to longer to get activated and showed significantly more activation when asked to make false statements, a pattern that did not show when she talked being innocent of poisoning her child (Spence, S.A. & Kaylor-Hughes, C.J, et.al, 2008) a pattern that does not show when people are speaking the truth (Hughes, C.J., Farrow, T.F.D., et.al 2005).

Undoubtedly, the more we can peek into the "Black-box" of the brain and observe its normal functioning and abnormal functioning directly, the better we will be able to distinguish normalcy from abnormality and hopefully, be able to separate it from criminal behavior. For now, abnormal behavior is defined as follows.

FIGURE 11.1 Letter from a Mental Patient to the Director of the State Hospital Where He Was Being Treated for a Severe Mood Disorder

Courtesy of Dr. Charles Lyons.

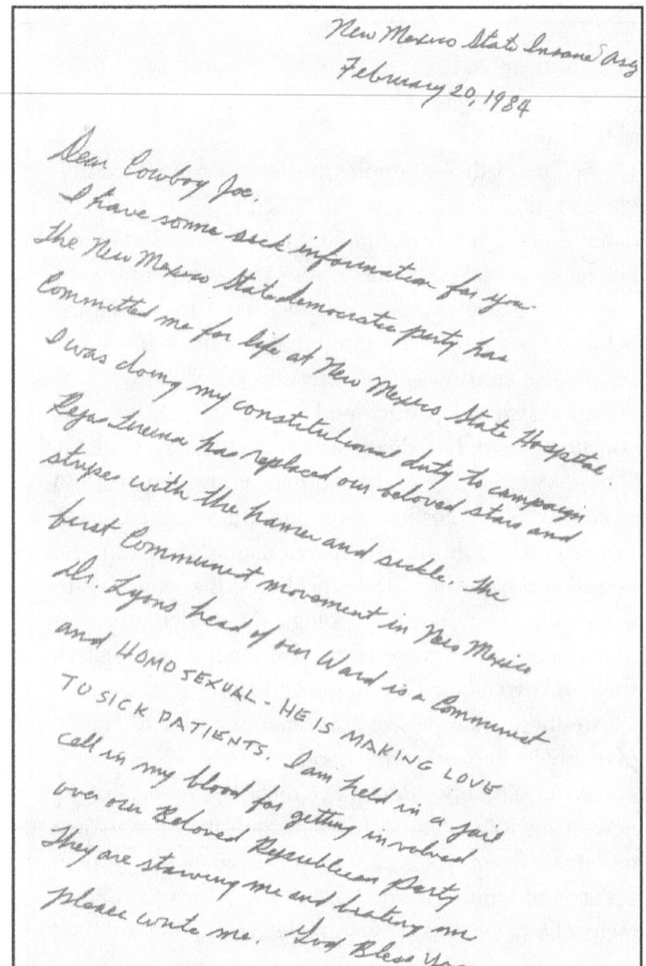

New Mexico State Insane Asy
February 20, 1984

Dear Cowboy Joe,
I have some sick information for you.
The New Mexico State democratic party has
Committed me for life at New Mexico State Hospital.
I was doing my constitutional duty to campaign
Reyes Lucena has replaced our beloved stars and
stripes with the hammer and sickle. the
first Communist movement in New Mexico
Dr. Lyons head of our Ward is a Communist
and HOMO SEXUAL - HE IS MAKING LOVE
TO SICK PATIENTS. I am held in a jail
cell in my blood for getting involved
over our Beloved Republican Party
They are starving me and beating me
Please write me. God Bless You

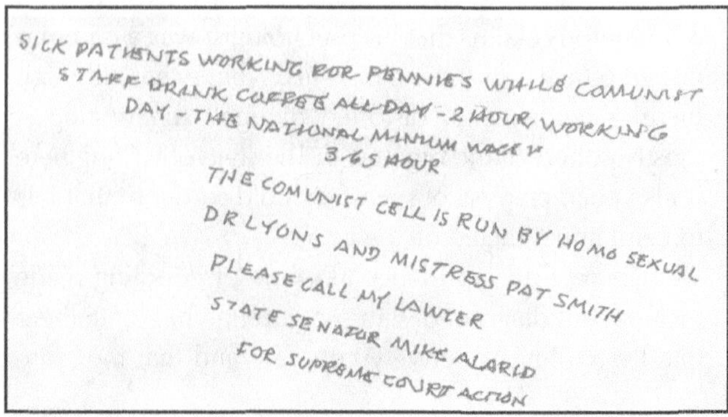

SICK PATIENTS WORKING FOR PENNIES WHILE COMUNIST
STAFF DRANK COFFEE ALL DAY - 2 HOUR WORKING
DAY - THE NATIONAL MINIMUM WAGE IS
3.65 HOUR
THE COMUNIST CELL IS RUN BY HOMO SEXUAL
DR LYONS AND MISTRESS PAT SMITH
PLEASE CALL MY LAWYER
STATE SENATOR MIKE ALARID
FOR SUPREME COURT ACTION

FIGURE 11.2 Doodling Produced by a Patient Diagnosed with Schizophrenia

Note references to Christianity and sex. **Courtesy of Dr. Charles Lyons.**

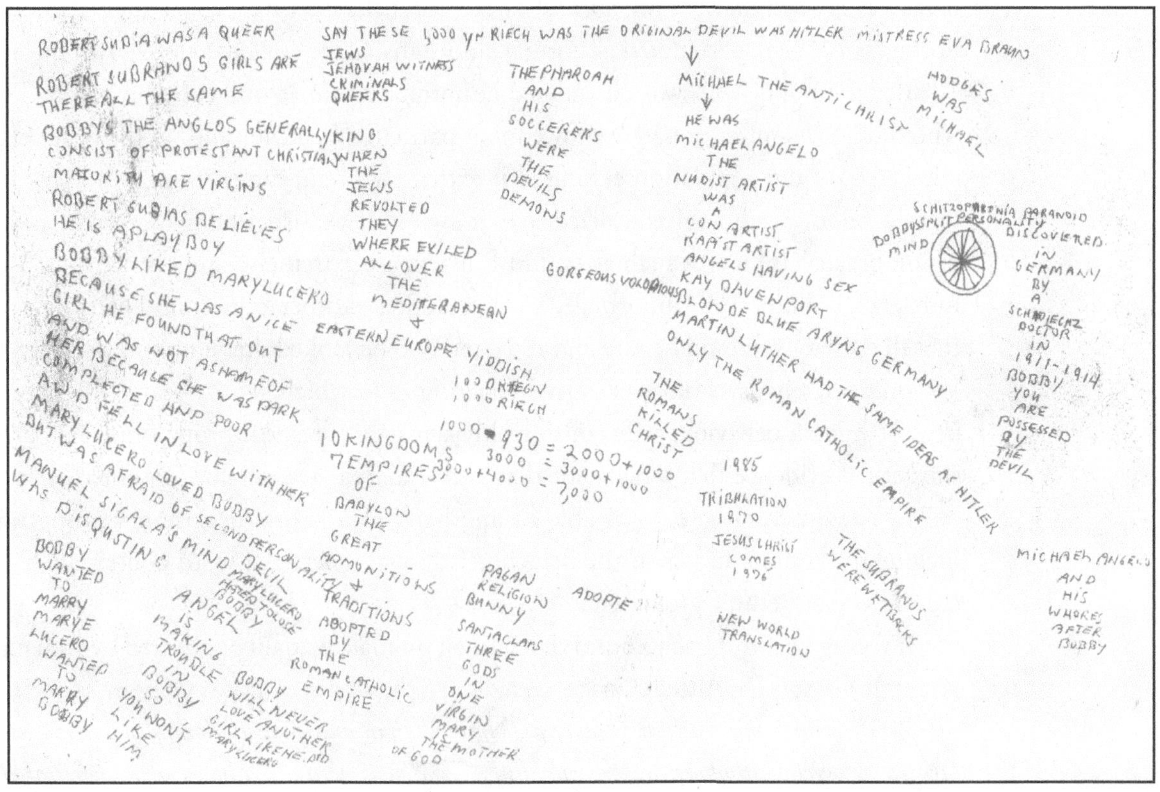

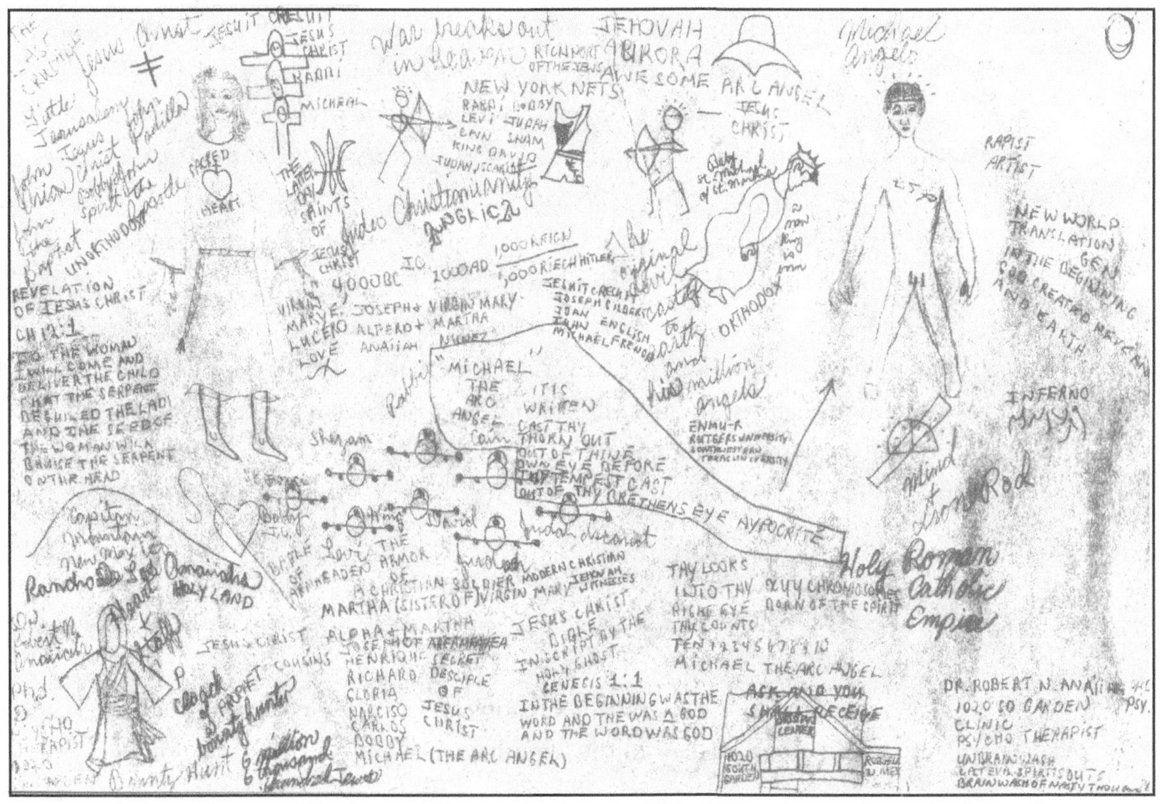

DEFINING ABNORMAL BEHAVIOR

Historically, the very first scientific definition of abnormal behavior was a statistical one, based on the *bell curve* or *the normal curve*. Any behaviors that fell at the tail ends of the normal curve were considered abnormal, and statistically, any behavior shown by less than 10% of the population was considered abnormal where at one extreme you had people who did not manifest or barely showed that particular behavior and on the other extreme, where 5% of the population exhibited it extremely often, often enough to make it seem bizarre. Soon, psychologists realized that going by the statistics alone was not a good definition because IQ scores such as that of Einstein are extremely rare, but we don't view his intellectual abilities as "abnormal", so they added another criterion. That criterion was that the behavior should be rare and it should also be looked down upon by society.

Immediately psychologists started debating as to which society was being referred to, because human behavior varies considerably across cultures. Anthropologists had provided substantial evidence that a behavior that is considered "respectable" in one society might be considered absolutely despicable in another. Hence the definition was modified to include the context in which the behavior is shown where the word context includes the culture, society, ethnic group, etc.

It was against this background that a book on male sexuality authored by Indiana University Professor, Dr. Alfred Kinsey, *brought to light the percentage of homosexual population.*

At the time, homosexuality was a behavior that was looked down in society and was labeled as psychopathology or "mental illness" and was actually labeled as a "Mental illness". Psychiatrists used to admit homosexuals to insane wards and even give them Electro-convulsive Shock Therapy and even chemical castration, in an effort to make them heterosexual (Smith,G., Bartlett, A.,& King, M., 2004; Kaplan,R.M., 2004).

Kinsey's findings known as Kinsey Reports, published in the 1950s gave a figure of 10% for white male college educated population and claimed that 37% of the males in the population he had studied, had reported at least one incident of homosexuality (Kinsey Institute, http://www.kinseyinstitute.org). Obviously if the percentage of homosexuals was so large, by definition, it could not be "abnormal"!

The above findings were very controversial and shocking because prior to the 1950s homosexuality was thought to be very rare, perhaps on the order of 1% of the population and homosexuality was listed as abnormal behavior well into the 1970s.

In the 1970s after much debate and research, the American Psychiatric Association decided to remove homosexuality as a category of abnormality from the Diagnostic Statistical Manual (DSM). The American Psychological Association followed suit. Psychologists and Psychiatrists would now treat a patient only if that patient was distressed about his/her homosexual orientation. *They would not help change that orientation but would help them live happily with the orientation they had a biological proclivity, to have.*

As discussed in the Motivation chapter, there is evidence that exclusive homosexuals have an undersized nucleus in the hypothalamus, and a search is on for a genetic explanation of this "Darwinian Paradox" (Clanl. A.C., Cermell, C., Zanzoto, G., 2008), however, *to date, a genetic link that causes homosexuality has not been found* (Ramagopalan, S.V., Dyment, D.A. et.al, 2010). *The fact remains, however, that Homosexuality has been removed from the list of Behavioral Disorders and is not to be found in DSM -5 which was released in May of 2013 (www.DSM5 org).*

Psychologists who specialize in studying abnormal behavior tend to emphasize a common core of four criteria that may be used to distinguish between normal and abnormal behavior. To be **labeled abnormal**, the behavior in question:

Abnormal behavior

Is behavior that is atypical, dysfunctional, distressful to self or others, and dangerous to self or others.

1. Must be rare or atypical.
2. Must be maladaptive, i.e., it must hamper the person from living a productive life.
3. Must cause distress either to the person or others.
4. Must be socially unacceptable.

Sometimes all four characteristics of abnormality are *not necessarily evident* in all behavioral disorders. Also since different societies have different cultural norms, a behavior that passes for normal in one society might be considered quite abnormal and be unacceptable in another. Even so, psychology professionals use a diagnostic method based on statistics and consensus, as described below.

CLASSIFYING BEHAVIORAL DISORDERS

The first widely accepted system for classifying behavioral disorders was published in 1952 by the American Psychiatric Association in the *Diagnostic and Statistical Manual of Mental Disorders,* conveniently shortened to *DSM-I.* Soon, it was replaced with a revised version known as *DSM-II,* followed by other revisions till in May 2013 they released the newest edition, the 5th one titled DSM -5. The World Health Organization (WHO) and the American Psychiatric Association (APA) jointly undertook the work of re-classification based on new research (Rey, J. 2010). They started he work in 1999 and finished the work in 2013, and several psychologists have already signed a petition to protest the categorization as done in DSM-5 on grounds that the scientific evidence provided for the changes is insufficient but the entire document is too new to be able to judge it adequately at this time, so time alone will tell us how things will work out. DSM-5 is said to have given more importance to cultural influences in the expression of disorders than before (Brown, R.J. & Lewis-Fernandez, R., 2011).

For most of the disorders DSM-5 requires that the symptoms be present for at least six months before a diagnosis is made.

The reason for specifying the length of time a symptom must persist before a diagnosis is made, is that we all have times when we are depressed, anxious, or somewhat disorganized in our thinking, the *key* to diagnosis of a behavioral disorder is the possession of a cluster of symptoms that are persistent rather than transitory.

Psychologists and Psychiatrists have used several models over the years to guide them in studying abnormal behavior. We will very briefly list all of the models used before we explore the subject further.

MODELS OF ABNORMAL PSYCHOLOGY

1. **THE SUPERNATURAL MODEL:** This prehistoric model that blamed disembodied spirits for abnormal behavior was discarded by scientists somewhere around the nineteenth century. DSM 5 has listed "Possession" which used to be thought of as a paranormal phenomenon, as Dissociative Identity Disorder, a non-paranormal but abnormal pattern of behavior.

2. **THE EARLY NURTURE MODEL:** This model was popular in the 1940s, and it got its start from the discovery of "psychosocial dwarfism," i.e., failure of children to develop because of emotional neglect or abuse by caretakers. This model got its start from the 1940s work of Dr. John Bowlby who worked with institutionalized children and connected their mental and often physical retardation to lack of affection or "mothering". His observations were later substantiated in the laboratory by Dr. Harry Harlowe, in now classic studies in which Rhesus monkeys were separated at birth from their natural mothers and were raised by "wire mothers". Most of the monkeys raised by these "cold" non-loving" mothers who fed the monkeys, but did not show affection or love for them, produced monkeys with abnormal behavior whereas monkeys raised in the lab by their natural mothers were perfectly normal. This model lost its importance when critics pointed out that most human mothers/parents take excellent care of their children and the number of children who grow up to suffer from disorders is disproportionately large to be due to parental neglect.

3. **THE SOCIAL MODEL** Expanded on the early nurture model by including the unhappy treatment given to a child by its entire family, the neighborhood, and the community in which the child grew up, and the effect of "labeling" by the family that becomes a source of relentless emotional pain which culminates in abnormality.

4. **THE MEDICAL MODEL** A model that is still current got its start from the discovery that penicillin prevented syphilitic patients from eventually developing insanity, by destroying the spirochetes and curing them of syphilis. Clearing the brain infection cleared up the abnormal behavior. Researchers using this model look for various bacteria or viruses that have infiltrated brain tissue and try to discover ways to destroy them.

Dissociative disorders

Group of disorders, including psychogenic amnesia, psychogenic fugue, and multiple personality, in which the thoughts and feelings that generate anxiety are separated or dissociated from conscious awareness.

Dissociative amnesia

Memory loss not attributable to disease or brain injury.

Dissociative identity disorder

A condition of separation in personality, or multiple personality, not attributable to disease or brain injury.

Dissociative fugue disorder

A dreamlike state of altered consciousness not attributable to disease, drug use, or brain injury.

5. **THE BIOCHEMICAL MODEL:** This model acquired its start from the discovery that insanity due to porphyria could be stemmed by providing Vitamin B-12. People who have Porphyria show bizarre behaviors primarily because oxygen does not reach their brains. Ordinarily the oxygen that we breathe-in, latches on to the hemoglobin circulating in the blood. It can do so because Vitamin B-12, a catalyst, is present. The oxygenated hemoglobin releases the oxygen in the brain where it becomes available for the proper functioning of the neurons. Lack of oxygen produces a whole host of symptoms in the victims of porphyria, the worst of which is insanity. Once this model came into existence, other bio-chemicals such as thyroid hormones, etc., were correctly implicated in various disorders.

6. **THE NEUROCHEMICAL MODEL:** This model fell in place with advancements in science, and it focuses on the imbalance in brain chemicals, primarily in the neurotransmitters, to be the cause of various disorders. The dopamine hypothesis of schizophrenia is one very strong piece of supporting evidence in favor of this theory. Numerous schizophrenics have been helped with anti-dopaminergic drugs.

7. **THE ECLECTIC MODEL:** This model came into existence as a fringe psychology born of the "New Age" movement. A few psychiatrists wrote bestsellers in which they presented case-histories that they claim as substantiating the supernatural model. The psychiatrists were careful in testing for and ruling out the medical, biochemical, and neurochemical models, to the extent that knowledge is available, and then gave in to the supernatural model only to find that it worked and their clients were cured of schizophrenia (Modi, 2000), multiple personality disorder (Whitton, 1986; Weiss, 1988), anxiety disorders or phobias when exorcisms were performed or when they were given past life therapy (Whitton, 1986; Weiss, 1988). This model is still a fringe model but can aid students in developing critical thinking skills, which is the reason for even mentioning it in this textbook. Although Psychology as a subject has veered towards Evolutionary Psychology, 42 percent of Americans believe in demon possession according to the 2005 Gallup Poll (Gallop News Service, http://home.sandiego.edu/~baber/logic/gallup.html).

Phobia

Any of a number of anxiety disorders that are characterized by a persistent fear of and consequent avoidance of a specific object or situation.

With DSM-5 classifying "Spirit Possession" as Dissociative Identity Disorder (DID) and Evolutionary Psychology becoming stronger than ever, chances are the Eclectic Model will vane and the medical, biochemical and neurochemical models will expand. Science is a slow process so we will have to wait and see how things go.

We end our discussion of each major category of disorder. Although every different perspective in psychology such as Freudian, Humanistic, Behavioristic, Cognitive, Neurobiological and Evolutionary, each have their theories, evidence from neuro-imaging studies is taking us in the direction of either anatomical problems, or neural connectivity problems or neuro-chemical problems. We will take a brief look at some of the Behavioral Disorders listed in DSM-5.

Neurodevelopmental Disorders

1. *"Intellectual Disability/ Intellectual Development Disorder":* This category used to be called "mental retardation". It is now called "Intellectual disability". This disorder applies to infants and children who fail to reach their developmental milestones on time and have low IQ score on tests but the diagnosis is based on the severity of adaptive functioning rather than the IQ score as such. Physical therapy to help with the physical milestones and educating the parents in the care of these special needs children is the standard treatment.

2. *Communication Disorders:* This category contains language disorders such as stuttering, which is now known as "Language Fluency Disorder", and "Language Expressive Disorder" in which the patients have phonological problems. Also included in this category is "Social Communication Disorder" in which the language user has persistent difficulty using socially acceptable words and gestures. Intensive speech therapy is given to children suffering from these disorders and there is some evidence that there is brain damage in the right hemisphere for the "Social Communication Disorder" and in the left hemisphere for some of the other language related disorders (Adams, C. Lockton, E. et. al, 2012).

The Neurodevelopmental Disorders category also contains Autism Spectrum Disorders, Attention Deficit Disorders, etc.

SCHIZOPHRENIA SPECTRUM AND OTHER PSYCHOTIC DISORDERS

Schizophrenia

Class of severe and disabling mental disorders that are characterized by extreme disruptions of perceptions, thoughts, emotions, and behavior. Types identified by *DSM-IV* include disorganized, catatonic, paranoid, undifferentiated, and residual schizophrenia.

1. *Schizophrenia: Is one of the most severe and disabling of all mental disorders, characterized by extreme disruptions of perceptions, thoughts, emotions, and behavior.* At any point in time it affects about 1 percent of people throughout the world, and it is estimated that as many as three out of every 100 people may experience this disorder at some time during their lives (American Psychological Association, 2003). Approximately 600,000 people receive treatment for schizophrenia annually in the United States. This disorder occurs with equal frequency in both sexes.

"Auditory Hallucinations" or "Hearing Voices" that mock and give commands to the patient were thought to be the "Hallmark" of Schizophrenia. However, that "Hallmark" seems to have been downplayed or removed from DSM-5! DSM-5 lists three symptoms as "core" symptoms of schizophrenia. They are: delusions, hallucinations and disordered speech. DSM-5 has done away with sub-types of schizophrenia such as "Paranoid Schizophrenia", "Catatonic Schizophrenia" etc. primarily because such labeling does not help

Delusion

An exaggerated and rigidly held belief that has little or no basis in fact.

Hallucination

False perception that lacks a sensory basis. Can be produced by hallucinogenic drugs, fatigue, or sensory deprivation. Often associated with severe psychotic disorders.

Paranoid schizophrenia

Subtype of schizophrenic disorder characterized by the presence of well-organized delusional thoughts.

Catatonic schizophrenia

Subtype of schizophrenia characterized by extreme psychomotor disturbances, which may range from stuporous immobility to wild excitement and agitation.

with the treatment. Lateralization anomalies and low activation of Inferior Frontal Gyrus (IFG) have been shown to correlate with the core symptom of thought disorder.

The term *schizophrenia* was coined by Eugene Bleuler (1950) to describe what he saw as the primary symptom of this disorder: a dissociation of thoughts from appropriate emotions caused by a splitting off (the Greek *schizo,* or split) of parts of the mind (Greek *phrenum,* for mind).

People often confuse schizophrenia with multiple personality, an entirely different disorder. *Whereas the split in* ***multiple personality disorder*** *is between different personalities,* ***all of which are capable of maintaining contact with reality, the split in schizophrenia is between thoughts and feelings***. The result is often bizarre behavior that is highly dysfunctional.

Schizophrenia is distinguished from other behavioral disorders primarily by the characteristically extreme disturbances in thinking that cause people to behave in maladaptive ways. In addition to these thought disturbances, constellations of other symptoms are used to diagnose this disorder. People diagnosed with schizophrenia may show considerable diversity of symptoms.

Delusions and Disturbances of Thought Thought disturbances associated with schizophrenia tend to be of two basic types: disturbances of content (that is, the actual ideas expressed), and disturbances of form (the manner in which ideas are organized).

Most individuals with schizophrenia demonstrate marked disturbances in the content of their thoughts. These disturbances may be evident from a few characteristic symptoms. One is a lack of awareness of some of the basic realities of life, such as what is going on around them and the nature of their condition. Another disturbance in the content of thought is delusions. Table 11.1 describes several varieties of delusional thoughts that may be associated with schizophrenia.

Disturbances in the form of thought may be evident in the incoherence of the ideas a person verbalizes. For example, consider the following account of a conversation between a schizophrenic patient and a clinician:

Therapist: How old are you?

Client: Why I am centuries old, sir.

Therapist: How long have you been here?

Client: I've been now on this property on and off for a long time. I cannot say the exact time because we are absorbed by the air at night, and they bring back people. They kill up everything: they can make you lie; they can talk through your throat.

Therapist: Who is this?

Client: Why, the air.

Therapist: What is the name of this place?

Client: This place is called a star.

Therapist: Who is the doctor in charge of your ward?

TABLE 11.1 Several Varieties of Delusional Thoughts That May Be Associated with Schizophrenia

Delusion of influence	A belief that others are influencing one by means of wires, TV, and so on, making one do things against one's will.
Delusion of grandeur	The belief that one is in actuality some great world or historical figure, such as Napoleon, Queen Victoria, or a religious figure like Jesus Christ.
Delusion of persecution	The belief that one is being persecuted, hunted, or interfered with by certain individuals or organized groups.
Delusion of reference	The belief that others are talking about one, that one is being included in TV shows or plays or referred to in news articles, and so on.
Delusion of bodily change	The belief that one's body is changing in some unusual way—for example, that the blood is turning to snakes or the flesh to concrete.
Delusion of nihilism	The belief that nothing really exists, that all things are simply shadows; also common is the idea that one has really been dead for many years and is observing the world from afar.

Client: A body just like yours, sir. They can make you black and white. I say good morning, but he just comes through there. At first it was a colony. They said it was heaven. These buildings were not solid at the time, and I am positive that this is the same place. They have others just like it. People die, and all the microbes talk over there, and prestigitis you know is sending you from here to another world. I was sent by the government to the United States to Washington to some star, and they had a pretty nice country there. Now you have a body like a young man who says he is of the prestigitis.

Therapist: Who was this prestigitis?

Client: Why, you are yourself. You can be prestigitis. They make you say bad things; they can read you; they bring back Negroes from the dead. (White, 1932, p. 228)

Neologisms

Literally, new words. Invention of neologisms is characteristic of schizophrenic disorder.

It is common for schizophrenics to invent new words, or **neologisms**, like the word "prestigitis" in the preceding passage. Another anomaly in the form of schizophrenic thoughts is *loose associations,* in which ideas shift from one topic to another so that it is very difficult for a listener to follow the train of thought.

Hallucinations and Disturbance of Perception A second primary symptom, disturbed perception, may include changes in how the body feels (including numbness, tingling, or burning sensations, or the feeling that organs are deteriorating or that parts of the body are too large or small), or a feeling of depersonalization that makes a person feel separated from his or her body. Research also demonstrates that schizophrenics have considerable difficulty properly focusing their attention as they process sensory stimulation and that

TABLE 11.2 Concordance Rates of Schizophrenia Between Identical and Fraternal Twins

		Identical Twins		Fraternal Twins	
Investigator	**Country**	**Number of Pairs in Sample**	**Percentage Concordance Rate**	**Number of Pairs in Sample**	**Percentage Concordance Rate**
Cardno et al.	England	106	82	118	19
Gottesman & Shields	England	22	40–50*	33	9–19
Pollin et al.	U.S.A.	95	14–27	125	4–8
Fischer	Denmark	21	24–48	41	10–19
Kringlen	Norway	55	23–38	90	4–10
Tienari	Finland	17	0–36	20	5–14

*The range in the concordance rate figures reflects different estimates of what would constitute a concordant pair, which vary depending on how narrowly or broadly schizophrenia is defined. The lower figure is for the narrower definition, which requires a majority of the major symptoms of schizophrenia to be present.

SOURCE: Figure of "Concordance Rates of Schizophrenia Among Identical and Fraternal Twins" from *Schizophrenia: The Epigenetic Puzzle* by Irving I. Gottesman and James Shields. Copyright ©by Irving I. Gottesman and James Shields.

they are often unable to filter out irrelevant information (Braff & Geyer, 1990; Grillon et al., 1990; Harris et al., 1990).

The most common altered perceptions in schizophrenia are hallucinations. Hallucinations may occur in any of the sense modalities, *but most often a schizophrenic person hears voices that seem to be coming from outside the person's head.* In contrast, people who have MPD, hear voices coming from inside their heads (North et.al., 1993). It has been suggested that at least some of the auditory hallucinations experienced by schizophrenics may be projections of their own thoughts (Bick & Kinsbourne, 1987). *These voices may give commands* ("take off your clothes"; "kill corrupting prostitutes") that are sometimes obeyed with disturbing or tragic consequences. More commonly the imagined voices may make insulting comments about the person's character or behavior (illustrated in the following account):

> A forty-one-year-old housewife heard a voice coming from a house across the road. The voice went on incessantly in a flat monotone describing everything she was doing with an admixture of critical comments. "She is peeling potatoes, got hold of the peeler, she does not want that potato, she is putting it back. ..." (Mellor, 1970, p. 16)

Disturbance in Emotional Expression: A third common symptom of schizophrenia is a disturbance in emotional expression. This symptom may take the form of a blunted or flat affect, characterized by a dramatic lack of emotional expression. *The person may stare vacantly with listless eyes, speak in a monotone, and show no facial expression.* Differing theories have been offered to explain this lack of affect, including the possibility that schizophrenic people may be so absorbed in responding to internal stimuli that they are unresponsive to outside stimuli (Venables & Wing, 1962). It has also been suggested that by turning themselves off, schizophrenics are able to protect themselves from stimuli with which they feel incapable of coping (Mednick, 1958).

Perhaps even more common than flat affect are inappropriate emotional responses, in which the emotional expression is incongruous with its context. For example, a schizophrenic person may laugh upon hearing of the death of a loved one, or may fly into a rage when asked an innocuous question such as, "Did you enjoy your dinner?" Mood states may shift rapidly for no discernible reason.

Disturbances in Speech: In addition to abnormal speech patterns (such as incoherence and loose associations) that result from thought disturbances, two verbal dysfunctions may be viewed as primary examples of speech disturbances linked with schizophrenia. In **mutism**, the person may not utter a sound for hours or days regardless of how much encouragement or prodding is provided. In the other disturbance, **echolalia**, a person might answer a question by repeating it verbatim or might repeat virtually every statement he or she hears uttered.

Mutism

Speech disturbance characteristic of schizophrenia in which an individual may not utter a sound for hours or days at a time.

Echolalia

Speech disturbance characteristic of some forms of schizophrenia in which people repeat virtually every statement they hear uttered.

Schizoaffective Disorder Is similar to schizophrenia but alternating with severe mood disturbances.

Brain Biochemistry: Researchers studying schizophrenia have focused considerable attention on biochemical abnormalities and mechanisms of drug action to explain schizophrenia. Although several different biochemical hypotheses have been proposed over the years the dopamine hypothesis appears to be the most promising. The dopamine hypothesis suggests that schizophrenia is caused either by abnormally high levels of the neurotransmitter dopamine or by above-normal reactivity to this chemical due to an increased number of receptors for dopamine (Barnes, 1987b; Grey et al., 1991; Wong et al., 1986).

The dopamine hypothesis is well supported by research. For example, it is known that the phenothiazines (drugs that alleviate some of the symptoms of schizophrenia) reduce the activity of dopamine by blocking postsynaptic dopamine receptors (Kimble, 1988; Lipper, 1985; Wolkin et al., 1989). Considered together, these findings provide strong evidence linking either excessive dopamine levels or abnormal sensitivity to dopamine because of increased dopamine receptors to schizophrenia (Abi-Dargham et al., 2003; Carlsson, 1977, 1995; Cortes et al., 1989; Glatt et al., 2003; Grey et al., 1991; Perez et al., 2003).

Brain Structural Abnormalities: There is also extensive evidence of structural *abnormalities in the brains of schizophrenics. These findings, considered in tandem* with data concerning biochemical irregularities, provide powerful evidence that schizophrenia is a brain disease (Johnson, 1989). Several of the new techniques for observing living brains, such as CAT and PET scans and magnetic resonance imaging, have provided evidence of various kinds of physical abnormalities in the brains of individuals diagnosed as having schizophrenia. These *structural abnormalities* include unusually large ventricles (Andreasen et al.,

FIGURE 11.3 PET Scans Comparing a Patient Diagnosed with Schizophrenia (left) with a Normal Subject (right)

Note the difference in activity in the frontal cortex. Some studies suggest that schizophrenics have lower levels of frontal cortex activity than normal subjects.

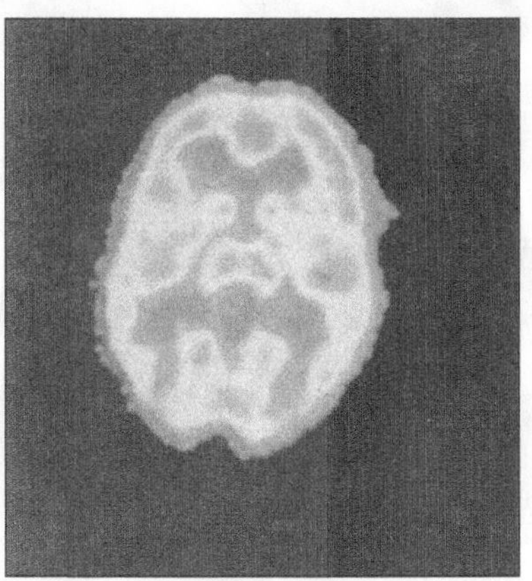

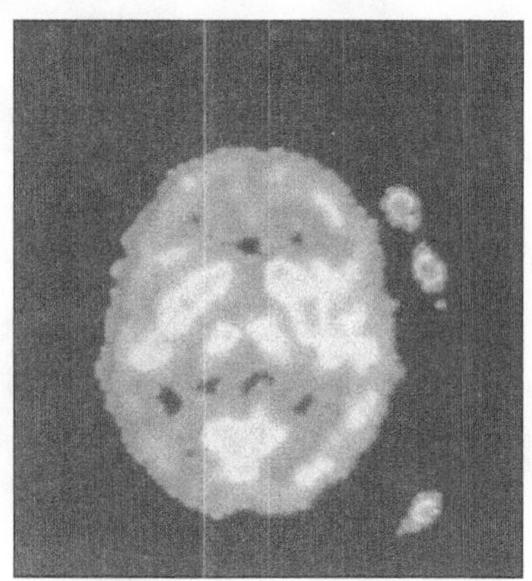

Psychosis

Term used until publication of *DSM-III* in 1980 to describe severe disorders that involve disturbances of thinking, reduced contact with reality, loss of ability to function socially, and often bizarre behaviors.

1990; Johnstone et al., 1989; Kaplan et al., 1990; Rossi et al., 1989a, 1989b; Weinberger et al., 1990; Woods et al., 1990), and reduced volume of temporal lobe gray matter (Rossi et al., 1990; Suddath et al., 1989; Weinberger et al., 1990). Likewise, Dr. Paul Thompson of UCLA has discovered that dramatic reduction in parietal lobe grey matter takes place during adolescence and then spreads to other outer regions of the cortex in about five years, based on resonance imaging MRI studies (Thompson, 2001), and unusually small corpus callosum (Ardekani et al., 2003; Rossi et al., 1989). The PET scans in Figure 11.5 show some of these abnormalities but how they relate to different symptoms displayed by patients in not known.

DEPRESSIVE AND BIPOLAR DISORDERS

Major depressive disorder

Type of mood disorder characterized by deep and persistent depression.

Bipolar (manic-depressive) disorder

Mood disorder characterized by intermittent episodes of both depression and mania (highly energized behavior).

1. *Major Depression:* is a form of psychosis in which a person is out of touch with reality and finds it near impossible to experience joy or pleasure. Patients feel worthless, fatigued and hopeless and have thoughts of suicide. They also experience changes in sleep patterns and appetite.

2. *Bipolar Disorder:* is a form of psychosis in which the patient suffers from depression or excessive sadness and mania, which is an excess of exuberance. When manicacal, a patient has too many thoughts which come at a rapid rate and are quite disconnected; the patient often becomes aggressive and belligerent and may experience elation and behave in a pompous or grandiose manner. People who are suffering from mania have been known to spend all their money in one bizarre shopping spree or go on a rampage.

Getty

Depression is the primary symptom of mood disorders.

ANXIETY

Generalized anxiety disorder

Chronic state of free-floating anxiety that is omnipresent.

1. Generalized Anxiety Disorder may be described as a generalized feeling of dread or apprehension typically accompanied by a variety of physiological reactions including increased heart rate, rapid shallow breathing, sweating, muscle tension, and drying of the mouth. Anxiety differs from fear in one important respect. Fear has an obvious cause, and once that cause is eliminated, the fear will subside. In contrast, *anxiety is less clearly linked to specific events or stimuli. Therefore, it tends to be more pervasive and less responsive to changes in the environment and is "future oriented", or is anticipatory of something but something that the patient is unaware of.*

We all experience occasional episodes of anxiety. For approximately one out of every eight Americans, however, anxiety is such a pervasive condition that they are said to suffer from an **anxiety disorder**. Anxiety disorders are fairly common in the United States (Narrow et al., 2002).

Anxiety disorder

Any of a number of disorders that produce pervasive feelings of anxiety.

2. Phobia is irrational fear of a specific object. If the object is removed from the victim's vicinity the fear subsides immediately and the person is calm and behaves normally again. This author has seen unexpected phobic reactions of people. They can be quite shocking. One was a successful gynecologist, who was enjoying a party till the hostesses' kitten came into the room. No sooner than she saw the cat, her eyes became as big as proverbial saucers, the tray of food she was holding slipped from her hands, she trembled and she screamed loudly enough to scare all the guests, till

TABLE 11.3 Concordance Rates for Major Depression and Bipolar Affective Disorder for Identical and Fraternal Twins

Study	Concordance Among Identical (MZ) Twins (%)	Concordance Among Fraternal (DZ) Twins (%)
Major Depression		
Allen, 1976	40	11
Kendler et al., 1992	48	42
Kendler et al., 1999	57	39
McGuffin et al., 1996	46	20
Bipolar Affective Disorder		
Allen, 1976	72	14
Bertelsen et al., 1977	79	19
Kendler, 1993	70	35
Kringlen, 1985	50	15
McGuffin et al., 2003	67	19

SOURCE: Table of "Concordance of Affective Mental Disorders" from *Handbook of Affective Disorders* by J. I. Numberger and E. S. Gershon, edited by E. S. Paykel. Copyright © 1982 by E. S. Paykel. Reprinted by permission of the Guilford Press.

> the little kitten was removed! No sooner than the kitten was removed, she calmed down, was shame-faced, apologized profusely and went about picking up the dropped food like any rational person would do.

Although Behaviorists claim that phobias are learned, either via operant conditioning or via classical conditioning, much like John Watson's subject little Albert learned to fear the Rabbit, there is a little bit of evidence that some phobias may be genetic as monozygotic (identical) twins show the same phobia far more often than do fraternal twins and even identical twins who were given up for adoption and raised in two completely different families seem to suffer from the same phobia. Furthermore, although there are quite a few different kinds of phobias, the objects of these phobias tend to be limited to a fairly narrow range of stimuli such as snakes or mice, etc. (Goldstein et.al, 1986). Today, we are exposed far more to motor vehicles and machines and even machine guns than we are to snakes. Why don't we develop proportionately more phobias to these objects? Proponents of Evolutionary Perspective answer this by saying that such fears were wired–in and inherited due to their survival or adaptive value and that may be a possibility but it is difficult to explain door-knob phobia of identical twins which was reported by Thomas Bouchard, the researcher famous for his Minnesota Twin Studies in which he studied identical twins given up for adoption and reared apart in two completely different families and found amazing similarities in their behaviors, choices, personality traits and yes, abnormalities like door-knob phobias! (Andorfer, G. & Skinner T. 1994).

Panic Disorders and Agoraphobia

Have you ever had an experience in which everything was fine one moment, and then for no apparent reason you suddenly felt an intense apprehension and overwhelming terror that caused your heart to pound, your breathing to become labored, and your hands to tremble? If your answer is yes, you have probably experienced a panic attack. There is good evidence that many people have occasional panic attacks. In one survey of over 2,000 college students, 12 percent of the sample had experienced at least one panic attack and 2.4 percent met the criteria for panic disorder (Telch, et al., 1989).

Panic Disorder

An Anxiety Disorder in which an individual experiences numerous panic attacks (four or more in a four-week period) that are characterized by overwhelming terror and often a feeling of unreality or of depersonalization.

Having an occasional panic attack does not necessarily mean that you suffer from a **panic disorder**. *DSM-5* stipulates that a person experience *recurrent, unexpected* or expected panic attacks and that the symptoms continue for at least six months before the diagnosis of Panic Disorder is made. The incidence of this disorder in America is estimated to be in the range of 1 to 2 percent of the population. Recently, researchers have described a link between panic attacks and smoking. Regular smokers with nicotine dependence are at a significantly greater risk of developing panic disorders than nonsmokers (Goodwin & Hamilton, 2002; Isensee et al., 2003).

Specific phobia

Anxiety disorder characterized by an irrational fear of specific situations or objects, such as heights, small closed places, or spiders.

Sometimes, people who suffer from panic attacks also develop **agoraphobia** *or fear of open or public places or places from which it might be difficult to escape.* Although they usually realize that their fear is far out of proportion to any actual danger, this understanding does little to reduce the fear.

In addition to agoraphobia which is classified as a Panic Disorder, DSM-5 provides diagnostic categories for social phobias and specific phobias.

Social Phobias

Social phobia

An anxiety disorder characterized by a persistent, irrational fear of performing some specific behavior (such as talking or eating) in the presence of other people.

A **social phobia** is a persistent, irrational fear of performing some specific behavior, such as talking, writing, eating, drinking, or using public lavatories, in the presence of other people. ***People with social phobias are compelled to avoid situations in which they may be observed behaving in an ineffective or embarrassing manner.*** Many social phobics are particularly fearful of interaction with authority figures such as teachers, employers, or police officers.

There are two kinds of social phobias. One kind, called *discrete performance anxiety,* reflects fear of specific situations—such as speaking or acting—in which the individual must perform before an audience. This kind of social phobia is manageable in that the individual can lead a relatively normal social life by simply avoiding such situations. However, a performance-oriented social phobia can limit career options or professional growth. The second type of social phobia, or **social anxiety disorder**, may impose more serious limitations by causing individuals to avoid all kinds of social situations in both professional and personal activities. Individuals with this phobia have difficulty making new acquaintances, interacting with peers and supervisors on the job, enjoying recreational pursuits with others, attending social functions, and so forth. "In extreme cases, victims fear contact with anyone outside their families" (Liebowitz, 1989). It is estimated that approximately 10 percent of the population will suffer from social phobia during their lifetime (Keller, 2003).

Obsessive-Compulsive and Related Disorders

If you have ever had the experience of not being able to get a catchy, melodious jingle out of your mind, or of needing to go back and make sure you have locked all the doors even though you are sure you have, you should have a sense of what it is like to have an **obsessive-compulsive disorder (OCD)**. Here, a person's profound sense of anxiety is reflected in persistent, unwanted, and unshakable thoughts (obsession) and/or irresistible, habitual repeated actions (compulsion).

Obsessive-compulsive disorder

Anxiety disorder characterized by persistent, unwanted, and unshakable thoughts and/or irresistible, habitual repeated actions.

Approximately 1.1 percent or 2.2 million Americans have Obsessive–Compulsive Disorder (www.nimh.nih.gov, 2013). People who have this disorder usually know that their obsessive thoughts or compulsive actions are irrational, they still cannot block out their thoughts or keep themselves from performing the repetitious act, often an extreme number of times and the illness begins in adolescence for many but the median age is 19 (www.nimh.nih.gov, 2013).

Women seem to be almost twice as vulnerable as men for OCD, even though compulsive urges are more common in men than in women (Mancini et al., 1999). There is one report of a woman who washed her hands over 500 times per day (Davison & Neale, 1990). Apparently men tend to be "checkers" rather than "cleaners," although there is no definitive answer as to why this gender difference exists. It may simply be due to societal expectations of the gender role. The senseless, repetitious behavior seems to ward off a flood of overwhelming anxiety that would result if the compulsive acts are terminated.

In the classic manifestation of this disorder, obsessive thoughts lead to compulsive actions. The following case illustrates this connection:

> Shirley K., a twenty-three-year-old housewife, came to the clinic with a complaint of frequent attacks of headaches and dizziness. During the preceding three months she had been disturbed by recurring thoughts that she might harm her two-year-old son, Saul, either by stabbing or choking him (the obsessive thought). She constantly had to go into his room, touch the baby, and feel him breathe in order to reassure herself that Saul was still alive (the compulsive act); otherwise she became unbearably anxious. If she read a report in the daily paper of the murder of a child, she would become agitated, since this reinforced her fear that she too might act on her impulse. Shirley turned to the interviewer and asked, with desperation, whether this meant that she was going crazy. (Goldstein & Palmer, 1975, p. 155)

In the case just described, it appears that by constantly checking on her son's well-being this woman was able to relieve temporarily the anxiety caused by her thoughts about harming her son. Most people who manifest this disorder demonstrate the components of both obsessions and compulsions. However, about 15 percent of cases experience only obsessive thoughts that are not accompanied by compulsive acts (March et al., 1989).

Body Dysmorphic Disorder This is a new addition in DSM-5. People who have a poor self-image with regard to their physical appearance, and who seek to correct what they perceive to be defects in their anatomy, even to the extent of undergoing elective plastic surgery repeatedly or obsess about their perceived defects in their body parts are included in this category.

Hoarding Disorder This is another new disorder that has been added in DSM 5 under Obsessive-Compulsive and Related Disorders Category. People with this disorder have extreme difficulty parting with their possessions and collect and hoard stuff till their living conditions become abominable. Although the symptoms sound similar to that of obsessive-compulsive behavior, this disorder is not just a variant of obsessive-compulsive disorder (OCD) because the neural correlates are different with higher activation of the ventromedial prefrontal cortex in people with Hoarding Disorder as compared to those with OCD and those who are normal (www.dsm5.org, 2013; An, S.K., Mataix-Cols, D. et.al, 2009).

Two other disorders named *Trichotillomania (hair-pulling disorder)* and Excoriation (skin-picking Disorder) are also grouped under OCD & Related Disorders and the names are descriptive enough so they don't warrant any further explanation. The stipulation that the symptoms persist for six months before a diagnosis is made applies to these disorders also.

Trauma and Stressor Related Disorders

Post-Traumatic Stress Disorder (PTSD) People who experience a profoundly traumatic event, such as an assault, an accident, or wartime combat, often exhibit a range of severely distressing symptoms as an aftermath to the occurrence. For example, a rape survivor may have vivid flashbacks of the attack in which she re-experiences all the terror of the assault, or war veterans may have flashbacks of traumatic war experiences as an aftermath of their participation in the conflict. A similar kind of reliving of the trauma often occurs among survivors of severe accidents. In one study, all 10 survivors of a plane crash that left 127 dead relived the tragedy over and over again in the form of dreams, nightmares, or panic attacks (Krupnick & Horowitz, 1981). Some people suffer from PTSD even if they themselves were not attacked but witnessed someone else's suffering.

Posttraumatic stress disorder (PTSD)

Anxiety disorder that typically follows a traumatic event or events, and is characterized by a reliving of that event, avoidance of stimuli associated with the event or numbing of general responsiveness, and increased arousal.

Characteristic symptoms of PTSD include recurrent distressing recollections or dreams of the traumatic event, acting or feeling as if the traumatic event were recurring, and intense distress associated with exposure to cues related to the traumatic event (American Psychiatric Association, 2003), changes in physiological arousal such as startle reflex and sleep problems and difficulty remembering some details of the traumatic incident (Okami, 2013, pg.632).

An Ethiopian boy soldier who suffers from posttraumatic stress disorder (PTSD).

Corbis

Posttraumatic stress disorder differs from other anxiety disorders in that it can be explained largely if not solely on environmental grounds. An examination of the life histories of people who have conditions such as phobias or obsessive-compulsive disorders does not reveal a consistent pattern of background factors. In contrast, all victims of PTSD, while certainly different from one another in many ways, share experiences with a profoundly traumatizing event(s).

For instance, war veterans most likely to manifest severe symptoms of PTSD are those who are exposed to frequent, intense combat and/or who participate in atrocities such as the killing of civilians (Breslau & Davis, 1987; Green et al., 1989). PTSD has also been diagnosed in veterans who were prisoners of war (POWs). A follow-up study of 62 former World War II POWs revealed that half experienced PTSD after repatriation, and that 18 (29 percent) continued to meet the criteria for PTSD 40 years later (Speed et al., 1989). More recently, the prevalence of PTSD in residents of Manhattan after the September 11, 2001 terrorist attacks was estimated to be as high as 20 percent (Galea et al., 2002). New information indicates that while a good 50%/60% of the US population is exposed to trauma, barely 1.3% of those who have been exposed to severe trauma develop PTSD, indicating genetic involvement (Okami, 2013 pg. 632) and those who have exposure to trauma and have a gene involved in methylation, a gene known as MAN2C1, are more likely to develop PTSD (Uddin, M., Galea, S. et.al, 2011), so environmental trauma alone might be an insufficient causal factor.

If certain people are biologically predisposed to some anxiety disorders, it follows that there may be a genetic basis for these disorders. The research program of Sapolsky and his colleagues at Stanford University, who have investigated the biology of stress and anxiety, represents one of the most fascinating new lines of evidence pertaining to this perspective. Data from a number of studies have led Sapolsky to believe that gene replacement therapy may be on the horizon for patients with severe anxiety disorders (Sapolsky, 2003a, 2003b, 2003c). Research in Sapolsky's laboratory has demonstrated that genetic manipulations can alter limbic function and an organism's reactions to stress. It is foreseeable that gene therapy might soon protect individuals from debilitating stress and anxiety.

Other evidence of a genetic link for anxiety disorders comes from studies examining the incidence of these disorders in families. One study measured the incidence of anxiety disorders among siblings, mothers, and fathers of three groups of subjects: agoraphobics, panic-disordered individuals, and a control group with no diagnosed anxiety disorders. As Table 11.4 shows, the relatives of both groups of anxiety-disordered subjects showed more than double the incidence of anxiety disorders that were found among relatives of the control group (Harris et al., 1983). Other research has also reported a higher than normal incidence of anxiety disorders among relatives of people with diagnosed panic disorders (Balon et al., 1989; Cloninger et al., 1981; Crowe et al., 1987). Recent research indicates that maternal but not paternal mood or anxiety disorders were highly correlated with that of adult offspring (Lowe, N. C.P., Dugas, E., 2012).

The studies just described suggest a genetic component in anxiety disorders. But does the evidence point clearly to a hereditary explanation, or is there another possible explanation for these findings? What other types of research besides family studies might provide more clear-cut evidence? Give these questions some thought before reading on.

Somatic Symptom and Related Disorders

The primary symptom of anxiety disorders is psychological distress, somatic disorders are expressed through *somatic* or physical symptoms. Dizziness, stomach pain, vomiting, breathing difficulties, difficulty in swallowing, impaired vision, inability to move the legs, numbness of the hands, and sexual dysfunctions are some of the common symptoms of somatoform disorders. *In all cases, however, the symptoms have no physiological basis that have been identified as of yet.* The old name, i.e. the one used in DSM IV was "Somatoform Disorder" and it included Hypochondriasis, Somatization Disorder, etc. which have been removed from DSM-5 not because people don't suffer from such disorders but because such labels encourage "Mind-body Dualism" (www.dsm5.org, 2013). The few disorders that DSM -5 now places in this category are:

Hypochondriasis

Somatoform disorder in which the individual is excessively fearful of contracting a serious illness or of dying.

TABLE 11.4 Risk for Several Types of Anxiety-Based Disorders in Siblings and Parents of Agoraphobics, Panic-Disordered, and Nonanxious Controls

	Patient Status		
	Agoraphobic	Panic	Controls
	Incidence (%) in first degree relatives for the disorder:		
Agoraphobia	8.6	1.9	4.2
Panic disorder	7.7	20.5	4.2
Generalized anxiety	5.1	6.5	5.3
Atypical anxiety	2.6	3.7	0.0
Social phobia	3.4	0.0	1.1
Specific phobia	2.6	0.0	0.0
Obsessive-compulsive	1.7	0.0	0.0
Total of all anxiety-based disorders	31.7	32.6	14.8

SOURCE: From Harris et al., 1983

Somatoform disorder

Class of disorders including somatization disorder, hypochondriasis, and conversion disorder that are manifested through somatic or physical symptoms.

1. *Somatic Symptom Disorder* A person with all the criteria that fit the DSM-IV list for **"somatization disorder" and who also has maladaptive thoughts, feelings and behaviors is said to have this "Somatic Symptom disorder"**.

Typically, such a patient has multiple and recurrent physical symptoms that have no physical cause, but for which medical attention is repeatedly sought. People who have this disorder commonly complain about chest, stomach, and back pain, headaches, heart palpitations, vomiting, dizziness, and fainting, and genitourinary symptoms. Patients typically present their complaints in such a convincing fashion that medications and medical procedures are provided, including unnecessary surgery in some cases. This disorder typically begins in the late teenage years, and is more common among women than men (Kroll et al., 1979). Recent data suggest that approximately one person in 250 manifests this disorder (Swartz et al., 1986).

Conversion disorder

Somatoform disorder that is manifested as a sensory or motor system disorder for which there is no known organic cause.

2. *Conversion Disorder (Functional Neurological Symptoms Disorder)* It is typically manifested as a sensory or motor-system disturbance for which there is no known organic cause. Unlike the two previous categories of somatoform disorders, conversion disorders are seldom confused with genuine physical disease *because their symptom patterns make no anatomical sense.* In the condition known as sensory conversion, for example, individuals may lose sensitivity in specific parts of their bodies in which the ***pattern of loss-of-feeling is neurologically impossible***. Other forms of sensory conversion may be reflected in loss of sensitivity to pain, impaired vision or hearing, and, in some cases, heightened sensitivity to touch. In another related condition, motor conversion, an individual may experience paralysis in some part of the body, usually a limb, or experience uncontrollable tremors or twitches.

Conversion disorders typically surface after a person has experienced serious stress or internal conflict, and the symptoms appear to allow the person to escape from or avoid that stress or internal conflict. This situation is apparent in the following case, in which a man developed a sensory conversion to escape from a nagging wife and mother-in-law:

> Phil, forty years of age, had a history of marginal work adjustment since his discharge from the Army at age twenty-five. In the fifteen years since discharge, he had depended on public assistance and financial aid from relatives to get by. He painted a very dismal picture of his married life, as one of almost constant harassment from his wife and mother-in-law. He had a history of minor illnesses involving his eyes, none of which had grossly affected his visual acuity.
>
> During the Christmas season his wife and mother-in-law were being more demanding than usual, requiring him to work nights and weekends at various chores under their foremanship. Three days before Christmas, while shopping with his wife and mother-in-law, Phil suddenly became blind in both eyes.
>
> Neurological and ophthalmological exams were essentially negative in accounting for his blindness, and a diagnosis of conversion disorder was made. At this time, *Phil did not seem greatly alarmed by his loss of sight, but instead displayed an attitude of patient forbearance.* Observers in the hospital noticed that Phil could get about in the ward better than expected for a totally blind man. He was not concerned with this, but felt hurt and unjustly accused when other patients pointed out the discrepancy to him. (Adapted from Brady & Lind, 1965, p. 162)

Phil's apparent lack of concern about his condition is fairly common among people with conversion disorders. The French psychiatrist Pierre Janet (1929) labeled this blasé attitude "*la belle indifference*", or the noble lack of concern. Observers may incorrectly assume that a person with a conversion disorder is malingering, or deliberately faking symptoms. However, unlike malingerers, who tend to be cautious about discussing their symptoms for fear that their pretense will be discovered, individuals with a conversion disorder appear eager to talk at great length about their symptoms. However, DSM-5 states that psychological causes are not always apparent during the neurological exam (www.dsm5.org, 2013), so diagnosing such illnesses is not as easy as it sounds.

Depersonalization/Derealization Disorders This category contains disorders which werre called **dissociative disorders in the past** and thoughts and feelings that generate anxiety seem to be separated, or *dissociated,* from conscious awareness by memory loss or a change in identity. These uncommon disorders usually take the form of *dissociative amnesia,* or *dissociative identity.* The most interesting aspect of these disorders is that these people have *intact procedural memory, intact semantic memory, and have no known organic brain abnormality.* The only problem they claim is loss of episodic memory, which is loss of those memories that allow them a continuous life story as to who they are, who they belong to, and what they have been up to, things which most normal ordinary people remember.

Dissociative Amnesia: The diagnosis of "dissociative Amnesia" is applied to a person who experiences sudden loss of episodic memory, usually after a particularly stressful, insoluble or unbearable event. The most typical manifestation is loss of episodic memory for all events for a specified period of time, as is seen in the following case of Patricia Lewis.

In 1996, on being indicted on fraud charges in connection with stealing over a million dollars via a business she worked for, Patricia Lewis became amnesic and was unable to recall any events of her life beginning with 1962 through 1996! She was tested by several forensic psychologists and they all agreed that Patricia had amnesia. After testing her memory extensively and indirectly, the forensic psychologists concluded that she was not faking it and was suffering from genuine dissociative amnesia but was competent to stand trial. The amnesia did not help her any because there was compelling evidence as to her involvement in the fraud, and she plead guilty to the charges on the basis of the extensive evidence, even though she had no recollection of committing the fraud (Welner, 1997).

In other similar cases, occasionally a person may develop total amnesia for all prior experiences, and will be unable to recognize relatives, friends, and familiar places. The individual usually retains reasoning and verbal abilities, talents such as the ability to play a musical instrument, and general knowledge. Episodes of dissociative amnesia may last from several hours to many years. They typically disappear as suddenly as they appeared, and they rarely recur.

Establishing a sense of safety helps many patients recover some, if not all, their memories and sometimes recovery is spontaneous. Some clinicians claim that these patients are highly hypnotizable and that hypnosis helps in recovery of memory. If the traumatic event that led to the amnesia can be discovered, it helps the patient overcome amnesia-related problems. Hirokazu, K. et.al (2010) report that they conducted fMRI studies on two patients with dissociative amnesia. One was a young man who could not recall four and a half years of his life beginning with the last year of his college, but could remember facts prior to the onset. There was no known trauma or any anatomical problems. The other was an older man who had lost 35 years of memories beginning with his high-school, and ending with the day he had been brought to the hospital for a diagnosis. He did have a very minor car accident in which he had superficial bruises, but there was no physical injury or any brain injury.

The researchers had them do a task where they viewed photos and responded by identifying the photo of a person they knew personally and recognized or they did know personally but claimed no memory for them and they included photos of people they could not have met and therefore not have known. Hirokazu and colleagues found that the prefrontal cortex was active but hippocampus was deactivated when viewing photos of people they knew but denied knowing, they also found the right dorsolateral prefrontal cortex was more active in dissociative amnesiacs when viewing photos of people they knew but denied knowing, so the "executive control" mechanisms of the right hemisphere seems to be involved in the suppression of the hippocampal retrieval process.

One of the Dissociative Amnesia patients had disappeared from home but had come back on his own. This type of disappearance used to be labeled "Fugue" and used to be considered a separate disorder, but it is no longer considered a disorder by itself and is seen as a symptom of dissociative amnesia in DSM-5.

Dissociative Identity Disorder

The book *Three Faces of Eve* (Thigpen, 1957) is thought to have brought this strange disorder, known as multiple personality disorder at the time, to the notice of lay people. **Dissociative identity disorder** (DID) or multiple personality disorder (MPD, former name of this disorder) is a very uncommon form of dissociative disorder in which *the individual alternates between an original or primary personality and one or more secondary or subordinate personalities.* Usually the subordinate personality is aware of the primary personality but not vice versa. Sometimes there are so many "alter personalities" that there simply isn't one "primary" personality, but in that case the psychiatrist simply labels the personality who first showed up for therapy as the "primary" personality (Putnam, 1986).

Most of us have opposing tendencies within ourselves but are able to find appropriate outlets for expressing different aspects of our personalities, and we do not lose the connectivity of our episodic memories or our sense of being the same old "self." However, not everyone is able to achieve a satisfactory synthesis. Multiple personality disorder (MPD) seems to provide an outlet for these different selves, by separating the conflicting parts and elaborating each into an essentially autonomous personality with a different "self." Frequently the separated personalities represent two extremes, from responsible and conforming to irresponsible and "naughty", to out-right fiendish and demon-like (North et.al 1993).

Some clinicians have reported patients who have several "fragmentary" personalities, for example, the famous case of Sybil from the 1970s (Schreiber, 1973). Sybil was supposed to have some 16 personalities, so obviously many of these personalities were not "opposites" but simply "composites." After both Sybil and her psychiatrist, Dr. Cornelia Wilbur, passed away, Dr. Herbert Siegel, one of the colleagues of Dr. Wilbur, charged that Sybil's MPD was created by Dr. Wilbur by having Sybil read *Three Faces of Eve* and giving her suggestions to manifest different personalities under hypnosis. Dr. Siegel has claimed that he had some tapes of the therapy sessions but had forgotten about them, and that these tapes clearly indicate that *Dr. Wilbur created the personalities via hypnotic suggestion* (Borch-Jacobson, 1997; Boynton, 1998). The real Sybil was just a "hysteric." The controversy is not quite over. Some psychiatrists also indicate that the claim of child abuse as the cause of MPD came into existence with Dr. Wilbur's Sybil case.

Ever since Sybil, almost all multiples have claimed child abuse or sexual molestation at the hands of relatives or care-givers as children (Spanos, 1996).

An analysis of 100 reported cases of multiple personality disorder revealed that 83 percent of these disturbed individuals had in common "histories of significant childhood trauma, primarily sexual abuse" (Putnam et al., 1986, p. 292; Putnam, 1993). The individuals in this sample also displayed a core of clinical symptoms including depression, substance abuse, insomnia, sexual dysfunction, and suicidal or other self-destructive behaviors.

Dissociative disorder seems to occur more frequently in women than men, with nine times more women affected than men (Putnam et al., 1986; Ross, 1989). It has been widely assumed that multiple personality is very rare: According to one estimate, only about 300 cases had been reported in the world's professional literature prior to 1970 (Bliss, 1984). In recent years, however, the reported incidence of this disorder has been on the rise (Boor, 1982; Putnam et al., 1986). One clinician reported seeing more than 100 cases of multiple personality between 1980 and 1984 (Bliss, 1984). Ross (1989) argues that this increasing trend may be the result of an increasingly sick society in which child abuse is increasing at a high rate. The incidence of child abuse of females is also much higher than for males. Although child abuse, particularly sexual abuse, appears to be associated with multiple personality disorder (Steele, H. 2003), not all psychologists agree that this is a causal connection.

Caution should also be exercised in diagnosing a dissociative disorder, especially when the diagnosis may produce secondary gains (Thigpen & Cleckley, 1984). This issue was brought to public attention by the case of Kenneth Bianchi (the Los Angeles "Hillside Strangler") who manifested what appeared to be a multiple personality disorder. The primary personality of Kenneth claimed no awareness of two underlying or subordinate personalities: "Steve," who claimed responsibility for a number of rape–murders, and "Billy," who was allegedly responsible for thefts and forgeries. At first, examining clinicians diagnosed Bianchi as having a genuine multiple personality disorder that would make him legally insane (Watkins, 1984). However, later findings (including a lack of consistency in the structure and content of the personalities over time and the inability of Bianchi's acquaintances to support his claims) led to the conclusion that Bianchi was feigning a multiple personality disorder in order to avoid the death penalty (Orne et al., 1984). Bianchi was diagnosed as having an antisocial (psychopathic) personality with sexual sadism, and the court held him responsible for his actions.

Dissociative identity disorder is still highly controversial primarily because to date there is no physiological evidence of any sort that allows the distinction of one personality from another (North et.al., 1993), and some psychologists believe that the disorder is completely iatrogenic that is, caused by a doctor or in these cases, by their psychiatrists and that the memories of child abuse claimed under hypnotic regression are totally false (Spanos, 1996).

DSM-5 considers "Spirit Possession" as a cultural variant of DID (www.dsm5.org, 2013). Relatively new research indicates that most DID patients do indeed show signs of relentless neglect and abuse (Steele, 2003). Although there are no anatomical abnormalities in the brain there are state differences in other bio-physiological measures such as heart rate, cerebral blood flow and activation and cardio-vascular responses when alters take over (Reinders et.al, 2006). Likewise, functional MRI (fMRI) studies indicate that there is bilateral suppression of hippocampi when the patient is switching from native to an alter personality and there is activation of the right hippocampus when switching from an alter personality to the main native personality (Guochuan, et.al, 1999). This is a highly controversial subject and the controversy will continue for some time to come, no doubt.

Theoretical Perspectives on Dissociative Disorders

Dissociative disorders are among the *least understood* of all behavioral disorders. Thus, explanations are highly speculative. Freudians claim that all three of the dissociative disorders we have discussed—dissociative amnesia, fugue (now subsumed under dissociative amnesia), and multiple personality (now called DID)—seem to provide support for Freud's view that excessive application of the defense mechanisms can lead to serious disorders.

Behavioral theory does *not offer* a well-developed and cohesive explanation for dissociative disorders either. A number of theorists within this perspective suggest, however, that the dissociative reactions may involve operant avoidance responses that are reinforced because they allow an individual to avoid anxiety associated with highly stressful events, such as early childhood abuse. There is *no evidence* that genetic factors or biological predispositions play a significant role in the development of dissociative disorders. In fact, *the preponderance of evidence suggests that it is strongly associated with childhood trauma* (Putnam, 1991, 1993). There are no genetic or biological explanations available at this time, and that makes these illnesses very interesting from a research point of view. Some researchers maintain that the various alters are different emotional states rather than autonomous entities capable of willful independent acts (Mercklebach, Devilly & Rassin, 2002) while others claim that they are more than brain states that they are indeed metaphysical entities (Stafford, B. 2005). All the dissociative disorders remain highly controversial and the debates are likely to continue till more objective evidence comes in.

PERSONALITY DISORDERS

Personality disorders

Diverse class of disorders that is collectively characterized by inflexible and maladaptive personality traits that cause either functional impairment or subjective distress.

We end our discussion of behavioral disorders with a brief look at the diverse array of disorders grouped under **personality disorders**. DSM-5 and DSM IV do not differ in their description and categorization of Personality Disorders. *DSM-IV* identifies 10 related personality disorders that are grouped into three clusters (A–C), outlined in Table 11.5. Cluster A disorders are all characterized by odd and/or eccentric behavior; Cluster B disorders are characterized by dramatic, emotional, or erratic behavior; and Cluster C disorders are characterized by anxious or fearful behavior.

The various personality disorders are linked by a number of shared characteristics. First, most tend to show up at an early age, usually no later than adolescence, and the characteristic

TABLE 11.5 Personality Disorders

Cluster A: Disorders of Odd or Eccentric Behavior	Cluster B: Disorders of Dramatic, Emotional, or Erratic Behavior	Cluster C: Disorders Involving Anxious or Fearful Behavior
Paranoid Personality Disorder Extreme and pervasive suspiciousness, mistrust, and envy of others; hypersensitivity and difficulty in getting along with others; restricted expression of emotion; inclined to avoid intimacy.	*Antisocial Personality Disorder* A continuous pattern of utter disregard for the rights of others and the rules of society; antisocial acts usually commence before age 15; often unable to perform adequately on the job or in relationships; a strong tendency to engage in exciting, impulsive behavior with little attention to the consequences.	*Avoidant Personality Disorder* Hypersensitive to the possibility of being rejected by others; a desire for close social relationships but unable to reach out to others because of fear of rejection; very low self-esteem.
Schizoid Personality Disorder Very cold, aloof, and socially isolated; unable to form close relationships; humorless; appears to be indifferent to praise or criticism.	*Borderline Personality Disorder* This condition is not associated with a characteristic pattern of behavior that is invariably present, and it is often associated with other personality disorders (hence the label "borderline"); instability in several areas including mood, self-image, behavior, and interpersonal relationships; a chronic inclination to be indecisive and uncertain about a variety of important life issues.	*Dependent Personality Disorder* Extremely poor self-image and a lack of self-confidence; depends upon others to make all major decisions; subordinates personal needs to avoid alienating people depended upon; unable to tolerate being alone.
Schizotypal Personality Disorder Oddities or eccentricities in thought, perception, speech, or behavior not severe enough to be diagnosed as schizophrenic; extreme social isolation; strong tendency toward egocentrism.	*Histrionic Personality Disorder* Overly dramatic behavior, frequently expressed as drawing attention to oneself and/or overreacting to minor events of small consequence; self-centered, self-indulgent, vain, manipulative, and inconsiderate; tendency to be dependent on others but poor interpersonal skills.	*Obsessive-Compulsive Personality Disorder* Excessive preoccupation with rules and regulations and the need to do things "by the book"; inflexible, stiff workaholic; limited ability to express tender emotions such as warmth, caring, and love.
	Narcissistic Personality Disorder Grandiose sense of self-importance; preoccupied with fantasies of great achievements; childish demands for constant attention and special favors; little empathy for others.	

SOURCE: Adapted table of "Personality Disorders" from *Diagnostic and Statistical Manual of Mental Disorders,* Third Edition, Revised, Washington, DC, American Psychiatric Association, 1987.

maladaptive behaviors often tend to become more deeply ingrained over the years. Another common feature is that very few individuals diagnosed as having a personality disorder ever seem to believe that there is something wrong with the way they are functioning. Third, there is a strong tendency for the various personality-disordered behaviors to be rigidly ingrained, highly repetitive, and ultimately *self-defeating.* Finally, the prognosis for overcoming any of the personality disorders is rather poor, perhaps because individuals with personality disorders are generally more inclined to refuse therapy than are people with the other behavioral disorders outlined in this chapter (Vaillant & Perry, 1985). The antisocial personality disorder has been the subject of more research and theorizing than any of the other personality disorders; therefore, it is the focus of our discussion.

Antisocial Personality Disorder

Antisocial personality disorder

Personality disorder characterized by disregard for rights of others, lack of remorse or guilt for antisocial acts, irresponsibility in job or marital roles, failure to learn from experience, and a profound poverty of deep and lasting emotions.

From the point of view of society at large, the most disruptive of the personality disorders is the **antisocial personality disorder**, also referred to as psychopathic or sociopathic personality disorder. Recent estimates indicate that antisocial personality is diagnosed in almost 3 percent of the population. *Six times as many men as women have this disorder* (Robins, 1987). The following list summarizes some of the most prominent characteristics of an antisocial personality.

1. A history dating back to before age 15 that demonstrates a repetitive and persistent pattern of behavior in which *either the basic rights of others or major age-appropriate societal norms or rules are violated.* Commonly occurring behavior includes intimidation of others, physical fights, use of weapons, thievery or robbery, physical cruelty to people and animals, rape, persistent lying, arson, vandalism, and/or truancy.
2. A pervasive pattern of disregard for the safety of self and others, and a *lack of remorse* for the mistreatment of others (American Psychiatric Association, 2003).

The most recent cases of Casey Anthony who went dancing and reported her child was with a nanny when the child was indeed dead for over 30 days seems to fit this bill! Likewise, Jodi Arias, who gave TV interviews proclaiming her innocence with great confidence and no trace of shame, guilt, or sadness for her dead boy-friend and was found guilty in 2013 come to mind. Both the cases were highly televised and public interest in them was astounding.

Theoretical Perspectives on Antisocial Personality Disorder

In spite of several decades of extensive research, we still do not have a clear understanding of the origins of the antisocial personality disorder. Child-hood maltreatment and poor quality mother-child or care-giver-child interaction seems to be a predictor of anti-social personality disorder (Zhenyu, S.et.al, 2012) where as others attribute antisocial or psychopathic personality to genetic inheritance. Two Dopamine genes DRD2 and DRD4 in particular are highly correlated with antisocial personality which supports a dopaminergic hypothesis for these disorders just like it does for Schizophrenia (Tong, W. & Barnes J.C., 2013).

Behavioral theorists propose a number of interpretations; perhaps the most prominent is the view that people with antisocial personality disorder act impulsively and repeatedly manifest antisocial misbehavior because they have not learned to avoid punishment. Such inappropriate behaviors persist despite repeated social and/or legal sanctions.

In this chapter we have defined, characterized, and discussed possible causes of the major behavioral disorders. Although considerable progress has been made in identifying causal factors in these disorders, this continues to be an active area of research from several theoretical perspectives. We can continue to expect that our understanding of these disorders will increase as this research progresses. In the next chapter we will see how psychologists and other professionals treat behavioral disorders.

SUMMARY

DEFINING ABNORMAL BEHAVIOR

1. While there is no universally accepted definition of abnormality, psychologists emphasize a common core of four criteria that distinguish between normal and abnormal behavior: Behavior that is rare or atypical, and which causes emotional discomfort to self or others, is maladaptive and socially unacceptable is considered to be abnormal.
2. Any given behavioral disorder may reflect only one or a combination of these four criteria.

CLASSIFYING BEHAVIORAL DISORDERS

3. DSM-5 was introduced in May 2013 and it has replaced DSM-IV. The DSM (Diagnostic Statistical Manual) is used throughout the world for diagnosing abnormal behavior and psychological disorders.
4. DSM-IV distinguishes two major mood disorders: major depressive disorder and bipolar (manic-depressive) disorder.

SCHIZOPHRENIA

5. A collection of primary or core symptoms that characterize many forms of schizophrenia includes disturbances in thought, perception, emotional expression, and speech, together with social withdrawal and diminished motivation.
6. An extensive body of research indicates that certain people are genetically predisposed to develop schizophrenia.
7. There is biochemical evidence that schizophrenia may be caused by elevated levels of dopamine or a heightened sensitivity to dopamine.
8. There is also substantial evidence of structural abnormalities in the brains of schizophrenics.

MOOD DISORDERS

9. Major depressive disorder is distinguished by deep depression. In contrast, bipolar disorder is characterized by intermittent episodes of both depression and mania (highly energized, euphoric behavior and excessive activity).
10. People with major depressive disorder typically manifest their symptoms over an extended period (minimum six months of persistence of symptoms required for diagnosis) are unable to function effectively, and experience a breakdown in interpersonal relationships.
11. In some cases of bipolar disorder, episodes of depression and mania may alternate regularly, with months or years of symptom-free normal functioning between the disordered mood states.

12. A manic episode often follows a course of accelerating intensity in which the individual's thinking and behavior become progressively more disorganized and psychotic-like.
13. There is compelling evidence linking altered brain chemistry to severe mood disorders.

SCHIZOPHRENIA

14. A collection of primary or core symptoms that characterize many forms of schizophrenia includes disturbances in thought, perception, emotional expression, and speech, together with social withdrawal and diminished motivation.
15. An extensive body of research indicates that certain people are genetically predisposed to develop schizophrenia.
16. There is biochemical evidence that schizophrenia may be caused by elevated levels of dopamine or a heightened sensitivity to dopamine.
17. There is also substantial evidence of structural abnormalities in the brains of schizophrenics.

OTHER DISORDERS

18. Generalized anxiety disorder is characterized by a chronic state of anxiety that is omnipresent across a wide range of situations.
19. A panic disorder is characterized by episodes of intense apprehension and overwhelming terror that occur as often as four or more times in a four-week period.
20. A specific phobia is an irrational fear of a specific situation or object such as closed places or spiders
21. Phobias, characterized by a persistent fear of and consequent avoidance of a specific object or situation, are among the most common behavioral disorders.
22. A social phobia is a persistent, irrational fear of performing some specific behavior in the presence of other people. A distinction is made between discrete performance anxiety and generalized social anxiety.
23. An obsessive-compulsive disorder is characterized by a profound sense of anxiety that is reflected in persistent, unwanted, and unshakable thoughts and/or irresistible habitual actions in which the individual repeatedly engages in some ritualistic act.
24. Posttraumatic stress disorder occurs after a person experiences a psychologically traumatic event (or events) outside the normal range of human experience. PTSD is characterized by vivid flashbacks and avoidance of stimuli associated with the traumatic event or numbing of general responsiveness.
25. A person with somatization disorder typically has multiple and recurrent physical symptoms for which medical attention is repeatedly sought, but that have no physical cause.
26. Conversion disorder is typically manifested as a sensory or motor system disturbance for which there is no known organic cause.
27. A person with psychogenic amnesia experiences sudden loss of episodic autobiographical memory, usually after a particularly stressful or traumatic event.
28. A person with a Dissociative Identity Disorder (DID) alternates between an original or primary (native) personality and one or more secondary or subordinate personalities known as "alters".
29. DSM-5 has not made any major changes to the criteria given in DSM-IV for diagnosis of Personality Disorders.
30. Common characteristics of antisocial disorder include a history dating back to or before age 15, lack of remorse or guilt over antisocial acts, repeated academic, vocational, and relationship failures, lack of insight, superficial charm, manipulative behavior, and extreme egocentricity.
31. Childhood neglect and maltreatment as well as inheriting some specific Dopaminergic genes is said to predict the development of a personality disorder by adolescence.

TERMS AND CONCEPTS

mood disorder
abnormal behavior
dissociative disorder
dissociative amnesia
dissociative identity disorder
dissociative fugue disorder
phobia
schizophrenia
delusion
hallucination
paranoid schizophrenia
catatonic schizophrenia
neologism
mutism
echolalia
psychosis
major depressive disorder
bipolar (manic-depressive) disorder
generalized anxiety disorder
anxiety disorder
panic disorder
specific phobia
social phobia
obsessive-compulsive disorder
posttraumatic stress disorder (PTSD)
hypochondriasis
somatization disorder
conversion disorder
personality disorder
antisocial personality disorder

CHAPTER 12

Treatment of Disorders

Corbis

The previous chapter discussed a variety of behavioral and psychological disorders. The treatment of these disorders is the topic of this chapter, which describes the kinds of therapeutic interventions used to help people overcome or at least better cope with behavioral problems. One focus in this chapter is on psychological therapies, or **psychotherapy**—*any nonbiological, noninvasive technique or procedure designed to improve a person's adjustment to life.*

The term *noninvasive* means that no attempt is made to alter body physiology or function, as occurs with biomedical therapies. Our other focus is with biological treatments—specifically drug therapy. We will discover that therapy may take many different forms; we will also see that these varied approaches share many common themes. Today, a variety of clinicians, including clinical psychologists, clinical social workers, psychiatrists, medical doctors, and family, marital, school, and pastoral counselors provide treatment for behavioral disorders and many disorders require both psychological therapy as well as drug therapy. We will begin with an overview of contemporary psychological therapies.

Psychotherapy

Any nonbiological, noninvasive psychological technique or procedure designed to improve a person's adjustment to life.

HEALTH, PSYCHOLOGY, AND LIFE

Guidelines for Seeking Professional Help

Many people are reluctant to seek professional help because they incorrectly believe that taking this step is an admission that they are weak and incapable of helping themselves. Quite the contrary, people who seek professional help demonstrate a high level of self-awareness and emotional maturity by recognizing that there are limitations to their ability to help themselves when faced with seriously disruptive psychological problems. If some day you find yourself seeking professional help, give yourself credit for having the wisdom to recognize that a skilled therapist can offer emotional support, a perspective other than your own, and perhaps recommend medication—all of which may help you make the desired changes in your life.

To help determine if a specific therapist will meet your needs, you may wish to establish the following points at your first meeting:

1. What do you want from therapy? You and your therapist should reach an agreement on goals. This agreement is sometimes referred to as the therapy contract.

2. Which approach does your therapist take and what kind of participation is expected of you? You can ask about the general process (what the therapist will do) during therapy sessions. You may also ask how long therapy is expected to last.

3. How do you feel about talking with the therapist? Therapy is not intended to be a light social interaction. It can be difficult. At times it may be quite uncomfortable for you to discuss personal concerns. However, for therapy to be useful, you want to have the sense that the therapist is trustworthy.

4. Is medication an option for you? Some individuals are reluctant to take medication because of their side effects or fear of addiction. Be sure to discuss these with your practitioner before commencing pharmacotherapy. Also discuss what kinds of improvements are typical and how long medication may be necessary.

5. Research your condition using the resources you have learned about in this course. What are the most effective treatment options for your particular condition? Be sure to discuss your research with your therapist.

While these suggestions may not ensure that you find a therapist who is a perfect fit for your needs, it is likely they will increase the odds that you will select a qualified therapist. If therapy doesn't appear to be progressing, discuss this with your therapist. If you feel at all uncomfortable with your sessions or your therapist, it may be time to select another.

PSYCHOLOGICAL THERAPIES

In the following pages we discuss several different forms of noninvasive therapy, including psychoanalysis, humanistic therapy, cognitive therapy, behavioral therapy, and therapies for interpersonal relationships and the most recently introduced ACT Therapy which draws on ancient meditative techniques from several ancient religions from various parts of the world (Harris, R. & Hayes, S.C. 2009). We begin this section with an overview of psychoanalysis, the oldest psychotherapy.

Psychoanalysis

Technique developed by Freud in which an individual's revelations of normally unconscious cognitions are interpreted.

Psychoanalysis

Sigmund Freud developed the first formal model of psychotherapy at the end of the last century. Freud's technique, which became known as **psychoanalysis** is based on a number of assumptions; the most fundamental is that *disordered behavior results from unconscious conflicts and repressed urges, most of which are rooted in childhood experiences.*

Freud professed that the human mind was a closed system and a human was not totally aware of all of its contents. In fact, the mind contained two compartments, the smaller of which was called the "Conscious" and we were aware of its contents. The larger compartment of the mind was called the "Unconscious" and we were not aware of its contents. This Unconscious contained three components of personality known as the *id*, the *ego* and the *superego*, which developed as a human baby developed.

Of these, the **id** was present at birth, and was a childish, selfish, and demanding component of personality that constantly demanded pleasure. The **ego** too was an inborn component of the personality, but it was a *rational* component, and its job was to negotiate reality so as to meet Id's demands. The third component, **superego**, was not present at birth, but fell into place as a child learned society's rules and regulations at the knee of his/her parents. The *superego was like a repository of "internalized" rules* or rules that held strong meaning and importance for a particular person, *important enough that a person tended not to break them.* This superego functioned very much like conscience does, and often prevented ego from meeting id's demands, such that over time the ego would get torn between the demands of id and the restrictions placed by superego and cave-in under the pressure, manifesting psychological disorders or neuroses as Freud termed them. *Those incidents in which the ego and the superego were at loggerheads were termed a* ***conflict****.* Most people maintained their sanity in spite of constant conflict between ego and superego by using techniques known as **defense mechanism** to dissipate tension.

A primary theme in many of these conflicts was the struggle between the id's sexual and aggressive impulses and the superego's moralistic commands. Freud professed that these conflicts generated anxiety, which the ego **defense mechanisms** were not always able to ward off. As the individual tried more desperate strategies, such as pushing unwanted thoughts or memories further into the unconscious, i.e., using a defense mechanism known as "repression" for coping with anxiety, symptoms of behavioral disturbances, such as phobias and conversion disorders, began to appear. At this point the person was likely to seek psychotherapy.

Freud believed that the only way to help people gain true relief from severe anxiety was to enter their unconscious, search out the anxiety-causing conflict(s), and help them gain *insight* or conscious awareness of the repressed conflict. Only then, he thought, could the conflict be resolved. Put another way, the aim of psychoanalysis is to make the unconscious conscious (Kutash & Wolf, 1986). To accomplish this goal, Freud developed a number of therapeutic techniques.

Techniques of Psychoanalysis

Classical Freudian psychoanalysis was organized around several major techniques. Probably the most important of these methods are free association, dream analysis, and interpretations of resistance etc. (Blum, 1986; Kutash & Wolf, 1986; Phares, 1988).

Free Association Freud encouraged his patients to lie on a couch and say whatever came into their mind, no matter how silly or frivolous it seemed.

Free association

Psychoanalytic technique developed by Sigmund Freud in which patients relax and say whatever comes to their minds

Freud believed that through this process of **free association**, he could obtain glimpses of the unconscious conflicts and desires boiling below the surface of conscious awareness. He also believed that the actual process of venting repressed feelings (*catharsis*) could result in at least a temporary reduction in tension. Freud maintained that free association was not an easy process, and that it often took several sessions before a person began to open up.

Dream analysis

Psychoanalytic technique involving the interpretation of dreams to learn about hidden aspects of personality.

Dream Analysis Freud placed great emphasis on **dream analysis**, or interpretation of dreams. He believed that dreams are the "royal road to the unconscious" and thus a rich source of information about the hidden aspects of personality.

Resistance

In psychoanalysis, a patient's unwillingness to describe freely some aspects of his or her life.

Resistance Freud believed that what a patient does not say is as important as what is verbalized. He noted that his patients often exhibited **resistance**, or an unwillingness to discuss freely some aspects of their lives. Freud believed that it was only natural to resist delving into certain areas, because it is often very painful to bring unconscious conflicts into conscious awareness. Resistance was thus viewed as a sign that the therapist was getting close to the problem and the unconscious was struggling to avoid giving up its secrets. One of the major goals of Freudian psychoanalysis was to detect and break through these resistances.

Interpretation To Freud it was important for analysts to interpret for patients the underlying meaning of their experiences, resistances, and dreams. He believed that such interpretations would help break through patients' defenses, providing them with insight into the causes of their neurotic behavior. This insight was also viewed as an excellent motivator to encourage a patient's active and willing participation in the therapeutic process.

Freudian therapists also gave importance to "slips of the tongue" or "Freudian slips" in which a person inadvertently used an incorrect word which "outed" his/her secret desires or wishes. For example, saying, "I would like to mate with you," instead of saying "meet," when making an appointment with someone.

A psychoanalytic therapist was not considered to be proficient in analyzing his/her patients he/she had been psychoanalyzed and had experienced the process firsthand. In a way, at least these psychotherapists knew exactly what they were putting their patients through!

The Present Status of Psychoanalysis

Earlier in this century psychoanalysis was the only form of psychotherapy available, and it remained the dominant force in psychotherapy until the early 1950s. Since that time, however, its popularity and influence have steadily declined, and today very few psychotherapists practice classical psychoanalysis as developed by Freud. *Contemporary psychoanalysts still attempt to help people gain insights into the unconscious roots of their problems, but early childhood conflicts are not emphasized as much. Psychoanalysis has mostly been replaced by* ***Psychodynamic Therapy, in which a client is asked to do free association but to restrict it to one main concern, rather than come up with free associations to unconnected issues.*** *The main issue of concern is determined by the patient and the therapist before the therapy starts. This type of therapy takes about two years, so it is much quicker than traditional psychoanalysis.*

Humanistic Therapy

In the 1950s Carl Rogers developed a therapy known as Client Centered Therapy. Rogers, like all humanistic psychologists believed that humans are basically good, they all want to better themselves, and if they only get unconditional positive regard, they will straighten themselves out. A Rogerian therapist does not tell the client what to do, he only given his full attention to the client to let the client speak whatever is on his/her mind and listens without being judgmental. You can try humanistic therapy if you log on to a program called Eliza and talk about your life. The program's responses are supposed to be similar to that of a humanistic psychologist! (http://psych.fullerton.edu/mbirnbaum/psych101/Eliza.htm).

Cognitive Therapies

Cognitive therapies

Approaches to therapy that are based on the premise that most behavioral disorders result from distortions in cognitions or thoughts.

The **cognitive therapies** (often called *cognitive-behavioral therapies)* are based on the premise that most behavioral disorders result from distortions in a person's cognitions or thoughts. Psychotherapists who operate within the cognitive framework attempt to demonstrate to their clients how their distorted or irrational thoughts have contributed to their difficulties, and they use a variety of techniques to help them change these cognitions to more appropriate ones. *Thus while the goal of therapy may be to change people's maladaptive behavior, the method is to change their thinking.*

Over the last two decades, many psychotherapists have incorporated a cognitive orientation into their therapy practices. The primary models for the cognitive focus are provided by Albert Ellis's rational-emotive therapy and Aaron Beck's cognitive behavior therapy.

RATIONAL-EMOTIVE THERAPY Rational-emotive therapy (RET) was developed in the 1950s by Albert Ellis (1962, 1984), who was originally trained as a psychoanalyst. After years of "being allergic to the passivity of psychoanalysis" (1984, p. 27) and frustrated in his efforts to reform the Freudian approach to therapy, Ellis began experimenting with new methods and discovered that *his clients get better when they start thinking differently about themselves and their problems. His efforts eventually culminated in his highly influential RET approach.*

Rational-emotive therapy (RET)

Approach to therapy based on the premise that psychological problems result when people interpret their experiences based on self-defeating, irrational beliefs.

Rational-emotive therapy (RET), *now known as rational-emotive behavioral therapy or REBT (Ellis, 1999), is based on the premise that behavioral problems result when people interpret their experiences on the basis of certain self-defeating, irrational beliefs.* Although the original incident called an "activating event" might have caused great emotional pain or hurt, it is the *irrational, self-defeating belief* of the person that causes the long-term grief or disability.

The REBT therapist's approach is to help people find the flaws in their thinking, to challenge or dispute these maladaptive cognitions (in Ellis's words, to "make mincemeat" of them), and *then to guide clients to substitute more logical or realistic thoughts.*

Ellis and other RET therapists take a much more active or directive role than either the psychoanalytic or humanistic therapists. To minimize a client's self-defeating outlook, *REBT therapists employ an eclectic, or highly varied, collection of therapeutic techniques, including such things as confrontation, persuasion, role playing, interpretation, behavior modification, and reflection of feelings.* The focus of therapy is on the here-and-now, rather than on the client's history. In most cases rational-emotive therapists use a rapid-fire directive approach, quickly pinning the client down to a few irrational beliefs. *The job of the REBT therapist is to dispute the client's irrational belief so that the client can enjoy the positive effects of rational beliefs* and be free of the distressing symptoms that brought the client to the therapist. A recent study linking irrational thoughts to daily hassles experienced by people supported Ellis's rational-emotive theory (Ziegler et al., 2003).

Cognitive behavior therapy

Cognitive therapy aimed at restructuring irrational thinking patterns such as the tendency to use negative self-labels.

COGNITIVE BEHAVIOR THERAPY Like the rational-emotive approach, **cognitive behavior therapy** approaches therapy with the premise that behavioral problems stem primarily from faulty thinking that causes people to behave and emote in maladaptive ways. *Aaron Beck, who developed cognitive behavior therapy, believes that disturbed people typically have very negative self-images based on highly* ***negative self-labels*** *(Beck, 1976).*

Beck believes that people who *do not value themselves* have a tendency to overgeneralize from their experiences, and *unconsciously seek out other experiences that will confirm their poor self-image.* Such people are likely to continue to be victimized by their own self-defeating behaviors unless salvaged through therapeutic intervention.

Like Ellis, Beck's aim is to get his clients to restructure their thinking, particularly their negative self-labels. His methods, however, tend to be less confrontational and more experiential. *A common strategy is for the therapist and client to make a list of the client's misguided self-impressions* (although, at this point, the client is not likely to consider them to be misguided), and then to agree on some *experiments to test these assumptions.* The therapist is interested in setting up experiments that will disprove rather than confirm the client's negative self-image. *The therapist also assists the client in replacing maladaptive thoughts and behaviors with ones that will lead to a more constructive, productive, and happy life.*

EVALUATING THERAPIES Smith & Glass (1977) concluded ***a meta-analysis on the effectiveness of seven different psychotherapies and found that they were all more or less equally effective.*** The therapies they looked at were psychoanalysis, transactional analysis, rational-emotive therapy, client-centered therapy, systematic desensitization, behavior modification, and imposition therapy. Each of these therapies was also successful in helping a client live a happier more productive life as compared to a client who received no therapy at all. The fact that there was very little or practically no difference in the effectiveness of such diverse therapies makes one wonder whether it is the therapy per se, or the fact that a person is *receiving therapy,* that helps the client. However, since a client's getting better is very subjective, it is very difficult to pin down the success or effectiveness of a therapy.

EVALUATING COGNITIVE THERAPIES Research on the outcomes of cognitive therapies suggests that, at least for some behavioral disorders, these methods can be quite effective. For instance, several studies evaluating therapy outcomes suggest that cognitive approaches are very effective in the treatment of moderate depression (Hollon & Garber, 1990; Kwon et al., 2003; Robinson et al., 1990). However, research on the effectiveness of cognitive therapy is less encouraging for more severe forms of depression (Parker et al., 2003). With severe depression, research supports the use of antidepressant medication along with psychotherapy (Thase et al., 1999) *but there are psychiatrists who report that antidepressant medication works no better than a placebo for people who have mild to moderate depression* (Fournier, J.C., et.al 2010) and that the prolific use of Anti-anxiety drugs, Anti-depressants, Anti-psychotics, etc. is due to the promotional efforts of the drug companies who promote the drugs for financial gain (Antonuccio, D. et.al, 2002; Harris R. & Hays.S, 2009; Rosenthal, M.B. et.al 2002)

Behavioral Therapies

Behavior therapy

Therapy based on the assumption that maladaptive behavior has been learned and can therefore be unlearned.

Traditional models of psychotherapy have emphasized the underlying causes of behavioral disorders, which are viewed as the result of either unresolved conflicts or disordered thought processes. **Behavior therapy** departs from this traditional conception. *Its central thesis is that maladaptive behavior has been learned and maintained by a history of reinforcement and/or punishment, and therefore it can be unlearned.* The same principles that govern the learning and maintenance of normal behavior also determine the acquisition and maintenance of abnormal behaviors. Behavior therapy draws heavily upon the extensive body of laboratory research on human and animal learning to *devise strategies for helping people to unlearn maladaptive behavior patterns at the same time that they learn more adaptive behavior patterns.*

For example, parents of children who fight or squabble incessantly might be shown how to extinguish these inappropriate behaviors by no longer providing the inadvertent reinforcers of paying attention to them. A person who responds sexually to inappropriate stimuli, such as small children, might be treated through repeated exposures to an aversive stimulus paired with the stimuli that elicit the deviant arousal pattern. The following paragraphs outline some of the more commonly employed behavior therapies.

Classical conditioning therapy

Any behavior therapy that involves classical conditioning. For example, systematic desensitization therapy.

CLASSICAL CONDITIONING THERAPIES In the chapter on learning, you learned that some phobias are learned via classical conditioning. It follows, then, that classical conditioning principles should also be able to help people unlearn fears—and this is the basic premise of **classical conditioning therapy**.

For example, suppose you are afraid of the dark as a result of a particularly frightening experience in a darkened room that occurred some years ago. Before this experience darkness (the conditioned stimulus) was a neutral or nonfrightening stimulus, but now due to the pairing of the CS with the frightening event (an unconditioned stimulus), fear has been learned as a conditioned response.

We know that repeated exposures to darkness without the association of a frightening experience would eventually cause a conditioned fear response to extinguish. However, you would probably be unwilling to expose yourself to solitary darkness long enough to extinguish your fear response. In view of this limitation, behavior therapists have devised a number of *counterconditioning* strategies in which a client learns a new response (one that is incompatible with fear) to the threatening stimulus, as described below.

Systematic desensitization

Behavior therapy using a classical conditioning technique that pairs the slow, systematic exposure to anxiety-inducing situations with relaxation training.

Systematic Desensitization Perhaps the most widely used behavioral therapy technique is **systematic desensitization**, a strategy developed in the late 1950s by Joseph Wolpe (1958, 1985) to treat people who respond to specific stimulus situations with excessive anxiety or phobic fear. Wolpe's therapy method is based on the premise that people cannot be both relaxed and anxious at the same time. Therefore, he reasoned, *if individuals can be trained to relax when confronted with fear-inducing stimuli, they will be able to overcome their anxiety. The key is to proceed slowly and systematically.*

For instance, in one case known to the authors, a young woman in her mid-twenties sought treatment at the urging of her husband, who was tired of sleeping "with a searchlight on every night." The woman had a deeply rooted fear of darkness that had generalized to situations other than just being in bed with the lights off. She was afraid to go anywhere if it was likely to be dark, particularly if she had to go alone.

The first step in treatment was to analyze her problem carefully, step by step. The goal of treatment was for the client to be unafraid of the dark no matter where she might encounter it—at home in bed, outside at night walking to a friend's house, and so forth. The next step was to construct a hierarchy of situations that triggered her fear of darkness, with the most intense fear-inducing situation at the top of the list and the least at the bottom.

The next phase of treatment was to teach her how to relax by training her first to recognize muscle tension in various parts of her body and then to relax all of the various muscle groups in a progressive fashion until she was in a state of complete, tranquil relaxation. Finally, when the client was fully relaxed, she was told to imagine as vividly as possible the scene at the bottom of her anxiety hierarchy. If at any time she found herself becoming anxious, she was instructed to signal, by raising a finger, her desire to switch off the image immediately, and to concentrate again on becoming deeply relaxed. When she was able to imagine this mildly threatening situation repeatedly without experiencing any anxiety, her attention was directed to the next image in the hierarchy. In this fashion, she was able to move up the hierarchy gradually and systematically until, after several sessions, she could imagine any of the scenes on her list with no discomfort.

The final phase of treatment was to instruct her to confront the anxiety-producing stimuli in the real world. Here again, she was encouraged to move slowly, starting with situations at the bottom of her anxiety hierarchy. As she received firsthand evidence that she was able to apply her newly acquired ability to relax in real life, she was encouraged to expose herself gradually to even the most fearful situation listed in the hierarchy and this technique was effective for her and has been found to be effective in treating phobias or specific fears, but has not been found effective in treating generalized anxiety disorder.

Virtual Reality Therapy One difficulty therapists encounter when applying systematic desensitization therapy is that patients find it difficult to imagine frightening or anxiety provoking scenes. Utilizing virtual reality simulations to generate a variety of stimuli for systematic desensitization therapy may be an effective method to overcome this difficulty (North et al., 2003). In a recent experiment 30 patients with a phobic fear-of-flying were randomly assigned to one of three treatment conditions. Group 1 received virtual reality exposure with physiological feedback; Group 2 received virtual reality exposure with no physiological feedback, and Group 3 received traditional systematic desensitization with imagined stimulus exposure. During a three-month period, following eight weeks of systematic desensitization, 18 of the 20 subjects receiving virtual reality exposure to flying reported an ability to fly in commercial airplanes without medication or alcohol. None of the 10 subjects in the imagined systematic desensitization group reported the ability to fly without medication (Wiederhold et al., 2003).

Aversive Conditioning Aversive conditioning is another variety of classical conditioning behavior therapy that is quite different from systematic desensitization. In aversion therapy the goal is to condition an aversion to some specific stimulus such as alcohol or cigarette smoking.

For example, an alcoholic's behavior is normally characterized by excessive attraction to the stimulus of alcoholic drinks. However, suppose a chronic drinker is given a drug like Disulfiram that induces nausea and vomiting when combined with alcohol. The drug alone will not make the person sick, but immediately after alcohol enters the system, the person experiences violent nausea and vomiting. It does not take many pairings of the CS, alcohol, and the UCS, sickness, before the alcohol begins to elicit an aversion response (CR). This conditioned aversion may generalize to a variety of alcohol-related stimuli including the taste and smell of alcohol and visual displays of containers of alcohol.

A number of studies have provided encouraging findings about the use of this therapeutic intervention in treating alcohol or nicotine addiction. For example, one study of 685 alcoholics who underwent an intensive aversive therapy program, followed by several booster treatments (additional conditioning trials) over a period of several months, showed that 63 percent still avoided alcohol one year later. Three years later this figure had changed to approximately one-third still abstaining (Wiens & Menustik, 1983; Akin, A.A. et.al, 2013). A 30 percent success rate over a period of four years is significant in an area of treatment characterized by high recidivism rates. Akin, et.al (2013) report an unusually high rate of 76.9% sustained remission in their patient population of 39 patients treated with Disulfiram (Akin, A.A. 2013).

OPERANT CONDITIONING THERAPIES We learned earlier that *our behaviors are strongly influenced by their consequences.* Reinforcers are powerful determinants of behavior,

Operant conditioning therapies

Behavior modification techniques that attempt to influence behavior by manipulating reinforcers.

and by manipulating contingencies of reinforcement; behavior therapists are often able to exert a strong influence on behavior. Three versions of **operant conditioning therapies** (sometimes called *behavior modification* techniques) include attempting to induce desired behavior through *positive reinforcement,* or striving to eliminate undesirable or maladaptive behavior through *extinction* or through *punishment.*

Positive Reinforcement The positive reinforcement therapy technique is based on the fact that people behave in ways that produce positive consequences or reinforcers. This approach to behavior therapy involves identifying the desired behavior and determining one or more reinforcers that will be effective in maintaining it. Reinforcers contingent upon the client's voluntarily manifesting the desired behavior are then provided consistently.

For instance, in one case reported by Arthur Bachrach and his associates (1965), a young anorexic woman had so drastically curtailed her eating that she was hospitalized, in danger of dying. When all else had failed, behavior therapy was applied to the woman, who now weighed only 47 pounds.

How would you apply positive reinforcement to ensure proper eating behavior in this severely emaciated person? What steps would you follow? Consider this question for a few moments before reading on.

In the first step of treatment, the therapist determined an appropriate reinforcer that could be made contingent upon eating. A social reinforcer was chosen: The therapist sat with her when a meal was delivered, and each time she swallowed a bite of food, the therapist reinforced her by talking to her and generally being attentive. If she refused to eat, the therapist left the room and she remained alone until the next meal was served. In this manner her eating behavior was gradually increased, and other reinforcers were introduced contingent upon her continuing to eat and gain weight. For example, other people joined her at mealtime, or having her hair done after an appropriate gain in weight, were reinforcing. This positive reinforcement method succeeded in inducing a dramatic gain in weight, and she was eventually discharged from the hospital.

Positive reinforcement is also a powerful tool for shaping desirable behaviors in everyday life. For example, a parent who wishes a child to use better table manners, or to be more responsible about room-cleaning chores, will probably find that reinforcing appropriate efforts in this direction will be a more effective agent of behavior change than punishment.

Extinction Technique: Just as positive reinforcement may be used to establish appropriate behaviors it may also be possible to eliminate undesired behaviors by eliminating the reinforcers that maintain them. For this technique to be effective, the behavior therapist must be able both to identify and to eliminate the reinforcer(s) maintaining the maladaptive behavior.

This procedure may not always be as easy as it sounds. An example is the case of Norma (not her real name), a 20-year-old woman known to one of the authors. Norma reluctantly sought help for a problem described by her parents as "compulsive face picking." According to both her parents and fiancé, Norma could not seem to keep her hands off her face. Whenever she found some little blemish or pimple, she would pick and scratch at it until it became a bleeding sore. As a result, several unsightly sores marked her face. This situation greatly distressed everybody but Norma, who seemed remarkably unconcerned. Both the parents and the fiancé had tried several tactics to get Norma to stop picking her face, including appealing to her vanity ("You are such an attractive person when your face is clear"), pleading ("I can't stand to see you do that to yourself"), and threats ("I won't be seen with you in public with your face in such a bad state").

What possible reinforcers could be maintaining Norma's behavior? Think about this question for a minute or two before reading on.

As mentioned previously, *attention can be a powerful reinforcer for behavior, even when the actual form of the attention may be negative.* In this case, too, the therapist determined that Norma's face picking was maintained by the considerable attention that both her parents and her fiancé directed toward this behavior. As long as Norma continued picking at her face, the pattern of inadvertent reinforcement was maintained, and she would likely remain the center of attention.

Realizing this pattern, the therapist instructed Norma's parents and fiancé *to ignore her face picking entirely.* They were cautioned that it would probably get worse before improving. (At the beginning of extinction training, people and other animals typically increase the intensity of no-longer-reinforced behaviors before discarding them.) True to prediction, Norma did exhibit a temporary increase in her face picking. However, it was quickly extinguished. (To prevent it from reappearing, the therapist encouraged both parents and fiancé to provide plenty of loving attention and support to Norma contingent upon a variety of healthy, adaptive behaviors.)

Punishment Aversive stimuli, such as electric shocks, can be used to punish voluntary maladaptive responses.

An example is the case of a nine-month-old infant, whose life was endangered by a chronic pattern of vomiting and regurgitating food (Lang & Melamed, 1969). From a six-month weight of 17 pounds, the infant had dropped to an emaciated 12 pounds. Attempts to feed him through a tube inserted through his nasal passage were a losing cause, since he continued to regurgitate his food within minutes. The behavior therapists assigned to this case carefully evaluated the vomiting behavior. Using electrical recordings of muscular activity, they found they could detect when the infant was about to vomit. On this basis they designed a treatment strategy. Each time electrical recordings signaled that the infant was about to vomit, the therapists delivered a brief shock to his leg. This electrical shock was immediately effective in reducing the vomiting, and after a few short training sessions the undesirable behavior had completely ceased. Within a relatively short period the child had gained considerable weight and was well enough to be discharged from the hospital. A follow-up one year later revealed continued healthy development, with no recurrences of the vomiting behavior.

Modeling Learning theorists have demonstrated that some kinds of learning appear to be learned through modeling. Modeling can be a helpful therapy technique for extinguishing irrational fears or for establishing new, more adaptive behaviors.

For example, suppose you are deathly afraid of the dark. Although this phobia might be treated by systematic desensitization as we described earlier, modeling might also be effective: You might observe others entering the dark with no visible adverse effects. Modeling may be live, or it may take place through films or videotapes. The beneficial, anti-phobia effects of modeling techniques may be enhanced even further if relaxation training is also used to ensure the client is in a calm, tranquil state while observing the models.

Modeling has wide application in treating people with phobias. In one study, children who were extremely fearful about undergoing a dental exam were first exposed to a 10-minute videotape in which a child model appeared to be happy and relaxed while experiencing several dental procedures such as X-rays and oral exams. The children who viewed the videotape exhibited markedly fewer signs of distress during the actual exam than a matched control group of children who were not exposed to the videotape or modeling procedure (Crooks, 1969).

Modeling may also be helpful in establishing new, more appropriate responses. In one study, modeling and active role-playing were found to be considerably more effective than cognitive therapy in establishing appropriate assertive behaviors (Gormally et al., 1975).

Token Economies Another way that reinforcement can be applied to maintain adaptive behavior patterns is through the use of tokens that can later be exchanged for desired objects or privileges. In a token economy patients are reinforced with tokens for demonstrating appropriate behavior. For instance, a patient may be reinforced with tokens for dressing appropriately and interacting with other patients and staff. These tokens can later be exchanged for the privilege of seeing a movie or having visitors. The major advantage of token economies is that appropriate behaviors can be immediately reinforced and there is little satiation to the reinforcer as there is with other primary reinforcers because the tokens can be exchanged for a wide variety of reinforcers which are selected by the patient. Although use of token economy is receding because of the difficulty of maintaining it on the part of the staff in psychiatric hospitals, it has been shown to be effective in many settings including normal College populations to induce the students to participate in classroom discussions (Boudewyns, P.A. et.al, 1986; Boniecki, K.A. et. al, 2003).

Family Therapy

Family therapy

Therapy in which family members meet together with a therapist.

Family therapy has gained steadily in popularity and respect over the last few decades. It differs from therapy with groups of unrelated individuals because family units bring to the experience a shared history of patterns of interrelationships. The family therapist is more likely to take an active role as model or teacher than other group leaders, who frequently define their role as facilitator rather than director (Yalom, 1975).

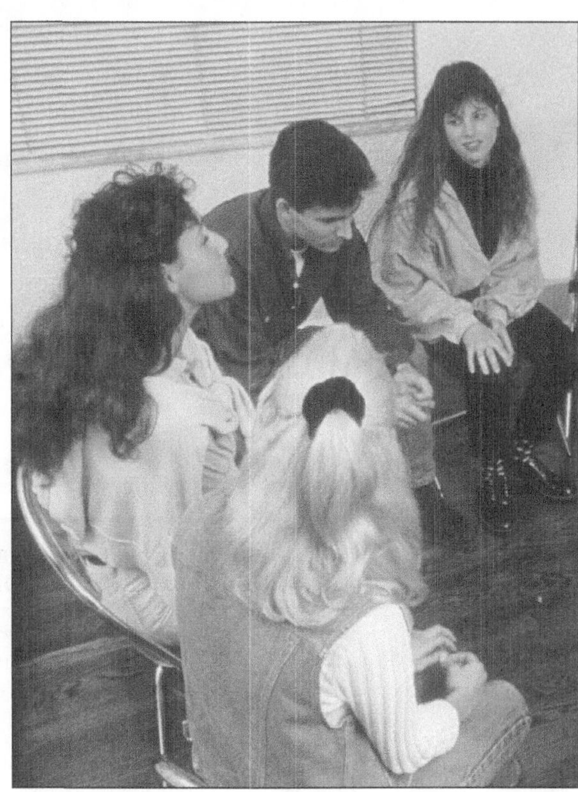

Family therapy uses a number of techniques to change maladaptive patterns in a disturbed family.

CMSP

Family therapy is based on the premise that an individual's behavioral adjustment is profoundly influenced by patterns of social interaction within the family unit. Families characterized by strife, poor communication, and pathological interaction patterns can foster behavioral difficulties in one or more individual members. The assumption that individual pathology has its roots in a disturbed family leads logically to the deduction that changing patterns of interaction in a disturbed family will affect those family members who have adjustment problems (Kutash & Wolf, 1986; Levene et al., 1990). Thus the task of the family therapist is to alter maladaptive relationship patterns so that symptoms of disturbed behavior diminish or disappear (Foley, 1984).

Family therapists use a number of techniques to change maladaptive patterns in a disturbed family. One strategy may be to alter patterns of alliances that are damaging to one or more family members. For instance, suppose an alliance has formed between a mother and her son, so that the father feels left out, angry, and depressed—feelings that may cause the father to display hostility toward his son and to withdraw from his wife. The therapist may seek to restructure patterns of family interaction by encouraging the father to take a more active interest in his son's experiences and to be more involved in making decisions that directly affect his son (Kendall & Norton-Ford, 1982).

Family therapists also aim to have all family members redefine problems as a family responsibility rather than projecting the blame onto only one member. For example, a teenage daughter's school truancy and drug use might be viewed as reflecting problem behavior of all family members. Perhaps she has reasoned that if she acts bad enough, her feuding parents will be forced to focus on her problems and thus stop battling with each other.

In summary, family therapists treat the entire family as the patient as they seek to educate all members about what kinds of maladaptive patterns are occurring within the family unit, how each member contributes to these problems, and what can be done to change the disruptive patterns to a more healthy system of interrelationships. Family therapy often tends to be relatively short term, consisting of once-a-week sessions for several weeks or a few months.

We have explored several approaches to psychotherapy, and Table 12.1 summarizes them. In the beginning of this chapter we reported the Smith & Glass meta-analysis that

TABLE 12.1 A Comparison of Several Different Forms of Therapy

Type of Psychotherapy	Primary Founder(s)	Interpretation of Cause(s) of Disorders	Focus/Goal of Therapy	Methods of Therapy
Psychoanalysis	Sigmund Freud	Disordered behavior results from unconscious conflicts and repressed urges, which are rooted in childhood experiences.	To enter the unconscious of disturbed people, search out the anxiety-causing conflict(s), and help these individuals gain insight or conscious awareness of the repressed conflicts.	Techniques include free association, dream analysis, and interpretation of resistance and transference.
Rational-Emotive	Albert Ellis	Psychological problems result when people interpret their experiences on the basis of certain self-defeating, irrational beliefs.	To help people find the flaws in their thinking, to challenge or dispute these maladaptive cognitions, and then to guide clients to substitute more logical or realistic thoughts.	Confrontation, persuasion, role-playing, interpretation, behavior modification, and reflection of feelings.
Cognitive Restructuring	Aaron Beck	Psychological problems stem primarily from a few irrational beliefs that cause people to behave and emote in maladaptive ways.	To help clients restructure their thinking, particularly their negative self-labels.	Structure certain "experiments" or experiences to disprove a client's misguided self-impressions.
Behavior	Joseph Wolpe, Albert Bandura, and others.	Disordered or maladaptive behaviors can be modified by conditioning.	To focus on people's current behaviors that are creating problems and help them unlearn maladaptive behavior patterns while learning more adaptive behavior.	Systematic desensitization, aversive conditioning, positive reinforcement, extinction, and punishment.
Biomedical	Antonio de Egas Moniz, James Watts, Ugo Cerletti, Lucino Bino, and others.	Many psychological problems result from biological abnormalities.	To eliminate symptoms of psychological disorders through biological intervention.	Drug treatment, psychosurgery, and electroconvulsive therapy.

found that there were no significant differences in the effectiveness of various therapies or that all the therapies were equally effective and their clients were better off receiving some treatment as compared to not receiving any treatment.

One possibility as to why so many diverse therapies seem to work well could be the client's perception that he/she is receiving help. On the other hand, it simply could be the fact that one positive change, whether it is in one's emotions, beliefs, attitudes, thoughts, behaviors, or brain processes brings about corresponding changes in all other processes, much like a stone thrown in any part of a well causes ripple effects all over the well, thus helping the patient.

Research indicates that the most effective psychotherapists are people who genuinely care about their clients and who are able to establish a warm, empathic relationship that helps to foster respect, trust, and the feeling of being cared for (Strupp, 1984; Williams & Chambers, 1990). A clinician who is reserved, aloof, and emotionally detached is not likely to provide the kind of warm, supportive atmosphere that is essential to therapeutic progress.

CURRENT TRENDS

Efforts to assess the relative success rates of various forms of psychotherapy may diminish in future years, in light of the current trend toward integrating the many diverse theoretical frameworks underlying the practice of American psychotherapy (Goldfried et al., 1990; Jensen et al., 1990).

Between one-third and one-half of currently practicing American psychotherapists do not consider themselves to be aligned with one particular type of psychotherapy, preferring instead to view themselves as eclectic in their application of psychotherapy (Beitman et al., 1989; Jayaratne, 1982; Norcross et al., 1988; Prochaska & Norcross, 1983; Watkins et al., 1986).

Research indicates that psychotherapists who are *eclectic* in their clinical practices tend to be older and more experienced. This finding suggests "with experience comes diversity and flexibility" (Beitman et al., 1989, p.139).

Even though the brain sciences and other hard sciences have moved towards accepting evolution and seeing the human mind as a biochemical product produced by a working brain and non-existent once the brain dies, Past-life therapy, a type of hypnotherapy has been found to be effective in several disorders (Marriott, J., 1984; Weiss, B.L., 2012).

Past-life Therapy is based on the long discarded Karma Theory which originated in ancient India and teaches Reincarnation and or transmigration of souls from one life to another, from one body to another, as a consequence of one's deeds in a current life. Illnesses and difficulties one faces are seen as consequences of deeds done in a lives lived before this one. Dr. Brian Weiss is a leading proponent of past-life therapy and is well-known for his first book titled "Many Lives Many Masters" which addressed the subject.

The newest therapy is ACT Therapy mentioned in the opening paragraph of this chapter. Its name is an acronym for Acceptance & Commitment Therapy. Its authors Harrison and Hayes, (2009) say that it draws from Buddhist meditative techniques, and from religious literature of the Hindus, Muslims, Jews and Christians, among others. They identify six different processes they feel are key, but the basic idea is to teach the patient Mind-fullness, or to pay full attention to the present moment rather than the past or the future, to mind one's inner speech and the language one uses in one's inner speech and to come up with a set of values the patient holds dear and then take committed action in order to live in keeping with those values. This Therapy is too new and does not come across as being "original" in any way, but is authored by a psychiatrist (Harris) and a psychologist (Hayes) in good standing.

These two above therapies are mentioned to provide food for thought to students who plan on becoming psychologists.

Common Features of Psychotherapeutic Approaches

Certain common features are shared by almost all styles of therapy. Researchers Jerome Frank (1982) and Marvin Goldfield (Goldfield & Padawer, 1982) have analyzed the commonalities of different psychotherapies extensively, and we explore some of their findings.

Combating the Client's Demoralization People who seek the services of a psychotherapist are typically demoralized by anxiety, depression, and a poor self-image, and they often have little hope for escaping from their misery. Virtually all effective psychotherapists, regardless of their particular methodology, tend to inspire in their clients a sense of hope and a belief that things will get better. These morale-boosting expectations may well contribute to a reduction in symptoms and an improved sense of well-being (Jacobson, 1968; Prioleau et al., 1983).

Providing a Rationale for Symptoms and Treatment Regardless of their theoretical orientation, virtually all therapists provide their clients with a plausible explanation for their symptoms and a logical scheme for alleviating them. As clients rethink the nature of their problems and possible solutions, they often acquire a new perspective on themselves as well as some fresh ideas about how to respond to their world more effectively. Acquiring a better understanding of oneself and one's problems, along with developing possible solutions, may contribute greatly to the healing process.

Providing a Warm, Supportive Relationship Effective therapists are individuals who are able to establish a caring, trusting, and empathic relationship with their clients. In one study, clients rated their personal relationship and interaction with their therapist as the most important part of their treatment (Sloane et al., 1975). Another study demonstrated that even paraprofessionals (laypeople trained by professionals) who were versed in how to engage in empathic listening were quite effective in helping people overcome behavioral problems (Berman & Norton, 1985). Thus it would seem that the nature of the client-therapist relationship has much to do with the success of the treatment (Henry et al., 1986; Kokotovic & Tracey, 1990). The fact that most therapists attempt to establish a warm, confiding, and empathic relationship with their clients may account, at least in part, for the comparable success rate reported for each method.

Providing a Professional Setting Good therapy does not usually take place over a cup of coffee, in the room of a private home that does double duty as a family room, or over the telephone. Instead, it usually takes place in a dignified, professional setting in a mental health clinic, hospital, or private office. This kind of setting may contribute much to the therapeutic process. An office that is quiet and professional is likely to provide a sense of security and safety that people may not experience in an informal setting, where the possibility of being overheard or interrupted may inhibit spontaneity. In addition, such a setting is likely to enhance the therapist's prestige and, by inference, to heighten the client's expectations for effective treatment.

BIOLOGICALLY-BASED THERAPIES

Many behavioral disorders result from biological abnormalities including altered brain structure and/or altered brain chemistry. Physiological intervention through surgery, electric shock, or drugs will alleviate or reduce the symptoms of such behavioral disorders.

Presently, only physicians with medical degrees may prescribe biomedical treatments. The American Psychological Association, however, is working towards legislation that would allow qualified licensed psychologists to prescribe psychoactive drugs for the treatment of certain psychological disorders. In this section we examine three types of biomedical treatment: psychosurgery, electroconvulsive (shock) therapy, and psychoactive drugs.

Psychosurgery

In the early decades of the last century mental hospitals throughout the Western world overflowed with severely disturbed patients, and there was a shortage of both professional staff and effective treatment strategies. During this time many mental health professionals became frustrated with what they perceived to be a general practice of using mental hospitals as little more than warehouses for severely disordered patients. In the effort to alleviate patient suffering and reduce problems of overcrowding, a number of psychiatrists were motivated to experiment with a variety of often-radical biological interventions. Lobotomy was one such radical surgery.

Lobotomy

Surgical procedure that severs the nerve tracts connecting the prefrontal cortex to lower brain areas that mediate emotional responses.

In 1941, Rosemary Kennedy, younger sister of John Kennedy was put through the newly discovered lobotomy at the tender age of twenty-three because of some mental/behavioral problems. Lobotomy did not help her and she was institutionalized for the rest of her life. Rosemary lived to be 96 years old.

Lobotomy, was originally performed by a very crude surgical procedure in which a hole was drilled through the skull on each side of the head, and a blunt instrument was then inserted and rotated in a vertical arc. The procedure was later refined by the transorbital lobotomy technique, in which an icepick-like instrument called a leucotome was inserted into the brain through an eye socket and rotated back and forth.

Lobotomized patients seemed more tranquil or calm after the operation, and thus more manageable. However, some observant clinicians began to raise questions. They suggested that the so-called calming effect was actually more a conversion of emotionally labile patients into lethargic, vegetative patients.

Furthermore, lobotomies were found to produce *no changes in the major manifestations of severe mental illness* other than reduction of emotional agitation (Barahal, 1958; Robbin, 1958, 1959). Such findings prompted several critics to call for a ban on all forms of psychosurgery. Although no formal prohibition was enforced, medical practitioners drastically curtailed their use of this method.

Psychosurgery did not die out completely. In fact, since the early 1970s there has been a growing interest in using surgical techniques to alter behavior when all other reversible treatment methods have failed. Newer surgical techniques produce only a small fraction of the brain damage associated with older procedures. For example, highly refined methods are now available for disconnecting the frontal cortex from lower brain centers (Shevitz, 1976). Other contemporary psychosurgery techniques involve destruction of limited amounts of tissue in precisely located sites within such brain structures as the amygdala, thalamus, and hypothalamus. These refined procedures are often effective in alleviating symptoms of severe depression, uncontrollable rage attacks, extreme anxiety, obsessive–compulsive disorders, schizophrenia, uncontrollable seizures, severe pain and sleep apnea and or epilepsy—all of which may have resisted more conventional forms of therapy—with very few serious side effects (Corkin, 1980; Donnelly, 1980; Mirsky & Orzacki, 1980; Kiloh et al., 1988; Sachdev et al., 1990; Valenstein, 1980; Foldvary-Schafer, N. et.al, 2008). Although these newer techniques are clearly an improvement over the lobotomies of the 1940s and 1950s, most contemporary clinicians believe that their use should be limited to patients whose problems are severe, persistent, and resistant to all other treatments.

Electroconvulsive Therapy

Electroconvulsive therapy (ECT)

Biomedical intervention in which electrical current applied to the brain induces a convulsive seizure. Used to treat depression.

Electroconvulsive therapy (ECT) is a procedure in which electrical current is applied to the surface of the head resulting in a convulsive seizure. Students often wonder how such a procedure could have come about to treat behavioral disorders. The story here is an interesting one.

In the early 1930s a Hungarian physician, Lazlo Von Meduna, noticed that hospitalized psychiatric patients often seemed to experience a remission or lessening of their psychotic symptoms after undergoing a spontaneous seizure of the type that occurs in epilepsy. Excited by this discovery, *Von Meduna began to experiment with different techniques for artificially inducing convulsions.* He first used intramuscular injections of camphor oil to elicit seizures. Although several patients were made physically ill by the injections, a number showed remarkable improvement. Von Meduna soon substituted synthetic camphor, Metrazol, which seemed to lessen the side effect of physical illness. The use of *pharmacoconvulsive therapy* (drug-induced seizures) quickly gained a foothold worldwide among psychiatrists desperate for a way to combat severe behavioral disorders.

Unfortunately, pharmacoconvulsive therapy was not without problems. Although the symptoms of behavioral disorders were often reduced, the procedure had other severe side effects, including painful preseizure spasms and uncontrollable convulsions that sometimes resulted in fractures and even death (Weiner, 1985). In the late 1930s two Italian neuropsychiatrists, Ugo Cerletti and Lucino Bini (1938), introduced a safer, better-controlled method for inducing seizures using electric shock. By 1940 electroconvulsive therapy had become a major component of psychiatric treatment strategies worldwide.

Early ECT sessions resembled a scene from a horror movie. A wide awake and often terrified patient was strapped to a table, electrodes were attached to each side of the forehead, and a current of roughly 100 volts was then passed between the electrodes for a fraction of a second, producing severe convulsions and a temporary loss of consciousness. Upon regaining consciousness the patient often seemed confused, distressed, and unable to remember events that happened both before and immediately after the procedure. In addition, the seizures induced by *the electric current often produced such a rapid and intense contraction of skeletal muscles that bone fractures, bruises, and other injuries sometimes resulted.* Altogether, this was not a pretty picture—but one that was repeated countless thousands of times due to compelling evidence that ECT was often amazingly effective in reducing symptoms of severe emotional distress, particularly depression.

Since the early days of the development of ECT, several modifications have been introduced to make this treatment safer and more humane. Today, patients are first put to sleep and administered a potent muscle relaxant before the shock is delivered. General anesthesia circumvents the terror many patients experienced in the early years of shock therapy. The patient typically wakes up in a half hour or so, with no recollection of the treatment. ECT is now often applied to only *one* of the cerebral hemispheres, usually the one that is not dominant. This unilateral treatment has significantly reduced the confusion and memory loss associated with ECT.

There is extensive evidence that ECT often produces a rapid and sometimes a dramatic reduction of the symptoms of major depression (Kalinowsky; 1980; Kramer, 1987; Scovern & Kilmann, 1980; Weiner, 1985; Yudofsky, 1982), and the treatment is sometimes effective in counteracting bipolar disorder (Berman & Wolpert, 1987). Research has generally shown ECT to be less effective in treating schizophrenia. The most common application of ECT today is for severely depressed patients who have not responded to antidepressant drugs or who cannot tolerate waiting for the slower acting drugs to take effect (Weiner, 1985).

One of the most perplexing aspects of electroconvulsive therapy is that no one is sure how the treatment works. We know that ECT alters the electrochemical processes in many central nervous system structures, but we still have not been able to determine which of these changes, if any, are linked with the antidepressant effects of ECT. One current proposal is that ECT increases the synthesis of thyrotropin-releasing hormone (TRH) in several limbic system regions. Increases in TRH are believed to suppress glutamate activity, which appears to be hyperactive in some depressed patients (Sattin, 1999). Electroconvulsive therapy may also increase serotonin activity either directly or by altering the serotonin transporter (Dremencov et al., 2003; Shen et al., 2003). It has even been suggested that the antidepressant effects of ECT can be explained by operant conditioning. According to this interpretation, a patient withholds or avoids depressed behaviors in order to prevent the aversive stimulus of ECT (Costello, 1976).

The questions and concerns raised by ECT will no doubt continue to be debated, and we can expect that ECT will continue to be used to treat approximately 80,000 Americans per year (Sackheim, 1985; Thompson & Blame, 1987). ECT is still being used on geriatric patients who are depressed and it is claimed that it does not induce any cognitive deficits (Haussner, et.al, 2011) and on women with Post-partum Depression in other countries where they claim almost immediate recovery, so it is in the best interest of the new-born (Babu, G. et.al, 2013).

Psychoactive Drugs

Psychoactive drugs

Drugs that have the effect of altering perceptions and behavior by changing conscious awareness.

The use of drugs to control symptoms of behavioral disorders became a primary strategy of psychiatric practice during the 1950s. Since then, *therapy with* ***psychoactive drugs*** *has become by far the most common biomedical treatment.* The use of psychoactive drugs has contributed both to a decline in the number of people hospitalized for behavioral disorders and to a significant reduction in the average duration of hospitalization.

Drugs are often so effective in controlling disruptive symptoms that many patients who might previously have required restraints or close observation in locked wards are now able to function reasonably effectively outside of a hospital setting. Even patients who still require hospitalization typically need less supervision than did their counterparts in the days before drugs were introduced. In other cases, drug therapy has been successfully used to calm patients so that psychological therapies can be applied.

The four major categories of psychoactive drugs that are used to control or alleviate symptoms of behavioral disorders are *antipsychotics, antidepressants, antimanics,* and *antianxiety drugs.* Table 12.2 lists several commonly used drugs in these categories. The various widely used psychoactive drugs differ considerably in their effects: Some calm, some energize, and some provide an emotional lift. However, they all share one common feature. Generally speaking, all psychoactive drugs merely help to control or manage symptoms rather than cure the disorder. When people cease taking these medications, symptoms tend to recur.

Besides dramatically enhancing the ability of psychiatrists to treat severely disordered patients, biomedical drug therapy has stimulated an abundance of research, resulting in some important new hypotheses linking many behavioral disorders to neurochemical factors.

TABLE 12.2 Major Categories of Psychoactive Drugs

Category	Used to Treat	Chemical Group	Generic Name	Trade Name
Antipsychotics	schizophrenic disorders, severe aggressive behavior	phenothiazines	chlorpromazine	Thorazine
			thioridazine	Mellaril
			trifluoperazine	Stelazine
		butyrophenones	haloperidol	Haldol
		thioxanthenes	chlorprothixene	Taractan
		dihydroindolones	molindone	Moban
		dibenzodiazepine	clozapine	Clozaril
Antidepressants	major depressive disorders, obsessive-compulsive behaviors	tricyclics	doxepin	Sinequan
			amitriptyline	Elavil
			imipramine	Trofranil
			nortriptyline	Aventyl
			protriptyline	Vivactil
		monoamine oxidase inhibitors	phenelzine	Nardil
			tranylcypromme	Parnate
			isocarboxazid	Marplan
		serotonin reuptake inhibitors	fluoxetine	Prozac
			paroxetine	Paxil
		dopamine agonists	bupropion	Welbutrin
Antimanics	bipolar disorder, mania	inorganic salts	lithium carbonate	Lithane
				Lithonate
			carbamazepine	Tegretol
Antianxiety	generalized anxiety, phobic anxieties, tension, sleep disorders	propanediols	meprobamate	Miltown
				Equanil
		benzodiazepines	chlordiazepoxide	Librium
			diazepam	Valium
			alprazolam	Xanax
			chlorazepate	Tranxene
			halazepam	Paxipam
			lorazepam	Ativan
			oxazepam	Serax
			prazepam	Centrax

Antipsychotic drugs

Drugs used to treat psychotic disorders such as schizophrenia.

ANTIPSYCHOTICS The **antipsychotic drugs**, sometimes called *neuroleptics* or *major tranquilizers,* were first used in the early 1950s to treat schizophrenia. As Table 12.2 shows, there are several varieties of these drugs. The most commonly employed are the *phenothiazine* derivatives. The most widely used drug in this group is chlorpromazine, sold under the name Thorazine. Chlorpromazine has been the number-one medication for treating schizophrenia since it was introduced to American psychiatry in 1952 (Duke & Nowicki,

1986). One effect of this drug and other neuroleptic drugs is to calm and quiet patients, reducing their responsiveness to irrelevant stimuli. In cases where patients are severely withdrawn or immobile, neuroleptic drugs tend to increase activity and responsiveness. The therapeutic effects of neuroleptics are believed to result from the fact that neuroleptic drugs block specific dopamine receptor sites in the brain, thus reducing dopamine activity in those locations. As we discussed in the previous chapter, schizophrenic symptoms appear to result from excessive dopamine activity or sensitivity in certain regions of the brain, perhaps mediated by the neurotransmitter glutamate (Carlsson et al., 1990, 1995; Davison & Neale, 1990; Gershon & Rieder, 1992; Grey et al., 1991).

Unfortunately, a sizable percentage (perhaps as many as 40 percent) of patients who take neuroleptic drugs develop a serious side effect called *tardive dyskinesia* (TD) (Bartzokis et al., 1989; Gureje, 1989; Haley, 1989; Stein, 1989; Yadalam et al., 1990). This neurological disorder, which may occur months to years after drug therapy has commenced or has stopped, is typically manifested as uncontrollable muscular movements of the jaw, lips, and tongue. The severity of the symptoms may range from barely noticeable chewing movements to involuntary biting of the tongue. Some psychiatrists are hopeful that the trend toward using lower dosages of neuroleptic drugs in treating severe behavioral disorders will significantly reduce the problem (Stein, 1989). Another way to reduce the occurrence of this negative side effect is the targeted strategy (Carpenter & Heinrichs, 1983; Herz et al., 1982). The application of this strategy involves discontinuation of neuroleptics during periods of relative remission and the reinstitution of medication when early signs of relapse appear (Kirkpatrick et al., 1989). Although the pharmaceutical companies have come up with newer drugs which are claimed to be safer and have fewer side-effects some psychiatrists claim that the older drugs like Haldol are still the best because the newer ones cause severe metabolic problems (Belmaker, 2012; Harris, 2009).

Antidepressant drugs

Drugs used to treat major depressive disorder.

ANTIDEPRESSANTS The **antidepressant drugs**, also introduced in the 1950s, consist of three main groups which are the *tricyclics* the *monoamine oxidase (MAO)* inhibitors, and *serotonin reuptake inhibitors* (see Table 12.2). These drugs are used to treat major depressive disorders, and they are often very effective in lifting the spirits of severely depressed patients. While it has been widely believed that these drugs act to increase the activity of the neurotransmitters norepinephrine and serotonin in certain areas of the brain, it is possible that their antidepressant effects may be related to increased sensitivity of the receptors for those two neurotransmitters. Hopefully, further research will clarify how and why the antidepressants are so effective.

A number of studies comparing treatment methods for depression have been conducted over the years. Perhaps the most ambitious study has been the Depression Collaborative Research Program sponsored by the National Institute of Mental Health (NIMH). The major findings from this study were similar to previous, smaller studies. Specifically, patients who receive drug treatment typically respond more quickly initially, but those receiving other forms of treatment often catch up towards the end of the treatment phase.

FIGURE 12.1 Comparison of the Four Treatment Methods Used in the NIMH Treatment of Depression Collaborative Research Program.

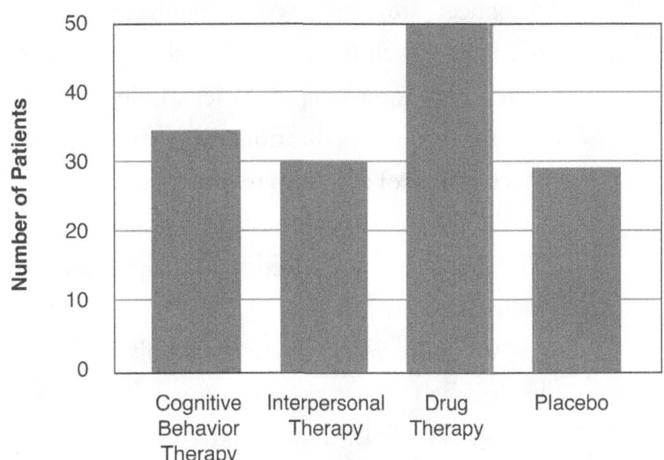

The results also revealed that no particular treatment method was superior to any other and the rates of relapse were similar. Figure 12.1 shows the relapse rates for the four treatment conditions eight weeks following treatment.

Of the major drugs listed in Table 12.2 to treat depression, the serotonin specific reuptake inhibitors (Prozac and Paxil) appear to be the most effective and tend to produce the least severe side effects. These drugs have become the most widely prescribed drugs for treatment for depression, with nearly 10 million people worldwide taking them. The newer Serotonin specific re-uptake inhibitors such as Vibryd (Vilazodone), approved for use in 2011 in the USA, are thought to have less serious side-effects such as nausea, diarrhea, indigestion, etc. but they are more expensive and are too new for a good body of research to determine their efficacy and any harm they might cause.

Antimanic drugs

Drugs used to control the manic symptoms of bipolar disorder.

ANTIMANICS In 1970 lithium carbonate was approved by the Food and Drug Administration for use as an **antimanic drug**. This medication, a simple inorganic salt, has been found to be the most effective drug for controlling the manic symptoms of bipolar disorder and has even been shown to help reduce depression associated with this disorder (Giannini et al., 1986; Murray, 1990). Lithium therapy appears to be less effective when applied to patients experiencing a state of mixed mania (in which both depressive and manic symptoms occur concurrently) (Schou, 1989). Its greatest benefit, however, seems to be as a prophylactic, reducing the frequency and severity of manic episodes or perhaps preventing them altogether (Lipper, 1985; Prien et al., 1984; Prien & Gelenberg, 1989; Schou, 1989). Neural mechanisms via which Lithium works are not understood and some researchers claim that Lithium works at the genomic level by altering gene expression (Ognian,C. et.al, 1999). Although the mechanism is still being researched there is enough literature to support the efficacy of Lithium as a mood stabilizer, especially in Mania.

Antianxiety drugs

Drugs used to reduce symptoms of anxiety and tension in disorders that are not severe enough to warrant hospitalization. Sometimes called minor tranquilizers.

ANTIANXIETY DRUGS The **antianxiety drugs**, sometimes called minor tranquilizers, are used to reduce symptoms of anxiety and tension in people whose behavioral disturbances are not severe enough to warrant hospitalization. These medications are particularly helpful in reducing the symptoms of generalized anxiety disorders, panic disorders, and some sleep disorders. Like most of the drugs we have discussed in this section, the antianxiety medications were introduced in the 1950s and widely used before their mechanisms of action were understood.

There are two major categories of minor tranquilizers: *propanediols* and *benzodiazepines.* The first to be introduced were the propanediols, the most common of which is meprobamate (Miltown).

Over the years the propanediols have become gradually less popular, and they have been largely replaced by the *benzodiazepines,* which were introduced in the 1960s. Like the propanediols, the benzodiazepines also have sedative and muscle-relaxing effects. In addition to these properties, the benzodiazepines, Librium and Valium being the first two benzodiazepines to be marketed, are known to facilitate the binding of the neurotransmitter GABA to its receptor sites (Julien, 2001). Currently, there are several benzodiazepines on the market and Xanax and Halcion, Klonopin, Ativan and Restoril are some of the well-known antianxiety agents that are also used as sleeping medications.

Throughout this chapter we have reviewed the major psychological and biological approaches to the treatment of behavioral disorders. It is important to remember that there is still considerable disagreement among professionals about causes and appropriate types of treatment for most of the disorders that we have discussed. While the fields of neuroscience and pharmacology have contributed considerably to our understanding and treatment of behavioral disorders, many professionals continue to apply therapy from an eclectic approach rather than focus on a single theoretical perspective. In the next chapter we shall examine social influences on behavior as well as factors that contribute to our social behavior.

SUMMARY

PSYCHOANALYSIS

1. Psychoanalysis is based on a number of assumptions; the most fundamental is that disordered behavior results from unconscious conflicts and repressed urges, most of which are rooted in childhood experiences.
2. Major techniques of psychoanalysis include free association, dream analysis, and interpretations of resistance.
3. Psychodynamic Therapy is a modern version of Psychoanalysis in which they give importance to internal conflicts and use free association but limit the associations to one major concern, making it a therapy that is quicker than psychoanalysis.

COGNITIVE THERAPIES

4. Cognitive therapies are based on the premise that most behavioral disorders result from distortions in a person's cognitions or thoughts.
5. Rational-emotive behavior therapy (REBT) is based on the belief that behavioral problems result when people interpret their experiences based on certain self-defeating, irrational beliefs. The goal of therapy is to eliminate these maladaptive cognitions.
6. Like REBT, cognitive restructuring therapy also aims to get clients to restructure their thinking, particularly negative self-labels, by arranging certain experiences that will disprove rather than confirm the client's negative self-image.

BEHAVIORAL THERAPIES

7. The central thesis of behavior therapy is that maladaptive behavior has been learned and that it can be unlearned; furthermore, the same principles that govern the learning of normal behavior also determine the acquisition of abnormal behavior.
8. The classical conditioning therapies, which include systematic desensitization and aversive conditioning, apply classical conditioning principles to help people to overcome maladaptive behavior.
9. Systematic desensitization involves training people to relax when confronted with fear-inducing stimuli.
10. In aversive therapy the goal is to associate aversive consequence to an inappropriate or harmful stimulus such as nicotine or alcohol.
11. The operant conditioning therapies, which include positive reinforcement, extinction, and punishment, focus on manipulating consequences of behavior as a way to overcome behavioral problems.
12. In positive reinforcement therapy the therapist first identifies desirable behavior and then provides appropriate reinforcers contingent upon the client voluntarily manifesting the desired behavior.
13. The extinction technique involves eliminating undesired behaviors by eliminating the reinforcers that maintain them.
14. In the punishment technique aversive stimuli are used to punish voluntary maladaptive responses.
15. Family therapy with entire family units is based on the premise that an individual's psychological adjustment is profoundly influenced by patterns of social interaction within the family.

EVALUATING PSYCHOTHERAPY

16. Research has also shown that no particular type of therapy is significantly superior to others.
17. Certain common features shared by almost all styles of therapy include combating the client's demoralization, providing a rationale for the client's symptoms and their treatment, providing a warm, supportive relationship, and providing a professional setting.

BIOLOGICALLY-BASED THERAPIES

18. Lobotomy was originally performed as a very crude surgical procedure.
19. Lobotomies eventually fell into disrepute when research revealed that they produced no changes in the major manifestations of severe mental illness and that many lobotomized patients had been transformed into lethargic, unmotivated, robot-like personalities.
20. Newer psychosurgery techniques produce only a small fraction of the brain damage associated with the older and cruder lobotomies. They have been shown to have some value in alleviating symptoms of severe disorders that have resisted more conventional forms of therapy.
21. There is extensive evidence that electroconvulsive therapy (ECT) often rapidly alleviates the symptoms of major depression. and post-partum depression.
22. Therapy with psychoactive drugs, by far the most common biomedical treatment, has contributed to both a decline in the number of people hospitalized for behavioral disorders and a significant reduction in the average duration of hospitalization.
23. The four major categories of psychoactive drugs that are used to control or alleviate symptoms of behavioral disorders are antipsychotics, antidepressants, antimanics, and antianxiety drugs.

TERMS AND CONCEPTS

psychotherapy
psychoanalysis
Psychodunamic therapy
free association
dream analysis
resistance
cognitive therapies
rational-emotive therapy (RET or REBT)
cognitive behavior therapy
behavior therapy
classical conditioning therapies
systematic desensitization
operant conditioning therapies
family therapy
lobotomy
electroconvulsive therapy (ECT)
psychoactive drugs
antipsychotic drugs
antidepressant drugs
antimanic drugs
antianxiety drugs

CHAPTER 13

Social Psychology

Corbis

Social psychologists study how people influence people, or the effect people have on other people, by devising experiments in which humans participate. They also study how individuals such as political leaders or cult leaders persuade people, and they study how ordinary individuals influence others in subtle ways.

Social psychologists have discovered that not only does the presence of other people have an effect on our behavior, but even the knowledge that someone else is present has a substantial effect on our behavior.

Many of the theories that social psychologists profess have their origin in real-life incidents that shocked the world for one reason or another. Numerous people wondered and several people probably pondered as to why the people in those situations behaved the way they did, but social psychologists went one step further. They not only wondered and pondered, but came up with a hypothesis and devised an experiment to truly understand the reasons for the behaviors shown in real life.

In 2004, after the abuse of Iraqi prisoners of war in what is well known as the Abu Ghraib incident came to light, a study conducted in 1971 by Phillip Zimbardo, and known as *The Stanford Prison Experiment,* came into sharp focus again, after a good thirty years! In the Stanford Prison Experiment, Phillip Zimbardo sought normal, healthy young men as volunteers in a simulated mock prison built on the Stanford Campus, only to discover that the "normal" young men behaved menacingly towards the prisoners in their roles as prison guards, in a matter of a few days! Likewise, the young men who were assigned to serve as "prisoners" in the experiment, very quickly behaved like prisoners do and showed signs of depression, guilt, shame, etc., when in reality, they had not committed any crimes and were not being punished for anything they had done, but were participants in an experiment! Based on that experiment Zimbardo concluded that we all play various roles in life and that ***societal expectations for the behaviors befitting a particular role guide our behavior.*** Zimbardo argued that *if we want prison guards to treat the prisoners better, we need to change our expectations as to what a prison guard is supposed to behave like!* (Carnahan & McFarland, 2007; Haney et. al., 1973).

Likewise, another study based on a real-life incident was conducted by John Darley and Bibb Latané (1968). Darley and Latané wanted to understand the behavior of several people who witnessed a now famous fatal stabbing, known as The Kitty Genovese murder which took place in 1964, in New York City (Hock, 1992). Kitty Genovese had returned from work and as she walked from her car to her

(continues)

apartment, a knife-wielding attacker stabbed her several times as she screamed. The attack lasted for about thirty minutes, at which point Kitty Genovese fell dead.

The police estimated that 38 of Kitty's neighbors watched the incidence in silence from their apartment windows, without moving a finger to help Ms. Genovese. They did not even dial the police! The murderer escaped and was never caught. The thought that Kitty would have been alive if only someone, anyone, had moved to help her or call the police a little earlier, drove New Yorkers crazy and appalled the Nation. It inspired several psychologists to conduct experiments, which studied the phenomenon of non-involvement, known as **Bystander Apathy**.

In one such experiment conducted by Darley and Latané (1968) students were told that there were five people in the discussion group, and each was going to get a private cubicle to sit in and would converse with the others but only over an intercom to ensure anonymity. Each student would have a microphone that would be activated for two minutes, when they were to share their stories, and then their mike would fall silent, and another student's mike would be activated, so each one of them would get a turn. In reality, this was the cover story told to the real subject. There were no other participants in the study, there were only taped voices that came on, making the student believe he/she was in a session with others.

The experiment began with the voice of what seemed to be one of the participants, hesitatingly describing the pressures he felt and the difficulties he was experiencing. The participant then went on to reveal in a halting, diffident way indicative of embarrassment that he was an epileptic and that he was prone to going into seizures when under stress.

Other participants then shared their woes, and within a very short time, it was the purported first participant's voice again, but this time he made it apparent that he was seizing. He fumbled for words, then appeared to be choking and pleaded for help, clearly saying he was having a seizure and needed help. Would a participant move to help the person who was seizing? Darley and Latané allowed the real subject four minutes to act. If within the four minutes the subject went in search of the experimenter to try to get help for the epileptic that was counted as helping. If the subject did not act in four minutes, the experiment was terminated.

What would you do, if you thought a person in one of the adjacent cubicles was having an epileptic attack? Did you say you would bolt right out of your seat and go tend to him?

Well . . . that's what we all *say*. But, what do we *do*? Darley and Latané discovered that a mere 31 percent of subjects offered help when they thought there were five other participants in the group! In contrast, 62 percent of subjects offered help when they thought there were two other participants, and 85 percent offered help when they thought they were the only ones aware of the epileptic's emergency!

Social psychologists use the term **diffusion of responsibility** or **"shared responsibility"** to explain Darley and Latané's findings (Hock, 1992). Our own sense of responsibility is diminished by the presence of other bystanders because we assume that they have as much responsibility to act as we have, we are less likely to intervene.

As we saw in the above experiment, *the mere knowledge of how many others are present in a given situation influences our behavior greatly.*

In this chapter we will focus on several variables that affect our ability to influence or be influenced. We begin with social perception.

SOCIAL PERCEPTION

Diffusion of responsibility

Tendency for an individual to feel a diminished sense of responsibility to assist in an emergency when other bystanders are present.

We encounter many people each day, from the clerk at the grocery store to the classmate sitting behind us to the mechanic who is servicing our car. Even if our interactions with these people are very brief, we form impressions or perceptions of them. The term **social perception** describes the ways we perceive, evaluate, categorize, and form judgments about the qualities of people we encounter. We then act or react in accordance with these perceptions. If, for example, you are hailed by a well-dressed person as you walk on the street, you are likely to stop to find out why he hailed you. On the other hand, if you are addressed by

Social perception

Way in which we perceive, evaluate, categorize, and form judgments about the qualities of other people.

a person dressed like a panhandler, you are more likely to walk off as if you did not hear him call out to you, or even hurry away from there. Your social perception of the well-dressed person has made you conclude that he/she is a decent person worthy of your attention.

Since these readings of other people are so important, it is worthwhile to know how we form them. *Three factors that influence our social perceptions are first impressions, schemas, and implicit personality theories. An implicit personality theory* is simply a collection of beliefs and assumptions that we hold about how certain traits are linked to other characteristics and behaviors of a person we know.

First Impressions

Primacy effect

Term used to describe the phenomenon that the first information we receive about a person often has the greatest influence on our perceptions of that person.

First impressions are the initial judgments we make about people, they have a lasting quality which is known as the **Primacy Effect** and they play an important role in social perceptions. Although first impressions may change as we get to know a person better, we often tend to hang on to them even in the face of contradictory evidence. Thus, initial opinions may have a strong impact on our future interactions with people.

Research indicates that *negative first impressions are often quickly formed and hard to overcome.* In contrast, the opposite tends to be true of positive first impressions. They are often hard to earn but easily lost (Rothbart & Park, 1986).

Person Schemas

What determines whether our first impression of a person is positive or negative?

Schemas are the conceptual frameworks we use to make sense out of our world. The concept of schemas helps explain how we perceive the people we meet. For example, you might have schemas of lawyers as aggressive and verbal, and of professors as brilliant but absent-minded. Social psychologists refer to these generalized assumptions about certain classes of people as **person schemas**.

Person schemas

Generalized assumptions about certain classes of people.

Person schemas provide a structure for evaluating the people we meet, allowing us to take shortcuts by concentrating on some facts and ignoring others. When we assess a person for the first time, we tend to pick up only the information that fits our existing schemas, ignoring the rest. This process is efficient, but, unfortunately, it is not always the most accurate way of forming impressions (Brigham, 1986). You may have experienced instances where first impressions were quite inaccurate.

Once we fit a person into a schema, we tend to use that schema as a general organizing principle for interpreting further information about the person. For example, if our first impression of a new neighbor is that she is unfriendly, we are likely to evaluate her failure to comment on our shiny new car as further evidence of unfriendliness. If she then acts in a way that does not fit the schema (for example, picking up our garbage after it has been scattered by the wind), we may dismiss that act by concluding that she picked up the mess only because she was worried that it would blow onto her lawn. In other words, of the new

Impression Management

Since first impressions are crucial when you are meeting a prospective life partner or a prospective employer, here are some tips that social psychologists say will help you form a good impression on the other person. The following tips might not work in a culture that is drastically different from the United States because each culture has different ideas and different norms for social behavior.

Techniques for making a good first impression in the United States:

1. Smile and shake hands warmly on introduction.
2. Look the other person in the eye when asking or answering a question.
3. Lean forward slightly and look at the person when he/she is talking.
4. Nod your head in agreement every now and then.
5. If the person has an accent, and you are good at mimicry, gently ease into using that person's accent. *The more similar the other person thinks you are to them, the more favorable the first impression will be.*
6. Adjust your body posture to reflect the body posture of the other person. Again, if your body language is similar, he/she will like you better and form a more favorable opinion of you.
7. Compliment the other person, especially if he/she is interviewing you for a job, but do it indirectly.
8. Show genuine appreciation if you feel it.
9. If being interviewed for a job, find out their dress code and conform to it.
10. Get as much information as you can about your prospective employer, before you are interviewed, so you come across as knowledgeable about them when you ask questions of them.

information available to us about a person, we seem to retain and integrate only that information that is consistent with our first impression of that person.

ATTRIBUTION THEORIES

An important part of social perceptions are the judgments we make about why people behave as they do. Our responses to other people are strongly influenced by these attributions, and we are constantly attempting to understand the reasons for other people's behavior.

Attribution theory
Theory that we attempt to make sense out of other people's behavior by attributing it to either dispositional (internal) causes or external (situational) causes.

According to **attribution theory people automatically try to ascertain the cause underlying a behavior as part of their need to understand or make sense of that behavior** (Heider, 1958; Jones, 1979; Kelley, 1971; Ross & Fletcher, 1985). We tend to attribute people's behavior either to dispositional (internal) causes, such as motivational states or personality traits, or to situational causes, such as environmental or external factors.

Most attributions have three dimensions: internal/external, stable/unstable, and controllable/uncontrollable. These six adjectives, which reflect the three dimensions, are found in any combination in an attribute. Let's take three students and their self-talk after receiving their grade on their first psychology test. Harry fails his first psychology test. Immediately Harry says to himself: "I blew it. I am dumb." Harry has attributed his failure to an internal, stable, and uncontrollable cause, i.e., his being "dumb," meaning "not very intelligent." Josh, on the other hand, fails his first psychology test and says, "This test was very hard!" Josh has attributed his failure to an external, unstable, uncontrollable cause. Had either of them said, "I could not study because the pizza made me sleepy," they would have attributed their failure to an external, unstable, controllable cause! Then there is Sheila. Sheila actually aces the test, and she says, "Oh! I was so lucky they asked the very questions I happened to know the answers to!" Sheila then has attributed her success to luck, which is external, unstable, and uncontrollable. *In general, people who attribute their successes to internal causes and failures to external causes tend to be more successful in life.*

The way we attribute our successes and failures, our behaviors, or even the behaviors of others, can have important effects on the course our lives take and on our relationships with people. For example, suppose you have recently begun dating someone you like very much, and the two of you spend a weekend visiting your date's parents. Much to your dismay, your friend acts like a different person—restrained and impersonal. If you attribute it to external factors (that your date is ill at ease around his or her parents) you are unlikely to feel that the relationship is seriously threatened. However, if you attribute the change to an internal cause (that he/she is ashamed of you or has taken a dislike for you) you might move in the direction of breaking the relationship!

Clearly, our attributions of the causes of people's behaviors have an important impact on relationships. How do we make these attributions? Two theories that attempt to explain this process are the correspondent inference theory and the covariation principle.

The Correspondent Inference Theory

Correspondent inference theory

Theory that the attributions we make about other people's behavior are influenced by a variety of conditions, such as the social desirability of that behavior or whether the behavior results from free choice.

The **correspondent inference theory** (Jones, 1979; Jones & McGillis, 1976) attempts to explain the attributions we make about people's behaviors by looking at the conditions under which we make those attributions. Theorists Edward E. Jones and his colleagues use the term correspondent inference to describe cases in which we attribute a person's behavior to an underlying disposition. For instance, suppose you witness a new neighbor behave raucously at a party. You might infer that the person has a loud and unpleasant disposition. However, we do not always make dispositional attributions based on the behaviors we observe. If you watch a television game show emcee behaving in a solicitous and charming manner to guest participants, you are unlikely to infer that the host is a genuinely warm and caring person. Why do we make correspondent inferences about people's dispositions in some cases but not in others? Jones and his associates suggest several factors.

One important variable is the *social desirability* or "expectedness" of behaviors we observe. Some common behaviors are so socially acceptable that they reveal virtually nothing about a person. For example, we expect politicians running for office to smile and shake hands with strangers. This expected behavior fits in nicely with our schema of a politician, but it does not tell us very much about the politician's disposition. True, the candidate might actually be a warm and friendly person, but it is equally possible that the smiles, handshakes, and baby kissing are due instead to the influence of social norms. Thus, we are unlikely to draw correspondent inferences about the politician.

ATTRIBUTIONS AND SOCIALLY UNDESIRABLE BEHAVIOR Do socially undesirable actions have the same impact on our attribution processes as socially acceptable behaviors? For instance, if you observe a tennis pro slam his racket on the court after a bad call are you more likely to make a correspondent inference about his or her disposition than if you observed polite and controlled behavior? If so, can you explain why unacceptable behavior would be more telling than desirable behavior? Consider this question before reading on.

Several experiments have demonstrated that we are more likely to make correspondent inferences from socially undesirable or norm-deviant behaviors than from socially desirable behaviors (Skowronski & Carlston, 1987). For example, in one study subjects listened to various versions of tapes of a man being interviewed for a job in which the interviewer opened the interaction by specifying the personality traits required for the job—traits such as independence and self-reliance. In one version, the applicant described himself in a way that closely matched the desired attributes, while in another version he described his traits as entirely different from those the interviewer was seeking. Most subjects indicated they were able to make confident judgments about the applicant's true character only when he had described himself as being the opposite of what the job demanded (Jones et al., 1961).

Such findings are consistent with the correspondent inference theory. Apparently, when a person's behavior fits external social expectations, we tend to discount it as a clue to a person's true nature. It is the unexpected behavior, which deviates from social desirability norms, that influences us to attribute actions to internal dispositions.

A second variable that determines whether we make correspondent inferences about a person's disposition is the degree to which his or her behavior is focused on achieving unique outcomes that would be unlikely to occur as a result of some other behavior. For example, suppose a friend of yours, a physics major, registers for a course in quantum mechanics. Will you be unimpressed, or will your image of your friend change? If you find out that the course is required for a degree in physics, you are likely to attribute your friend's action to external causes, since it accomplishes the unique or non-common outcome of obtaining a degree, a goal that could not have been achieved in any other way. If, on the other hand, you discover this course is an obscure offering that is neither required nor recommended for a physics major, you are more likely to make a dispositional attribution about your friend's great intellectual curiosity.

A third variable that influences correspondent inferences is whether or not we perceive a person's behavior as resulting from free choice. If we know that a person freely chose to behave in a particular manner, we probably assume that these actions reflect underlying dispositions. On the other hand, if that person was pressed to act in a certain way by situational forces, we are more inclined to attribute the behavior to external than internal causes.

Covariation Principle

A second theory of how people make attributions is based on our reckoning of cause-effect covariance, in the sense that we know that if a cause is altered, its effect will automatically change, so that causes and effects can be said to covary. According to Howard Kelley (1967, 1971, 1973), when we make attributions about people's behavior (the effect) we tend to look at three potential causes: the situation or context in which the behavior occurs, the persons involved, and the stimuli or objects toward which the behavior is directed. Kelley's theory is known as the **covariation principle**.

Covariation principle

Theory that our attributions about people's behavior are influenced by the situations in which the behavior occurs, the persons involved, and the stimuli or objects toward which the behavior is directed.

Kelley suggests that as we seek additional information to aid our interpretation of the causes of a person's behavior we act like social scientists, carefully, though informally, analyzing the data, paying particular attention to variations in situation, persons, and stimuli on each of the three following separate dimensions:

1. *Distinctiveness:* Relates to the degree to which other stimuli are capable of eliciting the same behavior from the person. We tend to attribute highly distinctive actions to situational causes.
2. *Consistency:* Relates to the degree to which the person exhibits the same behavior in response to the same stimulus on other occasions. Consistency is important for both dispositional and situational attribution.
3. *Consensus:* Relates to the degree to which other people exhibit the same response to the stimulus as the person in question. We tend to attribute low consensus responses to dispositional causes.

According to Kelley, we take in information about all of these dimensions and use it to determine whether the behavior we have observed is caused by an internal disposition or by the situation. All of this makes us sound very rational and methodical in judging other people. Unfortunately, our judgments are not always accurate. We often make errors in the inferences we draw from other people's behavior, and these errors can usually be traced to a few common attribution errors. We look at a few of these errors, including the fundamental attribution error, false consensus error, and the illusion of control.

Attribution Errors

FUNDAMENTAL ATTRIBUTION ERROR *One of the most common attribution errors is a tendency to overestimate dispositional causes and to underestimate situational causes when accounting for the behavior of others.* (Interestingly, we tend to do exactly the opposite when accounting for our own behaviors.) This inclination is so pervasive that it has been labeled the **fundamental attribution error** (Baron & Byrne, 1987; Ross, 1977). For example, when a casual acquaintance complains that she has just failed a history exam, do you attribute her poor performance to a tricky test or a lack of adequate preparation time (both situational causes), or are you more inclined to assume she is not very bright

Fundamental attribution error

Tendency to overestimate dispositional (internal) causes and to underestimate situational (external) causes of behavior.

(dispositional cause)? If you are like most of us, you probably tend to overestimate the latter cause and discount the former. Had you failed the same exam, however, the odds are good that you would look for situational causes.

Some researchers have found that attribution biases depend upon whether one is male or female. For instance, males tend to attribute their failures to situations ("I prepared poorly," or "it was a tricky exam") and their successes to dispositions ("I'm talented" or "smart"). On the other hand many females do just the opposite: They attribute success to situations ("I studied hard," or "I was lucky") and failure to dispositions ("I'm not very smart") (Erkut, 1983).

Consider another example: To what do you attribute the high degree of athletic ability we see in a professional athlete like Tiger Woods? If you are like most people, you attribute his ability to a disposition—his innate talent, not years of hard work. In fact, television commentators and sports writers continually comment about innate talent and instinct in athletes, when in reality it is years of hard work and training that determine performance.

Why are we so quick to attribute other people's behavior to their inner dispositions? At least part of the answer lies in the fact that while we know what situational factors affect our own behavior, we have far less information about how such factors affect other people. Thus, we take the easiest path and assume that they acted in a particular way because "that is the kind of people they are." As we get to know another person we begin to see how their behavior is influenced by situational variables and dispositional factors tends to dissipate in favor of situational factors in our attributions of their behavior, over time (Truchot et al., 2003).

FALSE CONSENSUS Another common attributional error is the assumption that most people share our own attitudes and behaviors (Goethals, 1986). This assumption is known as **false consensus bias**, and it influences us to judge any noteworthy deviations from our own standards as unusual or abnormal.

False consensus bias

Attribution bias caused by the assumption that most people share our own attitudes and behaviors.

For example, suppose you note that someone living in your apartment complex never laughs or even cracks a smile while listening to a certain television comedian you find hilarious. Consequently, you make a dispositional attribution: You assume that the other person has no sense of humor. This bias may be so strong that you do not stop to think that there are probably a number of people with good senses of humor who do not enjoy this comedian.

ILLUSION OF CONTROL Have you ever had a bad experience, such as being in an auto accident, and then later lamenting that if only you had left at a different time you could have avoided the situation? People often blame themselves or others for events that are beyond their control. *This attributional error, called the **illusion of control**, is the belief that we control events in our lives, even those that are actually influenced primarily or solely by external causes.* The illusion of control is reflected in the behavior of many gamblers, such as the slot player who thinks he can tell when a machine is ready to get hot by observing its patterns of payoff to other players.

Illusion of control

Attributional bias caused by the belief that we control events in our own lives that are really beyond our control.

Why do we hold on to the illusion that we are in control of such events? Most of us want to be in control of our own lives, and the feeling of being out of control can be very distressing, even when the uncontrollable event is highly negative. Thus, it may actually be less stressful to blame ourselves for losing a job in a round of company layoffs ("I should have seen it coming") than to acknowledge there was nothing we could do.

The illusion-of-control bias was demonstrated in an interesting experiment in which some subjects were given lottery tickets, and others were allowed to pick their own numbers. On the day of the lottery all subjects were urged individually to resell their tickets. Subjects who had not been permitted to choose their own tickets were more inclined to resell them. Furthermore, those subjects who had selected their own tickets and decided to resell them tended to demand higher resale prices than those who had not chosen their lottery numbers (Langer, 1975).

We have been talking about social perceptions and the inferences we make about other people's behavior. These perceptions all contribute to our attitudes about people, groups, and situations. Attitudes have been the subject of more research than any other topic in social psychology in attempts to both predict and explain human behavior. In the following section we explore this topic.

ATTITUDES

Many a student has heard an irritated teacher say: "You have a good head on your shoulders, but you have a bad attitude!" So, what exactly is an attitude? How does one acquire it, and how does one change it? *Basically, an attitude is a belief or an opinion to which a person aligns his/her behavior consistently over time.*

Attitude

Any learned, relatively enduring predisposition to respond in consistently favorable or unfavorable ways to certain people, groups, ideas, or situations.

Social psychologists Martin Fishbein and Icek Ajzen (1975) described **attitudes** as relatively enduring learned dispositions to respond in consistently favorable or unfavorable ways to certain people, groups, ideas, or situations. We use this definition because it points out that attitudes are learned, that they may change, and that they may predict behavior.

Acquiring Attitudes

How do we develop attitudes? As you might guess, attitudes are shaped by experiences, including our observations of behavior (both other people's and our own); classical and operant conditioning; and direct experiences with the *attitude object* (the people, ideas, or things about which we hold attitudes).

BEHAVIORAL OBSERVATION: We learn some behaviors by observing and imitating influential role models (Bandura, 1986). These same processes allow us to form our attitudes. Attitudes can be learned by the same process. Parents and peers have an especially strong influence on our attitudes. Thus, young people whose friends view adult authority figures with mistrust are likely to acquire this attitude, particularly if it serves a social adjustment function for them.

Observing Ourselves: Although it is commonly believed that attitudes cause behavior, the reverse may actually be more accurate. That is, our behaviors may determine our attitudes. Social psychologist Daryl Bem (1972) has proposed what he describes as a *self-perception theory*, which maintains that when we are not sure how we feel toward a particular attitude object, we sometimes infer our attitudes from our own behavior.

Attitudes can also be acquired via Classical conditioning or Operant conditioning (Inko & Melskon, 1969).

The Function of Attitudes

Whether we learn them from our own experiences or from observing others, attitudes serve a number of important functions in our lives (Brigham, 1986; DeBono, 1987; Tesser, 1990). **One is an understanding function:** *Attitudes provide a frame of reference that helps us structure and make sense out of the world and our experiences.* For example, your attitudes about what personal attributes you favor in a date provide you with a frame of reference for evaluating prospective romantic interests. If a person possesses behavioral dispositions you evaluate positively, you are likely to respond favorably to that individual.

Just as we rely on our own attitudes to evaluate unfamiliar situations or objects, we also rely on the attitudes of others. For instance, suppose a friend has just attended the first lecture in a class in which you are considering enrolling. Your first question to her will probably be something like, "Well, how did you like the class and the instructor?" If her attitude is positive, you will be more likely to sign up as well.

A second function of attitudes is a *social identification function.* The attitudes of others provide us with important information about what they are like, just as the attitudes we express tell others about us. That is why, when you date a person for the first time, you usually exchange information about favorite activities, food preferences, music interests, and so forth. Our overall assessment of other people is often strongly influenced by what we perceive to be their likes and dislikes.

A third function of attitudes is a *social adjustment function*. The attitudes we express sometimes allow us to identify with or gain approval from our peers.

All of the functions described above provide us with information about the probable consequences of our actions.

Do Attitudes Predict Behavior?

Attitudes, as you just learned, help you frame behavior, help you adjust socially, etc. However, do our attitudes always guide our actions? Consider the student who is strongly opposed to cheating but finds at exam time that she is doing so poorly in one course that her chances of acceptance into a graduate program are in jeopardy. In this situation, her motive to succeed coupled with her perceived failure may well have a stronger influence on her behavior than her attitude toward cheating.

To what extent do attitudes determine behavior? Social psychologists began investigating the relationship between attitudes and behavior over 70 years ago. In those early quasi-experiments the researchers found very little evidence to indicate a strong relationship between attitude and behavior. However, later research indicated that although any one particular behavior in any one particular situation might not reflect the influence of an attitude, several behaviors studied in several situations do show the influence of an underlying attitude. For example, in one study researchers measured people's attitudes toward environmental issues such as pollution control and conservation, and then observed subjects' behaviors over the next two months. Fourteen environmentally relevant behaviors were recorded, including recycling paper, picking up litter, and circulating petitions pertaining to clean environment issues. Considered individually, any one of these behaviors showed only a relatively small or moderate correlation with the subjects' environmental attitudes, but when these actions were treated collectively, attitudes and behaviors were strongly correlated (Weigel & Newman, 1976). *A clear implication of this finding is that in order to make an accurate judgment about someone's attitude toward a particular object, issue, or situation, we should observe as many attitude-reflective behaviors as possible.*

As we suspected from the start, studies using multiple behavior indices have suggested that attitudes are strong predictors of behavior. As the earlier example of attitudes toward cheating illustrated, however, our attitudes do not always predict our behaviors. What determines how influential our attitudes will be?

SOCIAL EXPECTATIONS AND BEHAVIOR One important variable is the degree to which other social factors influence our behavior. As long as other influences are minimized, our attitudes are likely to guide our behaviors. One influence that is particularly likely to mask the predictive relationship between attitudes and behavior is that of social expectations. For example, a young person who has a negative attitude toward drinking alcoholic beverages will usually say no when offered a drink, but might accept one when offered by prospective employers who have taken him to dinner after the interview. The need to conform to social expectations is particularly strong, and he may well have a glass of wine or a scotch despite his attitude toward alcohol consumption.

Another way that social expectations may influence our behavior is by augmenting our tendency to adopt stereotypical behavior of groups to which we belong. Could the stereotypes that black students perform more poorly on standardized academic tests as compared to Asians or Whites or that girls perform poorly as compared to boys in math skills may actually contribute to poor individual performance? Claude Steele of Stanford University has demonstrated that subjects do conform to negative group stereotypes by demonstrating poorer performance even when subjects are matched for ability. In several of his experiments black college students underperformed when compared to matched-ability white students on difficult verbal tests *when racial intellectual stereotypes were made salient.* This vulnerability of subjects to conform to negative stereotypes has been termed **stereotype threat** (Steele et al., 1995). Steele and others have observed a similar pattern of underperformance on math exams when testing similar-ability male and female students (Hunter et al., 2002).

Stereotype threat

A risk of confirming, as a self-characteristic, a negative stereotype about one's group. Stereotype threat may actually contribute significantly to poor academic performance by blacks and poor math performance by girls.

A number of studies have shown that attitudes are more strongly related to behavior when subjects recognize the relationship between their attitudes and their behavior (Snyder & Swann, 1976), or when they are made particularly self-conscious (Carver & Scheier, 1978; Diener & Wallbom, 1976). Studies in which subjects have repeatedly reminded themselves of their attitudes (for example, by filling out a series of attitude rating scales) have found that attitudes are more likely to predict behavior (Fazio, 1986; Powell & Fazio, 1984).

DOES OUR BEHAVIOR AFFECT OUR ATTITUDES? We have seen that our attitudes are often consistent with our behavior, but could this relationship exist because our attitudes are affected by our behavior? Several social psychologists suggest that our behavior may shape our attitudes (Chaiken & Stangor, 1987; Tesser, 1990).

A classic demonstration of the impact of actions on attitudes was provided by an experiment whose subjects were Duke University female students (Gergen, 1965). Initially, all subjects filled out a questionnaire rating their degree of self-esteem. Later, each subject was interviewed individually. Those in the first group were encouraged to provide honest and accurate self-descriptions; those in the second were urged to present themselves in a very positive light. Then after a reasonable time interval all the women again filled out the self-esteem questionnaire. Of those subjects who had provided presumably inflated descriptions of themselves, most showed a marked enhancement of their self-esteem. In contrast, the self-images of the women in the first group were unchanged. Apparently, even the brief experiences of role-playing a positive self-assessment actually boosted these women's attitudes about themselves.

Changing Attitudes

We have just seen that experiences such as taking a job or writing a glowing self-evaluation can produce a change in attitude, but how and why does this attitude change take place? *Part of the answer lies in our need for consistency.* Just as we attempt to fit new acquaintances into preexisting person schemas in order to minimize the differences between the familiar and the unfamiliar, we also are most secure when our attitudes are consistent both with other attitudes we hold and with our behavior. This is the basic idea behind the consistency theories, which see attitude change as "an attempt on the part of the individual to achieve cognitive equilibrium" (Penrod, 1986, p. 257). We consider two noteworthy consistency theories: balance theory and cognitive dissonance theory.

Balance theory

Theory that people are inclined to achieve consistency in their attitudes by balancing their beliefs and feelings about a particular issue, object, event, or situation against their attitudes about other people.

BALANCE THEORY **Balance theory** emerged from the writings of Fritz Heider (1946, 1958), who argued that people are inclined to achieve consistency in their attitudes by balancing their beliefs and feelings about a particular issue, object, event, or situation against their attitudes about other people. *According to this theory, the attitudes of other people play a significant role in determining whether we maintain our attitudes or change them.* For instance, suppose you are strongly opposed to abortion. Now, suppose a person you know named John also has a strong opinion about abortion. Balance theory predicts that if you like John, and if John also is opposed to abortion, you will feel no need to change your attitude because a balanced cognitive state will exist. Similarly, if you dislike John and John supports abortion, you will still be in a balanced state because your dislike of John will cause you to discount his opinions.

In contrast, you will be in an *unbalanced* state if you like John and discover that he supports abortion, or if you dislike John and find that he is firmly opposed to abortion, as you are. To restore balance, you might (1) decide that John is not such a good guy after all (which will then allow you to reject his opinions); (2) become a supporter of abortion so that you will not be identified with the viewpoint of someone you dislike; or (3) decide John is not such a bad guy after all.

Cognitive dissonance theory

Theory that people experience psychological discomfort or dissonance whenever two related cognitions or behaviors are in conflict.

COGNITIVE DISSONANCE THEORY Like balance theory, **cognitive dissonance theory** is concerned with the ways in which beliefs and attitudes are consistent or inconsistent with one another (Festinger, 1957). The cognitive dissonance model, however, focuses more closely on the internal psychological comfort or discomfort of the individual. *According to this theory, a person experiences a state of discomfort, or dissonance, whenever two related cognitions (thoughts or perceptions) are in conflict.* This discomfort motivates the person to achieve its reduction, either by realigning the key cognitive elements or by changing his/her attitude in the correct direction, in order to restore a state of consonance.

The theory of cognitive dissonance got its start from a real-life incident in which Leon Festinger, the originator of the theory, was involved. In the 1950s, Festinger investigated *a Dooms Day Christian cult* headed by a woman named Maria Keech, who was thought to be a prophet. The lady had handpicked a dozen of her followers and told them that God had revealed a secret to her, and if they promised to keep it, she would reveal it to them, her chosen people. All twelve promised. They were then told that God had said that he was angry with earthlings because they were sinning. *God had decided to obliterate all life on earth.* However, God was going to save the sinless prophet herself and her twelve faithful, if they wanted to be saved. He was going to send a spaceship for them so they could go live on a distant planet in a different galaxy! This *spaceship* was to come on Christmas Eve at midnight, and the thirteen of them kept a secret prayer vigil as they waited for the spaceship. However, the spaceship did not come. The prophet told the twelve faithful that God had contacted her again and told her that when He saw the thirteen of them praying so ardently, He had changed His mind, and He was not going destroy life on earth after all, so they were free to go home and live their lives as usual.

Since the prophecy had failed, Festinger thought that the church group would realize that the prophet was a hoax and that the church group would disband. *To his surprise, the members actually publicized the hitherto secret information and claimed that the prophet and her twelve faithful disciples had actually saved all mankind.* They actually recruited more people into their church! Newspapers, radio, and television stories now claimed that the Doom's Day cult had actually saved all mankind from a killer tidal wave that God was planning.

Festinger concluded that because it would have been emotionally very painful to admit that their leader was a fraud, the other eleven had changed their attitude and had strengthened their belief that the prophet and they themselves were to be thanked for their effort in saving all life.

Festinger later devised experiments to test his theory and the cognitive dissonance theory has been supported by numerous experimental studies. An example is a study of Princeton University men who had all indicated that they were opposed to banning alcohol from campus (Croyle & Cooper, 1983). These subjects were asked to write a letter that forcefully argued *in favor of* banning alcohol from campus. Half of these writers were reminded that their participation in this effort was purely voluntary; the other half was authoritatively ordered to register their arguments. At a later point, after the letter-writing process was completed, the researchers again assessed the subjects' attitudes toward the proposed ban.

As predicted by the cognitive dissonance theory, writing a letter in favor of a policy they opposed created cognitive dissonance in the Princeton subjects, most of whom reduced this dissonance by changing their attitudes. This shift in attitudes was more pronounced for those subjects who saw their participation as voluntary in nature. Apparently, if we act contrary to our prevailing attitudes, and if we cannot attribute our actions to coercion, we are more likely to see the rationale for what we are doing and we come to believe in it.

PERSUASION The balance theory and the cognitive dissonance theory help explain why we change our attitudes. They do not explain how a speaker can persuade members of an audience to change their attitudes, or why a talk with someone we respect can be enough to convert us to supporters of a particular cause.

We know that some persuasive efforts are more effective than others. What makes the difference? Carl Hovland and his colleagues at Yale University tackled this question in the 1950s, and found three elements to be particularly important in persuasive communications: the source of the message, the way in which the message is stated, and the characteristics of the message recipients (the audience) (Hovland et al., 1953).

The Communicator If a close friend you respect and trust becomes involved in a fringe religious movement and tries to persuade you to join, you are more likely to reevaluate your attitude toward such movements than if a person you did not like approached you. *Research demonstrates that the source or origin of a persuasive communication is a very important determinant of whether or not we change our attitude. The probability that persuasion will succeed is highest when the source of persuasion is seen as possessing any or all of the qualities of credibility, power, and attractiveness.*

A communicator with the quality of credibility is more likely to succeed in changing our attitude. **Two important elements of credibility are perceived expertise and trustworthiness.** Our perception *of expertise involves our assessment of the communicators' knowledge about a topic* and of his or her experience, education, and competence to speak authoritatively about it. For instance, when you watch the Super Bowl on television, you are less likely to dispute the views of a commentator who was once a football pro than those of your roommate, who has no athletic experience.

The second important element of credibility is *trustworthiness—our perception of a communicator as being basically honest.* Trustworthiness is important because we typically make attributions about why a person is advocating a particular position. As we might predict from the correspondent inference theory discussed earlier, our perception of trustworthiness is enhanced when the communicator seems to be arguing against his or her own best interests, or when the content of the message is not what we expect. For example, one investigation found that university students were more inclined to be persuaded by arguments against pornography if they perceived that the communicator was opposed to censorship than if the communicator favored censorship (Wood & Eagly, 1981).

Another factor that influences how persuasive a communicator will be is power. At least as it is measured by overt expression, attitude change is particularly likely to occur when these three conditions are met: (1) the communicator has the power to administer reinforcers or punishers to the target; (2) the communicator very much wants his or her message to have the desired effect on the target; and (3) the target knows the communicator will be able to evaluate whether or not she or he conforms to the message (McGuire, 1969; Rosenbaum & Rosenbaum, 1975). In view of these findings, it is not surprising that children often express attitudes similar to those of their parents, and that low-level management people may mirror the attitudes of higher-level executives.

A third strong influence on a communicator's effectiveness is attractiveness. A physically attractive communicator is often more effective than one whose appearance is either average or unattractive (Kelman, 1965; Mills & Aronson, 1965). *Attractiveness is influenced not only by physical looks, however, but also by likability, pleasantness, and perceived similarity to the audience.* A communicator who does not have these qualities is usually less effective in changing people's attitudes than one who does.

The Message Just as the source of a message has a strong influence on whether we are persuaded to change our attitude, the message itself is also a critical factor. One factor is the degree of discrepancy between the message and the audience's viewpoint. If the discrepancy is too great, the audience may discount or dismiss the message while too little discrepancy may result in the audience failing to perceive any difference of opinion or persuasive intent (Hovland et al., 1957; Peterson & Koulack, 1969). *Thus, attitude change is often greatest at moderate levels of discrepancy.*

In some cases, messages will be more effective if they appeal to emotion (particularly the emotion of fear) than if they appeal to logic. However, people who are well informed and personally concerned about a particular issue may be persuaded more effectively by logic than by emotional appeals (Petty & Cacioppo, 1986; Petty et al., 1983). Although appeals to fear are sometimes effective, the relationship between fear and persuasion is very complex and difficult to generalize.

For example, in one early study researchers used three separate messages to sway attitudes about oral hygiene. Subjects in the high-fear group were shown horrific color slides of rotting teeth and diseased gums and were told that these terrible conditions were the direct result of poor oral hygiene. Those in the moderate-fear group heard a message about the importance of good oral hygiene illustrated by pictures of mild gum infections and tooth decay. Finally, those in the low-fear group were simply told that failure to brush regularly could lead to tooth decay and gum disease; no pictures were used. The high-fear message was found to be the least effective in changing behavior (and presumably attitudes) whereas the low-fear message produced the greatest change in dental habits (Janis & Feshbach, 1953).

How can this result be explained? Researchers interpreted the results as indicating that fear may promote attitude change only up to a certain point. When tension becomes too great, however, people may attempt to reduce their anxiety by blocking out or discounting the message (McGuire, 1968a). Several later studies have demonstrated that, under some conditions, messages with moderate-fear appeal may be effective in changing attitudes and behavior. Researchers have also discovered that if the source had high credibility and if the fear-arousing message contained clear information about what to do to avoid the fearful consequences, people are more likely to be persuaded by the message (Leventhal & Nerenz, 1983; Rogers & Mewborn, 1976).

Novelty is another message characteristic that can make a difference. Generally speaking, messages that are presented in an unusual or novel fashion are more effective than time-worn arguments. People tend to tune out messages they have heard too many times before. Also, the expectation of something new or novel makes a message more attractive (Sears & Freedman, 1965).

Still another quality that helps determine how influential a message will be is whether it presents one or both sides of the issue. Interestingly, the effect of this variable seems to depend on the characteristics of the audience. A one-sided argument seems to be more effective if the audience is poorly educated and or unfamiliar with the issue (Chu, 1967; Hovland et al., 1949), whereas a two-sided presentation works better with a well-educated, well-informed audience (Lumsdaine & Janis, 1953). In fact, well-informed people may react strongly against one-sided arguments in order to protect their sense of free will or as a reaction against feeling coerced into adopting a particular view—a process called *psychological reactance* (Jones & Brehm, 1970).

The Audience We have just seen that an audience's intelligence and knowledge can make a difference in the effectiveness of tactics such as presenting one or both sides of an issue. A variety of other personality factors also seem to influence people's susceptibility to persuasion. For one, *the age of an audience seems to make a difference.* Researchers have found that teenagers and young adults, whose attitudes and opinions are not yet as well defined as those of older people, are more likely to shift their attitudes in response to a persuasive communication (Sears, 1979).

Another factor that may make a difference is the self-esteem of listeners. Studies conducted in the late 1960s indicated that people with high self-esteem seem generally less likely to yield to persuasion than those with low self-esteem (Cook, 1970; McGuire, 1969). This finding was interpreted as indicating that people with a very positive self-image have confidence in their opinions, which they may view as being more credible than those of the communicator. A more recent investigation, however, reported that people with high self-esteem are just as easily persuaded as those with a low self-image (Baumeister & Covington, 1985). More research is needed to clarify these mixed findings.

The evidence has also been unclear regarding the impact of listeners' intelligence on attitude change. For a persuasive message to be effective, an audience must both comprehend it and be willing to yield to the views of another.

When the persuader is able to get the audience to think seriously about the points he or she is making, the chances of attitude change are enhanced (Petty & Cacioppo, 1986). To the extent that the audience members are open to a particular viewpoint, getting them to think about and elaborate on the message in their own minds is likely to increase the probability of attitude change.

PREJUDICE

Prejudice

Negative, unjustifiable, and inflexible attitude toward a group and its members.

Stereotypes

Preconceived and oversimplified beliefs and expectations about the traits of members of a particular group that do not account for individual differences.

Discrimination

In classical and operant conditioning, the process by which responses are restricted to specific stimuli. In social psychology, the behavioral consequence of prejudice in which one group is treated differently from another group.

Prejudice *is a negative, unjustifiable, and inflexible attitude toward a group and its members that is based on erroneous information.* This definition contains three important elements. First, prejudice is characterized by very negative or hostile feelings toward all members of a group, often a minority, without any attention to individual differences among members of that group. Second, prejudice is based on inaccurate or incomplete information. The third element is its inflexibility. **Prejudice demonstrates great resistance to change even in the face of compelling contradictory evidence.**

Prejudice is built on **stereotypes**, preconceived and oversimplified beliefs and expectations about the traits of members of a particular group that do not account for individual differences. These stereotyped beliefs, coupled with hostile feelings, often predispose people to act in an abusive and discriminatory fashion toward members of a disliked or hated group. The widespread incidence of **discrimination** (the behavioral consequence of prejudice in which victims of prejudice are treated differently from other people) throughout the world reveals what a profoundly adverse impact prejudice has on human society. In almost every daily newspaper and every evening on the news there are reports of violence between groups fueled by prejudice. Ethnic groups within a nation war with each other and sometimes that leads to a catastrophe such as genocide, with which Human History is replete.

To devalue or feel contempt for women, overweight people, or homosexuals is to be prejudiced. To avoid hiring, associating with, renting to, or acknowledging the contributions of such people is to discriminate. How can prejudice be explained? We turn next to that question.

Out-groups, In-groups, and the Causes of Prejudice

Central to any explanation of prejudice is our inclination to define ourselves at least partly according to the particular group to which we belong. We all tend to categorize ourselves according to race, age, education, creed, economic level, and so forth—a process that inevitably leads us to categorize people who do not share the same characteristics as "different." The result is that we divide our world into two groups: us and "them" (Baron &

In-group

In social psychology, the group in which people include themselves when they divide the world into "us" and "them."

In-group bias

Tendency to see one's own group in a favorable light.

Out-group

The "them" group when individuals divide the world into "us" and "them."

Byrne, 1987). The very process of being in the "us" or **in-group** category tends to create an **in-group bias** (a tendency to see one's own group in a favorable light) while at the same time inducing a negative attitude or prejudice against the **out-group.**

A number of studies have demonstrated that in-group bias and prejudice toward the out-group often occur when experimental subjects are separated into we–they groups based on trivial factors that bear no relationship to real-life social categories (Tajfel, 1982; Tajfel & Turner, 1979; Turner, 1984; Wilder, 1981): *By perceiving their in-group as superior to an out-group, people seem to be attempting to enhance their self-esteem.*

COMPETITION BETWEEN GROUPS If we already tend to view the world in terms of us and them, the addition of another ingredient—*competition for jobs, power, or other limited resources*—adds to the likelihood that hostility and prejudice will develop. In such circumstances the more dominant group may exploit and discriminate against a less powerful group. This tendency was demonstrated during the development of America, when competition for land between European settlers and Native Americans led to prejudice, mistreatment, and extreme acts of discrimination against the minority Native Americans (Brigham & Weissbach, 1972). Today in the United States, competition for jobs contributes to prejudice between European-Americans and Hispanics, Native Americans and German immigrants, Asians and European-Americans, Cuban immigrants and other Floridians, and of course, African-Americans and European Americans.

Inter-racial and inter-ethnic tensions such as these *tend to increase during poor economic times and lessen as the economy improves.* Likewise, in a classic experiment, Muzafar Sherif and his colleagues (1961) documented how the introduction of competition between two clearly defined groups of boys transformed a harmonious atmosphere into one of prejudice and hostility, simply because of the competition between "us" and "them," even though they were all of the same ethnicity and belonged to the same cultural group.

FRUSTRATION, SCAPEGOATING, AND PREJUDICE Just as competition can lead to hostility and prejudice under certain conditions, so can frustration. *People who are frustrated by their lack of accomplishments or by adverse living conditions often* ***vent their frustration on scapegoats*** *whom they perceive as being less powerful than themselves, such as members of a minority group.* An example of how frustration may be tied to prejudice is provided by data relating economic conditions in the South from 1882 to 1930 to violence of whites toward blacks. *Research has shown that whenever the price of cotton decreased during this period, the lynching of blacks by whites increased (Hovland & Sears, 1940).*

The relationship between frustration and prejudice was also demonstrated in an experiment in which researchers first measured subject's attitudes toward a variety of minority groups, then frustrated the subjects by denying them a chance to see a good movie and making them complete a series of difficult tasks instead. The subjects' attitudes toward the same minority groups were measured a second time, after this frustrating experience. This time they demonstrated a marked increase in prejudice not exhibited by con-

Dr. Martin Luther King, Jr., marching for civil rights in an effort to eradicate social prejudice and injustice.

trol subjects who had not experienced the frustrating condition (Miller & Bugelski, 1948). In related experiments, students who are made to feel like failures have demonstrated an increased tendency to express negative attitudes toward others (Amabile & Glazebrook, 1982; Crocker et al., 1987).

SOCIAL LEARNING AND PREJUDICE We have seen that many of our attitudes are acquired by observing and emulating other people, particularly respected role models. Prejudice is also learned by this type of observational learning. For example, research has shown that children's racial attitudes are often closely aligned with those of their parents (Ashmore & Del Boca, 1976; Katz, 1976; Stephan & Rosenfield, 1978). Children may internalize the prejudices they observe in their parents and, in some cases, learning this lesson may earn the reward of approval from their parents or others. Sometimes, even children whose parents are relatively free of prejudice may acquire prejudicial attitudes from other influential sources such as peers, books, and the television and movie media, which often promote stereotypical beliefs and disparaging assessments of minority group members.

A "Prejudiced Personality"

We all have experienced competition and frustration, and most of us have probably observed incidents of prejudice and discrimination. Nevertheless, prejudice is not an attitude that we all adopt. *What kinds of qualities predispose a person to develop prejudices?* Some research in the late 1940s at the University of California at Berkeley sheds some light on this question. Here, researchers investigated the dynamics of *anti-Semitism* (prejudice against Jewish people) and ***ethnocentrism (general prejudice toward all out-groups).*** Their findings led them to describe a personality characterized by intolerance, emotional coldness, rigidity, unquestioning submission to higher authority, stereotyped thinking, and identification with power as particularly prone to developing prejudicial attitudes. A person possessing this cluster of characteristics was labeled an **authoritarian personality** (Adorno et al., 1950). These researchers developed a rating scale to detect people with authoritarian personalities, called the *Potentiality for Fascism Scale,* or *F Scale.* Table 13.1 presents some items from the F Scale with which an authoritarian personality would be likely to agree.

Authoritarian personality

Personality characterized by intolerance, emotional coldness, rigidity, submission to higher authority, stereotyped thinking, and identification with power.

How does an authoritarian personality develop? The researchers examined the backgrounds of subjects who scored high on the F Scale and found that such individuals shared certain common features in the manner in which they were reared. *Their parents tended to be harsh disciplinarians who used threats, physical punishment, and fear of reprisal to enforce desired behavior.* Children were not permitted to express aggressive behaviors themselves, and love was often withheld or made contingent on "being good." As a result, the children were inclined to grow up feeling hostile toward their parents but at the same time dependent on them. They were also fearful of authority figures and generally insecure.

We have seen how the people around us may change our feelings about certain people, groups, ideas, or situations. However, **social influence**—the efforts by others to alter our feelings, beliefs, and behavior—extends beyond merely changing how we feel about something. In this section we examine conformity, compliance, and obedience, all of which are forms of social influence that affect our behavior.

Social influence

Efforts by others to alter our feelings, beliefs, and behavior.

TABLE 13.1 Selected Items from the F Scale

1. America is getting so far from the true American way of life that force may be necessary to restore it.
2. Homosexuality is a particularly rotten form of delinquency and ought to be severely punished.
3. There are some activities so flagrantly un-American that, when responsible officials won't take the proper steps, the wide-awake citizen should take the law into his own hands.
4. Obedience and respect for authority are the most important virtues children should learn.

SOURCE: Adopted from Adorno et al., 1950.

SOCIAL INFLUENCES ON BEHAVIOR

Conformity

Conformity

Tendency to change or modify behaviors so that they are consistent with those of other people.

Conformity refers to a tendency to change or modify our own behaviors so that they are consistent with those of other people. Often these shifts in opinion or actions are accompanied, at least to some degree, by a perceived social pressure to conform. In the 1950s, a slew of experiments studied obedience, conformity, and the influence of authority primarily to understand the behavior of ordinary German folk during the Holocaust. Psychologists wanted to know why these people had obeyed and conformed to the Nazis led by Hitler and had shown such merciless behavior such as marching even innocent Jewish children to their deaths. Was this behavior unique to the Germans, or could any one of us, subjected to the similar circumstances, behave similarly? We will start the discussion of conformity with a classic experiment.

THE ASCH EXPERIMENTS In 1951, Solomon Asch conducted a now-classic experiment in which seven men sat around a table and were asked to make a series of comparison judgments on the length of various lines displayed on slides. Six of the men were confederates of the experimenter; the one subject was unaware that he was being set up (Asch, 1951). *None of the tasks was ambiguous; the correct answer was always readily apparent.* The experimental design called for each group member to provide his response in turn as Asch solicited answers sequentially from each man, moving from his left to right around the table. The naive subject was always located so that he was the sixth of the seven subjects to make his judgment. There were 18 such slides, one per trial, in all. On the first two trials, all seven chose the correct line. On 12 of the remaining 16 trials, however, the confederates unanimously chose the wrong comparison line.

The only real subject in the experiment was number 6; the others were confederates of the experimenter. *With five people having made an obviously incorrect choice regarding a line in plain view, how did the subject respond?* Generally, the subject showed signs of strain, leaning forward, straining, double-checking, and glancing around at the other group members, and *then conforming and giving the same incorrect answer the others had given.* About one in every three subjects adjusted his responses to match the incorrect judgments of the confederates in half or more of the 12 conformity trials. *Only 25 percent of the subjects completely resisted group pressure by making the correct response on all 12 trials.*

Asch interviewed the subjects after the experiment was completed. He found that in some cases subjects had gone along with the group consensus against their better judgment because they did not want to appear different from the others. However, some of the conforming subjects stated that they had thought that the majority opinion was probably correct and that their own perceptions were inaccurate. *Pressure to conform is pretty strong in a group situation because we don't want to be laughed at or be seen as oddballs.*

FIGURE 13.1 Line Comparison Task from Asch's Experiment

Which comparison line(s) is/are equal to the standard line?

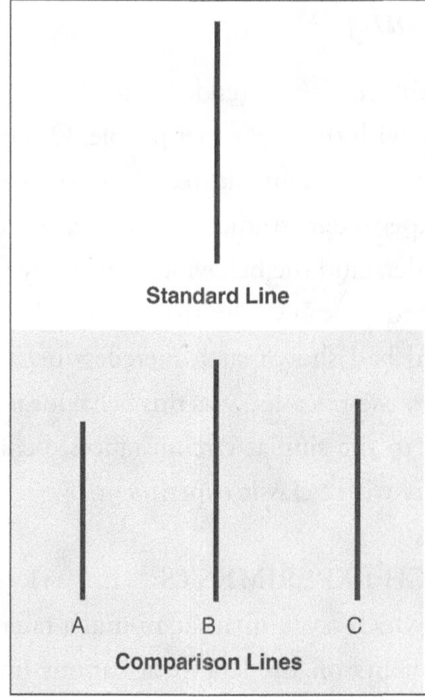

WHEN ARE WE MOST LIKELY TO CONFORM? In the years since Asch's classic study, numerous additional experiments have studied conformity. In general this research has found that our tendency to conform will be increased in situations in which some conditions are met. We list these conditions briefly as a conclusion to our discussion of conformity.

1. ***Unanimity of the majority group.*** We are much more likely to conform if the majority group is unanimous (Allen, 1965; Allen & Levine, 1969); *even one dissenter greatly reduces our inclination to conform.* Asch found that if one dissident agreed with the subject, the subject was almost 18 percent less likely to conform (Asch, 1951).

2. ***Perception that the majority of group members are acting independently.*** If we perceive that the other members of a group are acting independently of one another, we are more likely to conform than if we sense some collusion among them (Wilder, 1978).

3. ***Majority group size.*** The size of the group makes a difference. If there are at least three or four other people in the group, we are more likely to conform. Further increases in group size generally do not increase the likelihood of conformity, and may even decrease it (Gerard et al., 1968; Tanford & Penrod, 1984).

4. ***Familiarity with the attitude object.*** If we have no preconceived notions about the attitude object, we are more likely to act in a conforming manner than if this is not the case (Berkowitz, 1986).

5. ***Low self-esteem.*** People whose sense of personal self-worth is low (Santee & Maslach, 1982) or who are especially concerned about social relationships (Mullen, 1983; Thibaut & Strickland, 1956) are more likely to conform than people with higher self-esteem or less regard for social relationships.

6. ***Perceptions about other group members.*** We are more likely to conform if we consider the other group members to be of higher status than ourselves (Forsyth, 1983; Giordano, 1983), or if we have high regard for the other group members (Berkowitz, 1954, 1986). We are also more likely to conform if we perceive other group members as having power over us (in the sense of being able to administer reinforcers or punishers) (Berkowitz, 1986), or if we know that other group members will be able to observe our actions (Berkowitz, 1954).

Compliance

Compliance

Form of social influence in which people alter their behavior in response to direct requests from others, which usually involve a degree of coercion.

Although both conformity and compliance involve yielding to some pressure exerted by others, **compliance** involves an element of coercion as well, in that it takes place in situations where we alter our behavior in response to direct requests from others. Compliance is a very common form of social influence. We all experience a barrage of requests daily—ranging from friends, lovers, or family members asking us to change certain aspects of our behavior to requests by politicians or salespersons for votes or purchase of goods. Social psychologists have noted a number of techniques or forms of pressure that people use to increase the likelihood of compliance with their requests. Two of these methods are the foot-in-the-door technique and the door-in-the-face technique.

Foot-in-the-door technique

Technique for encouraging compliance in which a person is first asked to agree to a relatively minor request that serves as a setup for a more major request.

FOOT-IN-THE-DOOR TECHNIQUE Researchers have demonstrated that sometimes the best road to compliance is to begin by getting a person to agree to a relatively minor or trivial request that serves as a setup for a second, more major request (which is the actual goal). This so-called **foot-in-the-door technique** (Freedman & Fraser, 1966) is widely used by salespeople who attempt to produce a favorable attitude toward their product. For example, if a car salesperson can get you to comply with an initial request to "come in the office and we will run some numbers," you are more likely to develop the attitude that "I need that car." It has been suggested that the success of the foot-in-the-door technique is related to the fact that when people comply with a request, they begin to perceive themselves as "the kind of person who does this sort of thing." This self-perception then inclines them to make even greater commitments to a particular line of requests in order to be consistent with their perceived self-image (Eisenberg et al., 1987; Pliner et al., 1974).

DOOR-IN-THE-FACE TECHNIQUE Suppose you are moving to another apartment and you want your husky neighbor to help you move your piano. Anticipating a likely negative response to your request, you first ask if he would mind spending the afternoon helping you move all your stuff. As expected, he begs off, claiming a heavy study load. Next, you ask if he would have just a few minutes to help with the piano. How can he say no to such a reasonable request after he has already "slammed the door in your face" in response to the larger request? While some people might say no to both requests, research demonstrates that we are often more inclined to comply with a moderate request if we have already refused a larger one than if the smaller request is presented alone (Cialdini, 1985).

Door-in-the-face technique

Method for encouraging compliance in which an unreasonable request is followed by a more minor, reasonable request (which is the requester's goal in the first place).

This **door-in-the-face technique**, which is essentially the opposite of the foot-in-the-door method, was demonstrated in an interesting study in which college students were asked to serve as unpaid counselors to delinquent youth for two years at the rate of two hours per week. Predictably, none complied with this request. However, when presented with a second, far more moderate request to take the delinquents on a short outing to the zoo, 50 percent complied with this request. In contrast, only 17 percent of a control group of students agreed to this smaller request when it was presented alone (Cialdini et al., 1975).

Obedience

Obedience

Social influence in which we alter our behavior in response to commands or orders from people perceived as having power or authority.

All of us succumb routinely to social influence by conforming to behavioral standards established by others or by complying with the requests of associates. Less commonly, social influence takes the form of **obedience**, in which we alter our behavior in response to commands or orders from people we may perceive as having power or authority.

MILGRAM'S EXPERIMENTS ON OBEDIENCE TO AUTHORITY In the summer of 1961, social psychologist Stanley Milgram conducted a dramatic study to understand how many people obey authority and why they comply (1963). Milgram sought to determine if subjects would inflict considerable pain on others merely because an authority figure instructed them to do so. His all-male subjects thought they were participating in a study of the effects of punishment on learning. They were told to use an intercom system to present problems to another person (a total stranger who was actually an accomplice of the experimenter) who was strapped in a chair in another room, and to administer a shock each time the "learner" gave the wrong answer to a problem. Labeled switches on the "shock apparatus" ranged from a low of 15 volts to a high of 450 volts; subjects were instructed to increase the voltage with each successive error the learner made.

According to design, the learner made many errors. The result was a progressive escalation of shock intensity that posed a serious dilemma for the subjects, virtually all of whom exhibited high levels of stress and discomfort as they administered the shocks. Should they continue subjecting the learner to pain, or should they refuse to go on? Whenever they hesitated or protested, the experimenter pressured them to continue, using such commands as "It is absolutely essential that you continue" or "You have no other choice, you must go on."

Despite the fact that all subjects were volunteers, paid in advance, and obviously distressed, only a minority failed to exhibit total obedience. In fact, fully 65 percent proceeded to the final 450-volt level! A number of subsequent studies conducted with different research populations reported findings similar to those of Milgram (Kilham & Mann, 1974; Miller, 1986; Shanab & Yahya, 1977).

Why do people succumb to such destructive instances of obedience? This question has been explored and debated by both social scientists and laypersons. Social psychologists Robert Baron and Donn Byrne (1987) have outlined three reasons why people may respond to social influence in the form of destructive obedience. First, many people seem to believe that their personal accountability for their actions is somehow diminished or relieved by those authority figures who issue the commands.

In Milgram's research, subjects were told at the outset that the experimenter rather than the participants was responsible for the learner's well-being. Thus, we can see how they may have felt less responsible for their own actions. It is disheartening to know, however, that this same logic was employed by the Nazi war criminal Adolf Eichmann, and Lieutenant William Calley, who was court-martialed for the 1968 massacre of Vietnamese civilians at My Lai, both of whom justified their acts by claiming, "I was only following orders." In May of 2005, during the Iraq war, Lynndie England of Abu Ghraib Prison scandal notoriety said she caved in to peer-pressure. Her lawyers argued that she was only following orders from higher ups. Although she eventually did plead guilty of abusing prisoners of the Iraq war, a military judge threw out her guilty plea because he didn't think that, at that time she did it, she knew that what she was doing was illegal, or so he said. Some people were of the opinion that the judge may have rejected her plea because her immediate superior and boyfriend testified that they all were following orders from their superiors.

This goes to show that Adolf Eichmann and others like him a couple of generations ago were not all that different from Lynndie England or her boyfriend from today's youth.

A second factor contributing to obedience is that authority figures often possess highly visible symbols of their power or status that make it difficult to resist their dictates (symbols such as the white coat and title of a researcher, or the uniform and rank of a military officer). The impact of these external trappings of power was demonstrated in one experiment in which people were randomly stopped on the street and ordered to give a dime to a person in need of parking meter change. Subjects were decidedly more inclined to obey this order if it was issued by someone wearing a firefighter's uniform than if the source of the command was dressed in a business suit or laborer's clothes (Bushman, 1984).

Finally, people often comply with orders, even orders that are potentially destructive in nature, if they are sucked in by a series of graduated demands, beginning with seemingly innocuous or harmless orders. These orders then gradually escalate to orders of a more serious or potentially destructive nature. For example, a corporate executive might request that a supposedly loyal employee, who has a friend who works at a competitor company, ask the friend if his or her employer plans to introduce a new product line. Later, such requests might escalate to orders to ask specific questions about the nature of the products on the drawing board, followed by commands to conduct outright industrial espionage. In a sense, this escalation is what occurred with Milgram's subjects, who were first required to deliver only mild shocks followed by progressively more intense punishment. The problem with such a gradual escalation of demand intensity is that a person is often unable to distinguish a definite point at which disobedience is clearly a more appropriate course of action than obedience.

INTERPERSONAL BEHAVIOR: ATTRACTION AND AGGRESSION

Attraction

We have been exploring how we form perceptions of people, how we develop attitudes, and how other people influence our behavior. The most influential people in our adult lives are often the people to whom we are closest—our good friends and our partners in long-term intimate relationships. In this section we first analyze why we feel attracted to certain people as friends and lovers, and then we explore some of the causes of aggression.

FACTORS THAT CONTRIBUTE TO INTERPERSONAL ATTRACTION Have you ever had the experience of meeting a total stranger—at a party, on the first day of school, or in a bookstore—and feeling immediately that you liked one another? If so, you may have wondered what it was that made you feel close to the other person. This question has been the topic of research for over four decades, and the answers that social psychologists have found center on four primary variables: proximity, similarity, reciprocity, and physical attractiveness.

Proximity

Perceptual grouping principle whereby, all else being equal, we tend to organize perceptions by grouping elements that are the nearest to each other. In social psychology, the geographical nearness of one person to another, which is an important factor in interpersonal attraction.

Proximity Although most people overlook **proximity**, or geographical nearness, in listing factors that attracted them to a particular person, it is one of the most important variables. *We often develop close relationships with people whom we see frequently* in our neighborhoods, in school, at work, or at church or synagogue.

A classic study of the effect of proximity on attraction was conducted by Leon Festinger and his colleagues (1950). They evaluated friendship patterns among married MIT students living in a housing development consisting of 17 two-story buildings with five apartments per floor. All of the residents were asked to name their three best friends among residents of the housing development. These friends almost invariably lived in the same building, with next-door neighbors being the most likely to be named as a friend and the next most likely living two doors away. When the friendship ratings of all participants were pooled, certain people emerged as being widely liked (that is, included in the lists of many of the residents). The people who were "widely liked," lived in apartments close to heavily trafficked areas such as mailboxes, stairway entries, and exits. Not coincidentally, people with the fewest friends lived in more the out-of-the-way apartments.

The profound impact of proximity on interpersonal attraction has been confirmed by other research (Saegert et al., 1973; Segal, 1974). Why is it such a powerful factor? Research has shown that when we are repeatedly exposed to novel stimuli—whether they are unfamiliar musical selections, nonsense syllables, works of art, or human faces—our liking for such stimuli increases (Brooks & Watkins, 1989; Moreland & Zajonc, 1982; Nuttin, 1987; Zajonc, 1968, 1970). *This phenomenon, called the* **mere exposure effect**, *explains in part why we are attracted to people in close proximity to us.*

Mere exposure effect

Phenomenon by which repeated exposure to novel stimuli tends to increase an individual's preference for such stimuli.

Similarity A second factor attracting people to one another is **similarity**. Contrary to the old adage that opposites attract, *people who are attracted to one another often share common beliefs, values, attitudes, interests, and intellectual ability* (Byrne, 1971; Byrne & Griffitt, 1973; Byrne et al., 1966, 1968, 1986; Judd et al., 1983; Moreland & Zajonc, 1982; Wetzel & Insko, 1982). This tendency was demonstrated in one study in which 13 men expressed their attitudes independently on 44 separate issues prior to being housed together for 10 days in the close quarters of a fallout shelter. At intervals of one, five, and nine days of confinement, each subject was asked to list the three men in the group he would like to remain and the three he would most like to see removed from the shelter. The results provided consistent and clear indications that the participants wanted to keep the men who were most like them (judged by the earlier attitude assessments) and to get rid of those who were least like them (Griffitt & Veitch, 1974).

Similarity

In perception, the principle that we tend to group elements that are similar to each other. In social psychology, similarity of beliefs, interests, and values is recognized as a factor attracting people to one another.

Why do we feel drawn to people who are like us? For one thing, people with similar attitudes and interests are often inclined to enjoy participating in the same kinds of leisure activities. Even more important, however, we are more likely to communicate well with people whose ideas and opinions are similar to ours, and communication is a very important aspect of enduring relationships. It is also *reassuring to be with similar people, for they confirm our view of the world,* validate our own experiences, and support our opinions and beliefs (Arrowood & Short, 1973; Sanders, 1982). Thus, mutual reinforcement of behavior is important in maintaining close relations with others.

Reciprocity No doubt all of us have had personal experience (on both the delivery and recipient end) with the old adage "Flattery will get you everything." *People tend to react positively to flattery, compliments, and other expressions of liking and affection.* In the study of interpersonal attraction, this concept is reflected in ***the principle of reciprocity***, which holds that when we are the recipients of expressions of liking and loving, we tend to respond in kind, particularly if our own self-esteem is low (Byrne & Murnen, 1988; Jacobs et al., 1971). Furthermore, *when we are provided with indications that someone likes us, we tend to have warm feelings about these people and to respond positively to them*—a reaction that often influences them to like us even more (Curtis & Miller, 1988).

Reciprocity

The tendency to respond to others in a way similar to how they respond to, or treat us.

The key words in these descriptions of reciprocity are "tend to." We don't always like people who appear to like us. In some cases, some of us have experienced the often unsettling realization that we are the love object of someone who engenders only mildly positive feelings in us. Furthermore, when people perceive that expressions of liking directed toward them are merely part of a phony ingratiation strategy rather than genuine reflections of affection, reciprocity of liking and affection is unlikely to occur. These exceptions notwithstanding, ***undisguised, genuine expressions of liking or loving often serve as important stimulants to interpersonal attraction.***

Physical attractiveness

Physical features that persons of the opposite sex find appealing.

Physical Attractiveness **Physical attractiveness** may profoundly influence our impressions of the people we meet. In general, research reveals that *physically attractive people are more likely to be sought as friends.* Attractive people also impress potential employers favorably, and are more likely to be treated better, and to be perceived as more likable, interesting, sensitive, competent, and socially skilled than people of average or unattractive appearance (Baron, 1986; Cash & Janda, 1984; Dion & Berscheid, 1974; Dion & Dion, 1987; Hatfield & Sprechler, 1986; Lerner & Lerner, 1977; Snyder et al., 1977; Solomon, 1987).

But what determines physical attractiveness? Do you think that both sexes are equally influenced by physical attractiveness in forming impressions of people they meet and in selecting a mate?

A recent cross-cultural study of sex differences in human mate preferences provided strong evidence that men worldwide place greater value than women do on mates who are both young and physically attractive. In this study, conducted by University of Michigan psychologist David Buss (1989; 1990), over 10,000 subjects from 37 samples drawn from 33 countries on six continents and five islands (African, Asian, European, North and South American, and Oceanian cultures) were asked to rate the importance of a wide range of personal attributes in potential mates. These personal characteristics included such qualities as dependable character, good looks, good financial prospects, intelligence, sociability, and chastity.

In contrast to the apparent widespread male emphasis on youth and beauty, *women in these cultures are more inclined to place greater value on potential mates who are somewhat older, have good financial prospects, and are dependable and industrious.* This is not to say that physical attractiveness was unimportant in influencing mate selection among the women of these varied cultures. In fact, many of these women rated physical attractiveness as important, albeit less significant than earning potential.

What accounts for the apparent consistency across so many cultures in what males and females find attractive in a potential mate? *And why do males rate physical attractiveness and youth as most important while females rate earning potential and dependability most important?* According to Buss (1989; 1990), evolution has biased mate preferences in humans as it has in other animals. Males are attracted to younger, physically attractive females because these characteristics are good predictors of reproductive value. That is, a younger female has more reproductive years remaining than an older female. Physical attractiveness is important because characteristics such as smooth unblemished skin, good muscle tone, lustrous hair, and full lips are strong cues to reproductive value. On the other hand, females tend to find older established males more attractive because these characteristics are the best predictors of successful rearing of her offspring. That is, females prefer a mate with wealth, a better territory, or a higher rank. Youth and physical attractiveness are less important to females because male fertility is less age-related than it is for females.

Additional evidence that evolution may have biased our perceptions of attractiveness also comes from studies of young infants. A fascinating study conducted by Judith Langlois and her colleagues (1987) at the University of Texas at Austin revealed that infants from two to eight months old demonstrated marked preferences for attractive faces. When they were shown pairs of color slides of the faces of adult women previously rated by other adults for attractiveness, the infants demonstrated a marked inclination to look longer at the most attractive face in the pair. These findings challenge the commonly held assumption that standards of attractiveness are learned through gradual exposure to the current cultural standard of beauty and are merely "in the eye of the beholder" (p. 363).

Aggression

All of us, at some time or another, have been victimized by the aggressive behavior of others, whether it is by someone who knowingly initiates a false rumor about us, a parent who strikes us in a fit of anger, or a teammate who ridicules our athletic ability.

Interpersonal aggression

Any physical or verbal behavior intended to hurt another person.

Criminal violence is an extreme form of **interpersonal aggression**—*that is, any physical or verbal behavior intended to hurt another person.* Many instances of interpersonal aggression may not qualify as criminal acts, but they can nevertheless be very hurtful. Why do people behave aggressively? Explanations have focused on both biological and psychological processes. We look briefly at the evidence for each.

BIOLOGICAL BASES OF AGGRESSION The biological perspective has been approached by a number of researchers and theorists who seek to understand the biological factors that underlie social behaviors in all animal species, including humans.

There is considerable evidence that aggressive tendencies may be influenced by hormonal factors (Bell & Hepper, 1987). One study demonstrated that boys and girls who were exposed to high levels of androgens before birth were found to be significantly more aggressive than their same-sexed siblings who had normal hormonal exposure (Reinisch, 1981). Likewise, many studies have revealed strong correlations between testosterone or androgen levels and aggression in humans (Birger et al., 2003; Cashdan, E. 2003).

Other research has provided convincing evidence that aggressive behavior often results when certain regions within the limbic systems of the brains of humans and other animals are stimulated through implanted electrodes, lesions, or other abnormal physiological processes (Moyer, 1983).

Some researchers have also linked genetic factors with aggression. For example, Finnish psychologist Kirsti Lagerspetz (1979) selected the most and least aggressive animals from a large sample of mice, and then bred the fighters with one another and the nonaggressive mice with one another. *After 25 generations, she had two distinct strains of mice: a vicious, super-aggressive strain and a docile, passive strain.* Although such experiments suggest that human aggression may have a link with heredity, we must remember that behavioral patterns in nonhuman animals frequently show a stronger influence of nature than of nurture. There is, however, some provocative evidence from twin studies suggesting that human aggressiveness may be genetically influenced (Rushton et al., 1986; Rushton, 1988). These data demonstrate a much higher concordance rate among identical versus fraternal twins for behaviors such as violent tempers and inappropriate aggression. Recent research has reported that the heritability estimates for aggression are about 0.50, indicating that genetics accounts for about 50 to 70 percent of the variance in aggressive behavior in humans (Miles et al., 1997; Hudziak, J.J., 2003) and that aggression which is stable across different settings and situations is genetic (Haberstick, B.C., 2006).

Can we conclude from this research that biological factors contribute to aggressive behavior in humans? The answer here is a cautious yes. There is considerable evidence for biological dispositions to aggressive behavior in numerous animal species including humans. However, aggressive behavior is also heavily influenced by environmental factors. Behavior is the result of continuing interactions between the environment and genes, rather than additive contributions of each. In the next section we look at some important psychological factors that contribute to aggressive behavior.

PSYCHOLOGICAL BASES OF AGGRESSION Research on psychological contributions to aggression have focused on three major areas: the frustration-aggression hypothesis, social-learning theory, and the influence of media and movies on violence.

The Frustration-Aggression Hypothesis Over 50 years ago John Dollard and his colleagues (1939) proposed that there is a consistent link between frustration, the emotional state that results when something interferes with obtaining a goal, and aggression. In their widely influential **frustration-aggression hypothesis**, Dollard and his associates asserted that "Aggression is always a consequence of frustration" and that "Frustration always leads to aggression" (p. 1).

Frustration-aggression hypothesis

Theory that aggression is always a consequence of frustration, and that frustration leads to aggression.

A number of critics of the frustration-aggression hypothesis did not think so, and psychologist Neal Miller (1941) proposed that frustration could produce a number of possible responses, only one of which is aggression. Other responses to a frustrating situation may include withdrawal, apathy, hopelessness, and even increased efforts to achieve a goal. The response to a frustrating situation may be any behavior acquired through operant conditioning that eliminates or removes one from the aversive situation.

If aggression is only one of several responses to frustrating situations, then what circumstances will cause frustration to produce aggression? Social psychologist Leonard Berkowitz (1978) suggested that two conditions act together to instigate aggression. One is a readiness to act aggressively, which is often associated with the emotion of anger (Berkowitz, 1983, 1989, 1993) and the second factor, that of the presence of environmental cues such as the presence of others who accept aggressive behavior or the availability of weapons, etc. and of course, the presence of an acceptable target for aggression.

Thus, ***Berkowitz suggested that while we may respond to frustrating situations with anger, our anger is not likely to lead to aggressive behavior unless suitable environmental cues are present.*** A number of studies in which subjects experience frustration in either the presence or absence of suitable aggression cues has supported Berkowitz's prediction (Berkowitz, et al., 1966, 1976, 1993; Follingstad et al., 1992; Frodi, 1975; Gustafson, 1989; Leyens & Parke, 1975).

However, frustration is not the only cause of aggression. What about the grade school student who hits the schoolyard weakling because he has seen another admired classmate do the same thing? Learning theory also helps to explain some other instances of aggressive behavior where frustration might not be a factor.

Social-Learning Perspectives on Aggression Albert Bandura (1986) proposed that people may also learn to be aggressive by observing the behavior of others. A child who sees an adult or friend act aggressively may imitate this behavior, especially if he also witnesses the adult or friend reinforced for the aggressive behavior. There is extensive evidence that children raised by parents who behave aggressively are strongly inclined to be aggressive themselves. Children who are victimized by physically abusive parents often tend to behave in the same fashion toward their own children, maintaining an inter-generational continuity (Bandura, 1960, 1973; Feshbach, 1980; Garbarino & Gilliam, 1980; Kaufman et al., 1987; McCall et al., 1986; Straus et al., 1980). *This evidence suggests that each generation learns to be violent by being a participant in a violent family (Straus et al., 1980, p. 121).*

Parents and other significant role models can help to counteract the social roots of aggression by avoiding modeling aggressive actions such as physically punishing or verbally abusing children or engaging in aggressive or violent encounters with other adults. From very early in life, children can be encouraged to develop socially positive traits such as nurturance, tenderness, sensitivity, cooperation, and empathy. Parents and other adult socializing agents can employ the power of positive reinforcement to strengthen such prosocial qualities in children while at the same time discouraging inappropriate aggression and punishing aggressive behavior consistently but non-physically (Eron et al., 1984; Patterson, 1986; Patterson et al., 1982).

The Effects of Violence in the Media and on Film If children learn to behave aggressively by observing their parents, other adults, and their peers, what effect does viewing violence on film have on behavior? Most children in our society observe thousands upon thousands of murders and other acts of violence on television and in movies. The question of whether viewing violence actually increases a person's inclination to act aggressively has been the center of a lively debate. On one side of the issue, some psychologists (particularly psychodynamic psychologists) have argued that observing violence may be cathartic, for when we watch other people behaving violently we vent some of our own frustration and anger vicariously, so that we are *less likely* to behave aggressively.

Research evidence has not been very supportive of the catharsis hypothesis (Brigham, 1986; Evans, 1974; Lefkowitz et al., 1988; Singer, 1989; Tavris, 1982; Williams, 1986). Most psychologists who are familiar with the extensive research are convinced that *exposure to media violence increases the odds that the viewer will behave aggressively* (Berkowitz, 1986; Friedrich-Cofer, 1986; Jo et al., 1994; Penrod, 1986).

Yale University's Dorothy Singer (1989), a recognized authority on the behavioral consequences of television viewing, observed that longitudinal studies "effectively establish the link between television violence and aggressive behavior in children and adolescents" (p. 445). One longitudinal study recently completed by Rowell Huesmann and his colleagues at the University of Michigan *followed nearly 800 children between the ages of 6 and 10 for 15 years. Their study revealed that exposure to media violence at a young age predicted aggressive behavior as an adult nearly 15 years later (Huesmann et al., 2003).* Other studies have found that listening to music with violent lyrical content leads listeners to feel a greater sense of hostility and have more hostile thoughts than those who listened to less hostile music (Anderson et al., 2003).

However, not all psychologists support these interpretations of the effects of media violence. One dissenter, Jonathan Freedman (1984, 2003), has argued that *aggressive persons are inclined to select television programs with high violence content.* Even though this argument may be quite correct, experts caution that "violence on television may have other adverse effects such as increasing one's acceptance of aggressive behavior in others, *blunting one's sensitivity to violence,* and adopting 'mean world' attitudes that are consistent with television's portrayals of aggressive behavior" (Gadnow et al., 1989, p. 404).

Throughout this chapter we have examined the powerful influence of social conditions on our behavior. We have seen that our impressions of others, our tendency to conform, our prejudices, and human aggression are all greatly influenced by social circumstances. In addition, we discussed how social behaviors such as mate selection and aggression are influenced by biological and psychological factors.

SUMMARY

SOCIAL PERCEPTION

1. The term social perception describes the ways we perceive, evaluate, categorize, and form judgments about the characteristics of people we encounter. Three factors that influence our social perceptions are first impressions, schemas, and implicit personality theories.
2. Our first impressions about a person often seem to count the most, a phenomenon referred to as the primacy effect.
3. Person schemas, which are generalized assumptions about certain classes of people, provide a structure for evaluating the people we meet.
4. Attributions are the judgments we make about why people behave as they do. We tend to attribute people's behavior either to internal dispositional causes, or to external situational ones.
5. Two theories attempt to explain the process of making attributions in a rational, methodical manner. The correspondent inference theory suggests that we attribute a person's behavior to an underlying disposition. The covariation principle maintains that we make attributions by analyzing the manner in which causes and effects covary.
6. Biases in attribution processes include the fundamental attribution error (a tendency to overestimate dispositional causes and to underestimate situational causes when accounting for the behavior of others), false consensus bias (the assumption that most people share our own attitudes and behaviors), and the illusion of control (the belief that we control events in our lives).

ATTITUDES

7. Attitudes are learned, relatively enduring predispositions to respond in consistent ways to certain people, groups, ideas, or situations.
8. Attitudes are shaped by experiences, which include our observations of behavior (both other people's and our own) and classical and operant conditioning.
9. Attitudes serve a number of important functions in our lives, including an understanding function, a social identification function, a social adjustment function, and a value-expressive function.
10. Studies that have measured a variety of behaviors relevant to a given attitude have revealed a strong correlation between attitudes and behavior.
11. Attitudes are particularly strong predictors of behavior when other factors influencing behavior are minimized, when an attitude is highly relevant to the behavior being considered, and when we are quite conscious of our attitudes when we act.
12. Consistency theories suggest that we sometimes change our attitudes in an effort to maintain consistency both among attitudes we hold as well as between our attitudes and behaviors.
13. According to cognitive dissonance theory, people experience an unpleasant state of dissonance whenever they perceive a discrepancy between their actions and their attitudes. In such a situation, attitudes may be changed to be more consistent with behavior, thus resulting in a state of consonance or psychological comfort.
14. Three elements are particularly important in persuasive communications: the source of the message, the way the message is stated, and the characteristics of the message recipients.
15. The probability that persuasion will succeed is highest when the source of persuasion is seen as possessing any or all of the qualities of credibility, power, and attractiveness.
16. A message that is presented in an unusual or novel fashion is often more effective than time-worn arguments.

17. A one-sided argument seems to be more effective if the audience is poorly educated and/or unfamiliar with the issue, whereas two-sided arguments tend to work better with a well-educated, well-informed audience.
18. Teenagers and young adults are generally more susceptible than older people to persuasive communication. Research has been unclear about the impact of listeners' self-esteem and intelligence on their inclination to yield to persuasion.
19. Prejudice is a negative, unjustifiable, and inflexible attitude toward a group and its members that is based on erroneous information, often in the form of stereotypes (preconceived and oversimplified beliefs and expectations about the traits of members of a particular group that do not account for individual differences).
20. Prejudice often stems from a marked tendency of people to categorize themselves as belonging to an in-group (based on race, age, education, creed, economic level, etc.) and to have a negative attitude against people in out-groups who do not possess those characteristics. People seem to be enhancing their self-esteem by viewing their in-group as superior to other out-groups.
21. People who are frustrated by their lack of accomplishments or by adverse living conditions often vent their frustration in the form of prejudice against members of a minority group that they perceive as being less powerful than themselves.
22. Some evidence suggests that people raised in a harsh, authoritarian fashion may be inclined to develop prejudiced behaviors characterized by intolerance, emotional coldness, rigidity, unquestioning submission to higher authority, stereotyped thinking, and identification with power.

SOCIAL INFLUENCES ON BEHAVIOR

23. The realm of social influence (the effects of others on our behavior) encompasses the related phenomena of conformity, compliance, and obedience.
24. Conformity refers to a tendency to change or modify our own behaviors so that they are consistent with those of other people.
25. Whereas both compliance and conformity involve yielding to pressure exerted by others, compliance involves an element of coercion as well, in that it takes place in situations where we alter our behavior in response to direct requests from others.
26. Two methods employed by people who wish to increase the probability of compliance in others are the foot-in-the-door technique and the door-in-the-face technique.
27. Obedience occurs in situations in which people alter their behavior in response to commands or orders leveled by people they may perceive as having power or authority.
28. Psychologists have suggested three reasons why people may respond to social influence in the form of destructive obedience. First, people may believe that their personal accountability for actions is somehow diminished or relieved by those authority figures who issue the commands. Second, authority figures often possess highly visible symbols of power or status that make it difficult to resist their dictates. Finally, people often comply because they have first been "sucked in" by seemingly harmless commands.

INTERPERSONAL BEHAVIOR: ATTRACTION AND AGGRESSION

29. Factors known to contribute strongly to interpersonal attraction include proximity, similarity, reci-

procity, and physical attractiveness. We often develop close relationships with people whom we see frequently, who share similar beliefs, who seem to like us, and whom we perceive as being physically attractive.

30. Cross-cultural studies suggest that physical attractiveness and youth are more important for males selecting a potential mate than for females, who seek characteristics of wealth, status, and industriousness in potential mates.
31. Explanations for why people engage in interpersonal aggression (that is, any physical or verbal behavior intended to hurt another person) include both biological and psychological influences.
32. There is considerable evidence that aggressive behavior is at least partially determined by genetics but environmental influences play a significant role.
33. Social-learning theorists suggest that aggressive behavior is often learned by receiving reinforcement for aggressive acts and by observing and imitating the aggressive behavior of others.
34. Some psychologists have argued that observing television and film violence may be cathartic, providing a vicarious way to vent our own frustration and anger. However, the evidence has not provided much support for this hypothesis. Most psychologists believe that exposure to violence increases the odds that the viewer will behave aggressively.
35. Since aggressive behavior ultimately causes destruction and grief, parents can reduce aggressive behavior in their children by modeling nurturing, gentle behavior and by punishing their children's aggressive behavior by punishments that are not physical or violent.

TERMS AND CONCEPTS

diffusion of responsibility
social perception
primacy effect
person schemas
attribution theory
correspondent inference theory
covariation principle
fundamental attribution error
false consensus bias
illusion of control
attitude
impression management
stereotype threat
balance theory
cognitive dissonance theory
prejudice
stereotypes
discrimination
in-group
in-group bias
out-group
authoritarian personality
social influence
conformity
compliance
foot-in-the-door technique
door-in-the-face technique
obedience
proximity
mere exposure effect
similarity
reciprocity
physical attractiveness
interpersonal aggression
frustration-aggression hypothesis

Appendix

Statistics is one of the most commonly used mathematical tools in science. Without statistics it would be virtually impossible to present and interpret the results of scientific experiments. Two particularly useful types of statistics frequently used in psychology are descriptive statistics and inferential statistics. *Descriptive statistics,* as the name implies, are used to describe and summarize the results of research. *Inferential statistics* are used in making decisions about hypotheses and to make generalizations from research samples to larger populations.

DESCRIPTIVE STATISTICS

Measures of Central Tendency

Suppose your psychology instructor gives a sample test to 10 students who attended a study session. How would he or she describe the test results? One way would be to name all students and list their test scores—10 names and 10 scores. That would probably work nicely in a small class. But it would certainly be inefficient and confusing with a class of 500. Moreover, a listing of numbers does not indicate much of anything about the study group as a whole. It also would be helpful to know the average, typical, or most representative score. What is needed is a measure of *central tendency* for the group of scores, a number that represents the average. We shall describe three commonly used measures.

Mean
In descriptive statistics, the arithmetic average obtained by adding scores and dividing by the number of scores.

THE MEAN The **mean** (short for arithmetic mean) is computed by adding up all the scores and dividing by the number of scores. We can express this in mathematical form in the following formula:

$$\bar{X} = \frac{X}{N}$$

This formula introduces some elementary statistical symbols. The letter X refers to the independent variable, which can take on many different values. It could be anything—IQ, anxiety, or learning errors. The researcher measures the variable for each subject and assigns a score to each subject to represent the level of the variable for that subject. The capital Greek letter sigma (Σ) in the formula is a shorthand symbol for "add up these scores." We then divide this sum by the number of scores (symbolized by N) to arrive at the mean, which is symbolized by $\bar{X}$ (read "X bar").

We have made up a list of 10 test scores from students attending our hypothetical study session and computed their mean in Table A.1. To compute the mean, we add up the 10 scores and divide by 10 ($\overline{X} = 83$). Table A.1 also gives the number of hours each student in our study session studied during the previous week. To keep the variable of study time distinct from test score, we signify study times by Y. So ΣY tells us to add up the study times, which is also done in Table A. 1. Dividing this total by the number of scores gives us the mean study time of the students ($\overline{Y} = 8.35$ hours). We can express these steps in a shorthand formula.

$$\overline{Y} = \frac{Y}{N}$$

Now if we ask the teacher how the class performed on the test, the teacher could simply report the mean value of 83 points; if we ask how many hours these students studied, the teacher could report the mean from our group, which was 8.35 hours. This method is obviously much simpler than listing all the X and Y scores and it gives a better idea of the students' general performance as well as the hours of study time per week that are typical of these students.

Median

In descriptive statistics, the score that falls in the middle of a distribution of numbers arranged from the lowest to the highest.

THE MEDIAN The **median** is the *middle score* in a list of scores that have been arranged in increasing order. If there is an odd number of scores, then there will be one score exactly in the middle. Thus, if the class had 11 students, the score of the sixth student in order would be the median—there would be five scores higher and five scores lower. With an even number of scores, there is no single middle score; instead, there are two scores that determine the middle (one is above and one is below the theoretical midpoint). In our example of 10 test scores, the middle two scores are the fifth and sixth scores. Table A.2 shows the 10 test scores from Table A.1, but this time we have arranged them in order. The middle point is between the fifth and sixth scores (83). We average these two scores to obtain the median.

TABLE A.1 Computation of Mean Test Score and Study Time for 10 Students Enrolled in a Study Session

Student's Name	X (Test Score)	Y (Study Time)
Rita	85	9.2
Charles	78	8.1
Dawn	82	8.4
Bruce	74	7.2
Lauri	89	9.6
Marie	91	9.5
John	87	8.9
Randy	79	6.3
Jeff	81	7.7
Suzan	84	8.6
	$\Sigma X = 830$	$\Sigma Y = 83.5$
	$N = 10$	$N = 10$

The mean of test scores (X) is

$$\overline{X} = \frac{X}{N} = \frac{830}{10} = 83.0$$

The mean of study times (Y) is

$$\overline{Y} = \frac{Y}{N} = \frac{83.5}{10} = 8.35$$

TABLE A.2 Computation of the Median Test Score for 10 Students Enrolled in a Study Session

Name	X (Test Score)	
Marie	91	
Lauri	89	
John	87	
Rita	85	
Suzan	84	(The *median* is the average
Dawn	82	of the two middle scores)
Jeff	81	
Randy	79	
Charles	78	
Bruce	74	

The median in this case is the average of the two middle scores (84 and 82).

$$\frac{84 + 82}{2} = 83$$

Note that if we had an odd number of scores, the median would be the middle score.

The mean and the median are typically close, but not usually the same as they are in this case. They will be very close when the distribution of scores is symmetrical or equally balanced around the mean.

Now consider the set of test scores in Table A.3. Here we note that most of the 10 students from a study session didn't do very well—with the exception of two students who scored very high. This distribution of scores is asymmetrical and unbalanced. Technically, we call it skewed. The distribution of Table A.3 is skewed to the high end positively skewed). The mean score is 76 and the median is 72.

Mode

In descriptive statistics, the score that occurs most frequently in a distribution of numbers.

THE MODE The **mode** is the *most frequently occurring score.* In a small set of scores as in Tables A.1, A.2, and A.3, there is the possibility that no score will occur more than once and, thus, there is no mode. But suppose a psychologist gives an anxiety test to a group of 200 mental patients. With such a large group, it is convenient to set up a *frequency distribution* showing the various possible scores on the test and, for each possible score, how many people actually got that score. We have set up in Table A.4 such a frequency distribution for the anxiety scores from the 200 mental patients. Looking down the frequency column in Table A.4, we see that 27 is the highest frequency. That is, 27 people obtained a score of 15. Therefore, 15 is the *mode* or the *modal score.* Note that the sum of all the frequencies is equal to N, the number of people taking the test—in this case, 200.

Frequency distributions can also be represented graphically. Figure A.1 shows a frequency distribution from Table A.4. The horizontal axis of the graph represents the values of the variable X (the anxiety score) and the vertical axis represents the frequency of each score.

Measures of Variability

There are differences among people: Not everyone gets the same score on a test or is the same height. These *individual differences* among people are a fact of life. The variability among people

TABLE A.3 Comparison of the Mean and the Median for a Set of Test Scores for 10

Name	X (Test Score)	
Mike	99	
Julie	98	
Lynn	76	
Ryan	74	
Bill	72	(The *median* is the average
Lauri	72	of the two middle scores)
Kathy	69	
John	68	
Sue	68	
Bob	64	

The median test score is $\dfrac{72 + 72}{2} = 72$

The mean test score is $\overline{X} = \dfrac{X}{N} = \dfrac{760}{10} = 76$

TABLE A.4 A Frequency Distribution of the Anxiety Scores of 200 Mental Patients

Score (X)	Frequency (f)
20	10
19	10
18	12
17	15
16	20
15	**27**
14	15
13	21
12	22
11	12
10	10
9	8
8	7
7	5
6	3
5	0
4	2
3	1
2	0
1	0
	$\Sigma f = 200 = N$

The *mode,* the score that occurs most frequently, is equal to 15.

FIGURE A.1 A Frequent Distribution Based on the Data in Table A.4

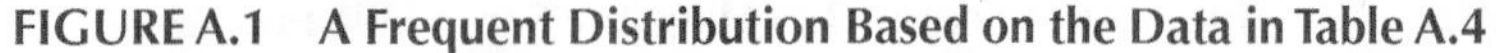

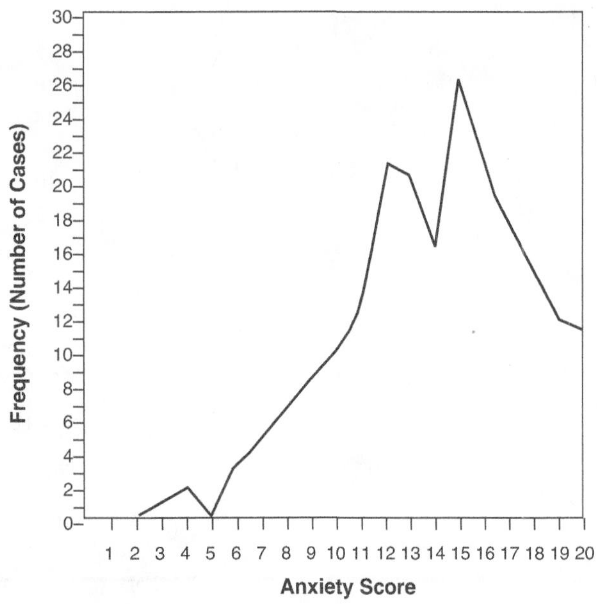

may be large when it comes to anxiety or test scores, but small when it comes to the number of fingers they have. How do we quantify the degree of variability in the scores?

Range

In descriptive statistics, a measure of variability that indicates the difference between the highest and lowest scores.

The quickest and least informative measure of the variability in a set of scores is the range. The **range** is defined as the *highest score minus the lowest score.* In Table A.4, we see that the patients' anxiety scores range from a high of 20 to a low of 3, and so the range would be 20 – 3 = 17. Although the range as a measure of variability is easy to compute, it is based on only two scores (the highest and the lowest) and, therefore, tells us little about the variability in the entire distribution. Better measures of variability are the variance and standard deviation, both of which reflect the degree of spread or fluctuation of scores around the mean.

Suppose we have a set of 10 scores with a mean of 20. Two such sets are shown in Table A.5. All but two of the scores in Set A cluster close to the mean. In Set B, we have the same mean, but the variability is higher, with several scores a long way from the mean. If we described both sets with a central tendency measure (such as the mean), the two sets would appear to be similar. If we described the variability of each set using the range, again the two sets would appear to be similar. To reflect the differences between the sets more accurately, we need a measure of variability that takes into account all the scores (not just the highest and lowest).

Variance

In descriptive statistics, a measure of variability that is the average of the squared distances of the scores from the mean.

The variance and the standard deviation are both measures of variability that are based on all of the scores in the sample. The **variance** is essentially the *average of the squared distances of the scores from the mean.* It is symbolized by: s^2.

To compute the variance, we first subtract the mean from each score as we have done in Table A.6. These differences are measures of each score's distance from the mean. Now why not just calculate the mean of these distance scores? The reason is that the mean of these distance scores will always be equal to zero, regardless of how variable the scores are. Instead, we square each score before adding them. These squared distance scores are also shown in Table

TABLE A.5 Two Sets of Scores That Have the Same Mean but Differ in Variability

SET A	SET B
36	36
22	32
21	28
21	24
20	20
20	20
19	16
19	12
18	8
4	4
$\Sigma X = 200$	$\Sigma X = 200$
$N = 10$	$N = 10$
$\bar{X} = \frac{200}{10} = 20$	$\bar{X} = \frac{200}{10} = 20$
Range = 36 – 4 = 32	Range = 36 – 4 = 32

A.6. Now we can add these scores up and divide by the number of scores. These steps are expressed in the following notational form:

$$s^2 = \frac{(X \quad \bar{X})^2}{N} = 52.4$$

Standard deviation

In descriptive statistics, a measure of variability that indicates the average extent to which all the scores in a distribution vary from the mean.

The **standard deviation** is simply the *square root of the variance.* This measure is somewhat easier to interpret because it is expressed in the same units as our independent variable, not a squared value like the variance. For this reason, the standard deviation is a more preferable measure of variability.

$$s = \sqrt{\frac{(X \quad \bar{X})^2}{N}} = 7.24$$

The standard deviation and the variance are better measures of variability than the range because they take all of the scores into account, not just the highest score and lowest score. If we compare the two data sets in Table A.6, we see that, even though the range is the same in the two sets, both the variance and the standard deviation reflect the smaller average spread of scores in Set A relative to Set B. Unlike Set B, most of the scores in Set A cluster close to the mean of 20. The variance in Set A is 52.4 and in Set B is 96.0. The standard deviation in Set A is 7.24 and in Set B is 9.80. The range is 32 (36 – 4) in both data sets.

Normal distribution

In descriptive statistics, a distribution in which scores are distributed similarly on both sides of the middle value, so that they have the appearance of a bell-shaped curve when graphed.

Normal Frequency Distributions

Earlier in this appendix, we introduced the *frequency distribution* and showed how it could be represented graphically. Figure A.2 presents the graph of what is called the **normal distribution** (or *normal curve*). This figure is not a graph of an actual data set (as in Figure A.1). Instead, this is a theoretical distribution defined by a mathematical equation. A normal distribution is sym-

TABLE A.6 Computation of the Variance and Standard Deviation for Two Sets of Scores

SET A			SET B		
X	$(X - \bar{X})$	$(X - \bar{X})^2$	X	$(X - \bar{X})$	$(X - \bar{X})^2$
36	16	256	36	16	256
22	2	4	32	12	144
21	1	1	28	8	64
21	1	1	24	4	16
20	0	0	20	0	0
20	0	0	20	0	0
19	–1	1	16	–4	16
19	–1	1	12	–8	64
18	–2	4	8	–12	144
4	–16	256	4	–16	256
Sums	0	524		0	960

SET A

$$x^2 = \text{variance} = \frac{(X \;\; \bar{X})^2}{N} = \frac{524}{10} = 52.4$$

$$s = \text{standard deviation} = \sqrt{s^2} = \sqrt{52.4} = 7.24$$

Range = 36 – 4 = 32

SET B

$$s^2 = \text{variance} = \frac{(X \;\; \bar{X})^2}{N} = \frac{960}{10} = 96.0$$

$$s = \text{standard deviation} = \sqrt{s^2} = \sqrt{96.0} = 9.80$$

Range = 36 – 4 = 32

metrical; if you fold it over at the mean, the two halves will overlap each other. Moreover, it is a bell-shaped curve (meaning it looks like a bell); scores near the mean are most common, and the frequency drops off smoothly as we move to the extremes. The normal distribution is very useful because many variables are "normally distributed"; that is, the graph of the distribution of the variable would be very similar in shape to the graph in Figure A.2. The variable of IQ is a good example. IQ is normally distributed with a mean of 100 and a standard deviation of 15; if we obtained IQ scores for everybody, the mean IQ would be 100 and the standard deviation would be 15. Furthermore, if we drew a graph representing the frequency of each of the possible IQ scores, it would show the characteristic bell shape of a normal distribution.

If we know that a variable such as IQ is normally distributed and if we know the mean and the standard deviation, we can use the mathematical properties of the normal distribution to deduce more information about the variable. We can do this because, in any normal distribution, the standard deviation can be used to divide the distribution into sections containing fixed percentages of the scores. Figure A.3 shows a normal distribution divided up in this way for the variable of IQ. The fixed percentages are printed in the various sections of the curve. For example, about 34 percent of the IQ scores lie between the mean and a score of 115; that

FIGURE A.2 The Normal Distribution of IQ Scores

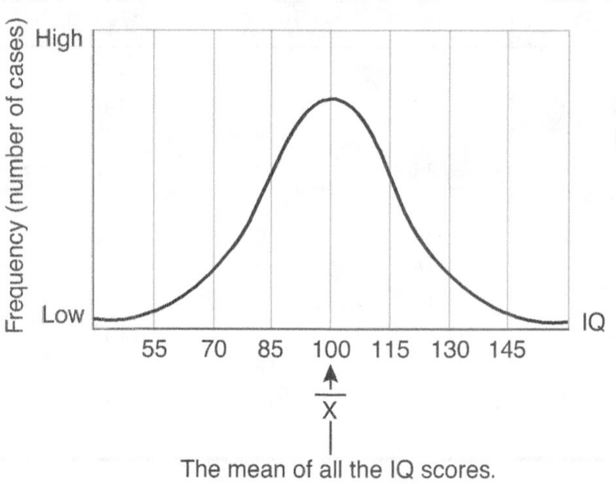

FIGURE A.3 The Normal Distribution Divided into Standard Deviation Units

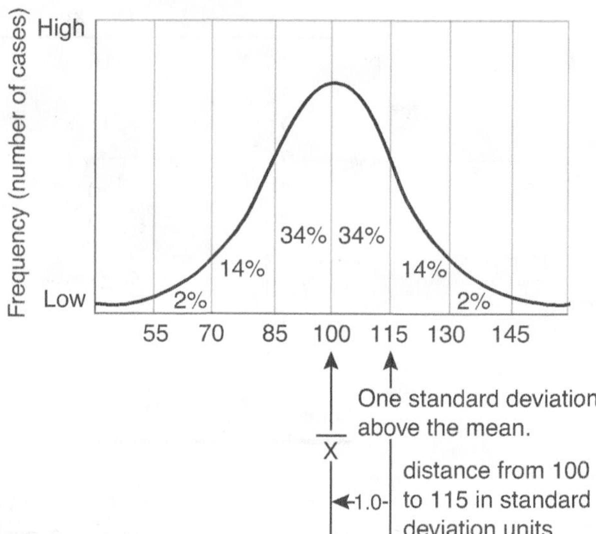

is, 34 percent of the people have IQs between the mean and one standard deviation above the mean. The standard deviation is a distance measure, and the "distance" from 115 to the mean of 100 is one standard deviation unit. An IQ of 130 would be two standard deviation units above the mean; an IQ of 145 would be three standard deviations above the mean. One standard deviation below the mean would be an IQ of 85; two standard deviations below the mean would be an IQ of 70; three standard deviations below the mean would be an IQ of 55. Regardless of the variable being measured, almost all of the scores will fall between three standard deviation units below the mean and three standard deviation units above the mean (for IQ scores, from 55 up to 145). Although it is theoretically possible to obtain scores outside of this range, scores more than three standard deviations from the mean are very rare. It is often convenient to convert the scores into standard deviation scores, called *z* scores, using the following formula:

$$z = \frac{X \quad \overline{X}}{s}$$

A major advantage of the *z* score is that it can be used as a common yardstick for all tests, allowing us to compare scores on different tests. For example, suppose you receive 80 on your history test, which has a class mean of 70 with a standard deviation of 10. On your psychology test, you got a 90, and the class mean was 85 with a standard deviation of 5. We also know that the distribution of test scores was approximately normal in each class. On which test did you do better? These test scores are not immediately comparable, but if you change each score into a *z* score using the mean and standard deviation for each test, you will discover that you did equally well on both tests in terms of where you stood in the class distribution (obtaining a *z* score of +1.00 on each test). Using the information in Figure A.3, we can infer that your score on each test puts you at approximately the 84th percentile—34 percent of the class scored between your score and the mean and another 50 percent of the class scored below the mean.

Figure A.4 again shows the IQ normal distribution, but this time we have two horizontal axes displayed. The upper one shows IQ scores, and the lower one shows the equivalent *z* scores. This figure shows that an IQ score of 115 is one standard deviation above the mean, and so the *z* score corresponding to 115 is +1.0. If your friend tells you that his *z* score in IQ is +2.0, you can see that he has an IQ of 130. If he tells you that his *z* score is + 3.0 (145), he is either very brilliant or he is pulling your leg.

From Figure A.4, suppose we ask you to figure out what percentage of the people have IQs between 85 and 115, which is the same as asking how many people have *z* scores between −1.0 and +1.0. The answer is 68 percent: 34 percent between 85 and 100, and another 34 percent between 100 and 115. If we know that the scores are distributed normally and we know the mean and standard deviation of the distribution, we can find the percentage of scores between *any* two points by using a simple table (the *Standard Normal table)* that can be found in almost any statistics textbook. An important thing to remember is that these percentages and the *z* score procedure apply to any normal distribution, not just the IQ distribution. The only difference between the IQ distribution and any other normal distribution of scores is that the other distributions probably have different means and different standard deviations. But if you know that something has a normal distribution and if you know the mean and standard deviation of it, you can set up a figure like the one in Figure A.4.

Suppose, for example, that we told you that waist size in American men is normally distributed with a mean of 34 inches and a standard deviation of 4 inches. You could now set up a normal frequency distribution as in Figure A.5. Almost all American men have a waist size within the range of 22 inches (*z* score of −3; 22 is 3 standard deviation units below the mean) to 46 inches (*z* score of +3; 3 units above the mean). Now can you fill in the percentages and answer the following questions?

1. what percentage of men have waist sizes less than 30 inches?
2. what percentage of men have waist sizes greater than 38?

FIGURE A.4 The Normal Distribution and *z* Scores

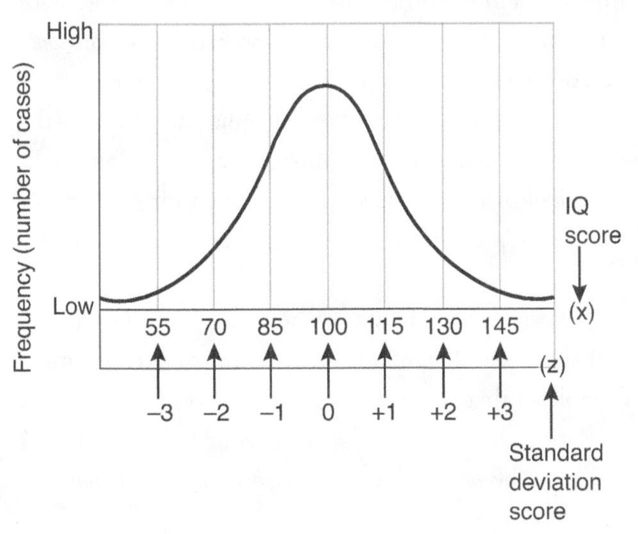

FIGURE A.5 The Normal Distribution of Waist Size in American Men (Hypothetical)

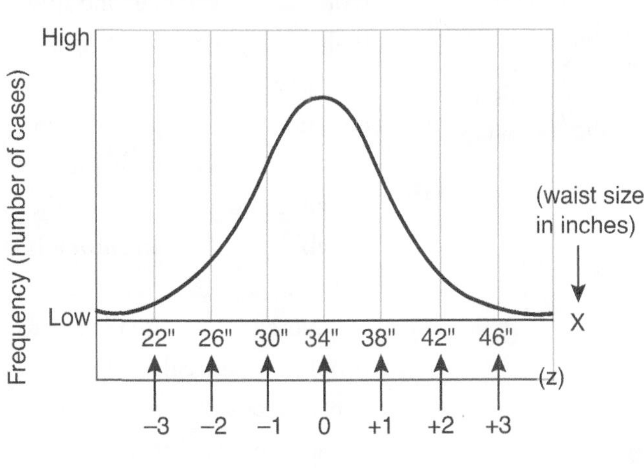

3. If Joe's waist size is 47, is he unusual?
4. If we randomly selected one man from the American population, what is the probability (how likely is it?) that his waist size will be equal to or greater than 38?

Probability

In statistics, the proportion of cases that fit a certain description.

This last question brings us to the notion of probability. **Probability** refers to the *proportion of cases that fit a certain description.* In general, the probability of A (the likelihood that a randomly drawn object will be an A object) is equal to the number of A objects divided by the total number of all possible objects. The number of A objects divided by the total number of objects is the *proportion* of objects that are A, and hence the probability is a proportion.

Suppose, as in question 4, we wanted to know the probability that a randomly selected American man will have a waist size equal to or greater than 38. To find the probability of selecting at random such an individual, we have to know what proportion of all men have waist sizes of 38 or greater. In Figure A.5, we can see that 14 percent of the men have waist sizes between 38 and 42 inches and an additional 2 percent are greater than 42, and so we add 14 percent and 2 percent and find that 16 percent of American men have waist sizes of 38 or greater. In proportion terms, this becomes .16 (we move the decimal point two places to the left to translate a percentage into a proportion). In summary, the probability of selecting a man with a waist size equal to or greater than 38 is .16. This means that 16 out of every 100 random selections would yield a man who fits this description.

Suppose that scores on an anxiety scale are normally distributed in the population of all American people with a mean of 50 and a standard deviation of 10. Calculate the probability that a randomly drawn person has an anxiety score that is equal to or less than 40. If you computed it correctly you should have obtained a probability of .16.

Correlation

Correlation coefficient

Statistic used to describe the degree of relationship between two or more variables. Positive correlations indicate that variables vary together in the same direction; negative correlations indicate the opposite.

The **correlation coefficient** was introduced in Chapter 2. The correlation coefficient does not describe a single variable as the mean or standard deviation does. Instead, it describes the degree of relationship between two variables. It is basically a measure of the degree to which the two variables vary together, or *covary.* Scores can vary together in one of two ways: (1) a *positive covariation,* in which high scores in one variable tend to go with high scores in the other variable (and low scores go with low scores), or (2) *negative covariation,* in which high scores in one variable tend to go with low scores in the other variable (and low scores go with high scores). when there is a positive covariation, we say that the two variables are *positively correlated,* and when there is a negative covariation, we say they are *negatively correlated.* A common example of positive correlation is the relationship between height and weight—the taller you are, the more you tend to weigh. A common example of negative correlation might be the relationship between the amount of alcohol a person has drunk in an evening and his or her ability to drive an automobile—the more the person has drunk, the lower his or her ability to drive.

Note that we used "tend to go with." Correlations are almost never perfect—not all tall people are particularly heavy, and not all short people are lightweights. In some cases, there may be a *zero correlation* between two variables—that is, no relationship between the variables. We might expect there to be a zero correlation, for example, between your height and your ability to learn psychology. So two variables can be *positively* or *negatively correlated* or *not cor-*

related at all, and the degree of correlation can be great or small. What we need is a statistic that conveniently measures the degree and the direction (positive or negative) of the correlation between two variables and this is what the correlation coefficient does.

Table A.7 shows the scores of 10 people on two tests: a test of anxiety and a test of happiness. The possible scores on each test ranged from 1 to 10. Larger scores represent more of the variable being measured. Hence, a high score on the anxiety measure represents a high level of anxiety; a low score represents a low level of anxiety. Intuitively, we would expect a negative correlation between the two variables of anxiety and happiness—the less anxious you are, the more happier you will be, and vice versa.

Table A.7 presents the anxiety and happiness scores for each of the 10 subjects. These data can be more easily visualized in a *scatter plot,* which we have set up in Figure A.6. In this scatter plot, the horizontal axis indicates the anxiety score, and the vertical axis indicates the happiness score. Each person is represented by a point on the graph that locates him or her on the two tests. For example, Clint had an anxiety score of 4 and a happiness score of 7. So we go over (to the right) to 4 on the anxiety scale and then up to 7 on the happiness scale, and we place a dot at that point to represent Clint's scores. The scores from all 10 people are represented in the graph. In this case, the 10 points all fall on a straight line, which means that the correlation is perfect. Further, the line slopes down to the right, which means that the correlation is negative in direction—high anxiety scores go with low happiness scores, and vice versa.

As we have said, however; correlations are almost never perfect. More often, the points are likely to be scattered all over the graph, hence the term "scatter plot." The closer the points are laying on a straight line, the higher the degree of correlation. If the points seem to cluster about a line that slopes downward to the right, then the correlation will be negative as in Figure A.6. If the points seem to cluster about a line that slopes upward to the right, the correlation will be positive. Figure A.7 shows four scatter plots. In panel A the two variables in question are negatively correlated; the points all seem to cluster about a straight line that slopes downward to the right. In panel B there is a positive correlation; the points again all seem to cluster about a line, but this time the line slopes upward to the right. In panel C there is no

TABLE A.7 The Correlation Between Anxiety and Happiness

Name	Anxiety (*X*)*	Happiness (*Y*)
Joan	1	10
Larry	2	9
Ralph	3	8
Clint	4	7
Sue	5	6
Sharon	6	5
Sam	7	4
Bonnie	8	3
Marsha	9	2
Harry	10	1

*Here we have arranged the anxiety scores in order. Note that the happiness scores are in reverse order. When these data are graphed in a scatter plot (see Figure A.6), all the points fall on a straight line, which indicates that the correlation IS perfect (in this case, –1.0).

FIGURE A.6 A Scatter Plot of the Data from Table A.7 Relating Anxiety to Happiness

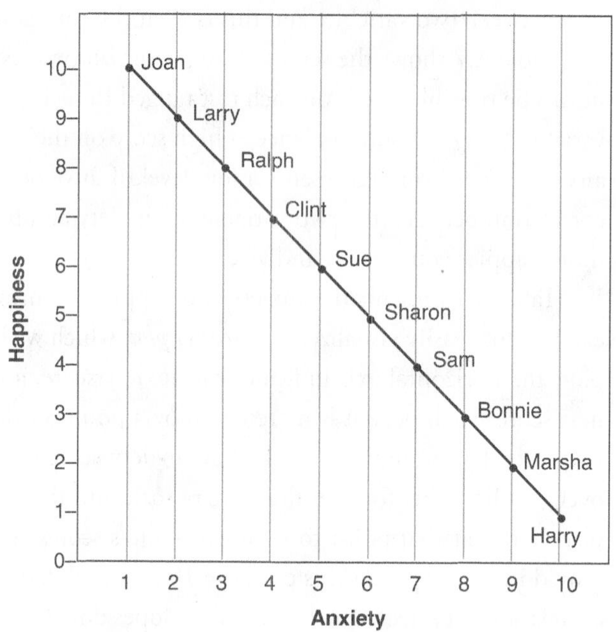

Pearson product-moment correlation coefficient

The most frequently used measure of correlation, ranging from −1.0 to +1.0. Correlations close to zero indicate little or no relationship between two variables; correlations close to +1.0 or −1.0 indicate more significant positive or negative relationships.

correlation; the points are scattered all over; and there is no line that fits them very well. Panel D presents an interesting case. The points do seem to cluster about a line, but it is a curved rather than a straight line. The scatter plot does suggest that there is a relationship between the variables, but it is not a simple relationship. Most correlation coefficients are designed to quantify a simple straight-line relationship and will give misleading results when applied to a complex relationship such as the one in panel D.

The **Pearson product-moment correlation coefficient** (symbolized r) is the most often used of several measures of correlation. It can take on any numerical value from −1.0 through 0.0 up to +1.0. A perfect negative product-moment correlation, as shown in Figure A.6, is equal to −1.0, and a perfect positive correlation is equal to +1.0. Correlations close to zero mean there

FIGURE A.7 Scatter Plots Showing Four Possible Relationships

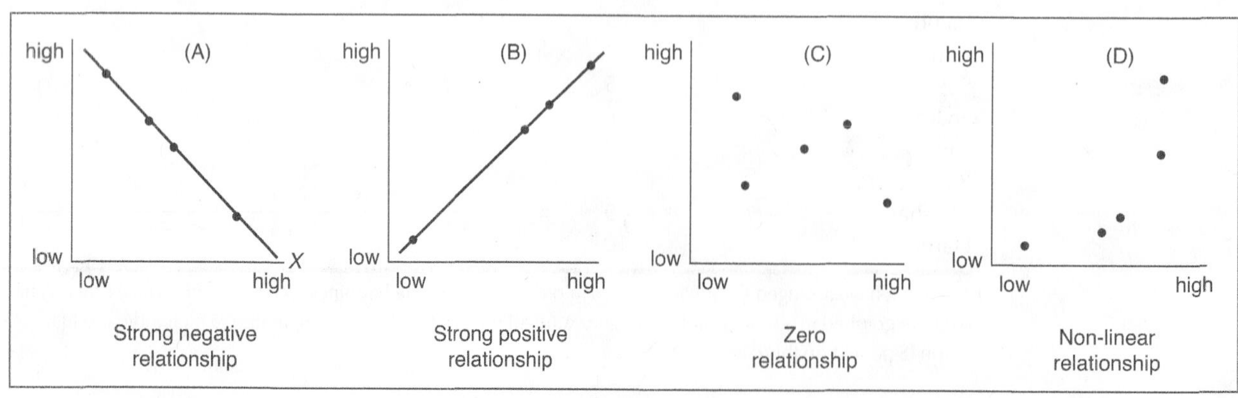

TABLE A.8 Calculating the Pearson Product-Moment Correlation Coefficient

Name	Anxiety (X)	X^2	Happiness (Y)	Y^2	XY (X times Y)
John	2	4	9	81	18
Ralph	5	25	6	36	30
Mary	9	81	4	16	36
Sue	1	1	3	9	3
Jan	3	9	2	4	6
Harvey	7	49	2	4	14
Jane	8	64	4	16	32
Joanne	6	36	5	25	30
$N = 8$ people	$\Sigma X = 41$	$\Sigma X^2 = 269$	$\Sigma Y = 35$	$\Sigma Y^2 = 191$	$\Sigma XY = 169$

$$r_{xy} \text{ (the correlation between } X \text{ and } Y) = \frac{N\ XY\ \ (\ X)(\ Y)}{\sqrt{[N\ X^2\ \ (\ X)^2][N\ Y^2\ \ (\ Y)^2]}}$$

$$\text{For these data: } r_{\text{ANXIETY}\,\bullet\,\text{HAPPINESS}} = \frac{(8)(169)\ \ (41)(35)}{\sqrt{[(8)(269)\ \ (41)^2][(8)(191)\ \ (35)^2]}} = \frac{1352\ \ 1435}{\sqrt{(2152\ \ 1681)(1528\ \ 1225)}}$$

$$= \frac{83}{\sqrt{(471)(303)}} = \frac{83}{\sqrt{142713}} = \frac{83}{377.77} = .219$$

is little or no relationship between the two variables X and Y. The size of the correlation (ignoring the sign) represents the degree of relationship. The sign of the correlation (positive or negative) tells us the direction of the relationship between the variables, but not the degree of the relationship. Thus a correlation of – .77 is just as strong a correlation as a correlation of +.77; the only difference is the direction. Table A.8 shows the steps for calculating the Pearson product-moment correlation coefficient in case you want to see exactly how it is done.

In all the examples so far, we have been correlating the scores of a person on two different tests, but we can use correlations in other ways. We might correlate the scores of a person on the same test taken at two different times. If the test measures a variable that should be stable, then the correlation between two administrations of the test would indicate an aspect of the reliability of the test—that is, how consistent are a person's scores on the same test given on two different occasions? A good test should be reliable. Another common use of correlation is to determine the test's validity—does the test measure what it is supposed to measure? For example, a test of intelligence should correlate positively with performance in school. If it did, it would help us argue that the test really did measure intelligence. (See Chapter 13 for a discussion of validity.)

Linear Regression

Linear regression

Using the general linear model $y = mx + b$ to predict values for y given values for x.

One important use of the correlational statistics is in a procedure called **linear regression**. A correlation coefficient tells us the degree to which a person's scores on two tests are related. Suppose, for example, that we try to predict your weight. We have no idea what to guess, because all we know about you is that you are reading this book. If we knew that the average person reading this book weighs 142 pounds, then that would be our best guess, and we would make the same guess for every reader. But if we knew your height, and we also knew the correlation between weight and height, then we could make a much more accurate guess of your weight. For example, if we knew that you were six feet, six inches tall, we would hardly guess 142 pounds. Someone that tall would almost certainly weigh more than 142 pounds. Likewise, if we knew you were four feet, two inches, 142 pounds would also be an inappropriate guess. We would adjust our prediction of your weight according to what we knew about your height. Linear regression is an accurate way of making this adjustment and allowing us to make as accurate a prediction as possible.

The higher the correlation between weight and height, the better we can predict a person's weight from knowing his or her height. If the correlation between the two variables is perfect (either +1.0 or –1.0), we can predict perfectly the value of one of the variables if we know the value of the other. But, because correlations are almost never perfect, our predictions are normally close, but usually not exactly correct. The lower the value of the correlation coefficient, the greater is the average error that will occur in the prediction.

Linear regression is used in many different settings. Many of you probably took the Scholastic Aptitude Test (SAT). From past research we know there is a positive correlation between scores on the SAT and success in college. Therefore, the SAT can now be given to college applicants and on the basis of their scores we can predict approximately how a person will do in college. These predictions are used to help decide whom to admit. Similar procedures are used to process applications for law school, medical school, graduate school, or a job. Using linear regression techniques, the psychologist predicts the applicant's success on the job or in school, and these predictions are used to determine whether or not to hire or admit the applicant. It is a serious business, and the decisions made on this basis are extremely important to the people involved.

Linear regression is based on a mathematical equation for a straight line (hence the term *linear*). What we are looking for is the straight line that comes closest to the most points on a scatter diagram (see Figure A.8). Figure A.8 shows two different hypothetical scatter plots relating scores on the SAT to grade point average in college (GPA). Each point in the diagram represents the SAT score and college GPA for one student. With data on SAT scores and college GPAs, we can proceed to use regression to make predictions for future students. First, we solve the equation for the best-fitting straight line (known as the *regression line*), a complex procedure we need not describe here. Then we draw the line on the scatter plot. Now we can use the line as a way to predict the GPA given a student's SAT score. For example, consider a student who scores 700 on the SAT; we draw a vertical line up from 700 until it intersects the regression line, and then we draw a horizontal line from this point to the Y axis and read off the predicted GPA. In this case, we come up with a prediction of 3.6 for the student's GPA.

This procedure will not give us perfect predictions. Not all students scoring 700 on their SAT had 3.6 averages in college; some were higher than 3.6 and some lower. As we have said, the main factor in determining the accuracy of the predictions is the degree of correlation between the two variables. If the variables are highly correlated, as depicted in panel A, all the points will cluster closer to the regression line, and none of the predictions is likely to be far off. In fact, if the correlation were perfect, all the points would be right on the line, and there would be no error. (All students with 700 SATs would get 3.6 GPAs.) On the other hand, with low correlations, the points will be widely scattered, and many of them will be a long way from the regression line, as depicted in panel B of Figure A.8. In such a case, the predictions can some-

FIGURE A.8 Scatter Plots Showing High (A) and Low (B) Correlations Between SAT Scores and College GPA

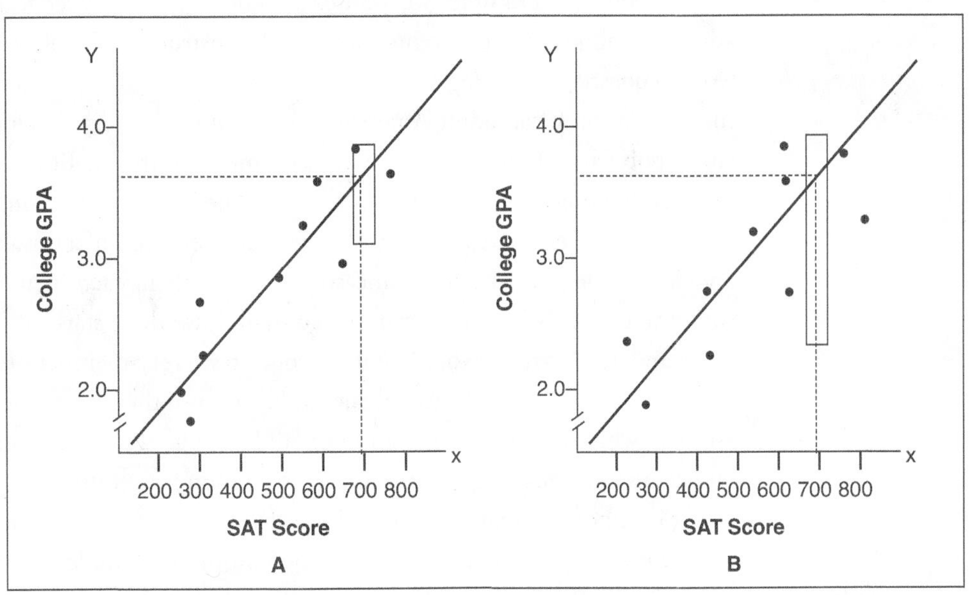

times be way off. Take a look at the GPAs of the students who scored around 700 on the SAT in the two panels; these points are boxed in on the graphs. In the left panel, which depicts a high correlation, you can see that all the students ended up with high college GPAs and all were fairly close to 3.6, the average we would predict using the regression line. In contrast, in the right panel, the students with 700 on the SAT varied widely in their GPAs, with some as low as 2.2 and others as high as 3.95. Regression would have predicted 3.6 for all of them, but this prediction would have been way off for some students. *The lower the correlation is between the two variables, the less precise will be our predictions.* In fact, if the correlation drops to zero, a regression equation will not improve our prediction at all—once again our best guess would be the mean. Given some degree of correlation, however, we can do better using regression than by simply guessing the mean, and the higher the correlation is, the better our predictions will be.

Multiple regression

Using more than one predictor variable to predict a response variable.

Often there is more than one variable that is correlated with the criterion (the number we are trying to predict). In such cases, a procedure called **multiple regression** can be used to improve and maximize the accuracy of our predictions. For example, in addition to SAT scores, we might also know each student's high school GPA and rank in his or her high school class. Rank, GPA, and SAT scores all could then be combined by using multiple regression to predict college GPA. Multiple regression techniques are also used by stockbrokers to predict the direction and amount of change in the price of a particular stock. As you can imagine, knowledge of an accurate set of predictor variables in this case could be quite valuable.

INFERENTIAL STATISTICS

Inferential statistics are used to make inferences from data, to draw conclusions, and to test hypotheses. Two of the basic concepts in inferential statistics are *estimation* and *hypothesis testing.*

Estimation

One use of inferential statistics is to estimate the actual value of some population characteristic. Suppose, for example, we wanted to know how knowledgeable, on average, American adults are about current events. We could construct a test of current events with carefully worded questions covering as many areas of current news as possible. Since we are interested in the population of all adult Americans, we could test every American age 18 and older (the entire population) and compute a mean score on our test. But it would be handy to have a short-cut method that did not require testing the entire population.

In order to estimate the mean and standard deviation of a variable in a population, we take a *sample* of the population and measure the variable in each member of the sample. We then compute the statistics on the sample scores and use these statistics to estimate what the mean and standard deviation would be if we could test every member of the population. For example, we might sample 200 American adults and use their scores on our current events test to estimate what the whole population of adults is like. Public opinion polls and the TV rating services use this sampling approach and estimation procedure.

It is important that the sample be *representative* of the population, which is usually done by making the sample a random selection from all possible members of the population. A **random sample** is one in which everyone in the specified population has the same chance of being in the sample. For example, it would not be a fair sample for estimating Americans' knowledge of current events if we measured only white female citizens of La Mirada, California. The second factor in sampling is sample size. Generally, the larger the sample, the more accurate the estimates. If you randomly chose one person from the phone book, scheduled him or her for our test of current events, got a score, and then estimated that this score was the mean for all American adults, you would almost certainly be off the mark. A sample larger than a single person is needed. But how many should there be in the sample? The amazing thing about sampling is that the size of the sample necessary to get a fairly accurate idea of the population is much smaller than you might guess. A sample of 200 American adults out of 150 million, if properly drawn, should provide a very accurate estimate of the entire population. There are ways of estimating how big a sample you need for a given level of accuracy. Of course, if the sample is not properly drawn and is not representative, then increasing the sample size will not improve the accuracy of estimation.

Random sample

Sample group of a larger population that is selected by randomization procedures. A random sample differs from a representative sample.

Hypothesis Testing

When we set out to do an experiment in psychology, we always begin with a hypothesis. For our brief discussion, we use the example of a psychologist who wants to know if breathing pure oxygen after strenuous exertion facilitates recovery. The psychologist carefully devises a test of recovery time that gives a consistent score (i.e., it is a reliable measure) and accurately predicts recovery in real life situations (i.e., it is a valid measure). The working hypothesis in the study is that athletes who breathe pure oxygen after exercise will recover more quickly than athletes who breathe normal air. The psychologist gets 30 athletes to volunteer for the experiment and randomly assigns them to one of two groups, 15 per group. The random assignment is designed to create two groups that are approximately equal in average recovery time at the start of the experiment. All of the subjects are then instructed to run 800 meters as quickly as they can. Immediately following each subject's run they are seated and fitted with a breathing mask that delivers either pure oxygen or normal air. Heart rate and respiration rates are measured to determine recovery time.

After all of the subjects are tested the psychologist finds that the mean recovery time for the athletes breathing pure oxygen was 118 seconds and the mean recovery time for athletes breathing normal air was 126 seconds. Can the psychologist conclude that breathing pure oxygen facilitates recovery? Think about your answer before reading on.

If the differences between the recovery times for the two groups was quite large (118 vs. 156 seconds) our psychologist could be confident that breathing pure oxygen does in fact facilitate recovery. Likewise, if the difference in recovery times was very small (118 vs. 119 seconds) we would be fairly confident that breathing pure oxygen had no effect. But what do we conclude about results that fall between these extremes?

There has to be an objective way to decide whether or not the psychologist's hypothesis can be accepted. We cannot leave it up to intuition. Here we can turn to inferential statistics. There are many different kinds of inferential statistics; in this case a ***t*-test** for comparing two sample means is appropriate.

***t*-test**

A statistical test used to compare two sample means.

We want to decide whether the difference between 118 (the mean recovery time for athletes breathing pure oxygen) and 126 seconds (the mean recovery time for the athletes breathing normal air) is a real difference or whether it can be attributed to chance or measurement error. In other words, is it a *statistically significant difference?* A difference is said to be statistically significant if it is very unlikely that it would happen by chance alone. The difference in mean recovery times for the two groups is 8 seconds (126 – 118 = 8).

For a moment, let's assume that oxygen has no effect on recovery times. This assumption is called the *null hypothesis.* Note that the null hypothesis predicts no difference, whereas our working hypothesis (that breathing pure oxygen facilitates recovery) does predict a difference. Specifically, the null hypothesis predicts that the variable being manipulated (the independent variable) will have no effect on the behavior being measured (the dependent variable). It is the null hypothesis that is actually tested with inferential statistics. We then draw conclusions about our working hypothesis on the basis of our findings regarding the null hypothesis.

What we need to know is if *the null hypothesis is true* (that breathing pure oxygen does not effect recovery time) what is the probability that the two samples will differ by eight seconds? If oxygen does not facilitate recovery, then any difference we find between our two groups will be just a chance difference. After all, we would not expect two random groups of 15 people to have exactly the same recovery times. Sample means will differ, and every once in a while there will be a difference of eight seconds by chance alone, with no help from oxygen. The question is how often will we get a difference this large? Or what is the probability of this difference occurring by chance alone?

In order to answer this question, we must know not only the mean values, but also the standard deviations in the two samples. We have to know how much variability between people there is in recovery times. Look at the three panels in Figure A.9. Each panel shows two frequency distributions, one for the oxygen group and one for the normal air group. Note that in each panel, the mean of the oxygen group is 118 and the mean of the normal air group is 126, but the three panels display quite different pictures in terms of variability in recovery times among people within each group. In the top panel, the variability within each group is very

FIGURE A.9 Comparisons of Three Outcomes in Variability

Each figure shows the same mean (118 vs. 126) with different amounts of variability.

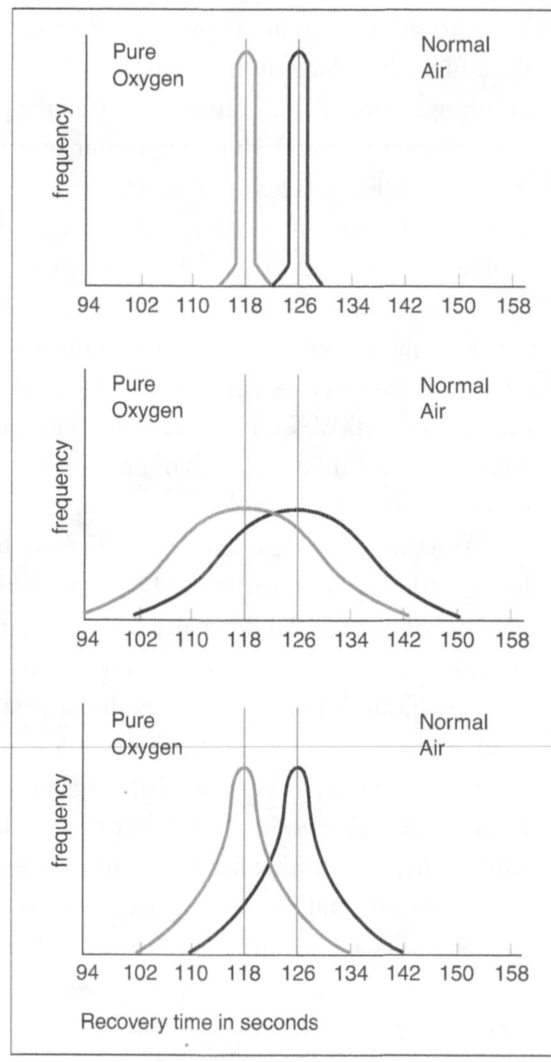

small (all of the recovery times are close to their respective means). In this case it looks as though the eight-second difference is a significant one.

In the middle panel, there is a great deal of variability in recovery times between people within each group. There is a lot of overlap in the two distributions. Many of the subjects breathing normal air recovered more quickly than the mean for the oxygen group. In fact, there is so much overlap in the two distributions that we would probably question whether the difference between 118 and 126 (the two means), which is very small compared to the variability, is just a chance difference. The two distributions look almost identical.

Situations like those depicted in the top panel are very rare indeed. Unfortunately, the middle panel is a more common outcome of an experiment—the means are so close together and there is so much overlap of scores that the groups appear to be indistinguishable on the dependent variable. The bottom panel represents the most common outcome of all. Here, the conclusion is less clear. The two distributions overlap somewhat, much more than in the top panel, but much less than in the middle panel. There is a moderate amount of variability among subjects within each group. Can we conclude whether the 118- to 126-second mean difference is a real one? Stated differently, is there a statistic ally significant difference between the means?

The *t*-test is designed to answer this question. The *t*-test is a ratio, the ratio of mean difference to an error term. A primary factor in the error term is the variability of scores within each group. In the top panel the difference is eight seconds, but the variability of scores within each group is very small. Therefore, the error term will be small. So if we divide the mean difference by this very small error term, we shall get a large number for the *t* ratio, and we then declare the difference to be significant. In the middle panel, the same eight-second difference will be divided by a very large error term, giving us a very small *t* ratio. We declare the difference insignificant. In the bottom panel, we have the borderline case. We divide the mean difference by a moderate-sized error term, and the *t* value obtained will be moderately large. What do we conclude? Fortunately for us, statisticians have prepared tables of the probability of various values of *t* occurring by chance. We compute the *t* ratio and then look it up in the statistical tables to find the chance probability of a *t* as large as the one we found. If the table tells us that the observed *t* ratio is unlikely to happen by chance, we conclude that what we have is not a chance effect but a real difference. Alternatively, most computer solutions to *t*-tests give the exact probability for each computed value oft. By convention, we use a cutoff probability of .05. That is, if the probability of obtaining a given *t* value is less than or equal to .05 we conclude that there is a significant difference between the two groups.

The null hypothesis says, "There is no difference in recovery times between groups breathing pure oxygen and those breathing normal air." If we obtain a significant *t* ratio, we conclude that the null hypothesis is wrong. Statistical inference is basically a procedure for drawing conclusions about the null hypothesis. Of course, our inference about the null hypothesis has implications for our working hypothesis. If we reject the null hypothesis and conclude that the observed difference between the groups is significant, then we can further conclude that breathing pure oxygen does facilitate recovery because the athletes in our study who used pure oxygen recovered more quickly than athletes who did not breathe pure oxygen.

We do not discuss the details of actually calculating a *t* ratio. You can find that information in any elementary statistics book Simply remember that when an experiment is done, the results will usually indicate some differences between the conditions in the study. The *t*-test, as well as many other types of inferential statistics, are used to help the experimenter decide whether the differences are large enough, relative to the variability, to allow rejection of the null hypothesis and support for the working hypothesis.

It is important to realize that statistical decisions are not always perfect; sometimes we make an incorrect decision on the basis of the data even though we have done everything correctly. There is always the chance, for example, that the samples are not truly representative of the populations from which they were drawn. There are two types of errors that can occur when we draw conclusions from experimental data, and these are depicted in Table A.9. A *Type I error* is made when we conclude that the independent variable has an effect on the dependent variable, when the truth of the matter is that it has no effect. A *Type II error* is made when we conclude that the independent variable has no effect on the dependent variable

TABLE A.9 Type I and Type II Errors in Decisions Based on Experimental Data

EXPERIMENTAL HYPOTHESES	
WORKING HYPOTHESIS	**NULL HYPOTHESIS**
Oxygen Facilitates Recovery	Oxygen Does Not Facilitate Recovery

DECISION ERRORS

TYPE I ERROR: REJECTING THE NULL HYPOTHESIS WHEN IT IS TRUE.

Example: Claiming oxygen facilitates recovery when in fact oxygen does not facilitate recovery.

TYPE II ERROR: ACCEPTING THE NULL HYPOTHESIS WHEN IT IS FALSE.

Example: Concluding that oxygen does not facilitate recovery when in fact *oxygen facilitates recovery.*

when, in fact, it does. Each type of error has a certain probability of occurring in any given experiment. By tradition, we require strong evidence for an effect of the independent variable on the dependent variable before we accept that such an effect exists. What this means is that we try to minimize the level of Type I error. However, you should note that Type I error and Type II error have an inverse relationship to one another—as one increases, the other decreases. Therefore, minimizing Type I errors will normally result in an increase in Type II errors. The task for the researcher is to balance these two types of errors, which requires a thorough understanding of research design and statistical procedures.

ADVANCED STATISTICAL TECHNIQUES

Analysis of Variance

The *t*-test is used when testing the difference between the means of two groups. But experiments may have more than two groups, and so the *t*-test is not used in such cases. Instead, a statistical procedure called **analysis of variance** is used. Analysis of variance is conceptually very similar to the *t*-test. The size of the mean difference between groups is compared to an error term that is, in part, a function of the variability within each group. In fact, the analysis of variance procedure and the *t*-test will lead to the same decision in the special case where there are just two groups. The test in analysis of variance is known as the *F*-test, named after the famous English statistician R. A. Fisher. Analysis of variance allows the experimenter to make inferences or draw conclusions about the differences among a set of means. It is a very common statistical procedure and you are likely to encounter the *F*-test if you read psychology journals.

Analysis of variance

A statistical test used to compare more than two sample means.

Factor Analysis

Factor analysis is a highly sophisticated correlational procedure that is used to identify the basic factors underlying a psychological phenomenon. The technique boils down to finding clusters of tests that correlate with one another. Suppose we administer the following six tests to 100 college students: (1) vocabulary, (2) ability to shoot baskets, (3) ability to write an essay on philosophy, (4) speed at running the 100-yard dash, (5) ability to understand statistics, and (6) speed at swimming 100 meters. Each person takes all six tests, and then we inter-correlate the tests. We correlate test 1 with 2, 1 with 3, 1 with 4, and so on. Suppose we find that tests 1, 3, and 5 correlate highly with one another and that 2, 4, and 6 correlate highly with one another, but that 1, 3, and 5 show little or no correlation with 2, 4, and 6. Why would this result be the case? Look at the tests: tests 1, 3, and 5 all involve thinking or knowledge—they all require "academic ability." On the other hand, tests 2, 4, and 6 all require "physical ability." So probably 1, 3, and 5 all are measuring something in common, which we might call Factor A. Would you guess that Factor A has something to do with intelligence? Tests 2, 4, and 6 also seem to be measuring something in common. We will call it Factor B. Because tests 1, 3, and 5 do not correlate with tests 2, 4, and 6, we conclude that Factor A, which we now have decided to call *intelligence,* is not the same thing as Factor B, which we might label *athletic ability.*

In short, we have isolated two factors that are involved in performance on our six tests; one we call intelligence, and the other we call athletic ability. Factor analysis is basically a correlational technique that allows us to separate performance on a large number of tests into factors, by isolating clusters of tests (even when the clustering is not as obvious as it is in the foregoing example). Correlations between tests are high within a cluster but low among clusters. We assume that the clusters then "represent" and measure psychological factors.

This technique has been used extensively in two areas of psychology—intelligence testing and personality assessment. Intelligence consists of many factors, as does personality. With factor analysis we can identify these factors and hope to learn more about intelligence and personality.

Glossary

Abnormal behavior Behavior that is atypical, maladaptive, socially unacceptable, and produces emotional discomfort.

Absolute threshold Minimum physical intensity of a stimulus that can be perceived by an observer 50 percent of the time.

Accommodation In vision, the focusing process in which the lens adjusts its shape, depending on the distance between the eye and the object viewed, in order to project a clear image consistently onto the retina. In Piaget's theory, the process of adjusting existing knowledge so that new information can fit more readily.

Acetylcholine (ACh) The neurotransmitter that is released from motor neurons onto muscle fibers to make them contract. Appears to also be involved in learning and memory.

Achievement need *See Need for achievement.*

Acquisition In classical conditioning, the process of learning to associate a conditioned stimulus with an unconditioned stimulus. In operant conditioning, the process of learning to associate responses with a reinforcer or punisher.

Acronym Meaningful arrangement of letters that provides a cue for recalling information; a mnemonic device.

Acrostics Sentences whose first letters serve as cues for recalling specific information; a mnemonic device.

Action potential Electrical signal that flows along the surface of the axon to the terminal buttons, initiating the release of neurotransmitters.

Active listening Technique in which person-centered therapists indicate their acceptance and understanding of what clients say.

Adaptation In perception, the decrease in the response of sensory receptors to stimuli when exposed to continual, unchanging stimulation.

Adolescent growth spurt Period of accelerated growth that usually occurs within about two years after the onset of puberty.

Adrenal glands Glands within the endocrine system, located just above the kidneys that influence emotional state, energy levels, and responses to stress by releasing hormones.

Aerial perspective *See Atmospheric perspective.*

Afferent neuron *See Sensory neuron.*

Age regression A phenomenon believed to be associated with hypnosis, in which the hypnotized subject appears to move back in time to reenact events that occurred in earlier years. Age regression seems to be role-playing of the subject's current conception of his or her past.

Agnosia Is a loss of ability to recognize objects, persons, sounds, shapes, or smells while the specific sense organ is not defective. It is generally due to loss in cortical areas that analyze the information received from the sense organ.

Agoraphobia An anxiety disorder characterized by an intense fear of being in places or situations from which escape might be difficult or in which help might not be available, such as stores, theaters, and trains. Agoraphobia often accompanies panic disorder.

Alcohol **A CNS** Depressant drug that acts to impair motor coordination, reaction time, thinking, and judgment.

Algorithm A problem-solving strategy that involves a systematic exploration of every possible solution; computers and people may use algorithms to find the correct answer.

All-or-none law Refers to the fact that once an Action Potential is triggered, there is no stopping it. It will be conducted to the end of the axon.

Altered state of consciousness state in which your consciousness is different from its NEA or Norma Everyday Awareness. Some of these states are natural, for e.g. sleep and some are brought on by deliberate efforts to change one's state of consciousness through drugs, meditation, or hypnosis.

Alzheimer's disease An incurable disease that destroys neural tissue resulting in an impaired capacity to remember, think, relate to others, and care for oneself. Generally seen in the elderly.

American Psychological Association (APA) The major professional organization of psychologists in the United States.

American Psychological Society (APS) Professional group of academic and research psychologists founded in 1988.

Amniocentesis A method of prenatal screening for fetal abnormalities in which a small sample of amniotic fluid is extracted from the uterus for chromosome analysis.

Amphetamines A group of powerful stimulants, including Benzedrine, Dexedrine, and Ritalin that dramatically increase alertness and promote feelings of euphoria.

Amygdala A small limbic system structure located next to the hippocampus in the brain that plays an important role in the storage and recall of traumatic memories.

Anal stage In Freud's theory of psychosexual development, the period between about 12 months and three years of age, during which the erogenous zone shifts from the mouth to the anal area.

Analysis of variance A statistical test used to compare more than two sample means.

Anandamide A naturally occurring substance that binds to THC receptors in the brain. Marijuana contains THC, which also binds to these receptors.

Androgens Male sex hormones the most common of which is testosterone.

Anorexia nervosa Eating disorder characterized by prolonged refusal to eat adequate amounts of food. This condition is most common among young females.

Anterograde amnesia Memory loss for information processed after an individual experiences brain trauma caused by injury or chronic alcoholism.

Antianxiety drugs Drugs used to reduce symptoms of anxiety and tension in disorders that are not severe enough to warrant hospitalization. These drugs are also known as minor tranquilizers.

Antidepressant drugs Drugs used to treat major depressive disorder.

Antimanic drugs Drugs used to control the manic symptoms of bipolar disorder.

Antipsychotic drugs Drugs used to treat the disorder known as schizophrenia.

Antisocial personality disorder Personality disorder characterized by disregard for rights of others, lack of remorse or guilt for antisocial acts, irresponsibility in job or marital roles, failure to learn from experience, and a profound poverty of deep and lasting emotions.

Anxiety Free-floating fear or apprehension that may occur with or without an easily identifiable source.

Anxiety disorder Any of a number of disorders that produce pervasive feelings of anxiety.

Aptitude test Test designed to predict an individual's ability to learn new information or skills.

Archetypes Powerful emotionally charged universal images or concepts in Carl Jung's theory of the collective unconscious. *See also Collective unconscious.*

Arousal A physiological state in which an individual is able to process information effectively and to engage in motivated behavior.

Artificial intelligence (AI) Field of specialization in which researchers develop computer models to simulate human cognitive processes and to solve problems.

Association cortex The largest portion of the cerebral cortex (about 75 percent), involved in integrating sensory and motor messages as well as processing higher functions such as thinking, interpreting, and remembering.

Associative learning Making a connection or association between two events, through either classical conditioning or operant conditioning.

Atmospheric perspective Monocular distance cue based on the fact that distant objects tend to appear more fuzzy and less clear than those close to the viewer due to dust and haze. Also known as Aerial perspective.

Attachment The emotional bond that typically forms between an infant and its caregiver, usually a parent.

Attention Psychological selection mechanism that determines which stimuli an organism responds to or perceives.

Attitude Any learned, relatively enduring predisposition to respond in consistently favorable or unfavorable ways to certain people, groups, ideas, or situations.

Attribution theory A theory which states that we attempt to make sense out of other people's behavior, by attributing it to either dispositional (internal) causes or external (situational) causes.

Auditory cortex Region of the temporal lobe that is involved in responding to auditory signals, particularly the sound of human speech.

Auditory localization Ability to locate the origins of sounds by differences from ear to ear in variables such as intensity and the time the sound arrives at each ear.

Auditory memory *See Echoic memory.*

Authoritarian Style of parenting in which parents rely on strictly enforced rules, leaving little room for children to discuss alternatives.

Authoritarian personality A personality characterized by intolerance, emotional coldness, rigidity, submission to higher authority, stereotyped thinking, and identification with power.

Authoritative Parenting Style of parenting in which parents delineate clear rules and standards but also show respect for children's opinions.

Autonomic nervous system Division of the peripheral nervous system that transmits messages between the central nervous system and the endocrine system as well as the smooth muscles of the heart, lungs, stomach, and other internal organs which operate without intentional control.

Availability heuristic Approach to decision making based on information assessed from memory. It assumes that the probability of an event is related to how frequently it occurred in the past, and that events occurring more frequently are easier to remember.

Aversive conditioning A behavior therapy approach which utilizes aversive stimuli to decrease the occurrence of a specific response. *See Punishment.*

Avoidance conditioning In operant conditioning, the learning of a response to a discriminative stimulus that allows an organism to avoid exposure to an aversive stimulus.

Awareness One's subjective sense of oneself, one's actions, and one's environment.

Axon Extension of a neuron that transmits an impulse from the cell body to the terminal buttons on the tip of the axon.

Balance theory Theory that people are inclined to achieve consistency in their attitudes by balancing their beliefs and feelings about a particular issue, object, event, or situation against their attitudes about other people.

Basal ganglia Neural structures involved in the initiation of motor movement and emotion.

Basic anxiety In Karen Horney's neoFreudian theory, the insecurity that results when children perceive their parents as indifferent, harsh, disparaging, or erratic in their responsiveness. *See also Basic hostility.*

Basic hostility In Karen Horney's neo-Freudian theory, a deep resentment associated with basic anxiety that motivates one of three ineffectual patterns of social interaction: moving against others, moving away from others, or moving toward others. *See also Basic anxiety.*

Basic level In a concept hierarchy, the classification that people naturally use when they think about an object.

Basilar membrane Membrane in the cochlea of the inner ear that vibrates in response to pressure waves, causing auditory hair cells on the adjoining organ of Corti to release neurotransmitters that activate neurons of the auditory nerve.

Behavior therapy Therapy based on the assumption that maladaptive behavior has been learned and can therefore be unlearned.

Behavioral medicine Study of how behavior patterns (smoking, drinking, lack of exercise, etc.) and emotions like stress and anxiety can contribute to physical diseases.

Behaviorism A school of thought that rejected the study of the mind or mental processes and focused on the study of observable behavior only.

Between-group differences Differences, or response variability, between treatment conditions.

Binocular cues Visual cues for depth or distance, such as binocular disparity and convergence that depend on both eyes working together.

Biofeedback Technique providing individuals with information (feedback) about their bodily processes that they can use to modify those processes.

Biological psychology Branch of neuroscience that focuses on the relationship between behavior and physiological events within the brain and the rest of the nervous system.

Biological rhythms Variations in biological function that repeat regularly after a certain amount of time has elapsed.

Biological rhythms Natural variations in biological functions, hormonal activity, temperature, and sleep that typically cycle every 24 to 25 hours. Also called circadian rhythms.

Biologically-based motives Motives such as hunger and thirst that are rooted primarily in body tissue needs; sometimes referred to as drives.

Bipolar disorder Mood disorder characterized by intermittent episodes of both depression and mania.

Body senses Term used to describe the two interrelated sensory systems of kinesthesis and equilibrium.

Brain stimulation Technique for studying the brain that involves stimulating precise regions with a weak electric current.

Brightness Intensity of light, measured by the number of photons, or particles of electromagnetic radiation, emitted by a light source.

Brightness constancy Element of perceptual constancy. We perceive objects that we see at night or in poor lighting to be the same brightness as they appear during the day.

Broca's area Region of the left frontal lobe that is the primary brain center for controlling speech.

Bulimia Eating disorder characterized by periodic episodes of binge eating followed by deliberate purging using either vomiting or laxatives.

Caffeine Stimulant found in coffee, tea, and chocolate that acts to increase arousal, heart rate, and blood pressure.

California Psychological Inventory Global personality assessment test designed specifically for use with normal populations.

Cannon-Bard theory Theory that emotions occur simultaneously with physiological changes, rather than deriving from body changes as the James-Lange theory suggests.

Cardinal trait In Gordon Allport's trait theory of personality, a powerful, dominating behavioral predisposition that is an organizing principle in a small number of people's lives. *See also Central trait and Secondary trait.*

Case study Method of research that involves in-depth study of one or more subjects who are examined individually using direct observation, testing, experimentation, and other methods.

Caudate nucleus A component of the basal ganglia involved with the control and initiation of motor movement. An area of the brain affected by Huntington's disease. Located adjacent to the putamen.

Cell body The largest part of a neuron, containing the nucleus as well as structures that handle metabolic functions.

Central nervous system (CNS) The part of the nervous system that consists of the brain and the spinal cord.

Central trait In Gordon Allport's trait theory of personality, a major characteristic such as honesty or sensitivity. *See also Cardinal trait and Secondary trait.*

Centration Inability to take into account more than one perceptual factor at a time. In Piaget's theory of cognitive development, centration is characteristic of the preoperational stage of development.

Cerebellum Brain structure located beneath the overhanging back part of the cerebral hemispheres which functions to coordinate and regulate motor movements.

Cerebral cortex Thin outer layer of the brain's cerebrum (sometimes called the gray matter) that is responsible for movement, perception, thinking, and memory.

Cerebral hemispheres The two sides (right and left) of the cerebrum.

Cerebrum The largest part of the brain, consisting of two cerebral hemispheres.

Chorionic villi sampling (CVS) Method of prenatal screening for fetal abnormalities in which threadlike protrusions on the membrane surrounding the fetus are extracted and cultured for chromosome analysis.

Chromosome A strand of DNA that contains the organism's genes.

Chunk Meaningful unit of short-term memory.

Chunking Process of grouping items into longer meaningful units to make them easier to remember.

Classical conditioning Learning that takes place when a neutral stimulus (the CS) is paired with a stimulus (UCS) that already produces a response (UCR). After conditioning, the organism responds to the neutral stimulus (CS) in some way. The response to the CS is called a conditioned response (CR).

Classical conditioning therapy Any behavior therapy that involves classical conditioning. For example, systematic desensitization therapy.

Climacteric Physiological changes, including menopause, that occur during a woman's transition from fertility to infertility.

Clinical psychology Area of specialization involved in the diagnosis and treatment of behavioral problems.

Closure Perceptual organizing principle that we tend to perceive incomplete figures as complete.

Clustering Mnemonic device involving grouping items into categories.

Cocaine Powerful central nervous system stimulant derived from the leaves of the coca shrub.

Cochlea Coiled, fluid-filled chamber in the inner ear with two flexible surfaces: the oval window and the round window.

Coefficient of correlation Statistic used to describe the degree of relationship between two or more variables. Positive correlations indicate that variables vary together in the same direction; negative correlations indicate the opposite.

Cognitive Abilities Test (CAT) Group intelligence test widely used in many school systems.

Cognitive behavior therapy Cognitive therapy aimed at restructuring irrational thinking patterns such as the tendency to use negative self-labels.

Cognitive dissonance theory Theory that people experience psychological discomfort or dissonance whenever two related cognitions or behaviors are in conflict.

Cognitive expectancies A learned expectancy of relationships between stimuli (in Pavlovian conditioning) and between responses and outcomes (in operant conditioning).

Cognitive learning Learning that involves processes such as thinking and reasoning.

Cognitive learning theory Theoretical perspective that attempts to study the role of thinking and memory processes in learning.

Cognitive map Internal representations of the relationship between events or spatial elements.

Cognitive psychology Approach to psychology focusing on the ways in which organisms process information. Investigates processes such as thinking, memory, language, problem solving, and creativity.

Cognitive therapies Approaches to therapy that are based on the premise that most behavioral disorders result from distortions in cognitions or thoughts.

Cohabitation Living together in a sexual relationship without being married.

Collective unconscious In Carl Jung's theory, a kind of universal memory bank that contains all the ancestral memories, images, symbols, and ideas that humans have accumulated throughout their evolvement. *See also Archetypes and Personal unconscious.*

Color constancy An element of perceptual constancy. We perceive objects that we see in the dark to be the same color as they appear during the day even though their retinal images change.

Compensatory model Decision-making model such as the additive model and the utility-probability model in which the desirable potential outcomes of alternative choices are weighed against undesirable potential outcomes.

Complex psychosocial motives Motives that demonstrate little or no relationship to biological needs, but are determined by learning.

Compliance Form of social influence in which people alter their behavior in response to direct requests from others, which usually involve a degree of coercion.

Computerized axial tomography (CAT) A procedure used to locate brain abnormalities that involve rotating an X-ray scanner around the skull to produce an accurate image of a living brain.

Concepts Cognitive categories for grouping events, objects, or processes.

Concordance Degree to which twins share a trait. Expressed as a correlation coefficient.

Concrete operations stage Third stage of cognitive development in Piaget's theory (ages 7 through 12), during which children begin to use logical mental operations or rules, mastering the concept of conservation.

Concurrent validity Type of criterion-related validity that involves comparing test performance to other criteria that are currently available. *See also Predictive validity.*

Conditioned reinforcer A stimulus that takes on reinforcing properties after being associated with a primary reinforcer. *See Secondary reinforcer.*

Conditioned response (CR) In classical conditioning, a learned response to a stimulus.

Conditioned stimulus (CS) In classical conditioning, a stimulus that elicits a response only after being associated with an unconditioned stimulus.

Conditioned taste aversion A learned aversion to a relatively novel taste or flavor that occurs following illness or nausea.

Conduction hearing loss Hearing loss caused by the failure of the outer and middle ear to conduct sound energy to the inner ear's receptors, sometimes due to infection or to buildup of ear wax.

Cones Photoreceptor cells distributed across the inner layer of the retina that play an important role in the perception of color.

Confirmation bias In problem solving, the tendency to seek out evidence that confirms a hypothesis and to overlook contradictory evidence.

Conformity Tendency to change or modify behaviors so that they are consistent with those of other people.

Connectionism The learning theory proposed by Thorndike that learning is the result of forming associations or connections between stimuli and responses. Modern connectionism is focused on discovering the neurobiological mechanisms underlying learned associations.

Consciousness State of awareness or alertness to processes that are going on inside or outside one's own body.

Conservation The understanding that changing the form of an object does not necessarily change its essential character. A key achievement in Piaget's theory of cognitive development. *See also Concrete operations stage.*

Consolidation Process by which information is transferred from short-term electrical activation of neuronal circuits to a longer-term memory coded by physical cell changes in the brain.

Continuous reinforcement schedule In operant conditioning, the presentation of a reinforcer for each occurrence of a specific behavior.

Control group In experimental psychology, a group of subjects who experience all the same conditions as subjects in the experimental group except for the key factor (independent variable) the researcher is evaluating.

Controlled drinking Technique for overcoming alcoholism through teaching skills that allow a person to drink in moderation.

Conventional morality Second level in Lawrence Kohlberg's theory of moral development, consisting of stages 3 and 4, in which the motivating force for moral behavior is the desire either to help others or to gain approval.

Convergence Binocular distance cue based on the fact that the two eyes must converge or rotate toward the inside to perceive objects closer than about 25 feet. The closer the object, the more rotation is necessary and the more muscle tension created.

Convergent thinking Thinking in which an individual responds to information presented in a problem by eliminating possibilities and narrowing his or her responses down to the single best solution.

Conversion disorder Somatoform disorder that is manifested as a sensory or motor system disorder for which there is no known organic cause.

Coronary heart disease (CHD) Any illness that causes a narrowing of the coronary arteries.

Corpus callosum Broad band of nerve fibers that connects the left and right hemispheres of the cerebral cortex.

Correlation coefficient *See Coefficient of correlation.*

Correlational method Research method that uses statistical techniques to determine the degree of relationship between variables.

Correspondent inference theory Theory that the attributions we make about other people's behavior are influenced by a variety of conditions, such as the social desirability of that behavior or whether the behavior results from free choice.

Counseling psychology Area of specialization involved in the diagnosis and treatment of problems of adjustment. Counseling psychologists tend to focus on less serious problems than do clinical psychologists; they often work in settings such as schools.

Couple therapy Therapy in which partners meet together with a therapist.

Covariation principle Theory that our attributions about people's behavior are influenced by the situations in which the behavior occurs, the persons involved, and the stimuli or objects toward which the behavior is directed.

Covert behavior Behavior that is unobservable in another person. Thinking is an example of covert behavior.

Crack Street name for a processed form of cocaine that takes effect more rapidly and is available at a cheaper price than powdered cocaine.

Creativity Ability to produce outcomes that are novel as well as useful or valuable.

Credibility Quality of trustworthiness and perceived expertise that increases the likelihood a communicator will persuade an individual to change his or her attitude.

Criterion-keyed test Assessment test in which each test item is referenced to one of the original criterion groups that were used in developing the test.

Criterion-related validity Method of assessing test validity that involves comparing peoples' test scores with their scores on other measures already known to be good indicators of the skill or trait being assessed.

Critical periods Periods in the developmental sequence during which an organism must experience certain kinds of social or sensory experiences in order for normal development to take place.

Cross-sectional design Research design in which groups of subjects of different ages are assessed and compared at one point in time, so that conclusions may be drawn about behavior differences which may be related to age differences.

Cross-sequential design Research design that combines elements of the cross-sectional and longitudinal designs. Subjects are observed more than once over a period of time.

Crowding Psychological response to a lack of space, characterized by subjective feelings of overstimulation, distress, and discomfort.

Crystallized intelligence Intelligence that results from accumulated knowledge, including knowledge of how to reason, language skills, and understanding of technology. *See also Fluid intelligence.*

Cultural mores Established customs or beliefs in a particular culture.

Cumulative curve A measure of the strength of an operant response; the more frequently an operant response takes place, the steeper the curve.

Cumulative record A chart recording of operant responses over time. Time increments are indicated along the horizontal axis and operant responses along the vertical axis. As response rate increases the slope of the record increases.

Dark adaptation Process by which an organism's vision gradually becomes more sensitive to minimal levels of light due to a chemical change in the rods and cones of the retina.

Declarative memory Recall of specific facts, such as information read in a book. *See also Procedural memory, Episodic memory, and Semantic memory.*

Defense mechanism In Freud's psychoanalytic theory, an unconscious maneuver that shields the ego from anxiety by denying or distorting reality.

Delayed conditioning In classical conditioning, learning that takes place when the conditioned stimulus is presented just before the unconditioned stimulus is presented and continues until the organism begins responding to the unconditioned stimulus.

Delusion An exaggerated and rigidly held belief that has little or no basis in fact.

Dendrite Branchlike extensions from a neuron with the specialized function of receiving messages from surrounding neurons.

Dependent variable In experimental research, the behavior that results from manipulation of an independent variable.

Depressants Psychoactive drugs, including opiates, sedatives, and alcohol that have the effect of slowing down or depressing central nervous system activity.

Descriptive statistics Mathematical/graphical methods for reducing data to a form that can be readily understood.

Developmental psychology Field of specialization in psychology concerned with factors that influence development and shape behavior throughout the life cycle, from conception through old age.

Difference threshold The minimum difference in intensity that we can distinguish between two stimuli 50 percent of the time. Also known as the just noticeable difference (JND).

Diffusion of responsibility Tendency for an individual to feel a diminished sense of responsibility to assist in an emergency when other bystanders are present.

Direct perception The interpretation of sensory information directly by the brain as opposed to perceptual interpretation resulting from cognitive processing.

Discrimination In classical and operant conditioning, the process by which responses are restricted to specific stimuli. In social psychology, the behavioral consequence of prejudice in which one group is treated differently from another group.

Discriminative stimulus In operant conditioning, a stimulus that controls a response by signaling the availability of reinforcement.

Dissociation theory A theory of hypnosis proposed by Hilgard in which our behaviors become separated from or dissociated from our awareness.

Dissociative amnesia Memory loss not attributable to disease or brain injury.

Dissociative disorders Group of disorders, including psychogenic amnesia, psychogenic fugue, and multiple personality, in which the thoughts and feelings that generate anxiety are separated or dissociated from conscious awareness.

Dissociative identity disorder A condition of separation in personality, or multiple personality, not attributable to disease or brain injury.

Divergent thinking Thinking in which an individual comes up with unusual but appropriate responses to questions, often associated with creativity.

Dizygotic twins *See Fraternal twins.*

DNA (deoxyribonucleic acid) Chemical substance whose molecules, arranged in varying patterns, are the building blocks of genes.

Dominant gene Gene that prevails when paired with a recessive gene, so that it is always expressed in the phenotype.

Dopamine A neurotransmitter involved with the initiation of motor movement, attention, and learning and memory. The dopamine system mediates reward and pleasure and it is the substance of addiction.

Door-in-the-face technique Method for encouraging compliance in which an unreasonable request is followed by a more minor, reasonable request (which is the requester's goal in the first place).

Dopamine A neurotransmitter substance released at terminal buttons of dopaminergic neurons in the brain. Dopamine is believed to be involved in movement and emotion. Abnormal levels of dopamine contribute to Parkinson's disease and schizophrenia.

Down syndrome Chromosomal disorder characterized by marked mental retardation as well as distinctive physical traits including short stature, a flattened skull and nose, and an extra fold of skin over the eyelid.

Dream analysis Psychoanalytic technique involving the interpretation of dreams to learn about hidden aspects of personality.

Drive Term commonly used to describe motives that are based on tissue needs, such as hunger and thirst.

Dual-code model of memory Theory that memories may be stored either in sensory codes or in verbal codes.

Echoic memory Auditory sensory memory; fleeting impressions of what we hear. Also known as auditory memory.

Echolalia Speech disturbance characteristic of some forms of schizophrenia in which people repeat virtually every statement they hear uttered.

Educational psychology Field of specialization in psychology concerned with the study and application of learning and teaching methods, focusing on areas such as improving educational curricula and training teachers.

Efferent neuron *See Motor neuron.*

Ego In Freud's psychoanalytic theory, the component of personality that acts as an intermediary between the instinctual demands of the id and the reality of the real world. *See also Id, Superego, and Reality principle.*

Egocentrism The tendency of young children to view the world as being centered on themselves.

Eidetic imagery Also known as photographic memory, the very rare ability to retain large amounts of visual material with great accuracy for several minutes.

Elaborative rehearsal System for remembering that involves using mnemonic devices; it is more effective than maintenance rehearsal.

Electrical recording Technique for studying the brain in which tiny wires implanted in the brain are used to record neural electrical activity.

Electroconvulsive therapy (ECT) Biomedical intervention in which electrical current applied to the brain induces a convulsive seizure. Used to treat depression.

Electroencephalography (EEG) Technique used to measure and record electrical activity of the cortex.

Embryo transfer Procedure in which a female donor is artificially inseminated with sperm, and approximately five days after fertilization the tiny embryo is removed from the woman donor and transferred surgically into the uterus of the mother-to-be, who then carries the pregnancy. Used in cases where a couple wishes to have a child, but the female partner carries a defective gene.

Embryonic stage Second stage of prenatal development, lasting from the beginning of the third week to the end of the eighth week after fertilization, characterized by fast growth and differentiation of the major body systems as well as vital organs.

Emotions An individual's subjective feelings and moods. The term applies to both physiological and behavioral responses to specific stimulus situations.

Empathic understanding Key element of person-centered therapy, referring to therapists' ability to see the world as the client sees it.

Empirical tests Tests in which scientists manipulate conditions or behaviors, for the purposes of testing a hypothesis, and observe the results.

Empiricism The philosophical position that all knowledge is obtained from direct experience.

Encoding In memory, the process of perceiving information, then categorizing or organizing it in a meaningful way so that it can be more easily stored and recalled.

Endocrine system System of ductless glands, including the pituitary, thyroid, parathyroid, adrenals, pancreas, and gonads, that secrete hormones directly into the bloodstream or lymph fluids.

Endorphins A class of neurotransmitter substances that function to inhibit the transmission of pain information. Morphine and other opiates act by facilitating endorphin transmission.

Engineering psychology Field of specialization concerned with creating optimal relationships among people, the machines they operate, and the environments they work in. Sometimes called human factors psychology.

Engram A neural representation of something learned.

Environmental psychology Field of specialization concerned with assessing the effects on behavior of environmental factors such as noise, pollution, or overcrowding.

Episodic memory Autobiographical memories about one's own experiences.

Equilibrium The sense of balance, localized within the inner ear and comprising two sensory receptors: the semicircular canals and the vestibular sacs.

Escape conditioning In operant conditioning, learning that takes place when an organism performs a response that will terminate an aversive stimulus.

Estrogens Hormones that influence female sexual development.

Ethology The scientific study of the evolution of animal behavior including humans.

Excitatory postsynaptic potentials (EPSPs) Effects that occur when excitatory neurotransmitters cause a graded potential to occur on the dendrite or cell body of a receiving neuron.

Exemplar theory Theory that the natural concepts we form in everyday life are structured around prototypes or typical representatives of categories (such as robins and jays as prototypes of the concept bird).

Experimental groups In experimental research, groups of subjects who are exposed to different varieties of independent variables, so that resulting behaviors can be compared.

Experimental psychology Field of specialization in which the primary activity is conducting research.

Experimental research Research conducted in precisely controlled laboratory conditions in which subjects are confronted with specific stimuli and their reactions are carefully measured to discover relationships among variables.

Expert system A computer program designed to solve a particular kind of problem. MYCIN is an expert system to aid physicians in making diagnoses.

Extinction In classical conditioning, the process by which a conditioned response is eliminated through repeated presentation of the conditioned stimulus without the unconditioned stimulus. In operant conditioning, the process of eliminating a response by discontinuing reinforcement for it.

Extroversion Personality trait manifested by sociability, friendliness, and interest in people and events in the external world. *See also Introversion.*

Facial feedback theory Theory that specific facial displays are universally associated with the expression of the emotions of fear, anger, happiness, sadness, surprise, interest, disgust, and shame.

Factor analysis A complex statistical procedure used to categorize or clump a group of related variables. A group of related variables is referred to as a factor.

False consensus bias Attribution bias caused by the assumption that most people share our own attitudes and behaviors.

False memory A memory of an event that never occurred.

Family therapy Therapy in which family members meet together with a therapist.

Fear of success Motivation to avoid achievement, especially among women, because of the potential negative consequences of success.

Fetal alcohol syndrome (FAS) Variety of developmental complications including spontaneous abortion, premature birth, infants born addicted to alcohol, and numerous developmental disabilities that are related to the mother's use of alcohol during pregnancy.

Fetal stage Third and final stage of prenatal development, extending from the beginning of the third month to birth, during which bone and muscle tissue form and the organs and body systems continue to develop.

Fetus Term used to describe an unborn infant during the period from the beginning of the third month after fertilization until birth.

Figure In perception, the part of an image on which we focus our attention.

Fixation In Freud's theory of psychosexual development, arrested development that results from exposure to either too little or too much gratification.

Fixed interval (FI) schedule Partial reinforcement schedule in operant conditioning wherein reinforcement is provided for the first response after a specified period of time has elapsed.

Fixed ratio (FR) schedule Partial reinforcement schedule in operant conditioning wherein reinforcement occurs after a fixed number of responses.

Flashbulb memory An apparent vivid recall for an event associated with extreme emotion or uniqueness, such as the assassination of a president or the bombing of Iraq.

Flextime Approach to scheduling work hours in which employees have some flexibility in picking starting and quitting times, as long as they are present during core work hours.

Fluid intelligence Ability to perceive and draw inferences about relationships among patterns of stimuli, to conceptualize abstract information, and to solve problems. *See also Crystallized intelligence.*

Foot-in-the-door technique Technique for encouraging compliance in which a person is first asked to agree to a relatively minor request that serves as a setup for a more major request.

Forensic psychology Field of specialization that works with the legal, court, and correctional systems to develop personality profiles of criminals, make decisions about disposition of convicted offenders, and help law enforcers understand behavioral problems.

Formal concepts Logical, clearly defined concepts with unambiguous rules specifying what features belong to that category.

Formal-operations stage Fourth and final stage in Piaget's theory of cognitive development (ages 12+), during which individuals acquire the ability to make complex deductions and solve problems by systematically testing hypotheses.

Fovea A small area near the center of the retina containing densely packed cones used for color vision and fine visual acuity.

Fraternal twins Twins produced when two ova are fertilized by two different sperm cells, so that their genetic codes are no more similar than those of any other siblings. Also known as dizygotic twins.

Free association Psychoanalytic technique developed by Sigmund Freud in which patients relax and say whatever comes to their minds.

Frequency theory of pitch discrimination Theory that perception of low tones depends on the frequency with which auditory hair cells in the inner ears organ of Corti trigger the firing of neurons in the auditory nerve.

Frontal lobe Largest, foremost lobe in the cerebral cortex; an important region for movement, emotion, and memory.

Frustration-aggression hypothesis Theory that aggression is always a consequence of frustration, and that frustration leads to aggression.

Functional fixedness Tendency to be so set in our perception of the proper function of a given object that we are unable to think of using it in a novel way to solve a problem.

Functional magnetic resonance imaging (*f*MRI) A method of magnetic resonance imaging that measures energy released by brain cells that are active during a specific task. *See magnetic resonance imaging.*

Functionalism Approach to psychology that emphasized the functional, practical nature of the mind. Influenced by Darwin's theory of natural selection, functionalists attempted to learn how mental processes, such as learning, thinking, and perceiving, helped people adapt.

Fundamental attribution error Tendency to overestimate dispositional (internal) causes and to underestimate situational (external) causes of behavior.

G-factor One of the two factors in Charles Spearman's conceptualization of intelligence, the g-factor consists of general intelligence, which is largely genetically determined. *See also S-factor.*

Gamete The reproductive cells, or sperm and ovum. Also known as germ cells.

Gamma-amino butyric acid (GABA) GABA is the major inhibitory neurotransmitter in the brain and spinal cord. It plays an important role in regulating arousal and anxiety.

Gate-control theory Theory that neural gates in the spinal cord allow passage of pain signals to the brain; these gates may be closed by the simultaneous firing of non-pain nerve fibers, so that pain is not perceived.

Gender identity An individual's subjective sense of being male or female.

Gender role Set of behaviors that is considered normal and appropriate for each sex in a society.

Genes The chemical blueprints of all living things. Genes are made of DNA molecules, and each chromosome contains thousands of genes.

Gene therapy *See Genetic engineering.*

General adaptation syndrome (GAS) Progressive responses to prolonged stress in which an organism mobilizes for action and compensates for stress.

Generalization Process by which an organism responds to stimuli that are similar to the conditioned stimulus, without undergoing conditioning for each similar stimulus.

Generalized anxiety disorder Chronic state of free-floating anxiety that is omnipresent.

Genital stage Fifth and final stage in Freud's theory of psychosexual development, beginning with puberty, during which sexual feelings that were dormant during the latency stage reemerge.

Gestalt psychology Approach to psychology that argues that the entirety or the whole of an experience is different from the sum of its parts. Gestalt psychology is an active force in current investigations of perceptual processes and learning as well as therapy, where it emphasizes the whole person.

Gestalt therapy Therapy approach that attempts to help individuals bring the alienated fragments of their personalities into an integrated, unified whole.

Gibson's theory of direct perception A theory of perception that argues that all information necessary for perception is available to the sensory system and no cognitive processing is necessary to complete the perceptual process.

Glia cells Specialized cells that form insulating covers called myelin sheaths around the axons of some neurons, increasing conductivity.

Glutamate (glutamic acid) An amino acid derived from glucose. This neurotransmitter plays an important excitatory function. MSG contains glutamate.

Glucostatic theory Theory that hunger results when glucoreceptors detect a lack of glucose, either because blood levels of glucose are low or because insulin is not available in sufficient quantity.

Glycogen A carbohydrate that can be synthesized from glucose for the storage of nutrients. Glycogen can also be converted into glucose for energy.

Gonadotropins Hormones released by the pituitary gland that stimulate production of testosterone in men and estrogen in women.

Gonads Glands within the endocrine system (ovaries in females and testes in males) that produce sex hormones that influence development of sexual systems and secondary sex characteristics as well as sexual motivation.

Good continuation Perceptual grouping principle that we are more likely to perceive stimuli as a whole or single group if they flow smoothly into one another than if they are discontinuous.

Graded potential Voltage change in a neuron's dendrites that is produced by receiving an impulse from another neuron or neurons. *See also Excitatory postsynaptic potentials and Inhibitory postsynaptic potentials.*

Ground In perception, the background against which the figure that we focus on stands. *See also Figure.*

Group therapy Therapy in which three or more clients meet simultaneously with a therapist.

Growth hormone Pituitary hormone that controls several metabolic functions including the rate of growth of the bones and soft tissues.

Gustation The sense of taste, which, like olfaction, is activated by chemical senses in the environment.

H-Y antigen Substance that appears to trigger the transformation of gonads into testes early in development

Hallucination False perception that lacks a sensory basis. Can be produced by hallucinogenic drugs, fatigue, or sensory deprivation. Often associated with severe psychotic disorders.

Hallucinogens Class of psychoactive drugs, like LSD and PCP that alter sensory perceptions, thinking processes and emotions, often causing delusions, hallucinations, and altered sense of time and space.

Halo effect Tendency to infer other positive or negative traits from our perception of one central trait in another person.

Health psychology Area of specialization concerned with the interaction between behavioral factors and physical health.

Hebb's cell assemblies Groups of neurons whose activities have been altered by learning.

Height on a plane Important monocular depth cue based on the fact that objects that are highest on one's plane of view appear to be farthest away.

Hebbian rule A neural mechanism for learning, which states that neurons that are simultaneously active develop an increase in the effectiveness of their synaptic connections.

Heritability An estimate ranging from 0 to 1.0 that indicates the proportion of variance in a trait that is accounted for by heredity.

Hermaphrodite Individual with ambiguous or contradictory sex characteristics resulting from abnormal differentiation of internal and external sex structures.

Heterozygous Genotype that contains different genes for a trait (for instance, both brown-eye and blue-eye genes).

Heuristics Rule-of-thumb (quick-fix) problem-solving strategies such as means-ends analysis and working backward.

Higher order conditioning In classical conditioning, the process by which a conditioned stimulus is used to condition the same response to other stimuli.

Hippocampus Structure in the brain's limbic system that seems to play an important role in memory.

Homosexual Primary erotic, psychological, and social interest in members of the same sex, even though that interest may not be expressed overtly.

Homozygous Genotype that consists of the same genes for a trait (for instance, brown-eye genes inherited from both parents).

Hormones Chemical messengers secreted by the endocrine glands that act to regulate the functioning of specific body organs.

Hospice Facility designed to care for the special needs of the dying, including love and support, pain control, and maintaining a sense of dignity.

Hue The color we perceive, determined partly by the wavelength of light and partly by the complex process by which an organism's visual system mixes wavelengths.

Humanistic psychology Approach to psychology that emphasizes the role of free choice and our ability to make conscious rational decisions about how we live our lives.

Huntington's disease Also known as Huntington's chorea, a genetically transmitted disease that progressively destroys brain cells in adults.

Hypertension Commonly referred to as high blood pressure; a condition of excessive blood flow through the vessels that can result in both hardening and general deterioration of the walls of the vessels.

Hypnosis State of altered consciousness characterized by a deep relaxation and detachment as well as heightened suggestibility to the hypnotist's directives.

Hypochondriasis Somatoform disorder in which the individual is excessively fearful of contracting a serious illness or of dying.

Hypothalamus Small structure located below the thalamus in the brain that plays an important role in motivation and emotional expression, as well as controlling the neuroendocrine system and maintaining the body's homeostasis. The hypothalamus is part of the limbic system.

Hypothesis Statement proposing the existence of a relationship between variables, typically as a tentative explanation for cause and effect. Hypotheses are often designed to be tested by research.

Iconic memory Visual sensory memory, including fleeting impressions of what we see. Also known as visual memory.

Id In Freud's psychoanalytic theory, the biological component of personality consisting of life instincts and death instincts. *See also Ego, Superego, Libido, and Pleasure principle.*

Identical twins Twins who share the same genetic code. Also known as one-egg or monozygotic twins.

Illusion False or inaccurate perception that differs from the actual physical state of the perceived object.

Illusion of control Attributional bias caused by the belief that we control events in our own lives that are really beyond our control.

Immune system A complex surveillance system that guards the body by recognizing and removing bacteria, cancer cells, and other hazardous foreign substances.

Implicit personality theories Assumptions people make about how traits usually occur together in other people's personalities.

Impression management Tendency of individuals to select carefully what information they reveal about their attitudes, depending on how they think such information will affect their image in the eyes of others.

Imprinting Process by which certain infant animals, such as ducklings, learn to follow or approach the first moving object they see. *See also Critical periods.*

Incentive Any external stimulus that can motivate behavior even when no internal drive state exists.

Independent variable Condition or factor that the experimenter manipulates in an experiment in order to determine whether changes in behavior (the dependent variable) result.

Indiscriminate attachment Attachment typically displayed by human infants during the first few months, when social behaviors are directed to virtually anyone. *See also Specific attachment and Separate attachment.*

Inductive reasoning Reasoning that draws broad conclusions by generalizing from specific instances. *See also Deductive reasoning.*

Industrial/organizational (I/O) psychology Field of specialization concerned with using psychological concepts to make the workplace a more satisfying environment for employees and management.

Inferential statistics Process of using mathematical procedures to draw conclusions about the meaning of research data.

Information processing Emerging approach to understanding psychology that uses computers to help develop models of cognitive processing of information.

Informational social influence One basis of conformity, in which we accept a group's beliefs or behaviors as providing accurate information about reality. *See also Normative social influence.*

In-group In social psychology, the group in which people include themselves when they divide the world into "us" and "them."

In-group bias Tendency to see one's own group in a favorable light.

Inhibitory postsynaptic potentials (IPSPs) A transitory state of hyperpolarization that occurs when inhibitory neurotransmitters inhibit the postsynaptic membrane of a receiving neuron. *See also Graded potential.*

Insight Sudden recognition of relationships that leads to the solution of a complex problem.

Insomnia Sleep disorder characterized by a consistent inability to get to sleep or by frequent awakenings during sleep.

Instincts Innate patterns of behavior that occur in every normally functioning member of a species under certain set conditions.

Intelligence An operational definition states simply that intelligence is what intelligence tests measure, although intelligence is commonly understood to include the abilities to think rationally and abstractly, act purposefully, and deal effectively with the environment.

Intelligence quotient (IQ) Intelligence measurement derived by dividing an individual's mental age by the chronological age, then multiplying by 100.

Interneurons Neurons of the central nervous system that function as intermediaries between sensory and motor neurons.

Interpersonal aggression Any physical or verbal behavior intended to hurt another person.

Interposition *See Overlap.*

Interview Method used in psychological studies in which an individual is asked questions. Interviews may be informal and unstructured or they may be highly structured.

Introversion Personality trait expressed as shyness, reclusiveness, and preoccupation with the inner world of thoughts, memories, and feelings. *See also Extroversion.*

Invariant Sensory information from the environment that is constant from one experience to the next. For example, texture is invariant because it is always finer at close distances than is at further distances.

James-Lange theory Theory that explains emotional states (such as fear) resulting from an organism's awareness of bodily responses to a situation, rather than from cognitions about that situation.

Job description index (JDI) Measure of job satisfaction that assesses five dimensions, including supervision, coworkers, promotions, pay, and the work itself.

Just noticeable difference (JND) *See Difference threshold.*

Karyotype Chart in which photographs of an individual's chromosomes are arranged according to size and structure.

Kinesthesis Bodily sense that provides information about perceptions of the location of various body parts in relation to other parts and about the position of the body in space.

Language acquisition device (LAD) According to the genetic or nativist view, the prewiring that gives humans the innate ability to learn and understand language.

Latency period Fourth state of psychosexual development in Freud's theory, extending from about age five to puberty, during which sexual drives remain unexpressed or latent.

Latent content In psychoanalysis theory, the hidden content or true meaning of dreams.

Latent learning Learning that is not demonstrated by an immediately observable change in behavior.

Lateral hypothalamus (LH) An area of the hypothalamus that is important for taste sensation, mediating digestive processes, and salivation.

Lateralization of function Degree to which a particular function, such as the understanding of speech, is controlled by one rather than both cerebral hemispheres.

Law of Effect Theory originally proposed by Edward Thorndike that is the foundation of the operant conditioning theory: Behavior followed by reinforcement will be strengthened while behavior followed by punishment will be weakened.

Leaderless group discussion Technique used in some assessment centers that places several job applicants in a group and asks them to solve a business problem while many realistic emergencies and interruptions occur.

Learned helplessness A response produced by exposure to unavoidable aversive stimuli. Characterized by the inability to learn an avoidance response.

Learning Relatively enduring change in potential behavior that results from experience.

Lesion production Technique for studying the brain that involves surgical damage to a precise region of the brain.

Libido In Freud's psychoanalytic theory, the energy that fuels the id and motivates all behavior.

Life review Process by which older people may retrospectively view their past, sorting out their accomplishments from their disappointments.

Light adaptation Process by which an organism's vision adjusts to bright lighting, due to a chemical change within the rods and cones of the retina.

Limbic system Collection of structures located around the central core of the brain that play a critical role in emotional expression as well as motivation, learning, and memory. Key structures of the limbic system include the amygdala, the hippocampus, the amygdala, and the hypothalamus.

Linear perspective Important monocular distance cue based on the fact that parallel lines converge when stretched into the distance.

Linear regression Using the general linear model $y = mx + b$ to predict values for y given values for x.

Linguistic-relativity hypothesis Notion that the language of a particular culture determines the content of thoughts among members of that culture, and the way these people perceive and think about their world.

Lipostatic theory Theory that explains long-term eating control as a result of a constant monitoring of levels of body fat, which is used as a barometer to regulate food intake. *See also Set point.*

Lobotomy Surgical procedure that severs the nerve tracts connecting the prefrontal cortex to lower brain areas that mediate emotional responses.

Longitudinal design Research design that evaluates a group of subjects at several points in time, over a number of years, to assess how certain characteristics or behaviors change during the course of development.

Long-term memory (LTM) The third memory system in the three-system model of memory. Information transferred from short-term to long-term memory may be stored for periods of time from minutes to years.

Long-term potentiation (LTP) An increase in a neuron's sensitivity to fire following a burst of signals to that neurons dendrites.

Loudness In hearing, the intensity of a sound as measured by decibels. Loudness is determined by the amplitude of a sound wave.

LSD (Lysergic acid diethylamide) Hallucinogenic drug derived from a fungus that grows on rye grass that produces profound distortions of sensations, feelings, time, and thought.

Lucid dreaming Process of being aware that one is dreaming and of influencing the content of one's own dreams.

Magnetic resonance imaging (MRI) Procedure for studying the brain that uses radio waves to excite hydrogen protons in the brain tissue, creating a magnetic field change.

Maintenance rehearsal System for remembering that involves repeatedly rehearsing information without attempting to find meaning in it. *See also Elaborative rehearsal.*

Major depressive disorder Type of mood disorder characterized by deep and persistent depression.

Manic-depression *See Bipolar disorder.*

Manifest content In psychoanalytic theory, the disguised version of the latent content, or true meaning, of dreams.

Marijuana Drug derived from the hemp plant *Cannabis sativa,* containing the chemical THC (delta 9-tetrahydrocannabinol), which is commonly classified as a hallucinogen, although it also may have depressant and stimulant effects.

Maturation Orderly unfolding of certain patterns of behavior, such as language acquisition or walking, in accordance with genetic blueprints.

MDMA Common name for 3, 4-methlenedioxy methamphetamines (also known as ecstasy); a designer drug chemically related to amphetamines that acts as a central nervous system stimulant.

Mean In descriptive statistics, the arithmetic average obtained by adding scores and dividing by the number of scores.

Means-ends analysis Common heuristic problem-solving strategy that involves identifying the difference between an original state and a desired goal, then progressing through a series of subgoals to reach the solution.

Measure of central tendency In descriptive statistics, a value that reflects the middle or central point of a distribution of scores. The three measures of central tendency are the mean, the median, and the mode.

Measure of variability In descriptive statistics, a value that reflects the middle or central point of a distribution of scores. The three measures of central tendency are the mean, the median, and the mode.

Median In descriptive statistics, the score that falls in the middle of a distribution of numbers arranged from the lowest to the highest.

Meditation Practice of deliberately altering one's state of consciousness in an effort to achieve a state of deep relaxation. Meditation is characterized by alpha brain waves as well as other physiological measures such as lowered respiration and heart rate.

Medulla Structure low in the brain that controls vital life support functions such as breathing, heartbeat, and blood pressure; it also regulates many reflexive functions such as coughing or sneezing.

Memory (1) Process or processes of storing newly acquired information for later recall; (2) recall for a specific experience, or the total collection of remembered experiences stored in our brains.

Menopause Cessation of menstruation that takes place during the climacteric.

Mental age In IQ testing, the chronological age of children who on the average receive a test score similar to that of the subject. For instance, a six year old whose composite score is equivalent to that of a nine year old has a mental age of nine.

Mental set In problem solving, a tendency to approach a problem or situation in a predetermined way, regardless of the requirements of the specific problem.

Mere exposure effect Phenomenon by which repeated exposure to novel stimuli tends to increase an individual's preference for such stimuli.

Mnemonic device Memory system, such as clustering or acrostics, that organizes material in a meaningful way to make it easier to remember.

Mode In descriptive statistics, the score that occurs most frequently in a distribution of numbers.

Modeling Learning process wherein an individual acquires a behavior by observing someone else performing that behavior. Also known as observational learning.

Monoamine theory The theory that attributes depression to abnormalities in brain the monoamines, norepinephrine and serotonin.

Monocular cues Distance cues such as linear perspective and height on a plane that can be used with just one eye.

Monozygotic twins *See Identical twins.*

Mood disorders Class of disorders including major depression and bipolar disorder that are characterized by persistent depression (which in bipolar disorder is accompanied by intermittent episodes of mania).

Morpheme Smallest unit of meaning in a given language.

Motion parallax *See Relative motion.*

Motivation Any condition that might energize and direct an organism's actions.

Motor cortex Region of the cerebral cortex that transmits messages to muscles. The motor cortex controls virtually all intentional body movement.

Motor neuron Neuron that transmits messages from the central nervous system to muscles or glands.

Multifactor motive Motive based on a combination of biological, psychological, and cultural factors.

Multifactorial inheritance Genetic transmission in which several gene pairs interact to produce a trait.

Multiple personality Form of dissociative disorder in which a person alternates between a primary personality and one or more secondary or subordinate personalities.

Multiple regression Using more than one predictor variable to predict a response variable.

Mutism Speech disturbance characteristic of schizophrenia in which an individual may not utter a sound for hours or days at a time.

Myelin sheath Insulating cover around some axons that increases a neuron's ability to transmit impulses quickly. Myelin sheaths are made of specialized cells called glia cells

Narcolepsy Sleep disorder characterized by falling asleep suddenly and uncontrollably.

Narcotics Also known as opiates, a class of depressant drugs that includes opium, morphine, codeine, and heroin.

Natural concepts Concepts that are commonly used in thinking about events and experiences, but that are more ambiguous than formal concepts.

Naturalistic observation Psychological research using the observational method that takes place in a natural setting, such as a subject's home or school environment.

Nature-nurture controversy Controversy over whether individual differences are the result of genetic endowment (nature) or of learning (nurture).

Need for achievement (nAch) Complex psychosocial motive to accomplish difficult goals, attain high standards, surpass the achievements of others, and increase self-regard by succeeding in exercising talent.

Negative afterimage The image that is seen after the retina is exposed to an intense visual image. A negative afterimage may consist of colors that are complements to those of the original image.

Negative reinforcement In operant conditioning, any stimulus that increases the probability of a response through its removal. For example, pounding on the wall (operant behavior) may be maintained by the termination of loud noise (negative reinforcer) in an adjoining room.

Neo-Freudians Psychologists who were in general agreement with Freud's basic interpretation of the structure of personality, his focus on the unconscious, and his emphasis on childhood experience, but dissented regarding other aspects of Freud's theory, such as his emphasis on aggressive impulses and unconscious sexual conflicts.

Neologisms Literally, new words. Invention of neologisms is characteristic of schizophrenic disorder.

Neural network model A model of the nervous system based on the connections among numerous neurons. Neural network models are believed to simulate real properties of neural connections.

Neuroleptic drugs Class of drugs that have the effect of calming and quieting patients with some psychotic disorders, most notably schizophrenia. Also known as antipsychotic drugs or major tranquilizers.

Neurometrics Technique for electrophysiological measurement of neural functioning. Neurometrics uses computer analysis of EEG patterns and evoked potentials to measure a variety of sensory, perceptual, and cognitive processes mediated by the brain.

Neuron Type of cell that is the basic unit of the nervous system. A neuron typically consists of a cell body, dendrites, and an axon. Neurons transmit messages to other neurons and to glands and muscles throughout the body.

Neurosis Term originally used by Freud to describe anxiety disorders, and widely used until publication of *DSM-III* to describe a range of disorders that are distressing and often debilitating, but are not characterized by a loss of contact with reality.

Neurotransmitter Chemical messenger that transmits an impulse across the synaptic gap from one neuron to another.

Nicotine Stimulant found in tobacco that acts to increase heart rate, blood pressure, and stomach activity and to constrict blood vessels.

Nightmare Bad dream that occurs during REM sleep.

Node of Ranvier Small gap or exposed portion of the axon of a neuron between the glia cells that form the myelin sheath.

Norepinephrine A major excitatory neurotransmitter in the brain. It is distributed throughout the central and peripheral nervous systems and is important in emotional arousal and stress.

Norm Standard that reflects the normal or average performance of a particular group of people on a measure such as an IQ test.

Normal distribution In descriptive statistics, a distribution in which scores are distributed similarly on both sides of the middle value, so that they have the appearance of a bell-shaped curve when graphed.

Normal state (of consciousness) State of consciousness in which a person is alert and aware of his or her environment, as contrasted to alternative or altered states of consciousness.

Normative social influence Social influence in which we conform not because of an actual change in our beliefs, but because we think we will benefit in some way (such as gaining approval). *See also Informational social influence.*

NREM sleep (Non-rapid eye movement sleep) Stages of sleep during which rapid eye movements typically do not occur. Dreaming occurs far less frequently during NREM sleep than during REM sleep.

Obedience Social influence in which we alter our behavior in response to commands or orders from people perceived as having power or authority.

Obese Condition in which an individual weighs 20 percent or more above the desirable weight for his or her height.

Object permanence Realization that objects continue to exist even when they are not in view. Piaget sees this awareness as a key achievement of the sensorimotor stage of development.

Observational learning *See Modeling.*

Observational method Method of psychological research in which subjects are observed as they go about their usual activities. The observational method provides descriptive information. *See also Naturalistic observation.*

Observer bias Tendency of an observer to read more into a situation than is actually there or to see what he or she expects to see. Observer bias is a potential limitation of the observational method.

Observer effect Tendency of subjects to modify behavior because they are aware of being observed.

Obsessive-compulsive disorder Anxiety disorder characterized by persistent, unwanted, and unshakable thoughts and/or irresistible, habitual repeated actions.

Occipital lobe Region at the rear of the cerebral cortex that consists primarily of the visual cortex.

Oedipus complex In Freud's theory of psychosexual development, the attraction a male child feels toward his mother (and jealousy toward his father) during the phallic stage.

Olfaction The sense of smell, which, like taste, is activated by chemical substances in the environment.

Olfactory bulb The end of the olfactory nerve that receives input from olfactory receptors.

One-egg twins *See Identical twins.*

Operant conditioning Learning process also known as instrumental conditioning by which an organism learns to associate its own behavior with consequences.

Operant conditioning Behavior modification techniques that attempt to influence behavior by manipulating reinforcers.

Operational definition Definition specifying the operations that are used to measure or observe a variable, such as a definition of obesity specifying a certain weight-height relationship.

Opiates *See Narcotics.*

Opponent-process theory of color vision Theory that explains color vision based on six primary colors, which are grouped into three pairs (red-green, blue-yellow, black-white). Receptors in the eye are sensitive to specific pairs, and the presence of one member of a pair inhibits vision of the other. *See also Trichromatic theory.*

Opponent-process theory of emotion Theory that when a strong emotional response to a particular stimulus disrupts emotional balance, an opposite emotional response is eventually activated to restore emotional equilibrium.

Optic disk A structure in the retina where the optic nerve exits; sometimes referred to as the blind spot.

Optimum level of arousal Level of arousal at which an individual's performance on a specific task is most efficient.

Oral stage According to Freud, the first stage of psychosexual development spanning birth through 12 to 18 months, during which the lips and mouth are the primary erogenous zone.

Organ of Corti Structure in the inner ear located directly above the basilar membrane, consisting of auditory hair cells, a tectoral membrane, and cilia.

Organ reserve Potential ability of organs such as the heart, lungs, and kidneys to increase their output to a level several times greater than normal under emergency conditions.

Organic amnesia Memory deficits caused by altered physiology of the brain, which might result from an accident or certain physical illnesses.

Ossicles Set of three tiny linked bones (the malleus, incus, and stapes) in the middle ear that receives a sound stimulus from the tympanic membrane and transfers it to the oval window of the inner ear.

Otis-Lennon School Ability Test (OLSAT) Group IQ test for children of all ages that is widely used in schools.

Outgroup The "them" group when individuals divide the world into "us" and "them."

Overlap Important monocular distance cue based on the fact that objects close to us tend to block out parts of objects that are farther away. Also known as interposition.

Overlearning Technique for memorizing material that involves rehearsing information after it has already been learned.

Panic disorder Anxiety disorder in which an individual experiences numerous panic attacks (four or more in a four-week period) that are characterized by overwhelming terror and often a feeling of unreality or of depersonalization.

Paper-and-pencil questionnaire In personality testing, an objective, self-report inventory designed to measure scientifically the variety of characteristics or traits that makeup personality.

Paranoid schizophrenia Subtype of schizophrenic disorder characterized by the presence of well-organized delusional thoughts.

Parasympathetic nervous system Division of the autonomic nervous system that functions to conserve energy, returning the body to normal from emergency responses set in motion by the sympathetic nervous system.

Parietal lobe Region of the cerebral cortex located just behind the central fissure and above the lateral fissure. The parietal lobe contains the somatosensory cortex as well as association areas that process sensory information received by the somatosensory cortex.

Partial reinforcement effect Behaviors that are acquired on partial instead of continuous reinforcement schedules tend to be established more slowly, but are more persistent when no reinforcement is provided.

Partial reinforcement schedule In operant conditioning, a schedule that reinforces behavior only part of the time, for example, a ratio or interval schedule.

Participant management Management strategy in which all levels of employees are included in decision-making.

Patient-controlled analgesia (PCA) Pain-reduction technique in which the patient uses a computerized program to self-administer analgesic medication through intravenous infusions.

PCP (Phencyclidine hydrochloride) Drug commonly known as "angel dust" that produces sensory distortions and hallucinations, as well as having stimulant, depressant, and painkilling properties. Side effects include unpredictable, violent behavior.

Pearson product-moment correlation coefficient The most frequently used measure of correlation, ranging from –1.0 to +1.0. Correlations close to zero indicate little or no relationship between two variables; correlations close to +1.0 or –1.0 indicate more significant positive or negative relationships.

Percentile Numbers from a range of data indicating percentages of scores that lie below them.

Perception Process of interpreting, organizing, and often elaborating on sensations.

Perceptual constancy The fact that objects are normally perceived to be constant in size, color or brightness, and shape, despite the fact that their retinal images change according to different conditions.

Perceptual grouping Tendency to organize patterns of stimuli into larger units according to proximity, similarity, and good continuation.

Perceptual organization Process by which we structure elementary sensations (such as the sight of lines, brightness, and points) into the objects we perceive.

Perceptual set Tendency to see, hear, smell, feel, or taste what we expect or what is consistent with our preconceived notions.

Periaqueductal gray area (PAG) A region of the brain stem that controls pain signals sent to higher brain centers. The PAG also receives signals from endorphin containing neurons for pain analgesia.

Peripheral nervous system (PNS) Portion of the nervous system that transmits messages to and from the central nervous system. Consists of the somatic nervous system and the autonomic nervous system.

Permissive Parenting style in which parents adopt a hands-off policy, making few demands and showing reluctance to punish inappropriate behavior.

Person schemas Generalized assumptions about certain classes of people.

Personal space Invisible boundary or imaginary circle of space with which individuals surround themselves, and into which others are not supposed to enter without invitation.

Personal unconscious In Carl Jung's theory, the part of the unconscious that is akin to Freud's concept of a reservoir of all repressed thoughts and feelings.

Personality Distinctive patterns of behavior, emotions, and thoughts that characterize an individual's adaptations to his or her life.

Personality disorders Diverse class of disorders that is collectively characterized by inflexible and maladaptive personality traits that cause either functional impairment or subjective distress.

Personality psychology Field of specialization that focuses on exploring the uniqueness of the individual, describing the elements that make up human personality, and investigating how personality develops and how it influences people's activities.

Person-centered therapy Therapeutic approach designed to help the client tap his or her own inner resources within a climate of genuineness, unconditional positive regard, and empathic understanding.

PET scan *See Positron emission tomography.*

Phallic stage According to Freud, the third phase of psychosexual development, spanning age three through age five or six, during which the focus of sexual gratification is genital stimulation.

Phenotype Characteristics that result from the expression of various genotypes (for instance, brown eyes or blond hair).

Phenylketonuria (PKU) Disease caused by a recessive gene that results in the absence of an enzyme necessary to metabolize the milk protein phenylalanine.

Pheromones Chemical substances that are secreted by an organism and detected by another organism. Pheromones may function to attract mates, define territories, and facilitate social behavior.

Phobia Any of a number of anxiety disorders that are characterized by a persistent fear of and consequent avoidance of a specific object or situation.

Phonemes Individual sounds (such as those represented by *s* and *sh* in the English spelling system) that are the basic structural elements of language.

Physical attractiveness Physical features that persons of the opposite sex find appealing.

Physiological dependence Addiction to a chemical substance in which withdrawal of that substance results in physiological symptoms such as cramps, nausea, tremors, headaches, or sweating.

Physiological psychology Field of specialization that studies the relationship between physiological processes and behavior. Also known as biological psychology.

Pitch Dimension of hearing that determines how high or low a sound is, measured in hertz. Pitch is determined by the frequency of a sound wave.

Pituitary gland Gland in the endocrine system, located directly below and connected to the hypothalamus. The pituitary gland produces a number of hormones, many of which trigger other endocrine glands to release hormones.

Place theory of pitch discrimination Theory that we discriminate different pitches because sound waves of different frequency displace different regions on the cochlea's basilar membrane.

Pleasure principle According to Freud, the principle guiding the id that seeks immediate gratification of all instinctive drives regardless of reason, logic, or the possible impact of behaviors.

Pons Brain structure located just above the medulla that functions in fine-tuning motor messages, programming species-typical behaviors, processing sensory information, and controlling respiration.

Positive psychology The study of human behavior aimed at discovering and promoting the positive strengths and attributes that enable individuals to thrive and to succeed.

Positive reinforcement therapy Behavior therapy technique that identifies the desired behavior then uses reinforcers to strengthen the behavior.

Positive reinforcement In operant conditioning, any stimulus presented after a response that increases the probability of the response.

Positron emission tomography (PET scan) Technique for studying the brain that involves injecting a subject with a glucose-like sugar tagged with a radioactive isotope that accumulates in brain cells in direct proportion to their activity level.

Posthypnotic suggestion Suggestion or instruction to a hypnotized person that motivates that person to perform an action or actions after returning to a normal state of consciousness.

Posttraumatic stress disorder (PTSD) Anxiety disorder that typically follows a traumatic event or events, and is characterized by a reliving of that event, avoidance of stimuli associated with the event or numbing of general responsiveness, and increased arousal.

Preconscious Mental state describing thoughts and memories that exist on the fringe of awareness, and that can be readily brought into consciousness.

Predictive validity Type of criterion-related validity assessed by determining the accuracy with which tests predict performance in some future situation. *See also Concurrent validity.*

Prejudice Negative, unjustifiable, and inflexible attitude toward a group and its members.

Premenstrual syndrome (PMS) Term used to describe a myriad of physical and psychological symptoms which precede each menstrual period for some women.

Preoperational stage According to Piaget, the second major stage of cognitive development (ages 2 to 6). Preoperational children can develop only limited concepts, and they are unable to evaluate simultaneously more than one physical dimension. *See also Centration.*

Primacy effect Term used to describe the phenomenon that the first information we receive about a person often has the greatest influence on our perceptions of that person.

Primary process thinking According to Freud, wish-fulfilling mental imagery used by the id to discharge tension.

Primary motor cortex The area of the frontal cortex that directly controls motor movement.

Primary reinforcer In operant conditioning, a stimulus that satisfies a biologically based drive or need (such as hunger, thirst, or sleep).

Primary visual cortex The region of the cortex that receives visual information directly from the visual system. *See also Occipital Cortex.*

Proactive interference In memory, the phenomenon that occurs when earlier learning disrupts memory for later learning.

Probability In statistics, the proportion of cases that fit a certain description.

Procedural memory Recall for how to perform skills such as bicycle riding or swimming. *See also Declarative memory.*

Programmed theory *See Genetic clock theory.*

Projection Defense mechanism in which an individual reduces anxiety created by unacceptable impulses by attributing those impulses to someone else.

Prototype Best or most typical representative of a category around which we often structure our concept of that category. *See also Exemplar theory.*

Proximity Perceptual grouping principle whereby, all else being equal, we tend to organize perceptions by grouping elements that are the nearest to each other. In social psychology, the geographical nearness of one person to another which is an important factor in interpersonal attraction.

Psychoactive drugs Drugs that have the effect of altering perceptions and behavior by changing conscious awareness.

Psychoanalysis Technique developed by Freud in which an individual's revelations of normally unconscious cognitions are interpreted.

Psychoanalytic approach Approach to psychology developed by Freud that emphasizes the dynamics among the three forces of personality, the id, ego, and superego; the importance of defense mechanisms; and the importance of dreams as the royal road to the unconscious.

Psychoanalytic theory Theory of personality that views people as shaped by ongoing conflicts between primary drives and the social pressures of civilized society.

Psychogenic amnesia Type of dissociative disorder characterized by sudden loss of memory, usually after a particularly stressful or traumatic event.

Psychogenic fugue disorder Type of dissociative disorder characterized by a loss of memory accompanied by a fugue state in which the individual travels from place to place with little social contact with other people.

Psycholinguistics Psychological study of how sounds and symbols are translated to meaning, and of the cognitive processes that are involved in the acquisition and use of language.

Psychological dependence Dependence on a chemical substance in which a person finds the substance so pleasurable or helpful in coping with life that he or she becomes addicted to its use.

Psychology Scientific study of the behavior of humans and other animals.

Psychoneuroimmunology The scientific study of the relationships between behavior and disease processes.

Psychophysics Study of the relationship between the physical aspects of external stimuli and our own perceptions of these stimuli.

Psychosexual development Stages of development, in Freud's perspective, in which the focus of sexual gratification shifts from one body site to another.

Psychosis Term used until publication of *DSM-III* in 1980 to describe severe disorders that involve disturbances of thinking, reduced contact with reality, loss of ability to function socially, and often bizarre behaviors.

Psychotherapy Any non-biological, noninvasive psychological technique or procedure designed to improve a person's adjustment to life.

Puberty Approximately two-year period of rapid physical changes that occur sometime between ages 7 and 16 in our society and culminate in sexual maturity.

Punisher Any stimulus whose presentation following a response decreases the strength or frequency of the response. *See also Punishment.*

Punishment A procedure in which the presentation of a stimulus following a response leads to a decrease in the strength or frequency of the response. *See also Punisher.*

Putamen A component of the basal ganglia involved with the control and initiation of motor movement. An area of the brain affected by Huntington's disease, located adjacent to the caudate nucleus.

Quantitative psychology Field of specialization that uses mathematical techniques and computer science to aid in understanding human behavior.

Radical behaviorism A strict approach to the study of behavior that emphasizes operant conditioning principles.

Random sample Sample group of a larger population that is selected by randomization procedures. A random sample differs from a representative sample.

Range In descriptive statistics, a measure of variability that indicates the difference between the highest and lowest scores.

Raphe system a group of serotonin-containing neurons extending from the raphe nuclei, located in the pons and medulla, throughout the limbic system and forebrain.

Rational-emotive therapy (RET) Approach to therapy based on the premise that psychological problems result when people interpret their experiences based on self-defeating, irrational beliefs.

Rationalization Defense mechanism in which an individual substitutes self-justifying excuses or explanations for the real reasons for behaviors.

Reaction formation Defense mechanism in which the ego unconsciously replaces unacceptable impulses with their opposites.

Reality principle According to Freud, the tendency to behave in ways that are consistent with reality. The reality principle governs the ego.

Recall In memory tests, a subject's ability to reproduce information that he or she was previously exposed to. Fill-in-the-blank and essay questions test recall.

Receptor Specialized protein molecule on the surface of a dendrite or cell body with which neurotransmitters or certain drugs bind.

Receptor cell Specialized cell that transduces sensory information into neural impulses. Photoreceptors in the retina are receptor cells.

Reciprocal determinism According to Albert Bandura, the principle that individual behaviors and thus personalities are shaped by the interaction between cognitive factors and environmental factors.

Reciprocity The tendency to respond to others in a way similar to how they respond to, or treat us.

Recognition In memory tests, a subject's ability to recognize whether he or she has been previously exposed to information. Multiple-choice and true/false questions test recognition.

Reflex An automatic response to a specific stimulus. An eye blink to a puff of air is a reflex.

Reinforcement In operant conditioning, any procedure where an event following a specific response increases the probability that the response will occur. *See also Reinforcer.*

Reinforcer In operant conditioning, any response contingent event that leads to an increase in the probability, or strength, of the response.

Relative motion Monocular distance cue based on the fact that moving objects appear to move a greater distance when they are close to the viewer than when they are far away. Also known as motion parallax.

Relative size Monocular distance cue based on the fact that objects of the same size appear to be smaller the farther they are from the viewer.

Relaxation response State of deep relaxation similar to meditation. Often used to reduce a stress response.

Relearning Technique for testing memory that involves measuring how much more quickly a person can relearn material that was learned at some previous time.

Reliability In testing, the dependable consistency of a test.

REM sleep State of sleep characterized by rapid eye movements, and often associated with dreaming.

Replication studies Research conducted for the purpose of verifying previous findings.

Representative heuristic Strategy for categorizing an object or situation based on one's preconceived notion of characteristics that are typical of that category.

Representative sample Sample in which critical subgroups are represented according to their incidence in the larger population that the researcher is studying. *See also Survey.*

Repression In psychoanalytic theory, the defense mechanism by which ideas, feelings, or memories that are too painful to deal with on a conscious level are banished to the unconscious.

Residual schizophrenia Term used to describe the residual phase of schizophrenic disorder, which is a recovery phase during which major symptoms are absent or markedly diminished.

Resistance In psychoanalysis, a patient's unwillingness to describe freely some aspects of his or her life.

Response contingency In operant conditioning, the occurrence of a specific response before a reinforcer is presented.

Resting potential State in which a neuron is not transmitting a nerve impulse. A neuron in this state has a net negative charge relative to its outside environment, and this state of potential energy prepares it to be activated by an impulse from an adjacent neuron.

Reticular activating system (RAS) *See Reticular formation.*

Reticular formation Set of neural circuits extending from the lower brain up to the thalamus that play a critical role in controlling arousal and alertness. Also known as the reticular activating system.

Retina Thin membrane at the back of the eye containing photoreceptors called rods and cones. The retina functions to record images.

Retinal disparity *See Binocular disparity.*

Retrieval Process by which information stored in memory is accessed.

Retroactive interference In memory, the phenomenon that occurs when a later event interferes with the recall of earlier information.

Retrograde amnesia Memory loss for certain details or events that occurred prior to experiencing brain trauma; a form of organic amnesia.

Reuptake The process by which neurotransmitter substance is taken back into the terminal button after its release.

Rhodopsin Photopigment contained in the retinal rods.

Rods Photoreceptor cells distributed across the inner layer of the retina that are important in peripheral vision and seeing in dim light.

Rorschach inkblot test Commonly used projective test in which the subject is asked to examine inkblots and say what they look like or bring to mind.

S-factor In Charles Spearman's two-factor theory of the structure of intelligence, s-factors are specific abilities or skills. *See also G-factor*

Saccadic eye movement Rapid movements of the eyes used to scan a visual scene.

Sample Selected segment of a larger population that is being studied in psychological research. Two kinds of samples are the representative sample and the random sample.

Schachter-Singer theory Theory that a given body state can be linked to a variety of emotions depending on the context in which the body state occurs.

Schedule of reinforcement The rule that determines the relationship between responses and reinforcement.

See also Fixed ratio, Variable ratio, Fixed interval, and Variable ratio schedules.

Schemas In reference to memory, conceptual frameworks that individuals use to make sense out of stored information. In Piaget's theory, the mental structures we form to assimilate and organize processed information.

Schizophrenia Class of severe and disabling mental disorders that are characterized by extreme disruptions of perceptions, thoughts, emotions, and behavior. Types identified by *DSM-IV* include disorganized, catatonic, paranoid, undifferentiated, and residual schizophrenia.

School psychology Field of specialization concerned with evaluating and resolving learning and emotional problems.

Scientific method Careful observation of events in the world, the formation of predictions based on these observations, and the testing of these predictions by manipulation of variables and systematic observation.

Seasonal affective disorder (SAD) Diagnostic category in which major depression or bipolar depression recurrently follows a seasonal pattern.

Secondary reinforcer Stimulus that acts as a reinforcer by virtue of its association with one or more primary reinforcers. Also known as a conditioned reinforcer.

Secondary sex characteristics Physical characteristics typical of mature males or females (such as facial, body, and pubic hair) that develop during puberty as a result of the release of testosterone or estrogen.

Second order conditioning A learned association between two conditioned stimuli (CS_2–CS_1) that can occur following conditioning to CS_1 and an unconditioned stimulus (US).

Secular growth trends Changes in human physical growth patterns (including height, weight, and rates of maturation) measured in sample populations throughout the world.

Sedatives Class of depressant drugs including tranquilizers, barbiturates, and nonbarbiturates that induce relaxation, calmness, and sleep.

Selective attention The process of focusing on one or a few stimuli of particular significance while ignoring others.

Selective perception A form of perceptual set; the tendency to perceive stimuli that are consistent with expectations and to ignore those that are inconsistent.

Self-efficacy Individual's belief that he or she can perform adequately and deal effectively with a particular situation.

Semantic memory General, non-personal knowledge about the meaning of facts and concepts.

Semantics Study of meaning in language.

Semicircular canals Three ring-shaped structures in the inner ear that provide information about the body's equilibrium or balance.

Senile dementia Collective term describing a variety of conditions sometimes associated with aging, including memory deficits, forgetfulness, disorientation for time and place, declining ability to think, and so forth.

Sensations Basic, immediate experiences that a stimulus such as a sound elicits in a sense organ such as the ear.

Sensation-seeking motive An explanation for the apparent need for certain levels of stimulation including the need to explore the environment and the need for sensory stimulation.

Sensorimotor stage In Piaget's theory, the period of development between birth and about age two during which infants learn about their worlds primarily through their senses and actions.

Sensorineural hearing loss Hearing loss caused by damage to either the hair cells of the inner ear or the auditory nerve.

Sensory cortex Regions of the cerebral cortex that is involved in receiving sensory messages. *Also see Association cortex.*

Sensory deprivation studies Experimental studies in which subjects lie motionless and are deprived of tactile, visual, and auditory sensations.

Sensory memory First system in the three-system model of memory, in which brief impressions from any of the senses are stored fleetingly, disappearing within a few seconds if they are not transferred to short-term memory. *See also Iconic memory and Echoic memory.*

Sensory neuron Neuron or nerve cell that carries messages to the CNS from receptors in the skin, ears, nose, eyes, and other receptor organs. Also known as afferent neuron.

Serial position effect Tendency to remember items at the beginning and end of a list more readily than those in the middle.

Serotonin A neurotransmitter involved in the control of the sleep/wake cycle, mood, and appetite. Deficiencies in serotonin are associated with sleep disorders, aggression, and depression.

Set point Physiologically preferred level of body weight for each individual.

Sex-linked inheritance Genetic transmission involving genes that are carried only on the X chromosome. (Females carry the XX chromosome pair; males carry the XY pair.)

Sexual orientation Sex to which an individual is attracted.

Shape constancy Element of perceptual constancy. We perceive objects as maintaining the same shape even though their retinal images change when we view them from different angles.

Shaping In operant conditioning, a technique in which responses that are increasingly similar to the desired behavior are reinforced, step by step, until the desired behavior occurs.

Short-term memory (STM) Immediate recollection of stimuli that have just been perceived; unless it is transferred to long-term memory, information in this memory system is usually retained only momentarily. Also called working memory.

Sign stimulus A stimulus to which all members of a species (occasionally of the same sex) respond to in a similar way. Elaborate rump feathers on some birds serve as a sign stimulus for mating.

Similarity In perception, the principle that we tend to group elements that are similar to each other. In social psychology, similarity of beliefs, interests, and values is recognized as a factor attracting people to one another.

Simultaneous conditioning In classical conditioning, learning that takes place when the conditioned stimulus is presented at the same time as the unconditioned stimulus.

Size constancy One form of perceptual constancy. Although the retinal image of an object becomes smaller as the object recedes into the distance (or larger as it approaches), the viewer adjusts for this change and perceives the object to be constant in size.

Skewed In descriptive statistics, the term describes an unbalanced distribution of scores.

Sleep Natural, periodically occurring state of rest characterized by reduced activity, lessened responsiveness to stimuli, and distinctive brain-wave patterns.

Sleep apnea Sleep disorder characterized by irregular breathing during sleep.

Sleep disorders Class of disorders that interfere with sleep, including insomnia, sleep apnea, sleep terrors, nightmares, and sleepwalking.

Sleep talking The production of speech or speech sounds associated with sleep without subjective awareness.

Sleep terror Sleep disorder in which a person suddenly awakens from Stage 4 sleep in a panic, typically with no recollection of a bad dream.

Sleepwalking Sleep disorder, also known as somnambulism, characterized by walking in one's sleep during Stage 3 or 4 of NREM sleep.

Social adjustment function One of the most important functions of our attitudes, which is to allow us to identify with or gain approval from our peers.

Social influence Efforts by others to alter our feelings, beliefs, and behavior.

Social isolation An environment lacking social interaction, such as one in which an elderly person lives alone.

Social learning theory Theory that emphasizes the role of observation in learning.

Social perception Way in which we perceive, evaluate, categorize, and form judgments about the qualities of other people.

Social phobia Anxiety disorder characterized by a persistent, irrational fear of performing some specific behavior (such as talking or eating) in the presence of other people.

Social psychology Field of specialization concerned with understanding the impact of social environments and social processes on individuals.

Social support An environment in which a person has close relatives or personal friends.

Socialization Process by which society conveys behavioral expectations to an individual, through various agents such as parents, peers, and school.

Sociobiology A specialization within biology that seeks to understand the biological factors that underlie social behaviors in all animal species, including humans.

Soma *See Cell body.*

Somatic nervous system Division of the peripheral nervous system that transmits messages to and from major skeletal muscles as well as from sensory organs to the CNS.

Somatization disorder Type of somatoform disorder characterized by multiple and recurrent physical symptoms that have no physical cause.

Somatoform disorder Class of disorders including somatization disorder, hypochondriasis, and conversion disorder that are manifested through somatic or physical symptoms.

Somatosensory cortex Area of the parietal lobe, directly across from the motor cortex in the frontal lobe, which receives sensory information about touch, pressure, pain, temperature, and body position.

Specific attachment Highly selective attachment often displayed by human infants sometime between six and 18 months, when increased responsiveness is displayed toward primary caregivers and distress may be displayed when separated from parents. *See also Indiscriminate attachment and Separate attachment.*

Specific phobia Anxiety disorder characterized by an irrational fear of specific situations or objects, such as heights, small closed places, or spiders.

Split-half reliability Measure of test reliability in which a subject's performance on a single administration of a test is assessed by comparing performance on half of the test items with performance on the other half of the test items.

Spontaneous recovery In classical conditioning, the spontaneous reappearance of a conditioned response after extinction has taken place.

Stage 1 sleep Light sleep that occurs just after dozing off, characterized by brain waves called theta waves.

Stage 2 sleep Stage of sleep that typically follows Stage 1 sleep, characterized by brief bursts of brain activity called sleep spindles as well as K-complex responses to stimuli such as noises.

Stage 3 sleep Stage of sleep that typically follows Stage 2 sleep, characterized by an EEG tracing 20 to 50 percent of which consists of delta waves. There are virtually no eye movements during Stage 3 sleep.

Stage 4 sleep Deepest level of sleep, characterized by an EEG tracing exceeding 50 percent delta waves and virtually no eye movements.

Standard deviation In descriptive statistics, a measure of variability that indicates the average extent to which all the scores in a distribution vary from the mean.

Standard score In descriptive statistics, a measure that indicates how far a score deviates from the average in standard units.

Standardization procedures Uniform and consistent procedures for administering and scoring tests, such as IQ or personality tests.

State-dependent memory Phenomenon wherein recall of particular events, experiences, or information is aided by the subject being in the same context or physiological state in which the information was first encoded.

Statistical significance Term used to describe research results in which changes in the dependent variable can be attributed with a high level of confidence to the experimental condition (or independent variable) being manipulated by the researcher.

Statistics Mathematical methods for describing and interpreting data. Two kinds of statistics are descriptive and inferential statistics.

Stereotypes Preconceived and oversimplified beliefs and expectations about the traits of members of a particular group that do not account for individual differences.

Stereotype threat A risk of confirming, as a self-characteristic, a negative stereotype about one's group. Stereotype threat may actually contribute significantly to poor academic performance by blacks and poor math performance by girls.

Stimulants Psychoactive drugs, including caffeine, nicotine, amphetamines, and cocaine that stimulate the central nervous system by increasing the transmission of neural impulses.

Stimulus contiguity In classical conditioning, the close pairing in time of the conditioned stimulus (CS) and the unconditioned stimulus (UCS). *See also Delayed conditioning.*

Stimulus contingency In classical conditioning, the correlation, or dependency, between a conditioned stimulus (CS) and an unconditioned stimulus (UCS).

Storage Process by which encoded material is retained over time in memory.

Stress Process of appraising events or situations as harmful, threatening, or challenging, of assessing potential responses, and of responding to those events. Also, a pattern of physiology that accompanies threatening events.

Stress-induced analgesia (SIA) Dramatically reduced sensitivity to pain that may occur under highly stressful conditions.

Structuralism Approach to psychology that attempted to break down experience into its basic elements or structures, using a technique called introspection, in which subjects provided scientific reports of perceptual experiences.

Sublimation Form of the defense mechanism displacement in which impulse-driven behaviors are channeled toward producing a socially valued accomplishment.

Substance P A peptide neurotransmitter that signals pain from peripheral nerve fibers to the spinal cord.

Subtractive color mixing Color mixing process that occurs when pigments are mixed, so that when light falls on the colored object some wavelengths are absorbed (or subtracted) and others reflected. *See also Additive color mixing.*

Superego According to Freud, the third system of personality that consists of an individual's conscience as well as the ego-ideal (the shoulds of behavior). *See also Id, Ego.*

Suprachiasmatic nucleus (SCN) An area of the hypothalamus that is located above the optic chiasm. The SCN exerts the main control over biological rhythms. The SCN is also referred to as the biological clock because damage to this area disrupts daily cycles in sleep and other biological functions.

Survey Research method in which a representative sample of people are questioned about their behaviors or attitudes. The survey provides descriptive information. *See also Sample.*

Syllogism Argument consisting of two or more premises, followed by a statement of conclusion that may or may not follow logically from the premises.

Sympathetic nervous system Division of the autonomic nervous system that functions to produce emergency responses such as increased heart rate, pupil dilation, and inhibited digestive activity. The sympathetic nervous system works in tandem with the parasympathetic nervous system.

Synapse Includes the synaptic gap and a portion of the presynaptic and postsynaptic membranes that are involved in transmitting a signal between neurons. *See also Synaptic gap.*

Synaptic facilitation An increase in the size of a post-synaptic potential to a weak stimulus resulting from neuronal changes that underlie learning and memory. Also see long-term potentiation.

Synaptic gap Space between transmitting and receiving neurons. *See also Synapse.*

Synaptic vesicle A microscopic sac that contains neurotransmitter substance located in the terminal button of a neuron.

Synesthesia A condition in which one type of sensory stimulation evokes the sensation of another as when, for example, the hearing of a sound produces the visualization of a color.

Syntax Set of language rules that govern how words can be combined to form meaningful phrases and sentences; grammar.

Systematic desensitization Behavior therapy using a classical conditioning technique that pairs the slow, systematic exposure to anxiety-inducing situations with relaxation training.

***t*-test** A statistical test used to compare two sample means.

Tardive dyskinesia A severe movement disorder often associated with long-term use of antipsychotic medication.

Taste bud A specialized receptor cell on the tongue.

Tectorial membrane Membrane located above the basilar membrane in the cochlea of the auditory system.

Template learning Learning that depends on a particular type of perceptual experience during a critical time in development. Examples would include imprinting and language learning.

Temporal contiguity In operant conditioning, the close relation in time between a response and a reinforcer.

Temporal lobe Region of the cerebral cortex located below the lateral fissure that contains the auditory cortex.

Terminal buttons Swollen bulb-like structure on the end of a neuron's axon that releases chemical substances known as neurotransmitters.

Territoriality Tendency to stake out certain areas with relatively fixed boundaries that others can enter only on invitation.

Testing hypotheses Problem-solving strategy that involves formulating specific hypotheses that generate relatively efficient approaches to solving a problem, then testing these hypotheses in a systematic fashion.

Test-retest reliability Method for evaluating test reliability by giving a subject (or subjects) the same test more than once.

Texture gradients Monocular distance cue based on the fact that textured surfaces (such as a grassy lawn) appear to be smoother, denser, and less textured when they are far from the viewer than when they are close.

Thalamus Structure located beneath the cerebrum in the brain that functions as a relay station, routing incoming sensory information to appropriate areas in the cerebral cortex. Also seems to play a role in regulating sleep cycles.

Thematic Apperception Test (TAT) Projective test for personality assessment in which the subject is shown cards depicting various scenes and is asked to describe what is happening in each scene.

Theories Tentative attempts to organize and fit into a logical explanatory framework all of the relevant data or facts scientists have observed regarding certain phenomena.

Thought Any cognitive processes directed toward problem solving, understanding language, memory retrieval, and perceiving patterns in sensory inputs.

Threshold Minimum level of intensity or strength of a stimulus that is sufficient to activate a sensory process (for instance, the minimum number of molecules that must be present in the air for us to smell a substance). *See Absolute Threshold.*

Thyroid gland Endocrine gland located in the neck that influences metabolism, growth, and maturation. Produces the hormone thyroxine.

Thyroxine The major hormone produced by the thyroid gland that regulates metabolism.

Timbre Quality of complex sound that is a product of the combination of fundamental frequency and additional frequency components called overtones.

Tolerance A decrease in responses caused by drugs resulting from cellular changes and classical conditioning.

Trace conditioning In classical conditioning, learning that takes place when presentation of the conditioned stimulus begins and ends before the unconditioned stimulus is presented.

Transduction Process by which sensory organs transform mechanical, chemical, or light energy into the electrochemical energy that is generated by neurons firing.

Transference In psychotherapy, a process in which a patient begins to relate to the therapist in much the same way as to another important person in his or her life (such as a parent).

Trial-and-error Problem-solving strategy that involves trying possible solutions, one by one, to see which one is correct.

Trichromatic theory of color vision Also known as the Young-Helmholtz theory, the postulation that the human eye contains three types of color receptors (for red, green, and blue), which form the basis for our perception of all colors. *See also Opponent-process theory of color vision.*

Two-egg twins *See Fraternal twins.*

Two-factor theory of learning A theory of avoidance learning that involves both classical and operant conditioning.

Tympanic membrane Membrane stretched across the end of the auditory canal that vibrates in response to sound waves. Also known as the eardrum.

Unconditional positive regard In person-centered therapy, the therapist's attitude of unconditional acceptance toward the client.

Unconditioned response (UCR In classical conditioning, an unlearned response or reflex caused by a stimulus.

Unconditioned stimulus (UCS) In classical conditioning, a stimulus that elicits an unlearned response or reflex.

Unconscious Level of mental awareness describing ideas, feelings, and memories that cannot easily be brought into consciousness.

Unconscious mind According to Freud's theory, the vast reservoir of the mind that holds countless memories and feelings that are repressed or submerged because they are anxiety-producing.

Variable interval (VI) **schedule** Partial reinforcement schedule in operant conditioning where opportunities for reinforcement occur at variable time intervals.

Variable ratio (VR) schedule Partial reinforcement schedule in operant conditioning where reinforcement is provided after an average of a specific number of responses occur.

Variance In descriptive statistics, a measure of variability that is the average of the squared distances of the scores from the mean.

Ventricle Fluid-filled chambers within the brain.

Ventromedial hypothalamus (VMH) A region of the hypothalamus in which damage results in faster gastric emptying and an increase in insulin production.

Virtual reality therapy A method of systematic desensitization therapy which utilizes computer simulation of situations similar to those which elicit intense fear in patient. *See systematic desensitization.*

Vestibular sacs Structures at the junction of the semicircular canals and cochlea of the middle ear that provide information about the head's position in space.

Visual cliff Device that produces the illusion of a cliff, allowing researchers to test the ability of animals to perceive and respond to depth cues.

Visual cortex Portion of the occipital lobe that integrates sensory information received from the eyes into electrical patterns that the brain translates into vision.

Visual memory *See Iconic memory.*

Volley theory Related to the frequency theory of pitch discrimination. Postulates that since single auditory neurons cannot fire rapidly enough to enable us to perceive tones in the 1,000 to 4,000 Hz range, pitch perception is made possible by groups of interrelated neurons firing in concert.

Wavelength The distance between adjacent waves. Used to measure electromagnetic energy. Colors of the visual spectrum are associated with different wavelengths.

Wear-and-tear theory *See Accumulating damages theory.*

Weber's fraction Ratio between a just noticeable difference and the intensity of a stimulus. *See also Weber's law.*

Weber's law One of the major principles of sensation, based on the fact that for various stimulus intensities, the difference threshold tends to be a constant fraction of the stimulus. As the strength of the original stimulus increases, the magnitude of the change must also increase in order for a just noticeable difference to be perceived.

Wechsler Adult Intelligence Scale (WAIS) Intelligence test developed by David Wechsler in the 1930s with sub-tests grouped by aptitude rather than age level.

Wernicke's aphasia A speech disorder associated with damage to Wernicke's area of the brain. Characterized by the production of meaningless speech and difficulties in speech perception.

Wernicke's area Area of the left temporal lobe that is the brain's primary area for understanding speech.

White matter Areas of the central nervous system that are predominantly axons covered with white myelin sheaths.

Withdrawal symptoms Symptoms associated with the abrupt discontinuation of drug use.

Within-group differences Differences or response variability, within treatment conditions.

Working backward Common heuristic problem-solving strategy that starts with describing the goal, then defines the step that directly precedes that goal, and works backward in this manner until the steps needed to reach the goal are defined.

Working memory *See Short-term memory.*

Yerkes-Dodson law Principle that the optimum level of arousal for peak performance will vary somewhat depending on the nature of the task.

Young-Helmholtz theory *See Trichromatic theory.*

Zygote Cell produced by the uniting of a sperm cell with an egg cell.

Zygote stage *See Germinal stage.*

Bibliography

Abraham, K. (1911). Notes on the psychoanalytical investigation and treatment of manic-depressive insanity and allied conditions. Originally written in 1911. In E. Jones (Ed.), *Selected papers of Karl Abraham, M.D.* London: Hogarth Press.

Abrahamson, A. C., Baker, L. A., & Caspi, A. (2002). Rebellious teens? Genetic and environmental influences on the social attitudes of adolescents. *Journal of Personality & Social Psychology, Dec; 83*(6), 1392–1408.

Abroms, I., & Bennett, J. (1981). Changing etiological perspectives in Down's syndrome: Implications for early intervention. *Journal of the Division for Early Childhood, 2*, 109–112.

Abu-Mostafa, Y., & Psalti, D. (1987). Optical neural computers. *Scientific American, 256*, 88–95.

Adams, J. (1977). *Understanding Adolescence*. Boston: Allyn & Bacon.

Ader, R., & Cohen, N. (1982). Behaviorally conditioned immunosuppression and murine systemic lupus erythematosus. *Science, 215*, 1534–1536.

Adler, A. (1930). Individual Psychology. In C. Murchinson (Ed.), *Psychologies of 1930*. Worcester, MA: Clark University Press.

Adler, A. (1927). *Practice and Theory of Individual Psychology*. New York: Harcourt, Brace & World.

Adler, A. (1917). *Study of Organ Inferiority and Its Physiical Compensation*. New York: Nervous and Mental Diseases Publishing Co.

Adorno, T., Frenkel-Brunswick, E., Levinson, D., & Sanford, R. (1950). *The Authoritarian Personality*. New York,: Harper & Row.

Aguiar, A., & Baillargeon, R. (2002). Developments in young infants' reasoning about occluded objects. *Cognitive Psychology, Sep; 45*(2), 267–336.

Aikawa, J. (1981). *Magnesium: Its Biological Significance*. Boca Raon, FL: CRC Press.

Ainsworth, M. (1989). Attachments beyond infancy. *American Psychologist, 44*, 709–716.

Ainsworth, M. (1981). Infant-mother attachment. *American Psychologist, 24*, 932–937.

Alain, M. (1989). Do what I say, not what I do: Children' s reactions to parents' behavioral inconsistencies. *Perceptual and Motor Skills, 68*, 99–102.

Alkon, D. (1989). Memory storage and neural systems. *Scientific American, July*, 42–50.

Alkon, D. L., Collin, C., Ito, E., Lee, C. J., Nelson, T. J., Oka, K., et al. (1992). Molecular and biophysical steps in the storage of associative memory. *Annals of the New York Academy of Sciences, Dec 20; 707*, 500–504.

Alexander, C. N., Chandler, H. M., Langer, E. J., Newman, R. I. & Davies J. L. (1989).Transcendental meditation, mindfulness, and longevity. An experimental study with the elderly. *Journal of Personality and Social Psychology*, 57,950–964.

Allen G. W. (1969). *William James*. New York: The Viking Press.

Allen, J. S., Damasio, H., Grabowski, T. J., Bruss, J., & Zhang, W. (2003). Sexual dimorphism and asymmetries in the gray-white composition of the human cerebrum. *NeuroImage, Apr; 18*(4), 880–894.

Allen, M. G. (1976). Twin studies of affective illness. *Archives of General Psychiatry, Dec; 33*(12), 1476–1478.

Allport, G. (1966). Traits revisited. *American Psychologist, 21*, 1–10.

Allport, G. (1965). *Letters from Jenny*. New York: Harcourt, Brace & World.

Allport, G. (1961). *Pattern and Growth in Personality*. New York: Holt, Rinehart and Winston.

Allport, G. (1937). *Personality: A Psychological Interpretation*. New York: Holt, Rinehart and Winston.

Allport, G., & Postman, L. (1947). *The Psychology of Rumor*. New York: Holt, Rinehart and Winston.

Altura, B. M., Altura, B. T., Gebrewold, A., Ising, H., & Gunther, T. (1984). Magnesium-deficient diets and microcirculatory changes in situ. *Science, 223*, 1315–1317.

Amabile, T., & Glazebrook, A. (1982). A negativity bias in interpersonal evaluation. *Journal of Experimental Social Psychology, 18*, 1–22.

American, Heart, & Asssociation. (1984). *Heart Facts.*Unpublished manuscript, Dallas.

American, Psychiatric, & Association. (2000). *Diagnostic and Statistical manual of Mental Disorders (4th ed. Rev.)*. Washington, DC
American Psychiatric Association.

American, Psychiatric, & Association. (1987). *Diagnostic and Statistical manual of Mental Disorders (3rd ed. Rev.)*. Washington, DC: American Psychiatric Association.

American, Psychological, & Association. (1988). *1998 APA Membership Register*. Washington, DC: American Psychological Association.

Amice, V., Bercovici, J., Nahoul, K., Hatahet, M., & Amice, J. (1989). Increase in H-Y antigen-positive lymphocytes in hirsute women: Effects of cyproterone acetate and estradiol treatment,. *Journal of Clinical Endocrinology and Metabolism, 68*, 58–62.

Anastasi, A. (1988). *Psychological Testing* (6th ed.). New York: Macmillan.

Anastasi, A. (1976). *Psychological Testing* (4th ed.). New York: Macmillan.

Anch, A., Browman, C., Mitler, M., & Walsh, J. (1988). *Sleep: A Scientific Perspective*. Englewood Cliffs, NJ: Prentice Hall.

Anderson, C., Carnagey, N., & Eubanks, J. (2003). Exposure to vioilent media: The effects of songs with vioilent lyrics on aggressive thoughts and feelings. *Journal of Personality and Social Psychology, 84*, 960–971.

Andreasen, N., Ehrhardt, J., Swayze, V., Alliger, R., Yuh, W., Cohen, G., et al. (1990). Magnetic resonance imaging of the brain in schizophrenia. *Archives of General Psychiatry, 47*, 35–44.

Angtrop, I., Roeyers, H., Oosterlaan, J., & Van Oost, P. (2002). Agreement between parent and teacher ratings of disruptive behavior disorders in children with clinically diagnosed ADHD. *Journal of Psychopathology & Behavioral Assessment, Mar; 24*(1), 67–73.

Antonov, I., Antonova, I., Kandel, E. R., & Hawkins, R. D. (2003). Activity-dependent presynaptic facilitation and hebbian LTP are both required and interact during classical conditioning in Aplysia. *Neuron, Jan 9; 37*(1), 135–147.

Apperloo, M. J. A., Van Der Stege, J. G., Hoek, A., & Weijmar Schultz, W. C. M. (2003). In the mood for sex: The value of androgens. *Journal of Sex and Marital Therapy, 29*(2), 87–102.

Ardekani, B. A., Nierenberg, J., . Hoptman, M. J., Javitt, D. C., & Lim, K. O. (2003). MRI study of white matter diffusion anisotropy in schizophrenia. *Neuroreport, Nov 14; 14*(16), 2025–2029.

Ariel, J., Craske, M. G., & Brown, M. (2001). Fear-related state dependent memory. *Cognition & Emotion, Sep; 15*(5), 695–703.

Arlow, J. (1984). Psychoanalysis. In R. Corsini (Ed.), *Current Psychotherapies*. Ithica, IL: Peacock.

Aronson, E., & Mills, J. (1959). The effect of seventy of initiation on liking for a group. *Journal of Abnormal Psychology and Social Psychology, 67*, 31–36.

Arrowood, J., & Short, J. (1973). Agreement, attraction and self-esteem. *Canadian Journal of Behavioral Science, 5*(242–252).

Arthur, A. (1987). Stress as a state of anticipatory vigilance. *Perceptual and Motor Skills, 64*, 75–85.

Asch, S. (1946). Forming impressions of personality. *Journal of Abnormal Psychology and Social Psychology, 41*, 258–290.

Asennsky, E., & Kleitman, N. (1953). Regularly occurring periods of eye motility and concomitant phenomena during sleep. *Science, 118*, 273–274.

Ashcraft, M., Fries, B., Nerenz, D., & Falcon, S. (1989). A psychiatric patient classification system: An alternative to diagnosis-related groups. *Medical Care, 27*, 543–557.

Ashmore, R., & Del Boca, E. (1976). Psychological approaches to understanding inter-group conflicts. In P. Katz (Ed.), *Towards the Elimination of Racism*. New York: Pergamon.

Aslin, R., Pisoni, D., & Jusczyk, P. (1983). Auditory development and speech perception in infancy. In M. Harth & J. Campos (Eds.), *Handbook of Child Psychology: Infancy and Developmental Psychobiology* (Vol. 2). New York: Wiley.

Athanasiou, R., Shaver, P., & Tavris, C. (1976). Sex. *Psychology Today, July*, 39–52.

Atkinson, R., & Shiffrin, R. (1971). The control of short-term memory. *Scientific American, 234*, 83–89.

Atkinson, R., & Shiffrin, R. (1968). Human memory: A proposed system and its control processes. In K. Spence & J. Spence (Eds.), *The Psychology of Learning and Motivation: Advances in Research and Theory* (Vol. 2). New York: Academic Press.

Aubert-Tulkens, G., Culee, C., & Rodenstein, D. (1989). Cure of sleep apnea syndrome after long-term nasal continuous positive airway pressure therapy and weight loss. *Sleep, 12*, 216–222.

Austrom, D., & Hanel. (1985). Psychological issues of single life in Canada: An exploratory study. *International Journal of Women's Studies, 8*, 12–23.

Austrom, D., & Hanel, K. (1985). Psychological issues of single life in Canada: An exploratory study. *International Journal of Women's Studies, 8*, 12–23.

Avison, W., & Speechley, K. (1987). The discharged psychiatric patient: A review of social, social-psychological and psychiatric correlates of outcomes. *American Journal of Psychiatry, 144*, 10–18.

Axel, R. (1995): The molecular logic of smell. *Scientific American*, October Issue, pp. 154–159.

Bachara, A., Damasio, H., & Damasio, A. R. (2003). Role of the amygdala in decision-making. *Annals of the New York Academy of Sciences, Apr; 985*, 356–369.

Bachrach, A., Erwin, W., & Mohn, J. (1965). The control of eating behavior in an anorexic by operant conditioning techniques. In L. Ullman & L. Krasner (Eds.), *Case Studies in Behavior Modification*. New York: Holt, Rinehart and Winston.

Baillargeon, R. (1987). Object permanence in 3 1/2 and 4 1/2-month-old infants. *Developmental Psychology, 33*, 655–664.

Baillargeon, R., & Wang, S. (2002). Event categorization in infancy. *Trends in Cognitive Sciences, Feb; 6*(2), 85–93.

Balon, R., Jordan, M., Pohl, R., & Yeragani, V. (1989). Family history of anxiety disordrs in control subjects with lactate-induced panic attacks. *The American Journal of Psychiatry, 146*, 1304j–1306.

Balota, D., & Lorch, R. (1986). Depth of automatic spreading activation: Medicated primary effects in pronunciation but not in lexical decision. *Journal of Experimental Psychology: Learning, Memory, and Cognition, 12*, 336–345.

Bancroft, J. (1984). Hormones and sexual behavior. *Journal of Sex and Marital Therapy, 10*, 3–21.

Bandura, A. (1986). *Social Foundations of Thought and Action: A Social Cognitive Theory*. Englewood Cliffs, NJ: Prentice-Hall.

Bandura, A. (1983). Temporal dynamics and decomposition of reciprocal determinism: A reply to Phillips and Orton. *Psychological Review, 90*, 166–170.

Bandura, A. (1982). Self-efficacy mechanism in human agency. *American Psychologist, 37*, 122–147.

Bandura, A. (1977). *Social Learning Theory*. Englewood Cliffs, NJ: Prentice-Hall.

Bandura, A. (1973). *Aggression: A Social Learning Analysis*. Englewood Cliffs: Prentice-Hall.

Bandura, A. (1971). *Social Learning Theory*. Morristown, NJ: General Learning Press.

Bandura, A. (1960). *Relationshiip of Family Patterns to Child Behavior Disorders: Progess Report, Project M-1734*. Stanford University, Stanford, CA: U. S. Public Health Service.

Bandura, A., & Mischel, W. (1965). Modification of self-imposed delay of reward through exposure to live and symbolic models. *Journal of Personality & Social Psychology, 2*, 698–705.

Bandura, A., Ross, D., & Ross, S. (1963). Limitation of the film-mediated aggressive models. *Journal of Abnormal Psychology and Social Psychology, 66*(3–11).

Bandura, A., & Walters, R. (1959). *Adolescent Aggression*. New York: Ronald Press.

Barahal, H. (1958). 1000 prefrontal lobotomies: Five-to-ten-year follow-up study. *Psychiatic Quarterly, 32*, 563–678.

Barber, T. (1975). Responding to "hypnotic" suggestions: An introspective report. *American Journal of Clinical Hypnosis, 18*, 6–22.

Barber, T., & Wilson, S. (1977). Hypnosis suggestions and altered states of consciousness. Experimental evaluation of a new cognitive-behavioral theory and the traditional trance-state therapy of "hynosis". *Annals of the New York Academy of Sciences, 296*, 430–433.

Barnes, D. (1987b). Biological isssues in schizophrenia. *Science, 235*, 430–433.

Baron, M., Gruen, R., Rainer, J., Kane, J., & Asnis, L. (1985). A famly study of schizophrenic and normal control probands: Implications for the spectrum concept of schizophrenia. *The American Journal of Psychiatry, 142*, 447–455.

Baron, M., Risch, N., Hamburger, R., Mandel, B., Kushner, S., Newman, M., et al. (1987). Genetic linkage between X-chromosome markers and bipolar affective illness. *Nature, 326*, 289–292.

Baron, R. (1986). Self-presentation in job interviews: When there can be "too much of a good thing". *Journal of Applied Social Psychology, 16*, 16–28.

Baron, R., & Byrne, D. (1987). *Social Psychology: Understanding Human Interaction* (5th ed.). Boston: Allyn & Bacon.

Bartels, M., Rietveld, M. J. H., Van Baal, G. C. M., & Boomsma, D. I. (2002). Genetic and environmental influences on the development of *intelligence. Behavior Genetics, Jul; 32*(4), 237–249.

Bartlett, E. (1932). *Remembering: A Study in Experimental and Social Psychology*. Cambridge, England: Cambridge University Press.

Bartusiak, M. (1980). Beeper man. *Discover, November*, 57.

Bartzokis, G., Hill, M., Altshuler, L., Cummings, J., Wirshing, W., & May, P. (1989). Tardive dyskinesia in schizophrenic patients: Correlation with negative symptoms. *Psychiatry Research, 28*, 145–151.

Bassey, E. J. (1998). Longitudinal changes in selected physical capabilities: muscle strength, flexibility and body size. *Age and Ageing, Dec; 27*(Suppl 3), 12–16.

Baumeister, R., & Covington, M. (1985). Self-esteem, persuasion, and retrospective distortion of initial attitudes. *Electronic Social Psychology, 1*, 1–22.

Baumrind, D. (1971). Current patterns of parental authority. *Developmental Monographs, 4*, 1–103.

Baumrind, D. (1964). Some thoughts on ethics of research after reading Milgram's "Behavioral study of obedience". *American Psychologist, 19*, 421–423.

Beal, G., & Muehlenhard, D. (1987). Getting sexually aggessive men to stop their advances: Information for rape prevention programs, *Association for Advancement of Behavior Therapy* (Vol. November). Boston.

Bechara, A., Damasio, H., & Damasio, A. R. (2003). Role of the amygdala in decision-making. *Annals of the New York Academy of Sciences, Apr; 985*, 356–369.

Beck, A. (1976). *Cognitive Therapy and Emotional Disorders*. New York: International Universities Press.

Beck, A., Brown, G., Berchick, R., Stewart, B., & Steer, R. (1990). Relationship between hopelessness and ultimate suicide: A replication with psychiatric outpatients. *The American Journal of Psychiatry, 147*, 190–195.

Beck, A., & Ward, C. (1961). Dreams of depressed patients: Characteristic themes in manifest content. *Archives of General Psychiatry, 5*, 462–467.

Beitman, G., Goldfried, M., & Norcross, J. (1989). The movement toward integrating the psychotherapies: An overview. *The American Journal of Psychiatry, 146*, 138–147.

Belec, L., Georges, A., Steenman, G., & Martin, P. (1989). Antibodies to human immunodeficiency virus in the semen of heterosexual men. *Journal of Infectious Diseases, 159*, 324–327.

Belickii, D., & Belicki, K. (1982). Nightmares in a university population. *Sleep Research, 11*, 116–121.

Bell, A., & Hepper, P. (1987). Catecholamines and aggression in animals. *Behavioral Brain Research, 23*, 1–21.

Bell, A., & Weinberg, M. (1978). *Homosexualities: A study of Diversity Among Men and Women*. New York: Simon & Schuster.

Bell, A., Weinberg, M., & Hammersmith, S. (1981). *Sexual Preference: Its Development in Men and Women*. Bloomington, IN: Indiana University Press.

Belsky, J., & Rovine, M. (1990). Patterns of marital change across the transition to parenthood: Pregnancy to three years postpartum. *Journal of Marriage and the Family, 52*, 5–19.

Bem, D. (1983). Further deje vu.

Bem, D. (1983). Further *deje vu* in the search for cross-situational consistency: A response to Mischel and Peake. *Psychological Review, 90*, 390–393.

Benbow, D., & Stanley, J. (1980). Sex differences in mathematical ability: Fact or artifact? *Science, 210*, 1262–1264.

Ben-Eliyahu, S., Yirmiya, R., Liebeskind, J., Taylor, A., & Gale, R. (1991). Stress increases metastatic spread of a mammary tumor in rats: Evidence for mediation by the immune system. *Brain, Behavior, and Immunity, 5*, June 193–205.

Benson, H., & Klipper, M. Z.(1976). *The Relaxation Response.* California: Harper Torch. ISBN: 0380006766

Benson, H. & Proctor, W. (1985): *Beyond the Relaxation Response.* Publisher: Berkley; ISBN: 0425081834.

Bergin, A., & Lambert, M. (1978). The evaluation of therapeutic outcomes. In S. Garfield & A. Bergin (Eds.), *Handbook of Psychotherapy and Behavior Change: An Empirical Analysis* (2nd ed.). New York: Wiley.

Berkowitz, L. (1993). Towards a general theory of anger and emotional aggression: Implications of the cognitive-neoassociationionists perspective for the analysis of anger and other emotions. In R. Wyer & T. Srull (Eds.), *Perspectives on Anger and Emoition. Advances in Social Cognition* (Vol. 6). Hillsdale, NJ: Erlbaum.

Berkowitz, L. (1989). Frustration—aggression hypothesis: Examination and reformulation. *Psychological Bulletin, 106*, 59–73.

Berkowitz, L. (1986). *A Survey of Social Psychology* (3rd ed.). New York: Holt, Rinehart and Winston.

Berkowitz, L. (1978). Aversively stimulated aggession: Some parallels and differences in research with animals and humans. *American Psychologist, 38*, 1135–1144.

Berkowitz, L. (1954). Group standards, cohesiveness, and productivity. *Human Relations, 7*, 509–519.

Berkowitz, L., & Geen, R. (1966). Film violence and cue properties of available targets. *Journal of Personality and Social Psychology, 43*, 525–530.

Berkowitz, L., & Lepage, A. (1976). Weapons as aggression-eliciting stimuli. *Journal of Personality & Social Psychology, 7*, 202–207.

Berlyne, D. (1971). *Aesthetics and Psychobiology*. New York: Appleton, Century, Crofts.

Berlyne, D. (1970). Novelty, complexity, and hedonic value. *Perception and Psychophysics, 8*, 279–286.

Berman, E., & Wolpert, E. (1987). Intractable manic-depressive psychosis with rapid cycling in an 18-year-old woman successfully treated with electroconvulsive therapy. *The Journal of Nervous and Mental Disease, 175*, 236–239.

Berman, J., & Norton, N. (1985). Does professional training make a therapist more effective? *Psychological Bulletin, 98*, 401–407.

Bern, D. (1972). Self-perception theory:. In L. Berkovitz (Ed.), *Advances in Experimental Social Psychology* (Vol. 6). New York: Academic Press.

Berndt, T. (1982). The features and effects of friendships in early adolescence. *Child Development, 53*, 1447–1460.

Bernstein, R. (1981). The Y chromosome and primary sexual differentiation. *Journal of the American Medical Association, 245*, 1953–1956.

Berry, D., & Philips, B. (1988). Sleep-disordered breathing in the elderly: Review and methodological comment. *Clinical Psychology Review, 8*, 101–120.

Besson, J., & Chaouch, A. (1987). Peripheral and spinal mechanisms of nociception. *Physiological Reviews, 67*, 67–186.

Best, J., & Suedfeld, P. (1982). Restricted environmental stimulation therapy and behavioral self-management in smoking cessation. *Journal of Applied Social Psychology, 12*, 408–419.

Bick, P., & Kinsbourne, M. (1987). Auditory hallucinations and subvocal speech in schizophrenic patients. *American Journal of Psychiatry, 144*, 222–225.

Binet, A., & Simon, T. (1905). *The Development of Intelligence in Children*. Baltimore: Williams & Wilkins.

Bird, E., Spokes, E., & Iverson, L. (1979). Brain norepinephrine and dopamine in schizophrenia. *Science, 204*, 93–94.

Birger, M., Swartz, M., Cohen, D., Alesh, Y., Grishpan, C., & Koteir, M. (2003). Aggression: The testosterone-serotonin link. *The Israel Medical Association Journal, 5*, Sep 653–658.

Birmahr, B., Baker, R., Kapur, S., & Quintana, H. (1992). Clozapine for the treatment of adolescents with schizophrenia. *Journal of the American Academy of Child and Adolescent Psychiatry, 31*, 160–164.

Bischoff, L. (1976). *Adult Psychology* (2nd ed.). New York: Harper & Row.

Bitterman, M. (1975). The comparative analysis of learning. *Science, 188*, 699–709.

Blander, A., & Wise, R. (1989). Anatomical mapping of brain stimulation reward sites in the anterior hypothalamic area: Special attention to the stria medullaris. *Brain Research, 483*, 12–16.

Blaney, P. (1986). Affect and memory: A review. *Psychological Bulletin, 99,* 229–246.

Blasi, A. (1980). Bridging moral cognition and moral action: A critical review of the literature. *Psychological Bulletin, 88,* 1–45.

Blass T. (2002). The Man Who Shocked the World. *Psychology Today.* NewYork. Document ID:1989.

Bleuler, E. (1950). *Dementia Praecox or the Group of Schizoiphrenias.* New York: International Universities Press.

Bliss, E. (1984). Spontaneous self-hypnosis in multiple personality disorder. *Psychiatric Clinics of North America, 7,* 135–148.

Bloch, S. (1979). Group Psychotherapy. In S. Bloch (Ed.), *An Introduction to the Psychotherapies.* Oxford, England: Oxford University Press.

Bloch, S. (1979). Group psychotherapy. In S. Bloch (Ed.), *An Introduction to the Psychotherapies.* Oxford, England: Oxford University Press.

Bloch, V., Hennevin, E., & Leconte, P. (1977). Interaction between post-trial reticular stimulation and subsequent paradoxical sleep in memory consolidation processes. In R. Drucker-Colin & J. McGaugh (Eds.), *Neurobiology of Sleep and Memory.* New York: Academic Press.

Blum, H. (1986). Psychoanalysis. In I. Kutash & A. Wolf (Eds.), *Psychotherapist's Casebook.* San Francisco: Jossey-Bass.

Bodamar, M. D., & Gardner, R. A. (2002). How cross-fostered chimpanzees (Pan troglodytes) initiate and maintain conversations. *Journal of Comparative Psychology, Mar; 116*(1), 12–26.

Bolter, A., Heminger, A., Martin, G., & Fry, M. (1976). Outpatient clinical experience in a community drug abuse program with phencyclidine abuse. *Clinical Toxicology, 9,* 593–600.

Borch-Jacobsen, M ,. (1997) Sybil: The Making of a Disease? An interview with Dr. Herbert Spiegel, *New York Review of Books.* Pg 60–64,Via Google On-line search.

Boring, E. J. (1950): A *History of Experimental Psychology,* Second Ed. New Jersey: Prentice Hall Inc. Publishers, ISBN #: 0-13-390039-8.

Borke, H. (1975). Piaget's mountains revisited: Changes in the egocentric landscape. *Developmental Psychology, 11,* 240–243.

Borkovec, T. (1970). Autonomic reactivity to sensory stimulation in psychopathic, neurotic, and normal juvenile delinquents. *Journal of Consulting and Clinicalk Psychology, 35,* 217–222.

Bouchard, T. (1984). Twins reared together and apart: What they tell us about human diversity. In S. Fox (Ed.), *Individuality and Determinism.* New York: Plenum.

Bouchard, T., Lykken, D., McGue, M., Segal, N., & Tellegen, A. (1990). Sources of human psychological differences: the Minnesota Study of twins reared apart. *Science, 250,* 223–228.

Bouchard, T., Lykken, D., McGue, M., Segal, N., & Tellegen, A. (1990). Sources of human psychological differences: The Minnesota study of twins reared apart. *Science, 250,* 223–250.

Bouchard, T., & McGu. (1981). Familial studies of intelligence: A review. *Science, 212,* 1055–1058.

Bouchard, T. J., Jr. (1998). Genetic and environmental influences on adult intelligence and special mental abilities. *Human Biology; an International Record of Research, Apr; 70*(2), 257–279.

Bouchard, T. J., Jr. (1997). The genetics of personality. In K. Blum & E. P. Noble (Eds.), *Handbook of psychiatric genetics* (pp. 273–296).

Bouchard, T. J., Jr, Segal, N. L., Tellegen, A., McGue, M., Keyes, M., et al. (2003). Evidence for the construct validity and heritability of the Wilson-Patterson Conservatism Scale: a reared-apart twins study of social attitudes. *Personality and Individual Differences, 34*(6), 959–969.

Bourne, L., Ekstrand, B., & Dominowski, T. (1971). *The Psychology of Thinking.* Englewood Cliffs, NJ: Prentice-Hall.

Bower, G. (1970). Analysis of a mnemonic device. *American Scientist, 58,* 496–510.

Bower, G., & Clark, M. (1969). Narrative stories as mediators for serial learning. *Psychonomic Science, 14,* 181–182.

Bower, G., & Mayer, J. (1985). Failure to replicate mood-dependent retrieval. *Bulletin of the Psychonomic Society, 23,* 39–42.

Bowlby, J. (1965). *Child Care and Growth of Love* (2nd ed.). Baltimore: Penguin.

Boyce, G., & Parker, G. (1988). Seasonal affective disorder in the southern hemisphere. *The American Journal of Psychiatry, 145,* 96–99.

Boyer, W., & Fieghner, J. (1992). An overview of paroxetine. *Journal of Clinical Psychiatry, 53,* 3–6.

Boyle, C., Berkowitz, G., & Kelsey, J. (1987). Epidemiology of premenstrual symptoms. *American Journal of Public Health, 77,* 349–350.

Boynton, R. S. (1998, Dec. 28) "Who was the real Sybil? The New York Antiques Show holds the key," *New Yorker,* p. 39–40.

Bradbury, T., & Fomcja, k. (1988). Individual difference variables in close relationships: A contextual model of marriage as an integrative framework. *Journal of Personality & Social Psychology, 54,* 713–721.

Brady, J., & Lind, D. (1965). Experimental analysis of hysterical blindness. In L. Ullman & L. Krasner (Eds.), *Case Studies in Behavior Modification.* New York: Holt, Rinehart, Winston.

Braff, D., & Geyer, M. (1990). Sensorimotor gating and schizophrenia. *Archives of General Psychiatry, 47,* 181–188.

Brannon, L., & Feist, J. (2004). *Health Psychology* (5th ed.). Belmont, CA: Wadsworth Publishing Company.

Brataas, A. (1989). Minnesota normals go national. *Oregonian* (October 5), A3.

Braun, K. A., Ellis, R., & Loftus, E. F. (2002). Make my *memory*: How advertising can change our memories of the past. *Psychology & Marketing, Jan; 19*(1), 1–23.

Braungart, J., Fulker, D., & Plomin, R. (1992). Genetic mediation of the home environment during infancy: A sibling adoption study of the HOME. *Developmental Psychology, 28,* 1048–1055.

Brecher, R., & Brecher, E. (1966). *An Analysis of Human Sexual Response.* New York: New American Library.

Breckles, S. (1984). Empirical validation of affect, behavior, and cognition as distinct components of attitude. *Journal of Personality & Social Psychology, 47,* 1191–2005.

Bredy, T., Weaver, I., Champagne, F. C., & Meaney, M. J. (2001). *Stress,* maternal care, and neural development in the rat. In C. A. Shaw & J. C. McEachem (Eds.), *Toward a theory of neuroplasticity* (pp. 288–300).

Breggin, P. (1979). *Electroschock: Its Brain-Disabling Effects.* New York: Springer.

Bremer, J. (1959). *Asexualization.* New York: Macmillan.

Bremmer, J. D., Vythilingam, M., Vermetten, E., Southwick, S. M., McGlashan, T., Nazeer, A., et al. (2003). MRI and PET study in deficits in hippocampal structure and function in women with childhood sexual abuse and posttraumatic stress disorder. *The American Journal of Psychiatry, May; 160*(5), 924–932.

Brennan, P. A., Hall, J., & Bor, W. (2003). Integrating biological and social processes in relation to early-onset persistent aggression in boys and gifls. *Developmental Psychology, 39*(2), 309–323.

Breslau, N., & Davis, G. (1987). Postraumatic stress disorder: The etiologic specificity of wartime stressors. *The American Journal of Psychiatry, 144,* 577–583.

Bretherton, I. (1992): The Origins of Attachment Theory: John Bowlby and Mary Ainsworth. *Developmental Psychology,* 28, 759–775.

Brett, J., Brief, A., Burke, M., George, J., & Webster, J. (1990). Negative affectivity and the reporting of stressful life events. *Health Psycholoigy, 9,* 57–68.

Brewster, D. (1854). North British Review, Quoted in J. Miller, *States of Mind.* New York: Pantheon Press.

Briddell, D., & Wilson, G. (1976). Effects of alcohol and expectancy set on male sexual arousal. *Journal of Abnormal Psychology, 85,* 225–234.

Brigham, J. (1986). *Social Psychology.* Boston: Little, Brown.

Brigham, J., & Weissbach, T. (Eds.). (1972). *Racial Attitudes in America: Analyses and Findings of Social Psychology.* New York: Harper & Row.

Brittain, C. (1963). Adolescent choices and parent-peer cross-pressures. *American Sociological Review, 23*, 385–391.

Brodbeck, A., & Irwin, O. (1946). The speech behavior of infants without families. *Child Development, 17*, 145–156.

Brooks, J., & Watkins, M. (1989). Recognition memory and the mere expossure effect. *Journal of Experimental Psychology: Learning, Memory, and Cognition, 15*, 968–976.

Brooks-Gunn, J., & Peterson, A. (1983). *Girls at Puberty: Biological and Psychosocial Perspectives*. New York: Plenum.

Brown, A., & Avery, C. E. Rationale and intervention techniques. In *Modifying Children's Behavior: A Book of Readings*. Springfield, IL: Thomas.

Brown, B., Clasen, D., & Eicher, S. (1986a). Perceptions of peer pressure, peer conformity dispositions, and self-reported behavior among adolescents. *Developmental Psychology, 22*, 521–530.

Brown, G., Lohr, M., & McClenahan, E. (1986b). Early adolescents' perceptions of peer pressure. *Journal of Early Adolescence, 6*, 139–154.

Brown, J. D., Steele, J. R., & Walsh-Childers, K. (Eds.). (2002). *Sexual teens, sexual media: investigating media's influence on adolescent sexuality*. Chapel Hill, NC: Univ of North Carolina.

Bruner, J., Goodnow, J., & Austin, G. (1956). *A Study of Thinking*. New York: Wiley.

Bruner, J., & Tagiuri, R. (1954). The perception of people. In G. Lindzey (Ed.), *Handbook of Social Psychology* (Vol. 2). Reading, MA: Addison-Wesley.

Buchsbaum, M., K, W., DeLisi, L., Holcomb, H., Hazlett, E., Cooper-Langston, K., et al. (1987). Positron emission tomography studies of basal ganglia and somatosensory cortex neuroleptic drug effects: Differences between normal controls and schizophrenic patients. *Biological Psychiatry, 22*, 479–494.

Buijs, R. M., Van Eden, C. G., Goncharuk, V. D., & Kalsbeek, A. (2003). The biological clock tunes the organs of the body: timing by hormones and the autonomic nervous system. *The Journal of Endocrinology, Apr; 177*(1), 17–26.

Bunker, S. J., Colquhoun, D. M., Esler, M. D., Hickie, I. B., Hunt, D., Jelinek, V. M., et al. (2003). "Stress" and coronary heart disease: psychosocial risk factors. *The Medical Journal of Australia, Mar 17; 178*(6), 272–276.

Bunney, W., Goodwin, E., & Murphey, D. (1972). The "Switch Process" in manic-depressive illness. *Archives of General Psychiatry, 27*, 312–317.

Burt, C. (1966). The genetic determination of differences in intelligence: A study of monozygotic twins reared together and apart. *British Journal of Psychology, 57*, 137–153.

Bushman, B. (1984). Perceived symbols of authority and their influence in compliance. *Journal of Applied Social Psychology, 14*, 501–508.

Buss, A., & Finn, S. (1987). Classification of personality traits. *Journal of Personality & Social Psychology, 52*, 432–434.

Buss, D. (1989). Sex differences in human mate preferences: Evolutionary hypotheses tested in 37 cultures. *Behavioral & Brain Sciences, 12*, 1–49.

Buss, D., Abbott, M., Angleitner, A., & Asherian, A. (1990). International preferences in selecting mates: A study of 37 cultures. *Journal of Cross Cultual Psychology, 21*(5–47).

Butler, R. (1961). Re-awakening interests. *Nursing Homes: Journal of American Nursing Home Associations, 10*, 8–19.

Byrne, D. (1971). *The Attraction Paradigm*. New York: Academic Press.

Byrne, D., Clore, G., & Smeaton, G. (1986). The attraction hypothesis: Do similar attitudes affect anything? *Journal of Personality & Social Psychology, 51*, 1167–1170.

Byrne, D., Clore, G., & Worchel, P. (1966). The effect of economic similarity-dissimilarity on interpersonal attraction. *Journal of Personality & Social Psychology, 4*, 259–271.

Byrne, D., & Griffin, W. (1973). Interpersonal attraction. *Annual Review of Psychology, 24*, 317–336.

Byrne, D., London, O., & Reeves, K. (1968). The effects of physical attactiveness, sex, and attitude similarity on interpersonal attraction. *Journal of Personality, 36*, 259–271.

Byrnes, D., & Murnen, S. (1988). Maintaining loving relationships. In R. Sternberg & M. Barnes (Eds.), *The Psychology of Loving*. New Haven, CT: Yale University Press.

Cadoret, R. (1978). Evidence for genetic inheritance of primary affective disorder in adoptees. *American Journal of Psychiatry, 135*, 463–466.

Cadoret, R., Troughton, E., & O'Gorman, T. (1987). Genetic and environmental factors in alcohol abuse and antisocial personality. *Journal of Studies on Alcohol, 48*, 1–8.

Cadwallader, M. (1975). Marriage as a wretched institution. In J. DeLora & J. DeLora (Eds.), *Intimate Lifestyles: Marriage and Its Alternatives*. Pacific Palisades, CA: Goodyear.

Caltech Media Relations (2005). Scientists Use fMRI to Catch Test Subjects in the Act of Trusting One Another. Caltech Media Release, On-line News. PR12671.html

Cameron, N. (1947). *The Psychology of Behavioir Disorders*. Boston: Houghton Mifflin.

Campbell, A. (1975). The American way of mating: Marriage Si, children only maybe. *Psychology Today*,(May), 37–43.

Campbell, C., & Davis, J. (1974). Licking rate of rats is reduced by intraduodenal and intraportal glucose infusion. *Psychology and Behavior, 12*, 357–365.

Campbell, D., & Specht, J. (1985). Altruism: Biology, culture, and religion. *Journal of Social and Clinical Psychology, 3*, 33–42.

Campbell, S. (1987). Evolutions of sleep structures following brief intervals of wakefulness. *Electroencephalographic Clinical Neurophysiology, 66*, 175–184.

Campbell, S. (1976). Double-blind psychometric studies on the effects of natural estrogen on post-menopausal women. In S. Campbell (Ed.), *The Management of the Menopausal and Post-Menopausal Years*. Baltimore: University Park Press.

Campbell, S., & Whitehead, M. (1977). Oestrogen therapy and the menopausal syndrome. *Clinical Obstetrical Gynecology, 42*, 31–47.

Cannon, W. (1927). The James-Lange theory of emotions: A critical examination and an alternative. *American Journal of Psychology, 39*, 106–124.

Cannon, W., & Washburn, A. (1912). An exploration of hunger. *American Journal of Physiology, 29*, 441–454.

Cantor, N., & Mischel, W. (1979). Prototypes in person perception. In L. Berkowitz (Ed.), *Advances in Experimental Social Psychology* (Vol. 12). New York: Academic Press.

Carden, S., & Coons, E. (1989). Diazepam modulates lateral hypothalamic self-stimulation but not stimulation-escape in rats. *Brain Research, 483*, 327–334.

Cardno, A. G., Marshall, E. J., Coid, B., Macdonald, A., Ribchester, T. R., Davies, N. J., et al. (1999). Heritability estimates for psychotic disorders: the Maudsley twin psychosis series. *Archives of General Psychiatry, Feb; 56*(2), 162–168.

Carelli, M., & Benelli, B. (1986). Linguistic development of t wins. *Eta Evolution, 24*, 107–116.

Carey, P., Howard, S., & Vance, M. (1988). Transdermal testosterone treatment of hypogonadal men. *Journal of Urology, 140*, 76–79.

Cargill, B. R., Clark, M. M., Pera, V., Niaura, R. S., & Abrams, D. B. (1999). Binge eating, body image, depression, and self-efficacy in an obese clinical population. *Obesity Research, 7*, 379–386.

Carlen, P., Penn, R., Fornazzari, L., Bennett, J., Wilkinson, D., Phil, D., et al. (1986). Computerized tomographic scan assessment of alcoholic brain damage and its potential reversibility. *Alcoholism: Clinical and Experimental Research, 10*, 226–232.

Carlson, L. E. et.al. (2003).Mindfulness-Based Stress Reduction in Relation to Quality of Life, Mood, Symptoms of Stress and Immune Parameters in Breast and Prostate Cancer. *Psychosomatic Medicine*, 65:571–581.

Carlson, N. (2003). *Physiology of Behavior* (8th ed.). Boston: Allyn & Bacon.

Carlsson, A. (1995). Neurocircuitries and neurotransmitter interactions in schizophrenia. *International Clinical Psychopharmacology, Sep; 10*(Suppl 3), 21–28.

Carlsson, M., & Carlsson, A. (1990). Schizophrenia: A subcortical neurotransmitter imbalance syndrome? *Schizophrenia Bulletin, 16*, 425–432.

Carnahan, T. & McFarland, S. (2007). Revisiting the Stanford Prison Experiment: Could Participant Self-Selection Have Led to the Cruelty? *Personality and Social Psychology Bulletin*, Vol. 33, No. 5, 603-614

Carpenter, W., & Heinrichs, D. (1983). Early intervention, time-limited, targeted pharmacotherapy of schizophrenia. *Schizophrenia Bulletin, 16*(534–542).

Carson, R., & Butcher, J. (1992). *Abnormal Psychology and Modern Life* (9th ed.). New York: HarperCollins.

Carver, C., & Glass, D. (1978). Coronary-prone behavior pattern and interpersonal aggression. *Journal of Personality and Social Psychology, 36*, 361–366.

Carver, C., & Scheier, M. (1978). Self-focusing effects on dispositional self-consciousness, mirror presence, and audience presence. *Journal of Personality and Social Psychology, 36*, 324–332.

Cash, T., & Janda, L. (1984). The eye of ghe beholder. *Psychology Today*(December), 46–52.

Castillo, M., & Butterworth, G. (1981). Neonatal localization of sound in visual space. *Perception, 10*, 331–350.

Castro, E., Newcomb, M., McCreary, C., & Baezcondo-Garbanati, L. (1989). Cigarette smokers do more than just smoke cigarettes. *Health Psychology, 8*, 107–129.

Cattell, R. (1982). *The Inheritance of Personality and Ability*. New York: Academic Press.

Cattell, R. (1973). Personality pinnned down. *Psychology Today*(July), 40–46.

Cattell, R. (1965). *The Scientific Analysis of Personality*. Baltimore: Penguin Books.

Cattell, R. (1950). *A Systematic Theoretical and Factual Study*. New York: McGraw-Hill.

Cavallaro, S., Schreurs, B. G., Zhao, W., D'Agata, V., & Aklon, D. L. (2001). Gene expression profiles during long-term memory consolidation. *The European Journal of Neuroscience, May; 13*(9), 1809–1815.

CDC Percentage of Obesity (2006): *Prevalence of overweight, obesity and extreme obesity among adults: United States, trends 1960–62 through 2005–2006* http://www.cdc.gov/nchs/fastats/overwt.htm

Ceci, S., Toglia, M., & Ross, D. (1988). On remembering...more or less: A trace strength interpretation of developmental differences in suggestibility. *Journal of Experimental Psychology: General, 117*, 201–203.

Centers, for, Disease, & Control. (1989). Results from the National Adolescent Student Health Survey. *Morbity and Mortality Weekly Report, 38*, 147–150.

Centers, for, Disease, & Control. (1987). Self-reported changes in sexual behaviors among homosexual and bisexual men from San Francisco City Clinic cohort. *Morbity and Mortality Weekly Report, 36*, 187–189.

Centers, for, Disease, & Control. (1984). Fetal alcohol syndrome: Public awareness week. *Morbity and Mortality Weekly Report, 33*, 1–2.

Cerletti, B., & Bini, I. (1938). L'elettroshock. *Archiva Generale Neurologia Psychiatria Psicoanalysia, 19*, 266.

Chaiken, S., & Stangor, C. (1987). Attitudes and attitude change. *Annual Review of Psychology, 38*, 375–630.

Charney, D., Heninger, G., & Sternberg, D. (1984). Serotonin function and the mechanism of action of antidepressant treatment. *Archives of General Psychiatry, 41*, 359–365.

Charney, D. S. (2003). Neuroanatomical circuits modulating fear and anxiety behaviors. *Acta Psychiatrica Scandinavica, Supplementum, Sep; 417*, 38–50.

Chase, M., & Morales, E. (1990). The atonia and myoclonia of active (REM) sleep. *Annual Review of Psychology, 41*, 557–584.

Chase, M., & Morales, E. (1983). Subthreshold excitatory activity and motor neuron discharge during REM periods of active sleep. *Science, 221*, 1195–1198.

Check, J., & Malamuth, N. (1983). Sex role stereotyping and reactions to depictions of stranger versus acquaintance rape. *Journal of Personality and Social Psychology, 45*, 344–356.

Chesno, E., & Kilman, P. (1975). Effects of stimulation intensity on sociopathic avoidance learning. *Journal of Abnormal Psychology, 84*, 144–151.

Chipuer, H., Rovine, M., & Plomin, R. (1990). LISREL modeling: Genetic and environmental influences on IQ revisited. *Intelligence, 14*, 1129.

Chomsky, N. (1980). The linguistic approach. In M. Piatelli-Palmarini (Ed.), *Language and Learning*. Cambridge, MA: Harvard University Press.

Chomsky, N. (1968). *Language and Mind*. New York: Harcourt Brace Jovanovich.

Chomsky, N. (1965). *Aspects of the Theory of Syntax*. Cambridge, MA: MIT Press.

Chozick, B. (1986). The behavioral effects of lesions of the amygdala: A review. *International Journal of Neuroscience, 29*, 205–221.

Christopher, E. (1988). An initial investigation into a continuum of premarital sexual pressure. *Journal of Sex Research, 25*, 255–266.

Christopher, E., & Cate, R. (1984). Factors involved in premarital decision making. *Journal of Sex Research, 2j0*, 363–376.

Chu, G. (1965). Prior familiarity, perceived bias, and one-sided versus two-sided communication. *Journal of Experimental Social Psychology, 3*, 243–254.

Cialdini, R. (1985). *Influence: Science and Practice*. Glenview, IL: Scott, Fofeman.

Cialdini, R., Vincent, J., Lewis, S., Catalan, J., Wheeler, D., & Darby, B. (1975). Reciprocal concessions procedure for inducing compliance: The door-in-the-face technique. *Journal of Personality and Social Psychology, 31*, 206–215.

Ciesielski, K., Beech, H., & Gordon, P. (1981). Some electrphysiological observations in obsessional states. *British Journal of Psychiatry, 138*, 479–484.

Cirignotta, F., Mondini, S., Zucconi, M., Lenzi, P., & Lugaresi, E. (1985). Insomnia: An epidemiological survey. *Clinical Neuropharmacology & Suppl, 1*, 549–554.

Clancy, S. A., McNally, R. J., Schacter, D. L., Lenzenweger, M. F., & Pitman, R. K. (2002). Memory distortion in people reporting abduction by aliens. *Journal of Abnormal Psychology, 111*(3), 455–461.

Clark, D., Salkovskis, P., Gelder, M., Koehler, M., Martin, M., Anastasiades, P., et al. (1988). Tests of a cognitive theory of panic. In I. Hand & H. Wittchen (Eds.), *Panic and Phobias*. Berlin: Spinger-Verlag.

Clark, G. A., Hawkins, R. D., & Kandel, E. R. (1994). Activity-dependent enhancement of presynaptic facilitation provides a cellular mechanism for the temporal specificity of classical conditioning in Aplysia. *Learning and Memory, Nov–Dec; 1*(4), 243–257.

Clarke, A. M., & Clarke, A. D. (1976). *Early Experience: Myth and Evidence*. London: Open Books.

Cleckley, H. (1970). *The Mask of Sanity* (5th ed.). St Louis: Mosby.

Clonnger, D., Martin, R., Clayton, P., & Guze, S. (1981). Blind follow-up and family study of anxiety neuroses. In D. Klein & J. Rabkin (Eds.), *Anxiety: New Research and Changing Concepts*. New York: Raven.

Cochran, S. (1988). *Paper presented*. Paper presented at the Annual American Psychological Association Convention, Atlanta.

Cohen, S., & Williamson, G. (1991). Stress and infectious disease in humans. *Psychological Bulletin, 109*, 5–24.

Colasanti, B. (1982). Anti-psychotic drugs. In C. Craig & R. Stitzel (Eds.), *Modern Pharmacology*. Boston: Little Brown.

Cole, D. (1989). Psychopathology of adolescent suicide: Hoplessness, coping beliefs, and depression. *Journal of Abnormal Psychology, 98*, 248–255.

Coleman, J. (1966). *Equality of Educational Opportunity*. Washington, DC: U S Government Printing Office.

Collins, A., & Quillian, M. (1969). Retrieval time from semantic memory. *Journal of Verbal Learning and Verbal Behavior, 8*, 240–247.

Colman, A. (1991). Expert psychological testimony in two murder trials in South Africa. *Issues in Criminological and Legal Psychology, 1*(17), 43–49.

Colwill, R., & Rescorla, R. (1986). Associative structures in instrumental learning. In G. Bower (Ed.), *The Psycholoigy of Learning and Motivation* (Vol. 20). New york: Academic Press.

Comery, T. A., Stamoudis, C. X., Irwin, S. A., & Greenough, W. T. (1996). Increased density of multiple-head dendritic spines on medium-sized spiny neurons of the striatum in rats reared in a complex environment. *Neurobiology of Learning and Memory, Sep; 66*(2), 93–96.

Condon, W., & Sander, L. (1974). Neonate movement as synchronized with adult speech: Interactional participation in language acquistion. *Science, 183*, 99–101.

Conningham, G., Cordero, E., & Thornby, J. (1989). Testosterone replacement with transdermal therapeutic systems. *Journal of the American Medical Association, 261*, 2525–2531.

Conrad, R. (1972). Short-term memory in the deaf: A test for speech coding. *British Journal of Psychology, 63*, 173–180.

Conrad, R. (1964). Accoustic confusions in immediate memory. *British Journal of Psychology, 55*, 75–84.

Cook, N. (1986). *The brain Code: Mechanisms of Information Transfer and the Role of the Corpus Callosum*. New York: Methuen.

Coope, J. (1976). Double-blind cross-over study of estrogen replacement. In S. Campbll (Ed.), *The Management of Menopausal and Post-Menopausal Years*. Baltimore: University Park Press.

Cooper, J. R., Bloom, F. E., and Roth, R. H. (2003). *The biochemical basis of neuropharmacology*, 8th Edition, New York: Oxford University Press.

Cooper, J. B., Jane, J. A., Alves, W. M., & Cooper, E. B. (1999). Right median nerve electrical stimulation to hasten awakening from coma. *Brain Injury, Apr; 13*(4), 261–267.

Cooper, R., & Zubec, J. (1958). Effects of enriched and resricted early environments on the learning abilities of bright and dull rats. *Canadian Journal of Psychology, 12*, 159–164.

Cooper, R., & Zubek, J. (1958). Effects of enriched and restricted early environment on the learning abilities of bight and dull rats. *Canadian Journal of Psychology, 12*, 159–164.

Coopersmith, S. (1980). *Antecedents of Self-Esteem*. San Francisco: Freeman.

Corkin, S. (1980). A prospective study of cingulatory. In E. Valenstein (Ed.), *The Psychosurgery Debate*. San Francisco: Freeman.

Corrigan, R. (1978). Language development as related to stage 6 object permanence development. *Journal of Child Language, 5*, 173–189.

Costello, C. (1976). Electroconvulsive therapy: Is further investigation necessary? *Canadian Psychiatric Association Journal, 21*, 61–67.

Costello, E. J., Mustillo, S., Erkanli, A., Keeler, G., & Angold, A. (2003). Prevalence and development of psychiatric disorders in childhood and adolescence. *Archives of General Psychiatry, Aug; 60*(8), 837–844.

Cotman, C., Monaghan, D., & Ganong, A. (1988). Excitatory amino acid neurotransmissioin: NMDA receptors and Hebb-type synaptic plasticity. *Annual Review of Neuroscience, 11*, 61–80.

Cox, J. (1936). Cholecystokinin interacts with prefeeding to impair runway performance. *Behavioral Brain Research, 21*, 29–36.

Craighead, L. (1990). Supervised exercise in behavioral treatment for moderate obesity. *Behavioir Therapy, 20*, 59–59.

Craik, E., & Tulving, E. (1975). Depth of processing and the retention of words in episodic memory. *Journal of Experimental Psychology: General, 104*, 268–294.

Craske, M., & Barlow, D. (1989). Nocturnal panic. *The Journal of Nervous and Mental Disease, 177*, 160–167.

Creekmore, C. (1985). Cities won't drive you crazy. *Psychology Today, 19*, 46–53.

Crick, E. (1989). The recent excitement about neural networks. *Nature, 337*, 129–132.

Crick, E., & Mitchison, G. (1983). The function of dream sleep. *Nature, 304*, 111–114.

Crockenberg, S. B., & Smith, P. (2002). Antecedents of mother-infant interaction and infant irritability in the first 3 months of life. *Infant Behavior & Development, 25*(1: 25th Anniversary), 2–15.

Crocker, J., Thompson, L., McGraw, K., & Ingerman, C. (1987). Downward comparison, prejudice, and evaluations of others. Effects of self-esteem and threat. *Journal of Personality and Social Psychology, 52*, 907–916.

Crook, L. S., & Dean, M. C. (1999). "Lost in a shopping mall"—a breach of professional ethics. *Ethics & Behavior, 9*(1), 39–50.

Crooks, R. (1969). Alleviation of fear in a dental setting via film-modeling. In *Report of Dental Education Summer Internship Program*. Chicago: American Association of Dental School.

Crossnoe, R., & Elder, G. H., Jr. (*2002*). Successful adaptation in the later years: a life course approach to *aging*. *Social Psychology Quarterly, Dec; 65*(4), 309–328.

Crowder, R. (1976). *Principles of Learning and Memory*. Hillsdale, NJ: Erlbaum.

Crowder, R. (1970). The role of one's own voice in immediate memory. *Cognitive Psychology, 1*, 157–178.

Crowe, R. (1974). An adoption study of antisocial personality. *Archives of General Psychiatry, 31*, 783–791.

Crowe, R., Noyes, R., Wilson, A., Elston, R., & Ward, L. (1987). A linkage study of panic disorder. *Archives of General Psychiatry, 44*, 933–937.

Croyle, R., & Cooper, J. (1983). Dissonance arousal: Physiological evidence. *Journal of Personality and Social Psychology, 45*, 782–791.

Csikszentmihalyi, M., & Larson, R. (1984). *Being Adolescent: Conflict and Growth in the Teenage Years*. New York: Basic Books.

Cumming, D., Cumming, C., Krausher, R., & Fox, E. (1991). Towards a definition of PMS II: A factor analytic evaluation of premenstrual changes in women with symptomatic premenstrual change. *Journal of Psychosomatic Research, 35*, 713–723.

Cummings, J. L. (2003). Toward a molecular neuropsychiatry of neurodegenerative diseases. *Annals of Neurology, Aug; 54*(2), 147–154.

Curtis, R., & Miller, K. (1988). Believing another likes or dislike you: Behavior making the beliefs come true. *Journal of Personality and Social Psychology, 51*, 284–290.

Dale, P. (1976). *Language Development*. New York: Holt, Rinehart and Winston.

Damasio, A. (1992). Aphasia. *New England Journal of Medicine, 326*, 531–539.

Damasio, A., & Demasio, H. (1992). Brain and language. *Scientific American, 267*, 88–95.

Damasio, A. R. (1998). Investigating the biology of consciousness. *Philosophical Transactions of the Royal Society of London. Series B: Biological Sciences, Nov 29; 353*(1377), 1879–1882.

Damasio, A. R. (1997). Brain and language: what a difference a decade makes. *Current Opinion in Neurology, Jun; 10*(3), 177–178.

Danks, H. (1992). Women never stopped trying to flee attacker. *The Oregonian* (December 4), A24.

Darly, J., & Latane, B. (1968). Bystander intervention in emergencies: Diffusion of responsibility. *Journal of Personality and Social Psychology, 8*, 337–383.

Darwin, C. (1872). *The Expression of Emotion in Man and Animals*. New York: Philosophical Library (reprinted in 1955 & 1965 by the University of Chicago Press).

Datan, N., & Thomas, J. (1984). Late adulthood: Love, work and the normal transitions. In D. Offer & M. Sabshin (Eds.), *Normality and the Life Cycle*. New York: Basic Books.

Davidson, G. (1984). Hypnotic augmentation of terminal care chemoanalgesia. *Australian Journal of Clinical and Experimental Hypnosis, 12*, 133–134.

Davidson, J. (1984). Response to "Hormones and sexual behavior" by John Bancroft, MD. *Journal of Sex and Marital Therapy, 1j0*, 23–27.

Davis, J., Wheeler, W., & Wiley, E. (1987). Cognitive correlates of obesity in a nonclinical population. *Psychological Reports, 60*, 1151–1156.

Davis, M. (1992). The role of the amygdala in fear and anxiety. *Annual Review of Neuroscience, 15*, 353.

Davis, M., Walker, D. L., & Myers, K. M. (2003). Role of the amygdala in fear extinction measured with potentiated startle. *Annals of the New York Academy of Sciences, Apr; 985*, 218–232.

Davis, P., & Schwartz, G. (1987). Repression and the inaccessibility of affective memories. *Journal of Personality and Social Psychology, 52*, 155–162.

Davis, S. R. (2001): Testosterone Treatment: Psychological and Physical Effects in Postmenopausal Women. *Menopausal Medicine*, Vol. 9, #2, pp. 1–6.

Davis, Wade (1997). *The Serpent and the Rainbow: A Harvard Scientist's Astonishing Journey into the Secret Societies of Haitian Voodoo, Zombies, and Magic.* Publisher: UK:Simon & Schuster ISBN: 0684839296. First edition 1986.

Davison, G., & Neale, J. (1986). *Abnormal Psychology* (4th ed.). New York: Wiley.

de Boysson-Bardies, B., DeBevoise, M., & (Trans). (1999). *How language comes to children: from birth to two years.*

De Colvenaer, L., Caemaert, J., Calliauw, L., & Martens, E. (1990). Spinal cord stimulation in chronic pain therapy. *The Clinical Journal of Pain, 6*, 51–56.

de Vilhers, P., & de Vilhers, J. (1979). *Easy Language*. Cambridge, MA: Harvard University Press.

DeBono, K. (1987). Investigating the social-adjustive and value-expressive functions of attitudes: Implication for persuasion processes. *Journal of Personality and Social Psychology, 52*, 279–287.

DeCasper, A., & Fifer, W. (1980). Of human bonding: Newborns prefer their mothers' voices. *Science, 208*, 1174–1176.

Dehaene-Lambertz, G. (2000). Cerebral specialization for speech and non-speech stimuli in infants. *Journal of Cognitive Neuroscience, May; 12*(3), 449–460.

Dehne, N., Mendenhall, D., Roselle, G., & Grossman, C. (1989). Cell-mediated immune responses associated with short term alcohol intake: Time course and dose dependency. *Alcoholism: Clinical and Experimental Research, 13*, 201–205.

Delahanty, L. M., Meigs, J. B., Hayden, D., Williamson, D. A., & Nathan, D. M. (2002). Psychological and behavioral correlates of baseline BMI in the diabetes prevention program (DPP). *Diabetes Care, Nov 1; 25*(11), 1992–1998.

Delamater, J., & MacCorquodale, P. (1979). *Premarital Sexuality: Attitudes, Relationships, Behavior.* Madison: University of Wisconsin Press.

Delgado, P., & Moreno, F. (1999). Antidepressants and the brain. *International Clinical Psychopharmacology, May; 14*(Suppl 1), S9–16.

Dembroski, T., MacDougall, J., Shields, J., Petitto, J., & Lushene, R. (1978). Components of the Type A coronary-prone behavior patterns and cardiovascular responses to psychomotor performance challanges. *Journal of Behavioral Medicine, 1*, 159–176.

Dement, W. (1972). *Some Must Watch While Some Must Sleep*. Stanford, CA: Stanford Alumni Association.

Dement, W. (1960). The effects of dream deprivation. *Science, 131*, 1705–1707.

Dement, W., & Kleitruan, N. (1957). Cyclic variations in EEG and their relation to eye movements, bodily motility, and dreaming. *Electroencephalographic Clinical Neurophysiology, j9*, 673–680.

Demos, E. V. (1993). Silvan *Thomkin's* theory of emotion. In M. E. Donnelly (Ed.), *Reinterpreting the legacy of William James* (pp. 211–219).

Denicoff, K., Joffe, R., Lakshmanan, M., Robbins, J., & Rubinow, D. (1990). Neuropsychiatric manifestations of altered thyroid state. *The American Journal of Psychiatry, 147*, 94–998.

Denmark, E., Russo, N., Frieze, I., & Sechzer, J. (1988). Guidelines for avoiding sexism in psychological research. *American Psychologist, 43*, 482–485.

Dennerstein, L., Burrows, G., Wood, C., & Hyman, G. (1980). Hormones and sexuality: The effects of estrogen and progesterone. *Obstectrics and Gynecology, 56*, 316–322.

Detera-Wadleigh, S., Berrettini, W., Goldin, L., Boorman, D., Anderson, S., & Gershon, E. (1987). Close linkage of c-Harvey-ras-I and the insulin gene to affective disorder is ruled out in three north American pedigrees. *Nature, 325*, 806–807.

Deutsch, J., & Folle, S. (1973). Alcohol and asymmetrical state-dependeancy: A possible explanation. *Behavioral Biology, 8*, 273–278.

Deutsch, M., & Gerard, H. (1955). A study of normative and informational influence upon individual judgment. *Journal of Abnormal and Social Psychology, 51*, 629–631.

DeValois, R., & DeValois, K. (1975). Neural coding of color. In E. Carterette & M. Friedman (Eds.), *Handbook of Perception* (Vol. 5). New York: Academic Press.

Devane, W. (1992). Isolation and structure of a brain constituant that binds to the cannabinoiid receptor. *Science, 258*, 1946–1949.

Devlin, B., Daniels, M., & Roeder, K. (1997). The heritability of IQ. *Nature, Jul 31; 388*(6641), 468–471.

Deykin, E., Levy, J., & Wells, V. (1987). Adolescent depression, alcohol and drug abuse. *American Journal of Public Health, 77*, 178–182.

Diamond, M. (1982). Sexual identity, monozygotic twins reared in discordant sex roles and a BBC follow-up. *Archives of Sexual Behavior, 11*, 181–186.

Diamond, M., & Sigmundson, H. K. (1999). Sex reassignment at birth. In S. J. Ceci & W. M. Williams (Eds.), *The nature-nuture debate: The essential readings. Essential reading in developmental psychology* (pp. 55–75).

Diener, E., & Wallbom, M. (1976). Effects of self-awareness on antinormative behavior. *Journal of Research in Personality, 10*, 107–111.

Dinsdale, J., & Moss. (1960). Plazma catecholamines levels in stress and exercise. *Journal of the American Medical Association, 243*, 340–342.

Dion, K., & Berscheid, E. (1974). Physical attractiveness and peer perception among children. *Sociometry, 37*, 1–12.

Dion, K., & Dion, K. (1987). Belief in a just world and physical attractiveness sterotyping. *Journal of Personality and Social Psychology, 52*, 775–780.

Dolezal, V., & Kasparova, J. (2003). Beta-amyloid and cholinergic neurons. *Neurochemical Research, Apr; 28*(3–4), 499–506.

Dollard, J., Doob, L., Miller, N., Mowrer, O., & Sears, R. (1939). *Frustration and Aggression*. New Haven, CT: Yale University Press.

Domos, E. V. (1993). Silvan *Tomkin's* theory of emotion. In M. E. Donnelly (Ed.), *Reinterpreting the legacy of William James* (pp. 211–219).

Donchin, E. (1975). On evoked potentials, cognition, and memory. *Science, 190*(1004–1005).

Donnelly, J. (1980). In H. Kaplan, A. Freedman & B. Sadock (Eds.), *Comprehensive Textbook of Psychiatry*. Baltimore: Williams & Wilkins.

Dorpat, T., & Ripley, H. (1967). The relationship between attempted suicide and committed suicide. *Comprehensive Psychiatry, 4*, 74.

Dosher, B. (1984). Discriminating preexperimental (semantic) from learned (episodic) associations: A speed-accuracy study. *Cognitive Psychology, 16*, 519–555.

Douglass, A., Harris, L., & Pazderka, E. (1989). Monozygotic twins concordant for the narcoleptic syndrome. *Neurology, 39*, 140–141.

Dremencov, E., Gur, E., Lerer, B., & Newman, M. E. (2003). Effects of chronic antidepressants and electroconvulsive shock on serotonergic neurotransmission in the rat hippocampus. *Progress in Neuropsychopharmacology & Biological Psychiatry, Aug: 27*(5), 729–739.

Driver, H. S., Rogers, G. G., Mitchell, D., Borrow, S. J., Allen, M., Luus, H. G., et al. (1994). Prolonged endurance exercise and sleep disruption. *Medicine and Science in Sports and Exercise, Jul; 26*(7), 903–907.

Dudley, R. (1991). IQ and heredity. *Science, 252*, 191–192.

Dudycha, G. (1936). An objective study of punctuality in relation to personalities and achievement. *Archives of Psychology, 204*, 1–53.

Dunham, R., Kidwell, J., & Wilson, S. (1986). Rites of passage at adolescence: a ritual process paradigm. *Journal of Adolescent Research, 1*, 139–154.

Eagly, A. (1981). Recipient characteristics as determinants of responses to persuasion. In R. Petty, T. Ostrom & T. Brock (Eds.), *Cognitive Responses in Persuasion*. Hillsdale, NJ: Erlbaum.

Eagly, A., & Warren, R. (1976). Intelligence, comprehension, and opinion change. *Journal of Personality, 44*, 226–242.

Eagly, A., Wood, W., & Chaiken, S. (1978). Causal inferences about communication and their effect on opinion change. *Journal of Personality and Social Psychology, 36*, 424–435.

Easterbrooks, M., & Goldberg, W. (1984). Toddler development in the family: Impact off father involvement and parenting characteristics. *Child Development, 55*, 740–752.

Ebbingham, H. (1913). *Memory: A Contribution to Experimental Psychology (translated by H. Ruger and C. Bussenius).* New York: Dover (Originally published in 1885).

Echterling, L., & Emmerling, D. (1987). Impact of stage hypnosis. *American Journal of Clinical Hypnosis, 29*, 149–154.

Eckholm, E. (1986). Researchers dispute tolling of genetic clock. *The Oregonian;*(June 19), F1–F2.

Edlund, M., Swann, A., & Clothier, J. (1987). Patients with panic attack and abnormal EEG results. *The American Journal of Psychiatry, 144*, 508–509.

Egeland, J., Gerhard, D., Pauls, D., Sussex, J., Kidd, K., & Allen, C. (1987). Bipolar affective disorders linked to DNA markers on chromosome 11. *Nature, 325*, 783–787.

Eibl-Eibesfeldt, I. (1991). *Human Ethology*. Hawthorne, NY: Aldine de Gruyter Publishers.

Eich, E., & Metcalfe, J. (1989). Mood dependent memory for internal versus external events. *Journal of Experimental Psychology: Learning, Memory, and Cognition, 15*, 443–455.

Eichorn, D., Hunt, J., & Honzik, M. (1981). Experience, Personality, and IQ: Adolescence to Middle Age. In D Eichorn, J. Clausen, N. Haan, M. Honzik & P. Mussen (Eds.), *Present and Past in Middle Age*. New York: Academic Press.

Eimas, P. (1975). Developmental studies of speech perception. In L. Cohen & P. Salapatek (Eds.), *Infant Perception: From Sensation to Perception* (Vol. 7). New York: Academic Press.

Eisenberg, N., Cialdini, R., McCreath, H., & Shell, R. (1987). Consistency-based compliance: When and why to children become velnerable? *Journal of Personality and Social Psychology, 52*, 1174–1181.

Ekinan, P. (1982). *Emotion and the Human Face* (2nd ed.). New York: Cambridge University Press.

Ekinan, P., & Friesen, W. (1984). *Unmasking the Face* (2nd ed.). Palo Alto, CA: Consulting Psychologists Press.

Ekinan, P., Levenson, R., & Friesen, W. (1983). Autonomic nervous system activity distinguishes among emotions. *Science, 221*, 1208–1210.

Ellis, A. (1984). Rational-emotive therapy. In R.Corsini (Ed.), *Current Pssychotherapies*. Itasca, IL: Peacock.

Ellis, A. (1975). *How to Live with a Neurotic*. N Hollywood, CA: Wilshire Books.

Ellis, A. (1962). *Reason and Emotion in Psychotherapy*. Secaucus, NJ: Lyle Stuart/Citadel Press.

Ellis, E., & Harper, R. (1975). *A New Guide to Rational Living*. N Hollywood, CA: Wilshire Books.

Ellis, L., & Ames, M. (1987). Neurohormonal functioning and sexual orientation: A theory of homosexuality-heterosexuality. *Psychology Bulletin, 101*, 233–258.

Ely, R., Gleason, J. B., MacGibbon, A., & Zaretsky, E. (2001). Attention to *language*: lessons learned at the dinner table. *Social Development, 10*(3), 355–373.

Emmerick, H. (1978). The influence of parents and peers on choices made by adolescents. *Journal of Youth and Adolescence, 7*, 175–180.

Emory, L. E., Cole, C. M., & Meyer, W. J., III. (1995). Use of Depo-Provera to control sexual aggression in persons with traumatic brain injury. *Journal of Head Trauma Rehabilitation, Jun; 10*(3), 47–58.

Engle, S., Zhang, X., & Wandell, B. (1997). Colour tuning in human visual cortex measured with functional magnetic resonance imaging. *Nature, 338*, 68–71.

Ennis, R. (1982). Children's ability to handle Piaget's propositional logic: A conceptual critique. In S. Modgil & C. Modgil (Eds.), *Jean Piaget: Consensus and Controversy*. New York: Praeger.

Epstein, A. (1960). Reciprocal changes in feeding behaviors produced by intrahypothalamic chemical injections. *American Journal of Physiology, 199*, 969–974.

Epstein, A., & Teitelbaum, P. (1967). Specific loss of the hypoglycemic control of feeding in recovered lateral rats. *American Journal of Physiology, 213*, 1159–1167.

Epstein, L., Wing, R., Koeskie, R., & Valoski, A. (1987). Long-term effects of family-based treatment of childhood obesity. *Journal of Consulting and Clinicalk Psychology, 55*, 91–95.

Epstein, R., Lanza, R., & Skinner, B. (1980). Symbolic communication between two pigeons. *Science*, 220–221.

Epstein, S. (1983). The stability of behavior across time and situations. In R. Zucker, J. Aronoff & A.Robin (Eds.), *Personality and the Prediction of Behavior*. San Diego, CA: Academic Press.

Erickson, E. (1963). *Childhood and Society* (2nd ed.). New York: Norton.

Erkut, S. (1983). Exploring sex differences in expectancy, attribution, and academic achievement. *Sex Roles, 9*, 217–331.

Erlenmeyer-Kimling, L., & Jarvik, L. (1963). Genetics and intelligence. *Science, 142*, 1477–1479.

Erlich, S., & Itabashi, H. (1986). Narcolepsy: A neuropathologic study. *Sleep, 9*, 126–132.

Eron, L., & Huesmann, L. (1984). The control of aggressive behaviors by changes in attitudes, values and the conditions of learning. In R. Blanchard & C. Blanchard (Eds.), *Advances in the Study of Aggression* (Vol. 1). Orlando, FL: Academic Press.

Eron, L., Huesmann, L., Lefkovitz, M., & Walder, L. (1972). Does television violence cause aggession? *American Psychologist, 27*, 253–263.

Esquirol, J. (1845). *Mental Maladies: Treatice on Insanity (translated by E Hunt)*. Philadelphia: Lea & Blanchard.

Estes, W. (1972). An associative basis for coding and organization in memory. In A. Melton & E. Martin (Eds.), *Coding Process in Human Memory*. Washington, DC: Winston.

Ettenberg, A., Raven, M. A., Danluck, D. A., & Necessary, B. D. (1999). Evidence for *Opponent-Process* actions of intravenous cocaine. *Pharmacology, Biochemistry & Behavior, Nov; 64*(3), 507–512.

Ettinger, R.H., Ettinger, W.F. and Harless, W. (1997) Active immunization with cocaine-protein conjugate attenuates cocaine effects. *Pharmacology, Biochemistry, and Behavior, 58*, 215–220.

Ettinger, R., Thompson, S., & Staddon, J. (1986). Cholecystokinin, diet palatability, and feeding regulation in rats. *Physiology and Behavior, 36*, 801–809.

European, Study, & Group. (1989). Risk factors for male to female transmission of HW. *British Medical Journakl, 298*, 411–415.

Evans, E. (1989). Hypnosis and chronic pain. *The Journal of Pain, 5*, 169–176.

Evans, R. (1974). A conversation with Konrad Lorenz about aggression, homosexuality, pornography, and the need for a new ethic. *Psychology Today* (November), 83ff.

Eveleth, P., & Tanner, J. (1976). *Worldwide Variation of Human Growth.* Cambridge, England: Cambridge University Press.

Everitt, B., Cador, M., & Robbins, T. (1989). Interactions between the amygdala and ventral striatum in stimulus-reward associations: Studies using a second-order schedule of sexual reinforcement. *Neuroscience & Biobehavioral Reviews, 30,* 63–75.

Everly, G. (1989). *A Clinical Guide to the Treatment of Human Stress Response.* New York: Plenum.

Everson, D., Bergmann, B., & Rechtschaffen, A. (1989). Sleep deprivation in the rat: III.Total sleep deprivation. *Sleep, 12,* 12–21.

Eysenck, H. (1990). Genetic and environmental contributions to individual differences: The three major dimensions of personality. *Journal of Personality, 58,* 245–226`.

Eysenck, H. (1952). The effects of psychotherapy: An evaluation. *Journal of Consulting Psychology, 16,* 319–324.

Fackelman, K. (1993). Marijuana and the brain. *Science News, 143,* 88–89.

Falloon, J., Eddy, J., Wiener, L., & Pizzo, P. (1989). Human immunodeficiency virus infection in children. *Journal of Pediatrics, 114,* 1–23.

Fantino, E. (1977). Conditioned reinforcement: Choice and information. In W. Honig & J. Staddon (Eds.), *Handbook of Operant Behavior.* Englewood Cliffs, NJ: Prentice-Hall.

Farley, E. (1986). The big T in personality. *Psychology Today*(May), 44–52.

Fava, M. (2003). The role of the serotonergic and noradrenergic neurotransmitter systems in the treatment of psychological and physical symptoms of depression. *The Journal of Clinical Psychiatry, 64*(Suppl 13), 26–29.

Fava, M., Copeland, P., Schweiger, U., & Herzog, D. (1990). Neurochemical abnormalities of anorexia nervosa and bulimia nervosa. *Annual Progress in Child Psychiatry and Child Development,* 368–386.

Fava, M., Copeland, P., Schweiger, U., & Herzog, D. (1989). Neurochemicakl abnormalities of anorexia nervosa and bulimia nervosa. *The American Journal of Psychiatry, 146,* 963–971.

Faymonville, M. E., Meurisse, M., & Fissette, J. (1999). Hypnosedation: a valuable alternative to traditional anaesthetic techniques. *Acta Chirurgica Belgica, Aug; 99*(4), 141–146.

Fazio, R. (1986). How do attitudes guide behavior? In R. Sorrentino & E. Higgins (Eds.), *The Handbook of Motivation and Cognition: Foundations of Social Behavior.* New York: :Guilford Press.

Fazio, R., Powell, M., & Herr, P. (1983). Toward a process model of the attitude-behavior relation: Assessing one's attitude upon mere observation of the attitude object. *Journal of Personality and Social Psychology, 44,* 723–735.

Fazio, R., & Zanna, M. (1981). Direct experience and attitude-behavior consistency. In L. Berkovitz (Ed.), *Advances in Experimental Social Psychology* (Vol. 14). New York: Academic Press.

Feather, N., & Raphelson, A. (1974). Fear of success in Australian and American student groups. Motive or sex-role stereotype? *Journal of Personality, 42,* 190–201.

Federmeier, K. D., Kleim, J. A., & Greenough, W. T. (2002). Learning-induced multiple synapse formation in rat cerebellar cortex. *Neuroscience Letters, Nov 8; 332*(3), 180–184.

Ferraro, K. F., Thorpe, R. J., Jr , , & Wilkinson, J. A. (2003). The life course of severe obesity: does childhood overweight matter? *The Journals of Gerontology. Series B, Psychological Sciences and Social Sciences, Mar; 58*(2), S110–119.

Ferster, C. (1965). Classification of behavior pathology. In L. Krasner & L. Ullman (Eds.), *Research in Behavior Modification.* New York: Holt, Rinehart and Winston.

Feshbach, N. (1985). Chronic maternal stress and its assessment. In J. Bucher & C. Speilberger (Eds.), *Advances in Personality Assessment* (Vol. 5). Hillsdale, NJ: Erlbaum.

Feshbach, S., & Weiner, G. (1982). *Personality.* Lexington, MA: Heath.

Festinger, L. (1957). *A Theory of Cognitive Dissonance.* Stanford, CA: Stanford University Press.

Festinger, L., Schachter, S., & Back, K. (1950). *Social Pressures in Informal Groups: A Study of Human Factors in Housing.* New York: Harper & Row.

Field, T. (1978). Interaction behaviors of primary versus secondary caretaker fathers. *Developmental Psychology, 14,* 182–184.

Fincham, E., Beach, S., & Baucom, D. (1987). Attribution processes in distressed and nondistressed couples: Self-partner attribution differences. *Journal of Personality and Social Psychology, 52,* 739–748.

Findlay, J., Place, V., & Snyder, P. (1989). Treatment of primary hypogonadism in men by the transdermal administration of testosterone. *Journal of Clinical Endocrinology and Metabolism, 68,* 369–373.

Fisch, H., Hyun, G., Golden, R., Hensle, T. W., Olsson, C. A., & Liberson, G. L. (2003). The influence of paternal age on down syndrome. *The Journal of Urology, Jun; 169*(6), 2275–2278.

Fischer, J., Sollie, D., & Morrow, B. (1986). Social networks in male and female adolescents. *Journal of Adolescent Research, 6,* 1–14.

Fishbein, M., & Ajzen, I. (1975). Belief Attitude, Intention, and Behavior: An Introductrion to Theory and Research. Reading, MA: Addison-Wesley.

Fisher, S., & Greenberg, R. (1977). *Scientific Credibility of Freud's Theories.* New York: Basic Books.

Flavell, J. (1985). *Cognitive Development* (2nd ed.). Englewood Cliffs, NJ: Prentice-Hall.

Flynn, J. (1987). Massive IQ gains in 14 nations: What IQ tests really measure. *Psychological Bulletin, 101,* 171–191.

Foley, J. (1984). Family therapy. In R. Corsini (Ed.), *Current Psychotherapies.* Itasca, IL: Peacock.

Follingstad, D., Kalichman, S., Cafferty, T., & Vormbrock, J. (1992). Aggression levels following frustration of abusing versus nonabusing college males. *Journal of Interpersonal Violence, 7,* 3–18.

Fontaine, R., Breton, G., Dery, R., Fontaine, S., & Elie, R. (1990). Temporal lobe abnormalities in panic disorder: An MRI study. *Biological Psychiatry, 27,* 304–310.

Ford, C., & Beach, E. (1951). *Patterns of Sexual Behavior.* New York: Harper & Row.

Ford, M. (1985). Two perspectives on the validation of developmental constructs: Psychometric and theoretical limitations in research on egocentrism. *Psychological Bulletin, 97,* 497–501.

Forsyth, D. (1983). *An Introduction to Group Dynamics.* Monterey, CA: Brooks/Cole.

Fosson, A., Knibbs, J., Bryant-Waugh, R., & Lask, B. (1987). Early onset anorexia nervosa. *Archives of Disease in Children, 62,* 114–118.

Foster, G., & Ysseldyke, J. (1976). Expectancy and halo effects as a result of artificially induced teacher bias. *Contemporary Educational Psychology, 1,* 37–45.

Fox, P., Mintun, M., Raichle, M., Miezin, E., Mlman, J., & Van Essen, D. (1986). Mapping human visual cortex with positon emission tomography. *Nature, 325,* 806–809.

Franco, P., Szliwowski, H., Dramaix, M., & Kahn, A. (1977). *Decreased autonomic responses to obstructive sleep events in future victims of sudden infant death syndrome* (Vol. Jul: 46).

Frank, J. (1982). Therapeutic components shared by all psychotherapies. In J. Harvey & M. Parks (Eds.), *The Master Lecture Series* (Vol. 1: Psychotherapy Research and Behavior Change). Washington, DC: American Psycholoigical Association.

Freedman, J. (2003). Media violence and its effects on aggression: Assessing the scientific evidence. *Canadian Psychology, 44,* 179–180.

Freedman, J., & Fraser, S. (1966). Compliance without pressure: The foot-in-the-door technique. *Journal of Personality and Social Psychology, 4,* 195–202.

Freeman, W., & Watts, J. (1950). *Psychosurgery.* Springfield, IL: Thomas.

Freud, S. (1936). *The Problem of Anxiety*. New York: Norton.

Freud, S. (1933). *New Introductory Lectures* (Vol. XXII The Standard Edition). London: Hogarth Press 1964.

Freud, S. (1919). *Mourning and melancholia. Orginally written in 1917 and later published in Collected Papers* (Vol. 4). London: Hogarth Press.

Freud, S. (1905). *Three Essays on the Theory of Sexuality. (Strachey, Ed and Translator)*. New York: Basic Books (1963: Originally published in 1905).

Freud, S. (1900). *The Interpretation of Dreams*. London: Hogarth Press.

Friederici, A. D., Ruschemeyer, S. A., Hahne, A., & Fiebach, C. J. (2003). The role of left inferior frontal and superior temporal cortex in sentence comprehension: localizing syntactic and semantic processes. *Cerebral Cortex, Feb; 13*(2), 170–177.

Friedman, H., Newton, C., & Klein, T. W. (2003). Microbial infections, immunomodulation, and drugs of abuse. *Clinical Microbiology Reviews, Apr; 16*(2), 209–219.

Friedman, M., & Rosenman, R. (1974). *Treating Type A behavior—and Your Heart*. New York: Knopf.

Friedrich-Cofer, L. (1986). Television violence and aggression: The debate continues. *Psychological Bulletin, 100*, 364–371.

Frodi, A. (1975). The effect of exposure to weapons on aggressive behavior from a cross-cultural perspective. *International Journal of Psychology, 10*, 283–292.

Frumkin, B., & Anisfeld, M. (1977). Semantic and surface codes in the memory of deaf children. *Cognitive Psychology, 9*, 475–493.

Fuhriman, A., & Burlingame, G. (1990). Consistency of matter: A comparative analysis of individual and group process variables. *The Consulting Psychologist, 18*, 6–63.

Furuhjelm, M., Karlgren, E., & Carstrom, K. (1984). The effect of estrogen therapy on somatic and physical symtoms in post-menopausal women. *Acta Obstetricia et Gynecologica Scandinavica, 63*, 655–661.

Gadnow, K., & Sprafkink, J. (1989). Field experiments of television violence: Evidence for an environmental hazard? *Pediatrics, 83*, 399–405.

Gafficy, E., Fenton, B., Lane, L., & Lake, C. (1988). Hemodynamic, ventilatory, and biochemical response of panic patients and normal controls with sodium lactate infusion and spontaneous panic attacks. *Archives of General Psychiatry, 45*, 53–61.

Gage, D., & Safer, M. (1985). Hemisphere differences in the mood state-dependent effect for recognition of emotional facres. *Journal of Experimental Psychology: Learning, Memory, and Cognition, 11*, 752–763.

Gaito, J. (1974). A biochemical approach to learning and memory: Fourteen yeatrs later. In G. Newton & A. Reisen (Eds.), *Advances in Psychobiology* (Vol. 2). New York: Wiley.

Gaitwell, N., Lonaux, D., & Chase, t. (1977). Plasma testosterone in homosexual and heterosexual women. *American Journal of Psychiatry, 134*, 117–119.

Galea, S., Ahern, J., Resnick, H., Kilpatrick, D., Bucuvalas, M., Gold, J., et al. (2002). Psychological sequelae of the *September 11* terrorist attacks in New York City. *New England Journal of Medicine, Mar; 346*(13), 982–987.

Galef, B. (1970). Aggression and timidity responses to novelty in feral Norway rats. *Journal of Comparative and Physiological Psychology, 70*, 370–373.

Gallagher, W. (1988). Sex and hormones. *Atlantic Monthly,*(March), 77–82.

Gallatin, J. (1980). Political thinking in adolescence. In J. Adelson (Ed.), *Handbook of Adolescent Psychology*. New York: Wiley.

Ganger, J. B. (2000). Genes and environment in *language* acquisition: a study of early vocabulary and syntactic development in *twins*. *Dessertation Abstracts International: Section B: The Sciences & Engineering, Dec; 61*(5–B), 2796.

Garbanino, J., & Gilliam, G. (1980). *Understanding Abusive Families*. Lexington, MA: Lexington Books.

Garber, J., & Seligman, M. (1980). *Human Helplessness: Theory and Application*. New York: Academic Press.

Garcia, J., Kimmeldorf, D., & Hunt, E. (1961). The use of ionizing radiation as a motivativatory stimulus. *Psychological Review, 68*, 383–385.

Garcia, J., & Koelling, R. (1966). Relation of cue to consequnces in avoidance learning. *Psychonomic Science, 4*, 123–124.

Gardner, A., & Gardner, B. (1975). Early signs of language in child and chimpanzee. *Science, 18*, 752–753.

Gardner, A., & Gardner, B. (1969). Teaching sign language to a chimpanzee. *Science, 165*, 644–673.

Gardner, H. (1999). *Intelligence reframed: multiple intelligences for the 21st century* (Vol. x).

Gardner, H. (Writer) (1990). Interview for program 16 *Discovering Psychology*, a 26-part telecourse from the Annenberg/CPB Project.

Gardner, H. (1983). *Frames of Mind: The Theory of Multiple Intelligence*. Englewood Cliffs, NJ: Prentice Hall.

Garlicki, J., Konturek, P., Majika, J., Kwiecien, N., & Konturek, S. (1990). Cholcystokinin.

Garlicki, J., Konturek, P., Majika, J., Kwiecien, N., & Konturek, S. (1990). Cholecystokinin receptors and vagal nerves in control of food intake in rats. *American Journal of Physiology, 258*, E40–E45.

Garvey, M., Wesner, R., & Godes, M. (1988). Comparison of seasonal and nonseasonal affective disorders. *The American Journal of Psychiatry, 145*, 100–102.

Gates, A. (1917). Recitation as a factor in memorizing. *Archives of Psychology,*(No. 40).

Gawin, E., & Kleber, H. (1984). Cocaine abuse treatment. *Archives of General Psychiatry, 41*, 903–909.

Gazzaniga, M.S. (1970): *The Bifurcated Brain*. New York: Plenum Press.

Geary, D. (1989). A model for representing gender differences in the pattern of cognitive abilities. *American Psychologist, 44*, 1155–1156.

Gehringer, W., & Engel, E. (1986). Effect of ecological viewing conditions on the Ames distorted room illusion. *Journal of Experimental Psychology: Human Perception and Performance, 12*, 181–185.

Geiselman, R. (1988). Improving eyewitness memory through mental restatement of context. In G. Davis & D. Thomson (Eds.), *Memory in Context: Context in Memory*. Chichester, England: Wiley.

Gelder, M. (1989). Panic disorder: Fact or Fiction? *Psychological Medicine, 19*, 277–283.

Gelderloos, P., Walton, K.G., Orme-Johnson, D.W., & Alexander C.N. (1991). Effectiveness of the Transcendental Meditation program in preventing and treating substance misuse: A review. *The International Journal of Addictions*, 26, 293–325.

George, C., & Main, M. (1979). Social interactions of young abused children: Approach, avoidance, and aggression. *Child Development, 50*, 306–318.

George, W. H., Lehman, G. L., Cue, K. L., Martinez, L., & al, e. (1997). Postdrinking *sexual* inferences: evidence for linear rather than curvilinear dosage effects. *Journal of Applied Social Psychology, Apr; 27*(7), 629–648.

Geracioti, T., & Liddle, R. (1989). Impaired cholecystokinin secretion in bulimia nervosa. *New England Journal of Medicine, 319*, 683–688.

Gerard, H., Wilhelmy, R., & Connolley, R. (1968). Conformity and group size. *Journal of Personality and Social Psychology, 8*, 79–82.

Gergen, K. (1965). The effects of interaction goals and personalistic feedback on the presentation of self. *Journal of Personality and Social Psychology, 1*, 413–424.

Gesell, A. (1928). *Infancy and Human Growth*. New York: Macmillan.

Getchell, T. (1986). Functional properties of vertebrate olfactory receptor neurons. *Physiological Reviews, 66*, 772–818.

Giannini, A., Pascarzi, G., Losiselle, R., Price, W., & Giannini, M. (1986). Comparison of clonidine and lithium in the treatment of mania. *American Journal of Psychiatry, 143*, 1608–1609.

Gibbs, J., Young, R., & Smith, G. (1973). Cholecystokinin elicits satiety in rats with open gastric fistulas. *Nature, 245*, 323–325.

Gibling, E., & Davies, G. (1988). Reinstatement of context following exposure to post-event information. *Journal of Psychology, 79*, 129–141.

Gibson, E., & Spelke, E. (1983). The development of perception. In J. Flavell & E. Markham (Eds.), *Handbook of Child Psychology: Cognitive Development* (Vol. 3). New York: Wiley.

Gibson, E., & Walk, R. (1960). The visual cliff. *Scientific American, 202*, 64–71.

Gibson, J. (1979). *The Ecological Approach to Visual Perception*. Boston: Houghton Mifflin.

Gillam, B. (1980). Geometrical illusions. *Scientific American, 242*, 102–111.

Gillie, O. (1976). Pioneer of IQ faked his research finding. *Sunday Times of London,*(October 29), H3.

Ginns, E. I., Ott, J., Egeland, J. A., Allen, C. R., Fann, C. S., Pauls, D. L., et al. (1996). A genome-wide search for chromosomal loci linked to bipolar affective disorder in the Old Order Amish. *Nature Genetics, Apr; 12*(4), 431–435.

Giordano, P. (1983). Sanctioning the higher-status deviant: An attributional analysis. *Social Psychology Quarterly, 46*(`), 329–342.

Glass, D. (1977). *Behavior Patterns, Stress and Coronary Disease*. Hillsdale, NJ: Erlbaum.

Glass, D., Snyder, M., & Hollis, J. (1974). Time urgency and the Type A coronary-prone behavior pattern. *Journal of Applied Social Psychology, 4*, 125–140.

Glass, D., Snyder, M., & Hollis, J. (1974). Time urgency and the Type A coronary-prone behavior pattern. *Journal of Applied Social Psychology, 4*, 125–140.

Glatt, S. J., Faraone, S. V., & Tsuang, M. T. (2003). Meta-analysis identifies an association between the dopamine D2 receptor gene and schizophrenia. *Molecular psychiatry, Nov; 8*(11), 911–915.

Gleason, J. (1990). Interview in program 6. *Discovering Psychology, a 26-part telecourse from the Annenbert/CPB Project*.

Gleason, J., & Ratner, N. (1993). *Psycholinquistics*. Fort Worth, TX: Harcourt Brace Jovanovich.

Glick, P. (1989). The family life cycle and social change. *Family Relations, 38*, 123–129.

Glucksberg, S., & Weisberg, R. (1966). Verbal behavior and problem solving: Some effects of labeling upon availability of novel functions. *Journal of Experimental Psychology:, 71*, 659–664.

Goethals, G. (1986). Fabricating and ignoring social reality: Self-serving estimates of consensus. In J. Olsen, C. Herman & M. Zanna (Eds.), *Relative Deprivation and Social Comparison: The Ontario Symposium* (Vol. 4). Hillsdale, NJ: Erlbaum.

Gold, P. (1987). Sweet memories. *American Scientist, 75*, 151–155.

Goldberg, S. (1983). Parent-infant bonding: Another look. *Child Development, 54*, 1355–1382.

Goldberger, L. (1982). Sensory deprivation and overload. In L. Goldberger & S. Bresnitz (Eds.), *Handbook of Stress: Theoretical and Clinical Aspects*. New York: Free Press.

Goldfarb, W. (1945). Psychological privation in infancy and subsequent adjustment. *American Journal of Orthopsychiatry, 15*, 247–255.

Goldfield, M., & Padawer, W. (1982). Current status and future directions in psychotherapy. In M. Goldfield (Ed.), *Converging Themes in Psychotherapy: Trends in Psychodynamic, Humanistic, and Behavioral Practice*. New York: Springer.

Goldfried, M., Greenberg, L., & Marmar, C. (1990). Individual psychotherapy: Process and outcome. *Annual Review of Psychology, 41*, 659–688.

Goldman-Rakic, P. S. (1999). The "psychic" neuron of the cerebral cortex. *Annals of the New York Academy of Sciences, Apr 30; 868*, 13–26.

Goldstein, M., & Palmer, J. (1975). *The Experience of Anxiety: A Casebook* (2nd ed.). New York: Oxford University Press.

Goleman, D. (1987). A reward mechanism for repression. *Psychology Today,*(March), 26–30.

Goodchilds, J., & Zellman, G. (1984). Sexual signaling and sexual aggression in adolescent relationships. In N. Malamuth & E. Donnestein (Eds.), *Pornography and Sexual Aggression*. Orlando: Academic Press.

Goodman, N. (2002). The serotonergic system and mysticism: could LSD and the nondrug-induced mystical experience share common neural mechanisms? *Jourrnal of Psychoactive Drugs, Jul–Sep; 34*(3), 263–272.

Goodwin, R., & Hamilton, S.P. (2002) Cigarette Smoking and Panic: The Role of Neuroticism *Am J Psychiatry* 159:1208–1213, July 2002.

Gooren, L. (1988). Hypogonadotropic hpogonadal men respond less well to androgen substitution treatment than hypergonadotropic hypogonadal men. *Archives of Sexual Behavior, 17*, 265–270.

Gopnik, A., Meltzoff, A., Kuhl, P. (1999). *The Scientist in the Crib: What Early Learning Tells Us About the Mind.* New York: Harper Collins.

Gormally, J., Hill, D., Otis, M., & Rainey, L. (1975). A microtraining approach in assertion training. *Journal of Conseling Psychology, 22*, 340–344.

Gormly, A., & Brodzinsky, D. (1989). *Lifespan Human Development* (4th ed.). New York: Holt, Rinehart and Winston.

Gorski, R. (1985). The 13th J.A.F. memorial lecture: Sexual differentiation of the brain: Possible mechanisms and implications. *Canadian Journal of Physiology and Pharmacology, 63*, 577–594.

Gotffredson, G. (1987). Employment setting, specialization, and patterns of accomplishments among psychologists. *Professional Psychology: Research and Practice, 18*, 452–460.

Gottesman, I., & Shields, J. (1982). *Schizoiphrenia: The Epigenetic Puzzle*. Cambridge, MA: Cambridge University Press.

Gottesman, I., & Shields, J. (1976). A critical review of recent adoption, twin, and family studies of schizophrenia: Behavior genetics perspective. *Schizophrenia Bulletin, 2*, 360–398.

Gottesman, L., McGuffin, P., & Farmer, A. (1987). Clinical genetics as clues to the "real" genetics of schizophrenia. *Schizophrenia Bulletin, 13*, 23–47.

Gough, H. (1957). *California Psychological Inventory: Manual* (rev. 1975 ed.). Palo Alto, CA: Consulting Psychologists Press.

Gough, J., & Marler, P. (1987). Learning by instinct. *Scientific American, 256*, 75–85.

Gould, S. J.(2000). Will We Figure Out How Life Began?. *Time* magazine, 155 (14): 92–93.

Greenberg, M., & Morris, N. (1974). Engrossment: The newborn's impact upon the father. *American Journal of Orthopsychiatry, 44*, 520–531.

Greenberg, R., & Pearlman, C. (1974). Cutting the REM nerve: An approach to the adaptive role of REM sleep. *Perspectives in Biology and Medicine, 17*, 513–521.

Greenough, W., & Green, E. (1981). Experience and the changing brain. In J. McGaugh, J. March & S. Kiesler (Eds.), *Aging: Biology and Behavior*. New York: Academic Press.

Gregory, R. (1978). *Eye and Brain: The Psychology of Seeing* (3rd ed.). New York: McGraw-Hill.

Griffiths, P., Merry, J., Browning, M., Eisinger, A., Huntsman, R., Polani, P., et al. (1974). Homosexual women: An endocrine and psychological study. *Journal of Endocrinology, 63*, 549–556.

Griffitt, W., & Veitch, R. (1974). Preacquaintance attitude similarilty and attraction revisited: Ten days in a fallout shelter. *Sociometry, 38*, 163–173.

Grillon, C., Courchesne, E., Ameli, R., Geyer, M., & Braff, D. (1990). Increased distractibility in schizophrenic patients: Electrophysiologic and behavior evidence. *Archives of General Psychiatry, 47 Feb*(2), 171–179.

Grilo, C., & Pogue-Geile, M. (1991). The nature of environmental influences on weight and obesity: A behavior genetic analysis. *Psychological Bulletin, 110*, 250–257.

Grochowicz, P., Schedlowski, M., Husband, A., King, M., Hibberd, A., & Bowen, K. (1991). Behavioral conditioning prolongs heart allograft survival in rats. *Brain, Behavior, and Immunity, 5*, 349–356.

Grosser, B. I., Monti-Bloch, L., Jennings-White, C., & Berliner, D. L. (2000). Behavioral and electrophysiological effects of androstadienone, a human pheromone. *Psychoneuroendocrinology, Apr; 25*(3), 289–299.

Grossman, M., & Stein, I. (1948). Vagotomy and the hunger producing action of insulin in man. *Journal of Applied Physiology, 1*, 263–269.

Groves, P., & Rebec, G. (1992). *Introduction to Biological Psychology*. Dubuque, IA: Wm. C. Brown Publishers.

Gruenewald, D. A., & Matsumoto, A. M. (2003). Testosterone supplementation therapy for older men: potential benefits and risks. *Journal of the American Geriatrics Society, Jan; 51*(1), 101–115.

Guilford, J. (1982). Cognitive psychology's ambiguities: Some suggested remedies. *Psychological Review*(89).

Guilford, J. (1977). *Way Beyond the I.Q.* Buffalo, NY: Creative Education Foundation and Bearly Unlimited.

Guilford, J. (1967). *The Nature of Human Intelligence*. New York: McGraw-Hill.

Gureje, O. (1989). The significance of subtyping tardive dyskinesis: A study of prevalence and associated factors. *Psychological Medicine, 19*, 121–128.

Gusella, J., Wexier, M., Conneally, P., Nayloi, S., Anderson, M., Tanzi, R., et al. (1983). A polymorphic DNA marker genetically linked to Huntington's disease. *Nature, 306*, 234–238.

Gustafson, G., & Harris, K. (1990). Women's responses to young infants' cries. *Developmental Psychology, 26*, 144–152.

Gustafson, R. (1989). Frustration and successful vs. unsuccessful aggression: A test of Berkowitz' completion hypothesis. *Aggressive Behavior, 15*, 5–12.

Gwirtsman, H., & Gerner, R. (1981). Neurochemical abnormalities in anorexia nervosa: Similarities to affective disorders. *Biological Psychiatry, 16*.

Halas, E., & Eberhardt, M. (1987). Blocking and appetitive reinforcement. *Bulletin of the Psychonomic Society, 25*.

Haley, J. (1989). The effect of long-term outcome studies on the therapy of schizophrenia. *Journal of Marital and Family Therapy, 15*, 127–132.

Hall, J. (1992). New theory on the origin of twins. *Science News, 142*, 84.

Hall, J. G. (1996). Twinning: mechanisms and genetic implications. *Current Opinion in Genetics & Development, Jun; 6*(3), 343–347.

Hall, W. (1987). Prenatal, perinatal and early postnatal aspects of behavioral development. *Annual Review of Psychology, 38*, 91–128.

Halonen J. S. and Santrock, J. W. (1999). *Psychology Contexts & Applications,* Third Edition. Chicago: McGraw-Hill College, ISBN #:0-697-37648-6

Halonen J. S., Santrock, J. W., Schneider S. A. and Ragade, A. R. (1996). *Instructor's Course Planner Psychology Contexts Of Behavior,* 2nd edition. Pp 20; Chicago: Brown & Benchmark. ISBN 0-697-14910-2

Halpen, D. (1989). The disappearance of cognitive gender differences: What you see depends on where you look. *American Psychologist, 44*, 1156–1158.

Halperin, J. M., Newcorn, J. H., Koda, V. H., Pick, L., McKay, K. E., & Knott, P. (1997). Noradrenergic mechanisms in ADHD children with and without reading disabilities: a replication and extension. *Journal of the American Academy of Child and Adolescent Psychiatry, Dec; 36*(12), 1688–1697.

Hamburg, D., & Takanishi, R. (1989). Preparing for life: The critical transition of adolescence. *American Psychologist, 44*, 825–827.

Hamilton, D., Katz, L., & Leirer, V. (1980). Memory for persons. *Journal of Personality and Social Psychology, 39*, 1050–1063.

Hamilton, J. (1943). Demonstrable ability of penile erection in castrate men with markedly low titers of urinary androgen. *Proceedings of the Society of Experimental Biology and Medicine, 54*, 309.

Hamilton, J., Gallant, S., & Lloyd, C. (1989). Evidence for a menstrual-linked artifact in determining rates of depression. *The Journal of Nervous and Mental Disease, 177*, 359–365.

Hampson, J. L., & Hampson, J. G. (1961). The ontogenesis of sexual behavior in man. In W. Young (Ed.), *Sex and Internal Secretions*. Baltimore: Williams & Wilkins.

Haney, C., & Zimbardo, P. (1977). The socialization into criminality: On becoming a prisoner and a guard. In J. Tapp & E. Levine (Eds.), *Law, Justice, and the Individual in Society: Psychological and Legal Issues*. New York: Holt, Rinehart and Winston.

Haney, Craig; Banks, Curtis; Zimbardo, Philip (1973) Interpersonal dynamics in a simulated prison. *International Journal of Criminology & Penology.* Vol 1(1), Feb 1973, 69–97.

Hanna, G. (1988). Gender differences in mathematics achievement among eighth graders: Results from twenty countries. Paper presented at the annual meeting of the American Association for the Advancement of Science. In. Boston, February.

Harbuz, M. (2003). Neuroendocrine-immune interactions. *Trends in Endocrinology and Metabolism: TEM, Mar; 14*(2), 51–52.

Hardy, J., Stolwijk, J., & Hoffman, D. (1968). Pain following step increase in skin temperature. In D. Kenshalo (Ed.), *The Skin Senses*. Springfield, IL: Thomas.

Hare, R. (1975). Psychophysiological studies of psychopathy. In D. Fowles (Ed.), *Clinical Applications of Psychophysiology*. New York: Columbia University Press.

Hare, R. (1970). *Psychopathy: Theory and Research*. New York: Wiley.

Hare, R., Frazelle, J., & Cox, D. (1978). Psychopathy and physiological responses to threat of an aversive stimulus. *Psychophysiology, 15*, 165–172.

Harlow, E., Harlow, M., & Meyer, D. (1950). Learning motivated by a manipulative drive. *Journal of Experimental Psychology: 40*, 228–234.

Harlow, H., & Harlow, M. (1966). Learning to love. *American Scientist, 54*, 244–272.

Harlow, H., Harlow, M., & Suomi, S. (1971). From thought to therapy: Lessons from a primate laboratory. *American Scientist, 59*, 538–549.

Harlow, H., & Zimmerman, R. (1958). The development of affectional responses in infant monkeys. *Proceedings of the American Philosophical Society, 102*, 501–509.

Harris, A., Benedict, R., & Leek, M. (1990). Consideration of pigeon-holing and filtering as dysfunctional attention strategies in schizophrenia. *British Journal of Clinical Psychology, 29*, 23–35.

Harris, E., Noyes, R., Crowe, R., & Chaudhry, D. (1983). Family study of agoraphobia. *Archives of General Psychiatry, 4j0*, 1061–1069.

Harris, I. M., & Miniussi, C. (2003). Parietal lobe contribution to mental rotation demonstrated with rTMS. *Journal of Cognitive Neuroscience, Apr 1; 15*(3), 315–323.

Hartman, E., Russ, D., Oldfield, M., Sivan, I., & Cooper, S. (1987). Who has nightmares? *Archives of General Psychiatry, 44*, 49–56.

Hartman, E., Russ, D., van der Kolk, B., Falke, R., & Oldfield, M. (1981). A preliminary study of the personality of the nightmare sufferer: Relationship to schizophrenia and creativity? *American Journal of Psychiatry, 138*, 794–797.

Hartshorne, H., & May, M. (1928). *Studies in the Nature of Character* (Vol. 1, Studies in Deceit). New York: Macmillan.

Harvard, Medical, & School. (1989). Group therapy Part I. *The Harvard Medical School Mental Health Letter, 5*, 1–4.

Harvich, L., & Jameson, D. (1957). An opponent process theory of color vision. *Psychological Review, 64*, 384–404.

Haseltine, E., & Ohno, S. (1981). Mechanisms of gonadal differentiation. *Science, 21*, 1272–1278.

Hatcher, R., Guest, E., Stewart, E., Stewart, G., Trussell, J., Bowen, S., et al. (1988). *Contraceptive Technologies 1988–1989* (14th ed.). New York: Irvington.

Hatfield, E., & Sprechler, S. (1986). *Mirror, Mirror..The Importance of Looks in Everyday Life.* Albany: State University of New York Press.

Hathaway, S., & McKinley, J. (1942). *Minnesota Multiphasic Personality Inventory.* Minneapolis: University of Minnesota.

Hawn, P., & Harris, L. (1983). Laterality in manipulatory and cognitive related activity. In G. Young, S. Segalowitz, C. Corter & S. Trehub (Eds.), *Manual Specialization and the Developing Brain.* New York: Academis Press.

Hayes, C. (1951). *The Ape in Our House.* New York: Harper & Row.

Hayflick, L. (1974). The strategy of senescence. *The Gerontologist, 14,* 37–45.

Hearnshaw, L. (1979). *Cyril Burt: Psychologist.* Ithaca, NY: Cornell University Press.

Hearst, N., & Hulley, S. (1988). Preventing the heterosexual spread of MDS. *Journal of American Medical Association, 259,* 2428–2432.

Heath, D. L., & Vink, R. (1999). Improved motor outcome in response to magnesium therapy received up to 24 hours after traumatic diffuse axonal brain injury in rats. *Journal of Neurosurgery, Mar; 90*(3), 504–509.

Heath, R., McCarron, K., & O'Neil, C. (1989). Antiseptal brain antibody in IgG schizophrenic patients. Biological Psychiatry, 25, 725–733. (1989). Antiseptal brain antibody in IgG schizophrenic patients. *Biological Psychiatry, 25,* 725–733.

Heath, R. (1972). Pleasure and brain activity in man. *Journal of Nervous and Mental Disease, 154,* 3–18.

Hebb, D. (1955). Drives and the CNS. *Psychological Review, 62,* 243–254.

Hebb, D. (1949). *The Organization of Behavior.* New York: Wiley.

Heider, E., & Oliver, D. (1972). The structure of the color space in naming and memory for two languages. *Cognitive Psychology, 3,* 337–354.

Heider, F. (1958). *The Psychology of Interpersonal Relations.* New York,: Wiley.

Heider, F. (1946). Attitudes and cognitive organization. *Journal of Psychology, 21,* 107–112.

Heider, K. (1976). Dani sexuality: A low energy system. *Man, 11,* 188–201.

Heim, N. (1981). Sexual behavior of castrated sex offenders. *Archives of Sexual Behavioir, 10,* 11–19.

Helfand, S. L., & Rogina, B. (2003). Molecular genetics of aging in the fly: is this the end of the beginning? *BioEssays, Feb; 25*(2), 134–141.

Hem, K. (1989). Commentary on adolescent acquired immunodeficiency syndrome: The nextr wave of immunodeficiency virus epidemic? *Journal of Pediatrics, 114,* 144–149.

Henderson, N. (1982). Human behavior genetics. *Annual Review of Psychology, 33,* 403–440.

Heninger, G., Charney, D., & Menkies, D. (1983). Receptor sensitivity and the mechanism of action of antidepressant treatment. In P. Clayton & J. Barrett (Eds.), *Treatment of Depression: Old Controversies and New Approaches.* New York: Raven.

Henkel, V., Bussfeld, P., Moller, H. J., & Hegerl, U. (2002). Cognitive-behavioural theories of helplessness/hopelessness: valid models of depression? *European Archives of Psychiatry and Clinical Neuroscience, Oct; 252*(5), 240–249.

Henly, A., & Williams, R. (1986). Type A and B subjects' self-reported cognitive/affective/behavioral responses to descriptions of potentially fustrating situations. *Journal of Human Stress, 12,* 168–174.

Henry, W., Schacht, T., & Strupp, H. (1986). Structural analysis of social behavior: Application to a study of interpersonal processes in differential psychotherapeutic outcome. *Journal of Consulting and Clinicalk Psychology, 54,* 27–31.

Henson, G. , Venturelli, P.J., Fleckenstein, A. E. (20000). *Drugs and Society,* Sixth Ed. Boston: Jones and Bartlett Publishers. ISBN 0-7637-1391-0

Herdt, G., & Davidson, J. (1988). The Sambia "Turnim-man": Sociocultural and clinical aspects of gender formation in male pseudo-hermaphrodites with 5-alpha-reductase deficiency in Papua, New Guinea. *Achives of Sexual Behavior, 17,* 33–56.

Herman, J., & Roffwarg, H. (1983). Modifying ocularmotor acitivity in awake subjects increases the amplitude of eye movement during REM sleep. *Science, 220,* 1075–1076.

Herz, M., Szymanski, H., & Simon, J. (1982). Intermittent medication for stable schizophrenic outpatients: An alternative to maintenance medication. *The American Journal of Psychiatry, 139,* 918–922.

Hess, W. (1957). *Functional Organization of the Diencephalon.* New York: Grune & Stratton.

Hesse-Biber, S. (1989). Eating patterns and disorders in a college population: Are college women's eating problems a new phenomenon? *Sex Roles, 20,* 71–84.

Heston, L., & Shields, J. (1968). Homosexuality in twins. *Archives of General Psychiatry, 13,* 149–160.

Hilgard, E. (1977). *Divided Consciousness: Multiple Controls in Human Thought and Action.* New York: Wiley-Interscience.

Hilgard, E. (1975). Hypnosis. *Annual Review of Psychology, 26,* 19–44.

Hobson, A. (1989). Dream theory: A new view of he brain-mind. *The Harvard Medical School Mental Health Letter, 5,* 3–5.

Hock, R. R.: (1992): To Help or Not to Help, in *Forty Studies That Changed Psychology Explorations Into the History of Psychological Research,* Third Ed; pp. 295–303; New Jersey: Prentice Hall Publisher, ISBN 0-13-922725-3

Hockett, C. (1960). The origin of speech. *Scientific American, 203,* 89–96.

Hodgkins, J. (1988). Everything you always wantd to know about sex. *Naturé, 331,* 300–301.

Hodgkins, J. (1962). Influence of age on the speed of reaction and movement in females. *Journal of Gerontology, 17,* 385–389.

Hodgkinson, S., Sherrington, R., Gurling, H., Marchbanks, R., Reeders, S., Mallet, J., et al. (1987). Molecular genetic evidence for heterogeneity in manic depression. *Nature, 325,* 805–806.

Hofferth, S., Kahn, J., & Baldwin, W. (1987). Premarital sexual activity among U.S. teenage women over the past three decades. *Family Planning Perspectives, 19,* 46–54.

Hoffman, L. (1979). Maternal employment: 1979. *American Psychologist, 34,* 359–365.

Hoffman, L. (1974). Effects of maternal employment on the child: A review of the research. *Developmental Psychology, 10,* 204–228.

Hoffman, L., & Manis, J. (1979). The value of children in the United States: A new approach to the study of fertility. *Journal of Marriage and the Family, 41,* 583–596.

Hohmann, G. (1966). Some effects of spinal cord lesions on experienced emotional feelings. *Psychophysiology, 3,* 143–156.

Holiday, H. (1987). X-chromosome reacitivation. *Nature, 327,* 661–662.

Holinger, P. (1979). Violent deaths among the young: Recent trends in suicide, homicides, and accidents. *American Journal of Psychiatry, 136,* 1144–1147.

Hollinger, P. (1980). Violent deaths as a leading cause of mortality. *Journal of American Psychiatry, 137,* 472–476.

Hollon, S., DeRubeis, R., & Evans, M. (1987). Causal mediation of change in treatment for depression: Discriminating between non-specificity and noncausality. *Psychological Bulletin, 102,* 139–149.

Hollon, S., & Garber, J. (1990). Cognitive therapy for depression: A social cognitive perspective. *Personality & Social Psychology Bulletin, 16,* 58–73.

Holmes, D., & Jorgensen, B. (1971). Do personality and social psychologists study men more than women? *Representative Research in Social Psychology, 2,* 71–76.

Holmes, J., & Boon, S. (1990). Developments in the field of close relationships: Creating foundations for intervention stategies. *Personality & Social Psychology Bulletin, 16,* 23–41.

Holmes, T., & Rahe, R. (1967). The social readjustment rating scale. *Journal of Psychosomatic Research, 11*, 213–218.

Holway, A., & Boring, E. (1941). Determinants of apparent visual sight with distant variant. *American Journal of Psychology, 54*, 21–37.

Horney, K. (1950). *Neurosis and Human Growth*. New York: Norton.

Horney, K. (1945). *Our Inner Conflicts*. New York: Norton.

Horney, K. (1939). *New Ways in Psychoanalysis*. New York: Norton.

Hopkins, B., & Palthe, T. (1987). The development of the crying state during infancy. *Developmental Psychobiology, 20*, 165–175.

Horn, J. (1982). The aging of human abilities. In B. Wolman (Ed.), *Handbook of Developmental Psychology*. Englewood Cliffs, NJ: Prentice-Hall.

Horn, J., & Donaldson, G. (1980). Cognitive development in adulthood. In O. Brim & J. Kagan (Eds.), *Constancy and Change in Human Development*. Cambridge, MA: Harvard University Press.

Host, L. (1979). The antisocial character. *American Journal of Psychoanalysis, 39*, 235–249.

Houston, J. (1985). *Motivation*. New York: Macmillan.

Houston, M., & Hay, I. (1990). Practical management of hyperthyroidism. *American Family Physician, 41*, 909–916.

Hovland, C., Harvey, D., & Sherif, M. (1957). Assimilation and contrast effects in reactions to communication and attitude change. *Journal of Abnormal and Social Psychology, 55*, 244–252.

Hovland, C., Janis, I., & Kelley, H. (1953). *Communication and Persuasion*. New Haven, CT: Yales University Press.

Hovland, C., Lumsdaine, A., & Sheffield, E. (1949). *Experiments on Mass Communication*. Princeton, NJ: Princeton University Press.

Hovland, C., & Sears, R. (1960). Minor studies in aggression, VI: Correlations of lynchings with economic indices. *Journal of Personality, 9*, 301–310.

Howard, A., Pion, G., Gottfredson, G., Flattau, P., Oskamp, S., Pfaftin, S., et al. (1986). The changing face of American psychology. *American Psychologist, 41*, 1311–1327.

Howard, A., Pion, G., Sechrest, L., Cordray, D., Kaplan, L., Hall, J., et al. (1987). Membership opinions about reorganizing APA. *American Psychologist, 42*, 763–779.

Hubbard, T. (1990). Cognitive representation of linear motion: Possible direction and gravity effects in judged displacement. *Memory and Cognition, 18*, 299–309.

Hubel, D., & Wiesel, T. (1979). Brain mechanisms of vision. *Scientific American, 241*, 150–162.

Hublin, C., Kaprio, J., Partinen, M., & Koskenvuo, M. (1999). Nightmares: familial aggregation and association with psychiatric disorders in a nationwide twin cohort. *American Journal of Medical Genetics, Aug 20; 88*(4), 329–336.

Huessman, L. R., Moise-Titus, J., Podolski, C.-L., & Eron, L. D. (2003). Longitudinal relations between children's exposure to TV violence and their aggressive and violent behavior in young adulthood: 1977–1992. *Developmental Psychology, 39*(2), 201–221.

Hull, C. (1943). *Principles of Behavior Theory*. New York: Appleton, Century, Crofts.

Hull, C. (1920). Quantitative aspects of the evolution of concepts. *Psychological Monographs, Whole No. 123.*

Hurvich, L. (1978). Two decades of opponent process. In E. Bilmeyer & G. Wyszecki (Eds.), *Color 77*. Bristol, England: Adam Hilger.

Hutchings, B., & Mednick, E. (1974). Registered criminality in the adoptive and biological parents of registered male adoptees. In S. Mednick, E. Schulsinger, J. Higgins & B. Bell (Eds.), *Genetics, Environment and Psychopathology*. New York: Elsevier.

Hutton, M., Perez-Tur, J., & Hardy, J. (1998). Genetics of Alzheimer's disease. *Essays in Biochemistry, 33*, 117–131.

Hyde, J. (1981). How large are cognitive gender differences? A meta-analysis using W^2 and d. *American Psychologist, 36*, 892–901.

Hyde, J., Fennema, E., & Lamon, S. (1990). Gender differences in mathematics performance: A meta-analysis. *Psychological Bulletin, 107*, 139–155.

Hyde, J. G. (1997). *Gender differences* in cognition: results from meta-analyses. In P. J. Caplan, M. Crawford & e. al (Eds.), *Gender differences in human cognition. Counterpoints: Cognition, memory and language* (pp. 30–51).

Hyde, J. S., & Frost, L. A. (1993). Meta-analysis in the psychology of women. In F. L. Denmark & M. Paludi (Eds.), *Psychology of Women: A handbook of issues and theories* (pp. 67–103).

Hyde, J. S., & Linn, M. C. (1988). *Gender differences* in verbal ability: a meta-analysis. *Psychological Bulletin, Jul; 104*(1), 53–69.

Imperato-McGinley, J., Peterson, R., Gautier, T., & Sturla, E. (1979). Androgens and the evolution of the male-gender identity among male pseudohermaphrodites with 5-reductase deficiency. *New England Journal of Medicine, 300*, 1233–1237.

Insko, C., & Melson, W. (1969). Verbal reinforcement of attitude in laboratory and nonlaboratory contexts. *Journal of Personality, 37*, 25–40.

Isensee, B., Wittchen, H. U., Stein, M. B., Hofler, M., & Lieb, R. (2003). Smoking increases the risk of panic: findings from a prospective community study. *Archives of General Psychiatry, Jul; 60*(7), 692–700.

Izard, C. (1990). Facial expression and the regulation of emotions. *Journal of Personality and Social Psychology, 58*, 487–498.

Jacobs, B. L., & Fornal, C. A. (1999). Activity of serotonergic neurons in behaving animals. *Neuropsychopharmacology, Aug; 21*(2, Suppl), 9S–15S.

Jacobs, L., Berscheid, D., & Walster, E. (1971). Self-esteem and attraction. *Journal of Personality and Social Psychology, 17*, 84–91.

Jacobson, E. (1932). The electrophysiology of mental activities. *American Journal of Psychology, 44*, 677–694.

Jacobson, G. (1968). The briefest psychiatric encounter. *Archives of General Psychiatry, 18*, 718–724.

Jacques, J., & Chason, K. (1979). Cohabitation: Its impact on marital success. *Family Coordinator, 28*, 35–39.

James, E., Large, R., & Beale, I. (1989). Self-hypnosis in chronic pain. *The Clinical Journal of Pain, 5*, 161–168.

James, W. (1890). *Principles of Psychology* (Vol. 2 vols). New York: Holt, Rinehart and Winston.

James, W. (1884). What is an emotion? *Mind, 9*, 188–205.

Janet, J. (1929). *The Major Symptoms of Hysteria* (2nd ed.). New York: Macmillan.

Janis, I., & Feshbach, S. (1953). Effects of fear-arousing communication. *Journal of Abnormal and Social Psychology, 48*, 78–92.

Janowitz, H., & Grossman, M. (1950). Hunger and appetite: Some definitions and concepts. *Journal of Mount Sinai Hospital, 16*, 231–240.

Janus, C. (2003). Vaccines for Alzheimer's disease: how close are we? *CNS Drugs, 17*(7), 457–474.

Jayaratne, S. (1982). Characteristics and theoretical orientations of clinical social workers: A national survey. *Journal of Social Service Research, 4*, 17–30.

Jemmott, J., Borysenko, J., Borysenko, M., McClelland, C., Chapman, R., Meyer, D., et al. (1983). Academic stress, power motivation, and decrease in salivary secretory immunoglobulin A secretion rate. *Lancet, 1*, 1400–1402.

Jensen, J., Bergin, A., & Greaves, D. (1990). The meaning oif eclectiscism: New survey and analysis of components. *Professional Psychology: Research and Practice, 21*, 124–130.

Jensvold, M. L. A., & Gardner, R. A. (2000). Interactive use of sign *language* by cross-fostered chimpanzees (Pan troglodytes). *Journal of Comparative Psychology, Dec: 114*(4), 335–346.

Jo, E., & Berkovitz, L. (1994). A priming effect analyssis of media influences: An update. In J. Bryant & D. Zillman (Eds.), *Media Effects: Advances in Theory and Research*. Hillsdale, NJ: Erlbaum.

Joe, G., & Simpson, D. (1987). Mortlity rates among opioid addicts in a longitudinal study. *American Journal of Public Health, 77*, 347–348.

Johansson, C., Willeit, M., Levitan, R., Partonen, T., Smedh, C., Del Favero, J., et al. (2003). The serotonin transporter promoter repeat length polymorphism, seasonal affective disorder and seasonality. *Psychological Medicine, Jul: 33*(5), 785–792.

Johnson, D. (1989). Schizophrenia as a brain disease. *American Psychologist, 44*, 553–555.

Johnson, M. and Ettinger, (2000) R.H. Active immunization attenuates cocaine's discriminative properties. *Experimental and Clinical Psychopharmacology*, 8, 163–167.

Johnstone, E., Owens, D., Bydder, G., Colter, N., Crow, T., & Friith, C. (1989). The spectrum of structural brain changes in schizophrenia: Age of onset as a predictor of cognitive and clinical impairments and their cerebral correlates. *Psychological Medicine, 19*, 91–103.

Joiner, T. E., Jr;, Lewinsohn, P. M., & Seeley, J. R. (2002). The core of loneliness: lack of pleasurable engagement—more so than painful disconnection—predicts social impairment, depression onset, and recovery from depressive disorders among adolescents. *Journal of Personality Assessment., Dec; 79*(3), 472–491.

Jones, E. (1979). The rocky road from acts to dispositions. *American Psychologist, 34*, 107–117.

Jones, E., Davis, K., & Gergen, K. (1961). Role playing variations and their informational value on person perception. *Journal of Abnormal and Social Psychology, 63*, 302–310.

Jones, E., & McGillis, D. (1970). Correspondent inferences at the attribution cube: A comparative reappraisal. In J. Harvey, W. Ickes & R. Kidd (Eds.), *New Directions in Attrbution Research* (Vol. 1). Hillsdale, NJ: Erlbaum.

Jones, H., & Conrad, H. (1933). The growth and decline of intelligence: A study of a homogeneous group between the ags of ten and sixty. *Genetic Psychology Monographs, 13*, 223–294.

Jones, M. (1958). A study of socialization patterns at the high school level. *Journal of Genetic Psychology, 93*, 87–111.

Jones, M. (1957). The later careers of boys who were early- or late-maturing. *Child Development, 28*, 115–128.

Jones, M., & Mussen, P. (1958). Self-conceptions, motivations, and interpersonal attitudes of early- and late-maturing girls. *Child Development, 29*, 491–501.

Jones, R., & Brehm, J. (1970). Persuasiveness of one- and two-sided communications as a function of awareness: There are two sides. *Journal of Experimental Social Psychology:, 6*, 46–56.

Jones, W., & Anderson, J. (1987). Short- and long-term memory retrieval: A comparison of the effects of information load and relatedness. *Journal of Experimental Psychology: General, 116*, 136–153.

Judd, C., Kenny, D., & Krosnick, J. (1983). Judging the positions of political candidates: Models of assimilation and contact. *Journal of Personality and Social Psychology, 44*, 952–963.

Julien, R. (2001). *A Primer of Drug Action* (9th ed.). New York: W H Freeman and Company.

Jung, C. (1953). *Collected Works*. Princeton, Nj: Princeton University Press.

Jung, C. (1933). *Modern Man in Search of a Soul*. New York: Harcourt, Brace & World.

Jung, C. (1916). *Analytical Psychology*. New York: Moffat.

Kagan, J. (1987). Perspectives on infancy. In J. D. Osofsky (Ed.), *Handbook of infant development (2nd ed.)* (pp. 1150–1198): Wiley.

Kagan, J., Kearsley, R., & Zelazo, P. (1978). *Infancy: Its Place in Human Development*. Cambridge, MA: Harvard University Press.

Kagan, J., & Klein, R. (1973). Cross-cultural perspectives on early development. *American Psychologist, 28*, 947–961.

Kahn, J., Komfeld, D., Frank, K., Heller, S., & Hoar, P. (1980). Type A behavior and blood pressure during coronary artery bypass surgery. *Psychosomatic Medicine, 42*, 407–414.

Kalat, J. (1992). *Biological Psychology* (2nd ed.). Belmont CA: Wadsworth Publishing Company.

Kales, A., Caldwell, A., Preston, T., Healey, S., & Kales, J. (1976). Personality patterns in insomniacs: Theoretical implications. *Archives of General Psychiatry, 33*, 1128–1134.

Kales, J., Tan, T., Kollar, E., Naitoh, P., Preston, T., & Malmstrom, E. (1970). Sleep patterns following 205 hours of sleep deprivation. *Psychosomatic Medicine, 32*(189–200).

Kalinowsky, L. (1980). Convulsive therapies. In A. F. H. Kaplan, & B. Sadock (Ed.), *Comprehensive Textbook of Psychiatry*. Baltimore: Williams & Wilkins.

Kalinowsky, L. (1975). Psychosurgery:. In H. Kaplan, A. Freeman & B. Sadok (Eds.), *Comprehensive Textbook of Psychiatry*. Baltimore: Williams & Wilkins.

Kamin, L. (1974). *The Science and Politics of IQ*. Potomac, MD: Erlbaum.

Kamin, L. (1969). Predictability, surprise, attention, and conditioning. In B. Campbell & R. Church (Eds.), *Punishment and Aversive Behavior*. New York: Appleton, Century, Crofts.

Kandel, E., & Hawkins, R. (1992). The biological basis of learning and individuality. *Scientific American, 267*, 78–86.

Kandel, E. (1983). A cellular mechanism of classical conditioning in Aplysia: Activity dependent amplification of postsynaptic facilitation. *Science, 219*, 400–405.

Kane, J. (1992b). Clinical efficacy of clozapine in treatment-refractory schizophrenia: An overview. *British Journal of Psychiatry, 160*, 41–45.

Kane, J. (1992a). New developments in the pharmacological treatment of schizophrenia. *Bulletin of the Menninger Clinic, 56*, 62–75.

Kanin, B. (1967). Reference groups and sex conduct norms. *Sociological Quarterly, 8*, 495–504.

Kaplan, G., Salonen, J., Cohen, R., Brand, R., Syme, S., & Puska, P. (1988). Social connections and mortality from all causes and from cardiovascular disease: Prospective evidence from eastern Finland. *American Journal of Epidemiology, 128*, 370–380.

Kaplan, M., Lazoff, M., Kelly, K., Lukin, R., & Garver, D. (1990). Enlargement of cerebral third ventricle in psychotic patients with delayed response to neuroleptics. *Biological Psychiatry, 27*, 205–214.

Kaprio, J., Koskenvuo, M., & Rita, H. (1987). Mortality after bereavement: A prospective study of 95,647 widowed persons. American Journal of Public Health, 77, 283–287. (1987). Mortality after bereavement: A prospective study of 95,647 widowed persons. *American Journal of Public Health, 77*, 283–287.

Karni, A. (1992). *REM sleep and memory consolidation. Paper presented at the annual meeting of the Society for Neuroscience.*Unpublished manuscript, Anaheim, CA.

Katschnig, K., & Shepherd, M. (1978). Neurosis: The epidemiological perspective. In H. v. Prang (Ed.), *Research in Neurosis*. New York: Spectrum Publications.

Katz, P. (1976). The acquisition of racial attitudes in children. In P. Katz (Ed.), *Towards the Elimination of Racism*. New York: Pergamon.

Katzman, R., Aronson, M., Fuld, P., Kawas, C., Brown, T., Morgenstern, H., Frishman, W., Gidez, L., Eder, H., & Ooi, W. (1989). Development of dementing illnesses in an 80-year-old volunteer cohort. Annals of Neurology, 25, 317–324. (1989). Development of dementing illnesses in an 80-year-old volunteer cohort. *Annals of Neurology, 25*, 317–324.

Kaufman, A. S. (2001). WAIS-III IQs, Horn's theory, and generational changes from young adulthood to old age. *Intelligence, Mar–Apr; 29*(2), 131–167.

Kaufman, L., & Rock, I. (2000). The *moon illusion*. In S. Yantis (Ed.), *Visual perception: Essential readings. Key readings in cognition* (pp. 233–242).

Kauftnan, J., & Zigler, E. (1987). Do abused children become abusive parents? *American Journal of Orthopsychiatry, 57*, 186–192.

Keating, D. (1980). Thinking processes in adolescence. In J. Adelson (Ed.), *Handbook of Adolescent Psychology*. New York: Wiley-Interscience.

Kebbell, M. R., & Wagstaff, G. F. (1998). Hypnotic interviewing: the best way to interview eyewitnesses? *Behavioral Sciences & the Law, Winter; 16*(1), 115–129.

Keegan, D., Bowen, R., Blackshaw, S., & Saleh, S. A comparison of fluoxetine and amitriptyline in the treatment of major depression. I. *International Clinical Psychopharmacology, 6*, 117–124.

Keel, P. K., Mitchell, J. E., Miller, K. B., Davis, T. L., & Crow, S. J. (1999). Long-term outcome of bulimia nervosa. *Archives of General Psychiatry, Jan; 56*(1), 63–69.

Keicott-Glaser, J., & Glaser, R. (1988). Psychological inlfuences on immunity. *American Psychologist, 43*, 892–898.

Keller, M. B. (2003). The lifelong course of social anxiety disorder: a clinical perspective. *Acta Psychiatrica Scandinavica, Supplementum, Sep; (417)*, 85–94.

Kellerman, H., & (ed.). (1987). *The Nightmare: Psychological and Biological Foundations*. New York: Columbia University Press.

Kelley, H. (1973). The process of causal attribution. *American Psychologist, 28*, 107–128.

Kelley, H. (1967). Attribution theory in social psychology. In D. Levine (Ed.), *Nebraska Symposium on Motivation*. Lincoln: University of Nebraska Press.

Kellner, R. (1994). Psychosomatic syndromes, somatization and somatoform disorders. *Psychotherapy and Psychosomatics, 61*(1–2), 4–24.

Kellner, R. (1990). Somatization: Theories and research. *The Journal of Nervous and Mental Disease, 178*, 150–160.

Kellogg, W., & Kellogg, L. (1933). *TheApe and the Child*. New York: McGraw-Hill.

Kelsoe, J., Ginns, E., & Egeland, J. (1989). Reevaluation of the linkage relationship between chromosome 11p loci and the gene for bipolar affective disorder in the Old Order Amish. *Nature, 342*, 238–243.

Kendall, P., & Norton-Ford, J. (1982). *Clinical Psychiatry*. New York: Wiley.

Kendler, K. (1986). Genetics of schizophrenia. In A. Francis & R. Hales (Eds.), *Psychiatry Update: American Psychiatric Association Annual Review* (Vol. 5). Washington, DC: American Psychiatric Press.

Kendler, K., Gruenberg, A., & Tsuang, M. (1985). Psychiatric illness in first-degree relatives of schizophrenics and surgical control patients: A family study using DSM-III criteria. *Archives of General Psychiatry*, p. 770–779.

Kendler, K. S., Pedersen, N., Johnson, L., Neale, M. C., & Mathe, A. A. (1993). A pilot Swedish twin study of affective illness, including hospital- and population-ascertained subsamples. *Archives of General Psychiatry, Sep; 50*(9), 699–700.

Kendler, K. S., Pedersen, N. L., Farahmand, B. Y., & Persson, P. G. (1996). The treated incidence of psychotic and affective illness in twins compared with population expectation: a study in the Swedish Twin and Psychiatric Registries. *Psychological Medicine, Nov; 26*(6), 1135–1144.

Kendler, K. S., & Prescott, C. A. (1999). A population-based twin study of lifetime major depression in men and women. *Archives of General Psychiatry, Jan; 56*(1), 39–44.

Kennedy, J., Giuffra, L., Moises, H., Cavalli-Sforza, L., Pakstis, A., Kidd, J., Castiglione, C., Sjogren, B., Wetterberg, L., & Kidd, K. (1988). Evidence against linkage of schizophrenia to markers on chromosome 5 in a northern Swedish pedigree. *Nature, 336;*, 167–170.

Kennedy, K., Fortney, J., & Sokal, D. (1989). Breastfeeding and HIV. *Lancet, 1*, 333.

Kessler, S. (1980). The genetics of schizophrenia: A review. *Schizophrenia Bulletin, 6*, 404–416.

Kety, S., Rosenthal, D., Wender, P., Schulsinger, F, & Jacobsen, B. (1975). Mental illness in the biological and adoptive families of adopted individuals who have become schizophrenic: A preliminary report based upon psychiatric interviews. In R. Fieve, D. Rosenthal & H. Brill (Eds.), *Genetic Research in Psychiatry*. Baltimore: John Hopkins University Press.

Kety, S. (1975). Biochemistry of the major psychoses. In A. Freedman, H. Kaplan & B. Sadock (Eds.), *Comprehensive Textbook of Psychiatry*. Baltimore: Williams & Wilkins.

Kierkegaard, S. (1844). *The Concept of Anxiety* (2nd ed.). Princeton, NJ: Princeton University Press (revised printing 1980).

Kiernan, J., & Taylor, V. (1990). Coercive sexual behavior among Mexican-American college students. *Journal of Sex and Marital Therapy, 16*, 44–50.

Kilham, W., & Mann, L. (1974). Level of destructive obedience as a function of transmitter and executant roles in the Milgram obedience paradigm. *Journal of Personality and Social Psychology, 29*, 696–702.

Kiloh, L., Smith, J., & Johnson, G. (1988). *Physical Treatments in Psychiatry*. Melbourne: Blackwell Scientific Publications.

Kimura, D. (1992). Sex differences in the brain. *Scientific American, 267*, 118–125.

King, B., & Liston, E. (1990). Proposals for the mechanism of action of convulsive therapy: A synthesis. *Biological Psychiatry, 27*, 76–94.

Kinsey, A., Pomeroy, W., & Martin, C., and Gebhard, P. (1953). *Sexual Behavior in the Human Female*. Philadelphia: Saunders.

Kinsey, A., Pomeroy, W., & Martin, C. (1948). *Sexual Behavior in the Human Male*. Philadelphia: Saunders.

Kirkpatnck, B., Buchanan, R., Waltrip, R., Jauch, D., & Carpenter, W. (1989). Diazepam treatment of early symptoms of schizophrenic relapse. *The Journal of Nervous and Mental Disease, 177*, 52–53.

Klagsbrun, E. (1985). *Married People: Staying Together in the Age of Divorce*. New York: Bantam.

Klaich, D. (1974). *Woman Plus Woman: Attitudes Towards Lesbianism*. New York: Simon & Schuster.

Klaus, M., & Kennell, J. (1982). *Parent-Infant Bonding*. (2nd ed.). St. Louis: Mosby.

Klein, D. (1981). Anxiety reconceptualized. In D. Klein & J. Rabkin (Eds.), *Anxiety: New Research and Changing Concepts*. New York: Raven.

Kleinhauz, M., & Eli, I. (1987). Potential deleterious effects of hypnosis in the clinical setting. *American Journal of Clinical Hypnosis, 29*, 155–159.

Kleinmuntz, B. (1982). *Personality and Psychological Assessment*. New York: St. Martin's Press.

Klineberg, O. (1935). *Negro Intelligence and Selective Immigration*. New York: Columbia University Press.

Knackstedt, L. A., Samimi, M. M., & Ettenberg, A. (2002). Evidence for *opponent-process* actions of intravenous cocaine and cocaethylene. *Pharmacology, Biochemistry & Behavior, Jul; 72*(4), 931–936.

Knittle, J., & Hirsch, J. (1968). Effect of early nutrition on the development of rat epididymal fat pads: Cellularity and metabolism. *Journal of Clinical Endocrinology and Metabolism, 47*, 2001–2098.

Knussmann, R., Christiansen, K., & Couwenbergs, C. (1986). Relations between sex hormone levels and sexual behavior in men. *Archives of Sexual Behavior, 15*, 429–445.

Ko, G., Zhang, L., Yan, W., Zhang, M., Buchner, D., Xia, Z., Wyatt, R., & Jeste, D. (1989). The Shahghai 800: Prevalence of tardive dyskinesia in a Chinese psychiatric hospital. *The American Journal of Psychiatry, 146*, 387–389.

Kohlberg, L., & Candee, D. (1984). The relationship of moral judgement to moral action. In W. Kurtins & L. Gewirtz (Eds.), *Morality, Moral Behavior, and Moral Development*. New York: Wiley.

Kohlberg, L. (1981b). *The Psychology of Moral Development: Essays on Moral Development* (Vol. II). San Francisco: Harper & Row.

Kohlberg, L. (1981a). *The Philosophy of Moral Development: Essays on Moral Development* (Vol. 1). San Francisco: Harper & Row.

Kohlberg, L., & Gilligan, C. (1971). The adolescent as a philosopher: The discovery of the self in a postconventional world. *Daedalus*, Fall, 1051–1056.

Kohlberg, L. (1969). Stage and sequence: The cognitive-developmental approach to socialization. In D. Goslin (Ed.), *Handbook of Socialization Theory and Research*. Chicago: Rand McNally.

Kohlberg, L. (1968). The child as a moral philosopher. *Psychology Today, 2*, 25–30.

Kohlberg, L. (1964). The development of moral character and moral ideology. In M. Hoffman & L. Hoffman (Eds.), *Reviews of Child Development Research* (Vol. I). New York: Russell Sage Foundation.

Kohn, A. (1987). Making the most of marriage. *Psychology Today*, December, 6–8.

Kohn, Y., & Lerer, B. (2002). Genetics of schizophrenia: a review of linkage findings. *The Israel Journal of Psychiatry and Related Sciences, 39*(4), 340–351.

Kokotovic, A., & Tracey, T. (1990). Working alliance in the early phase of counseling. *Journal of Counseling Psychology, 37*, 16–21.

Koss, L., Gidycz, C., & Wisniewski, N. (1987). The scope of rape: Incidence and prevalence of sexual aggression and victimization in a national sample of higher education students. *Journal of Consulting and Clinical Psychology, 55*, 162–170.

Kraemer, G., & McKinney, W. (1979). Interactions of pharmacological agents which alter biogenic amine metabolism and depression. *Journal of Affective Disorders, 1*, 33–54.

Kraeplin, E. (1918). *Dementia Praecox*. London: Livingstone.

Kramer, B. (1987). Electroconvulsive therapy use in geriatric depression. *The Journal of Nervous and Mental Disease, 175*, 233–235.

Krantz, D., Grunberg, N., & Baum, A. (1985). Health psychology. *Annual Review of Psychology, 36*, 349–383.

Krantz, D., & Manuck, S. ((1984). Acute psychophysiologic reactivity and risk of cardiovascular disease: A review and methodological critique. *Psychological Bulletin, 96*, 435–464.

Krantz, D., & Durel, A. (1983). Psychobiological substrates of the Type A behavior pattern. *Health Psychology, 2*, 393–412.

Kringlen, E. (1985). Depression research: a review with special emphasis etiology. *Acta Psychiatrica Scandinavica, Supplementum, 319*, 117–130.

Kripke, D., & Sonnenschein, D. (1978). A biologic rhythm in waking fantasy. In K. P. J. Singer (Ed.), *The Stream of Consciousness: Scientific Investigations into the Flow of Human Experience*. New York: Plenum.

Kroll, N., & Ogawa, K. (1988). Retrieval of the irretrievable: The effect of sequential information on response bias. In P. M. M. Gruneberg, & R. Sykes (Ed.). Chichester, England: Wiley.

Kroll, P., Chamberlain, P., & Halpern, D. (1979). The diagnosis of Briquet's syndrome in a male population. *Journal of Mental Disorders, 34*, 423–428.

Ku, L., Sonenstein, F. L., Lindberg, L. D., Bradner, C. H., Boggess, S., & Pleck, J. H. (1998). Understanding changes in sexual activity among young metropolitan men: 1979–1995. *Family Planning Perspectives, 30*(6), 256–262.

Kuehnel, J., & Liberman, R. (1986). Behavior modification. In I. Kutash & A. Wolf (Eds.), *Psychotherapist's Casebook*. San Francisco: Jossey-Bass.

KuHa, A. (1972). Attributional determinants of achievement-related behavior. *Journal of Personality and Social Psychology, 21*, 166–174.

Kulik, J., & Mahler, H. (1989). Social support and recovery from surgery. *Health Psychology, 8*, 221–238.

Kurtines, W., & Greif, E. (1974). The development of moral thought: Review and evaluation of Kohlberg's approach. *Psychological Bulletin, , 81*, 453–470.

Kushida, C., Bergmann, B., & Rechtschaffen, A. (1989). Sleep deprivation in the rat: IV. Paradoxical sleep deprivation. *Sleep, 12*, 22–30.

Kutash, I., & Wolf, A. (eds.). (1986). *Psychotherapist's Casebook*. San Francisco: Jossey-Bass.

Kwon, S. M., & Oei, T. P. (2003). Cognitive change processes in a group cognitive behavior therapy of depression. *Journal of Behavior Therapy and Experimental Psychiatry, Mar: 34*(1), 73–85.

Lacey, J. (1967). Somatic response patterning and stress: Some revisions of activation theory. In M. Appley & R. Trumball (Eds.), *Psychological Stress*. New York: McGraw Hill.

Lagerspetz, K., & Engblom, P. (1979). Immediate reaction to TV violence by Finnish preschool children of different personality types. *Scandinavian Journal of Psychology, 20*, 43–53.

Lamb, M. (1982). Second thoughts on first touch. *Psychology Today*, April, 9–11.

Lamb, M. (1981). The development of father-infant relationships. In M. Lamb (Ed.), *The Role of the Father in Child Development* (2nd ed.). New York: Wiley.

Landesman, S., Minkoff, H., & Willoughby, A. (1989). HW disease in reproductive age women: A problem of the present:. *Journal of the American Medical Association, 261*, 1326–1327.

Lang, A. J., Craske, M. G., & Brown, M. (2001). Fear-related state dependent memory. *Cognition & Emotion, Sep; 15*(5), 695–703.

Lang, P., Melamed, B. (1969). Case report: Avoidance conditioning therapy of an infant with chronic ruminative vomiting. *Journal of Abnormal Psychology, 74*, 1–8.

Lange, C. (1885). *The Emotions* (1922 ed.). Baltimore: Williams & Wilkins, (originally published in 1885).

Langer, D., Brown, G., & Docherty, J. (1981). Dopamine receptor supersensitivity and schizophrenia: A review. *Schizophrenia Bulletin, 7*, 273–280.

Langer, E. (1975). The illusion of control. *Journal of Personality and Social Psychology, 32*, 311–328.

Langlois, J., Roggman, L., & Rieser-Danner, L. (1990). Infants' differential social responses to attractive and unattractive faces. *Developmental Psychology., 26*, 153–159.

Langlois, J., Roggman, L., Casey, R., Ritter, J., Rieser-Danner, L., & Jenkins, Y. (1987). Infant preferences for attractive faces: Rudiments of a stereotype? *Developmental Psychology, 23*, 363–369.

Langlois, J., Kalakanis, K., Rubenstein, A., Larson, A., Hallam, M., & Smoot, M. (2000). Maxims or myths of beauty? A meta-analytic and theoretical review. *Psychological Bulletin, 126*, 290–423.

Langois, J., & Roggman, L. (1990). Attractive faces are only average. *Psychological Science, 1*, 115–121.

Lanzetta, J., Cartwnght-Smith, J., & Kleck, R. (1976). Effects of nonverbal dissimulation on emotional experience and autonomic arousal. *Journal of Personality and Social Psychology, 33*, 354–370.

LaPiere, R. (1934). Attitudes vs. action. *Social Forces, 13*, 230–237.

Lara, M. E., & Klein, D. N. (1999). Psychosocial processes underlying the maintenance and persistence of depression: implications for understanding chronic depression. *Clinical Psychology Review, Aug; 19*(5), 553–570.

Lashley, K. (1950). In search of the engram. *Symposia of the Society for Experimental Biology, 4*, 454–482.

Lashley, K. (1929). *Brain Mechanisms and Intelligence*. Chicago: University of Chicago Press.

Latane', B., & Darley, J. (1970). *The Unresponsive Bystander: Why Doesn't He Help?* New York: Appleton-Century-Crofts.

Lauer, J., & Lauer, R. (1985). Marriages made to last. *Psychology Today, 19*, 22–26.

Lavie, P. (1987). Ultrashort sleep-wake cycle: Timing of REM sleep. Evidence for sleep-dependent and sleep-independent components of REM cycle. *Sleep, 10*, 62–68.

Lawrence, J., Kelly, J., Hood, H., & Brasfield, T. (198). Behavioral intervention to reduce AIDS risk activities. *Journal of Consulting and Clinical Psychology, 57*, 60–67.

Lazarus, R. (1993). Coping theory and research: Past, present, and future. *Psychosomatic Medicine, 55*(3), 234–247.

Lazarus, R., & Folkman, S. (1984b). Coping and adaptation. In W. Gentry (Ed.), *The Handbook of Behavioral Medicine.* New York: Guilford.

Lazarus, R., & Folkman, S. (1984a). Stress, Appraisal, and Coping. New York: Springer. (1984a). *Sttress, Appraisal, and Coping.* New York: Springer.

Lazarus, R. (1981). Little hassles can be hazardous to health. *Psychology Today, 15*, 58–62.

Lazarus, R. S. (1999). *Stress and emotion: A new synthesis.*

Leconte, P., Hennevin, E., & Bloch, V. (1972). Increase in paradoxical sleep following learning in the rat: Correlation with level of conditioning. *Brain Research, 42*, 552–553.

LeDoux, J. (2003). The emotional brain, fear, and the amygdala. *Cellular and Molecular Neurobiology, Oct; 23*(4–5), 727–738.

LeDoux, J. (1992). Brain mechanisms of emotion and emotional learning. *Current Opinion in Neurobiology, 2*, 191.

LeDoux, J., Wilson, D., & Gazzaniga, M.421. (1977). A divided mind: Observations of the conscious properties of the separated hemispheres. *Annals of Neurology, 2*, 417–421.

LeDoux, J., Wilson, D., & Gazzaniga, M. (1977). A divided mind: Observations of the conscious properties of the separated hemispheres. *Annals of Neurology, 2*, 417–421.

Lee, A. L., Ogle, W. O., & Sapolsky, R. M. (2002). Stress and depression: possible links to neuron death in the hippocampus. *Bipolar Disorders, Apr; 4*(2), 117–128.

Lee, E. (1951). Negro intelligence and selective migration: A Philadelphia test of Klineberg's hypothesi. *American Sociological Review, 61*, 227–233.

Lee, S. H., Lee, S., Jun, H. S., Jeong, H. J., Cha, W. T., Cho, Y. S., et al. (2003). Expression of the mitochondrial ATPase6 gene and Tfam in Down syndrome. *Molecules and Cells, Apr 30; 15*(2), 181–185.

Lefkowitz, M., Eron, L., & Walder, L. (1988). *Growing Up To Be Violent: A Longitudinal Study of the Development of Aggression.* New York: Pergamon Press.

Lehne, G. K., & Money, J. (2000). The first case of paraphilia treated with Depo-Provera: 40-year outcome. *Journal of Sex Education & Therapy, 25*(4), 213–220.

Lemon, B., Bengston, V., & Peterson, J. (1972). An exploration of the activity theory of agmg: Activity types and life satisfaction among in-movers to a retirement community. *Journal of Gerontology, 27*, 511–523.

Leon, B., & Roth, L. (1977). Obesity: Psychological causes, correlations, and speculations. *Psychological Bulletin, 84*, 117–139.

Lerner, R., & Spanier, G. (1980). *Adolescent Development: A Life-Span Perspective.* New York: McGraw-Hill.

Lerner, R., & Lerner, J. (1977). Effects of age, sex, and physical attractiveness on child-peer relations, academic performance, and elementary school adjustment. *Developmental Psychology, 13*, 585–590.

Lester, D., & Smith, B. (1989). Applicability of Kübler-Ross's stages of dying to the suicidal individual: A review of the literature. *Psychological Reports, 64*, 609–610.

Lester, D. (1989). Suicide among psychologists and a proposal for the America Psychological Association. *Psychological Reports, 64*, 65–66.

Levene, J., Newman, E, & Jeffries, J. (1990). Focal family therapy: Theory and practice. *Family Processes, 29*, 73–86.

Leventhal, H., & Tomarken, A. (1986). Emotion: Today's problems. *Annual Review of Psychology, 37*, 565–610.

Leventhal, H., & Nerenz, D. (1983). A model for stress research with some implications for the control of stress disorders. In D. Meichenbaum & M. Jaremko (Eds.), *Stress Reduction and Prevention.* New York: Plenum.

Lewin, J., & Gambosh, D. (1973). Increase in REM time as a function of the need for divergent thinking. In W. Koella & P. Lewin (Eds.), *Sleep: Physiology, Biochemistry, Psychology, Pharmacology, Clinical Implications.* Basel, Switzerland: Karger.

Lewinsohn, P. (1974). A behavioral approach to depression. In R. Friedman & M. Katz (Eds.), *The Psychology of Depression: Contemporary Theory and Research.* Washington, DC: Winston/Wiley.

Lewinsohn, P., & Libet, J. (1972). Pleasant events activity schedules and depression. *Journal of Abnormal Psychology, 79*, 291–295.

Lewinsohn, P. M., Gotlib, I. H., & Seeley, J. R. (1997). Depression-related psychosocial variables: are they specific to depression in adolescents? *Journal of Abnormal Psychology, Aug; 106*(3), 365–375.

Lewis, C. (1981). The effects of parental firm control: A reinterpretation of findings. *Psychological Bulletin, 90*, 547–563.

Lewis, E., Baird, R., Leverenz, E., & Koyama, H. (1982). Inner ear: Dye injection reveals peripheral origins of specific sensitivities. *Science, 215*, 1641–1643.

Lewis, J. (1988). The transition to parenthood: Stability and change in marital structure. *Family Processes, 27*, 273–283.

Lewontin, R. (1976). Race and intelligence. In N. Block & G. Dworkin (Eds.), *The IQ controversy.* New York: Pantheon.

Lewy, A., Sack, R., Miller, L., & Hoban, T. (1987). Antidepressant and circadian phase-shifting effects of light. *Science., 235*, 352–354.

Lewy, A. J., Ahmed, S., Jackson, J. M., & Sack, R. L. (1992). Melatonin shifts human circadian rhythms according to a phase-response curve. *Chronobiology International, Oct; 9*(5), 380–392.

Lewy, A. J., Sack, R. L., Singer, C. M., White, D. M., & Hoban, T. M. (1988). Winter depression and the phase-shift hypothesis for bright light's therapeutic effects: history, theory and experimental evidence. *Journal of Biological Rhythms, Summer; 3*(2), 121–134.

Leyens, J., & Parke, R. (1975). Aggressive slides can induce a weapons effect. *European Journal of Social Psychology, 5*, 229–236.

Li, J., Johansen, C., & Olsen, J. (2003). Cancer survival in parents who lost a child: a nationwide study in Denmark. *British Journal of Cancer, Jun 2; 88*(11), 1698–1701.

Lieberman, M., & Coplan, A. (1970). Distance from death as a variable in the study of aging. *Developmental Psychology., 2*, 71–84.

Liebowitz, M. (1989). Is there a drug treatment for social phobia? *The Harvard Medical School Mental Health Letter, 5*, 8.

Liebowitz, M., Fyer, A., Gorman, J., Dillon, D., Appleby, I., Levy, G., Anderson, S., Levitt, M., Palij, M., Davies, S., & Klein, D. (1984). Lactate provocation of panic attacks: Clinical and behavioral findings. *Archives of General Psychiatry, 41*, 764–770.

Lifson, A., Rutherford, G., & Jaffe, H. (1988). The natural history of human immunodeficiency virus infection. *Journal of Infectious Diseases, 158*, 1360–1366.

Lindgren, H., & Suter, W. (1985). *Educational Psychology in the Classroom* (7th ed.). Monterey, CA: Brooks/Cole.

Linn, M., & Hyde, J. (1989). Paper presented at the annual meeting of the American Association for the Advancement of Science. (April).

Livson, N., & Peskin, H. (1980). Perspectives on adolescence from longitudinal research. In J. Adelson (Ed.), *Handbook of Adolescent Psychology.* New York: Wiley.: Wiley.

Loehlin, J., Willerman, L., & Horn, J. (1988). Human behavior genetics. *Annual Review of Psychology, 39*, 101–133.

Loehlin, J., Lindzey, G., & Spuhler, J. (1975). *Race Differences in Intelligence.* San Francisco: : Freeman.

Loftus, E. (1994). The repressed memory controversy. *The American Psychologist, 49,* 443–445.

Loftus, E., & Burns, T. (1982). Mental shock can produce retrograde amnesia. *Memory and Cognition, 10,* 318–323.

Loftus, E., & Loftus, G. (1980). On the permanence of stored information in the human brain. *American Psychologist, 35,* 409–420.

Loftus, E., Miller, D., & Burns, H. (1978). Semantic integration of verbal information into a visual memory. *Journal of Experimental Psychology, 4,* 19–31.

Loftus, E. (1975). Leading questions and the eyewitness report. *Cognitive Psychology, 7,* 560–572.

Loftus, E., & Palmer, J. (1974). Reconstruction of automobile destruction: An example of interaction between language and memory. *Journal of Verbal Learning and Verbal Behavior, 13,* 585–589.

Loftus, E. F. (1997). Creating childhood memories. *Applied Cognitive Psychology, 11*(Special issue), S75–S86.

Loomis, A., Harvey, E., & Hobart, G. (1937). Cerebral status during sleep as studied by human brain potentials. *Journal of Experimental Psychology, 21,* 127–144.

Lorenz, K. (1974). *The Eight Deadly Sins of Civilized Man.* New York: Harcourt Brace Jovanovich.

Lorenz, K. (1937). The companion in the bird's world. *Auk, 54,* 245–273.

Lourea, D., Rila, M., & Taylor, C. (1986). *Sex in the age of AIDS. Paper presented at the Western Region Annual Conference of the Society for the Scientific Study of Sex,* . Scottsdale, Arizona, January.

Lovass, O. (1987). Behavioral treatment and normal educational and intellectual functioning in young autistic children. *Journal of Consulting and Clinical Psychology, 55,* 3–9.

Lovass, O. (1973). *Behavioral Treatment of Autistic Children.* Morristown, NJ: General Learning Press.

Luborsky, L., Singer, B., & Luborsky, L. (1975). Comparative studies of psychotherapies. *Archives of General Psychiatry, 32,* 995–1008.

Luce, G. (1965). *Current Research on Sleep and Dreams.*: Health Service Publication No. 1389, U.S. Department of Health, Education and Welfare.

Luchins, A., & Luchins, E. (1959). *Rigidity of Behavior.* Eugene, OR: University of Oregon Press.

Lumsdaine, A., & Janis, I. (1953). Resistance to "counter-propaganda" produced by one-sided and two-sided "propaganda" presentations. *Public Opinion Quarterly, 17,* 311–318.

Lykken, D. (1957). A study of anxiety in the sociopathic personality. *Journal of Abnormal and Social Psychology, 57,* 6–10.

Lynch, G. (1984). A magical memory tour. *Psychology Today*, April, 70–76.

Maccoby, E., & Jacklin, C. (1987). Gender segregation in childhood. In H. Reese (Ed.), *Advances in Child Behavior and Developmen* (Vol. 20). New York: Academic Press.

Maccoby, E. (1985). Address presented at a Symposium on Issues in Contemporary Psychology, Reed College, Portland, Oregon May.

Maccoby, E. (1980). *Social Development: Psychological Growth and the Parent-Child Relationship.* New York: Harcourt Brace Jovanovic.

Maccoby, E., & Jacklin, C. (1974). *The Psychology of Sex Differences.* Stanford, CA: Stanford University Press.

Macdonell A. A. (1971). *A History of Sanskrit Literature.* 2nd ed. Delhi, India: Motilal Banarasidass Publisher.

MacDonald, R., Weddle, M., & Gross, R. (1986). Benzodiazapine, b-carboline, and barbiturate actions on GABA responses. *Advances in Biochemical Psychopharmacology, 41,* 67–78.

MacPhillamy, D., & Lewinsohn, P. (1974). Depression as a function of levels of desired and obtained pleasure. Journal of Abnormal Psychology, 83, 651–657. (1974). Depression as a function of levels of desired and obtained pleasure. *Journal of Abnormal Psychology, 83,* 651–657.

MacPhillamy, D., & Lewinsohn, P. (1974). Depression as a function of levels of desired and obtained pleasure. *Journal of Abnormal Psychology, 83,* 651–657.

Maddison, S. (1977). Intraperitoneal and intracranial cholecystokinin depresses operant responding for food. *Physiology and Behavior, 19,* 819–824.

Madhavananda Swami (1975): *Brhadaranyka Upanishad;* Calcutta, India: Advaita Ashrama, pp 449.

Magnusson, A., & Boivin, D. (2003). Seasonal affective disorder: an overview. *Chronobiology International, Mar; 20*(2), 189–207.

Mahone, C. (1960). Fear of failure and unrealistic vocational aspiration. *Journal of Abnormal and Social Psychology, 60,* 253–261.

Mahowald, M., & Schenck, M. (1989). REM sleep behavior disorders. In M. Kryger, T. Ruth & W. Dement (Eds.), *Principles and Practice of Sleep Medicine.* Philadelphia: Saunders.

Malberg, J. E., & Duman, R. S. (2003). Cell proliferation in adult hippocampus is decreased by inescapable stress: reversal by fluoxetine treatment. *Neuropsychopharmacology, Sep; 28*(9), 1562–1571.

Malmstrom, P., & Silva, M. (1986). Twin talk: Manifestations of twin status in the speech of toddlers. *Journal of Child Language, 13,* 293–304.

Mancini, F., Gragnani, A., Orazi, F., & Peitrangeli, M. G. (1999). Obsessions and compulsions: normative data on the Padua Inventory from an Italian non-clinical adolescent sample. *Behavior Research and Therapy, Oct; 37*(10), 919–925.

Manning, C. G., & Loftus, E. F. (1996). Eyewitness testimony and memory distortion. *Japanese Psychological Research, 38*(1), 5–13.

Mannion, K. (1981). Psychology and the lesbian: A critical view of the research. In S. Cox (Ed.), *Female Psychology: The Emerging Self* (2nd ed.). New York: St. Martin's Press.

Manson, J., Stampfer, M., Hennekens, C., & Willett, W. (1987). Body weight and longevity. *Journal of the American Medical Association, 257,* 353–358.

Manuck, S., Craft, S., & Gold, K. (1978). Coronary-prone behavior patterns and cardiovascular response. *Psychophysiology, 15,* 403–411.

Markman, E. (1987). How children constrain the possible meanings of words. In U. Neisse (Ed.), *Concepts and Conceptual Development: Ecological and Intellectual Factors in Categorization.* New York: Cambridge University Press.

Marler, P. (1967). Animal communication signals. *Science, 157,* 769–774.

Marmor, J., & (ed.). (1980). *Homosexual Behavior.* New York: New York: Basic Books.

Marshall, D. (1971). Sexual behavior on Mangaia. In D. Marshall & R. Suggs (Eds.), *Human Sexual Behavior: Variations in the Ethnographic Spectrum.* Englewood Cliffs, NJ: Prentice-Hall.

Marshall, G., & Zimbardo, P. (1979). Affective consequences of inadequately explained physiological arousal. *Journal of Personality and Social Psychology, 37,* 970–988.

Martin, D., & Lyon, P. (1972). *Lesbian Women.* New York: Bantam.

Maslow, A. (1971). *The Farther Reaches of Human Nature.* New York: Viking.

Maslow, A. (1970). *Motivation and Personality* (2nd ed.). New York: Harper & Row.

Maslow, A. (1968). *Toward a Psychology of Being* (2nd ed.). Princeton, NJ: Van Nostrand Reinhold.

Maslow, A. (1965). A philosophy of psychology: The need for a mature science of human behavior. In E. Severin (Ed.), *Humanistic Viewpoints in Psychology.* New York: McGraw-Hill.

Masters, W., & Johnson, V. (1966). *Human Sexual Response.* Boston: Little, Brown.

Matas, L., Arend, R., & Sroufe, L. (1978). Continuity of adaptation in the second year: The relationship between quality of attachment and later competence. *Child Development, 49,* 547–556.

Matlin, M. (1989). *Cognition* (2nd ed.). Fort Worth, TX: Holt, Rinehart and Winston.

Max, L. (1937). An experimental study of the motor theory of consciousness: IV. Action-curved responses in the deaf during awakening, kinaesthetic imagery and abstract thinking. *Journal of Comparative Psychology, 24,* 301–344.

Mayer, J. (1955). Regulation of energy intake and body weight. The glucostatic and the lipostatic hypothesis. *Annals of the New York Academy of Sciences, 63,* 15–43.

Mayer, R. (1982). Different problem-solving strategies for algebra word and equation problems. *Journal of Experimental Psychology: Learning, Memory, and Cognition, 8,* 448–462.

Mayer-Gross, w., Slater, E., & Roth, M. (1969). *Clinical Psychiatry* (3rd ed.). Baltimore: Williams & Wilkins.

Mayleas, D. (1980). The impact of tiny feet on love. *Self,* August, 105–110.

Mazzoni, G., & Memon, A. (2003). Imagination can create false autobiographical memories. *Psychological Science, Mar; 14*(2), 186–188.

McCall, G., & Shields, N. (1986). Social and structural factors in family violence. In M. Lystad (Ed.), *Violence in the Home: Interdisciplinary Perspectives.* New York: Brunneri Mazel.

McCarley, R. W., and Hobson J. A. (1977). The neurobiological origins of psychoanalytic dream theory. *Am J Psychiatry* 1977; 134: 1211–1221

McClelland, D. C. (1987): *Human Motivation* (Foreword, pg vi). Cambridge University Press, New York.

McClelland, D. (1985). *Human Motivation.* Glenview, IL: Scott.

McClelland, D., & Pilon, D. (1983). Sources of adult motives in patterns of parent behavior in early childhood. *Journal of Personality and Social Psychology, 44,* 564–574.

McClelland, D., Atkinson, J., Clark, R., & Lowell, E. (1976). *The Achievement Motive* (2nd ed.). New York: Irvington.

McClelland, D. (1961). *The Achieving Society.* Princeton, NJ: Van Nostrand.

McClelland, D. (1953). *The Achievement Motive.* New York: Appleton, Century, Crofts.

McClintock, M. K. (1998). On the nature of mammalian and human pheromones. *Annals of the New York Academy of Sciences, Nov 30; 855,* 390–392.

McCloskey, M., & Zaragoza, M. (1985b). Postevent information and memory: Reply to Loftus, Schooler, and Wagenaar. *Journal of Experimental Psychology: General, 114,* 381–387.

McCloskey, M., & Zaragoza, M. (1985a). Misleading postevent information and memory for events: Arguments and evidence against memory impairment hypothesis. *Journal of Experimental Psycholog: General, 114*(3–18).

McConnell, J. (1983). *Understanding Human Behavior.* New York: Holt, Rinehart and Winston.

McConnell, J. (1962). Memory transfer through cannibalism in planarians. *Journal of Neuropsychiatry, 3,* 542–548.

McCourt, K., Bouchard, T. J., Jr, Lykken, D. T., Tellegen, A., & Keyes, M. (1999). Authoritarianism revisited: Genetic and environmental influences examined in twins reared apart and together. *Personality and Individual Differences, Nov; 27*(5), 985–1014.

McCrae, R. (1984). Situational determinants of coping responses: Loss, threat, and challenge. *Journal of Personality and Social Psychology, 46,* 919–928.

McDonald, C., & Murphy, K. C. (2003). The new genetics of schizophrenia. *The Psychiatric Clinics of North America, Mar; 26*(1), 41–63.

McDonough, R., Madden, J., Falek, A., Shafer, D., Pline, M., Gordon, D., Bokos, P., Kuehnle, J., & Mendelson, J. ((1980). Alteration of T and null lymphocyte frequencies in the peripheral blood of human opiate addicts: In vivo evidence for opiate receptor sites on T lymphocytes. *Journal of Immunology, 125,* 2539–2543.

McGaugh, J.L. (2003). *Memory and Emotion: The Making Of Lasting Memories.* New York: Columbia University Press: 2003.

McGillivary, B., Bassett, A., Langlois, S., Pantzar, T., & Wood, S. (1990). Familial 5q 11.2®q13.3 segmental duplication cosegregating with multiple anomalies, including schizophrenia. American Journal of Medical Genetics, 35, 10–13. (1990). Familial 5q 11.2®q13.3 segmental duplication cosegregating with multiple anomalies, including schizophrenia. *American Journal of Medical Genetics, 35,* 10–13.

McGinty, D. (1969). Effects of prolonged isolation and subsequent enrichment on sleep patterns in kittens. *Electroencephalography and Clinical Neurophysiology, 26,* 335.

McGrath, M., & Cohen, D. (1978). REM sleep facilitation of adaptive waking behavior: A review of the literat. *Psychological Bulletin, 85,* 24–57.

McGraw, M. (1940). Neural maturation as exemplified in achievement of bladder control. *Journal of Pediatrics, 16,* 580–589.

McGue, M., Bouchard, T. J., Jr, Iacono, W. G., & Lykken, D. T. (1993). Behavioral genetics of cognitive ability: a life-span perspective. In R. Plomin & G. E. McClearn (Eds.), *Nature, Nuture & Psychology* (pp. 59–76).

McGuffin, P., Katz, R., Watkins, S., & Rutherford, J. (1996). A hospital-based twin register of the heritability of DSM-IV unipolar depression. *Archives of General Psychiatry, Feb; 53*(2), 129–136.

McGuffin, P., Rijsdijk, F., Andrew, M., Sham, P., Katz, R., & Cardno, A. (2003). The heritability of bipolar affective disorder and the genetic relationship to unipolar depression. *Archives of General Psychiatry, May; 60*(5), 497–502.

McGuffin, P., Rijsdijk, F., Andrew, M., Sham, P., Katz, R., & Cardno, A. (2003). The heritability of bipolar affective disorder and the genetic relationship to unipolar depression. *Archives of General Psychiatry, May; 60*(5), 497–502.

McGuffin, P., Tandon, K., & Corsico, A. (2003). Linkage and association studies of schizophrenia. *Current Psychiatry Reports, Jun; 5*(2), 121–127.

McGuire, W. (1969). The nature of attitudes and attitude change. In G. Lindzey & E. Aronson (Eds.), *Handbook of Social Psychology* (2nd ed.). Reading, MA: Addison-Wesley.

McGuire, W. (1968b). Personality and susceptibility to social influence. In E. Borgotta & W. Lambert (Eds.), *Handbook of Personality Theory and Research.* Chicago: Rand McNally.

McGuire, W. (1968a). Theory of the structure of human thought. In R. Abelson, E. Monson, W. McGuire, T Newcomb, M. Rosenberg & P. Tannenbaum (Eds.), *Theories of Cognitive Consistency: A Sourcebook.* Chicago: Rand McNally.

McHugh, M., Koeske, R., & Frieze, I. (1986). Issues to consider in conducting nonsexist psychological research. *American Psychologist, 41,* 879–890.

McIntosh, T., Vink, R., Yamakami, I., & Fadon, A. (1989). Magnesium protects against neurological deficit after brain injury. *Brain Research, 482,* 252–260.

McKim, W. A. (1991) *Drugs and Behavior An Introduction To Behavioral Pharmacology.* Second Edition. New Jersey: Prentice Hall Publishers, ISBN 0-13-221532-2

McKoon, G., Ratchff, R., & Dell, G. (1986). A critical evaluation of the semantic-episodic distinction. *Journal of Experimental Psychology: Learning, Memory, and Cognition, 12,* 295–306.

McLeod, P., & Brown, R. (1988). The effects of prenatal stress and post-wearnng housing conditions on parental and sexual behavior of male Long-Evans rats. *Psychobiology, 16,* 372–380.

Mead, M. (1963). *Sex and Temperament in Three Primitive Societies.* New York: Morrow.

Meade, M. L., & Roediger, H. L. (2002). Explorations in the social contagion of memory. *Memory and Cognition, Oct; 3 0*(7), 995–1009.

Meador, B., & Rogers, C. (1984). Person-centered therapy. In R. Corsini (Ed.), *Current Psychotherapies.* Itasca, IL: Peacock.

Meaney, M. (1990). Interview in Program 4, *Discovering Psychology*, a 26-part telecourse from the Annenberg/CPB Project.

Meaney, M., Aitken, D., VanBerkel, C., Bhatnagar, S. (1988). Effect of neonatal handling on age-related impairments associated with the hippocampus. *Science, 239*, 766–768.

Mednick, S., Gabrielli, W., & Hutchings, B. (1984). Genetic influences in criminal convictions: Evidence from adoption cohort. *Science, 224,* 891–894.

Mednick, S., Pollock, V., Volavka, J., & Gabrielli, W. (1982). Biology and violence. In M. Wolfgang & N. Weiner (Eds.), *Criminal Violence.* Beverly Hills, CA: Sage.

Mednick, S., Volavka, J., Gabrielli, W., & Itil, T. (1981). EEG as a predictor of antisocial behavior. *Criminology, 19*, 219–231.

Mednick, S. (1958). A learning theory approach to schizophrenia. *Psychological Bulletin, 55*, 316–327.

Mefford, I., Baker, T., Boehme, R., Foutz, A., Ciaranello, R., Barchas, J., & Dement, W. (1983). Narcolepsy: Biogenic amine deficits in an animal model. *Science, 220*, 629–632.

Megargee, E. (1972). *The California Psychological Inventory Handbook.* San Francisco: JosseyBass.

Meichenbaum, D. (1977). *Cognitive-Behavioral Modification: An Integrative Approach.* New York: Plenum.

Meichenbaum, D., & Fitzpatrick, D. (1993). A constructive narrative perspective on stress and coping: Stress inoculation applications. In L. Goldberger & S. Breznitz (Eds.), *Handbook of stress: Theoretical and clinical aspects* (2nd ed., pp. 706–723).

Meilman, P., Leibrock, L., & Leong, E. (1989). Outcome of implanted spinal cord stimulation in the treatment of chronic pain: Arachnoiditis versus single nerve root injury and mononeuropathy. *The Clinical Journal of Pain, 5*, 189–193.

Mellor, C. (1970). First rank symptoms of schizophrenia. *British Journal of Psychiatry, 117*, 15–23.

Melman, S. A. (1995). Use of Prozac in Animals for Selected Dermatological and Behavioral Condition.s *Veterinary Forum,* August 1995.

Meltzoff, A., & Moore, M. (1983). Newborn infants imitate adult facial gestures. *Child Development, 54*, 702–709.

Melville, J. (1977). *Phobias and Obsessions.* New York: Coward, McCann & Geoghegan.

Melzack R. (1992). *The Gate Control Theory of Pain.* Canadian Health Research: A Salute to Excellence: web:

Menec, V. H. (2003). The relation between everyday activities and successful *aging*: a 6-year longitudinal study. *Journals of Gerontology: Series B: Psychological Sciences & Social Sciences, Mar; 58B*(2), S74–S82.

Merckelbach, H., Devilly, G.J., Rassin, E. (2002): Alters in dissociative identity disorder: Metaphors or genuine entities? *Clinical Psychology Review* Volume 22, Issue 4, May 2002, Pages 481–497

Messenger, J. (1971). Sex and repression in an Irish folk community. In D. Marshall & R. Suggs (Eds.), *Human Sexual Behavior: Variations in the Ethnographic Spectrum.* Englewood Cliffs, NJ: Prentice-Hall.

Meyer-Bahlburg, H. (1977). Sex hormones and male homosexuality in comparative perspective. *Archives of Sexual Behavior, 6*, 297–325.

Michel, K. (1987). Suicide risk factors: A comparison of suicide attempters with suicide completers. *British Journal of Psychiatry, 150*, 78–82.

Milavsky, J., Kessler, R., Stipp, H., & Rubens, W. (1982). Television and aggression: Results of a panel study. In D. Pearl, L. Bouthilet & J. Lazer (Eds.), *Television and Behavior: Ten Years of Scientific Progress and Implications for the Eighties* (Vol. II Techncal Reviews). Rockville, MD: National Institute of Mental Health.

Miles, C. (1977). Conditions predisposing to suicide. *Journal of Nervous and Mental Disease, 164*, 231–246.

Miles, D., & Carey, G. (1997). Genetic and environmental architecture of human aggression. *Journal of Personality and Social Psychology, 72*, 207–217.

Milgram, S. (1964). Issues in the study of obedience: A reply to Baumrind. *American Psychologist, 19*, 848–852.

Milgram, S. (196). Behavioral study of obedience. *Journal of Abnormal and Social Psychology, 67*, 371–378.

Miller, G., Galanter, E., & Pribram, K. (1960). *Plans and the Structure of Behavior.* New York: Holt, Rinehart and Winston.

Miller, M., & Bowers, K. (1993). Hypnotic analgesia: Dissociated experiences or dissociated control? *Journal of Abnormal Psychology, 102*, 29–38.

Miller, N., & Bugelski, R. (1948). Minor studies of aggression, II: The influence of frustration imposed by the in-group on attitudes expressed toward out-groups. *Journal of Psychology, 25*, 437–452.

Miller, N. (1941). The frustration-aggression hypothesis. *Psychological Review, 48*, 337–342.

Miller, S. (1986). The treatment of sleep apnea. *Journal of the American medical Association, 256*, 348.

Mills, J., & Aronson, E. (1965). Opinion change as a function of communicator's attractiveness and desire to influence. *ournal of Personality and Social Psychology, 1*, 173–177.

Milner (1985). Memory and the human brain. In: *How We Know* (Shafto,.ed.), Harper & Row, San Francisco, , pp.: 31–59.

Milner, P. (1989). A cell assembly theory of hippocampal amnesia. *Neuropsychologia, 27*, 23–30.

Milnwe, V. (1966). Amnesia following operation on the temporal lobes. In C. Whitty & O. Zangwill (Eds.), *Amnesia.* London: Butterworth.

Mirsky, A., & Duncan, C. (1986). Etiology and expression of schizophrenia: Neurological and psychosocial factors. *Annual Review of Psychology, 37*, 291–319.

Mirsky, A., & Orzacki, M. (1980). Two retrospective studies of psychosurgery. In E. Valenstein (Ed.), *The Psychosurgery Debate.* San Francisco: Freeman.

Mischel, W., Shoda, Y., & Rodriquez, M. (1989). Delay of gratification in children. *Science, 44*, 933–938.

Mischel, W., Shoda, Y., & Rodriquez, M. (1989). Delay of gratification in children. *Science, 44*, 933–938.

Mischel, W. (1986). *Introduction to Personality* (4th ed.). New York: Holt, Rinehart and Winston.

Mischel, W. (1984). Convergences and challenges in the search for consistency. *American Psychologist, 39*, 351–364.

Mischel, W. (1979). On the interface of cognition and personality. *American Psychologist, 34*, 740–754.

Mischel, W. (1968). *Personality Assessment.* New York: Wiley.

Mischel, W., Shoda, Y., & Mendoza-Denton, R. (2002). Situation-behavior profiles as a locus of consistency in personality. *Current Directions in Psychological Science, Apr; 11*(2), 50–54.

Mita, T., Dermer, M., & Knight, J. (1977). Reversed facial images and the mere-exposure hypothesis. *Journal of Personality and Social Psychology, 35*, 597–601.

Moffett, M. (1990). Dance of the electronic bee. *National Geographic, 177*, 134–140.

Mohs, M. (1982). I.Q. *Discover, September*, 18–24.

Mohsenin, N., Mostofi, M. T., & Mohsenin, V. (2003). The role of oral appliances in treating obstructive sleep apnea. *The Journal of the American Dental Association, Apr; 134*(4), 442–449.

Moller, S. (1991). Carbohydrates, serotonin, and atypical depression. *Nordisk Psykiatrisk Tidsskrif, 45*, 363–366.

Money, J. (1988). *Gay, Straight, and In-Between.* New York: Oxford University Press.

Money, J. (1975). Ablatio penis: Normal male infant sex-reassigned as a girl. *Archives of Sexual Behavior, 4*, 65–72.

Money, J., & Ehrhardt, A. (1972). *Man and Woman, Boy and Girl.* Baltimore: Johns Hopkins University Press.

Money, J., Ehrhardt, A., & Masica, D. (1968). Fetal feminization by androgen insensitivity in the testicular feminizing syndrome: Effect on marriage and maternalism. *Johns Hopkins Medical Journal, 123*, 105–114.

Money, J. (1968). *Sex Errors of the Body: Dilemmas, Education, Counseling.* Baltimore: Johns Hopkins Press.

Money, J. (1965). Psychosexual differentiation. In J. Money (Ed.), *Sex Research: New Developments.* New York: Holt, Rinehart and Winston.

Money, J., Hampson, J., & Hampson, J. (1955). An examination of some basic sexual concepts: The evidence of human hermaphrodism. *Bulletin of Johns Hopkins Hospital, 97*, 301–319.

Moore, C., Williams, J., & Gorczynska, A. (1987). View specificity, array specificity, and egocentrism in young children's drawings. *Canadian Journal of Psychology, 41*, 74–79.

Monk, T., & Folkard, S. (1983). *Circadian Rhythms and Shiftwork, Stress and Fatigue in Human Performance.* Ed. Robert Hockey. N.Y: John Wiley and Sons, ISBN 0-471-10265-2

Mora, F., & Ferrer, J. (1986). Neurotransmitters, pathways and circuits as the neural substrates of self-stimulation of the prefrontal cortex: Facts and speculations. *Behavioural Brain Research, 22*, 127–140.

Morden, B., Mitchell, G., and Dement, W. (1967). Selective REM sleep deprivation and compensation phenomena in the rat. *Brain Research, 5*, 339–349.

Moreland, J., & Gebhart, G. (1980). Effect of selective destruction of serotoninergic neurons in nucleus raphe magnus on morphine-induced antinociception. *Life Sciences, 27*, 2627–2632.

Moreland, R., & Zajonc, R. (1982). Exposure effects in person perception: Familiarity, similarity, and attraction. *Journal of Experimental Social Psychology, 18*, 395–415.

Morgan, C., & Morgan, J. (1940). Studies in hunger: The relation of gastric denervation and dietary sugar to the effect of insulin upon food intake in the rat. *Journal of Genetic Psychology, 57*, 153–163.

Morris, J. (1969). Propensity for risk taking as a determinant of vocational choice: An extension of the theory of achievement motivation. *Journal of Personality and Social Psychology, 3*, 328–335.

Morris, N., Khan-Dawood, E, & Dawood, M. (1987). Marital sex frequency and midcycle female testosterone. *Archives of Sexual Behavior, 7*, 157–173.

Morrison, A. (1983). A window on the sleeping brain. *Scientific American, 248*, 94–102.

Moses, N., Bavilivy, M., & Lifshitz, E. (1989). Fear of obesity among adolescent girls. *Pediatrics, 83*, 393–398.

Mott, E., & Haurin, R. (1988)). Linkages between sexual activity and alcohol and drug use among American adolescents. *Family Planning Perspectives, 20*, 128–137.

Moyer, K. (1983). The physiology of motivation: Aggression as a model. In C. Scheier & A. Rogers (Eds.), *G. Stanley Hall Lecture Series* (Vol. 3). Washington, DC: American Psychological Association.

Moynihan, J. (2003). Mechanisms of stress-induced modulation of immunity. *Brain, Behavior, and Immunity*, Feb 17, Supl 11 S11–16.

Moynihan, J. A. (2003). Mechanisms of stress-induced modulation of immunity. *Brain, Behavior, and Immunity, Feb; 17*(Suppl 1), S11–16.

Muehlenhard, C., & Hollabaugh, L. (1988). Do women sometimes say no when they mean yes? The prevalence and correlates of women's token resistance to sex. *Journal of Personality and Social Psychology, 54*, 872–879.

Muehlenhard, C. (1988). Misinterpreting dating behaviors and the risk of date rape. *Journal of Social and Clinical Psychology, 6*, 20–37.

Muehlenhard, C., & Linton, M. ((1987). Date rape and sexual aggression in dating situations: Incidence and risk factors. *Journal of Consulting Psychology, 34*(.), 186–196.

Muehlenhard, C., Felts, A., & Andrews, S. (1985). Men's attitudes toward the justifiability of date rape: Intervening variables and possible solutions. Paper presented at the Midcontinent Meeting of the Society for the Scientific Study of Sex, Dallas, June.

Muehlenhard, C., & Andrews, S. (1985). Open communication about sex: Will it reduce risk factors related to rape? Paper presented at the Annual Meeting of the Association for Advancement of Behavior Therapy, Houston.

Mullen, B. (1983). Operationalizing the effect of the group on the individual: A self-attentive perspective. *Journal of Experimental Social Psychology, 19*, 295–322.

Murakami, S., & Johnson, T. E. (1998). Life extension and stress resistance in Caenorhabditis elegans modulated by the tkr-1 gene. *Current Biology: CB, Sep 24; 8*(19), 1091–1094.

Murdock, B. (1974). *Human Memory: Theory and Data.* New York: Wiley.

Murray, G., Allen, N. B., & Trinder, J. (2003). Seasonality and circadian phase delay: prospective evidence that winter lowering of mood is associated with a shift towards Eveningness. *Journal of Affective Disorders, Sep: 76*(1–3), 15–22.

Murray, H. (1938). *Exploration in Personality.* New York: Oxford University Press.

Murray, J. (1990). New applications of lithium therap. *The Journal of Psychology, 124*, 55–73.

Mussen, P., & Jones, M. (1957). Self-conceptions, motivation, and interpersonal attitudes of late- and early-maturing boys. *Child Development, 28*, 243–256.

Mutlu-Turkoglu, U., Ilhan, E., Oztezcan, S., Kuru, A., Aykac-Toker, G., & Uysal, M. (2003). Age-related increases in plasma malondialdehyde and protein carbonyl levels and lymphocyte DNA damage in elderly subjects. *Clinical Biochemistry, Jul; 36*(5), 397–400.

Muuss, R. (1985). Adolescent eating disorder: Anorexia nervosa. *Adolescence, 79*, 525–536.

Muzur, A., Fabbro, F., Clarici, A., Braun, S., & Bava, A. (1998). Encoding and recall of parsed stories in hypnosis. *Perceptual and Motor Skills, Dec; 87*(3 Pt 1), 963–971.

Mwamwenda, T., & Mwamwenda, B. (1989). Formal operational thought among African and Canadian college students. *Psychological Reports, 64*, 43–46.

Mwamwenda, T. S. (1999). Undergraduate and graduate students' combinatorial reasoning and formal operations. *Journal of Genetic Psychology, Dec; 160*(4), 503–506.

Mwamwenda, T. S. (1993). Formal operations and academic achievement. *Journal of Psychology, Jan; 127*(1), 99–103.

Myers, B. (1984). Mother-infant bonding: The status of the critical period hypothesis. *Developmental Review., 4*, 240–274.

Naeser, M., Helm-Estabrooks, N., Haas, G., Auerbach, S., & Srinivasan, M. (1987). Relationship between lesion extent in "Wernicke's area" on computed tomographic scan and predicting recovery of comprehension in Wernicke's aphasia. *Archives of Neurology, 44*, 73–82.

Narrow, W. E., Rae, D. S., Robins, L. N., & Regier, D. A. (2002). Revised prevalence based estimates of mental disorders in the United States: using a clinical significance criterion to reconcile 2 surveys' estimates. *Archives of General Psychiatry, Feb; 59*(2), 115–123.

Nathan, M., & Guttman, R. (1984). Similarities in test scores and profiles of kibbutz twins and singletons. *Acta Geneticae Medicae et Gemellologiae, 33*, 213–218.

Nathan, P. J., Burrows, G. D., & Norman, T. R. (1999). Melatonin sensitivity to dim white light in affective disorders. *Neuropsychopharmacology, Sep; 21*(3), 408–413.

National, Institute, of, Mental, & Health. (1982). *Television and Behavior: Ten Years of Scientific Progress and Implication for the Eighties* (Vol. U.S. Government Printing office). Washington, DC: U.S. Government Printing office.

Neely, J., & Durgunoglu, A. (1985). Dissociative episodic and semantic priming effects in episodic recognition and lexical decision tasks. *Journal of Memory and Language, 24*, 466–489.

Neisser, U. (1982). Memory: What are the important questions? In U. Neisser (Ed.), *Memory Observed.* San Francisco: Freeman.

Neisser, U. (1967). *Cognitive Psychology.* New York: Appleton, Century, Crofts.

Nemiah, J. (1981). A psychoanalytic view of phobias. *American Journal of Psychoanalysis, 41,* 115–120.

Neugarten, B., & Hagestad, G. (1976). Age and the life course. In H. Binstock & E. Shanas (Eds.), *Handbook of Aging and the Social Sciences.* New York: Van Nostrand Reinhold.

Neugarten, B. (1972). Personality and the aging process. *The Gerontologist, 12,* 9–15.

Neugarten, B., Havighurst, R., & Tobin, S. (1965). Personality and patterns of aging. In B. Neugarten (Ed.), *Middle Age and Aging.* Chicago: University of Chicago Press.

Newell, A. (1992). Precis of unified theories of cognition. *Behavioral and Brain Sciences, 15,* 425–492.

Newell, A., & Simon, H. (1972). *Human Problem Solving.* Englewood Cliffs, NJ: Prentice-Hall.

Nicassio, P., Mendlowitz, D., Fussel, J., & Petras, L. (1985). The phenomenology of the pre-sleep state: The development of the pre-sleep arousal scale. *Behavior Research and Therapy, 23,* 263–271.

Nichols, C. D., Garcia, E. E., & Sanders-Bush, E. (2003). Dynamic changes in prefrontal cortex gene expression following lysergic acid diethylamide adminstration. *Brain Research. Molecular Brain Research, Mar 17; 111*(1–2), 182–188.

Niedermeyer, E. (2003). Electrophysiology of the frontal lobe. *Clinical Electroencephalography, Jan; 34*(1), 5–12.

Nield, T. (1987). Lest you forget. *New Scientist*(May 7), 63.

Niemcryk, S., Jenkins, D., Rose, R., & Hurst, M. (1987). The prospective impact of psychosocial variables on rates of illness and injury in professional employees. *Journal of Occupational Medicine, 29,* 119–125.

Nisbet, J. (1957). Intelligence and age: Retesting with twenty-four years interval. *British Journal of Educational Psychology, 27,* 190–198.

Nisbett, R., & Wilson, I. (1977). The halo effect: Evidence for unconscious alteration of judgments. *Journal of Personality and Social Psychology, 35,* 250–256.

Nisbett, R., Caputo, C., Legant, P., & Maracek, J. (1973). Behavior as seen by the actor and as seen by the observer. *Journal of Personality and Social Psychology, 27,* 154–164.

Nolen-Hoeksema, A. (1987). Sex differences in unipolar depression: Evidence and theory. *Psychological Bulletin, 101,* 259–282.

Norcross, J., Strausser, D., & Faltus, E. (1988). The therapists' therapist. *American Journal of Psychotherapy, 42,* 53–66.

Norman, R., Penman, I., Kolb, H., Jones, J., & Daley, S. (1984). Direct excitatory interactions between cones of different spectral types in the turtle retina. *Science, 224,* 625–627.

North C. S., Ryall, J.M., Ricci, D. A., Wetzel, R. D. (1993): *Multiple Personalities, Multiple Disorders Psychiatric Classification and Media Influence,* Oxford University Press, New York, Oxford. ISBN 0-19-508095-5

North, M. M., North, S.M., & Coble, J.R. (1997). Virtual reality therapy: an effective treatment for psychological disorders. *Studies in Health Technology and Informatics, 44,* 59–70.

Norton, G., Dorward, J., & Cox, B. (1986). Factors associated with panic attack in non-clinical subjects. *Behavior Therapy, 17,* 239–252.

Norton, G., Harrison, B., Hauch, J., & Rhodes, L. (1985). Characteristics of people with infrequent panic attacks. *Journal of Abnormal Psychology, 94,* 216–221.

Novak, M., & Harlow, H. (1975). Social recovery of monkeys isolated for the first year of life: I. Rehabibtation and therapy. *Developmental Psychology, 11,* 453–465.

Novin, D. (1976). Viceral mechanisms in the control of food intake. In D. Novin, W. Wyrwicka & G. Bray (Eds.), *Hunger: Basic Mechanisms and Clinical Implications.* New York: Raven.

Nutt, D. J. (2002). The neuropharmacology of serotonin and noradrenaline in depression. *International Clinical Psychopharmacology, Jun: 17*(Suppl 1), S1–12.

Nuttin, J. (1987). Affective consequences of mere ownership: The name letter effect in twelve European languages. *European Journal of Social Pychology, 17,* 381–402.

Offer, D., & Offer, J. (1975). *From Teenage to Young Manhood.* New York: Basic Books.

Ohman, A. (1979). Fear relevance, autonomic conditioning, and phobias: A laboratory model. In P. Sjoden, S. Bates & W. Dockens (Eds.), *Trends in Behavior Therapy.* New York: Academic Press.

Oishi, K., Nishio, N., Konishi, K., Shimokawa, M., Okuda, T., Kuriyama, T., et al. (2003). Differential effects of physical and psychological stressors on immune functions of rats. *Stress, Feb; 6 1*(33–40).

Ojemann, G. A. (2003). The neurobiology of language and verbal memory: observations from awake neurosurgery. *International Journal of Psychophysiology, May; 48*(2), 141–146.

Oldbridge, N. (1982). Compliance and exercise in primary and secondary prevention of coronary heart disease: A review. *Preventive Medicine, 11,* 56–70.

Olds, J. (1973). Commentary on positive reinforcement produced by electrical stimulation of septal areas and other regions of rat brain. In E. Valenstein (Ed.), *Brain Stimulation and Motivation: Research and Commentary.* Glenview, IL: Scott, Foresman.

Olds, J. (1956). Pleasure centers in the brain. *Scientific American, 193,* 105–116.

Olds, M., & Forbes, J. (1981). The central basis of motivation: Intracranial self-stimulation studies. *Annual Review of Psychology, 32,* 523–574.

O'Leary, A. (1990). Stress, emotion, and human immune function. *Psychological Bulletin, 108,* 363–382.

O'Neal, J. (1984). First person account: Finding myself and loving it. *Schizophrenia Bulletin, 10,* 109–110.

Oomura, Y. (1976). ignificance of glucose insulin and free fatty acid on the hypothalamic feeding and satiety neurons. In D. Novin, W. Wyrwicka & G. Bray (Eds.), *Hunger: Basic Mechanisms and Clinical Implications.* New York: Raven.

Ophardt, C. E. (2003). *Prostaglandins in Virtual Chembook,* Elmhrust College, Web Tutotial, Website: http://www.elmhurst.edu/~chm /vchembook/555prostagland.html

Orlansky, H. (1949). Infant care and personality. *Psychological Bulletin, 46,* 1–48.

Orne, M., Dinges, D., & Orne, E. (1984). On the differential diagnosis of multiple personality in the forensic context. *International Journal of Clinical and Experimental Hypnosis, 32,* 118–169.

Orne, M., & Scheibe, K. (1964). The contribution of nondeprivation factors in the production of sensory deprivation effects: The psychology of the panic button. *Journal of Abnormal and Social Psychology, 68,* 3–12.

Ornstein, P., & Naus, M. (1978). Rehearsal processes in children's memory. In P. Ornstein (Ed.), *Memory Development in Children.* Hillsdale, NJ: Erlbaum.

Osaka, T., & Matsumura, H. (1994). Noradrenergic inputs to sleep-related neurons in the preoptic area from the locus coeruleus and the ventrolateral medulla in the rat. *Neuroscience Research, Feb; 19*(1), 39–50.

Osborne, R. (1960). Racial differences in mental growth and school achievement: A longitudinal study. *Psychological Reports, 7,* 233–239.

Paivio, A., & Lambert, W. (1981). Dual coding and bilingual memory. *Journal of Verbal Learning and Verbal Behavior, 20,* 532–539.

Paivio, A. (1971). *Imagery and Verbal Processes.* New York: Holt, Rinehart, and Winston.

Palca, J. (1989). Sleep researchers awake to possibilities. *Science, 245,* 351–352.

Palermo-Neto, J., de Oliveira Massoco, C., & Robespierre de Souza, W. (2003). Effects of physical and psychological stressors on behavior, macrophage activity, and Ehrlich tumor growth. *Brain, Behavior, and Immunity, Feb; 17*(1), 43–54.

Parker, G., Roy, K., & Eyers, K. (2003). Cognitive behavior therapy for depression? Choose horses for courses. *The American Journal of Psychiatry, May: 160*(5), 825–834.

Parrot, A., & Allen, S. (1984). Acquaintance rape: Seduction or crime? Paper presented at the Eastern Regional Annual Conference of the Society for the Scientific Study of Sex, Boston, April. (1984). Acquaintance rape: Seduction or crime? Paper presented at the Eastern Regional Annual Conference of the Society for the Scientific Study of Sex, Boston, April.

Patel, S. N., Clayton, N. S., & Krebs, J. R. (1997). Spatial learning induces neurogenesis in the avian brain. *Behavioral Brain Research, Dec; 89*(1–2), 115–128.

Patterson, G. (1986). Performance models for antisocial boys. *American Psychologist, 41*, 432–444.

Patterson, G., Chamberlain, P., & Reid, J. (1982). A comparative evaluation of parent training procedures. *Behavior Therapy, 13*, 638–650.

Paulsen, K., & Johnson, M. (1983). Sex-role attitudes and mathematical ability in 4th, 8th, and 11th grade students from a high socioeconomic area. *Developmental Psychology, 19*, 210–214.

Penfield, W., & Perrot, P. (1963). The brain's record of auditory and visual experience. *Brain, 86*, 595–696.

Penrod, S. (1986). *Social Psychology* (2nd ed.). Englewood Cliffs, NJ: Prentice-Hall.

Perez, V., Catafau, A. M., Corripio, I., Martin, J. C., & Alvarez, E. (2003). Preliminary evidence of striatal D2 receptor density as a possible biological marker of prognosis in naive schizophrenic patients. *Progress in Neuropsychopharmacology & Biological Psychiatry, Aug: 27*(5), 767–770.

Perley, M., & Guze, S. (1962). Hysteria—the stability and usefulness of clinical criteria. *The New England Journal of Medicine, 266*, 421–426.

Perloff, R. M., & Lamb, M. E. (1981). The development of *gender roles*: an integrative life-span perspective. *Catalog of Selected Documents in Psychology, Aug; 11*(MS 2294), 52.

Perls, E. (1948). Theory and technique of personality integration. *American Journal of Psychotherapy, 2*, 656–686.

Perls, F. (1973). *The Gestalt Approach.* Palo Alto, CA: Science and Behaviour Books.

Persky; H., L., H., Strauss, D., Miller, W., & O'Brien, C. (1978). Plasma testosterone level and sexual behavior of couples. *Archives of Sexual Behavioir, 7*, 157–173.

Peskin, H. (1973). Influence of the developmental schedule of puberty on learning and ego functioning. *Journal of Youth and Adolescence, 2*, 273–290.

Peskin, H. (1967). Pubertal onset and ego functioning. *Journal of Abnormal Psychology, 72*, 1–15.

Peterman, T., Cates, W., & Curran, J. (1988). The challenge of human immunodeficiency virus (HIV) and acquired immunodeficiency syndrome (AIDS) in women and children. *Fertility and Sterility, 49*, 571–581.

Peterson, A. (1979). Female pubertal development. In M. Sugar (Ed.), *Female Adolescent Development.* New York: Bruner/Mazel.

Peterson, C., & Seligman, M. (1984). Causal explanations as a risk factor for depression: Theory and evidence. *Psychological Review, 91*, 347–374.

Peterson, P., & Koulack, D. (1969). Attitude change as a function of latitudes of acceptance and rejection. *Journal of Personality and Social Pychology, 11*, 309–311.

Petty, R., Cacioppo, J., & Petty, R., Schumann, D. (1983). Central and peripheral routes to advertising effectiveness: The moderating role of involvement. *ournal of Consumer Research, 10*, 135–146.

Petty; R., C., J. (1986). The elaboration likelihood model of persuasion. In L. Berkowitz (Ed.), *Advances in Experimental Social Psychology* (Vol. 19). Orlando, FL: Academic Press.

Phares, E. (1988). *Clinical Psychology: Concepts, Methods, & Profession.* Chicago: Dorsey.

Piaget, J. (1977). *The Development of Thought: Equilibrium of Cognitive Structures.* New York: Viking Press.

Piaget, J. (1972). Intellectual evolution from adolescence to adulthood. *Human Development, 15*, 1–12.

Piaget, J. (1970). Piaget's theory. In P. Mussen (Ed.), *Carmichael's Manual of Child Psychology* (Vol. 1). New York: Wiley.

Piaget, J., & Inhelder, B. (1969). *The Psychology of the Child.* New York: Basic Books.

Pihl, R., & Parkes, M. (1977). Hair element content in learning disabled children. *Science, 198*, 204–206.

Pittenger, C., & Kandel, E. R. (2003). In search of general mechanisms for long-lasting plasticity: Aplysia and the hippocampus. *Philosophical Transactions of the Royal Society of London. Series B: Biological Sciences, Apr 29; 358*(1432), 757–763.

Pliner, P., Hart, H., Kohl, J., & Saari, D. (1974). Compliance without pressure: Some further data on the foot-in-the-door technique. *Journal of Experimental Social Psychology, 10*, 17–22.

Pliszka, S. R., McCracken, J. T., & Maas, J. W. (1996). Catecholamines in attention-deficit hyperactivity disorder: current perspectives. *Journal of the American Academy of Child and Adolescent Psychiatry, Mar; 35*(3), 264–272.

Plomin, R., Pederson, N., McClearn, G., & Nesselroade, J. (1988). EAS temperaments during the last half of the life span: Twins reared apart and twins reared together. *Psychology and Aging, 3*, 43–50.

Plomin, R., & Defries, J. (1980). Genetics and intelligence: Recent data. *Intelligence, 4*, 15–24.

Plomin, R., & Bergeman, C. (1991). The nature of nurture: Genetic influence on "environmental" measures. *Behavioral and Brain Sciences, 14*, 373–427.

Plutchik, R. (1980). *Emotion: A Psychoevolutionary Synthesis.* New York: Harper & Row.

Pomeroy, W. (1965). Why we tolerate lesbians. *Sexology, May*, 652–654.

Posner, M. (1973). *Cognition: An Introduction.* Glenview, IL: Scott, Foresman.

Powell, M., & Fazio, R. (1984). Attitude accessibility as a function of repeated attitudinal expression. *Personality and Social Psychology Bulletin, 10*, 139–148.

Prange, A., Wilson, I., & Lynn, C. (1974). L-tryptophan in mania: Contributions to a permissive amine hypothesis of affective disorders. *Archives of General Psychiatry, 30*, 56–62.

Premack, A. J., & Premack, D. (1991). Teaching *language* to an ape. In W. S.-Y. Wang (Ed.), *The emergence of language: Development and evolution: Readings from "Scientific American"* (pp. 16–27).

Premack, D. (1971). Language in chimpanzees. *Science, 172*, 808–822.

Prioleau, L., Murdock, M., & Brody, N. (1983). An analysis of psychotherapy versus placebo studies. *The Behavioral and Brain Sciences, 6*, 275–310.

Prochaska, J., & Norcross, J. (1983). Contemporary psychotherapies: A national survey of characteristics, practices, orientation, and attitudes. *Psychotherapy: Theory, Research and Practice, 20*, 161–173.

Putnam, F., Guroff, J., Silberman, F., Barban, L., & Post, R. (1986). The clinical phenomenology of multiple personality disorder: Review of 100 recent cases. *Journal of Clinical Psychiatry, 4*, 285–293.

Putnam, F. W. (1993). Dissociative disorders in children: behavioral profiles and problems. *Child Abuse and Neglect, Jan–Feb; 17*(1), 39–45.

Putnam, F. W. (1991). Recent research on multiple personality disorder. *The Psychiatric Clinics of North America, Sep; 14*(3), 488–502.

Pylyshyn, Z. (1984). *Computation and Cognition: Toward a foundation for cognitive science.* Cambridge, MA: MIT.

Pylyshyn, Z. (1973). What the mind's eye tells the mind's brain: A critique of mental imagery. *Psychological Bulletin, 80*, 1–24.

Pylyshyn, Z. W. (2002). Mental *imagery*: In search of a theory. *Behavioral & Brain Sciences, Apr; 25*(2), 157–238.

Rachlin, H., Logue, A., Gibbon, J., & Franlel, M. (1986). Cognition and behavior in studies of choice. *Psychological Review, 93*, 33–45.

Ragade, A. R.(1996). *Teaching about Diversity Stages of Sleep, in Instructor's Course Planner, adjunct to Psychology Contexts of Behavior,* Second Ed. Prepared by Steven A. Schneider. Pp 36–37. Chicago: Brown & Benchmark.

Rahe, R., & Arthur, R. (1978). Life changes and illness reports. In K. Gunderson & R. Rahe (Eds.), *Life Stress and Illness.* Springfield, IL: Thomas.

Ramachandran, V. S., & Hubbard, E. M. (2003). Hearing color, tasting shapes. *Scientific American, May*, 53–59.

Rapoport, J. (1991). Recent advances in obsessive-compulsive disorder. *Neuropsychopharmacology, 5*, 1–10.

Rapoport, J. (1989). The biology of obsessions and compulsions. *Scientific American*, March 83–89.

Rasmussen, P. (1996). The congenital insensitivity-to-pain syndrome (analgesia congenita): report of a case. *Int J Paediatr. Dent.* Jun;6(2):117-22.

Ratchif, R., & McKoon, G. (1986). More on the distinction between episodic and semantic memories. *Journal of Experimental Psychology: Learning, Memory, and Cognition, 12*(312–313.).

Raynor, J. (1970). Relationships between achievement-related motives, future orientation, and academic performance. *Journal of Personality and Social Psychology, 15*, 28–33.

Rechtschaffen, A., Gilliland, M., Bergmann, B., & Winter, J. (1983). Physiological correlates of prolonged sleep deprivation in rats. *Science, 221*, 182–184.

Register, P., & Kihlstrom, J. (1988). Hypnosis and interrogative suggestibility. *Personality and Individual Differences, 9*, 549–558.

Reichard, S., Livson, E, & Peterson, P. (1962). *Aging and Personality: A Study of 87 Older Men.* New York: Wiley.

Reilly, R., & Lewis, E. (1983). *Educational Psychology: Applications for Classroom Learning and Instruction.* New York: Macmillan.

Reinisch, J. (1981). Prenatal exposure to synthetic progestin increases potential for aggression in humans. *Science, 211*, 1171–1173.

Reinke, B., Holmes, D., & Harris, R. (1985). The timing of psychosocial changes in women's lives: The years 25 to 45. *Journal of Personality and Social Psychology, 48*, 456–471.

Reker, G., Peacock, E., & Wong, P. (1987). Meaning and purpose in life and well-being: A life-span perspective. *Journal of Gerontology, 42*, 44–49.

Rescorla, R. (1988b). Behavioral studies of Pavlovian conditioning. *Annual Review of Neuroscience, 11*, 329–352.

Rescorla, R. (1988a). Pavlovian conditioning: It's not what you think it is. *American Psychologist, 43*, 151–160.

Rescorla, R. (1987). A Pavlovian analysis of goal-directed behavior. *American Psychologist, 42*, 119–129.

Rescorla, R. (1968). Probability of shock in the presence and absence of CS in fear conditioning. *Journal of Comparative and Physiological Psychology, 66*, 1–5.

Rescorla, R. (1967). Pavlovian conditioning and its proper control procedures. *Psychological Review, 74*, 71–80.

Restak, R. (1988). *The Mind.* New York: Bantam.

Ribble, M. (1943). *The Rights of Infants: Early Psychological Needs and Their Satisfaction.* New York: Columbia University Press.

Richards, J., & Rader, N. (1981). Crawling-onset age predicts visual cliff avoidance in infants. *Journal of Experimental Psychology: Human Perception and Performance, 7*, 382–387.

Riche, M. (1988). Postmarital society. *American Demomaphics*, November, 60.

Rieber, R. W.; and Robinson D. K. Eds. (2001). *Wilhelm Wundt In History. The Making of Scientific Psychology.* New York: Plenum Publishers. ISBN #: 0-306-46599

Rips, L., Shoben, E., & Smith, E. (1973). Semantic distance and the verification of semantic relations. *Journal of Verbal Learning and Verbal Behavior, 12*, 1–20.

Robbin, A. (1959). The value of leucotomy in relation to diagnosis. *Journal of Neurology, Neurosurgery, and Psychiatry, 22*, 132–136.

Robbin, A. (1958). A controlled study of the effects of leucotomy. *Journal of Neurology, Neurosurgery, and Psychiatry, 21*, 262–269.

Roberts, M. (1987). No language but a cry. *Psychology Today*, June, 57–58.

Roberts, S.C. & Gosling, L.M. (2003): Genetic Similarity and quality interact in mate choice decisions by female mice. *Nature,* http://www.nature.com/naturegenetics on link: httpp://www.liv.ac.jk/www/evolpsyc/2003_nat_genetics.pdf

Robins, L. (1987). The epidemiology of antisocial personality. In J. Cavenar (Ed.), *Psychiatry.* Philadelphia: Lippincott.

Robinson, L., Berman, J., & Neimeyer, R. (1990). Psychotherapy for the treatment of depression: A comprehensive review of controlled outcome research. *Psychological Bulletin, 108*, 30–49.

Robinson, S. R., Bishop, G. M., & Munch, G. (2003). Alzheimer vaccine: amyloid-beta on trial. *Bioessays, Mar; 25*(3), 283–288.

Rocchi, A., Pellegrini, S., Siciliano, G., & Murri, L. (2003). Causative and susceptibility genes for Alzheimer's disease: a review. *Brain Research Bulletin, Jun 30; 61*(1), 1–24.

Roediger, H. L., III, Meade, M. L., & Bergman, E. T. (2001). Social contagion of memory. *Psychonomic Bulletin & Review, Jun; 8*(2), 365–371.

Rogers, C. (1987). Sex roles in education. In D. Hargraves & A. Colley (Eds.), *The Psychology of Sex Roles.* New York: Hemisphere.

Rogers, C. (1986). Client-centered therapy. In I. Kutash & A. Wolf (Eds.), *Psychotherapist's Casebook.* San Francisco: Jossey-Bass.

Rogers, C. (1980). *A Way of Being.* Boston: Houghton Mifflin.

Rogers, C. (1977). *On Personal Power: Inner Strength and Its Revolutionary Impact.* New York: Delacorte.

Rogers, C. (1961). *Becoming a Person: A Therapist's View of Psychotherapy.* Boston: Houghton Mifflin.

Roggman, L., Langlois, J., & Hubbs-Tait, L. (1987). Mothers, infants, and toys: Social play correlates of attachment. *Infant Behavior and Development, 10*, 233–237.

Rohrbaugh, J. (1979). *Women: Psychology's Puzzle.* New York: New York.

Rollins, B., & Galligan, R. (1978). The developing child and marital satisfaction of parents. In R. Levner & G. Spanier (Eds.), *Child's Influences on Marital and Family Interaction: A Lifespan Perspective.* New York: Academic Press.

Romano-Spica, V., Mettimano, M., Ianni, A., Specchia, M. L., Ricciardi, G., & Savi, L. (2003). Epidemiology of essential hypertension: the role of genetic polymorphism. *European Journal of Epidemiology, 18*(3), 211–219.

Romeo, R. D., Richardson, H. N., & Sisk, C. L. (2002). Puberty and the maturation of the male brain and sexual behavior: recasting a behavioral potential. *Neuroscience & Biobehavioral Reviews, May; 26*(3), 381–391.

Roper, W. G. (1996). The etiology of male homosexuality. *Medical hypotheses, Feb; 46*(2), 85–88.

Rosch, E. (1988). Coherences and categorization: A historical view. In F. S. Kessel (Ed.), *The Development of language and language researchers: Essays in honor of Roger Brown* (pp. 373–392).

Rosch, E. (1988). Principles of categorization. In A. M. Collins & E. E. Smith (Eds.), *Readings in Cognitive Science. A Perspective from Psychology and Artificial Intelligence* (pp. 312–322).

Rosch, E. (1978). Principles of categorization. In E. Rosch & B. Lloyd (Eds.), *Cognition and Categorization.* Hillsdale, NJ: Erlbaum.

Rosch, E., Mervis, C., Gray, W., Johnson, E., & Boyes-Braem, P. (1976). Basic objects in natural categories. *Cognitive Psychology, 8*, 382–439.

Rosch, E. (1975). Cognitive representations of semantic categories. *Journal of Experimental Psychology: General, 104*, 192–253.

Rosch, E. (1973). Natural categorie. *Cognitive Psychology, 4*, 328–350.

Rose, J., & Fantino, E. (1978). Conditioned reinforcement and discrimination in second-order schedules. *Journal of the Experimental Analysis of Behavior, 29*, 393–418.

Rose, J., Brugge, J., Anderson, D., & Hind, J. (1967). Phase-locked responses to low-frequency tones in single auditory nerve fibers of the squirrel monkey. *Journal of Neurophysiology, 30*, 769–793.

Rosenbaum, L., & Rosenbaum, W. (1975). Persuasive impact of a communicator where groups differ in apparent co-orientation. *Journal of Psychology, 89*, 189–194.

Rosenhan, D. (1973). *Moral Development*: CRM-McGraw-Hill Films.

Rosenthal, D. (1977). Searches for the mode of genetic transmission in schizophrenia: Reflections of loose ends. *Schizophrenia Bulletin, 3*, 268–276.

Rosenthal, D., Wender, P, Kety, S., Welner, J., & Schulsinger, E. (1971). The adopted away offspring of schizophrenics. *American Journal of Psychiatry, 128*, 307–311.

Rosenthal, D. (1971). *Genetics of Schizophrenia*. New York: McGraw-Hill.

Rosenthal, D. (1970). *Genetic Theory and Abnormal Behavior*. New York: McGraw-Hill.

Rosenthal, N., Sack, D., Carpenter, C., Parry, B., Mendelson, W., & Wehr, T. (1985). Antidepressant effects of light in seasonal affective disorder. *The American Journal of Psychiatry, 142*, 163–170.

Rosenzweig, M. (1966). Environmental complexity, cerebral change, and behavior. *American Psychologist, 21*, 321–332.

Rosenzweig, M. R., & Bennett, E. L. (1996). Psychobiology of plasticity: effects of training and experience on brain and behavior. *Behavioural Brain Research, Jun: 78*(1), 57–65.

Roses, A., Pericak-Vance, M., Clark, C., Gilbert, J., Yarnaoka, L., Yaynes, C., Speer, M., Gaskell, P., Hung, W., Trofatter, J., Earl, N., Lee, J., Alberts, M., Dawson, D., Bartlett, R., Siddique, T., Vance, J., Conneally, P., & Heynian, A. (1990). Linkage studies of late-onset familial Alzheimer's disease. *Advances in Neurology, 51*, 185–196.

Roses, A., Pericak-Vance, M., & Haynes, C. (1987). Linkage analysis in late onset familial Alzheimer's disease. *Cytogenetics and Cell Genetics, 46*, 684.

Ross, H., & Taylor, H. (1989). Do boys prefer daddy or his physical style of play? *Sex Roles, 20*, 23–33.

Ross, L. (1977). The intuitive psychologist and his shortcomings: Distortions in the attribution process. In L. Berkowitz (Ed.), *Advances in Experimental Social Psychology*. New York: Academic Press.

Ross, M., & Fletcher, G. (1985). Attribution and social perception. In G. Lindzey & E. Aronson (Eds.), *Handbook of Social Psychology*. New York: Random House.

Rossi, A., Stratta, P., D'Albenzio, L., Tartaro, A., Schiazza, G., di Michele, V., Bolino, E, & Casacchia, M. (1990). Reduced temporal lobe areas in schizophrenia: Preliminary evidences from a controlled multiplanar magnetic resonance imaging study. *Biological Psychiatry, 27*, 61–68.

Rossi, A., Stratta, P., Gallucci, M., Passariello, R., & Casacchia, M. (1989). Quantification of corpus callosum and ventricles in schizophrenia with nuclear magnetic resonance imaging: A pilot study. *The American Journal of Psychiatry, 146*, 99–101.

Rossi, A., Stratta, P., D'Albenzio, L., DiMichele, V., Seno, A., Giordano, L., Petruzzi, C., & Casacchia, M. (1989). Quantitative computed tomographic study in schizophrenia: Cerebral density and ventricle measures. *Psychological Medicine, 19*, 337–342.

Rothbart, M., & Park, B. (1986). On the confirmability and disconfirmability of trait concepts. *Journal of Personality and Social Psychology, 50*, 131–142.

Rothblum, E. (1988). More on reporting sex differences. *American Psychologist, 43*, 1095.

Rotter, J. (1966). Generalized expectancies for internal versus external control of reinforcement. *Psychological Monographs, 80*, No. 601.

Rotter, J. (1954). *Social Learning and Clinical Psychology*. Englewood Cliffs, NJ: Prentice-Hall.

Rouche, B. (1980). *The Medical Detectives*. New York: Truman Talley Books.

Rowley, H., Lowenstein, D., Rowbotham, M., & Simon, R. (1989). Thalamomesencephalic stroke after cocaine abuse. *Neurology, 39*, 428–430.

Rubenstein, A., Langlois, J., & Roggman, L. (2002). What makes a face attractive and why: The role of averageness in defining facial beauty. In G. Rhodes, L. Zebrokwitz & A. Leslie (Eds.), *Facial attractiveness: Evolutionary, cognitive, and social perspectives. Advances in visual cognition* (Vol. 1). Westport, CT: Ablex Publishing.

Rubin, J., Provenzano, E, & Luria, Z. (1974). The eye of the beholder: Parents views on sex of newborns. *American Journal of Orthopsychiatry, 44*, 512–519.

Rumbaugh, D. (1977). *Language Learning by Chimpanzee The Lana Project*. New York: Academic Press.

Rumbaugh, D. M., Beran, M. J., & Hillix, W. A. (2000). Cause-effect reasoning in humans and animals. In C. Heyes & L. Huber (Eds.), *The evolution of cognition. Vienna series in theoretical biology* (pp. 221–238).

Rushton, J. (1988). Altruism and aggression. *Aggressive Behavior, 14*, 35–50.

Rushton, J., Fulker, D., Neale, M., Nias, D., & Eysenck, H. (1986). Altruism and aggression: The heritability of individual differences. *Journal of Personality and Social Psychology, 50*, 1192–1198.

Rushton, J. P. (2002). New evidence on Sir Cyril Burt: his 1064 speech to the Association of Educational Psychologists. *Intelligence, 30*(6), 555–567.

Russell, D. (1984). *Sexual Exploitation: Rape, Child Sexual Abuse, and Workplace Harassment*. Beverly Hills, CA: Sage.

Rutkow I. M. (2000). Trephination How Did They Do It? *Arch. Surg.* 2000;135:1119.

Sachdev, P., Smith, J., & Matheson, J. (1990). Is psychosurgery antimanic? *Biological Psychiatry, 27*, 363–371.

Sack, R., Lewy; A., White, D., Singer, C., Fireman, M., & Vandiver, R. (1990). Morning vs. evening light treatment for winter depression. *Archives of General Psychiatry, 47*, 343–351.

Sackheim, J. (1985). The case for ECT. *Psychology Today, June*, 36–40.

Sadker, M., & Sadker, D. (1985). Sexism in the school room of the 80s. *Psychology Today, 19*, 54–57.

Sager, C. (1986). Couples therapy with marriage contracts. In I. K. A. Wolf (Ed.), *Psychotherapist's Casebook*. San Francisco: Jossey-Bass.

Sakai, K. L., Homae, F., & Hashimoto, R. (2003). Sentence processing is uniquely human. *Neuroscience Research, Jul; 46*(3), 273–279.

Sanders, G., & Cairns, K. (1987). Loss of sexual spontaneity. *Medical Aspects of Human Sexuality, 92*, 94–96.

Sanders, G. (1982). Social comparison as a basis for evaluating others. *Journal of Research in Personality, 16*, 21–31.

Sano, K. (1962). Sedative neurosurgery. *Neurologia, 4*, 112–142.

Santee, R., & Maslach, C. (1982). To agree or not to agree: Personal dissent amid social pressure to conform. *Journal of Personality and Social Psychology, 42*, 690–700.

Santrock, J. W. (2003): *Psychology 7*, Publishers: McGraw Hill, Boston. ISBN: 0-07-249412-3.

Sapolsky, R. (2003). Taming stress. *Scientific American, Sep; 289*(3), 86–95.

Sapolsky, R. M. (2003). Gene therapy for psychiatric disorders. *The American Journal of Psychiatry, Feb; 160*(2), 208–220.

Sapolsky, R. M. (2003). Altering behavior with gene transfer in the limbic system. *Physiology & Behavior, Aug; 79*(3), 479–486.

Sattin, A. (1999). The role of TRH and related peptides in the mechanism of action of ECT. *The Journal of ECT, Mar: 15*(1), 76–92.

Savage-Rumbaugh, E., Pate, J., Lawson, J., Smith, S., & Rosenbaum, S. (1983). Can a chimpanzee make a statement? *Journal of Experimental Psychology: General, 112*, 457–492.

Savage-Rumbaugh, E., Rumbaugh, D., & Boysen, S. (1980). Do apes use language? *American Scientist, 68*, 49–61.

Sawaguchi, T., Franco, P., Kato, I., Shimizu, S., Kadhim, H., Groswasser, J., et al. (2002). Interaction between apnea, prone sleep position and gliosis in the brainstems of victims of SIDS. *Forensic Science International, Sep 14; 130*(Suppl), S44–52.

Scammell, T. E. (2003). The neurobiology, diagnosis, and treatment of narcolepsy. *Annals of Neurology, Feb; 53*(2), 154–166.

Scarr, S. (1986). Intelligence: Revisiting. In R. Sternberg & D. Detterman (Eds.), *What Is Intelligence.* Norwood, NJ: Ablex.

Scarr, S. (1984). What's a parent to do? *Psychology Today*, May, 58–63.

Scarr, S. (1981). Testing for children: Assessment and the many determinants of intellectual competence. *American Psychologist, 63*, 1159–1166.

Schacheve, K. (1990). Attachment between working mothers and their infants: The influence of family processes. *American Journal of Orthopsychiatry, 60*, 19–34.

Schachter, S., & Latané, B. Schachter, S., & Latané, B. (1964). Crime, cognition, and the autonomic nervous system. In D. Levine (Ed.), *Nebraska Symposium on Motivation.* Lincoln: University of Nebraska Press.

Schachter, S., & Singer, J. (1962). Cognitive, social, and physiological determinants of emotional state. *Psychological Review, 69*, 379–399.

Schacter, D. L. (1995). *Implicit memory*: A new frontier for cognitive neuroscience. In M. S. Gazzaniga (Ed.), *The Cognitive Neurosciences* (pp. 815–824).

Schaffer, H., & Emerson, P. (1964). The development of social attachments in infancy. *Monographs of the Society for Research in Child Development, 20*, Whole No. 94.

Schaie, K. (1975). Age changes in intelligence. In D. Woodruff & J. Birren (Eds.), *Aging: Scientific Perspectives and Social Issues. New York: Van Nostrand.* New York: Van Nostrand.

Schare, M., Lisman, S., & Spear, N. (1984). The effects of mood variation on state-dependent retention. *Cognitive Therapy and Research, 8*, 387–408.

Schein, E. (1956). The Chinese indoctrination program for prisoners of war: A study of attempted brainwashing. *Psychiatry, 19*, 149–172.

Schiffman, H. (2000). *Sensation and Perception* (5th ed.). New York: John Wiley & Son.

Schiffman, S. S. (1999). Chemosensory impairment and appetite commentary on "Impaired sensory functioning in elders: the relation with its potential determinants and nutritional intake". *The Journals of Gerontology. Series A, Biological sciences and medical sciences, Aug; 54*(8), B332–335.

Schildkraut, J. (1970). *Neuropsychopharmacology of the Affective Disorders.* Boston: Little, Brown.

Schlegel, R., Wellwood, J., Copps, B., Gruchow, W., & Sharratt, M. (1980). The relationship between perceived challenge and daily symptom reporting in Type A vs. Type B postinfarct subjects. *Journal of Behavioral Medicine, 3*, 191–204.

Schluppeck, D., & Engel, S. A. (2002). Color opponent neurons in V1: a review and model reconciling results from imaging and single-unit recording. *Journal of Vision, 2*(6), 480–492.

Schneidman, E. (1987). At the point of no return. *Psychology Today*, March, 55–58.

Schneidman, E. (1974). *Deaths of Man.* Baltimore: Penguin Books.

Schneidman, E., Faberow, N., & Litman, R. (eds.), . (1970). *The Psychology of Suicide.* New York: Jason Aronson.

Schou, M. (1989). Lithium prophylaxis: Myths and realities. *The American Journal of Psychiatry, 146*, 573–576.

Schreiber, F. R. (1973). *Sybil.* Warner Books Inc. N.Y. ISBN 0-446-35940-8

Schroeder, D., & Costa, P. (1984). Influence of life event stress on physical illness: Substantive effects or methodological flaws? *Journal of Personality and Social Psychology, 46*, 853–863.

Schulsinger, E. (1972). Psychopathy: Heredity and environment. *International Journal of Mental Health, 1*, 190–206.

Schumacher, M., Coirini, H., & McEwen, B. (1989). Regulation of high-affinity GABAA receptors in the dorsal hippocampus by estradiol and progesterone. *Brain Research, 487*, 178–183.

Schvaneveldt, R., & Meyer, D. (1973). Retrieval and compassion processes in semantic memory. In S. Komblum (Ed.), *Attention and Performance IV.* New York: Academic Press.

Schwartz, P. J., Rosenthal, N. E., & Wehr, T. A. (1998). Serotonin 1A receptors, melatonin, and the proportional control thermostat in patients with winter depression. *Archives of General Psychiatry, Oct: 55*(10), 897–903.

Schwartz, P. J., Turner, E. H., & Garcia-Borreguero, D., Sedway, J.; Vetticad, R.G.; Wehr, T.A.; Murphy, D.L.; Rosenthal, N.E. (1999). Serotonin hypothesis of winter depression: behavioral and neuroendocrine effects of the 5-HT(1A) receptor partial agonist ipsapirone in patients with seasonal affective disorder and healthy control subjects. *Pyschiatry Research, Apr 19; 86*(1), 9–28.

Scovern, A., & Kilmann, P. (1980). Status of electroconvulsive therapy: Review of the outcome literature. *Psychological Bulletin, 87*, 260–303.

Scribner, S. (1977). Modes of thinking and ways of speaking: Culture and logic reconsidered. In P. Johnson-Laird & P. Wason (Eds.), *Thinking: Readings in Cognitive Science.* New York: Cambridge University Press.

Seagall, M., Campbell, D., & Herskovits, M. (1966). *The Influence of Culture on Visual Perceptio.* New York: Bobbs-Merrill.

Searle, J. (1990). Is the brain's mind a computer program? *Scientific American, 262*, 26–31.

Sears, D. (1979). Life stage effects upon attitude change, especially among the elderly. *Paper presented at the Workshop on the Elderly of the Future, Committee on Aging, National Research Council, Annapolis, Maryland*, May.

Sears, D., & Freedman, J. (1965). Effects of expected familiarity of arguments upon opinion change and selective exposure. *Personality and Social Psychology, 2*, 420–425.

Sears, P., & Barbee, A. (1977). Career and life situations among Terman's gifted women. In J. Stanley, W. George & C. Solano (Eds.), *The Gifted and the Creative: A Fifty-Year Perspective.* Baltimore: Johns Hopkins University Press.

Sears, R. (1977). Sources of life satisfaction of the Terman gifted men. *American Psychologist, 32*, 119–128.

Sechzer, P. (1968). Objective measurement of pain. *Anesthesiology, 29*, 209–210.

Segal, M. (1974). Alphabet and attraction: An unobtrusive measure of the effect of propinquity in a field setting. *Journal of Personality and Social Psychology, 30*, 654–657.

Segal, N. (1985). Monozygotic and dizygotic twins: A comparative analysis of mental ability profile. *Monozygotic and dizygotic twins: A comparative analysis of mental ability profile., 56*, 1051–1058.

Seiden, R. (1974). Suicide: Preventable death. *Public Affairs Report, 15*, 1–5.

Seligman, M., Abramson, L., & Semmel, A. (1979). Depressive attributional style. *Journal of Abnormal Psychology, 88*, 242–247.

Seligman, M. (1975). *Helplessness: On Depression, Development and Death.* San Francisco: Freeman.

Seligman, M., & Maier, S. (1967). Failure to escape traumatic shock. *Journal of Experimental Psychology, 75*, 1–9.

Seligman:, M. (1971). Phobias and preparedness. *Behavior Therapy, 2*, 307–320.

Selye, H. (1976). *Stress in Health and Disease.* Woburn, MA: Butterworth.

Selye, H. (1974). *Stress Without Distress.* Philadelphia: Lippincott.

Selye, H. (1956). *The Stress of Life.* New York: McGraw-Hill.

Selye, H. (1936). A syndrome produced by diverse nocuous agents. *Nature, 138*, 32.

Sem-Jacobsen, C. (1968). *Depth-Electrographic Stimulation of the Human Brain.* Springfield, IL: Thomas.

Semple, M., & Kitzes, L. (1987). Binaural processing of sound pressure level in the inferior colliculus. *Journal of Neurophysiology, 57,* 1130–1147.

Serbin, L. (1980). Interview in NOVA. The Pinks and the Blues. Boston: WGBH Transcripts.

Seyfarth, R., & Cheney, D. (1992). Meaning and mind in monkeys. *Scientific American, 12,* 122–128.

Shanab, M., & Yahya, K. (1977). A behavioral study of obedience in children. *Journal of Personality and Social Psychology, 35,* 530–536.

Shapiro, C., Bortz, R., Mitchell, D., Bartel, P, & Jooste, P. (1981). Slow-wave sleep: A recovery after exercise. *Science, 214,* 1253–1254.

Shea, M. T., Elkin, I., Imber, S. D., Sotsky, S. M., Watkins, J. T., Collins, J. F., et al. (!992). Course of depressive symptoms over follow-up. Findings from the National Institute of Mental Health Treatment of Depression Collaborative Research Program. *Archives of General Psychiatry, Oct: 49*(10), 782–787.

Sheehan, P. (1988). Confidence, memory and hypnosis. In H. Pettinati (Ed.), *Hypnosis and Memory.* New York: Guilford.

Sheffield, E. (1966). A drive induction theory of reinforcement. In R. Haber (Ed.), *Current Research in Motivation.* New York: Holt, Rinehart and Winston.

Sheffield, E., Wulff, J., & Backer, R. (1951). Reward value of copulation without sex drive reduction. *Journal of Comparative and Physiological Psychology, 44,* 3–8.

Shen, H., Numachi, Y., Yoshida, S., Fujiyama, K., Toda, S., Awata, S., et al. (2003). Electroconvulsive shock increases serotonin transporter in the rat frontal cortex. *Neuroscience Letters, May 1; 341*(2), 170–172.

Shepard, R., & Metzler, J. (1971). Mental rotation of three-dimensional objects. *Science, 171,* 701–703.

Shepherd, R., & Cooper, L. (1982). *Mental Images and Their Transformation.* Cambridge, MA: MIT Press.

Sherif, M., Harvey, O., White, B., Hood, W., & Sherif, C. (1961). *Intergroup Cooperation and Competition: The Robbers Cave Experience.* Norman, OK: University Book Exchange.

Sherif, M. (1937). An experimental approach to the study of attitudes. *Sociometry, 1,* 90–98.

Sherrington, R., Brynjolfsson, J., Petursson, H., Potter, M., Dudleston, K., Barraclough, B., Wasmuth, J., Dobbs, M., & Gurling, H. (1988). Localization of a susceptibility locus for schizophrenia on chromosome 5. *Nature, 336,* 336.

Sherwin, B., & Gelfand, M. (1987). Individual differences in mood with menopausal replacement therapy: Possible role of sex hormone-binding globulin. *Journal of Psychosomatic Obstetrics and Gynaecology, 6,* 121–131.

Sherwin, B., Gelfand, M., & Brender, W. (1985). Androgen enhances sexual motivation in females: A prospective crossover study of sex steroid administration in the surgical menopause. *Psychosomatic Medicine, 47,* 339–351.

Shettleworth, S. (1983). Memory in food-hoarding birds. *Scientific American, 248,* 102–110.

Shevitz, S. (1976). Psychosurgery: Some current observations. *The American Journal of Psychiatry, 133,* 266–270.

Shiffrin, R., & Atkinson, R. (1969). Storage and retrieval processes in long-term memory. *Psychological Review, 76,* 179–193.

Shoda, Y., LeeTieman, S., & Mischel, W. (2002). *Personality* as a dynamical system: emergency of stability and distinctiveness from intra- and interpersonal interactions. *Personality & Social Psychology Review, 6*(4), 316–325.

Shoda, Y., & Mischel, W. (1996). Toward a unified, intra-individual dynamic conception of personality. *Journal of Research in Personality, Sep; 30*(3), 414–428.

Shodand, R., & Goodstein, L. (1983). Just because she doesn't want to doesn't mean it's rape: An experimentally based causal model of the perception of rape in a dating situation. *Social Psychology Quarterly, 46,* 220–232.

Siegel, D. (1982). Personality development in adolescence. In B. Wolman (Ed.), *Handbook of Developmental Psychology.* Englewood Cliffs, NJ: Prentice-Hall.

Siegel, M. (1987). Are sons and daughters treated more differently by fathers than by mothers? *Developmental Review., 7,* 183–209.

Siegel, S., Hinson, R., & Krank, M. (1978). The role of pre-drug signals in morphine analgesic tolerance: Support for a Pavlovian conditioning model of tolerance. *Journal of Experimental Psychology: Animal Behavior Processes, 4,* 188–196.

Simkin, J., Simkin, A., Brien, L., & Sheldon, C. (1986). Gestalt therapy. In I. Kutash & A. Wolf (Eds.), *Psychotherapist's Casebook.* San Francisco: Jossey-Bass.

Singer, D. (1989). Children, adolescents, and television—1989. *Pediatrics, 83,* 445–446.

Singer, L., Brodzinsky; D., Ramsay, D., Stein, M., & Waters, F. (1985). Mother-infant attachment in adoptive families. *Child Development, 56,* 1543–1551.

Skinner, B. (1987). *Upon farther reflection.* Englewood Cliffs, NJ: Prentice Hall.

Skinner, B. F. (1976). *About Behaviorism* London: Vintage ISBN: 0394716183

Skinner, B. (1974). *About behaviorism.* New York: Alfred Knopf.

Skinner, B. (1957). *Verbal Behavior.* Englewood Cliffs, NJ: Prentice-Hall.

Skinner, B. (1953). *Science of Human Behavior.* New York: Macmillan.

Skowronski, J., & Carlston, D. (1987). Social judgment and social memory: The role of diagnosticity, positivity, and extremity biases. *Journal of Personality and Social Psychology, 52,* 689–699.

Skre, I., Onstad, S., Torgersen, S., Philos, D. R., Lygren, S., & Kringlen, E. (2000). The heritability of common phobic fear: a twin study of a clinical sample. *Journal of Anxiety Disorders, Nov–Dec; 14*(6), 549–562.

Slade, A. (1987). Quality of attachment and early symbolic play. *Developmental Psychology, 23,* 78–85.

Slater, E., & Shields, J. (1969). Genetic aspects of anxiety. In M. Lader (Ed.), *Studies of Anxiety.* Ashford, England: Headley Brothers.

Slater, F., & Cowie, V. (1971). *The Genetics of Mental Disorders.* London: Oxford University Press.

Sloane, R., Staples, F, Cristol, A., Yorkston, N., & Whipple, K. (1975). *Psychotherapy versus Behavior Therapy.* Cambridge, MA: Harvard University Press.

Slot, L. A. B., & Colpaert, F. G. (2003). A persistent opioid-addiction state of memory. *Behavioural Pharmacology, Mar; 14*(2), 167–171.

Smith, C. (1996). Pluralistic ignorance: An integration of perception of difference. *Dissertation Abstracts International: Section B: The Sciences & Engineering, 56,* 5227.

Smith, K. (1947). The problem of stimulation deafness. Histological changes in the cochlea as a function of tonal frequency. *Journal of Experimental Psychology, 37,* 304–317.

Smith, M. L., & Glass G. V. (1977): Meta-analysis of psychotherapy outcome studies in *Forty Studies that Changed Psychology,* ed. Hock, R.R. Third ed., 1992, New Jersey: Prentice Hall Publishers, ISBN 0-13- 922725-3, pp. 259–260.

Smith, M., Glass, G., & Miller, R. (1980). *The Benefits of Psychotherapy.* Baltimore: Johns Hopkins University Press.

Smith, P., & Langoff, G. (1981). The use of Sternberg's memory scanning technique. *Human Factors, 23,* 701–708.

Smith, S., Brown, H., Toman, J., & Goodman, L. (1947). The lack of cerebral effects of I-Tubercurarine. *Anesthesiology, 8,* 1–14.

Snarey, J. (1987). A question of morality. *Psychology Today,* June, 6–8.

Snyder, M. (1983). The influence of individuals on situation: Implications for understanding the links between personality and social behavior. *Journal of Personality, 51,* 497–516.

Snyder, M., Tanke, E., & Berscheid, E. (1977). Social perception and interpersonal behavior: On the self-fulfilling nature of social stereotypes. *Journal of Personality and Social Psychology, 35*, 691–712.

Snyder, M., & Swann, W. (1976). When actions reflect attitudes: The politics of impression management. *Journal of Personlity and Social Psychology, 34*, 1034–1042.

Snyder, S. (1986). *Drugs and the Brain.* San Francisco: Freeman.

Snyder, S. (1984). Drug and neurotransmitter receptors in the brain. *Science, 224*, 22–31.

Solomon, R. (1982). The opponent-process in acquired motivation. In D. Pfaff (Ed.), *The Physiological Mechanisms of Motivation.* New York: Springer-Verlag.

Solomon, R. (1980). The opponent-process theory of acquired motivation: The costs of pleasure and the benefits of pain. *American Psychologist, 35*, 691–712.

Solomon, R., & Corbit, J. (1974). An opponent-process theory of motivation. *Psychological Review, 81*, 119–145.

Solso, R. (1991). *Cognitive psychology* (3rd ed.). Boston: Allyn and Bacon.

Solso, R. L. (2000). *Cognitive Psychology* (6th ed.): Allyn & Bacon.

Sorenson, R. (1973). *Adolescent Sexuality in Contemporary America.* New York: World.

Spanos, N. P .(1996). Multiple Identities & False Memories: A Sociocognitive Perspective. N.Y.: American Psychological Association. ISBN 155983402

Spanos, N., Williams, V., & Gwynn, M. (1990). Effects of hypnotic, placebo, and salicylic acid treatments on wart regression. *Psychosomatic Medicine, 52*, 109–114.

Spanos, N., Perlini, A., & Robertson, L. (1989). Hypnosis, suggestion, and placebo in the reduction of experimental pain. *Journal of Abnormal Psychology, 98*, 285–293.

Spearman, C. (1904). General intelligence objectively determined and measured. *American Journal of Psychology, 15*, 201–229.

Speed, N., Engdahl, B., Schwartz, J., & Eberly, R. (1989). Posttraumatic stress disorder as a consequence of the POW experience. *The Journal of Nervous and Mental Disease, 177*, 147–153.

Spencer, S., Steele, C., & Quinn, D. (2002). Stereotype threat and women's math performance. In A. Hunder & C. Forden (Eds.), *Readings in the pssychology of gender: Exploring our differences and commonalities.* Needham Heights, MA: Allyn & Bacon.

Sperling, G. (1960). The information available in brief visual presentations. *Psychological Monographs, 74*, 1–29.

Sperry, R. (1968). Hemispheric deconnection and the unity of conscious experience. *American Psychologist, 23*, 723–733.

Spielberger, C., Johnson, E., Russell, S., Crane, R., Jacobs, G., & Worden, T. (1985). The experience and expression of anger. In M. Chesney, S. Goldston & R. Rosennian (Eds.), *Anger and Hostility in Behavioral Medicine.* New York: Hemisphere/McGraw-Hill.

Spitz, R., & Wolff, K. (1946). Anaclitic depression: An inquiry into the genesis of psychiatric conditions in early childhood: II. In A. Freud (Ed.), *he Psychoanalytic Study of the Child* (Vol. 2). New York: International Universities Press.

Spitz, R. (1945). Hospitalism: An inquiry into the genesis of psychiatric conditions in early childhood. *Psychoanalytic Study of the Child, 2*, 313–342.

Sroufe, L. (1985). Attachment classification from the perspective of infant-caregiver relationships and infant temperament. *Child Development, 56*, 1–14.

Sroufe, L., Fox, N., & Pancake, V. (1983). Attachment and dependency in a developmental perspective. *Child Development, 54*, 1615–1627.

Stastny, J., Konstantinidis, A., Schwarz, M. J., Rosenthal, N. E., Vitouch, O., Kasper, S., et al. (2003). Effects of tryptophan depletion and catecholamine depletion on immune parameters in patients with seasonal affective disorder in remission with light therapy. *Biological Psychiatry, Feb 15; 53*(4), 332–337.

Steele, C., & Aronson, J. (1995). Stereotype threat and the intellectual test performance of African Americans. *Journal of Personality and Social Psychology, 69*, 797–811.

Steele, C., Spencer, S., & Aronson, J. (2002). Contending with group image: The psychology of sterotype and social identity threat. In M. Zanna (Ed.), *Advances in Experimental Social Psychology.* San Diego, CA: Academic Press.

Steele, H. (2002). State of the art: *Attachment* theory. *Psychologist, Oct; 15*(10 The changing family), 518–522.

Stein, L. (1989). The effect of long-term outcome studies on the therapy of schizophrenia: A Critique. *Journal of Marital and Family Therapy, 15*, 133–138.

Stein, L., & Wise, C. (1971). Possible etiology of schizophrenia: Progressive damage to the noradrenergic reward system by 6-hydroxy dopamine. *Science, 171*, 1031–1036.

Stellar, E. (1954). The physiology of motivation. *Psychological Review, 61*, 5–22.

Stephan, W., & Rosenfield, D. (1978). Effects of desegregation on racial attitudes. *Journal of Personality and Social Psychology, 36*, 36.

Steriade, M., & Timofeev, I. (2003). Neuronal plasticity in thalamocortical networks during sleep and waking oscillations. *Neuron, Feb 20; 37*(4), 563–576.

Sterlitz, J. (2003). Aron Ralston Sacrifices His Right Arm to Save His Life, *The Aspen Times, On-line.*

Stern, D. (1986). *The Interpersonal World of the Infant.* New York: Basic Books.

Stern, J., Brown, M., Ulert, G., & Sletten, I. (1977). A comparison of hypnosis, acupuncture, morphine, valium, aspirin, and placebo in the management of experimentally induced pain. *Annals of the New York Academy of Sciences, 296*, 175–193.

Sternberg, R. (1986). *Intelligence Applied: Understanding and increasing Your Intellectual Skills.* San Diego, CA: Harcourt Brace Jovanovich.

Sternberg, R. (1985). *Beyond IQ: A Triarchic Theory of Human Intelligence.*

Sternberg, R. (1984). Testing intelligence without IQ tests. *Phi Delta Kappan, 65*, 694–698.

Sternberg, R. (1982). Reasoning, problem solving, and intelligence. In R. Sternberg (Ed.), *Handbook of Human Intelligence.* New York: Cambridge University Press.

Sternberg, R., Conway, B., Ketron, J., & Bernstein, M. (1981). People's conceptions of intelligence. *Journal of Personality and Social Psychology, 41*, 37–55.

Sternberg, R. (1981). Testing and cognitive psychology. *American Psychologist, 36*, 181–1189.

Sternberg, R. (1979). The nature of mental abilities. *American Psychologist, 34*, 214–230.

Sternberg, R. J. (2003). Construct validity of the theory of special *intelligence.* In R. Sternberg & J. Lautrey (Eds.), *Models of intelligence: International perspectives.* (pp. 55–77). Washington, DC: American Psycological Association.

Sternberg, R. J., Forsythe, G. B., Hedlund, J., Horvath, J. A., Wagner, R. K., Williams, W. M., et al. (2000). *Practical intelligence in everyday life* (Vol. xiv).

Stevenson, H. (1992). Learning from Asian schools. *Scientific American, 12*, 70–76.

Stevenson, H. (1983). Making the Grade: School Achievement in Japan, Taiwan, and the United States. *Stanford, CA: Center for Advanced Study in the Behavioral Sciences, Annual Report.*

Stevenson, J., Graham, P., Fredman, G., & McLoughlin, V. (1987). A twin study of genetic influences on reading and spelling ability and disability. *Journal of Child Psychology and Psychiatry, 28*, 229–247.

Stocks, J. T. (1998). Recovered memory therapy: a dubious practice technique. *Social Work, Sep; 43*(5), 423–436.

Straus, B., & Yalow, R. (1979). Cholecystokinin in the brains of obese and nonobese mice. *Science, 203*, 68–69.

Straus, M., Gelles, R., & Steinmetz, S. (1980). *Behind Closed Doors: Violence in the American Family*. Garden City, NY: Anchor Press.

Strupp, H. (1984). Psychotherapy research: Reflections on my career and the state of the art. *Journal of Social and Clinical Psychology, 2*, 3–24.

Stunkard, A., Sorenson, T., Hanis, C., Teasdale, I, Chakraborty, R., Schall, W., & Schulsinger, E . (1986). An adoption study of human obesity. *The New England journal of Medicine, 314*, 193–198.

Stunkard, A., Sorensen, T, Hanis, & Teasdale, T. (1986). "An adoption study of human obesity". Reply. *New England Journal Medicine, 315*, 130.

Subotnik, R. F., Karp, D. E., & Morgan, E. R. (1989). High IQ children at midlife: an investigation into the generalizability of *Terman's* genetic studies of genius. In *Roeper Review* (Vol. 11(3), pp. 139–144): US: Roeper School.

Suddath, R., Casanova, M., Goldberg, T., Daniel, D., Kelsoe, J., & Weinberger, D. (1989). Temporal lobe pathology in schizophrenia: A quantitative magnetic resonance imaging study. *The American Journal of Psychiatry, 146*, 464–472.

Suomi, S., & Harlow, H. (1978). Early experience and social development in Rhesus monkeys. In M. Lamb (Ed.), *Social and Personality Development*. New York: Holt, Rinehart and Winston.

Suomi, S., & Harlow, H. (1972). Social rehabilitation of isolate-reared monkeys. *Developmental Psychology, 6*, 487–496.

Swaab, D. F., Chun, W. C., Kruijver, F. P., Hofman, M. A., & Ishunina, T. A. (2002). Sexual differentiation of the human hypothalamus. *Advances in Experimental Medicine and Biology, 511*, 75–100; discussion 100–105.

Swann, W., Wenziaff, R., Krull, D., & Pelham, B. (1992). Allure of negative feedback: Self-verification strivings among depressed persons. *Journal of Abnormal Psychology, 101*, 293–306.

Swartz, M., Blazer, D., George, L., & Landerman, R. (1986). Somatization disorder in a community population. *American Journal of Psychiatry, 143*, 1403–1408.

Swets, J., Tanner, W., & Birdsall, T. (1961). Decision processes in perception. *Psychological Review, 68*, 301–340.

Syndulko, K. (1978). Electrocortical investigations of sociopathy. In R. Hare & D. Schalling (Eds.), *Psychopathic Behavior: Approaches to Research*. Chichester, England: Wiley.

Tajfel, H. (1982). *Social Identity and Intergroup Relations*. New York: Cambridge University Press.

Tajfel, H., & Turner, J. (1979). An integrative theory of intergroup conflict. In W. Autin & S. Worchel (Eds.), *The Social Psychology of Intergroup Relations*. Monterey, CA: Brooks/Cole.

Takeuchi, T., Ogilvie, R. D., Murphy, T. I., & Ferrelli, A. V. (2003). EEG activities during elicited sleep onset REM and NREM periods reflect different mechanisms of dream generation. Electroencephalograms. Rapid eye movement. *Clinical Neurophysiology, Feb; 114*(2), 210–220.

Tambs, K., Sundet, J., & Magnus, P. (1984). Heritability analysis of the WAIS subtests: A study of twins. *Intelligence, 8*, 283–293.

Tan, Y., Gan, Q., & Knuepfer, M. M. (2003). Central alpha-adrenergic receptors and corticotropin releasing factor mediate hemodynamic responses to acute cold stress. *Brain Research, Apr 4; 968*(1), 122–129.

Tanford, S., & Penrod, S. (1984). Social influence model: A formal integration of research on majority and minority influence processes. *Psychological Bulletin, 95*, 189–225.

Tavris, C. (1982). *Anger: The Misunderstood Emotion*. New York: Simon & Schuster.

Telch, M., Lucas, J., & Nelson, P. (1989). Non-clinical panic in college students: An investigation of prevalence and symptomatology. *Journal of Abnormal Psychology, 98*, 300–306.

Tellegen, A., Lykken, D., Bouchard, T, Wilcox, K., Segal, N., & Rich, S. (1988). Personality similarity in twins reared apart and together. *Journal of Personality and Social Psychology, 54*, 1031–1039.

Terman, L. (1954). Scientists and nonscientists in a group of 800 gifted men. *Psychological Monographs, 68*, 1–44.

Terman, L. (1925). Mental and physical traits of a thousand gifted children. In L. Terman (Ed.), *Genetic Studies of Genius*. Stanford, CA: Stanford University Press.

Terman, L. (1921). In Symposium: Intelligence and its measurement. *Journal of Educational Psychology, 12*, 127–133.

Terman, M. (1988). On the question of mechanism in phototherapy: Considerations of clinical efficacy and epidemiology. *Journal of Biological Rhythms, 3*, 155–172.

Terman, M., Lewy, A. J., Dijk, D. J., Boulos, Z., Eastman, C. I., & Campbell, S. S. (1995). Light treatment for sleep disorders: consensus report IV. sleep phase and duration disturbances. *Journal of Biological Rhythms, Jun; 10*(2), 135–147.

Terrace, H., Petitto, L., Sanders, R., & Bever, T. (1979). Can an ape create a sentence? *Science, 206*, 891–902.

Terrace, H. (1979). How Nim Chimsky changed my mind. *Psychology Today*, November, 63–91.

Tervsky, A., & Kahneman, D. (1981). The framing of decision and the psychology of choice. *Science, 211*, 453–458.

Tesser, A. (1990). Attitudes and attitude change. *Annual Review of Psychology, 41*, 479–523.

Thase, M. E., & Friedman, D. S. (1999). Is psychotherapy an effective treatment for melancholia and other severe depressive states? *Journal of Affective Disorders, Jul: 54*(1–2), 1–19.

Thatcher, R., Walker, R., & Giudice, S. (1987). Human cerebral hemispheres develop at different rates and ages. *Science, 236*, 1110–1113.

Thibaut, J., & Strickland, L. (1956). Psychological set and social conformity. *Journal of Personality and Social Psychology, 25*, 115–129.

Thigpen, C., & Cleckley, H. (1984). On the incidence of multiple personality disorder. *The International Journal of Clinical and Experimental Hypnosis, 32*, 63–66.

Thigpen, C. & Cleckley, H. (1957). *The 3 Faces of Eve*. New York: Fawcett.

Thomas, A., & Chess, S. (1977). *Temperament and Development*. New York: Bruner/Masel.

Thompson, C., & Isaacs, G. (1988). Seasonal affective disorder—a British sample: Symptomatology in relation to mode of referral and diagnostic subtype. *Journal of Affective Disorders, 14*, 1–11.

Thompson, J., & Blame, J. (1987). Use of ECT in the United States in 1975 and 1980. *American Journal of Psychiatry, 144*, 557–562.

Thompson, J., Jarvie, G., Lahey, B., & Cureton, K. (1982). Exercise and obesity: Etiology, physiology, and intervention. *Psychological Bulletin, 91*, 55–79.

Thompson, P. (2001). UCLA Researchers Map How Schizophrenia Engulfs Teen brains Dramatic Images Hold Hope for early Diagnosis, Treatment of Devastating Disease. Contact: Dan Page, UCLA Health Sciences Communications http://www.loni.ucla.edu/~thompson /MEDIA/PNAS/Press_release.html

Thompson, R. (1986). The neurobiology of learning and memory. *Science, 233*, 941–947.

Thompson, R. (1985). *The Brain*. San Francisco: Freeman.

Thorndike, E. (1911). *Animal intelligence*. New York: Macmillan.

Thorndike, R., Hagen, E., & Sattler, J. (1986). *The Stanford-Binet intelligence Scale* (Fourth ed.). Chicago, IL: Riverside Publishing Company.

Thornhill, R.; Gangestad, S. W.; Miller, R.,; Scheyd, G.; McCollough, J.K.; Franklin, M. (2003): Major histocompatibility complex genes, symmetry, and body scent attractiveness in men and women *Behavioral Ecology* Vol. 14 No. 5: 668–678.

Thurstone, L. (1938). *Primary Mental Abilities*. Chicago: University of Chicago Press.

Thurstone, L. C. A. J. o. S., 52, 39–40. (1946). Comment. *American Journal of Sociology, 52*, 39–40.

Tolchin, M. (1989). Suicide rate among elderly increases 25% from 1981 to 1986. *The Oregonian*(July 23), Al5.

Tolman, D. L., & Diamond, L. M. (2001). Desegregating sexuality research: cultural and biological perspectives on *gender* and desire. *Annual Review of Sex Research, 12*, 33–74.

Tolman, E. (1967). *Purposive Behavior in Animals and Man.* New York: Irvington.

Tolstedt, B., & Stokes, J. (1983). Relation of verbal, affective, and physical intimacy to marital satisfaction. *Journal of Counseling Psychology, 30*, 573–580.

Tomkins, S. (1963). *Affect, Imagery, and Consciousness: The Negative Effects* (Vol. 2). New York: Springer.

Tomkins, S. (1962). *Affect, Imagery, and Consciousness: The Positive Effects* (Vol. 1). New York: Springer.

Toran-Allerand, C. D., Singh, M., & Setalo, G., Jr. (1999). Novel mechanisms of estrogen action in the brain: new players in an old story. *Frontiers in Neuroendocrinology, Apr; 20*(2), 97–121.

Tourney, G. (1980). Hormones and homosexuality. In J. Marmor (Ed.), *Homosexual Behavior.* New York: Basic Books.

Treisman, A. (1964). Monitoring and storage of irrelevant messages in selective attention. *Journal of Verbal Learning and Verbal Behavior, 3*, 449–459.

Treisman, A. (1960). Contextual cues in selective listening. *Quarterly Journal of Experimental Psychology, 12*, 242–248.

Troll, L. (1975). *Early and Middle Adulthood.* Monterey, CA: Brooks/Cole.

Truchot, D., Maure, G., & Patte, S. (2003). Do attributions change over time when the actor's behavior is hedonically relevant to the perceiver? *Journal of Social Psychology, 143*, 202–208.

Trujillo, K., Belluzzi, J., & Stein, L. (1989). Effects of opiate antagonists and their quaternary analogues on nucleus accumens self-stimulation. *Behavioural Brain Research, 33*, 181–188.

Tryon, R. (1940). *Genetic differences in maze-learning ability in rats* (Vol. In 39th Yearbook, National Society for the Study of Education). Chicago: University of Chicago Press.

Tulving, E. (1986). What kind of a hypothesis is the distinction between episodic and semantic memory? *Journal of Experimental Psychology: Learning, Memory, and Cognition, 12*, 307–311.

Tulving, E. (1983). *Elements of Episodic Memory.* New York: Oxford University Press.

Tulving, E. (1977). Cue-dependent forgetting. In I. Janis (Ed.), *Current Trends in Psychology.* Los Altos, CA: Kaufmann.

Tulving, E. (1972). Episodic and Semantic Memory. In E. Tulving & W. Donaldson (Eds.), *Organization of Memory.* New York: Academic Press.

Tulving, E., & Schacter, D. L. (1990). Priming and human memory systems. *Science, Jan; 247*(4940), 301–306.

Turk, D., & Rudy, T. (1986). Assessment of cognitive factors in chronic pain: A worthwhile enterprise? *Journal of Consulting and Clinical Psychology, 54*, 760–768.

Turkkan, J. (1989). Classical conditioning: The new hegemony. *Behavioral and Brain Sciences, 12*, 121–179.

Turner, J. (1984). Social identification and psychological group formation. In H. Tajfel (Ed.), *The Social Dimension.* Cambridge, England: Cambridge University Press.

Turner, S., Beidel, D., & Nathan, R. (1985). Biological factors in obsessive-compulsive disorders. *Psychological Bulletin, 97*, 430–450.

Tversky, A., & Kahneman, D. (1973). On the psychology of prediction. *Psychological Review, 80*, 237–251.

Tversky, B., & Tuchin, M. (1989). A reconciliation of the evidence on eyewitness testimony: Comments on McCloskey and Zaragoza. *Journal of Experimental Psychology: General, 118*, 86–91.

Ueker, A., Reiman, E. M., Schacter, D. L., Polster, M. R., Cooper, L. A., Yun, L. S., et al. (1997). Neuroanatomical correlates of *implicit* and explicit *memory* for structurally possible and impossible visual objects. *Learning and Memory, Nov–Dec; 4*(4), 337–355.

Ullman, L., & Krasner, L. (1975). *A Psychological Approach to Abnormal Behavior* (2nd ed.). Englewood Cliffs, NJ: Prentice-Hall.

Ullman, M., Krippner, & Vaughan, A. (1973.) *Dream Telepathy: Experiments in Nocturnal Extrasensory Perception (Studies in Consciousness)* First published in 1973, 2nd publication 2002. New York: Hampton Roads Publishing Co. ISBN 1-57174-321-9

Vaillant, G., & Perry, J. (1985). Personality disorders. In H. Kaplan & B. Sadock (Eds.), *Comprehensive Textbook of Psychiatry* (4th ed.). Baltimore: Williams & Wilkins.

Valenstein, E. (1980). *The Psychosurgery Debate: Scientific, Legal, and Ethical Perspectives.* San Francisco: W. H. Freeman and Co.

Valenstein, E. (1973). *Brain Control.* Toronto: John Wiley & Sons.

Valian, V. (1986). Syntactic categories in the speech of young children. *Developmental Psychology, 22*, 562–579.

Van Egeren, L., Sniderman, L., & Roggelin, M. (1982). Competitive two-person interaction of Type-A and Type-B individuals. *Journal of Behavioral Medicine, 5*, 55–66.

Vega-Lahr, N., & Field, 1. (1986). Type A behavior in preschool children. *Child Development, 57*, 1333–1348.

Venables, P., & Wing, J. (1962). Level of arousal and the subclassification of schizophrenia. *Archives of General Psychiatry, 7*, 114–119.

Vink, R., McIntosh, 1, Demediuk, P., Weiner, M., & Faden, A. (1988). Decline in intracellular free Mg^{2+} is associated with irreversible tissue injury following brain trauma. *Journal of Biological Chemistry, 263*, 757–761.

Vink, R., O'Conner, C. A., Nimmo, A. J., & Heath, D. L. (2003). Magnesium attenuates persistent functional deficits following diffuse traumatic brain injury in rats. *Neuroscience Letters, Jan 9; 336*(1), 41–44.

Visintainer, M., Seligman, M., & Volpicelli, J. (1983). Helplessness, chronic stress, and tumor development. *Psychosomatic Medicine, 45*, 75–76.

Vogel, G. (1975). A review of REM sleep deprivation. *Archives of General Psychiatry, 32*, 749–761.

von Bekesy, G. (1960). *Experiments in Hearing.* New York: McGraw-Hill.

von Frisch, K. (1974). Decoding the language of the bee. *Science, 185*, 663–668.

Wadden, T., & Anderton, C. (1982). The clinical use of hypnosis. *Psychological Bulletin, 91*, 215–243.

Wade, A. R., Brewer, A. A., Rieger, J. W., & Wandell, B. A. (2002). Functional measurements of human ventral occipital cortex: retinotopy and colour. *Philosophical Transactions of the Royal Society of London. Series B: Biological Sciences, Aug 29; 357*(1424), 963–973.

Wahba, N., & Bridwell, L. (1976). Maslow reconsidered: A review of research on the need hierarchy theory. *Organization Behavior and Human Performance, 15*, 212–240.

Waldvogel, J. (1990). The bird's eye view. *American Scientist, 78*, 342–353.

Wallach, M., & Wallach, L. (1985). How psychology sanctions the cult of the self. *Washington Monthly*, February, 46–56.

Wallach, M., & Wallach, L. (1983). *Psychology's Sanction for Selfishness: The Error of Egoism in Theory and Therapy.* New York: Freeman.

Walling, M., Andersen, B., & Johnson, S. (1990). Hormonal replacement therapy for postmenopausal women: A review of sexual outcomes and related gynecologic effects. *Archives of Sexual Behavior, 19*, 119–137.

Walster, E., Aronson, E., & Abrahams, D. (1966). On increasing the persuasiveness of a low prestige communicator. *Journal of Experimental Social Psychology, 2*, 375–342.

Walters, J., Apter, M., & Sveback, S. (1982). Color preference, arousal, and the theory of psychological reversals. Motivation and Emotion, 6, 193–215. (1982). Color preference, arousal, and the theory of psychological reversals. *Motivation and Emotion, 6*, 193–215.

Walters, R., & Willows, D. (1968). Imitation of behavior of disturbed children following exposure to aggressive and nonaggressive models. *Child Development, 39*, 79–91.

Wangensteen, O., & Carlson, A. (1931). Hunger sensation after total gastrectomy. *Proceedings of the Society for Experimental Biology, 28*, 545–547.

Wapshott, N. (2003). Trapped climber cuts off arm with penknife. World News, *Times On-line.*

Wardle, J., Waller, J., & Rapoport, L. (2001). Body dissatisfaction and binge eating in obese women: the role of restraint and depression. *Obesity Research, Dec 1; 9*(12), 778–787.

Warga, C. (1987). Pain's gatekeeper. *Psychology Today*, August, 51–56.

Wason, P. (1968). On the failure to eliminate hypothesis—a second look. In P. Wason & P. Johnson-Laird (Eds.), *Thinking and Reasoning.* Baltimore: Penguin.

Waters, E., Wippman, J., & Sroufe, L. (1979). Attachment, positive affect, and competence in the peer group: Two studies in construct validation. *Child Development, 50*, 821–829.

Waters, H., & Huck, J. (1989). Networking wome. *Newsweek*, March 13, 48–54.

Watkins, C., Lopez, E, Campbell, V., & Himmell, C. (1986). Contemporary counseling psychology: results of a national survey. *Journal of Counseling Psychology, 33*, 301–309.

Watkins, J. (1984). The Bianchi (L.A. Hillside Strangler) case: Sociopath or multiple personality? *International Journal of Clinical and Experimental Hypnosis, 32*, 67–101.

Watkins, M., Ho, E., & Tulving, E. (1976). Context effects in recognition memory for faces. *Journal of Verbal Learning and Verbal Behavior, 15*, 505–518.

Watkins, S. S. (2000). *Opponent process* and nicotine addiction: Perpetuation of dependence through negative reinforcement processes. *Dissertation Abstracts International: Section B: The Sciences & Engineering, Sep; 61*(3–B), 1689.

Watson, J. (1930). *Behaviorism.* New York: Norton.

Watson, J. (1925). *Behaviorism.* Chicago: The University of Chicago Press.

Watson, R., & DeMeo, P. (1987). Premarital cohabitation vs. traditional courtship and subsequent marital adjustment: A replication and follow-up. *Family Relations, 36*, 193–197.

Watters, P. A., Martin, F., & Schreter, Z. (1997). Caffeine and cognitive performance: the nonlinear Yerkes-Dodson Law. *Human Psychopharmcology Clinical & Experimental, May–Jun; 12*(3), 249–257.

Weaver, C. (1993). Do you need a "flash" to form a flashbulb memory? *ournal of Experimental Psychology: General, 122*, 39–46.

Wechsler, D. (1944). *The Measurement of Adult Intelligence* (3rd ed.). Baltimore: Williams & Wilkins.

Wehr, T., & Rosenthal, N. (1989). Seasonality and affective illness. *The American Journal of Psychiatry, 146*, 829–839.

Wehr, T., Giesen, H., & Schulz, P. (1989). Summer depression: Description of the syndrome and comparison with winter depression. In N. Rosenthal & N. Blehar (Eds.), *Seasonal Affective Disorder and Phototherapy.* New York: Guilford Press.

Weigel, R., & Newman, L. (1976). Increasing attitude-behavior correspondence by broadening the scope of the behavioral measure. *Journal of Personality and Social Psychology, 33*, 793–802.

Weilburg, J., Bear, D., & Sachs, G. (1987). Three patients with concomitant panic attacks and seizure disorder: Possible clues to the neurology of anxiety. *The American Journal of Psychiatry, 144*, 1053–1056.

Weiner, R. (1985). Electroconvulsive therapy. In J. Walker (Ed.), *Essentials of Clinical Psychiatry.* Philadelphia: Lippincot.

Weiss, B. L. (1988). *Many Lives, Many Masters: The True Story of a Prominent Psychiatrist, His Young Patient, and the Past-Life Therapy That Changed Both Their Lives.* Publisher: Fireside, ISBN 0671657860

Weiss, R. (2004). "Ecstasy" Use Studied to Ease Fear in Terminally Ill. *Washington Post* Monday, December 27, 2004; Page A11, Staff Writer.

Weissman, M., Kierman, G., Markowitz, J., & Quellette, R. (1989). Suicidal ideation and suicide attempts in panic disorder and attacks. *New England Journal of Medicine, 321*, 1209–1214.

Weissman, M., Kierman, G., & Paykel, E. (1971). Clinical evaluation of hostility in depression. *American Journal of Psychiatry, 128*, 261–266.

Weissman, M., & Paykel, E. (1974). *The Depressed Woman.* Chicago: University of Chicago Press.

Welin, C. L., Rosengren, A., & Wilhelmsen, L. W. (1995). Behavioural characteristics in patients with myocardial infarction: a case-control study. *Journal of Cardiovascular Risk, Jun; 2*(3), 247–254.

Welner, M. (1997). Despite Amnesia, Fraud Defendant Competent to Plead Guilty Strong Evidence of Guilt Obviates Fair Trial Issue. *The Forensic Echo,* Vol. 1, Issue 3, On-line Journal. http://echo.forensicpanel.com/toc/more

Wetzel, C., & Insko, C. (1982). The similarity-attraction relationship: Is there an ideal one? *Journal of Experimental Social Psychology, 18*, 253–276.

Wetzler, S. (1985). Mood state-dependent retrieval: A failure to replicate. *Psychological Reports, 56*, 759–765.

Wever, E. (1949). *Theory of Hearing.* New York: Wiley.

White, L., & Booth, A. (1986). Children and marital happiness. *Journal of Family Issues, 7*, 131–147.

White, P. (1985). The poppy. *National Geographic, 167*, 143–188.

White, W. (1932). *Outlines of Psychiatry.* New York: Nervous and Mental Disease Publishing Company.

Whitman, E., & Diamond, M. (1986). *A preliminary report on the sexual orientation of homosexual twins.* Paper presented at the Western Region Annual Conference of the Society for the Scientific Study of Sex, Scottsdale, Arizona, January.

Whorf, B. (1956). Science and linguistics. In J. Carroll (Ed.), *Language, Thought, and Reality: Selected Writings of Benjamin Whorf.* Cambridge, MA: MIT Press.

Wicker, A. (1969). Attitudes versus actions: The relationship of verbal and overt behavioral responses to attitude objects. *Journal of Personality and Social Psychology, 33*, 793–802.

Widom, C. (1989). Does violence beget violence? A critical examination of the literature. *Psychological Bulletin, 106*, 3–28.

Wiederhold, B. K., Jang, D. P., Gevirtz, R. G., Kim, S. I., Kim, I. Y., & Wiederhold, M. D. (2002). The treatment of fear of flying: a controlled study of imaginal and virtual reality graded exposure therapy. *IEEE Transactions on Information Technology in Biomedicine, Sep; 6*(3), 218–223.

Wiens, A., & Menustik, C. (1983). Treatment outcome and patient characteristics in an aversion therapy program for alcoholism. *American Psychologist, 38*, 1089–1096.

Wilder, D. (1981). Perceiving persons as a group: Categorization and intergroup relations. In D. Hamilton (Ed.), *Cognitive Processes in Stereotyping and Intergroup Behavior.* Hillsdale, NJ: Erlbaum.

Wilder, D. (1978). Homogeneity of jurors: The majority's influence depends upon their perceived independence. *Law and Human Behavior, 2*, 363–376.

Willeit, M., Praschak-Rieder, N., Neumeister, A., Zill, P., Leisch, F., Stastny, J., et al. (2003). A polymorphism (5-HTTLPR) in the serotonin transporter promoter gene is associated with DSM-IV depression subtypes in seasonal affective disorder. *Molecular psychiatry, Nov; 8*(11), 492–496.

William, K., & Chambers, D. (1990). The relationship between therapist characteristics and outcome of in vivo exposure treatment for agoraphobia. *Behavior Therapy, 21*, 111–116.

Williams, D., Buder, M., & Overmier, J. (1990). Expectancies of reinforcer location and quality as cues for a conditional discrimination in pigeons. *Journal of Experimental Psychology: Animal Behavior Processes, 16,*(3–13).

Williams, P., & Smith, M. (1979). *Interview in The First Question.* London: British Broadcasting System Science and Features Department film.

Williams, T. (1986). *The Impact of Television: A Natural Experiment in Three Communities.* New York: Academic Press.

Wilmore, J., & Costill, D. (1988). *Training for Sport and Activity.* Dubuque, IA: C. Brown.

Wilson, B., & Lawson, D. (1976). Effects of alcohol on sexual arousal in women. *Journal of Abnormal Psychology, 85,* 489–497.

Wilson, E. (1978). *On Human Nature.* Cambridge, MA: Harvard University Press.

Wilson, E. (1975). *Sociobiology: The New Synthesis.* Cambridge, MA: Harvard University Press.

Wilson, M. (1984). Female homosexuals' need for dominance and endurance. *Psychological Reports, 55,* 79–82.

Wilson, R. (1986). Continuity and change in cognitive ability profile. *Behavioral Genetics, 16,* 45–60.

Winterbottom, M. (1958). The relation of need for achievement to learning experiences in independence mastery. In J. Atkinson (Ed.), *Motives in Fantasy, Action and Society.* Princeton, NJ: Van Nostrand.

Wolfe, J. (1936). Effectiveness of token rewards for chimpanzees. *Comparative Psychological Monographs, 12,* Whole No. 5.

Wolff, G. (1987). Body weight and cancer. *American Journal of Clinical Nutrition, 45,* 68–180.

Wolpe, J. (1985). *The Practice of Behavior Therapy* (3rd ed.). New York: Pergamon Press.

Wolpe, J. (1958). *Psychotherapy by Reciprocal Inhibition.* Stanford: Stanford University Press.

Wolvetang, E. W., Bradfield, O. M., Tymms, M., Zavarsek, S., Hatzistavrou, T., Kola, I., et al. (2003). The chromosome 21 transcription factor ETS2 transactivates the beta-APP promoter: implications for Down syndrome. *Biochimica et Biophysica Acta, Jul 28; 1628*(2), 105–110.

Women. (1975). *Channeling Children: Sex Stereotyping on Prime Time TV.* Princeton, NJ: Author.

Wong, D., Wagner, H., Tune, L., Dannals, R., Pealson, G., Links, J., Tamminga, C., Broussolle, E., Ravert, H., Wilson, A., Toung, J., Malat, J., Williams, J., O'Tuama, L., Snyder, S., Kuhar, M., & Gjedde, A. (1986). Positron emission tomography reveals elevated D2 dopamine receptors in drug-naive schizophrenics. *Science, 234,* 1558–1563.

Wood, J., & Bootzin, R. (1990). The prevalence of nightmares and their independence from anxiety. *Journal of Abnormal Psychology, 99,* 64–68.

Wood, W., & Eagly, A. (1981). Stages in the analysis of persuasive messages: The role of causal attributions and message comprehension. *Journal of Personality and Social Psychology, 40,* 246–259.

Woods, B., Yurgelun-Todd, D., Benes, E, Frankenburg, E, Pope, H., & McSparren, J. (1990). Progressive ventricular enlargement in schizophrenia: Comparison to bipolar affective disorder and correlation with clinical course. *Biological Psychiatry, 27,* 341–352.

Wozniak, R.H. (1999). Oskar Pfungst: Clever Hans (The Horse of Mr. von Osten) (1907; English 1911) Extracted From: *Classics in Psychology* ISBN 1 85506 703 X, http://www.thoemmes.com/psych /pfungst.htm

Wu, C., & Shaffer, D. (1987). Susceptibility to persuasive appeals as a function of source credibility and prior experience with the attitude object. *Journal of Personality and Social Psychology, 53,* 677–688.

Wu, J., Kramer, G. L., Kram, M., Steciuk, M., Crawford, I. L., & Petty, F. (1999). Serotonin and learned helplessness: a regional study of 5-HT1A, 5-HT2A receptors and the serotonin transport site in rat brain. *Journal of Psychiatric Research, Jan–Feb; 33*(1), 17–22.

Wurtman, R., Blusztajn, J., Ulus, I., Coviella, I., Buyukuysal, L., Growdon, J., & Slack, B. (1990). Choline metabolism in cholinergic neurons: Implications for the pathogenesis of neurodegenerative diseases. *Advances in Neurology, 51,* 117–125.

Wurtman, R., & Wurtman, J. (1989). Carbohydrates and depression. *Scientific American,* January, 68–75.

Wurtman, R. (1983). Behavioral effects of nutrients. *Lancet, 1,* 1145–1147.

Wurtman, R. (1982). Nutrients that modify brain function. *Scientific American, 246,* 50–59.

Yadalam, K., Korn, M., & Simpson, G. (1990). Tardive dystonia: Four case histories. *Journal of Clinical Psychiatry, 51,* 17–20.

Yalom, I. (1975). *The Theory and Practice of Group Psychotherapy* (2nd ed.). New York: Basic Books.

Yarrow, L., Goodwin, M., Manheimer, H., & Milowe, I. (1973). Infancy, experience and cognitive and personality development at ten years. In L. Stone, H. Smith & L. Murphy (Eds.), *The Competent Infant.* New York: Basic Books.

Yerkes, R., & Dodson, J. (1908). The relation of strength of stimulus to rapidity of habit formation. *Journal of Comparative Neurological Psychology, 18,* 459–482.

Youniss, J., & Ketrerlinus, R. (1987). Communication and connectedness in mother- and father-adolescent relationships. *Journal of Youth and Adolescence, 16,* 265–280.

Yudofsky, S. (1982). Electroconvulsive therapy in the eighties: Techniques and technology. *American Journal of Psychiatry, 36,* 391–398.

Zabin, I., Hirsch, M., Smith, E., & Hardy, J. (1984). Adolescent sexual attitudes and behavior: Are they consistent? *Family Planning Perspectives, 16,* 181–185.

Zajonc, R. (1970). Brainwash: Familiarity breeds comfort. *Psychology Today,* February, 32–35, 60–62.

Zajonc, R. (1968). Attitudinal effects of mere exposure. *Journal of Personality and Social Psychology, 9,* Monograph Supplement No. 2, Part 2.

Zajonc, R. (1965). Social facilitation. *Science, 149,* 269–274.

Zaragoza, M., & McCloskey, M. (1989). Misleading postevent information and the memory impairment hypothesis:. *Journal of Experimental Psychology: Learning, Memory, and Cognition, 13,* 36–44.

Zaragoza, M., & Koshmider, J. (1989). Misled subjects may know more than their performance implies. *Journal of Experimental Psychology: Learning, Memory, and Cognition, 15,* 246–255.

Zelnick, M., & Kantner, J. (1977). Sexual and contraceptive experiences of young unmarried women in the United States, 1976 and 1979. *Family Planning Perspectives, 9,* 55–71.

Ziegler, D. J., & Leslie, Y. M. (2003). A test of the ABC model underlying rational emotive behavior therapy. *Psychological Reports, Feb: 92*(1), 235–240.

Ziegler, J. (1984). Scientists ponder drinkers, drunks, differences. *The Oregonian,* July 5, B4–B5.

Zigler, E., & Seitz, V. (1982). Social policy and Intelligence. In R. Sternberg (Ed.), *Handbook of Human Intelligence.* Cambridge, England: Cambridge University Press.

Zilbergeld, B. (1983). *The Shrinking of America: Myths of Psychological Change.* Boston: Little, Brown.

Zimbardo, P. (1975). Transforming experimental research into advocacy for social chaange. In M. Deutsh & H. Hornstein (Eds.), *Applying Social Psychology: Implications for Research, Practice and Training.* Hillsdale, NJ: jErlbaum.

Zimmer, D. (1983). Interaction patterns and communication skills in sexually distressed, maritally distressed, and normal couples. *Journal of Sex and Marital Therapy, 9,* 251–265.

List of Recommended Web Sites

Chapter. 4
Take the Ishihara Test for Colorblindness (free) at
http://www.toledo-bend.com/colorblind/Ishihara.html

To see what the world looks like to colorblind people, check out:
http://www.mcw.edu/cellbio/colorvision/cvb.htm (page 1)

Source: Neuroscience for kids
(http://faculty.washington.edu/chudler/neurok.html) :(Note this is a source so we might need permission to display their table, though slightly modified. (Page)

ARTIFICIAL VISION (For more information see Dr. William Dobelle's web-site at: http://www.dobelle.com/index.html) (page 17)

To see a bunch of tomatoes like they look to you, versus what they look like to a dog, check out the following neat web site:
http://www.mcw.edu/cellbio/colorvision/colorvision.pdf (pg 18)

Want more information? Check out Davis's article at:
http://www.gi.alaska.edu/ScienceForum/ASF2/278.html

Hot bird-seed http://www.hotbirdseed.com/html/faq.html

Chapter 5
http://edition.cnn.com/2004/TECH/11/02/brain.dish/

http://www.theage.com.au/articles/2004/12/06/1102182227308.html?oneclick=true

Sleepwalking:
http://edition.cnn.com/2005/WORLD/europe/03/18/britain.sleepwalk/

Chapter 10
Pfungst, check out the following web-site:
http://www.thoemmes.com/psych/pfungst.htm

Chapter 13
Psychological Disorders check this neat link by Dr. John Grohol:
http://www.psychcentral.com

Index

A

B

C

I

J

L

M

N

O

P

Q

R

S

T

U

V

W

Y

Z

BVT Publishing

Better textbooks, better prices.

Digital Access

Product Key: K1357310

Understanding Psychology, Ragade & Ettinger

Instructions:

1. Visit BVTLab.com, enter your product key (printed above) and click on the orange *"redeem a product key"* button.
2. Follow the instructions to create an account. A verification email will be sent to you. (If you do not receive an email, please check your junk mail folder.)
3. Verify your email address by entering the code from that verification email.
4. Create a password and complete the creation of your account.
5. If you have an online class click on *"go to your classroom"* and enter the course section code that your instructor provides.

Understanding Psychology

Fourth Edition

Student study resources are available
at www.BVTLab.com

Product Key on Reverse Side

This product is non-returnable and non-refundable once packaging has been opened